EEC LAW

AUSTRALIA
The Law Book Company Ltd.
Sydney : Melbourne : Brisbane

GREAT BRITAIN
Sweet & Maxwell Ltd.
London

INDIA
N. M. Tripathi Private Ltd.
Bombay

ISRAEL
Steimatzky's Agency Ltd.
Jerusalem : Tel Aviv : Haifa

MALAYSIA : SINGAPORE : BRUNEI
Malayan Law Journal (Pte.) Ltd.
Singapore

NEW ZEALAND
Sweet & Maxwell (N.Z.) Ltd.
Wellington

PAKISTAN
Pakistan Law House
Karachi

U.S.A. AND CANADA
Matthew Bender & Co. Inc.
New York

EEC LAW

by

ANTHONY PARRY, B.A.(CANTAB.)

Licencié spécial en droit européen (Brussels)
of the Middle Temple, Barrister

and

STEPHEN HARDY, B.A.(CANTAB.)

Licencié spécial en droit européen (Brussels)

LONDON   NEW YORK
SWEET & MAXWELL   MATTHEW BENDER
1973

Published in 1973
in Great Britain by
Sweet & Maxwell Ltd. of
11 New Fetter Lane, London

Published in the U.S.A. by
Matthew Bender & Co. Inc. of
235 East 45th Street,
New York, New York 10017.

Printed in Great Britain by
The Eastern Press Ltd. of
London and Reading.

SBN   Hardback   421   17390   4
　　　Paperback   421   17410   2

Library of Congress Catalog Card No. 72-96578

PREFACE

DENMARK, Ireland and the United Kingdom acceded to the three European Communities on January 1, 1973. This book attempts to give a concise picture of the whole range and scope of EEC law as it stood immediately prior to accession, whilst discussing where appropriate the accession arrangements themselves. In analysing Community law we have attempted to place it in its "European" context, rather than to examine its impact on existing United Kingdom law; that impact is as yet impossible to assess, although likely to be considerable. It is hoped that the present work will provide at least some of the answers to questions raised by those concerned with, or affected by, Community law, and will suggest lines of further research to those seeking more detailed answers. The reader will no doubt appreciate that a discussion of an entire system of law, albeit only fifteen years old, in 400-odd pages cannot cover every aspect in detail.

The book is divided into eight Parts and thirty-eight chapters. In Part I the general structure of the European Economic Community and its governing Treaty are described, while its institutions are examined in Parts 2 and 3, Part 2 covering the Council, Commission, European Parliament and the various consultative bodies, Part 3 the Court of Justice. There are chapters on each of the main heads of jurisdiction of the Court under the EEC Treaty, and the important topics of supremacy and direct applicability of Community law are each given a separate chapter. We have throughout placed considerable emphasis upon discussion of the case law of the Court of Justice.

In Part 4 are discussed the so-called four freedoms fundamental to the EEC customs union—freedom of movement for goods, persons, capital and transport. Somewhat unconventionally, in terms of the order in which the topics are discussed in the Treaty, the chapter on social policy (Chapter 24) is placed next to the chapter on the worker and the Community (Chapter 23), since the subjects are closely related. In Chapter 22 we have attempted to cover the vast topic of Community agricultural law.

The ensuing chapters analyse the various topics of Community economic law. By and large the order of the Treaty articles has been adopted, but in view of the importance of the subject-matter, separate chapters are devoted to company law, to the approximation of laws in general, and to regional policy, none of which forms the subject-matter of a single part of the Treaty. The chapters on competition law, taxation and economic policy attempt to give comprehensive surveys of the more conventional topics of Community economic law.

Rather more general legal questions are discussed in Chapters 35 and 36, dealing notably with the manner in which the Community and its institutions are financed, with the personality of the Community in international and in domestic law, with the Community's privileges and immunities, and with its legal liability, both contractual and non-contractual.

In Chapter 37 we have attempted to give an account of the commercial policy of the Communities, and of its external relations. Most if not all the other topics of discussion in this book are at least theoretically familiar; for instance, most readers will be aware that the Community has a taxation policy, of which one manifestation is the valued added tax, but it is felt that the topic of external relations is relatively unfamiliar, if only because there is something of a dearth of literature on the subject. It is hoped by this chapter to redress the situation somewhat.

The European Communities Act 1972 is described in Chapter 38. In keeping with the overall approach of the book, the Act is examined with a view to seeing how Community law is received into English law. The effects of Community law on English law being as yet uncertain, they are left to be discussed by others with the benefit of hindsight.

After some heart-searching it was decided not to annex the Community Treaties or the European Communities Act to the book, since the extra material would make the book unacceptably bulky and indeed costly. These documents are of course available individually, and, we would add, in a convenient single volume, put out by our own publishers, under the title *Sweet and Maxwell's European Community Treaties.*

A. P.
S. H.

January 5, 1973.

TABLE OF CONTENTS

PROVISIONS OF THE TREATIES GOVERNING THE INSTITUTIONS

MANY of the provisions relating to the institutions are identical in the two Rome Treaties, as also are the provisions of the Protocols on the Statute of the Court of Justice. The lists below indicate which are the identical provisions in question. Throughout this book the EEC provision alone is cited, but the provision so cited is designated with an asterisk.(*)

The Assembly

EEC	Euratom
137	107
138†	108†
139	109
140	110
141	111
142	112
143	113
144	114

The Court of Justice

EEC	Euratom
164	136
165†	137†
166†	138†
167†	139†
168	140
169	141
170	142
171	143
172	–
–	144
–	145
173	146
174	147
175	148
176	149
[177]	[150]
178	151
179	152
180	–
181	153
182	154
183	155
184	156
[185]	[157]
186	158
187	159
188	160

The Council

EEC	Euratom
[145]	[115]
146‡	116‡
147‡	117‡
148†	118†
149	119
150	120
151‡	121‡
152	122
153	–
154‡	123‡

Common Provisions

EEC	Euratom
189	161
190	162
191	163
[192]	[164]

The Commission

EEC	Euratom
[155]	[124]
156‡	125‡
[157]‡	[126]‡
158‡	127‡
159‡	128‡
160‡	129‡
[161]‡	[130]‡
162‡	131‡
163‡	132‡
–	133
–	134†
–	135

Economic and Social Committee

EEC	Euratom
[193]	[165]
194†	166†

Key
[ ] Corresponding Article serves same purpose, but is not identical.
† Article amended by Act of Accession.
‡ Article repealed by Merger Treaty.
– No corresponding Article.
N.B. Articles varying only in so far as they cite other articles in the relevant Treaty (e.g. Article 144 EEC, citing Article 158 EEC, corresponding to Articles 114 and 127 Euratom) are for these purposes assimilated to the provisions which are word for word the same in the two Treaties.

*Economic and Social
Committee—cont.*

EEC	Euratom
195	167
196	168
[197]	[169]
198	170

*The Protocols on the Statute of
the Court of Justice*

EEC	Euratom
1	1
2	2
3	3
4	4
5	5
6	6
7	7
8	8
9	9
10	10
11	11
12	12
13	13
14	14
15	15
16	16
17	17
18	18
19	19
–	20

*The Protocols on the Statute of
the Court of Justice—cont.*

EEC	Euratom
20	21
21	22
22	23
23	24
24	25
25	26
26	27
27	28
28	29
29	30
30	31
31	32
32	33
33	34
34	35
35	36
36	37
37	38
38	39
39	40
40	41
41	42
42	43
43	44
44	45
45	46
46	47

COMMUNITY TREATIES

COMMUNITY ACTS

INTERNATIONAL AGREEMENTS

NATIONAL CONSTITUTIONS AND LAWS

TABLE OF CASES

ALPHABETICAL LIST OF CASES

Wirtschaftsvereinigung Eisen- und Stahlindustrie v. High Authority, 13/57
Witt v. HZA Lüneburg, 28/70
Wöhrmann v. Commission, 31 & 33/62
Wöhrmann v. HZA Bad Reichenhall, 7/67
Wünsche v. EVSt, 50/71

Zuckerfabrik Watenstedt GmbH v. Council, 6/68

COMMISSION DECISIONS ON COMPETITION

NATIONAL COURTS

ABBREVIATIONS

AASM	Associated African States and Malagasy
AETR	Accord européen relatif au travail des équipages des véhicules effectuant des transports internationaux par route. Also: ERTA
A.F.D.I.	*Annuaire Français de Droit International*
AG	Aktiengesellschaft
A.J.C.L.	*American Journal of Comparative Law*
A.J.I.L.	*American Journal of International Law*
Ann.Eur.	*Annuaire Européen*—European Yearbook
Art.	Article
BGBl.	Bundesgesetzblatt
B.J.E.	*Bulletin des Juristes Européens*
BKA	Bundeskartellamt
BLEU	Belgo-Luxembourg Economic Union
Brinkhorst and Schermers	*Judicial Remedies in the European Communities*, A case book, by L. J. Brinkhorst and U. G. Schermers, Kluwer, Deventer, Stevens, London, 1969
Bulletin	Bulletin of the European Communities. EC Commission, monthly
CAP	Common agricultural policy
CCH	Commerce Clearing House
CCT	Common customs tariff
C.D.E.	*Cahiers de Droit Européen*
C.E.D.	*Cahiers économiques de Bruxelles*
CET	Common external tariff
Cie	Compagnie
Cin.L.Rev.	*Cincinnati Law Review*
C.M.L.Rev.	*Common Market Law Review*
Cmnd.	Command Paper
COCOR	Comité de Coordination
COREPER	Committee of Permanent Representatives to the European Communities (in fact abbreviation of comité des représentants permanents)
D.E.T.	*Droit Européen des Transports*
EAEC	European Atomic Energy Community
ECE	Economic Commission for Europe
ECMT	European conference of Ministers of Transport
ECSC	European Coal and Steel Community
EDF	European Development Fund
EEC	European Economic Community
EFTA	European Free Trade Association
EIB	European Investment Bank
EP (or PE) doc.	European Parliament document
ERTA	European Agreement concerning the work of crews of vehicles engaged in International Road Transport. Also: AETR
ESF	European Social Fund
E.T.L.	*European Transport Law*
Eur.	*Europarecht*
Euratom	European Atomic Energy Community
Europe Bulletin	Daily bulletin produced by Agence Europe, Brussels-Luxembourg
EVSt	Einfuhr- und Vorratstelle
FA	Finanzamt
FAO	Food and Agriculture Organisation
FEOGA	Fonds européen d'orientation et de garantie agricole (European agricultural guidance and guarantee fund)
GATT	General Agreement on Trade and Tariffs
GmbH	Gesellschaft mit beschränkter Haftung
GNP	Gross national product
H.A.	High Authority of the ECSC

xlv

H.I.L.J.	*Harvard International Law Journal*
H.M.S.O.	Her Majesty's Stationery Office
HZA	Hauptzollamt
I.C.L.Q.	*International and Comparative Law Quarterly*
ILO	International Labour Organisation
J.C.M.S.	*Journal of Common Market Studies*
J.O.	*Journal officiel* (des Communautés Européennes)
J.T.	*Journal des Tribunaux* (Belgium)
J.W.T.L.	*Journal of World Trade Law*
K.G.	Kommanditgesellschaft
K.S.E.	*Kölner Schriften zum Europarecht*
L.G.D.J.	Librairie Général de Droit et de Jurisprudence
Misc.	Miscellaneous series of treaties published by H.M.S.O.
Mod.L.Rev.	*Modern Law Review*
NATO	North Atlantic Treaty Organisation
N.J.W.	*Neue juristische Wochenschrift*
NV	Naamloze Vennootschap
OECD	Organisation for Economic Co-operation and Development
OEEC	Organisation for European Economic Cooperation
OHG	Offene Handelsgesellschaft
PE (or EP) doc.	European Parliament document
R.B.D.I.	*Revue Belge de Droit International*
R.C.A.D.I.	*Recueil des Cours de l'académie de droit international*
R.D.E.	*Rivista di Diritto Europeo*
Rec.	*Recueil de la jurisprudence de la cour de justice des communautés européennes*
R.G.D.I.P.	*Revue générale de droit international public.*
R.I.D.C.	*Revue International de Droit Comparé*
R.M.C.	*Revue du Marché Commun*
R.T.D.E.	*Revue Trimestrielle de Droit Européen*
SA	Société anonyme
S.a.r.L.	Société à responsabilité limitée
S.E.W.	*Sociaal-economische Wetgeving*
Soc.	Société
S.p.A.	Società per Azioni
S.P.R.L.	Société de personnes à responsabilité limitée
Stan.L.Rev.	*Stanford Law Review*
Tex.L.Rev.	*Texas Law Review*
u.a.	unit of account
U.N.	United Nations Organisation
UNESCO	United Nations Educational, Scientific and Cultural Organisation
Valentine	*The Court of Justice of the European Communities.* 2 Vols. 1965. Stevens
VAT	Value Added Tax
Wash.L.Rev.	*Washington Law Review*
WEU	Western European Union
WHO	World Health Organisation
Y.L.J.	*Yale Law Journal*

Part 1

INTRODUCTORY

INTRODUCTORY

SCOPE AND METHOD OF THIS BOOK

1–01 EUROPEAN integration has been a constant theme in Western Europe since the end of the last world war, and the United Kingdom has throughout been more or less closely associated with such efforts as have been made in this direction. Nevertheless, it is only with her accession to the European Communities, envisaged by the Treaty of Accession of January 22, 1972 and by the Decision of the Council of the European Communities of the same date [1] that the United Kingdom becomes a member of the organisations in which this integration is most advanced.

The debate concerning the accession of the United Kingdom to the European Communities has continued over most of the past decade, and it is not proposed to recapitulate its vicissitudes or the history of European integration in general, these subjects being covered elsewhere.[2] Similarly it is felt that the economic arguments for and against entry are now relatively familiar, as indeed is the economic background in general.[2] It is exclusively with legal questions relating to the European Communities that this book is concerned, and since the European Economic Community (or EEC) is more important than the other two Communities, both because of its much more immediate impact for the individual, and because the matters over which it has jurisdiction are much more extensive, the discussion of Community law in the ensuing chapters of this book relates primarily to the law of the EEC.

1–02 This book sets out to touch on all major aspects of EEC law. The order of discussion by and large follows that in which matters are dealt with by the EEC Treaty. It is felt, however, that an understanding of the workings of the Community institutions is an important prerequisite to any analysis of the rules laid down by the Treaty governing the various sectors of the economy. The Community institutions are therefore discussed first. This is followed by an examination of the heads of jurisdiction of the Court of Justice and of the nature of Community law in general. The various provisions of the Treaty governing economic activity are then discussed more or less *seriatim*. The various chapter headings are self-explanatory. Company law and regional policy are not covered by specific chapter headings of the Treaty, but are nevertheless of such importance that they merit extensive treatment. In Chapter 36, "Particular legal questions relating to the Communities," are gathered various matters which relate neither to economic law as such, nor yet

---

[1] *Infra*, Chap. 2.   [2] See bibliography at end of book.

purely to the administrative law of the Court of Justice, but rather to the institutions of the Communities generally.

A matter of particular importance to the Community is the conduct of external relations. All aspects of external relations, including commercial policy, are therefore discussed together in Chapter 37, " External relations."

In the last chapter, Chapter 38, the European Communities Act 1972 is examined. The Act makes the necessary changes in domestic law to enable the United Kingdom to ratify the Treaty of Accession, and to deposit its instrument of accession to the European Coal and Steel Community.

Changes made to the Community Treaties, and the secondary legislation made thereunder, by the Treaty of Accession, the Decision of the Council concerning accession and by the Act of Accession (" the accession instruments ") are referred to throughout this book. The reader should bear in mind, however, that not every technical adaptation contained in the annexes to the Act of Accession is of sufficient importance to merit express mention.

" WHERE TO FIND YOUR LAW "

1–03 It is not possible in a book of this length to go into every aspect of Community law in full detail. Suggestions for further reading are given in the Bibliography at the end of the book.

Details are given here of the basic materials referred to in the text.

1. *The treaties*

1–04 The main treaties governing the three European Communities are the following [2a]:

1. *Treaty Establishing the European Coal and Steel Community,* Paris, April 18, 1951—Misc. No. 4 (1972), Cmnd. 4863.

2. *Treaty Establishing the European Economic Community,* Rome, March 25, 1957—Misc. No. 5 (1972), Cmnd. 4864.

3. *Treaty Establishing the European Atomic Energy Community,* Rome, March 25, 1957—Misc. No. 6 (1972), Cmnd. 4865.

4. *Treaty Establishing a Single Council and a Single Commission of the European Communities,* Brussels, April 8, 1965—Misc. No. 7 (1972), Cmnd. 4866.

5. *Treaty amending certain Budgetary Provisions of the Treaties establishing the European Communities and of the Treaty establishing a Single Council and a Single Commission of the European Communities,* Luxembourg, April 22, 1970—Misc. No. 8 (1972), Cmnd. 4867.

6. *Treaty concerning the Accession of the Kingdom of Denmark, Ireland, the Kingdom of Norway and the United Kingdom of*

[2a] Cmnd. 4862–4867 will be re-published in the Treaty Series, with new Cmnd. numbers.

Great Britain and Northern Ireland to the European Economic Community and the European Atomic Energy Community (with Final Act) and Decision of the Council of the European Communities concerning the Accession of the said States to the European Coal and Steel Community, Brussels, January 22, 1972—Misc. No. 3 (1972), Parts I and II, Cmnd. 4862—I and II.

All but the ECSC Treaty were originally drawn up in the four languages of the original Member States—Dutch, French, German and Italian, and are now available in authentic texts in English (the Command texts as above) and Danish, the French text remaining the only authentic text of the ECSC Treaty.

Other treaties relating to the Communities have been published in the *Official Journal (q.v. infra)* and in English in *European Communities, Treaties and Related Instruments,* 10 volumes, H.M.S.O., 1972.

2. *Acts of the institutions of the Communities*

1–05   Acts of the institutions of the Communities [3] are published in the *Official Journal (q.v. infra).* Most of those issued before November 10, 1971 and expected to be in force for the United Kingdom upon accession were published in English in *European Communities, Secondary Legislation,* 42 volumes, H.M.S.O. 1972 (later acts have been published in supplementary parts).[4] Those in force on accession are to be published in authentic English texts in special editions of the *Official Journal.*

Citation: The legislative acts of the institutions are referred to as follows:

Regulations: Regulation number followed by year; thus—Regulation 1009/68. (Prior to 1963; thus—Regulation 17 of 1962 (*or* 17/62).)

Decisions: ECSC—Council of Ministers; date only prior to 1968, thereafter as for EEC and Euratom decisions.
High Authority; as for Regulations.
EEC and Euratom year followed by decision number; thus—64/221. (Prior to 1963; by date only.)

Directives: As for EEC and Euratom decisions.

ECSC Recommendations: as for Regulations.

Other instruments are generally referred to by date, although many are in fact numbered. See *infra* on citation of the *Official Journal.*

3. *Judgments of the Court of Justice*

1–06   The judgments of the Court of Justice are published in all four of the original Community languages, the French version of the reports

---

[3] The nature of these is discussed in Chap. 8.

[4] Quotations from Community instruments are from these texts unless otherwise stated.

being entitled *Recueil de la Jurisprudence de la Cour de Justice des Communautés Européennes.* Only the text in the "language of procedure"[5] is authentic. Official translations of the judgments given after accession will be available in English and Danish. Earlier judgments will be available in official translations at a later stage. In the meantime, translations of the principal judgments (along with translations of judgments of domestic courts on Community questions) are published in English in the *Common Market Law Reports* (published by Common Law Reports, London) and in the *Common Market Reporter* (published by Commerce Clearing House, Chicago). Both series begin with judgments given in December 1961.

> *Citation*: Judgments of the Court of Justice are in this book cited as follows: 7/61, *Commission* v. *France*, Rec. VII 633, [1962] C.M.L.R. 39. The number preceding the name of the case is the case number given to the case by the Court. It is by this number that cases may be most rapidly identified. *Rec.* refers to the French *Recueil*, the number in roman figures following it to the appropriate volume number (it is important to indicate to which language version one is referring, since the pagination varies somewhat). Where possible a reference is given to the *Common Market Law Reports*, cited as in the example. Commerce Clearing House reports are not referred to.

The Official Journal

1–07   Most Community instruments are published in the *Official Journal,* which appears more or less daily. Not all instruments so published are legislative in character (see *infra,* § 8–01 as to the obligation to publish). The *Official Journal* of the European Coal and Steel Community appeared between December 30, 1952 and April 19, 1958. The *Official Journal* of the European Communities replaced it as from April 20, 1958. As from January 1, 1968 the *Official Journal* was divided into two parts: *Legislation* (L) and *Communications* (C).

> *Citation*: References are to the French text of the *Official Journal*—whether of the ECSC or of all three Communities. It is cited as follows:
>
> | 1952–June 30, 1967 | : *e.g.* J.O. 1961, 408 [6] |
> | July 1, 1967–December 31, 1967 | : *e.g.* J.O. 1967, 295/6 |
> | January 1, 1968 onwards | : *e.g.* J.O. 1968, L 148/1 |
> | | and J.O. 1968, C 22/3 |
>
> (Pagination was continuous within each year until July 1, 1967, when the system was adopted of paginating within each daily part only.)

---

[5] See § 9–15, *infra.*
[6] References to the J.O. of 1958 differentiate between the ECSC Journal and the Journal of the three Communities, which started again at p. 1.

In the L part are published notably Community acts referred to in Article 189 EEC * ⁶ᵃ (*infra*, § 8–01) and international agreements. The C part contains reports of the sessions of the European Parliament, including written questions and answers, and notices of proceedings of the Court of Justice. It also contains Commission proposals and opinions thereon, besides various other types of notices and opinions. An annual index volume appears, which covers both the L and the C parts.

The *Official Journal* appears in all four of the original languages, the French version being entitled " *le Journal officiel des Communautés Européennes.*" It will also appear in English and Danish (see *supra,* § 1–05).

Other Community publications ⁷

1–08   The Community institutions publish a vast amount of material on all aspects of the Communities. Most of these publications are produced by the Commission.

Particularly useful are the monthly *Bulletin of the European Communities* (separate editions for the ECSC and for the EEC prior to 1968) and the annual *General Report* (separate editions for each Community prior to 1968). Both publications appear in English as well as in the original official languages.

The *Bulletin* contains documents and articles or studies on the Communities, a general survey of Community activities, and, in effect, a monthly index to the *Official Journal.* To the *Bulletin* are annexed various supplements, containing longer documents or Commission proposals.

> *Citation*:
> Bulletin, followed by number and year.
> Supplement to Bulletin, followed by number and year.
> Bulletin Supplement, followed by number and year.

The annual *General Report* contains a rather more detailed survey of the main achievements of the year.

> *Citation*: *e.g.* Fifth General Report (1971) p. 60.

Of importance also are the reports presented to the European Parliament by the various committees and sub-committees. These are referred to as session documents.

> *Citation*: Usually by name of *rapporteur*, followed by *e.g.* session doc. 65–66 No. 54; or session doc. 1971 No. 1.

---

⁶ᵃ For an explanation of the asterisk (*) see the notes to the table of Provisions of the Treaties Governing the Institutions, *ante*, p. ix.

⁷ See generally *Catalogue des Publications 1952–1971*, Vol. 1, European Communities, Brussels-Luxembourg, 1972. Information on how to obtain Community publications is available from European Communities Information Service, 23 Chesham Street, London S.W.1, tel. 01-235 4904.

Documents referred to with a code number (*e.g.* Sec (71) 600 Final) are cyclostyled on A4-size paper. They are not generally produced in more permanent form, being generally proposals or plans, but they sometimes appear in whole or in part in the *Bulletin* supplements or in the C part of the *Official Journal*.

Other sources of information on Community law

1–09   The reader is referred to the bibliography at the end of this book for further reading on Community law in general. So far as jurisprudence is concerned, the *Répertoire de la Jurisprudence relative aux traités instituant les Communautés Européennes*, edited by H. J. Eversen and H. Sperl (1966 and annual supplements, KSE, Karl Heymanns, Cologne) is a very useful key to the decisions of the Court of Justice as well as to national jurisprudence relating to Community law: against each Treaty article or Community instrument is listed the relevant jurisprudence. The indexes are cumulative. Each volume of the *Recueil* and of the *Common Market Law Reports* have keys to discussions of given Treaty articles etc., also, but that in C.M.L.R. is non-cumulative. The most recent volume of the *Recueil* with a cumulative index was Volume XIII (1967).

Norway and the Accession Instruments

1–10   As the long title of the Treaty of Accession, referred to above, itself indicates, the Kingdom of Norway was to accede to the European Communities. Following the negative result of a consultative referendum held in October 1972, however, Norway announced that she would not after all be acceding to the Communities. Such a contingency is in fact provided for by the Treaty of Accession and by the Decision of the Council (see *infra*, § 2–08) but the necessary adaptations to the accession instruments have yet to be decided upon, although it is clear at the very least that changes in the institutional structure will be called for. In view of the uncertainty as to the exact changes to be made, the institutional provisions of the accession instruments are discussed as though Norway was still to accede. Adaptations relating solely to Norway, however, are on the whole passed over in silence.

Accommodation will be made for Norway by means of a trade agreement similar to those already signed with the EFTA non-candidate countries (*infra*, § 37–56).

CHAPTER 2

EUROPEAN COMMUNITIES—GENERAL NATURE

2–01 THERE are three European Communities, the Coal and Steel Community (ECSC) set up by the Treaty of Paris of April 18, 1951 (Cmnd. 4863), and the Economic Community (EEC) and the Atomic Energy Community (EAEC or Euratom) set up by the two Treaties of Rome of March 25, 1957 (Cmnd. 4864 and 4865). The signatories of the Treaties and original Members of the Communities were Belgium, France, the Federal Republic of Germany, Italy, Luxembourg, and the Netherlands.

The enlargement of the EEC and of Euratom to include Denmark, Ireland, Norway and the United Kingdom is envisaged by the Treaty of Accession signed at Brussels on January 22, 1972 (Cmnd. 4862). These same States are also to accede to the ECSC. This is envisaged by the Decision of January 22, 1972, of the Council (Cmnd. 4862, p. 133). In October, 1972, Norway announced that she would not now accede (*supra*, § 1–10).

Each Community is a distinct legal entity, but all three are closely allied; from their inception the EEC and Euratom have shared a common Court of Justice and a common parliamentary Assembly with the ECSC, these institutions taking the place of those created for the ECSC by virtue of the Convention on Certain Institutions Common to the European Communities (Cmnd. 4864, p. 144). The same Convention provided for an Economic and Social Committee common to the EEC and to Euratom. The close alliance between the three Communities was further consolidated by the Treaty signed at Brussels on April 8, 1965, establishing a single Commission and a single Council for all three Communities (Cmnd. 4866).

Of the three Communities, the EEC, extending as it does to very broad spheres of economic and social activity, is far the most important, the other two being essentially specialised. It is with the EEC, therefore, that this book is primarily concerned. It is beyond its scope to go into a detailed description of the workings of the ECSC and the EAEC, and the discussion of these latter Communities is limited to those aspects having an importance for the three Communities as a group.

THE EUROPEAN ECONOMIC COMMUNITY

General structure

2–02 The EEC Treaty (also commonly known as the Treaty of Rome) is set out in 248 Articles, and divided up into a Preamble and six Parts. It is further subdivided into Titles and Chapters. There are in addition a number of annexes and annexed Protocols and Conventions, followed by a Final Act, together with a series of declarations.

The way in which the Treaty provisions are arranged is not entirely logical, but the broad divisions follow on naturally from one another.

2–03   The intention to set up a European Economic Community is stated in the Preamble, while the first Part, entitled " Principles " (Arts. 1 to 8) gives substantive effect to this intent, in fact setting up the Community (Art. 1). The tasks and activities of the Community are then set out (Arts. 2 and 3). Article 4 provides for four institutions of the Communities: an Assembly; a Council; a Commission; and a Court of Justice. Articles 5 to 7 are of general application, in particular requiring Member States to ensure fulfilment of their obligations, and to abstain from activities which could jeopardise the attainment of the objectives of the Treaty (Art. 5); this provision may be compared in its intention with the full faith and credit clause of the United States Constitution. Article 6 calls for economic co-operation, and requires the institutions to take care not to prejudice the financial stability of the Member States. Article 7 contains a non-discrimination clause. Article 8 sets out a timetable for the establishment of the Economic Community.

2–04   Part Two, " Foundations of the Community " (Arts. 9 to 37) contains the provisions which are considered fundamental to an Economic Community, or Common Market. Article 9, in some sense the key Article, bases the system upon a customs union. In contrast to a Free Trade Area, a customs union provides for a Common Customs Tariff *vis à vis* third countries in addition to a prohibition on customs duties on imports and exports as between Member States. A customs union does not, on the other hand, go as far as an economic union, in that the latter implies a common economic policy rather than simple approximation of separate policies.

The Economic Community is said to embody the four freedoms of movement of goods, of persons, of services and of capital. Effect is given to these four freedoms in the Foundations of the Community: the principle of free movement of goods is stated in and defined by Article 9, the principle being worked out in the provisions for the customs union (Arts. 12 to 29). These involve elimination of customs duties between Member States (Arts. 12 to 17) and the setting up of the Common Customs Tariff (CCT—sometimes referred to as the Common External Tariff: CET). In addition Member States are required to eliminate quantitative restrictions (quotas) as between themselves (Arts. 30 to 37). The provisions relating to agriculture (Arts. 38 to 47) are assembled under a distinct Title. They are separate from, but related to, the provisions on the free movement of goods.

Free movement of persons, services and capital are provided for in Articles 48 to 73, which make up the third Title. The four freedoms are then in some sense tied together by a Common Transport Policy in the fourth Title (Arts. 74 to 84).

2–05   The provisions of Part Three, " Policy of the Community " (Arts. 83 to 130) seek to ensure that conditions are equal as between Member States and that wide divergences in national policies may be eliminated. Accordingly, the Part contains rules on competition between undertakings on dumping and on state aids or subsidies (Arts. 85 to 94); provisions on taxation (Arts. 95 to 99); provisions on the approximation (or harmonisation) of differing national laws (Arts. 100 to 102); and provisions on economic policies in general (Title II, Arts. 103 to 116) and on external trade policy in particular (Arts. 110 to 116). Further, there are provisions on social policy (Arts. 117 to 128). Regional policy is not the subject of a separate section in the Treaty, but Articles 129 to 130 on the European Investment Bank touch specifically on problems of regional underdevelopment and decline in the Community. The sections in the Treaty on social policy, aids and transport all have some bearing on regional questions.

2–06   Part Four (Arts. 131 to 136) deals exclusively with association of those overseas countries and territories which have particular links with Member States of the Community.

Part Five (Arts. 137 to 209) sets up the four institutions of the Community referred to in Article 4—the Assembly, the Council, the Commission and the Court of Justice—and provides generally for their functioning and financing. The Economic and Social Committee is set up by Articles 193 to 198.

Part Six, " General and Final Provisions " (Arts. 210 to 248) covers a multitude of questions, notably status and certain powers of the institutions; unification of laws (Art. 220); foreign relations (Arts. 228 to 231, 234, 237, 238); the entry into force of the Treaty; and the setting up of the institutions.

Modifications

2–07   The Community Treaties have, since 1957, been modified by a number of later agreements and other instruments, notably by the Merger Treaty of April 8, 1965, establishing a single Council and a single Commission (Cmnd. 4866) and the so-called Budget Treaty of April 22, 1970, amending certain budgetary provisions of the Community Treaties (Cmnd. 4867). Most recently the Community Treaties have been modified by the Treaty of Accession of January 22, 1972 (Cmnd. 4862) providing for the accession of Denmark, Ireland, Norway and the United Kingdom to the EEC and Euratom, and by the Decision of the Council providing for the accession of those same States to the ECSC. The Treaty of Accession and the Council Decision, together with the annexed Act of Accession and its annexes make adjustments to the original Community Treaties and subordinate instruments to take account of the enlarged membership, but do not otherwise modify the existing Communities. A brief examination of the accession arrangements is appropriate at this point, for the discussions of the original Treaties in the ensuing Chapters will assume an understanding of the relationship between those arrangements and the original Treaties.

THE ACCESSION INSTRUMENTS

2-08 The Treaty of Accession to the EEC and to Euratom (Cmnd. 4862–I, p. 1) is a short document in three Articles, providing in principle for accession to the Communities by deposit of instruments of ratification before January 1, 1973, conditional upon deposit of instruments of accession to the ECSC upon that date. All the original Member States must ratify the Treaty before it can enter into force. Accession to all three Communities is to take place on January 1, 1973; there is no provision for acquiring membership of some but not all of the Communities; indeed this is expressly excluded. It is not, however, necessary for all the applicant States to accede at the same time; " . . . the Treaty shall come into force for those [of the intending new Member] States which have deposited their instruments " in time (Art. 2, para. 3, of the Treaty and of the Decision).

2-09   There is annexed to both the Treaty of Accession and the Council Decision what is styled an Act of Accession (Cmnd. 4862–I, p. 9), laying down the conditions of accession and effecting the modifications requisite in the earlier Treaties and subsidiary instruments. This Act, to which there are appended various annexes and Protocols and an exchange of notes, is completed by a Final Act (Cmnd. 4862–I, p. 111), to which five joint declarations are annexed. The Final Act records that note was taken of a German declaration on Berlin, and of the arrangements regarding the procedure for adopting decisions and other measures to be taken by the Community during the period preceding accession (*i.e.* providing for consultations between the Community and the acceding States during that period). Lastly, five unilateral declarations are annexed to the Final Act.

The Act of Accession itself is divided into five Parts: (1) Principles; (2) Adjustments to the Treaties; (3) Adaptations to Acts Adopted by the Institutions; (4) Transitional Measures; and (5) Provisions Relating to the Implementation of the Act. These Parts are subdivided into Chapters and Titles, the whole Act being made up of 161 Articles.

Contents of the Act of Accession

2-10   The specific provisions of the Act of Accession providing for adaptation to the EEC structure are discussed in relation to that part of the EEC structure, but an outline of their general effect is given here for the sake of convenience.

Part One—Principles (Articles 1 to 9)

2–11   Articles 1 to 9 lay down a series of general rules, governing the rest of the Act of Accession.

From the date of accession the provisions of the original Treaties (defined in Article 1 as meaning the Paris and Rome Treaties, as supplemented or amended by Treaties or other acts which entered into force before accession), and the acts adopted by the institutions of the Communities are to be binding on the new Member States, and are to apply in those States under the conditions laid down in the original Treaties and in the Act of Accession (Art. 2).

The provisions of various international agreements concluded between the Six and relating to or connected with the Community are either made binding on the new Member States, or else the new Member States are required to accede to them (Arts. 3 and 4 (2) and (3)), subject in some cases, to adaptations consequential upon enlargement.

2–12   The new Member States stand in the same relationship to non-binding acts of the Council and similar acts adopted by common agreement of the Member States which concern the Communities as the original Member States; they will accordingly observe the principles and guidelines deriving from them and are to take steps to implement them where necessary (Art. 3 (3)).

Further, the new Member States are required to accede to such international agreements or conventions with third States and international organisations concluded by the Community and the Six acting jointly (Art. 4 (2)). International agreements concluded by the Community alone are binding under the conditions laid down in the original Treaties and in the Act of Accession (Art. 4 (1)). The new Member States are in addition required to adjust their existing international obligations and relations in a manner appropriate to their Community commitments (Arts. 5 and 4 (4)).

Articles 6 to 8 contain various saving clauses, making it clear that the Act of Accession can only be amended or repealed in the manner laid down for the revision of the original Treaties, but that the adjustments made by the Act to existing acts of the institutions of the Communities do not affect the status of those instruments in law in any way.

Article 9 provides in principle for a transitional period of five years, running from the entry into force of the accession arrangements on January 1, 1973, to the end of 1977. At the end of this period the original Treaties and all the subsidiary acts are to apply integrally in all the Member States. But it should be noted that, on specific matters, the period for which transitional arrangements are envisaged varies from the period laid down in Article 9.

Part Two—Adjustments to the Treaties (Articles 10 to 28)

2–13   Articles 10 to 28 make adaptations to the Treaties reflecting the increase in the number of Member States and a wider territorial application. Articles 10 to 23 revise the membership of the Assembly (Art. 10), the Council (Arts. 11 to 14), the Commission (Arts. 15 and 16), the Court of Justice (Arts. 17 to 20), the Economic and Social Committee (Art. 21), the ECSC Consultative Committee (Art. 22), and the Scientific and Technical Committee (Art. 23). Articles 24 to 28 make adaptations to the definitions contained in the Treaties of the territories to which they apply.

Part Three—Adaptations to Acts (Articles 29 and 30)

2–14   Articles 29 and 30 provide for technical adaptation of Community acts, consequential upon accession of the new Members; these acts relate not to the institutional structure of the Community, but to the whole range of Community activity. Annex I to the Act, referred to in Article 29, contains adaptations made by the Act itself, while Annex II, referred to in Article 30, lists the acts to be adapted later, with an indication as to the nature of the adaptation to be made.

Part Four—Transitional Measures (Articles 31 to 138)

2–15   This Part is divided into seven Titles: (1) Free Movement of Goods (Arts. 31 to 49); (2) Agriculture (Arts. 50 to 107); (3) External Relations (Arts. 108 to 116); (4) Association (Arts. 117 to 119); (5) Capital Movements (Arts. 120 to 126); (6) Financial Provisions (Arts. 127 to 132); and (7) Other Provisions (Arts. 133 to 138).

The first six Titles make provision for transition to the Community system and for consequential adaptations in the existing texts. Title VII contains miscellaneous transitional provisions, relating *inter alia* to certain ECSC matters, to safeguards and to dumping.

Part Five—Implementation of the Act (Articles 139 to 161)

2–16   Part Five, on the implementation of the Act, is divided into three Titles: Title I, " Setting up the Institutions " (Arts. 139 to 148) gives effect to the new membership provisions contained in Articles 10 to 23, and makes adjustments to various committees (Arts. 146 to 148: and see Chapter 7 on committees in general).

2–17   Under Title II, on the applicability of the acts of the institutions (Arts. 149 to 157), the new Member States are as from the date of accession assimilated to the original addressees of such of the existing binding decisions, directives and recommendations of the three Communities as were addressed to all the Member States (Art. 149). Article 149 also makes it clear that the new Member States are considered to have been notified of the acts in question, in accordance with the requirements of Articles 191 EEC* and 15 ECSC. EEC and Euratom regulations are not included in Article 149, since they are directly applicable in accordance with the terms of Article 189 EEC* and thus apply automatically in the new Member States by virtue of Article 2 of the Act of Accession, which makes acts of the institutions binding on the new Member States under conditions laid down in the original Treaties. Existing regulations are not required to be notified to the new Member States in the way that the latter are notionally notified of other existing binding acts, for regulations take effect on publication rather than upon notification.

The application of certain Community acts is deferred until dates after the date of accession (Arts. 150 and 151) but otherwise the new Member States are required to put into effect the measures necessary to enable them to comply from the date of accession with the provisions of all acts of the types referred to in Article 149 (Art. 152). The second limb of Article 152 does, however, admit of later compliance where this is provided for elsewhere in the Act of Accession or in the list in Annex X. (This provision highlights a somewhat unsatisfactory feature of the Act of Accession, for it contains various articles which annex a whole series of acts, making adaptations to them, and/or deferring their application; *cf.* Articles 29 and 30, Articles 32 (2) (*b*) and (3), and 36 and 39, Article 107, Article 133, Article 150, and Article 152 itself. This arrangement does not make for clarity or ease of use. What is really required is an index to all the instruments referred to, listing them in numerical order.)

2–18   Article 153 makes it clear that technical adaptations not effected by the Act of Accession or its Annexes can be made by the Council before accession, to enter into force on accession. Such adaptations may of course be made after accession, in the usual way that the act in question would be revised, but not so as to affect the transitional arrangements.

Article 154 represents an exception to Article 3 (3) of the Act (which makes it clear that the new Member States are in the same position as the original Member States in respect of non-binding acts) by applying to the new Member States the terms of the resolution of the Representatives of the Member States of October 20, 1971 (J.O. 1971, C 111/1, see generally, § 8–13, *post*) in suitably adapted form only as from July 1, 1973.

Article 155 requires texts of existing Community acts that are drawn up in the new official languages (as to which see *infra*) before accession to be published in the *Official Journal* if the original was published, the new texts to have equal authority with the originals.

Article 156, referring to ECSC competition questions, requires agreements coming within the scope of Article 65 ECSC to be notified to the Commission within three months of accession. The notification requirement for similar EEC matters is contained in Regulation 17/62

(J.O. 1962, 204), and thus Article 156 of the Act is mirrored in respect of the EEC by a technical adaptation to that regulation, consisting in inserting a new Article 25, containing a six-month time-limit (see Cmnd. 4862–II, p. 74).

Article 157, referring to the obligation contained in Article 33 Euratom to notify the Commission of municipal rules relating to protection of health against the danger arising from ionising radiations, requires the new Member States to effectuate a similar notification within three months of accession.

2–19   The Final Provisions (Arts. 158 to 161, Title III of Part Five of the Act) make the Annexes and Protocols and the Exchange of Letters an integral part of the Act (Art. 158) and also annex the Rome Treaties and amending treaties in authentic texts in each of the languages of the acceding States. Texts of the Paris and Rome Treaties in the original languages are to be transmitted to the acceding States in certified copy (Art. 159 and 160, first para.). It will be noted that these provisions do not *ipso facto* make the "new" languages official languages of the Community; this is achieved by a technical adaptation to Regulation 1 of 1958 (J.O. 1958, 385) determining the official languages to be used by the EEC. (See Cmnd. 4862–II, p. 134, and Regulation 857/72, J.O. 1972, L 101/1.) Of the languages of the new Member States, only Irish does not become an official language under this adaptation.

The structure of the Communities together with the controlling texts having been examined in outline, it is appropriate to turn to an analysis of the workings of the Community institutions, for an understanding of the institutional aspect of the Communities is essential to any consideration of the law and practice of the EEC.

Part 2

INSTITUTIONS OTHER THAN THE
COURT OF JUSTICE

CHAPTER 3

THE INSTITUTIONS OF THE EUROPEAN COMMUNITIES

PROVISIONS FOR INSTITUTIONS

3–01 THE Treaties of Rome provide that the tasks entrusted to the Community shall be carried out by an Assembly, a Council, a Commission and a Court of Justice, each acting within the limits of the powers conferred upon it by the relevant Treaty (Art. 4 (1) EEC, Art. 3 (1) Euratom). Article 7 of the ECSC Treaty simply states that the institutions of that Community consist of a High Authority, a common Assembly, a special Council of Ministers and a Court of Justice. Although the institutions of all three Communities are constituted on broadly similar lines, and exercise broadly similar functions, the Rome Treaties did not provide that the institutions of the ECSC should serve the EEC and Euratom equally, but chose rather to provide for separate Commissions and Councils, acting independently of each other and of the organs of the already established ECSC. Provision for an Assembly and a Court of Justice is made on a rather different basis; pursuant to the Convention on Certain Institutions Common to the European Communities, concluded simultaneously with the Rome Treaties (Cmnd. 4864, p. 144), the powers and jurisdiction conferred in the Rome Treaties on the Assembly and on the Court of Justice were to be exercised by a single Assembly and a single Court of Justice from the inception of the EEC and of Euratom (Arts. 1 and 3). Upon taking up their duties these institutions took the place of their ECSC predecessors (Arts. 2 and 4). Article 5 of the same Convention provides that the functions conferred on the Economic and Social Committee in the Rome Treaties should be exercised by a single such Committee. The Coal and Steel Community Consultative Committee was not amalgamated with the Economic and Social Committee, but continues its separate existence, under Article 18 ECSC.

3–02 The first few years of experience with three European Communities indicated that the interests of the region would be better served if not by the creation of a single Community, embracing all three existing ones (an aim adumbrated in the Preamble to the Merger Treaty, and in its Article 33), then at least in the short-term by the creation of a single Council and a single Commission for all three Communities. The Treaty establishing a single Council and a single Commission (Cmnd. 4866, commonly known as the Merger or Fusion Treaty) achieving this result, and making consequential amendments to the three original Treaties, was signed on April 8, 1965, and came into force on July 1, 1967. Since that date a single Commission has exercised the functions of the High Authority of the ECSC and of the two Commissions, and a single Council has exercised those of the three Councils of Ministers.

The Merger Treaty clearly represents a step towards the eventual merging of the three Communities. Consequential features of the merger of the Councils and Commissions are provision for a common budget (Arts. 20 *et seq.* of the Merger Treaty) and provision that officials and other servants of the three Communities should form part of a single administration of those Communities (Art. 24). In addition, new provision is made in respect of privileges and immunities of all three Communities (Article 28 of the Merger Treaty, and the annexed Protocol on the Privileges and Immunities of the European Communities).

No further progress towards setting up what would in law amount to a single European Community has been made, and the accession of new states to the Communities as they now stand has postponed, rather than accelerated, the possibility of such a development, for it will hardly be feasible to carry out a revision of the Community Treaties until the transitional provisions of the accession arrangements are spent. The provisions of those arrangements have, it is true, some effect on the institutional structure of the Communities, but only in so far as they operate to enable the new Member States to participate in the activities of the institutions of the Community.

THE NOTION OF " INSTITUTION "

3–03   It is to be noted that the relevant Article of each of the three Treaties provides for four institutions only. The better view would appear to be that the notion of Community " institution " is to be confined to those four bodies alone, and does not for example include the Economic and Social Committee. The point is not entirely free from doubt, but this view is supported by the fact that the Economic and Social Committee and the European Investment Bank are for certain purposes expressly assimilated to the institutions: *cf.* 79/70, *Müllers* v. *Economic and Social Committee,* Rec. XVII 689. The distinction between the institutions proper and the subsidiary bodies is potentially of importance, for only the institutions of the Community (and bodies assimilated thereto) may be represented before the Court of Justice pursuant to Article 17 of the Protocols to the EEC and Euratom Treaties on the Statute of the Court, and its equivalent in the ECSC Protocol, Article 20. The Court has not yet been called upon to give an express ruling on the status of bodies which might otherwise fairly be described as institutions, but it has held that clearly subsidiary bodies such as the Commission Secretariat are not institutions (see *e.g.* 66/63, *Netherlands* v. *H.A.,* Rec. X 1047, [1964] C.M.L.R. 522). Some guidance as to the attitude the Court would be likely to take if faced with a less clear-cut case is perhaps to be derived from those cases where the question of the designation of the Community defendant has been discussed; the Court has always referred to the institution appointing the official concerned as being the appropriate defendant (see *e.g.* 79 and 82/63, *Reynier* v. *Commission*, Rec. X 511).

THE RELATIONSHIP BETWEEN THE INSTITUTIONS

3–04   The Treaties setting up the Communities do not elaborate on the nature of the relationship between the institutions *inter se*, and a brief comparative analysis of the institutions is therefore necessary before going on to examine each institution individually. The institutions play broadly similar roles in each of the Communities, although the relative importance of each institution varies; this must be borne in mind in what follows.

The Council in relation to the other institutions

3–05   The Council, consisting of representatives of the Member States, constitutes the final expression of the political will of the Member States constituting the Community. Under the ECSC Treaty the scope left for political control of the running of the Community is apparently quite limited. Most of the decisions of ECSC policy require no more than the prior assent of the Council, administrative authority at least resting almost invariably with the Commission, although the Council, by its very power to withhold assent, in fact exercises considerable influence. The difference in the position of the Council under the ECSC Treaty on the one hand, and the EEC Treaty on the other, is thus not perhaps very great, the two systems having if anything grown more alike over the years. The wording of the Articles of the Euratom Treaty, defining the duties of the Council and of the Commission (Arts. 115 and 124 respectively), suggests that the position of the Council under this Treaty is similar to its position under the ECSC Treaty, but in practice the position under the Euratom Treaty is closely assimilated to that under the EEC Treaty. The Council is, under the latter, invested with the major share of political and regulatory power; and can, not wholly inaccurately, be described as the Community legislature. No new departure or important decision (with the possible exception of action on competition matters) can be taken without the agreement of the Council. Some idea of the power of the Council over the Commission is provided by the fact that the former has a large degree of control in the drawing up of the Community budget although final control here is now to be in the hands of the Assembly (Art. 203 EEC, as amended by Article 4 of the Budget Treaty, Cmnd. 4867); and to some extent over expenditure (Art. 206). The Council also has the final word in international negotiations (Arts. 111, 113, 228 and 238). The powers specified in Article 160,* enabling the Council to suspend a Commissioner and to replace him, pending an application to the Court of Justice for his compulsory retirement on grounds of misconduct or that he no longer fulfils the conditions required for the performance of his duties have been repealed by the Merger Treaty (Art. 19), and no significance is to be attached in this context to Article 152,* enabling the Council to request that proposals be made to it by the Commission; for it is not a power of coercion, but rather a provision for mutual co-operation.

The position of the Commission

3–06   If the Council is the legislature, then the Commission is the executive of the Communities. Under the ECSC Treaty it has very wide powers, and is not only able to propose policy, but to promote it as well. It is subject to relatively limited control by the Council in its activities, and its independence is guaranteed. The Commission's powers under the EEC Treaty (and under the Euratom Treaty) are materially narrower than those that it enjoys under the ECSC Treaty. Its own power of decision is limited in the main to executive matters. There is no doubt, however, that the Commission is the motor of the EEC and of Euratom, in that virtually all important decisions taken by the Council must be on the basis of proposals made by the Commission.

The Assembly (European Parliament)

3–07   The Assembly, now officially called the European Parliament, pursuant to its own resolution, is not a parliament in the true sense of the term, in that it possesses no direct legislative powers. It must, however, be consulted on certain matters, and in practice the Commission refers to it the vast majority of its proposals of any importance where these are made public. It is to this body alone that the Commission is responsible (Art. 144 EEC*).

The Court of Justice of the European Communities

3–08   The Court of Justice can most nearly be compared to a municipal administrative court; indeed its practice and powers are closely modelled upon those of the French Conseil d'Etat. It has jurisdiction in relation to matters concerning individuals, the institutions and the Member States. In an institutional context it is relevant to note that it has jurisdiction to rule upon the *vires* of the acts of the institutions of the Communities, and it can compulsorily retire members of the Commission.

THE INSTITUTION ANALYSED

3–09   The discussion in the following Chapters is devoted to an examination of the Commission, the Council and the European Parliament in turn. This is followed by an examination of the various other organs of the

Communities. Chapter 8 discusses provisions common to the institutions, and is primarily devoted to the power of decision of the institutions. The Court of Justice is discussed in Chapters 9 *et seq.*

CHAPTER 4

THE COMMISSION

THE FUNCTIONS OF THE COMMISSION

4–01 THE Commission of the European Communities combines the role of initiator of action with that of an executive. In this its functions do not differ from those of a national central administration, acting with the Government of the day, but the Commission is exceptional, in that it acts as a proposer of policy not simply as a matter of practice, but in the execution of its prescribed duties. The duties of the Commission under the EEC Treaty are set out in Article 155, and under the Euratom Treaty in Article 124. In order to ensure the proper functioning and development of the common market and of nuclear energy the Commission is, in virtue of these Articles, which are, *mutatis mutandis*, in identical terms:

> (a) to ensure that the provisions of the Treaties and the measures taken by the institutions pursuant thereto are applied;
>
> (b) to formulate recommendations or deliver opinions on matters dealt with in the Treaties, if they expressly so provide or if the Commission considers it necessary;
>
> (c) to have its own power of decision and to participate in the shaping of measures taken by the Council and by the Assembly in the manner provided for in the Treaties;
>
> (d) to exercise the powers conferred on it by the Council for the implementation of the rules laid down by the latter.

Each point will be taken in turn.

(a) The Commission as watch-dog of the Treaties

4–02 The function of the Commission as watch-dog of the application of the Treaties divides into two distinct parts: detection of breaches of the Treaties and remedial action.

So far as detection is concerned, Member States are under a general duty to facilitate the achievement of the Community's tasks (Arts. 5 EEC, 192 Euratom, and *cf.* Art. 86 ECSC). In addition a number of Articles impose specific obligations to give information of one kind or another (*e.g.* Arts. 14 (6), 15 (1), 31, 72, 73 (2), 93 (3), 109 (2), 111 (5) and 115 EEC). Various items of Community secondary legislation also call for the supply of information of all kinds (see *e.g.* Reg. 17/62). A Member State cannot, however, be obliged to supply information the disclosure of which it considers contrary to the essential interests of its security (Art. 223 (1) (*a*)).

On a general level, Article 213 EEC (187 Euratom) empowers the Commission to collect any information and to carry out any checks required for the performance of the tasks entrusted to it, subject to limits and conditions laid down by the Council in accordance with the provisions of the Treaties. No general rules have as yet been laid down, but the Article has been used as the legal basis for statistical exercises and the like (*e.g.* Dir. 64/475, J.O. 1964, 2193). Specific powers of control are contained in Articles 79 and 89 EEC, relating respectively to transport and competition. Otherwise, some check on fraud is provided by rules on origin of goods, designed to ensure that Community rules on free circulation are not evaded. Additionally, a certification system designed to combat fraud is associated with agricultural support measures. This still did not, according to press reports, prevent enterprising traders selling the Vatican improbable quantities of butter. (See Written Question 18/71, J.O. 1971, C 47/3, and *cf.* Question 357/70, J.O. 1970, C 22/1.)

Matters may also come to the attention of the Commission through complaints from Member States, by way of written question from the European Parliament (as provided for in Article 140 EEC,* Article 20 ECSC) and by way of complaints of individuals—whether informal or under specific provisions—*e.g.* complaints procedure under Article 3 (2) of Regulation 17/62 (competition). This would not appear to exhaust the matter; the attention of the Commission was initially drawn to the celebrated Quinine Cartel by the activities of the U.S. Department of Justice anti-trust division (see cases 41, 44 and 45/69).

4-03   Where an individual has committed a breach of a Treaty provision, it will usually be a Member State which will take steps to punish the offender, but the Commission itself has certain powers to punish breaches, notably under Regulation 17/62 (competition) and Regulation 11/60 (transport). These powers have not been widely used. The Euratom Treaty itself contains provisions for sanctions in Articles 83 and 145.

In case of a breach of a Treaty provision by a Member State, the Commission was originally able to take direct action, notably under Article 97 EEC and (possibly) Article 89 (2) EEC, but these provisions are now spent for all practical purposes.

The usual procedure by which the Commission takes action against a Member State is contained in Article 169,* providing for the issue of a reasoned opinion on the matter; in the event of non-compliance, the matter can be brought before the Court of Justice (see further, Chap. 11). Often, however, threat of proceedings will have the desired effect, or else the action may be dropped at the opinion stage or even later. (See Fourth General Report, p. 404, and Fifth General Report, p. 440. Of the seventy or so cases which got as far as the issue of an opinion between 1958 and 1971, only about twenty cases went to the Court.)

Responsibility for the preparation of "infraction dossiers" lies with the legal service of the Commission, the same service also dealing with the preparation of cases for the Court of Justice, and generally taking the case before the Court itself.

(b) The Commission as guide of national, and therefore of Community action through the power of recommendation

4-04   Article 155 EEC, second hyphen, enables the Commission to formulate recommendations or to deliver opinions if the Treaty expressly so provides, or if the Commission considers it necessary. In so far as Article 189 * confers on the Commission the facility to make recommendations or deliver opinions in accordance with the provisions of the Treaty, the first limb of Article 155, second hyphen, duplicates that facility.

A number of substantive Articles (notably Arts. 14, 15, 27, 35, 37, 64, 71, 72, 81, 91, 102, 111 and 118) provide for recommendations or opinions. The real interest of the relevant sub-paragraph of Article 155, however, lies in the fact that the recommendatory power conferred shall be exercisable where "the Commission considers it necessary." In so far as this power is general, it contributes to the influence the Commission may exercise in the direction of integration, despite the fact that it is not a provision for the issue of binding acts. In practice its greatest utility probably lies in the fact that it enables the Commission to prepare the ground for the promulgation of a binding act by way of preliminary recommendation or opinion, whether under a substantive provision of the Treaty, or under Article 235 (the residual decision-making power). The power in effect provides a diplomatic way of making proposals where a formal proposal would be inappropriate, or where a formal power is not provided in the Treaty.

(c) The Commission as decision-maker and as participant in the shaping of measures taken by the Council and by the Assembly

1. The Commission as decision-maker

4-05   Under Article 189 * the Commission is to make Regulations, issue Directives, take Decisions, make recommendations or deliver opinions in order to carry out its task. On the face of Article 189 * the Council has a coextensive facility to issue such acts. (The nature of these acts is considered *infra*, § 8–01.) In reality, however, the power of the Commission is much narrower than that of the Council. The competence of the Commission (and indeed of the Council) is one of attribution (see *e.g.* 12/63, *Schlieker* v. *H.A.*, Rec. IX 173, [1963] C.M.L.R. 281, and 44/65, *Hessische Knappschaft* v. *Singer*, Rec. XI 1191, [1966] C.M.L.R. 82), and the Commission may issue one of the binding acts referred to in Article 189 * only where a substantive Article of the Treaty confers upon it the power so to do. This state of affairs is implicitly recognised by Article 189 * itself, referring to the issue of the types of acts mentioned " in accordance with the provisions of this Treaty."

The distinction between the "power of decision" referred to in Article 155, and the power to "take decisions," conferred by Article 189 * is quite clear-cut; the former expression describes the power to issue any of the types of acts listed in Article 189 *; it amounts to a power to take action of any kind. A decision *stricto sensu* is a particular kind of act (see further, § 8–11, *infra*).

2. The Commission as participant in the shaping of measures

4-06   The reference in Article 155 to the Commission participating in the shaping of measures requires some clarification. The measures referred to are acts of the Council and of the Assembly. In the nature of things the most important part of this work relates to the decision-making power *sensu lato* of the Council, exercised in accordance with the substantive provisions of the Treaty. In the vast majority of cases Decisions thus provided for are required to be taken on the basis of proposals of the Commission; the Commission can thus be described as the initiator of the Community decision-making process, and therefore as the motor of Community action. The power in question is not simply a legislative initiative, since under Article 149 * the Council cannot, where it is required to act on a proposal of the Commission, amend that proposal except by unanimous agreement; the Commission on the other hand can, if the Council has yet to act, alter its original proposal, in particular where the Assembly has been consulted on that proposal (Art. 149,* second para.).

In the formulation of its proposals, the Commission is not to be taken as acting *in vacuo*; Article 15 of the Merger Treaty (replacing Art. 162 EEC *; *cf.* Art. 26 ECSC) requires mutual consultation between Council and Commission, and also the working out of methods of co-operation on the basis of a common accord. Despite the resolution on the point, contained in the Luxembourg Accords of January 31, 1966 (Bulletin 3, 1966, p. 5) no formal arrangement has emerged, although, of course, *de facto* forms of co-operation exist. Co-operation is also aimed at by Article 152,* enabling the Council to request the Commission to undertake studies or to submit proposals. This does not impinge on the Commission's powers; rather it provides for a two-way flow of ideas.

4-07   The members of the Commission are required to be selected so as to ensure that they will fulfil their functions in full independence and will not be influenced by partisan views in the formulation of Community policies, relatively secure tenure of office itself apparently ensuring a continuity of policy line in their proposals to the Council. (It is true that the Commissioners are appointed only for four years at a time, but provision is made for renewal of term, and renewal is the rule rather than the exception.) In the formulation of its proposals the Commission may be conceived of as having the role of honest broker. The Accords of Luxembourg (*supra*) opined that consultation with the Governments of the Member States through their permanent representatives was desirable before the adoption of proposals of special importance. Practice, however, goes considerably beyond this, in that the Commission in fact has contacts with national administrations direct.

In addition, the Commission is obliged in a limited number of cases to refer to consultative bodies in the formulation of its proposals. Thus Article 107 requires consultation of the Monetary Committee set up by Article 105, and Article 118 requires consultation of the Economic and Social Committee.

4–08   In practice the European Parliament is at least kept fully informed of all important Community proposals, whether or not it is officially consulted. The information processes are freer and wider ranging than formal consultations, and indeed if such formal consultations were demanded on all occasions this would constitute a curtailment of the powers of the Commission and the Council. The Parliament asked for prior consultations on Commission proposals as a general rule in the early 1960s, but the Commission resisted such a move, as derogating from its autonomy and authority.

Apart from consultations with bodies set up by the Treaties, the Commission is advised by various committees of experts on specific topics; their views are not necessarily binding on it. (See notably " Management Committee procedure " described at § 22–08.)

4–09   *Where no proposal power is provided.* In relation to certain matters the Commission has no formal power of proposal, but has power to intervene in the decision-making process in some other way. Article 8 (3) required a report from the Commission, Article 109 (3) requires a Commission opinion, Article 113 (3) requires recommendations of the Commission, Article 195 (2) requires consultation of the Commission, Article 203 (4), second sub-para., required discussion with the Commission, and Article 212 requires the co-operation of the Commission.

Still other provisions enable the Council to act without any intervention at all from the Commission, *e.g.* Article 28, first sentence.

4–10   *Other proposals.* Even in the absence of formal powers the Commission may suggest to the Council that it is opportune to take action. This may be done informally or on the basis of recommendations or opinions under Article 155, second hyphen, second limb.

More formally the Commission may make proposals under Article 235 (Article 203 Euratom—Article 95 of the ECSC requires the unanimous assent of the Council to the proposed action by the High Authority), which enables the Council to take appropriate measures if action by the Community should prove necessary to attain, in the course of the operation of the common market, one of the objectives of the Community, and the Treaty has not provided the necessary powers. This Article is now frequently used by the Community, in particular where new policies are being mapped out.

Otherwise the Commission is, on its own admission (see reply to Written Question 140/64, J.O. 1964, 898), closely associated with the preparation and elaboration of the Decisions of the Representatives of the Member States meeting in Council and similar acts (see generally *infra*, § 8–13).

4–11   *Other powers of communication with the Council.* The specific provisions discussed above do not exhaust the possibilities of contact with the Council. Apart from informal contacts, the Commission *inter alia* addresses communications, memoranda and reports to the Council. These have no official status as part of the decision-making process, but are nevertheless a significant part of that process, in that they express the Commission's thinking and describe Commission action in various fields.

(d) The Commission as agent of execution of the Treaty

4–12   The Commission's executive functions fall into two parts: it has powers conferred directly by the Treaties, and also by the Council for the execution of decisions of the Council.

Execution of Council Decisions

4–13   The power specified in Article 155 (Art. 124 Euratom, fourth hyphen), enabling the Commission to exercise the powers conferred on it by the Council for the implementation of the rules laid down by the latter, is the only provision for delegation by the Council contained in the Treaties themselves. In principle it is the Council which must ensure that the objectives of the Treaty are attained and to this end it has a power to take decisions (Art. 145 EEC). In practice, however, the Council has no means of executing the details of its decisions, and does not set up the machinery for their implementation. These two tasks are generally left to the Commission. In a number of areas the Commission acts on its own initiative, albeit generally within Council guidelines; *e.g.* setting agricultural levies under market organisation regulations (*e.g.* Reg. 120/67, Art. 13 (5), J.O. 1967, 2269 (cereals)).

Other provisions require the Commission to act in liaison with the national authorities (*e.g.* Directive of October 23, 1962, Art. 11 (2), J.O. 1962, 2645 (food standards)).

Yet other provisions require the Commission to seek the opinion of a committee (*e.g.* Reg. 17/62, J.O. 1962, 204; committee on agreements and dominant positions).

A very common procedure is the so-called management committee procedure (discussed *infra*, § 22–08. See *e.g.* Reg. 120/67, *supra*, Art. 26).

Most agricultural market organisation regulations provide for action by the Commission on the basis of a request of a Member State in connection with safeguard clauses (*e.g.* Art. 20, Reg. 120/67, *supra*). The Commission decides upon the necessary measures at the request of the Member States where imports or exports in one or more of the products covered by the market organisation cause or threaten to cause a serious disturbance which may endanger the objectives set out in Article 39 of the EEC Treaty. A Member State affected by the measures decided upon by the Commission (which are immediately applicable) may refer them to the Council within three working days following the day on which the measures are communicated. The Council may amend or repeal them.

The Commission acts with the agreement of the interested Member States in certain cases, as in the establishment of the list of frontier communes provided for in Regulation 3/64, Article 3, J.O. 1964, 50.

Execution of the Treaty pursuant to powers conferred by the Treaty

4–14   The chief powers of execution conferred on the Commission by the Treaty are contained in Chapter 1 of Title I of Part II, on the establishment of the customs union, and in Chapter 1 of Title I of Part III, on competition. Other provisions in the Treaty are of a less general nature. Particular responsibilities are, however, conferred on the Commission in its role as watch-dog of the application of the Treaty, and for receiving information for various purposes. In addition the Commission has a largely exclusive control over Community finance and over the application of safeguard provisions. Systematic description of the powers of execution of the Commission serves no particular purpose except to establish that they exist. Discussion of these powers is accordingly to be found in the context of the relevant Community activity.

THE COMMISSION UNDER THE ECSC TREATY

4–15 The Commission of the European Communities, which, by Article 9 of the Merger Treaty (Cmnd. 4866) took the place of the High Authority of the European Coal and Steel Community, and which now exercises the powers and jurisdiction conferred on that institution by the ECSC Treaty, fulfils in relation to the Coal and Steel Community the same role that it fulfils in respect of the Rome Treaties, but its duties are expressed rather differently; it is the High Authority (*i.e.* now the Commission) whose primary duty it is to ensure that the objectives of the Treaty are attained in accordance with the provisions thereof (Art. 8 ECSC), whereas it is the Council that has this duty under Article 145 EEC, 115 Euratom. This in itself indicates that the High Authority was intended to play a leading role in the ECSC, and indeed it was provided with much broader powers of execution than were the Commissions under the Rome Treaties, and it enjoys much wider residual powers. The attribution of such greater general powers to the High

Authority than to the Commissions is accounted for by the fact that the ECSC has relatively limited, and therefore well defined, objectives, and that the ECSC Treaty is much more detailed than are the Rome Treaties in setting out the powers and duties of the institutions. The position of the ECSC executive in the day-to-day running of the Community is thus much stronger than that of the Commissions under the Rome Treaties, and since most decisions taken under the ECSC Treaty are taken by the Commission, and not by the Council (although many are taken with the assent of the Council), this strength is apparently reinforced (see § 5–10). True, the powers of the High Authority are, as under the other two Treaties, only powers of attribution, but the Court of Justice has held that the High Authority nevertheless enjoys a certain autonomy in relation to deciding on measures of execution called for in order to realise the objectives of the Treaty (8/55, *Fédéchar* v. *H.A.,* Rec. II 199; see further, § 5–11).

4-16   The discussion above of the powers of the Commission centred upon the terms of Article 155 of the EEC Treaty (Art. 124 Euratom); the ECSC Treaty contains no directly comparable clause, but within the sphere of operations of the ECSC the High Authority fulfils much the same roles of watch-dog, adviser and honest broker, and initiator, of legislation, subject to the limitation, contained in Article 5 ECSC, that the task of the Community is to be carried out with a limited measure of intervention. Such a limitation is comprehensible in a Treaty setting up a Community with limited objectives. With these reservations, then, this discussion applies generally to the role of the Commission under the ECSC Treaty. The similarities in the institutional structure (discussed below) are even greater.

Whether, on the general level, the Commission is a more independent body under the ECSC Treaty than it is under the Rome Treaties is a moot question. The difference is probably more apparent than real (see § 5–10).

COMPOSITION OF THE COMMISSION

4-17 Article 157 (1) of the EEC Treaty as originally formulated provided for a Commission of nine members, to be chosen on the grounds of their general competence and whose independence is beyond doubt (Art. 9 ECSC is to similar effect). Article 126 (1) of the Euratom Treaty provided for a five-member Commission to be chosen on a similar basis, having regard to the objectives of that Treaty. On the merger of the executives as from July 1, 1967, provision was made initially for fourteen Commissioners, this number to be reduced to nine within three years (Art. 32, together with Art. 10 of the Merger Treaty). The operative provision of the Merger Treaty, Article 10 (1), itself amended by Article 15 of the Act of Accession, provides for a Commission of fourteen as from the accession of the new Member States. No Member State may appoint more than two Commissioners, and all appointees must be nationals of Member States (Art. 157 EEC, Art. 126 Euratom and Art. 9 ECSC, replaced by Art. 10 of the Merger Treaty). In practice the four largest States of the Community will have two Commissioners each, and the others one each.

The device of a small number of Commissioners "acting by a majority of the number of members provided for in Article 10" of the Merger Treaty (Art. 17) was felt to have considerable advantages, further reinforced by the secrecy in which Commission decisions are taken. The Commission is able to present a united front to the outside and takes collective responsibility for its acts. Internal consultation between Commissioners is considered to have worked well. Some doubts are expressed as to whether the same smooth working will be possible with a larger number of Commissioners, provided for by the Act of Accession. No real difficulties appear to have developed during the previous period (1967-70) during which there were fourteen Commissioners, however.

4-18   Commission members are nominated by common accord of the Governments of the Member States under Article 158 EEC * (Art. 10 ECSC was a little different) now replaced by Article 11 of the Merger Treaty. In practice the usual procedure is for members to be appointed by accord of the Representatives of the Member States meeting in Council (appointment by the Council itself would suggest dependence on that body). In general Member States do not oppose the candidates of other Member States, but a certain amount of mutual consultation takes place before final nominations are made.

The terms of office of members of the Commission are not staggered in the same way, for example, as those of members of the U.S. Senate (the only exception to this being the pre-merger provisions of Article 10 ECSC) but rather the mandate of the Commission as a whole is for four years, and is renewable. Vacancies caused by resignation, compulsory retirement or death are filled for the remainder of the mandate unless the Council decides, unanimously, to leave the post vacant until the end of the mandate (Art. 159 EEC,* replaced by Art. 12 of the Merger Treaty).

Provision is made for the appointment of a President and Vice-Presidents of the Commission, the current provision being Article 14 of the Merger Treaty, amended by Article 16 of the Act of Accession, providing for one President and five Vice-Presidents, to be appointed from among the members of the Commission for a renewable term of two years in accordance with the same procedure as that laid down for the appointment of members of the Commission. Save where the entire Commission is replaced, such appointments are required to be made after consultation of the Commission. This consultation has limited scope, however, in that the person selected has already been appointed a Commissioner.

Position of the Commission

4–19   The key provision relating to the status of the Commission is Article 10 (2) of the Merger Treaty (replacing Art. 157 (2) EEC, Art. 126 (2) Euratom, and Art. 9 ECSC), which provides that the members of the Commission shall, in the general interest of the Community, be completely independent in the performance of their duties. The independence of the Commission is reinforced by the injunction to the members in the same article neither to seek nor take instructions from any Government or from any other body. They are to refrain from any action incompatible with their duties (the ECSC Treaty, Art. 9, described these duties as having a supranational character). Each Member State undertakes to respect these principles and not to seek to influence the members of the Commission in the performance of their tasks. The Commissioners for their part further undertake (Art. 10 (2), third sub-para., of the Merger Treaty) not to engage during their term of office in any other occupation (the French is more specific here; the term used is *activités professionelles*), whether gainful or not. The interpretation of " occupation " is not altogether without difficulty. Teaching work is not, apparently, considered to be excluded. Acceptance of a parliamentary seat would be considered to be incompatible, but perhaps not the act of taking part in an election campaign. Signor Malfatti (President of the Commission from 1970 to 1972) nevertheless resigned before the start of the Italian election campaign of 1972. Retention of political interests, and even of a seat in local government is apparently acceptable. By the same paragraph the Commissioners are required to give a solemn undertaking to respect the obligations arising from their duties and to behave with integrity and discretion as regards the acceptance of certain appointments or benefits after they have ceased to hold office. The Court of Justice can punish breaches of this undertaking, either by making an order for compulsory retirement under Article 13 of the Merger Treaty or by stopping pension rights, etc. Article 13 of the Merger Treaty (replacing Art. 160 EEC,* Art. 12 ECSC) provides for compulsory retirement on application by the Council or the Commission where any member of the Commission no longer fulfills the conditions required for the performance of his duties, or has been guilty of serious misconduct.

4–20   It is certain that none of the restraints placed upon members of the Commission can deny them the right to promote the European idea or the general right of comment. An attempt was made on at least one occasion to restrain the Commission in its criticisms of national policy, but the Council came to recognise that it could not legitimately take any action in the matter.

Individual compulsory retirement aside, the Assembly may pass a motion of censure on the Commission as a whole. If this be carried on a two-thirds majority of members, the Commission resigns as a body,

33

remaining in office only to complete current business (Art. 144 EEC,*
Art. 24 ECSC). This provision is to be contrasted with Article 12,
third para., of the Merger Treaty which provides that save in the case of
compulsory retirement under the provisions of Article 13, members of
the Commission shall remain in office until they have been replaced.
Article 12 therefore covers the case of end of mandate as well as
individual retirement.

Salaries, privileges, etc.

4-21   The salaries, allowances and pensions of the President and members
of the Commission are fixed by the Council acting by qualified majority
(Art. 6 of the Merger Treaty, replacing Art. 154 EEC,* Art. 29 ECSC).
The Commissioners enjoy the privileges and immunities specified in the
Protocol on Privileges and Immunities (see Chap. 36).

Internal organisation of the Commission

4-22   By virtue of Article 16 of the Merger Treaty (replacing Art. 162
EEC,* second para., and Art. 13 ECSC, second para.) the Commission
adopts its own Rules of Procedure so as to ensure that both it and its
departments operate in accordance with the provisions of the Treaty.
The rules are published in the *Official Journal* (J.O. 1963, 181 and J.O.
1967, 147/1). Salient points are majority decision-making, and the facts
that discussions and meetings are held *in camera.*

Decisions are often not in fact discussed by the Commissioners face
to face, a written procedure playing an important role here. Proposals
of any single Commissioner are circulated, and are deemed adopted
unless objection is lodged within a week (Art. 11 of the Rules of Procedure). For purely administrative matters the President and Vice-
Presidents have the control of current business. Here too a written
procedure is much used.

These methods of decision-making are not generally considered to
amount to delegation of responsibility, but delegation of responsibility
is made to individual Commissioners (with the possibility of sub-
delegation in some cases) in certain relatively limited areas (Arts. 24
to 27 of the Rules). The Commission may not effect a complete delegation of its responsibilities (66/63, *Netherlands* v. *H.A.*, Rec. X 1047,
[1964] C.M.L.R. 522). There can never be a delegation of more than
predetermined and controlled executive powers (*cf.* 9 & 10/56, *Meroni*
v. *H.A.*, Rec. IV 9 and 51).

This is not the place to discuss the position of the Secretariat of
the Commission, but it goes without saying that the prohibition on
delegation of responsibilities does not prevent the Commission from
entrusting the task of preparation of action to its own staff. In practice
each Commissioner has responsibility for groups of departments, and
its officials are responsible to him.

Chapter 5

THE COUNCIL

5–01   The merger of the Councils of the European Communities was in some sense a less radical departure than the merger of the Commissions and the High Authority. The Councils had always tended to have rather similar methods of operation, and had from the inception of the EEC and Euratom shared a single Secretariat. Although, therefore, merger meant, as it did for the Commissions, a changeover to a single system, effectively that of the EEC, where three systems had existed previously, the changeover was more one of form than of substance for the Council.

The Council consists of representatives of the Member States. It acts not merely as a group of representatives of Member States, however; its mission is to ensure that the objectives of the Treaty are attained (Art. 145 EEC) and in fact the Council can be said to work in two distinct ways; on the one hand, it acts as the representative of Community interests, and on the other, it brings together national interests. It follows that it further acts as a forum for the confrontation of national and Community interests and ideas.

5–02   The individuals who attend meetings of the Council are generally ministers. The Treaty provides that each Government shall delegate to the Council " one of its members," but the Treaty does not define the latter phrase. It is accepted in practice that representation is not confined to *e.g.* cabinet ministers, but will include *secretaires d'état* with political responsibility. In terms of British practice a Permanent Under-Secretary would probably be excluded, but a Minister of State or a Parliamentary Under-Secretary would be considered eligible to attend meetings of the Council discussing matters falling within his field of activity. It is also permissible to send a non-voting alternate, in which case the member of the Council absenting himself may depute another member to vote on his behalf (Art. 150 EEC *). A proxy may vote on behalf of one absentee only (same Article).

The individual sent to any particular meeting of the Council may vary with the subject-matter of the meeting; thus ministers of agriculture will go to meetings on the Common Agricultural Policy, transport ministers to meetings on the Common Transport Policy, and so forth. It is also possible to arrange Council meetings at which the Member States are represented jointly by, for example, ministers of agriculture and ministers of finance; this would be appropriate where matters concerning the financing of the CAP are under discussion. The foreign ministers, apart from attending meetings on external relations, generally attend sessions on the directions of Community policy in general, being naturally the ministers with the main national responsibility for the European Communities. It has been suggested that there should be ministers for Europe, who would deal with all aspects of national policy at the Community level.

5-03   Meetings of the Council are presided over by a President. Under Article 11 of the Act of Accession, which amends Article 2 of the Merger Treaty, the office of President is to be held for a term of six months by each member of the Council in turn; the order in which this is to take place is the " absolute " alphabetical order of States, that is to say, the order that they would be listed, were the name of each State written in the national language or languages; thus, Belgique-België, Danmark, Deutschland, and so on. The President is frequently relieved of the duty of representing the viewpoint of his own State, so as to be enabled to devote himself to the tasks of co-ordination of viewpoint, but it is recognised that whether or not he is so relieved, the incumbent of the office can be relied upon, in greater or lesser degree, to defend and express the Community point of view rather than the purely national one, particularly in contacts with third countries. This has greatly reinforced the institutional identity of the Council.

Internal functioning of the Council

5-04   The Council meets when convened by its President, or at the request of one of its members, or of the Commission (Art. 3, Merger Treaty). There is no exact calendar for these meetings, but there is generally at least one meeting each month.

The meetings of the Council are, in the terms of the Council's own Rules of Procedure,[1] held *in camera* (Art. 3) but the rule is not an absolute one. In the first place, the Council may decide otherwise by unanimous vote. Secondly, the Commission is, again subject to contrary decision, invited to attend. Thirdly, the members of the Council and of the Commission may bring officials with them, to assist them in their work, provided the Council so decides by unanimous vote. As a matter of practice such officials are usually admitted to Council meetings, but there is a tendency for the numbers attending to burgeon. Periodic attempts have been made to reduce the numbers to the minimum commensurate with the smooth running of the sessions.

5-05   The course of business follows an agenda drawn up in accordance with the Rules of Procedure (Art. 2) by the President and fixed by the Council. The voting procedure depends in theory on the type of

---

[1] There is no officially published version of the Council Rules of Procedure, but the provisions at present operative are those set out for the EEC and Euratom Councils in Houben, *Les Conseils de Ministres des Communautés Européennes* at p. 227. See also *Dictionnaire du Marché Commun.*

instrument to be voted upon, and the majority stipulated in the governing primary source of law. As stated in Article 148 (1) EEC,* the normal rule is that the Council should act by simple majority, but special majorities are in fact more frequently required than not. Thus certain Articles of the Treaties require the Council to reach a decision by a qualified majority, others by a unanimous vote.

The authors of the Treaty clearly intended that unanimity should be the rule at first, but that more " European " voting majorities should be used later in the development of the Communities. Thus quite a number of Articles provide initially for unanimity, and for *e.g.* qualified majority subsequently. It is in keeping with this aim that there should be no rule preventing members from abstaining. In some circumstances abstention will, however, block the adoption of acts requiring unanimity under the ECSC Treaty (*cf*. Art. 8, Merger Treaty).

Article 148 EEC * as amended by Article 14 of the Act of Accession sets out the procedure for voting by qualified majority, which really amounts to a weighting of votes, giving the greatest *appui* to the largest States—France, Germany, Italy and the United Kingdom all being on an equal footing in this respect.

Where acts of the Council are required to be adopted by a qualified majority on a proposal from the Commission, forty-three votes in favour are required (Art. 14, Act of Accession). On this basis, the measure can be carried by a minimum of five States. Where the act in question is required to be carried by qualified majority other than on proposal from the Commission at least six States are required to concur. Article 28 ECSC as amended by Article 7 of the Merger Treaty and by Article 12 of the Act of Accession, achieves similar result, but the weighting is in terms of value of coal and steel output. The purpose of these formal requirements, quite apart from the obvious purpose of preventing States losing sight of reality, is to ensure that the will of the larger States shall not prevail over that of the smaller States, and vice versa.

5–06 The formal position as regards voting in the Council is as set out above. The question arises how far the voting procedures of the Council were affected by the so-called Accords of Luxembourg, and how far the formal position reflects the reality.

The Accords of Luxembourg (Bulletin 3, 1966, p. 5) constitute the political settlement which terminated the crisis in the Communities of 1965. The work of the Communities came to a virtually complete standstill for a period of months during which the French absented themselves from the Council. Part of the " price " for the return of the French was the Luxembourg Communiqué, known as the Accords of Luxembourg, dealing with many of the complaints of the French about the running of the Communities. " Accord " is something of a misnomer; to some extent the communiqué amounts to an agreement to disagree.

One of the matters on which the French delegation pressed for a statement related to the Council voting procedures. The statement of the Council as a whole was to the effect that:

> "where, in the case of decisions which may be taken by majority vote on a proposal of the Commission, very important interests of one or more partners are at stake, the Members of the Council will endeavour, within a reasonable time, to reach solutions which can be adopted by all the Members of the Council while respecting their mutual interests and those of the Community, in accordance with Article 2 of the Treaty."

To this the French delegation added a rider to the effect that it considered that:

> "where very important interests are at stake the discussion must be continued until unanimous agreement is reached."

The six delegations as a group noted that there was a divergence of views on what should be done in the event of a failure to reach complete agreement.

5–07　　　It is generally accepted that the Accords have no force in law. The British Government has attached some importance to the Accords, but this is in recognition of their political reality rather than of their binding force. It must in any case be noted that the Council rarely in fact votes on a proposal, decisions in effect being taken by consensus. Where matters coming before the Council are controversial, and are not likely to meet with general acceptance, it is the practice to remit the issue to the Committee of Permanent Representatives or to a special working group to try to work out a solution which will be acceptable to all. It is only when the issue is ripe for decision that the Council will take a formal decision.

In order to expedite the discussion of matters before it, the Council resorts to two principal devices:

1. a division of the agenda into " A " and " B " points; and
2. the use of a written procedure.

Under the system of dividing the agenda into " A " and " B " points, the items submitted as " A " points are the points upon which the delegations of the Member States have already reached agreement in principle. At the political level of the Council very little remains to be done in relation to these matters except to approve the action proposed. If any difficulties arise, discussion is postponed. " B " points are the points presented to the Council on which an attempt to reach agreement is to be made in discussion at the Council meeting itself. These form the substantive part of the discussions.

The written procedure is generally reserved for matters which are urgent, and which require a simple affirmative (*cf*. Art. 6 of the Rules of Procedure).

5–08   As has already been indicated in the discussion of the Commission (§ 4–06, *supra*) the vast majority of Council decisions require, under the Rome Treaties, to be taken on the basis of Commission proposals. The Commission thus exercises a decisive influence over the subject-matter of Council discussions, except where the Council is empowered to act on its own initiative. Although it can request that proposals be submitted to it (Art. 152 EEC *) the Council cannot amend a Commission proposal except by unanimous vote (Art. 149 *), a circumstance which theoretically makes it easier to adopt a proposal than to amend it. On the other hand, the Commission may alter its original proposal as long as the Council has not acted, in particular where the Assembly has been consulted on that proposal (Article 149 * : *i.e.* where the Assembly has suggested acceptable and desirable amendments). This provision is double-edged, in that it enables the Commission to keep improving its proposals, but it also enables it to act as a conciliatory body, mediating between national positions. This latter role was at the fore-front in the adoption of the package of agricultural reform proposals in March and April 1972.

The arrangements under the ECSC Treaty are rather different, in that it is in general the Commission (High Authority) which takes the decision, but there are many circumstances in which the Council must first approve the Commission's proposal. There is much to be said for the argument that the difference between prior approval (or disapproval) and decision-making by the Council is more apparent than real (*cf.* § 4–15, *supra* and see *infra*).

Apart from the proposal and approved mechanisms, there are, as already mentioned, various provisions in all three Treaties authorising action by the Council of its own motion. These represent the exception rather than the rule, and in no case do they relate to major questions of Community policy-making, but relate primarily to national policy and politics (see *e.g.* Arts. 84 (2), 136 and 217).

5–09   Clearly, when a proposal comes before the Council a vast amount of work has to be done behind the scenes to reconcile points of view, and at least part of this work is done by the Commission, but the Commission is not in reality the body best adapted to reconciling national positions if it is to retain its position of independence. It is through Council machinery, therefore, that the task of attempting to arrive at a consensus amongst the Member States is undertaken before the Council itself votes upon the proposal. The body which in fact carries out the preparatory work is the Committee of Permanent Representatives of the Member States (see § 7–01, *infra*). In addition, the Council is assisted by various committees and working groups, whether set up under specific Articles of the Treaties, or otherwise, and of course by a Secretariat General, which initially served the ECSC special Council of Ministers, and was then expanded to serve the other two Councils. This body carries out the technical back-up work for the Council.

At least some assistance to the decision-making process should derive from the provision for mutual consultation under Article 15 of the Merger Treaty, but no institutionalised arrangement has as yet emerged. The consultation provided for under Article 26, second para., of the ECSC Treaty is, however, quite similar on its face, and many of the plans which fall within the autonomous powers of the High Authority are submitted to the Council under this provision through the Committee of Permanent Representatives, so that its eventual decision will reflect the general consensus of views. This type of consultation, which certainly does not amount to an abnegation of existing High Authority powers (for the submission is to discussion, and not to decision or approval), does not differ materially in kind from that existing in fact within the ambit of the Rome Treaties between the Commission and the Committee of Permanent Representatives.

Powers of the Council

5-10   As has already been explained, the powers of the Council under the ECSC Treaty on the one hand, and the EEC and Euratom Treaties on the other, are dissimilar, in that the Council ostensibly plays a secondary role to the High Authority under the ECSC Treaty, while it is the dominant body under the Rome Treaties.

Under the EEC and Euratom Treaties (Arts. 145 and 115 respectively) the Council is entrusted with tasks of co-ordination and with powers of decision. Under the ECSC Treaty it possesses similar responsibilities and powers (Arts. 26 and 28) with the difference that it in general agrees with Commission proposals, rather than decides on them. Nevertheless, the High Authority has a large measure of independence, and the real limitation on this independence is not the veto of the Council, but the fact that, as must inevitably be the case in a Community with limited aims, the Member States have considerable concurrent powers.

5-11   The powers of the Council under the Rome Treaties are from all points of view much wider, and it is through the Council that all important decisions on a vast range of topics must be channelled. The powers of the Communities themselves are nevertheless powers of attribution, so the powers of the Council ultimately have limits set to them by the Member States. The Court of Justice has recognised that under the ECSC Treaty the Council has implied powers enabling it to execute specific requirements of the Treaty, even when methods of execution are not provided (8/55, *Fédéchar* v. *H.A.*, Rec. II 199). It seems evident that this principle would apply equally to the single Council of the Communities, but it is not clear how far it would go. Some indication is given by the *AETR* case (22/70, *Commission* v. *Council*, Rec. XVII 263, [1971] C.M.L.R. 335) which suggests that where the Community has laid down common rules, the Member States are no longer entitled *inter alia* to conclude treaties with third States which would impinge upon those rules. Such a line of reasoning is open to considerable extension, but could in no circumstances enable the Community to act, for example by regulation, where only a power of recommendation is granted.

5-12 The jurisdiction of the Council under the ECSC Treaty is not defined in the clear way that the functions of the Commission are set out in Article 155 EEC, and indeed it is questionable how far an attempt to define the areas of responsibilities of the Council can serve any purpose. There are three factors involved here; in the first place, the Council itself possesses the power of decision if not perhaps in the absolute majority of instances, certainly nearly always where a decision going beyond the merely technical is concerned. Secondly, the Council is in any case the repository of any residual powers which may lie with the Community. A fair illustration of this is to be found in Article 235, which provides that it is for the Council to decide upon appropriate measures where the necessary powers to attain one of the objectives of the Community are not available. Lastly, even assuming it were possible to provide a definitive list of Council powers by inspection, nevertheless the *AETR* case (*supra*) suggests that these powers are capable of expansion, while practice indicates that they may not always be as wide as they may at first sight appear. Thus Article 238 states that association agreements are to be concluded by the Council, but three out of the seven extant agreements were concluded by the Council together with the Member States. This intervention, which does not appear to be provided for by the text of the Treaty, is justified legally by the fact that the subject-matter of these three agreements extended beyond the powers of the Community. The justification is not perhaps entirely convincing (see generally Chap. 37, *infra*) but there is here a clear indication that the powers of the Council are neither totally clear-cut nor unchanging.

5-13 It is possible to indicate a number of areas in which the Council has primary responsibility for action under the EEC Treaty, even though it may only be able to act upon a proposal from the Commission. Thus Article 145, which itself sets out the Council's responsibilities, states that the Council is to ensure the co-ordination of the general economic policies of the Member States, and there are a number of other Articles involving co-operation and co-ordination for which the Council bears some responsibility, although generally acting on proposals from the Commission where a power of action is given; *e.g.* Articles 6, 56 (2), 57 (2), 70 (1), 103, 105, 112, 116 (220). Secondly, it is invariably for the Council to lay down the rules for the expansion of Community activity: the Treaty itself contains guidelines, and the Council is to expand upon these on the basis of Commission proposals, or on its own motion in certain cases (*e.g.* Arts. 84 (2), 126 (*b*), 136, 217, 223 (3), 227 (2), 228, 237 and 238). Thirdly, there are a group of powers exercised by the Council either of its own motion or on proposals from the Commission, which are of an *ad hoc* nature, generally involving discretionary powers to combat economic difficulties at a national level, and requiring the political, rather than the purely administrative touch (*e.g.* Arts. 8 (3), 8 (5), 25 (1), 28, 45 (3), 70 (2), second sub-para., 73, 76, 93 (2), 98, 108, 109 (3). Arts. 115 and 226 are conspicuous by their absence from this list, but both are concerned with essentially temporary situations).

CHAPTER 6

THE EUROPEAN PARLIAMENT

6–01 As already mentioned (§ 3–01, *supra*) the Assemblies provided for in the three Treaties (Arts. 7 and 20 *et seq.* ECSC, Arts. 4 and 137 *et seq.** EEC, and Arts. 3 and 107 *et seq.* Euratom) are constituted by a single Assembly. Provision for a single Assembly is made by Articles 1 and 2 of the Convention on Certain Institutions Common to the European Community (Cmnd. 4864, p. 144), adopted at the same time as the Rome Treaties, and entering into force on the same date. The Convention provides that the powers and jurisdiction conferred upon the Assembly by the Rome Treaties are to be exercised by a single Assembly, taking the place of the ECSC Common Assembly, and exercising its powers and jurisdiction. After the establishment of the Rome Treaty Communities the Assembly initially called itself the European Parliamentary Assembly (Resolution of March 20, 1958, J.O. 1958, 6) but now calls itself the European Parliament (Resolution of March 30, 1962, J.O. 1962, 1045).

6–02 Article 137 EEC * provides that the Assembly is to exercise the advisory and supervisory powers conferred upon it by the Treaty. Article 20 ECSC omits mention of any advisory capacity, but such is implicit, inasmuch as the Assembly is required to be consulted in various contexts.

If a parliament is to be defined as an elected legislature with real powers of decision, the European Parliament does not as yet qualify. True, it is in an indirect sense an elected body, but it is certainly not a legislature, and although it is an autonomous institution, its powers are not extensive.

Article 137 EEC,* Article 20 ECSC, state that the Assembly is to consist of representatives of the peoples of the States brought together in the Community. This phrase indicates that representatives are to be more than mere national nominees and it also contains a germ of the idea of direct election to the European Parliament, but in fact members are designated by their respective national parliaments from among the members of those parliaments in accordance with a procedure laid down by each Member State (Art. 138 (1) EEC *). Article 10 of the Act of Accession, amending Article 138 (2) EEC,* gives six delegates to Luxembourg, ten each to Denmark, Ireland and Norway, fourteen each to Belgium and Holland, and thirty-six each to the Big Four, Germany, France, Italy and the United Kingdom (total 208). It will be noted that the number of seats allotted to each State has not been altered to take account of the acceding States; all that has been done is to allocate new seats on a proportional basis to the new Member States.

6–03 The European Parliament has already elaborated proposals for election to itself by direct universal suffrage, under Article 138 (3) EEC.* The Council, which is required, acting unanimously, to lay down the appropriate provisions to be recommended to the Member States for adoption in accordance with their respective constitutional requirements, has failed to take any effective initiative on these proposals. It is in any case probable that such recommendations would require to be adopted not as a Community act in the sense of Article 189 EEC,* but rather in Treaty form—as indeed was envisaged by the proposals made in 1960 for a convention on the subject. The report of the Vedel Committee on the future role of the Parliament, which appeared in March 1972 (Bulletin, Supplement, 4, 1972), does, it is true, suggest a general expansion of the powers of that body, and in that context advocates provision for direct suffrage at a later stage, but whether this will meet with the approval of the Council remains to be seen. In the meantime membership of the Parliament continues on a basis which is not truly representative, with the result that minority and dissident groups are largely excluded from participation, since the methods of designation of delegates are fixed by national procedures. There are, however, movements, notably in Germany and Italy, to provide unilaterally for direct elections to the European Parliament.

DELEGATES

6–04 The position of the individual parliamentarian of the European Parliament is, for the time being at least, inescapably linked with his status as a member of a national parliament (*cf.* Art. 138 EEC *). He can be selected to fulfil the role of European parliamentarian only if he already holds a seat in the national parliament. The Rules of Procedure of the European Parliament (J.O. 1962, 2437 and 1967, 240/3 and 280/1, and 1971, C 55) do provide for scrutiny of the credentials, so to speak, of those designated (Art. 3). It must be admitted that this scrutiny is more in the nature of a symbolic function, affirming the independence of the European Parliament, than anything else.

The Treaties do not contain any provision as to the length of mandate of the Members of the Parliament, and in practice this question is regulated nationally, the length tending towards that of the normal national parliamentary mandate. The mandate of the Members of the Parliament expires with the expiration of the mandate conferred, on death, resignation or invalidation of appointment, or through loss of the requisite seat in the national parliament (Art. 4, Rules of Procedure). Where the Member loses his seat at home, he may, if his " European Mandate " has not expired, retain his seat in the European

Parliament until his successor is appointed (Art. 4 (2)). This rule has the obvious advantage that its other aspect is that a re-elected national parliamentarian whose European mandate has not expired retains the latter position, and difficulties over re-appointment are avoided. There are no objections in principle to a European parliamentarian being made a Minister at home: this seems natural enough to the English constitutionalist but, the matter being governed by the applicable municipal rule, a French delegate would be forced to resign, ministerial status being incompatible in France with that of Deputy.

SESSIONS OF THE PARLIAMENT

6–05 The Rules of Procedure, which in this regard more or less follow the applicable Treaty dispositions (Arts. 22 ECSC, 139 EEC,* replaced as to their first paragraphs by Art. 27 (1) of the Merger Treaty), provide for a single annual session of the Assembly, meeting without requiring to be convened on the second Tuesday in March. The Assembly may also meet in extraordinary session at the request of a majority of its members, or at the request of the Council or of the Commission (same Articles). In practice the Parliament meets about ten times a year for up to a week or more at a time, but a continuity in its working is preserved as a result of the fact that its standing committees work during the intervals. The standing committees are responsible primarily for the preparation of debates on topics falling within their terms of reference (foreign affairs, agriculture, social policy, transport etc.) but they may also report on any other matters coming before the Parliament which they may consider to be of concern.

The Parliament has its seat in Strasbourg, meeting in the chamber of the Consultative Assembly of the Council of Europe, but it may, exceptionally, decide to hold one or more sessions elsewhere (Art. 2 (2), Rules of Procedure). Its General Secretariat and Departments are located in Luxembourg pursuant to Article 4 of the Decision of the Representatives of April 8, 1965 (Cmnd. 4866, p. 23) on the Provisional Location of Certain Institutions and Departments of the Communities.

The running of the Parliament

6–06 The Assembly elects its own President and officers from amongst its Members (Art. 140 EEC *). It had, before enlargement, a President and eight Vice-Presidents allotted on a national basis; whether any change is to be made remains to be seen. The President, as is usual in the Community bodies, provides much of the direction to the work of the Parliament. Unlike the President of the Council, however, the President of the Parliament is required to act with total impartiality, and in the chamber fulfils many of the functions fulfilled by the Speaker of the House of Commons. Day to day running of the Parliament is conducted by its officers, assisted by a Secretariat. The running of the

Parliament is governed generally by the Rules of Procedure, laid down by the Parliament itself under Article 142 EEC,* and not subject to any confirmation, *e.g.* by the Council. The Rules represent in some sense a synthesis of the national procedures of the Six. The proceedings of the Parliament are published, pursuant to the same Article, in the manner laid down by the Rules of Procedure. All the written questions (provided for under Art. 140 EEC *) appear, with their answers, in the Communications and Information (C) section of the *Official Journal of the European Communities*, as do minutes of all its debates, which are required to be published in the *Official Journal* within one month. The full debates appear in a separate annex to the *Official Journal*, entitled " Debates."

Political groupings

6-07   The sittings of the Parliament follow the form of the sittings of a normal parliamentary body. The delegates do not, however, sit as members of national political parties, but rather as members of political groupings which are supposed to transcend national frontiers. The political groupings are constituted on a formal basis, fourteen adherents being required to form a political grouping (Art. 36, Rules of Procedure). In general the groups, besides sitting together, are represented by a spokesman speaking for the whole group. The Presidents of the groups have a certain official status. The Parliament at present contains four political groups, sitting from left to right: Socialists, Christian-Democrats; Liberals; and the European Democratic Union (the smallest group, consisting of French Gaullist representatives). The Socialists have the greatest cohesion apart from the Gaullist group, while the Liberal group which contains a number of non-aligned members does not form an integrated political entity. Members of the Parliament are not required to be members of a political group, although the vast majority are.

POWERS OF THE PARLIAMENT

6-08   Article 137 * describes the Assembly as exercising advisory and supervisory powers. Its advisory powers are those enabling it to give its opinion on projects which must (or may) be submitted to it before the Council takes a decision thereon.

The right to be consulted for an opinion

6-09   The power to give an opinion, which is more accurately expressed as the right to be consulted, stems from a large number of provisions in the Treaties, and in particular in the EEC Treaty: *e.g.* Articles 7, 14, 43, 54, 56, 57, 63, 75, 87, 100, 126, 127, 201, (203), (203a), 212, 228, 235 236, 238. Each of these provisions confers a power of decision on the Council, but the exercise of that power is made in each case dependent upon prior consultation with the Parliament for its opinion. The Commission is not generally required to consult the Parliament, but under certain provisions of the ECSC Treaty, it is so obliged (*cf.* Art. 95 and budget provisions). Quite apart from any obligation to this effect, however, the Commission of all three Communities has found it convenient to consult the Parliament more or less informally on a wide range of topics, although without ever going so far as to concede the demands of the Parliament itself, which has expressed the desire to be consulted on all matters. The Commission has held out against this, arguing correctly that this would amount to a usurpation of its decision-making and proposal powers, which would in effect be *ultra vires*. A limitation was in any case placed on informal consultations by the Accords of Luxembourg of January 1966, which *inter alia* forbade the publication of Commission proposals before their communication to the Council (see generally § 5–06, *supra*).

6–10   Whether or not the Parliament is consulted formally (and it is clear that even where there is no duty to consult, it may nevertheless be consulted and give an opinion), the opinion of the Parliament is without binding force. Decisions must refer to any proposals or opinions which are required to be obtained pursuant to the Treaties (Art. 190 EEC *) but it is open to the Council to ignore the substance of the opinion, and the Commission may even alter its proposals after the Parliament has been consulted, although this liberty is subject to certain limits (*cf.* 41/69, *ACF Chemiefarma* v. *Commission*, Rec. XVI 661, and Jozeau-Marigné report, session doc. 110/67).

Nevertheless, the functions of the Parliament are not confined merely to giving opinions on matters on which it is consulted, for it may discuss any matter it chooses, and its resolutions have not been without influence on matters which would otherwise have been outside its sphere of competence. The Parliament has now acquired the last word on the adoption of the Community budget, but the relevant provisions of the Budget Treaty only become operative for the adoption of the budget for the years 1975 and following (see generally Chap. 35, *infra*).

Supervisory powers

6–11   Apart from its new powers in budgetary matters, which contain a supervisory element, the Parliament has a degree of supervisory power over the other Community institutions. For, in the first place, the Commission is required to submit to the Assembly an annual General Report on the three Communities (Article 18 of the Merger Treaty, replacing Article 17 ECSC, Article 156 EEC,* Article 125 Euratom) and the Assembly discusses it in depth (Art. 24 ECSC, Art. 143 EEC *). Secondly, in so far as the Parliament may discuss any matter and issue an opinion on any matter, a spontaneous discussion of a matter, subsequently brought to the attention of the Council or Commission, involves a supervisory element. Thirdly, the Commission is required to reply orally or in writing to questions put to it by the Assembly or by its members (Art. 140 EEC *) and in practice, the subject-matter of such questions is of enormous range. Questions are also asked of the Council, but the Council, which "shall be heard by the Assembly in accordance with the conditions laid down by the Council in its rules of procedure" is not under the same obligation to reply. Members of the Commission have a right to be heard on behalf of the Commission, and may attend all meetings of the Assembly (same Article). Both the Council and the Commission are expected to keep abreast of Parliamentary affairs. In so far as this requires the two institutions to follow its activities fairly closely, the Parliament itself is able to engage in a process of dialogue with them, which, if not involving an element of control, at least enables the three bodies to form an idea of each others' thinking. This dialogue is in some degree institutionalised by annual colloquies between all the institutions, but the exchange is perhaps of too formal a character to be of any real value.

6–12   The final supervisory power of the Parliament consists in the motion of censure. Provision is made (Art. 144 EEC,* Art. 24 ECSC, as amended by Art. 27 of the Merger Treaty) for the tabling of motions of censure on the activities of the Commission. The Assembly may not vote thereon until at least three days after such a motion has been tabled and then only by open vote. If the motion is carried by a two-thirds majority of the votes cast, representing a majority of the members of the Assembly, the members of the Commission must resign as a body, but they are to continue to deal with current business until replaced. The 1967 amendments to the Rules of Procedure take account of the Merger of the Commissions and High Authority, and the motion of censure is thus brought against the Commission of the three Communities; it is not possible to censure the Commission as to one Community only. (*Cf.* Art. 21 of the Rules of Procedure.) The device of the motion on censure has only once been used; the tabling of such a motion in December 1972 and its subsequent withdrawal only emphasised, however, that it is far too crude a means of controlling the day-to-day activities of the Commission. It is doubtful whether the existence of the power has even deterrent force.

CONCLUSIONS

6–13 Clearly then the powers exercised by the Parliament are decidedly limited; but, as appears from their enlargement in the Budget Treaty (Cmnd. 4867), it is not as though they are incapable of expansion. For the moment however the powers of the Parliament are confined to deliberation. Any reality of control which there may be over the executive of the Community is exercised as much by informal contact on internal lines as in formal debate. The judgment that the influence of the Parliament is about as telling as that of an annual general meeting of a joint stock company seems, however, unduly harsh. There are, moreover, moves afoot to enlarge the powers of the European Parliament.

CHAPTER 7

OTHER CONSULTATIVE BODIES

THE COMMITTEE OF PERMANENT REPRESENTATIVES OF THE MEMBER STATES

7–01 THE responsibilities of the Committee of Permanent Representatives, generally known as COREPER, in abbreviation of the French *Comité de Representants Permanents,* are stated in Article 4 of the Merger Treaty (Cmnd. 4866) to be the preparation of the work of the Council and the execution of the tasks assigned to it by the Council.

COREPER was not set up by any of the Community Treaties, but a similar body, known as COCOR (*Commission de Coordination*) was established under Article 10 of the ECSC Council Rules of Procedure, permitting the creation of Commissions. Article 151 EEC * provided for the creation of a similar committee for the Rome Treaty Communities, its task and powers to be defined by the Council. COCOR, and the single COREPER which had served the Councils of the EEC and Euratom, have been combined in a single COREPER, whose existence is recognised rather than provided for by Article 4 of the Merger Treaty. In so far as that Article sets out the responsibilities of COREPER, it does no more than institutionalise Article 16 of the EEC Council Rules of Procedure and does not clarify the Committee's legal position. Article 16 of the Council Rules of Procedure thus still provides the basis of the powers and duties of the Committee. Its powers are primarily confined to the preparation of the work of the Council, but it may set up working groups to do preparatory work or to undertake studies. Co-operation with the Commission is built-in, for the Commission is normally to be invited to be represented at the Committee and on its working groups.

7–02 The internal workings of the Committee are described as being at the pre-political stage, that is to say that its function is to narrow and clarify areas of dispute and difficulty, and to prepare issues for eventual political decision. Its members are diplomats rather than politicians and, as is indicated by the name of the Committee, they are the Permanent Representatives of the Member States to the Community. In this capacity they constitute an integral part of the Community decision-making machinery. Some doubt has been expressed as to the possibility of delegation of powers to the Committee. Although one of the functions of the Committee is to carry out the tasks entrusted to it by the Council, it would seem that no delegation of substantial powers is possible. The Committee is not a group of alternates for the Council, and its members have no voting power when acting as substitutes. In the same way the Committee, not being a politically responsible body, cannot be and is not entrusted with powers of decision. Its prime function must rather be to provide the element of continuity between Council meetings, and to prepare the way for the actual decision-making process by exploring the area of possible compromise, or at least through informal contacts.

7–03   Specific aspects of the work of the Committee are dealt with by special committees or working groups, set up by COREPER itself. Other special committees are set up directly by the Council and stand in the same relationship to the Council as COREPER. The most important of these are the Special Agriculture Committee, initially set up under Article 5, para. 4, of the first acceleration decision of May 12, 1960 (J.O. 1960, 1217, see § 21–12, *infra*) and the so-called Article 113 Committee, successor to the Article 111 Committee (see §§ 37–15 *et seq.* for the interrelationship of these two Articles), set up under Article 111 (2), third sub-para., now Article 113 (3) third sub-para., and appointed by the Council to assist the Commission in the negotiation of tariff agreements.

The regular aspects of the work of the Committee are directed by the President of the Committee, who presides over it, and gives it considerable directional force. The office of President rotates with the office of President of the Council, thus emphasising the close links between the two bodies.

7–04   The meetings of the Committee do not follow the form of Council meetings, for the purpose of its meetings, which may be of a quite informal nature, is to attempt to arrive at a general consensus with the assistance of national experts and with the Commission (the outcome going down as "A" points on the Council agenda—which can be agreed upon by the Council without discussion), rather than to take preliminary decisions by some system of majority vote. Nevertheless, the conclusions arrived at by the Committee have considerable decisional force. This decision-making process, carried out by a body which is not politically responsible to an elected body, has been questioned in some quarters, but the Commission has officially stated that the function of co-ordination played by the Committee is most valuable (Hallstein, " *L'Evolution des Communautés Européennes,*" Ann. Eur. Vol. VI, p. 8) and it is undoubtedly this function which justifies the existence of the Committee.

ECSC CONSULTATIVE COMMITTEE [1]

7–05   As already mentioned, the Communities are assisted in various ways by a proliferation of other committees. Perhaps the most important of these are the Economic and Social Committee common to the EEC and

---

[1] Rules of Procedure J.O. 1960, 513.

Euratom, and the Consultative Committee, discharging substantially similar functions in the context of the ECSC.

7–06 The ECSC Consultative Committee is set up by Articles 18 and 19 of the ECSC Treaty, its membership (expanded by the appointment of " additional " members: Art. 144, Act of Accession) comprising equal numbers of producers, of workers and of consumers and dealers, appointed by the Council. The members, although to greater or less extent nominees of representative organisations (*cf.* Art. 18), enjoy independence of those bodies in the exercise of their functions.

The conduct of the Committee is in the hands of a chairman and officers, elected for one year, assisted by a Secretariat. The Committee itself has four standing committees on general objectives, on markets and prices, on labour and on research and development. *Ad hoc* committees can also be appointed for special problems.

THE ECONOMIC AND SOCIAL COMMITTEE [2]

7–07 In the same way that the Consultative Committee of the ECSC is singled out for special mention in Article 7 of the Treaty of Paris, so the Economic and Social Committee receives individual mention in the Treaties of Rome: Article 4 (2) EEC, Article 3 (2) Euratom; both Articles state that the Council and the Commission are assisted by an Economic and Social Committee acting in an advisory capacity. It is clear that there is here in question only one Economic and Social Committee, for this is one of the common bodies in terms of Article 5 of the Convention on Certain Institutions Common to the European Communities (Cmnd. 4864, p. 144).

The Committee is set up by Article 193 EEC, 165 Euratom, which gives it an advisory status. It consists of representatives of the various categories of economic and social activity (particularised in the EEC Treaty as including producers, farmers, carriers, workers, dealers, craftsmen, professional occupations and representatives of the general public). Members of the Committee may not be bound by any mandatory instructions whatsoever (Art. 194 EEC,* third para.). Members are appointed by the Council, on the basis of lists produced by the Member States, after consultation with the Commission (Art. 195 EEC *). There is also the possibility (same Article) of obtaining the opinion of European bodies which are representative of the various economic and social sectors to which the activities of the Communities are of concern. This facility has not been extensively used. Article 21 of the Act of Accession, amending Article 194 EEC,* first para., fixes the number of members of the Committee at six for Luxembourg; nine each for Denmark, Norway and Ireland; twelve each for Belgium and Holland, and twenty-four each for the Big Four. (Total 153. It is to be noted that the

---

[2] Rules of Procedure J.O. 1968, L 42/1.

number of seats allotted to the original Member States remains the same except in the case of Luxembourg, which receives an additional seat.) In allotting seats account is to be taken of the need to ensure adequate representation of the various categories of economic and social activity (Art. 195 (1) EEC *). In practice the system of representation by category works well, and there is considerable solidarity within the groups.

7–08   The internal structure of the Committee, based upon its Rules of Procedure (J.O. 1968, L. 42/1) is similar to that of the Consultative Committee, but the mandate of chairman and officers is for two years instead of one (Art. 196 EEC *). The most notable new feature lies in the institutionalised creation of specialised sections of the Committee for the principal fields covered by the Treaties, in particular for transport and agriculture (Art. 197 EEC, 169 Euratom). The sections can be consulted only through the main committee.

Sub-committees can also be created within the Committee for the preparation of draft opinions for the Committee itself.

In addition, members of the Committee may form groups representative of the various categories of economic and social life (Art. 19, Rules of Procedure). In practice on the basis of this provision the Committee is divided into three groups: employers; workers; and " others." These groups serve primarily as *fora* within which common positions to be taken in plenary meetings are elaborated, but the groups do not, with the exception possibly of the workers' group, display any marked cohesion.

7–09   The Committee must be consulted by the Council or the Commission wherever the Treaties so provide (Art. 198 EEC *). It may be consulted in all cases which are considered appropriate (Art. 198 *). Where a specialised section of the Committee is seised of the question by the Committee, that section's opinion goes forward with that of the plenary Committee (Art. 44, Rules of Procedure).

The Economic and Social Committee is in theory weaker than the Consultative Committee, in that its rules of procedure are subject to approval by the Council (as are the rules of procedure of all the committees provided for in the EEC Treaty (Art. 153)), and in that it cannot convene its own sessions (Art. 196 EEC *). Nevertheless, it enjoys greater influence than its ECSC counterpart, and in practice the second of the above difficulties is overcome in that the Committee can indicate that it is interested in a question, whereupon a reference will generally be made to it under Article 198 EEC *. Additionally, under Article 20, third para., of its own Rules of Procedure, the Committee may, with the prior approval of the Council or of the Commission, be convened to make a study of matters on which, under the Treaties, it must or may be consulted.

The Committee is nevertheless not an autonomous institution of the Communities and does not possess any powers of its own, but it has proved most valuable as a platform for discussion.

OTHER COMMITTEES

(a) Set up under the Treaties

EEC

7-10   Transport Advisory Committee: Article 83.
"Article 113 Committee": Article 111, now 113.
Monetary Committee: Article 105.
European Social Fund Committee: Article 124.
Audit Board: Article 206.

Euratom

Arbitration Committee: Article 18.
Group of Experts: Article 31.
Scientific and Technical Committee: Article 134.
Audit Board: Article 180.

ECSC

(Study Committees including Economic Study Committee: Article 16).

(b) Set up in the context of the Treaties

7-11   Apart from the committees, etc., set up under specific provisions of the Treaties, there is a large number of others, set up in the context of the Treaties. A fairly comprehensive list of these is contained (for the purposes of Article 148 of the Act of Accession) in Annexes VIII and IX to the Act of Accession (Cmnd. 4862–I, pp. 71, 72); to these may be added:

The Committee on Short Term ("Conjunctural") Economic Policy,
Decision of March 9, 1960, J.O. 1960, 764.
Special Agricultural Committee,
Decision of May 12, 1960 (first acceleration decision) J.O. 1960, 1217.
Consultative Committee on Agreements and Monopolies,
Regulation 17/62, J.O. 1962, 204.
Standing Committee on Agricultural Structures,
Decision of December 4, 1962, J.O. 1962, 2892.
FEOGA Committee,
Regulation 17/64 (Article 24) J.O. 1964, 586.
Committee on Medium Term Economic Policy,
Decision 64/247, J.O. 1964, 1031.
Committee on Budgetary Policy,
Decision 64/299, J.O. 1964, 1205.
Committee of the Governors of the Central Banks,
Decision 64/300, J.O. 1964, 1206.

Committee on Seeds and Planting Material,
 Decision 66/399, J.O. 1966, 2289.
Standing Committee on Food Standards,
 Decision 69/414, J.O. 1969, L291/9.
Standing Committee on Employment,
 Decision 70/532, J.O. 1970, L273/25.
Customs Regulation Committees,
 e.g. Regulations 802/68, 803/68, 97/69, 542/69, Dir. 69/73.
Further, a number of committees have been set up in the context of the Association agreements and other agreements with third States, and also by Decisions of the Representatives of the Member States (*e.g.* Mines and Safety and Health Commission, J.O. 1967, 487, J.O. 1965, 698).

 The lists given above do not pretend to be exhaustive; they are merely illustrative of scale.

CHAPTER 8

PROVISIONS COMMON TO SEVERAL INSTITUTIONS

ACTS OF THE INSTITUTIONS OF THE COMMUNITIES

8–01 ARTICLE 189 EEC * provides:

" In order to carry out their task the Council and the Commission shall, in accordance with the provisions of this Treaty, make regulations, issue directives, take decisions, make recommendations or deliver opinions.

A regulation shall have general application. It shall be binding in its entirety and directly applicable in all Member States.

A directive shall be binding, as to the result to be achieved, upon each Member State to which it is addressed, but shall leave to the national authorities the choice of form and methods.

A decision shall be binding in its entirety upon those to whom it is addressed.

Recommendations and opinions shall have no binding force."

Article 189,* quoted in full above, defines the various types of acts that both the Council and Commission may issue in order to carry out their tasks. The Article does not in itself give power to issue an act; this must be sought in an express conferment of power elsewhere in the Treaty. The Article merely lists the types of acts that either institution may issue as being Regulations, Directives, Decisions, recommendations and opinions. The definition of each such act is not complete, for while the Article describes the effect that the act issued will have, no other means of identification is provided. By Article 190,* Regulations, Directives and Decisions (*i.e.* the acts which have binding force) are required to state the reasons on which they are based and to refer to any proposals or opinions which were required to be obtained under the terms of the Treaty article giving the power of decision (decision *lato sensu*, as opposed to decision *stricto sensu*—defined in Article 189,* fourth para.: the broad power of decision is often referred to by its German appellation—*Beschluss*—for purposes of clarity, the specific instrument being an *Entscheidung*). This does not of itself help to define the acts. Nor do the provisions of Article 190 * take the matter any further. This Article makes entry into force of regulations dependent upon publication in the *Official Journal*, and provides that directives and decisions shall take effect upon notification to those to whom they are addressed. The formal requirements laid down for the binding acts in Articles 9 to 15 of the Council's provisional Rules of Procedure are likewise of limited assistance. (See Houben, *Les Conseils de Ministres des Com-*

munautés Européennes, p. 227, and *Encyclopédie du Marché Commun* for text, which is not officially published.) Primarily the provisions of the Rules of Procedure amplify Articles 190 * and 191 * of the Treaty, and require regulations, decisions and directives to bear those names, but these matters go to form rather than to substance.

8–02 The provisions of the ECSC Treaty conferring powers of decision on the High Authority (*i.e.* now the Commission) are similar to but not identical with the provisions of the two Rome Treaties. Article 14 ECSC provides for decisions, which are binding in their entirety (corresponding both to EEC decisions and regulations), recommendations, which are binding as to the aims to be pursued but leaving the choice of the appropriate methods for achieving these aims to those to whom the recommendations are addressed (these correspond to EEC directives), and opinions, which have no binding force.

Article 14 ECSC further provides that where the High Authority is empowered to take a decision, it may confine itself to making a recommendation. There is no parallel provision in the EEC and Euratom Treaties, and in the absence of such provision the better view appears to be that a " lesser " act than that provided for (*i.e.* a directive or decision, instead of a regulation) may not be issued, although recommendations and opinions may be issued by the Commission whenever considered necessary (Art. 155 EEC). The point is, however, rather academic as the number of Articles providing only for regulations is extremely limited, the commonest type of provision being that which leaves open the method of execution (see Arts. 7, 8 (3), 10 (2), 17 (4), 20, 21 (1), 22, etc.).

8–03 The list of available forms of Community act contained in Article 189 * is probably not exhaustive; various types of rules of procedure exist, and use is made *inter alia* of communications, memoranda, guidelines and general programmes. None of these instruments is binding in the sense of Article 189,* but decisions of the representatives of the Member States meeting in Council present greater difficulty. Ostensibly they are binding agreements. It will be noted that Article 3 (1) of the Act of Accession merely states that the new Member States " accede by this Act " to such decisions and agreements. In the same way the Act of Accession does not pass upon the binding force or otherwise of " declarations or resolutions of, or other positions taken up by, the Council and . . . those concerning the European Communities adopted by common agreement of the Member States "; the new Member States are simply described as being in the same situation in relation to these acts as the original Member States, and " they will accordingly observe the principles and guidelines deriving from those declarations, resolutions or other positions and will take such measures as may be necessary to ensure their implementation " (Art. 3 (3), Act of Accession).

The differences between the various types of non-binding act, whether or not provided for in the Treaty, are probably not very significant, the names of several types of non-binding act being descriptive of content rather than importing particular consequences. The number of types of such act is potentially limitless, but unless the act fulfils the criteria set out in Article 189 * for one of the types of binding acts, it is doubtful whether it will entail any legally binding consequences. Thus in 90 and 91/63, *Commission* v. *Luxembourg and Belgium*, Rec. X 1217, [1965] C.M.L.R. 58, a resolution of the Council was held to have no binding force, since it was a statement of intent and no more. In 22/70, *Commission* v. *Council*, Rec. XVII 263, [1971] C.M.L.R. 335, on the other hand, the Court held Council " deliberations " to be susceptible of annulment, since, looked at from the point of view of substance, they were clearly designed to bind the Member States. The differences between the several types of binding act are more fundamental, for upon the category into which an act in question falls depends the availability or otherwise of actions brought by individuals, and the extent of applicability of that act within the Member States.

The rules for the classification of Community acts were first elaborated in relation to ECSC decisions.

ECSC Decisions

8-04   It has already been noted (§ 8-02, *supra*) that ECSC decisions correspond not only to decisions under the Rome Treaties, but also to regulations. Where a given ECSC decision is assimilable to a regulation, in that it is intended to have general application and to be binding in its entirety and directly applicable in all Member States, it is described as a general decision. ECSC decisions addressed to undertakings or associations, and thus having a more limited character, are described as individual decisions.

The concept of individual act derives not so much from Article 14 ECSC or from Article 15 and Decision 22/60, J.O. 1960, 1250, implementing it, requiring decisions and recommendations which are individual in character to be notified to the party concerned and in all other cases to be published, but rather from the jurisprudence of the Court in relation to Article 33. The latter Article refers on the one hand to decisions concerning undertakings or associations which are individual in character, and on the other to general decisions; undertakings and associations may attack individual decisions under Article 33 on any of the four grounds of illegality there set out, but may attack general decisions for misuse of powers only.

8-05   The Court has defined general decisions as being quasi-legislative acts originating with a public authority and having a normative effect *erga omnes* (18/57, *Nold* v. *H.A.*, Rec. V 89, see also 8/55, *Fédéchar* v. *H.A.*, Rec. II 199). Identification of a given act will not generally depend upon the form of the act (because, for example, a decision which is in fact an individual decision may of course have been published) but upon the object and content—*e.g.* 20/58, *Phoenix-Rheinrohr* v. *H.A.*, Rec. V 163; 22 and 23/60, *Raymond Elz* v. *H.A.*, Rec. VII 357; 23, 24, 52/63, *Usines Henricot* v. *H.A.*, Rec. IX 439, [1964] C.M.L.R. 119. If the act does not create rights and obligations, it is not a decision at all, nor will it constitute a decision if it does not contain substantially all the elements of a binding decision. Thus an instrument issued by the services of the High Authority or Commission, rather than by the collegiate body of the Commission itself, will not amount to a decision (*Usines Henricot*), nor will an instrument which fails to give adequate reasoning.

Pursuant to Decision 22/60 (*supra*), an ECSC act must state whether it is a Decision, recommendation or opinion. The matters which may go into a Decision are not dictated by Article 14 so much as by specific enabling provisions of the Treaty. Where the decision is a general decision, it will have general validity in all the Member States. An individual decision will normally only be binding upon the addressee.

EEC Regulations

8–06 " A regulation shall have general application. It shall be binding in its entirety and directly applicable in all Member States " (Art. 189,* second para.).

EEC regulations correspond to ECSC general decisions, and may not be attacked by individuals for illegality; Article 173,* second para., permits an individual plaintiff to attack only a decision addressed to him, or one which although in the form of a regulation or a decision addressed to another person, is of direct and individual concern to him. Disputes under this provision thus relate primarily to attempts to prove the element of direct and individual concern.

In examining the question whether a regulation or a decision is or is not of direct and individual concern to the plaintiff, the Court must in the first place take account of the object and content of the act; the basis for the distinction between a regulation and a decision which directly and individually concerns a plaintiff is to be sought in the general *scope* of the act, and not in the particular *appellation* of the act in question. (*Cf.* case 16 & 17/62, *infra*, [1963] C.M.L.R. at p. 175 uses " application " rather than " appellation "—this appears to be an accurate translation of the original, but even if that word was intended, which is doubted, the general drift of the passage is better reflected by " appellation.")

Regulations were, in 16 & 17/62, *Confédération Nationale des Producteurs de Fruits et Légumes* v. *Council*, Rec. VIII 901, [1963] C.M.L.R. 160, described as being essentially normative in character, applicable to situations assessed objectively, and involving immediate legal consequences in all the Member States for categories of persons envisaged in a general and abstract manner (see generally actions for annulment, Chap. 13 *infra*).

There is no difference in law between regulations adopted by the Council, and those adopted by the Commission. Nor is it material whether the act was adopted by the Council alone, on proposal from the Commission, by the Commission acting alone, etc., although it will be material to mention any opinions or proposals which were required in the circumstances in the reasons at the beginning of the regulations.

8–07   Article 189 * states that regulations are directly applicable in the Member States (as to this notion, see Chap. 18). The phrase " a regulation shall have general application " (Art. 189,* second para.) implies that regulations have normative effect, or effect *erga omnes.* The notion of the effect *erga omnes*, or the non-individual nature of a regulation, is extremely wide, and an individual will probably only be individually and directly concerned by an act, thus enabling him to impugn it, if he can show that he was already identifiable and identified before the act was even issued (see generally on actions for annulment Chap. 13). There is no requirement that regulations should have to do with circumstances in all the Member States, nor that they should treat all situations alike (*cf.* cases 63/69, 64/69 and 65/69). All that is required is an objective determination of a Community problem without reference to individuals who may be concerned as individuals. The regulation is then legally binding in all Member States, although practical effects may occur only in one.

The nature and authority of Community law in general (see supremacy of Community law, Chap. 17) involves that regulations, although directly applicable in the Member States, are law *in* the Member States, rather than the law *of* the Member State. Regulations are stated to be binding in their entirety, however, and this raises the question whether Member States are permitted to take national legislative action in relation to regulations. In theory there should be no need, but in practice a number of regulations requires, *e.g.* legislative action, or entry by the Member States into bilateral accords (*cf.* Reg. 3, J.O. 1958, 561, Art. 52), but these measures must not hinder or affect the operation of the regulation—*cf.* 27/69, *Caisse de Maladie des C.F.L. " Entr'aide Médicale "* v. *A.G.*, Rec. XV 405, [1970] C.M.L.R. 243, and 74/69, *HZA Bremen-Freihafen* v. *Krohn*, Rec. XVI 451, [1970] C.M.L.R. 466. The formula used in Regulation 1463/70, J.O. 1970, L. 164/1 (Art. 21 (1)), which is of a fairly usual type, is:

> " Member States shall, in good time and after consulting the Commission, adopt such laws, regulations or administrative provisions as may be necessary for the implementation of this Regulation. Such measures shall cover, inter alia, the organisation of, procedure for and means of control, and the penalties to be imposed in case of breach."

It is not usual for regulations to legislate on methods of control or execution inside the Member States, nor to provide for penalties (the main exceptions being Regulations 11/60 and 17/62), this being left to the States to implement, subject to the supervision of the Commission.

The regulation is the prime means of achieving a uniformity of rules throughout the Community and this type of instrument has been resorted to far more than any other, just short of three thousand per year now being issued.

8–08   The formal requirements for the issue of a regulation are basically the same as those for decisions and directives, in that all three types of act must state the reasons on which they are based and must refer to any proposals or opinions which were required to be obtained pursuant to the Treaty (Art. 190 *). Further, the majority of the more detailed requirements set out in the Council's provisional Rules of Procedure for regulations apply equally to decisions and directives (Art. 14, Rules of Procedure, Houben, *Les Conseils*, p. 227; *Encyclopédie du Marché Commun*). Even those requirements set out for regulations which are not made applicable to the issue of decisions and directives are in practice complied with. Thus although only regulations are required to be numbered and published in the *Official Journal* (*cf.* § 8–01) directives and decisions are in fact also numbered and are usually published. Similarly directives and decisions are usually dated and signed, although this is a formal requirement only for regulations. The only material difference in form between regulations on the one hand and directives and decisions on the other seems to be that regulations alone carry a formula describing their legal effects; they are required to carry the formula " this regulation is binding in its entirety and directly applicable in all Member States," a phrase taken directly from Article 189,* second paragraph.

There are no provisions comparable to these in the Commission Rules of Procedure, but the practice in relation to Commission acts is much the same.

Directives

8–09   " A directive shall be binding, as to the result to be achieved, upon each Member State to which it is addressed, but shall leave to the national authorities the choice of form and methods " (Art. 189,* third para.).

Directives are thus not a direct instrument for achieving precise legislative uniformity throughout the Member States, and have been used primarily where uniformity is unnecessary or where national political interests prevent the adoption of a Community rule, or else where the aim is to lay down a standard (quality, packaging, etc.) rather than a procedure. Legislation by directive is always something of an exceptional procedure because of the relatively limited efficiency of the instrument for laying down common rules, and regulations have always been issued in much greater numbers. It is to be noted, however, that the directive is now relatively less common than it was as a vehicle for legislation of more than a routine nature.

The ECSC recommendation corresponds broadly to the EEC directive, with the difference that the former may be directed to undertakings and associations.

8–10   The legal nature of a directive is still somewhat unclear. Article 173 * does not enable an individual to attack a directive, but on the other hand a number of cases refer to directives laying down cut-off dates in directly applicable terms (see generally, § 18–13). Whether the substantive part of a directive could be held to be directly applicable, so as to enable an individual to invoke Article 173 * in relation to it is uncertain. On the face of it a directive must leave to the national authorities the choice of form and methods for the implementation of the intended result. But if the date for implementation is once passed, and the terms of the directive are such that it could in the light of the jurisprudence of the Court be considered directly applicable, then it might be argued that the directive, or a particular provision of a directive, becomes directly applicable even in the absence of legislative implementation. It would appear, however, that apart from a municipal action (possibly resulting in a reference under Article 177 EEC) the only means of compelling compliance with it would be by an action under Article 169 * or 170 * (actions against Member States for a finding of a failure to fulfil a Community obligation).

Decisions

8–11   " A decision shall be binding in its entirety upon those to whom it is addressed " (Art. 189,* fourth para.).

In 25/62, *Plaumann* v. *Commission*, Rec. IX 197, [1964] C.M.L.R. 29, the Court held that an act is to be considered to be a decision if it is addressed to a particular person, and has binding effect *vis-à-vis* that person alone. The criteria for identifying a decision under the Rome Treaties are *mutatis mutandis* the same as those applicable under the ECSC Treaty: see *Usines Henricot, supra,* § 8–05 and 8–11/66, *Cimenteries CBR*, Rec. XIII 93, [1967] C.M.L.R. 77.

For a decision to be attackable by individuals under Article 173 EEC,* it must be addressed to the plaintiff or be of direct and individual concern to him. It was held in 9/70, *Grad* v. *Finanzamt Traunstein*, Rec. XVI 825, [1971] C.M.L.R. 1 and related cases that it would be incompatible with the binding effect attributed to decisions by Article 189 * to exclude in principle the possibility that persons affected might invoke the obligations imposed by a decision. The factors that were persuasive in this case were the fact that the decision-making power, Article 75, enabled the Community to take any type of binding act, and that the decision in question was addressed to all Member States.

If one may attempt to summarise the Court's approach, the content rather than the form is to be looked to; if the act be normative in character, then it is potentially directly applicable.

Reasons

8–12   As already mentioned, the binding acts of the Council and of the Commission must state the reasons on which they are based and must refer to any proposals or opinions which were required to be obtained pursuant to the Treaty (Art. 190 EEC *). The manner of recital of these matters is laid down in Articles 11 and 14 of the Council's provisional Rules of Procedure (see Houben, *Les Conseils*, p. 227, and *Encyclopédie du Marché Commun* for text); Commission acts in practice comply with the same rules. By Article 11 a Council act must indicate the dispositions in virtue of which it is adopted in a paragraph preceded by the words " having regard to," and must similarly refer to any proposals or opinions which were required to be obtained, these references being followed by the reasons on which the act is based, introduced by the word " whereas " and concluded with the formula " has adopted this " regulation, directive or decision.

The requirement of recital of reasons applies only to binding acts in the EEC, but it extends equally to non-binding acts under Article 15 of the ECSC Treaty.

The Court has held that the rule requiring reasons to be given for a decision is not based merely upon formal considerations, but is designed also to enable parties to protect their rights, to enable the Court to exercise its functions of control and to apprise the Member States as well as any nationals of the Member States affected of the manner in which the Council or Commission has applied the Treaty. For these purposes it is sufficient if the act sets out the main points of law and of fact on which it is based and which are necessary for an understanding of the reasoning which led the Community institution to act. The reasons may be brief, provided they are clear and to the point: in 24/62, *Germany* v. *Commission*, Rec. IX 129, [1963] C.M.L.R. 347; 1 & 14/57, *Soc. tubes de la Sarre* v. *H.A.*, Rec. III 201; 18/57, *Nold* v. *H.A.*, Rec. V 89; in 16/65, *Schwarze* v. *EVSt.*, Rec. XI 1295, [1966] C.M.L.R. 172 the Court elaborated its views, holding that the reasoning in an earlier, fully reasoned decision could, if expressly invoked, be relied upon to justify later decisions dealing with similar matters on a day-to-day basis (*in casu* free to frontier prices). It also held that the duty to provide reasons is to be interpreted in the light of the practical realities and the time and technical facilities available for making a decision. (See also 5/67, *Beus* v. *HZA München-Landesbergerstrasse*, Rec. XIV 125, [1968] C.M.L.R. 131, and 18/62, *Barge* v. *H.A.*, Rec. IX 539, [1965] C.M.L.R. 330.)

The failure to provide adequate reasoning constitutes an infringement of an essential procedural requirement, and an act not containing such may be annulled under Articles 173 * and 174.*

Decisions of the representatives of the Member States meeting in Council

8–13   Many decisions relating to the Communities have been taken not by the Council itself, but by the representatives of the Member States to the Council meeting in Council. (See list given in reply to question 336/68, J.O. 1968, C38/5, and that annexed to the Burger Report—EP session doc. 215/69. Decisions of this sort currently in force are contained in the list appendixed to the Act of Accession, Cmnd. 4862–I, at p. 137.)

Most, if not all, of these acts are either measures taken in execution of Community obligations or measures taken to complement the provisions of Community law (cf. acceleration decisions of 1960, J.O. 1960, 1217, and 1962, J.O. 1962, 1284). Their exact nature is, however, uncertain. The majority of them are described as being decisions of the representatives of the Member States, or as agreements of the representatives, the latter being generally supplementary to Association Agreements, etc. (e.g. agreements in connection with the Association Agreement with Greece—July 9, 1961, J.O. 1963, 350, 352). There are other minor variations in terminology which are probably immaterial in law. Nevertheless, the contents of the acts vary considerably, some amounting to little more than extracts from the Council minutes. Others resemble fully fledged decisions, and indeed were in some cases taken at the suggestion of the Commission. The vast majority are published, as any ordinary Community act. Still others of these acts, on the other hand, resemble ordinary multilateral treaties. Thus, it would appear that the weight to be attributed to a particular instrument will depend upon its content and not upon its form. But it would be wrong to draw conclusions as to the nature of an act purely from its subject-matter; whether or not the subject-matter is one in which the Community already has powers, and whether the act executes the Treaty or enlarges upon it must be examined together with the question whether a binding obligation is intended.

The Court of Justice has not yet had occasion to pronounce upon the nature of these acts; a very few of them specifically confer jurisdiction on the Court of Justice, but most are silent on the point. The Commission, in answer to written question 336/68 (supra) described these acts as having the character of international agreements, a view which is generally accepted. This suggests that they may be outside the jurisdiction of the Court, but the point is far from certain. In 90 & 91/63, Commission v. Luxembourg and Belgium, Rec. X 1217, [1965] C.M.L.R. 58, the Court held that a resolution of the Council, not provided for by Article 189,* was not a binding act. It was to this case that the Commission pointed when asked about the legal nature of these acts—Written Question 109/65, J.O. 1965, 678. But it seems now that the test the

Court would adopt will not be whether the act is in the form of one of the types of acts referred to in Article 189,* but rather whether in substance it can be said to be intended to produce legal effects: 22/70, *Commission* v. *Council* (the *AETR* case), Rec. XVII 263, [1971] C.M.L.R. 335.

8–14   There has been some question as to whether acts of the representatives can derogate from Treaty obligations, or even effectuate Treaty revisions. The generally accepted view is that this is not possible, since revision is only possible subject to certain clearly defined conditions, and indeed if one accepts the view that the Court could in appropriate circumstances take jurisdiction over these acts, then it would seem to follow that the Court would be obliged to ensure that the terms of the Treaty were respected. Where, however, the subject-matter of the decision of the representatives in question is strictly outside the powers and obligations set out in the Treaty or in binding acts in the sense of Article 189,* the Court might possibly be forced to come to the conclusion that it had no jurisdiction, even though the act had the characteristics of, for example, a decision.

Many of the decisions of the representatives have been ratified in accordance with the applicable national constitutional requirements. The question thus arises whether, assuming that the Court of Justice could be said to have jurisdiction over these acts coming within the criteria set out in the *AETR* case, ratification within the Member States negates the "Community character" of the act for the purposes of that jurisdiction. No clear answer can of course be given to this question, but it may be pointed out that the Court of Justice referred explicitly to the acts of ratification deposited by the Member States as being the starting point for consideration of the autonomous nature of Community law in 9/65, *San Michele* v. *H.A.*, Rec. XIII 1. It would appear therefore that ratification ought not to impair the Community nature of decisions of the representatives, although it may make it difficult to accept that a given decision of the representatives has the characteristics of, for example, a regulation once ratified.

SOURCES OF LAW OUTSIDE THE COMMUNITY TREATIES

1. International law

8–15   The Court of Justice has held the Community to constitute a new legal order in international law: 26/62, *Van Gend en Loos* v. *Nederlandse Administratie der Belastingen*, Rec. IX 1, [1963] C.M.L.R. 105. It is undoubtedly an emanation of international law, but the question arises how far the Community Treaties exclude the application of legal principles which are not founded upon those Treaties.

The Court has in a number of cases applied principles of international law, notably in 10/61, *Commission* v. *Italy* (radio valves case), Rec. VIII

1, [1962] C.M.L.R. 187, and 8/55, *Fédéchar* v. *H.A.*, Rec. II 199, but these were arguably principles of interpretation. Apart from specific references in the Community Treaties to other international agreements, as in Article 31 EEC (OEEC quota liberalisation list) it has been doubted how far the Court may refer to international law or apply it. 28/68, *Caisse Régionale* v. *Torrekens*, Rec. XV 125, [1969] C.M.L.R. 377, where the Court refused to interpret the Franco-Belgian Protocol of 1948 on social security, is cited in support of the proposition that the Court may never interpret an international Treaty, but it seems that the correct inference to be drawn from that case is that the Court will not interpret Treaties which are extraneous to the Community system. This is no bar to the Court's applying international law in the appropriate circumstances. (*Cf.* similar approach in relation to application of municipal law, when expressly called upon to do so: 24/71, *Meinhardt-Forderung* v. *Commission*, Rec. XVIII 269.) Some support for this view is to be drawn from 22/70, *Commission* v. *Council*, Rec. XVII 263, [1971] C.M.L.R. 335, where the Court indicated that Community action in relation to non-Community treaties could be limited by Community commitments. Action violative of those commitments could be struck down by the Court. The Court considered the applicable international law relating to extraterritorial jurisdiction in 48/69, *I.C.I.* v. *Commission* and related cases [1972] C.M.L.R. 557, but evidently considered its power to consider international law to be beyond question, for the difficulties here discussed were not alluded to. Similarly in 21–24/72, *International Fruit Co.* v. *Produktschap voor Groenten en Fruit*, not yet reported, the Court, asked to give a preliminary ruling upon the compatibility of a rule of international law (Art. XI of the GATT) with a Community act, stated that it might, under Article 177 EEC, examine any alleged ground of invalidity of a Community act and went on to consider whether the Community is bound by the GATT and whether Article XI could be held to be directly applicable.

2. General principles of law

8–16   Article 215, second para., relating to the non-contractual liability of the Communities, is the only provision to refer to the general principles common to the laws of the Member States, but the Court frequently has recourse to such principles: 7/56 & 3–7/57, *Algera* v. *Assembly*, Rec. III 81 at p. 115. Of these principles may be mentioned the principle of legal certainty: 42 & 49/59, *SNUPAT* v. *H.A.*, Rec. VII 101, and *e.g.* 24/69, *Nebe* v. *Commission*, Rec. XVI 145; the principle of good faith: 43, 45 & 48/59, 44/59, *Lachmüller*, and *Fiddelaar* v. *Commission*, Rec. VI 933 and 1077; and the principle of proportionality of administrative acts: 8/55, *Fédéchar* v. *H.A.*, Rec. II 199, and *e.g.* 25/70, *EVSt* v. *Köster, Berodt and Co.*, Rec. XVI 1161, [1972] C.M.L.R. 255. The Court has also held that fundamental rights have an integral part in the general principles of law, respect for which it assures: 29/69, *Stauder*

v. *Ulm Sozialamt*, Rec. XV 419, [1970] C.M.L.R. 112, 25/70, *Köster, Berodt, supra,* and 11/70, *Internationale Handelsgesellschaft* v. *EVSt,* Rec. XVI 1125, [1972] C.M.L.R. 255.

8–17   The application of general principles of law is not to be confused with the actual application of Community law to national law. This the Court has rightly refused to proceed to do; first because such application would be incompatible with Community law, and secondly because it does not have the jurisdiction to apply or interpret law in the Member States, but only Community law. (See, *e.g.* 1/58, *Stork* v. *H.A.,* Rec. V 43 and 28/70, *Witt* v. *HZA Lüneburg,* Rec. XVI 1021, [1971] C.M.L.R. 163; 24/71, *Meinhardt* v. *Commission,* Rec. XVIII 269, makes extensive references to the German law of divorce, but this was for the purpose of applying Community law (the Staff Regulations) to a Community servant. The case is not therefore an exception to the other authorities. The Court has held in two cases: 49/71, *Hagen* v. *EVSt,* Rec. XVIII 23, and 50/71, *Wünsche* v. *EVSt,* Rec. XVIII 53, that in the absence of a *renvoi,* whether explicit or implied, to national law, the legal concepts used by Community law must be interpreted and applied in a uniform fashion throughout the Community.

Part 3

THE COURT OF JUSTICE OF THE EUROPEAN COMMUNITIES

CHAPTER 9

THE COURT OF JUSTICE OF THE EUROPEAN COMMUNITIES

9–01 As already mentioned (§ 4–19, *supra*) the Courts of Justice provided for in the three Treaties (Arts. 7 and 31 *et seq.* ECSC; Arts. 4 and 164 * *et seq.* EEC; Arts. 3 and 136 *et seq.* Euratom) are constituted by a single Court of Justice, which exercises the jurisdiction of the EEC and Euratom Courts of Justice, and that of the ECSC Court of Justice which it replaces (*cf.* Arts. 3 and 4 of the Convention on Certain Institutions Common to the European Communities, Cmnd. 4864, p. 144). In recognition of the fact that the Court of Justice is the judicial arm for all three Communities, it describes itself as the Court of Justice of the European Communities. The existence of a single Court of Justice rather than of three separate such institutions is conducive to the achievement of a unity of jurisprudence and the easy resolution of any jurisdictional conflicts between the Treaties.

COMPOSITION OF THE COURT OF JUSTICE

9–02 Article 17 of the Act of Accession, which partially replaces Article 165 EEC * and Article 32 ECSC, provides for a Court of Justice of eleven members, assisted by three Advocates-General (Art. 18, Act of Accession, amending Art. 32 (*a*) ECSC and Art. 166 EEC *).

Article 167 EEC * provides that the judges and Advocates-General shall be chosen from persons whose independence is beyond doubt, and who possess the qualifications required for appointment to the highest judicial office in their respective countries, or who are jurisconsults of recognised competence. They are appointed by common accord of the Governments of the Member States in the same way that the Members of the Commission are chosen (*cf.* § 4–18, *supra*), the independence of the Court from the Council, which might otherwise be expected to appoint its members, being thereby underlined.

One of the most notable features of the composition of the Court is considered to be that in contrast to the position under the provisions relating to the Commission (*cf.* Art. 10 of the Merger Treaty) there is no requirement (a) that all Member States be represented on the Court, or (b) that the nominees of the Member States should all be nationals of Community countries. This formal omission has not, however, affected practice in the matter; all the Member States are represented upon the Court, and in fact by their own nationals. Similarly, the posts of Advocates-General have up until the time of writing always been filled by French and German nationals. With the accession of the new Member States, the United Kingdom will also nominate an Advocate-General.

9–03   The judges and Advocates-General are each appointed for a term of six years, but to ensure a continuity of composition, first six then three judges are to be replaced alternately every three years. The terms of office of the Advocates-General are similarly staggered (Art. 19 of the Act of Accession, partially replacing Art. 167 EEC *). Retiring judges and Advocates-General are, however, eligible for reappointment (Art. 167 *) and there is no upper age limit for appointment.

The relatively short term of office provided for has been criticised as not safeguarding judicial independence sufficiently. There is some force in the criticism, which is not fully met by the reply that independence is inherent, and that the judges and Advocates-General are themselves required to be independent.

As already stated, the judges and Advocates-General must be chosen from persons whose independence is beyond doubt (Art. 167 *) and the Advocates-General, in making their submissions, must act with complete impartiality and independence.

More precision is given to these provisions by the Statutes of the Court of Justice contained in Protocols annexed to the three Treaties (Cmnd. 4863, p. 132; Cmnd. 4864, p. 150; Cmnd. 4865, p. 85).

9–04   Before taking up their duties, the judges and Advocates-General are required to take an oath in open court to perform their duties impartially and conscientiously, and to preserve the secrecy of the deliberations of the Court (Art. 2 EEC Statute,* Art. 2 ECSC Statute; the form of the oath is set out in Art. 3 of the Rules of Procedure, J.O. 1960, 17 and 1962, 1113). Judges and Advocates-General are debarred from holding any political or administrative office (Art. 4 EEC Statute,* Art. 4 ECSC Statute) and, in virtue of the same provision, they are disabled from engaging in any occupation, whether gainful or not, unless exemption is exceptionally granted by the Council. But they are apparently permitted to engage in teaching. The restrictions placed upon outside activities are similar to those placed on Members of the Commission (see § 4–19, *supra*).

Upon taking up their duties, the judges and Advocates-General are required to give a solemn undertaking (in addition to the oath above, and immediately after having taken it: Art. 3, para. 3, Rules of Procedure) that, both during and after their term of office, they will respect the obligations arising therefrom, in particular the duty to behave with integrity and discretion as regards acceptance, after they have ceased to hold office, of certain appointments or benefits (Art. 3, para. 3, Rules of Procedure). The ECSC Statute is more specific, prohibiting acceptance for a minimum period of three years after relinquishing office of any appointment in the coal and steel industries. In all cases the Court of Justice is the final arbiter of what is or is not permissible.

9–05   A judge or Advocate-General may be deprived of his office or of his right to a pension or other benefits in its stead only if, in the unanimous opinion of his fellow judges and Advocates-General of the Court, he no longer fulfils the requisite conditions or meets the obligations arising from his office (Art. 6 EEC Statute *). This provision for discipline by internal means is itself a guarantee of independence, although the judge affected has no right to vindicate himself in public, but only to present his comments at a private hearing (Art. 5, Rules of Procedure).

The provisions discussed above do, therefore, go some way towards mitigating the lack of security of tenure, and further provisions relating to privileges and immunities afford some additional protection. The judges also receive some measure of protection from the fact that no dissenting judgments are pronounced, so that no individual judge can be singled out for his views. Curiously enough, the Treaty contains no provision that the judges and Advocates-General shall neither seek nor take instructions from any Government or from any other body (*cf.* Art. 10 (2), second sub-para., of the Merger Treaty in relation to the Commission) but the seeking or taking of such instructions would manifestly be incompatible with the judicial function, and would bring into operation the disciplinary provisions of the Statutes (Art. 6 EEC,* Art. 7 ECSC).

The President

9–06   Pursuant to Article 167 EEC,* final paragraph, the judges elect the President of the Court of Justice from among their number for a term of three years. He may be re-elected. The election takes place after the appointment of the judges themselves, and is valid for the period until the next partial election (*cf.* Art. 6, Rules of Procedure).

The President directs the work and the running of the Court (Art. 7, Rules of Procedure), and in particular decides upon matters of distribution, timetable and so forth. He presides over the sittings of the Court whether in open court or in private session, and the ancillary services of the Court are under his authority.

The President has in addition a certain jurisdiction which is exclusive to himself. Thus he adjudicates alone on applications by way of summary procedure to suspend execution (Art. 36, EEC Statute *) and it is to him that applications are made for orders to ensure that inspections pursuant to Article 81 of the Euratom Treaty are carried out compulsorily.

The Advocates-General

9–07   As will have emerged from the above discussion, the status of the Advocates-General is for virtually all practical purposes identical with that of the judges. The function of the Advocates-General is to make, in open court, reasoned submissions on cases brought before the Court of Justice, in order to assist the Court in the performance of its task of ensuring that the law is observed in the interpretation and application of the Treaties (Art. 166 EEC *). The Advocates-General are also called upon to give opinions on the various steps the Court may take, but their primary function is to provide submissions for the guidance of the Court (whether sitting in chambers or in plenary session) in making its judgments. As a matter of procedure, the submissions of the Advocates-General are given orally, after the close of the oral hearing of the parties, and before judgment is given. They are reproduced after the judgments of the Court in the *Recueil de la Jurisprudence de la Cour*, as also in the reports in the other official languages.

The system of submissions of Advocates-General is unknown to the English legal system, being apparently taken from the practice of the French Conseil d'Etat, where the officer involved is called *Commissaire du Gouvernement*; his function is essentially to set out the matter under examination and to discuss the law applicable to the case, finally suggesting what should be the outcome. The detail into which he will go into any question will depend upon the importance and difficulty of the case. The nature of his submissions is best compared to the judgment of a Court in a common law jurisdiction; judgments of Courts following the French tradition tend to be short and epitomised to the point of being upon occasion rather oracular, while the judgments of Courts following our own traditions tend to go into the facts, examine the history of the legal point, and thereby justify the final decision. The submissions of the Advocates-General are of this nature, in contrast to the judgments of the Court of Justice, which, while not as peremptory as those of some Continental courts, tend to pronounce without going into elaborate discussion.

The Registrar of the Court

9-08   Provision is made for the appointment of a Registrar in Article 168 * of the EEC Treaty, and the existence of the office is confirmed, rather than provided for, in Articles 9 * to 11 * of the EEC Statute. The Registrar is required to take an oath identical to that of the judges and Advocates-General. It is to the Registrar that the officials and other servants attached to the Court are responsible, and he is thus the head of the ancillary services of the Court, but his most obvious public function is to handle the paper work of the Court: *cf.* Instructions to the Registrar, provided for in Article 14 of the Rules of Procedure (J.O 1960, 1417 and J.O. 1962, 1114).

THE HEARING OF THE CASE

Chambers

9-09   Article 165 EEC,* second para., sets out the general proposition that the Court of Justice sits in plenary session. It goes on to provide, however, that it may form chambers, each consisting of three or five judges, either to undertake certain preparatory inquiries or to adjudicate on particular categories of cases in accordance with rules laid down for this purpose. Two such smaller Courts have been set up for the purpose of undertaking preparatory inquiries, each consisting of three judges (Art. 24, Rules of Procedure). It will be noted that chambers which are called upon to exercise adjudicatory jurisdiction are established separately, although the composition may of course coincide (*cf.* Art. 95, Rules of Procedure). Cases are automatically assigned to one of the two chambers on filing, and a judge is appointed from within it to act as rapporteur (Art. 24, Rules of Procedure). After the closing of the written procedure the Rapporteur Judge presents a preliminary report on whether preparatory inquiries are needed (Art. 44, Rules of Procedure). The Court itself decides the point, having heard the Advocate-General. It will be seen that preparatory inquiries are not automatically carried out, but the mechanism for instituting them functions more or less automatically. If it is decided that preparatory inquiries are necessary, the case is either remitted to a chamber, or the Court may itself carry them out. If the Court itself decides to carry out the inquiries, it will " determine what measures for calling evidence it considers suitable " (Art. 45, para. 1, Rules of Procedure) and may itself give effect to these measures, or delegate this duty to the Rapporteur Judge (same Article, para. 3). Where the chamber is carrying out the inquiries, it exercises the relevant powers of the full Court, its President exercising those of the President of the full Court (Art. 46 of the Rules of Procedure).

9–10 The term " preparatory inquiries " which is used in relation to the functions of the chambers is not without its difficulties. The term which it translates is the French *mesures d'instruction*, which has a definite technical meaning, but which has no exact equivalent in English legal terminology. The idea of having a separate judge or group of judges to carry out preparatory inquiries is alien to the strictly adversary system of English civil procedure, but an examining magistrate fulfils similar functions in relation to criminal cases under English criminal procedure. The concept is only partially reflected by the use of the term " taking of evidence," which is sometimes used instead of " preparatory inquiries," for the former fails to put over the idea that the inquiries may also embrace more active investigation by a court.

9–11 Apart from their instructional function, chambers may also decide on legal aid and on recoverable costs, and may try certain types of cases, subject to the rule laid down in Article 165 EEC,* third para., that the Court must invariably sit in plenary session for cases brought by a Member State or an institution, and for references for preliminary rulings under Article 177 EEC. The contentious jurisdiction of the chambers relates to actions brought by servants and agents of the institutions (*cf.* Art. 95 of the Rules of Procedure). The chamber may refer the case to the full Court for decision (same Article, para. 2).

General procedural considerations

9–12   A number of points must be borne in mind in considering the nature of the procedure of the Court of Justice. These relate to the composition of the Court, and the manner in which judgment may be given.

In the first place, the provisions of Article 20 of the Act of Accession, which replace the second paragraph of Article 18 of the ECSC Statute and Article 15 of the EEC Statute,* stipulate that " decisions of the Court shall be valid only when an uneven number of its members is sitting in deliberations." This Article goes on to provide for a quorum of seven judges in the case of judgments of the full Court, and of three in the case of decisions of the chambers.

9–13   Article 16 of the EEC Statute * provides that " no judge or Advocate-General may take part in the disposal of any case in which he has previously taken part . . ." in any capacity whatsoever. The Court is itself the final arbiter in case of doubt on this point, but a judge or Advocate-General may disqualify himself for a particular case on his own motion, or else the President may notify him that he should not take part. The fact that a judge or Advocate-General has previously heard a case before the Court of Justice, involving the same parties and same subject-matter will not of course automatically disqualify him.

Although an individual could conceivably challenge a judge on grounds of partiality, Article 16 of the EEC Statute * provides that " a party may not apply for a change in the composition of the Court or of one of its chambers on the grounds of either the nationality of a judge or the absence from the Court or from the chamber of a judge of the nationality of that party " (last paragraph). This is in keeping with the Community spirit, and is in contrast with the system of *ad hoc* judges provided for by Article 31 of the Statute of the International Court of Justice. (The Statute of the latter Court is otherwise followed quite closely where appropriate.)

9–14   As already indicated, decisions of the Court are taken by a majority of the judges, but the deliberations of the Court are, and remain, secret (Art. 32, EEC Statute *). Each judge taking part is nevertheless required to give a reasoned opinion in voting for or against the case (Art. 27. para. 3, Rules of Procedure).

The Court of Justice and its ancillary services are located in Luxembourg, this state of affairs being confirmed by Article 3 of the Decision of the Representatives on the Provisional Location of the Institutions (Cmnd. 4866, p. 23). The original Court of Justice of the ECSC likewise had its seat in Luxembourg, and its successor took over that location.

9–15   The proceedings of the Court may be conducted in any one of the languages of the Community (Art. 29 of the Rules of Procedure), the Court itself bearing the cost of translations for its own purposes, since it is deemed to be multilingual. The plaintiff or appellant selects the language to be employed, but the parties may by agreement employ some other language, if the Court consents. If, however, the defendant is a Member State, the language of the proceedings must be its official language. These rules are, however, flexible; parties other than the institutions of the Communities may be authorised to use another language for some or all purposes of the case, while witnesses may be heard in any language at all.

Finally, members of the Court are at liberty to use an official language other than the procedural language for virtually all purposes during the oral phase, but the judgment of the Court must be in the procedural language, and texts drawn up in that language are the authentic texts (Art. 31 of the Rules of Procedure).

Representation

9–16   A State or an institution of the Community is represented by an agent appointed for each case, who may be assisted by an adviser or by a lawyer entitled to practise before a court of a Member State (Art. 17, EEC Statute *). In the practice of the institutions it is usually the legal service which conducts a case from beginning to end, and a member of this service who appears before the Court.

Other parties, *i.e.* individuals, corporations, etc. must be represented by a lawyer entitled to practise before a court of a Member State.

The EEC Statute (Art. 17,* fifth para.) makes it clear that university teachers having a right of audience at home will have a right of audience to the same extent before the Court of Justice.

The Court of Justice itself has disciplinary jurisdiction over agents, advisers and lawyers appearing before it, and may waive the rights and immunities which they otherwise enjoy for the independent exercise of their duties before the Court (same Article).

THE PROCEDURE BEFORE THE COURT

9–17 It would be out of place in a book of this length to go into the procedure of the Court in any great detail, but salient features of that procedure should be noted; actions before the Court go through a written and an oral stage: the written stage follows much the same course as that of an English civil action, with exchanges of pleadings and rejoinders. At the end of the written stage, a Rapporteur judge reports to the full Court on the general nature of the case, and on whether any further evidentiary points need to be brought out—whether any preparatory inquiries are necessary. If these are necessary, the Court may either remit the case to a chamber, or itself take measures. The oral hearing normally follows the instruction procedure (although further preparatory inquiries may be carried out at any time). The oral procedure tends not to be the occasion for great oratory, since most of the arguments will have been gone into extensively during the written stage. It is, however, the occasion upon which questions of doubt and detail may be cleared up. When the parties have argued, the Advocate-General makes his submissions, and then the Court gives a reserved judgment at a later stage.

It will be noted that this procedure is not purely adversary as is that in English civil proceedings, but that, on the contrary, the Court may itself step in to direct the case, and in practice does so.

THE RULES OF PROCEDURE

9-18 The Rules of Procedure of the Court of Justice are divided into three Titles, the first relating to the organisation of the Court; the other two relating to procedure *stricto sensu* and to special types of procedure.

Title 2: Procedure

9-19 Title 2 of the Rules of Procedure, headed " Procedure " is divided into nine Chapters of varying length:
  (1) Written Procedure,
  (2) Procedure of Inquiry (*i.e.* preparatory inquiries),
  (3) Oral Procedure,
  (4) Judgments,
  (5) Costs,
  (6) Free Legal Aid,
  (7) Withdrawals,
  (8) Service, and
  (9) Time-Limits.

Written procedure [1]

9-20 The written procedure, which consists in the communication to the parties and to the institutions of the Community whose decisions are in dispute of applications, statements of case, defences and observations, and of replies if any, as well as of all papers and documents in support or of certified copies of them (Art. 18, EEC Statute *) does not vary substantially from the procedures of municipal courts.

There are fairly strict rules about introducing fresh arguments after service of the statement of claim (Art. 42, para. 2, Rules of Procedure).

After the final reply has been submitted, the President of the Court fixes a date on which the judge acting as Rapporteur is to present his preliminary report on whether " procedure of inquiry " on the case is required. The Court having heard the Advocate-General on the point, itself decides whether preparatory inquiries are in fact required (Art. 44).

Procedure of inquiry—calling of evidence [2]

9-21 The Court itself determines the measures which it considers appropriate for calling of evidence, by an order setting out the facts to be proved (Art. 45). Such, for example, include:

---

[1] Arts. 37–44, Rules of Procedure.   [2] Arts. 45–54.

(a) the personal appearance of the parties;
(b) a request for information and production of documents;
(c) evidence by witnesses;
(d) expert examination and report; and
(e) a visit to the scene (*i.e.* a view).

A correlation of Articles 44 and 45 indicates that these measures will be carried out by the Court itself, by the chamber, or by a Rapporteur judge. Later Articles set out the way in which the evidence is to be taken.

Oral procedure [3]

9–22   Cases are heard in the order in which the procedure of inquiry has been completed (Art. 55). The President conducts the proceedings (Art. 55) and he and the other judges and the Advocates-General may address questions to agents and lawyers (Art. 57). The Court may at any time order a (further) measure of inquiry (Art. 60) or reopen the oral procedure (Art. 61) but as a matter of principle, it is desirable that all questions of doubt should be settled beforehand, so that the oral procedure tends not to be a lengthy affair involving persuasive oratory.

Judgments [4]

9–23   Article 63 sets out certain formal requirements for judgments. The judgment is delivered in open court (Art. 64). There are provisions for publication of the judgment (Art. 68), for its revision for clerical errors and the like, and also for failure to rule on a given count or on costs (Art. 66 and 67).

Costs [5]

9–24   The normal rule is that costs follow the event, unless costs have been incurred by vexatious behaviour, in which case the successful party may be ordered to pay costs.

The proceedings before the Court are in principle free, but the Court may require the amount of costs needlessly incurred to be refunded (Art. 72).

Free Legal Aid [6]

9–25   Eligibility for legal aid is decided by the chamber to which the judge acting as Rapporteur appointed to the case belongs, having regard to means and likelihood of success. The sums advanced by way of legal aid are deducted from the costs as ordered by the Court.

Withdrawals [7]

9–26   These Articles provide for the striking-out of actions.

[3] Arts. 55–62.
[4] Arts. 63–68.
[5] Arts. 69–75.
[6] Art. 76.
[7] Arts. 77 and 78.

Service [8]

9-27   Parties are obliged to designate an address for service in Luxembourg. It is at this address that documents are served on the parties.

Time-Limits [9]

9-28   These Articles contain rules for the computation of time-limits laid down in other parts of the Rules of Procedure.

Title 3: Special Forms of Procedure

9-29   Title 3 of the Rules of Procedure, entitled "Special Forms of Procedure" is divided into eleven Chapters:
(1) Suspension of enforcement and other interim measures,
(2) Preliminary points of procedure,
(3) Intervention,
(4) Judgment by default and retrial,
(5) Proceedings by servants of the Communities,
(6) Exceptional forms of recourse,
(7) Appeals against decisions of the Euratom Arbitration Committee,
(8) Interpretation of judgments,
(9) Preliminary rulings,
(10) Special Euratom procedures, and
(11) Opinions of the Court.

Most of the Chapter-headings are self-explanatory, but on others elaboration may be helpful:

Suspension of enforcement and other interim measures [10]

9-30   Provision is made for suspension of enforcement and for interim measures by way of summary proceedings in these Articles.

Preliminary points of procedure [11]

9-31   These Articles provide for the trial of preliminary issues and separate points.

Intervention [12]

9-32   Parties wishing to intervene must first establish an interest. The request must be submitted before the opening of the oral procedure at the latest. Intervenors are entitled to receive copies of all documents, but must take the case as they find it.

Proceedings by servants of the Communities [13]

9-33   Actions brought by servants of the Community are heard and judged by a chamber appointed annually for the purpose. The chamber may

---

[8] Art. 79.
[10] Arts. 83-90.
[12] Art. 93.

[9] Arts. 80-82.
[11] Arts. 91 and 92.
[13] Arts. 95 and 96.

remit any case to the full Court (*cf.* 44/59, *Fiddelaar* v. *Commission*, Rec. VI 1077).

Exceptional procedures [14]

9–34   The exceptional procedures referred to are applications to have a judgment retried and modified, or to have it revised.

Interpretation [15]

9–35   In giving its ruling on a request for interpretation, the Court is required to act by way of judgment. The record of the interpretative judgment is annexed to the record of the judgment so interpreted.

Opinions [16]

9–36   This Chapter makes provision for the giving of opinions under Article 228 EEC (optional request for opinion as to compatibility of Treaties with third States, etc.) and under Article 95 ECSC (*petite révision*).

[14] Arts. 97–100.
[15] Art. 102.
[16] Arts. 106–108.

CHAPTER 10

THE COURT OF JUSTICE—SCOPE OF JURISDICTION

10–01 ARTICLE 219 EEC states that Member States undertake not to submit disputes concerning the interpretation or application of the Treaty to any method of settlement other than those provided therein. (Article 193 Euratom is identical. Article 87 ECSC is to similar effect.) This provision creates a jurisdictional closed circuit, in that such questions of interpretation and application can only be decided in certain defined ways. In the vast majority of cases it is the Court of Justice which has jurisdiction, and generally exclusive jurisdiction, to decide the question, although Article 183 * states that, save where jurisdiction is conferred on the Court by the EEC Treaty, disputes to which the Community is a party shall not on that ground be excluded from the jurisdiction of the courts or tribunals of the Member States. However, Article 4 EEC (*cf.* Art. 3 ECSC) which states that each institution of the Communities shall act within the limits of the powers conferred on it by the Treaties, makes it clear that the jurisdiction of the Court of Justice is one of attribution, *i.e.* that its jurisdiction is limited to that conferred (see 12/63, *Schlieker* v. *H.A.*, Rec. IX 173, [1963] C.M.L.R. 281, and 44/65, *Hessische Knappschaft* v. *Singer*, Rec. XI 1191, C.C.H., p. 8042, [1966] C.M.L.R. 82). Whether the Court of Justice has jurisdiction in any particular circumstance cannot therefore be ascertained by a reference to general principles, but only by inspection of the relevant Treaty provisions (see schematic list of types of jurisdiction under the EEC, ECSC and Euratom Treaties immediately below).

Admittedly, Article 164 * states that the Court of Justice shall ensure that in the interpretation and application of the Treaty the law is observed, but this is not the same as conferring jurisdiction to decide such questions; it defines the Court's role without specifying when and how it is to be implemented.

It is not feasible in a book of this size to discuss all the possible bases of jurisdiction of the Court of Justice, and the following discussion is accordingly by and large restricted to those contained in the EEC Treaty.

BASES OF JURISDICTION CONTAINED IN THE EEC TREATY

10–02   The EEC Treaty contains the following bases of jurisdiction [1]:

Legal Basis	Grounds of Jurisdiction	Plaintiff	Defendant
Article 93 (2), 2nd para.	Direct reference in derogation from Articles 169 and 170 for failure to comply with a decision of the Commission on abolition of aids	Commission, any interested State	Member State
Article 157 (2), 3rd para. repealed by Article 19 of the Merger Treaty, but re-enacted by Article 10 of the same	Application for a ruling that a Commission Member be compulsorily retired under Article 160 (Article 13 of the Merger Treaty) or be deprived of pension rights or other benefits	Council, Commission	(Commission Member)
Article 160, repealed by Article 19 of the Merger Treaty, but re-enacted as to first paragraph by Article 13 of the same	Application for compulsory retirement of Commission Member (power of provisional suspension not re-enacted)	Council, Commission	(Commission Member)
Article 169	Action for failure to fulfil an obligation	Commission	Member State
Article 170	Same	Member State	Member State
Article 172	Jurisdiction in regard to penalties laid down in regulations	(Any party)	(Commission)
Article 173, 1st para.	Action seeking review of legality binding acts of Council or Commission	Member State, Council, Commission	Council, Commission
Article 173, 2nd para.	Same, the category of acts being restricted to decisions addressed to the plantiff or acts of direct and individual concern to him	Any natural or legal person	Council, Commission
Article 175, 1st para.	Action for failure to act	Member State, the other institutions	Council, Commission
Article 175, 3rd para.	Action for failure to address to the plaintiff a binding act	Any natural or legal person	Council, Commission

---

[1] Plaintiffs and defendants listed in brackets are not referred to as such explicitly in the relevant Article.

Legal Basis	*Grounds of Jurisdiction*	*Plaintiff*	*Defendant*
Article 177	Application for a preliminary ruling	(Reference by municipal court)	—
Article 178	Jurisdiction in disputes relating to the compensation for damage provided for in Article 215, 2nd para.	(Any party)	(Community institutions)
Article 179	Jurisdiction in disputes between the Community and its servants	(Servants, Community institutions)	(Community institutions, Servants)
Article 180	Jurisdiction in relation to the European Investment Bank	—	—
Article 180 (*a*)	Article 169-type action	Board of Directors of the Bank	Member State
Article 180 (*b*)	Article 173-type action	Member State, Commission, Board of Directors of the Bank	Board of Governors of the Bank
Article 180 (*c*)	Article 173-type action for non-compliance with the procedure laid down in Article 21 (2), (5), (6) and (7) of the Statute of the Bank	Member State, Commission	Board of Directors of the Bank
Article 181	Jurisdiction pursuant to any arbitration clause in a contract concluded by or on behalf of the Community	(Any party) (Community institution)	(Any party) (Community institution)
Article 182	Jurisdiction in disputes submitted under a special agreement	Member State	Member State
Article 184	Plea (or exception) of illegality	Any party	Council, Commission
Article 225, 2nd para.	Direct reference in derogation from Articles 169 and 170, for improper use of Articles 223 and 224 (defence etc.)	Commission, Member State	Member State
Article 228 (1), 2nd sub-para.	Opinion of the Court as to whether an agreement envisaged is compatible with the provisions of the Treaty	(Reference by Council, Commission or Member State)	—

BASES OF JURISDICTION IN THE ECSC TREATY

10–03

Legal Basis	Grounds of Jurisdiction	Plaintiff	Defendant
Article 10, 11th para. repealed by Article 19 of the Merger Treaty	Declaration of annulment of abusive use of veto on appointments to the High Authority	A Government	A Government
Article 12, repealed by Article19 of the Merger Treaty, replaced by Article 10 of the same	Application for compulsory retirement of High Authority Members	High Authority, Council	(High Authority Member)
Article 33, 1st para.	Action seeking review of legality	Member State, Council	High Authority
Article 33, 2nd para.	Same, category of acts being limited to individual decisions, and to general decisions involving misuse of powers affecting the plaintiff	Undertakings or Associations	High Authority
Article 34	Proceedings for damages for failure to comply with judgment of annulment of act involving a fault rendering the Community liable	(Undertakings or groups of undertakings)	High Authority
Article 35	Action for failure to act or for abstention from acting	(Any party)	High Authority
Article 37	Action against express or implied decision refusing to recognise a situation potentially of a nature to provoke fundamental and persistent disturbances in the economy	(Member State)	High Authority
Article 38	Application for declaration of nullity of Assembly or Council act	Member States, High Authority	Assembly, Council
Article 40, as amended by Article 26 of the Merger Treaty	Jurisdiction to order reparation from the Community	(Any party)	(Community institution)

Legal Basis	Grounds of Jurisdiction	Plaintiff	Defendant
Article 41	Jurisdiction to give preliminary rulings on the validity of High Authority or Council acts	(Reference by national court or tribunal)	—
Article 42	Equivalent to Article 181 EEC		
Article 43, 1st para.	Jurisdiction where provided for in any provision supplementing the Treaty	—	—
Article 43, 2nd para.	Jurisdiction where conferred by the law of a Member State	—	—
Article 47, 4th para.	Actions for compensation under Article 40 for breach of professional secrecy by the High Authority	(Any party)	High Authority
Article 63	Right of action impugning restriction or prohibition on dealings imposed following finding of discrimination by the High Authority	Purchaser	High Authority
Article 66 (5), 2nd para.	Unlimited jurisdiction, by way of derogation from Article 33, to assess whether transaction amounts to concentration	Any person directly concerned	High Authority
Article 88, 2nd para.	Action against a decision establishing a failure to fulfil an obligation	Member State	High Authority
Article 88, 4th para.	Action against decisions taken by way of sanction	Member State	High Authority
Article 89, 1st para.	Provision for (optional) jurisdiction of the Court where no other procedure for settlement provided	Member State	Member State
Article 89, 2nd para.	Equivalent to Article 182 EEC		
Article 95	Submission of proposed amendments to the Treaty for opinion of the Court (*petite révision*)	Council and the High Authority	—

BASES OF JURISDICTION IN THE EURATOM TREATY

10–04

Legal Basis	Grounds of Jurisdiction	Plaintiff	Defendant
Article 12, 4th para.	Application to the Court in licensing matters	Licensee	Commission
Article 18, 2nd para.	Appeals against the decisions of the arbitration committee	The parties	The parties
Article 21, 3rd para.	Reference to the Court for failure to grant a licence	Commission	Member State
Article 38, 3rd para.	Direct reference to the Court by way of derogation from Articles 141 and 142 for failure to comply with Commission directives on radioactivity levels	Commission, Member State	Member State
Article 81, 3rd para.	Power of President to issue decision ordering compulsory inspection	(Application by Commission)	—
Article 82, 4th para.	Direct reference to the Court by way of derogation from Articles 141 and 142 for failure to comply with Commission directive calling on Member States to end infringements relating to records on nuclear materials	Commission, Member State	Member State
Article 83 (2)	Special provisions in relation to actions impugning sanctions	Persons, Undertakings, (and Commission or any Member State)	Commission
Article 126	Equivalent to Article 157 EEC		
Article 129	Equivalent to Article 160 EEC		
Article 141	Equivalent to Article 169 EEC		
Article 142	Equivalent to Article 170 EEC		
(Article 144)	(Unlimited jurisdiction given in relation to Articles 12 and 83)	—	—
Article 145	Action to establish infringement of the Treaty to which Article 83 does not apply	Commission	Persons, Undertakings

Legal Basis	*Grounds of Jurisdiction*
Article 146	Equivalent to Article 173 EEC
Article 148	Equivalent to Article 175 EEC
Article 150	Equivalent to Article 177 EEC
Article 151	Equivalent to Article 178 EEC
Article 152	Equivalent to Article 179 EEC
Article 153	Equivalent to Article 181 EEC
Article 154	Equivalent to Article 182 EEC
Article 156	Equivalent to Article 184 EEC

10–05   Of the bases of jurisdiction contained in the EEC Treaty listed above, Articles 157 * and 160 * as re-enacted have already been discussed in relation to the Commission (§ 4–19, *supra*). Articles 178,* 179 * and 181 * are discussed in relation to the legal liability of the Communities (Chap. 36). Article 228 is discussed in connection with the exterior relations of the Community (Chap. 37, *infra*). The remaining Articles are discussed in the immediately following Chapters under the following heads.

(1) Actions against Member States for failure to fulfil an obligation (Arts. 169 * and 170,* Arts. 93, 180 (*a*), 182 * and 225).

(2) Actions relating to penalties (Art. 172).

(3) Review of legality of Council and Commission acts (Arts. 173 * and 180 (*b*) and (*c*)).

(4) Actions against the Commission or the Council for failure to act (Art. 175 *).

(5) Requests for preliminary rulings (Art. 177).

(6) The so-called plea of illegality (Art. 184 *).

THE ROLE OF THE COURT OF JUSTICE

10–06   Article 164 EEC * states that the role of the Court is to ensure that in the interpretation and application of the Treaties the law is observed. The formula of Article 31 ECSC is rather wider in that the Court is, additionally, under that Treaty, to fulfil the same functions in relation to the rules laid down for the implementation thereof. Nevertheless, it is clear that the Court has the same functions under the Paris and Rome Treaties, for Article 173 EEC * provides for review by the Court of Justice of the legality of binding acts of the Council and the Commission, or, in other words, the rules laid down for the implementation of the Treaties. Despite the broad similarity of the general rule laid down, however, the actual scope of the jurisdiction of the Court varies as between the Treaties. (See 27–29/58, *Cie. des Hauts Fourneaux de Givors* v. *H.A.*, Rec. VI 501: inapplicability of the rules of regional policy contained in Article 80 (2) EEC (transport) to transport of ores coming under the ECSC Treaty.)

10–07   Under the jurisdictional provisions contained in the Community Treaties the Court is variously called upon to deliver judgments, opinions and decisions. The vast majority of these provisions call for a judgment, and indeed applications resulting in a formal judgment make up the bulk of the work of the Court. In no circumstance, however, may the Court act without first having been seised of the question. Once seised, the Court must in fact give a judgment (or opinion or decision, where applicable), but in general only within the limits of the submissions of the parties in the case. The judgments of the Court are not subject to appeal.

Actions brought before the Court of Justice do not *ipso facto* suspend the application of any act attacked (Art. 185 EEC) but the Court of Justice may in fact order such suspension if it considers that the circumstances so require. The Court of Justice may also prescribe any necessary interim measures (Art. 186 EEC *).

EFFECTS OF JUDGMENTS OF THE COURT OF JUSTICE

1. Enforceability

10–08   Judgments of the Court of Justice are in terms only enforceable within the fairly narrow limits laid down in the Treaty (*cf.* Art. 187 *). Thus under Article 192 the decisions of the Court are only enforceable where they impose a pecuniary obligation on persons other than States. In such cases enforcement is governed by the rules of civil procedure in force in the State in the territory of which it is carried out. Enforcement is carried out at the national level without any formality other than that of verifying the authenticity of the decision of the Court of Justice, to which is appended the order for its enforcement (*la formule exécutoire*).

2. Effects in absence of enforceability

10–09   Where the judgment of the Court of Justice is not in terms enforceable, there is nonetheless generally an obligation to comply with it. Thus Member States found guilty of a failure to fulfil an obligation under the Treaty are required to take the necessary measures to comply with the judgment of the Court (Art. 171 EEC *), and similarly, an institution whose act has been declared void or whose failure to act has been declared contrary to the Treaty is required to take the necessary measures to comply with the judgment (Art. 176 *). The jurisdiction to give preliminary rulings does not give rise to a judgment susceptible of enforcement, and there is accordingly no necessity for having a provision similar to Articles 171 * and 176 * for the purposes of Article 177. Article 5 imposes the obligation on Member States to "take all appropriate measures . . . to ensure fulfilment of the obligations . . . resulting from action taken by the institutions of the Community " (see generally, Chaps. 18 and 20).

NATURE OF THE JUDGMENT

Action for failure to fulfil an obligation

10–10   A judgment of the Court of Justice takes the form, under Articles 169 * and 170,* of a finding that a Member State has failed to fulfil an obligation, the judgment specifying the nature of the failure. The Member State is required to take the necessary measures to comply with the judgment (Art. 171 *) but a further failure to fulfil this obligation under Article 171 * does not open the way for sanctions, as it does under the equivalent provision of the ECSC Treaty (Art. 88). In terms of express Treaty provisions, redress for failure to fulfil an obligation under Article 171 * of the EEC Treaty may therefore only be obtained by way of a further application under Article 169 * or 170.* No such second action has as yet been brought, but the Court of Justice had cause to remark on Italy's failure to put itself in order after the judgment in 7/69, *Commission* v. *Italy*, Rec. XVI 111, [1970] C.M.L.R. 97; 18/71, *Eunomia* v. *Italian Ministry of Public Instruction*, Rec. XVII 811, [1972] C.M.L.R. 4. (*Cf.* also 43/71, *Politi* v. *Italian Ministry of Finance*, Rec. XVII 1039, esp. at 1048.) Excuses of difficulties with national legislature are not sufficient; *e.g.* 45/64, *Commission* v. *Italy*, Rec. XV 433.

Review of legality of Community acts

10–11   If the Court of Justice finds an action seeking review of the legality of Community acts to be well founded, it is required, by Article 174 EEC,* to declare "the act concerned " void. "In the case of a regulation, however, the Court of Justice shall if it considers this necessary, state which of the effects of the regulation which it has declared void shall be considered as definitive." Under Article 176 EEC,* the institution whose act has been declared void is required to take the necessary measures to comply with the judgment of the Court of Justice.

It is settled that the judgment of the Court declaring a Community act to be void has effect *erga omnes*, and not simply as between the parties. Since as a general rule invalidity runs from the time of issue of the Community act, it was necessary to make provision for declaring certain effects of Regulations definitive, as otherwise undue hardship might result for those who reasonably relied upon the Community act. There is probably no need for such a provision in relation to directives, for redress must be sought against the national legislation, enacted in execution of the directive. Similarly, such a provision is unnecessary in relation to decisions, for the effects can be dealt with on an individual basis, if indeed the decision can be taken to have individual application. The tendency to issue decisions of general application would appear to raise the question whether such a decision ought to be dealt with in such a case in the same manner as a Regulation. Cases 9/70, *Grad* v. *Finanzamt Traunstein*, Rec. XVI 825, [1971] C.M.L.R. 1; 20/70, *Transports Lesage* v. *HZA Freiburg*, Rec. XVI 861, [1971] C.M.L.R. 1 and 33/70, *SACE* v. *Ministry of Finance*, Rec. XVI 1213, [1971] C.M.L.R. 123, holding decisions of general application to be directly applicable in some circumstances, suggest that this view might be adopted.

Since the decision of invalidity takes effect *ab initio*, it will generally be necessary for the Community institution concerned to make arrangements to recall the act impugned, and to eliminate the consequences, where appropriate paying compensation.

An interesting variant on the action for illegality arose in 10 & 18/68, *Eridania* v. *Commission*, Rec. XV 459, where the Court held that the procedures of Article 173 * could not be used to attack an implied decision of refusal; the latter could only be attacked under Article 175 * (actions for failure to act) because the action for illegality relates to the existence of acts, but not their absence.

Actions for failure to act

10–12   Where the Court of Justice declares a failure to act on the part of a Community institution to be contrary to the Treaty, the institution concerned is required to take the necessary measures to comply with the judgment (Art. 176 *). It may be asked how far, for example, the Commission could be held responsible for failure to take the necessary measures where the original failure concerns an obligation imposed on the Community as a whole, and Commission action is dependent upon action taken by the Council. It seems that the Court would be unlikely to entertain such an excuse sympathetically (*cf. e.g.* 45/64, *Commission* v. *Italy*, § 10–10, *supra*) but such an excuse might be acceptable in respect of an obligation placed upon the Commission alone. Either way, a further Article 175 * action is the only method of enforcing compliance with Article 176.*

Preliminary rulings

10–13   Article 177 EEC, giving the Court of Justice jurisdiction to give preliminary rulings on questions referred to it by national courts, offers no guidance as to the nature and effect of its judgment—for judgment it is, not a mere opinion—with the result that there is a certain amount of controversy particularly as to the scope of the judgment.

It is quite certain that the judgment of the Court of Justice is binding on the Court that refers the question: *cf.* 29/68, *Milch- Fett- und Eierkontor* v. *HZA Saarbrücken*, Rec. XV 165, [1969] C.M.L.R. 390, and 20/64, *Albatros* v. *SOPECO*, Rec. XI-3 1, [1965] C.M.L.R. 159, but doubted in *Internationale Handelsgesellschaft* v. *Einfuhr- und Vorratstelle für Getreide und Futtermittel (EVSt)* (Verwaltungsgericht, Frankfurt am Main) [1972] C.M.L.R. 177 at p. 186. But the judgment is not required to be, and cannot in fact be, adopted *in toto* by the national court in giving its final judgment, for it is expressed in general terms, and is deliberately drawn up so as to ensure that the Court of Justice cannot be accused of applying the law to the substantive facts, which is the responsibility of the relevant municipal jurisdiction. The municipal judge is thus free to draw from the judgment of the Court of Justice the legal conclusions appropriate to the case before him.

10–14   Although the judgment of the Court of Justice given under Article 177 is in quite general terms, it is not at all clear whether that judgment can be said to have a validity *erga omnes* in the way that judgments under Articles 173 * and 175 * EEC have such validity. Arguments for such an interpretation are based primarily on the abstract form of the judgment; against this it is argued that the judgment is nevertheless inextricably bound up with the given fact situation, and that another tribunal is free to ask the same question, to which it will receive a reply, the implication of this in turn being that the question is not closed, and that the Court is not bound by its previous decisions. The latter argument assumes that the civil law never recognises the value of precedent, and for that matter that the doctrine of precedent, characteristic of the common law, requires automatic application of previous decisions. The two approaches to case law differ greatly in theory, but are not dissimilar in practice. This being so, it would appear that the question whether a decision of the Court of Justice has validity *erga omnes* is perhaps without very much substance; admittedly, the Court of Justice may go back on the interpretation of the law given in a previous case, and admittedly it may be asked for a further interpretation, which may in effect vary the earlier interpretation, but until such a variation is carried out, the earlier interpretation on the point remains the law, and indeed is the law.

10–15   To illustrate this, it is perhaps useful to provide an example: thus in 26/62, *Van Gend en Loos* v. *Nederlandse Administratie der Belastingen*, Rec. IX 1, [1963] C.M.L.R. 105, the Court of Justice held Article 12 of the EEC Treaty to be directly applicable in internal law, a result which at the time was probably not necessarily to be expected. The Court of Justice was, however, only giving a preliminary ruling, and thus it could be said that the judgment had binding effect only as between the parties in the case. As a matter of fact, however, the Court of Justice had created a precedent; it had settled the law. Admittedly, the Court of Justice could later reverse itself, although this is unlikely, but until it does so it is very hard to avoid the conclusion that an interpretation of Article 12 of the EEC Treaty, different from the one given, would be contrary to the Treaty. Admittedly, the Court of

Justice does not possess any powers to enforce its interpretation, but national courts will generally be under some constraint to observe it. Faced with a question of interpretation of Article 12, a national court may certainly take *Van Gend en Loos* into account and hold the Article to be directly applicable, but the situation is rather different if it holds otherwise. A final court of appeal is under a more or less complete obligation (see Chap. 15 as to the extent of this obligation) to refer any "question" of Community law to the Court of Justice under Article 177. It cannot be doubted that a court failing to make a reference under that Article where it questioned the decision in *Van Gend en Loos*, would be in breach of its obligations under Article 177, for if it wished to take a different line, *i.e.* wished to interpret Article 12 differently, there would undoubtedly be a "question" of Community law, which must be settled by the Court of Justice. Until such a reference is made, the conclusion is inescapable that the interpretation given in *Van Gend en Loos* was the correct one, and a domestic court will in fact be wrong in law in applying another interpretation. The Court of Justice has in a number of cases pointed to its earlier rulings as containing the correct interpretation; see notably 28–30/62, *Da Costa en Schaake* v. *Nederlandse Administratie der Belastingen*, Rec. IX 59, [1963] C.M.L.R. 224, questioning *Van Gend en Loos*; and 28/67, *Molkerei-Zentrale* v. *HZA Paderborn*, Rec. XIV 211, [1968] C.M.L.R. 187, questioning 57/65, *Lütticke* v. *HZA Saarelouis*, Rec. XII 293, [1971] C.M.L.R. 674.

10–16 In none of these cases did the Court of Justice reject the new request out of hand, but it directly reminded the applicants of the terms of its earlier judgment. In other words, the Court of Justice reiterated that the correct interpretation, the law, was as stated in the earlier case, the necessary implication from this being that the law would remain as it was until the Court changed its interpretation, or until the effects of any such decision were legislated away. It thus seems that the question whether a decision of the Court of Justice has validity *erga omnes* is probably without content; on a narrow interpretation, the judgment has no such validity, for it is always open to the Court of Justice to change its view, but until it does so that decision stands. If one must attach labels, then it has relative validity.

A decision on the validity of a Community act, as opposed to its interpretation, presents greater difficulties; it is doubtful whether the Court of Justice can annul an invalid act under Article 177, but this does not appear to detract from the general validity of the judgment, as defined above.

CHAPTER 11

ACTIONS AGAINST MEMBER STATES FOR FAILURE
TO FULFIL AN OBLIGATION

ARTICLES 169 * AND 170 * EEC

11–01   ARTICLE 169 * states that:

> " If the Commission considers that a Member State has failed
> to fulfil an obligation under this Treaty, it shall deliver a reasoned
> opinion on the matter after giving the State concerned the
> opportunity to submit its observations.
>
> " If the State concerned does not comply with the opinion within
> the period laid down by the Commission, the latter may bring the
> matter before the Court of Justice."

Article 170 * enables other Member States equally to bring such
matters before the Court of Justice, subject to bringing the matter to the
attention of the Commission.

This procedure, known in the French shorthand of Community law
as *recours en constatation de manquement*, is best described in English
as the action against Member States for failure to fulfil an obligation.
A similar procedure exists under Article 88 of the ECSC Treaty.

The nature of the obligation not fulfilled may be:

    (a) one arising from the Treaty directly;

    (b) from secondary legislation thereunder; or

    (c) possibly a failure to observe general principles of law implied
         by Community law (*cf.* 29/69, *Stauder* v. *Ulm Sozialamt*,
         Rec. XV 419, [1970] C.M.L.R. 466).

The procedure is not necessarily, however, a contentious procedure, and
may be set in motion with a view to obtaining an interpretation on a
point not otherwise entirely clear.

Articles 169 * and 170 * set out the basic principles of the action,
but it is subject to certain special procedures under various Articles of
the Treaties; thus Article 180 (*a*) enables the procedure to be operated
by the Board of Directors of the European Investment Bank, and
Articles 93 (2), 225 EEC and 38 and 82 Euratom provide for direct
reference to the Court without the administrative procedure provided
in Article 169,* first para., being required, since these Articles contain
comparable safeguards of their own. These Articles do not, however,
preclude use of Article 169 * even where they apply.

11–02   The role of the Commission is pivotal in the procedure, but a
Member State may itself initiate what amount to parallel proceedings

(see *infra*) even though it may have no direct interest in the case other than a desire to see that the law is observed (such proceedings have in fact been initiated, but the cases did not come to trial). The Commission is under some obligation to set the Article 169 * procedure in motion, this being its principal way of discharging its watchdog duties under Article 155 in cases of failure to fulfil an obligation. It has, however, a wide measure of discretion in the method of applying that Article. It is concerned to bring the matter before the Court only if the Member State fails to comply with the reasoned opinion. There is no compulsion to bring an action, only an obligation to give a reasoned opinion once it has reached the conclusion that the Member State has failed to fulfil an obligation. (Between 1968 and 1971 the Commission issued some seventy-odd opinions under Article 169,* but only about twenty cases came before the Court. See § 4–03, *supra*.) Failure to issue an opinion cannot be considered to be an actionable failure (unless in the case where the failure results from a failure of the Commission to carry out its duty to guard against breaches of the Treaty).

This emerges from case 48/65, *Lütticke* v. *Commission*, Rec. XII 27, [1966] C.M.L.R. 378. Lütticke had asked the Commission to initiate Article 169 * proceedings against Germany, claiming that the compensatory turnover tax on imported dairy products levied by the Federal Republic was incompatible with EEC Article 95. The Commission services did not agree that Germany was in breach of the Treaty, and it was against this reply that Lütticke directed an action,

(a) alleging that the reply constituted a decision susceptible of annulment under Article 173 EEC,* and

(b) complaining of the Commission's failure to act, under Article 175 EEC.*

The plaintiff failed on both counts, the Court holding:

(a) that neither the reply nor any other act adopted by the Commission under Article 169 * constituted a binding act susceptible of such annulment; and

(b) that the Commission could not be held to have failed to act for the purposes of Article 175,* since it had in fact replied.

It is generally agreed, however, that the Court could have rejected the action for failure to act on the narrower ground that since the act requested was a non-binding act, it did not come within the category of acts appealable by a natural or legal person under Article 175 EEC,* or alternatively that the act in question was not one in which the plaintiff had a sufficient interest to request its issue.

11–03   Although an individual cannot therefore compel the opening of the Article 169 * procedure, he may be able to obtain the same result by bringing a domestic action followed by a question under Article 177: *cf.* 57/65, *Lütticke* v. *Hauptzollamt Sarrelouis*, Rec. XII 293, [1971] C.M.L.R. 674. This impossibility of forcing the Commission to act is one of the chief differences between the EEC procedure and the ECSC procedure under Article 88 (see discussion below). But an indirect attack under Article 177 EEC (preliminary ruling on the validity and interpretation of acts of the institutions) is permissible. The Court of Justice rejected the opposite view out of hand in 26/62, *Van Gend en Loos* v. *Nederlandse Administratie der Belastingen*, Rec. IX 1, [1963] C.M.L.R. 105. Since the Article 169 * opinion is not a binding act, it is doubtful whether it could be annulled under Article 173,* once given.

The procedure

11–04   The Article 169 * procedure falls into two parts; what may be described as the pre-contentious procedure under the first paragraph, and the reference to the Court under the second paragraph.

Pre-contentious procedure

11–05   " If the Commission considers that a Member State has failed to fulfil an obligation under this Treaty, it shall deliver a reasoned opinion on the matter after giving the State concerned the opportunity to submit its observations."

The giving of at least the opportunity to be heard is fundamental to the procedure and cannot be dispensed with, although certain Articles, which contain their own safeguards (see § 11–01, *supra*) provide for direct reference to the Court.

The Member State is informed of the opening of the Article 169 * procedure by letter, which must clearly state the grounds of complaint, but should not contain the full reasoning of the opinion, which may be required later. The Member State is usually given one month in which to reply, but this period can be extended with a fair degree of flexibility. If the State fails to reply, the Commission may issue its opinion without further delay. In fact, however, a reply is the rule rather than the exception, and indeed many cases have been settled at this stage without the necessity for an opinion.

The reasoned opinion

11–06   Again, the reasoned opinion is essential to the procedure. It states the Commission's position as to the failure, and requests the Member State to put itself in order. The opinion does not itself have any legal force, nor does it make a determination that there has been a failure as does the decision taken in similar circumstances under Article 88 ECSC. This is a function of the Court: *cf.* 48/65, *Lütticke* v. *Commission*, Rec. XII 27, [1966] C.M.L.R. 378, *supra*, and 6 & 11/69, *Commission* v. *France*, Rec. XV 523, [1970] C.M.L.R. 43. But the difference is one of form, not of substance, for while the Commission's act is here non-binding, it is for it to seise the Court. Under the ECSC Treaty, its decision is binding, and the Member State may seise the Court if aggrieved.

As a matter of general practice, the Commission takes some care to provide exhaustive reasoning in its opinion. The reasoning is an essential element of legal security, and is required even though the facts of the case will be well known to all parties by this stage. On the other hand, the opinion need not as a matter of law contain more than a certain minimum of information. In case 7/61, *Commission* v. *Italy* (the pork imports case), Rec. VII 613, [1962] C.M.L.R. 59, the Italian Government claimed *inter alia* that the letter sent by the Commission as a reasoned opinion did not conform to the requirements of Article 169,* first para., since it did not examine the relevance of the arguments advanced by the Italian Government. The Court held that:

> " Article 169 of the Treaty considers an opinion to be reasoned when it contains, as in the present case, a coherent statement of the reasons which convinced the Commission that the State in question failed to fulfil one of its obligations under the Treaty. The above-mentioned letter of December 21, 1960, although not drawn up in the required form, nevertheless complies with this requirement." (Trans. [1962] C.M.L.R. 39 at p. 54.)

Further, it is clear that the Commission is in no sense prevented from altering its reasons between the time of the initial complaint and the issue of the reasoned opinion.

11–07 The question remains what effect a lack of reasoning would have on a case brought under Article 169,* second para. As emerges from 7/61, *Commission* v. *Italy*, it is probable that the Court would, in such circumstances, hold the reference to be inadmissible.

All this assumes, however, that the Member State fails to comply with the opinion. The Commission must give the State concerned time to comply with its opinion, and should give indications of what will constitute compliance, unless this is obvious from the context.

If the Member State takes action designed to achieve compliance, but which does not in fact do so, the Commission may well be obliged to start an entirely fresh Article 169 * procedure: 7/69, *Commission* v. *Italy*, Rec. XVI 111, [1970] C.M.L.R. 97.

Reference to the Court

1–08 If the Member State fails to comply, the Commission may seise the Court. It has a discretion in this matter, limited only by its duty under Article 155 to secure observance of the Treaty. There is no time-limit on making the reference—although the Court frowns on interminable delay in bringing any action (see generally § 36–29, *infra*, on limitation of action).

On the other hand, the Member State cannot engage in delaying tactics, *e.g.* by introducing a request for safeguards under Article 226 EEC (now expired), as happened in 7/61, *Commission* v. *Italy*, since this is part of an entirely separate procedure. Such attempts were specifically rejected in cases 2 & 3/62, *Commission* v. *Belgium and Luxembourg*, Rec. VIII 813, [1963] C.M.L.R. 199 (" the *Gingerbread* case "), and case 7/61, *Commission* v. *Italy*. Belgium and Luxembourg also argued in the *Gingerbread* case that since the Commission was itself allegedly at fault, there was no need to comply until the Commission had regularised its own position. This was rejected by the Court, as was a rather similar argument in 48/65, *Lütticke* v. *Commission*. Nor, for that matter, may a Member State excuse its failure to act by pointing to a failure to act on the part of one of its constitutionally independent institutions, such as the legislature: 45/64, *Commission* v. *Italy*, Rec. XV 433; 8/70, *Commission* v. *Italy*, Rec. XVI 961; 77/69, *Commission* v. *Belgium*, Rec. XVI 237.

11–09   A further issue raised by 7/61, *Commission* v. *Italy*, was whether the Commission could justifiably pursue its complaint although, between the reference to the Court and the hearing, Italy had in fact complied with the opinion. The Court held that the Commission had a valid interest in the proceedings, which, as it pointed out, were not designed to condemn the failure, but rather to obtain " a judgment at law as to whether the failure has or has not occurred." The Court appears, however, to have changed its position since that date, and will now examine whether a sufficient interest can be shown: 26/69, *Commission* v. *France*, Rec. XVI 565, [1970] C.M.L.R. 444. In that case, the sufficient interest lay in the fact that the decision of the Court would govern a number of similar cases.

A slightly different point was raised in 7/69, *Commission* v. *Italy*, Rec. XVI 111, [1970] C.M.L.R. 97, where the Commission argued that the alleged breach of obligation had not been cured by a legislative modification subsequent to the reference to the Court. Referring to the need to protect the legal right of parties to be heard, the Court rejected the application, in effect saying that new facts would require a fresh Article 169 * procedure. 45/64, *Commission* v. *Italy* involved in this respect rather similar facts, but the action was allowed to go forward apparently because the subsequent legislative modification did not affect the nature of the breach.

Procedure under Article 170 *

11–10   " A Member State which considers that another State has failed to fulfil an obligation under this Treaty may bring the matter before the Court of Justice " (Article 170,* first para.). But before it takes such action, it must bring the matter before the Commission for a reasoned opinion, delivered after hearing the parties. Here again, the same exceptions to the obligation to submit to the pre-contentious procedure apply (see § 11–01, *supra*). In this case, the pre-contentious procedure involves two or more States rather than one.

The opinion given by the Commission will now be rather different from that given under Article 169 *; in the first place, the Commission can find that there is, in its opinion, *no* failure, and secondly, if it does find that there is a failure, it confines itself to that and little more. It seems likely, however, that if it does find a failure, the Commission will have to initiate an Article 169 * procedure in addition, for the first paragraph of Article 169 * leaves it no discretion in the matter.

The introduction of a case under Article 170 * is not dependent on an opinion of the Commission; the fourth paragraph makes it clear that its absence is not a bar to the action, but it must at least be asked for, and assuming that an opinion is given, there is similarly no bar on introducing an action, whether the opinion is positive or negative.

PROCEDURE UNDER THE ECSC TREATY

1–11   Article 88 of the ECSC Treaty provides for a procedure somewhat similar to that under Article 169,* the first paragraphs of both Articles being to largely similar effect, with the difference that the Commission's opinion is here a decision. Under the second paragraph of Article 88 ECSC, however, it is for the Member State to institute proceedings before the Court, effectively to attack the decision concluding that there is a failure, for it is here the Commission that establishes the failure and not the Court. (It is clear that the decision can only record a failure, and is not used to state that there is no failure.)

If the Commission fails to take a decision, it can under this Treaty, in contrast to the EEC and Euratom procedure, be attacked for failure to act under Article 35 (1) ECSC: 7 and 9/54, *Groupement des Industries Sidérurgiques Luxembourgeoises* v. *High Authority*, Rec. II 53; 17/57, *Gezamenlijke Steenkolenmijnen in Limburg* v. *H.A.*, Rec. V 9, and 30/59, *Gezamenlijke Steenkolenmijnen in Limburg* v. *H.A.*, Rec. VII 1. The decision that is taken is only declaratory, and may not impose new obligations, although it can suggest how the situation can be corrected: 20/59, *Italy* v. *H.A.*, Rec. VI 663, and 25/59, *Netherlands* v. *H.A.*, Rec. VI 723; here again, Member States cannot excuse their failure by pointing to a failure of the Commission: *cf.* cases 20/59 and 25/59.

Unlike Article 169,* Article 88 ECSC provides for the application of sanctions against the Member State if it has not fulfilled its obligation within the time-limit, or if it brings an action which is dismissed, and the Council acting by a two-thirds majority assents. The Member State affected may appeal against the sanctions, but not against the original decision.

ARTICLE 182 *

1–12   Article 182 * provides that:

   " The Court of Justice shall have jurisdiction in any dispute between Member States which relates to the subject-matter of this Treaty if the dispute is submitted to it under a special agreement between the parties."

Article 154 Euratom is identical. Article 89, second para., ECSC is *mutatis mutandis* identical.

Article 182 EEC * is in some sense an extension of Article 170,* for it includes within its ambit not only disputes relating to fulfilment of Treaty obligations, but the undefined area of disputes relating to the subject-matter of the Treaty. Article 170 * in effect provides for compulsory jurisdiction, however, while Article 182 * provides only for submission of disputes by both parties on an agreed basis. There is some analogy to be drawn here with the compulsory and voluntary jurisdictions of the International Court of Justice, but the analogy is not to be pushed too far, although Article 182 * does offer a type of jurisdiction not unlike that of a more conventional international tribunal.

11–13   There is no case law on the application of Article 182,* so that any conclusions must be essentially speculative, but there is some question as to whether Article 182 * covers disputes concerning the *application* of the Treaty, given that Article 89, first para., ECSC established a separate head of jurisdiction in respect of such disputes, while providing for jurisdiction in respect of disputes relating to the *subject-matter* of the ECSC Treaty in the second paragraph of the same Article. On the other hand, Member States undertake by Article 219 EEC not to submit disputes concerning the *interpretation* or *application* of the Treaty to any method of settlement other than those provided for therein, and it must be considered that the term " subject-matter " (French *objet*, German *Gegenstand*) used in Article 182 * is to have a wide meaning, which would include disputes as to the application of the Treaty, although there is conceivably an area of disputes outside *interpretation* and *application* which are still within *subject-matter*. It may be doubted, however, whether it was intended that these should be settled by judicial measures otherwise than before the Court of Justice.

Essentially, however, Article 182 * is never likely to be a primary method for the settlement of disputes in the Community context, for actions between the Member States and the Commission are likely to resolve most questions, and Article 170 * is perhaps likely to be resorted to before Article 182.* The type of dispute which might result in a special agreement under Article 182 * is probably more readily settled at the political level, given the close ties between the Member States within the Community.

CHAPTER 12

ACTIONS RELATING TO PENALTIES

12–01 ARTICLE 172 EEC provides that Regulations made by the Council pursuant to the provisions of that Treaty may give the Court of Justice unlimited jurisdiction in regard to the penalties provided for in such Regulations. The Council is given a specific power to issue Regulations under four Articles only: Article 43 (2), third sub-para. (agricultural policy); Article 49 (free movement of workers); Article 87 (1) (rules on competition); Article 94 (authorisation of state aids) (*cf.* also Art 209); but this certainly does not exhaust its power to make Regulations, for a fairly large number of Articles enable the Council to " lay down provisions " or otherwise to act, without the mode of action being limited. Pursuant to Article 189,* the Council can, where it has a power to act, adopt any one of the types of acts referred to in that Article (and in practice other types besides) subject only to limitations contained in the enabling power. The most general of the enabling provisions is Article 235, which enables the Council to adopt " the appropriate measures " where the Treaty has not provided the necessary powers.

12–02 There are at present three Regulations imposing penalties and conferring jurisdiction upon the Court, namely Regulation 17/62 (J.O. 1962, 204) on competition, and Regulation 11/60 (J.O. 1960, 1121) on transport and Regulation 1017/68 (J.O. L 175/1) on competition in transport. Regulation 11 is based upon Article 79 of the EEC Treaty, Regulation 17 upon Article 87 and Regulation 1017/68 upon Articles 75 and 87.

Article 17 of Regulation 17 and Article 24 of Regulation 1017/68 provide that:

> " The Court of Justice shall have unlimited jurisdiction within the meaning of Article 172 of the Treaty to review decisions whereby the Commission has fixed a fine or periodic penalty payment; it may cancel, reduce or increase the fine or periodic penalty payment imposed."

Article 25 (2) of Regulation 11 provides that:

> " Pursuant to Article 172 of the Treaty, the Court of Justice shall have unlimited jurisdiction in regard to any penalty imposed under Articles 17 and 18 [of the Regulation]. The Commission may not proceed with the enforcement of a penalty until the period allowed for appeal has expired."

It is to be noted that Article 172 to some extent duplicates the provisions of Article 173,* second para., which enables a natural or legal person to institute proceedings against a decision addressed to himself

101

or of direct and individual concern to him within a period of two months. Article 172 is not so limited by time, but it is difficult to avoid the conclusion that the plaintiff under the latter provision would equally have to show an interest to be able to sue, and would have to sue within a reasonable time.

12–03   The phrase " unlimited jurisdiction " is a translation of the French term *pleine jurisdiction*, which is to be contrasted with a limited type of jurisdiction, *e.g.* merely to annul. It is clear that by the reference to unlimited jurisdiction it was intended that the Court should be able to decide not only upon the validity of a penalty or its amount, but also upon the validity of the decision imposing the penalty, and that the applicant should be able to rely upon any of the four grounds of illegality mentioned in Article 173 *—cf. 9/56, Meroni* v. *H.A.*, Rec. IV 9—if the action is brought in time. Alternatively, he might be able to rely upon the exception of illegality (see generally, Chap. 16).

Chapter 13

REVIEW OF LEGALITY OF COUNCIL AND COMMISSION ACTS (ACTION FOR ANNULMENT)

13–01 ARTICLE 173 * of the EEC Treaty requires the Court to review the legality of acts of the Council and the Commission other than recommendations or opinions. Unlike the jurisdiction under Article 171,* this jurisdiction only enables the Court to find the Community act illegal and to declare it void (*cf.* Art. 174,* first para.). The Court may not therefore substitute a decision of its own for the Community act which it could not have made in the first place.

Article 173,* first para., EEC gives a definition of what type of act may be impugned under its provisions. In referring to acts other than recommendations and opinions, the authors of the Treaty intended that only binding acts in the sense of Article 189 * should be attackable. There are, however, two qualifications on this:

(1) an act couched in the form of a recommendation but as a matter of fact having the effect of a binding act in the sense of Article 189 * would, it seems, be open to annulment in appropriate circumstances: 22/70, *Commission* v. *Council* (the *AETR* case), Rec. XVII 263, [1971] C.M.L.R. 335;

(2) it is not entirely clear what would be the reaction of the Court of Justice to a request for annulment of a decision of the representatives of the Member States, but here again *AETR* suggests that the Court might be amenable to such a request in appropriate circumstances.

The status of decisions of the representatives of the Member States is somewhat uncertain (see generally, § 8–13), but it would be difficult to describe such an instrument as an " act of the Council," and an action under Article 173 * impugning such an instrument could most easily be dismissed on this ground alone. An approach under Article 177 (preliminary rulings) might be more profitable, but here too it could be argued that such decisions are not acts of one of the institutions, and therefore that the Court has no jurisdiction to give a preliminary ruling on the validity of such acts, let alone on their interpretation.

13–02 The first paragraph of Article 173 * enables parties to attack a Community act on any of four grounds:

(1) lack of competence (*incompétence*);

(2) infringement of an essential procedural requirement (*violation des formes substantielles*);

103

(3) infringement of the Treaty or of any rule of law relating to its application; or

(4) misuse of powers (*détournement de pouvoirs*).

The four terms used are taken more or less directly from French administrative law and thus the terms were already terms of art with definite meanings, which are only imperfectly conveyed by their literal translation. It is not, however, the case that these terms should only be understood in relation to French law. Whatever their origin, they are now terms of Community law and must be taken in that context alone (49/71, *Hagen OHG* v. *EVSt*, Rec. XVIII 23, and 50/71, *Wünsche* v. *EVSt*, Rec. XVIII 53). The same terms are used in the comparable article of the ECSC Treaty (Art. 33) and a considerable jurisprudence has been built up which is by and large applicable to Article 173 EEC.* The only other outside source of which the Court may avail itself for their interpretation would be the general principles of law prevailing in the Member States.

GROUNDS OF ACTION

1. Lack of competence

13–03   When the Treaty refers to lack of competence, it is clear that what is to be understood is a lack of powers to do the act complained of; it is in a sense an *ultra vires* act. Thus in 9/56, *Meroni* v. *H.A.*, Rec. IV 43, the Court held that a delegation of discretionary powers of the High Authority to another body was invalid, the delegation provided for relating only to powers of execution. In 20/59, *Italy* v. *H.A.*, Rec. VI 663, and in 25/59, *Netherlands* v. *H.A.*, Rec. VI 723, the Court annulled decisions of the High Authority because the ECSC Treaty conferred no decision-making power for the implementation of Article 70.

2. Infringement of an essential procedural requirement

13–04   By "infringement of an essential procedural requirement" is meant infringement of a requirement which goes beyond the merely procedural and vitiates the very basis of the act which purports to be issued; without that element it is not truly an act. Thus there are throughout the Treaties provisions setting out decision-making powers subject to certain formalities which are all substantial procedural requirements. An opinion which is required to be reasoned, and which is not in fact reasoned can be attacked under this heading: 1 & 14/57, *Soc. Usines à Tubes de la Sarre* v. *H.A.*, Rec. III 201. Similarly, parts of a decision which is to some extent reasoned but which lacks the necessary clarity and is vague and contradictory have been annulled: 24/62, *Federal Republic of Germany* v. *Commission*, Rec. IX 129, [1963] C.M.L.R. 347, *cf.* 18/57, *Nold* v. *H.A.*, Rec. V 89; 36–38 and 40/59, *Präsident*

v. *H.A.*, Rec. VI 857; 2/56, *Geitling* v. *H.A.*, Rec. III 9; and 6/54, *Netherlands* v. *H.A.*, Rec. I 201. But an unreasoned decision which explicitly refers to an earlier fully reasoned decision as being the controlling act has been upheld: 16/65, *Schwarze* v. *EVSt*, Rec. XI 1081, [1966] C.M.L.R. 172. The amount of reasoning required will in fact depend upon the importance, difficulty and urgency of the matter to be regulated (*Schwarze* v. *EVSt, supra*) and the type of act in question: 8-11/66, *Cimenteries CBR* v. *Commission*, Rec. XIII 93, [1967] C.M.L.R. 77; and 5/67, *Beus* v. *HZA München Landsberger-strasse*, Rec. XIV 125, [1968] C.M.L.R. 131.

3. Infringement of the Treaty

13-05   The ground of action constituted by infringements of the Treaty, or of any rule of law relating to its application, overlaps to some extent with the previous head, in that a good number of such essential procedural requirements (*e.g.* as to reasoning) are laid down in the Treaty. The Court's jurisprudence reflects this in the sense that it has not always distinguished the two cases (see *e.g.* 2/54, *Italy* v. *H.A.*, Rec. I 73). Infringement of the Treaty etc. may of course be an infringement of any kind, including a failure to take a Treaty Article into account. (*Cf.* 8/57, *Groupement des Hauts Fourneaux et Aciéries Belges* v. *H.A.*, Rec. IV 223, where the Court held that Article 3 of the ECSC Treaty could not be applied without taking Articles 2, 4 and 5 into account as well. *Cf.* also 1/54, *France* v. *H.A.*, Rec. I 7.) A failure to observe the stipulation of a Community act would also of itself be such a violation.

It is not clear what is the meaning to be attributed to the phrase " rule of law relating to its application," but it would seem at least to embrace an application of general principles of law.

Infringement of the Treaty undoubtedly overlaps also with misuse of powers (below), the distinguishing line, if one can be drawn, lying in the degree of discretion enjoyed by the Community. If there is no discretion, there will probably be a violation of the Treaty. If there is complete discretion, there will probably be misuse of powers, but this distinction cannot be taken too far; the actual dividing line, if any, will depend on practice, not on an objective test.

4. Misuse of powers

13-06   The term " misuse of powers " describes the action of the administrative authority in applying powers which it has for one purpose to other unauthorised situations: 6/54, *Netherlands* v. *H.A.*, Rec. I 201; 8/55, *Fédéchar* v. *H.A.*, Rec. II 199; 15/67, *Hauts Fourneaux de Chasse* v. *H.A.*, Rec. IV 155. The illegal objective may not in fact be achieved, or else the objective may not itself be illegal, but an act which is based upon power given for other purposes will nevertheless be voidable. It seems, however, that a decision which incidentally does something for which powers were not provided will not be struck down provided the essential purpose for which the powers were provided is not infringed: 8/55, *Fédéchar* v. *H.A.*, *supra*; 1/54, *France* v. *H.A.*, Rec. I 7; and 2/57, *Hauts Fourneaux de Chasse* v. *H.A.*, Rec. IV 129.

The standard of proof of misuse of powers is clearly very high: 10/55, *Mirossevich* v. *H.A.*, Rec. II 365. But the plaintiff need not necessarily produce evidence of a motive wrongful in itself, although the test of misuse depends on motive, if misuse be a reasonable implication from the facts (*res ipsa loquitur*): 8/55, *Fédéchar* v. *H.A.*, Rec. II 199. This has permitted a number of plaintiffs to allege misuse of powers where matters appear merely marginally out of the ordinary, or, to the plaintiff at least, obscure. But this is to put the hurdle of admissibility too low; there must be at least some evidence that the Community was acting illicitly: *cf.* 8/57, *Groupement des Hauts Fourneaux et Aciéries Belges* v. *H.A.*, Rec. IV 223. Misuse of powers is probably the most important of the bases of illegality in the three Treaties.

The relevance of misuse of powers to actions for annulment is clear; the ground of action is used to impugn the act complained of because its foundations are illegal. The ground of action is not therefore strictly relevant to the act itself, but rather to the motives for which it was done.

ACTION FOR REVIEW OF LEGALITY

13–07 With the exception of Article 172 (jurisdiction in regard to penalties) the provisions in relation to jurisdiction so far discussed permit Member States or Community institutions alone to bring actions. By contrast, Article 173 * (and Art. 175 *) gives natural or legal persons rights at least similar to, although not identical with those of Member States and the institutions.

Article 173,* second para., enables any natural or legal person to institute proceedings against a decision addressed to that person, or against a decision which, although in the form of a Regulation or a decision addressed to another person, is of direct and individual concern to the former.

Essentially, therefore, the right of action of individuals is limited; only decisions, or acts which are really decisions, may be attacked. Any attempt at widening this right of action must therefore be directed to proving that acts in the form of a Regulation are of direct and individual concern to the plaintiff, and lack the generality of a true Regulation. It is only by this means that an individual can aspire to attack a general act.

13–08 For the purposes of the second paragraph of Article 173 * the definition of a Regulation contained in Article 189 *: " a Regulation shall have general application. It shall be binding in its entirety and directly applicable in all Member States " is not sufficient. Some criterion is required by which the general act may be distinguished from the act which is essentially individual in character, but is disguised in the form of the general act. The Court of Justice draws a distinction between general and individual decisions for the purposes of Article 33 of the ECSC Treaty, and this has been developed for the purposes of application to EEC situations. (*Cf.* 16 & 17/62, *Confédération Nationale des Producteurs de Fruits et Légumes* v. *Commission*, Rec. VIII 901, [1963] C.M.L.R. 160; and 25/62, *Plaumann* v. *Commission*, Rec. IX 197, [1964] C.M.L.R. 29.) It emerges that a Regulation is essentially legislative (*normatif*) in character, and is applicable not merely to specific addressees but to categories in the abstract and in general. It has a validity *erga omnes*, while a decision is limited in its validity to those to whom it is addressed (*Confédération Nationale, supra*). Thus, in 41 and 44/70, *International Fruit Company* v. *Commission*, Rec. XVII 411, a Regulation ultimately addressed to a group of persons who were identified in advance, was held to be a bundle of individual decisions. But in 63/69, *Cie. Française Commerciale et Financière* v. *Commission*, Rec. XVI 205, [1970] C.M.L.R. 369, and 65/69, *Cie. d'Approvisionnement* v. *Commission*, Rec. XVI 229, [1970] C.M.L.R. 369, the Court held that the fact that individuals were affected in different ways did not affect the general nature of the Regulation. 64/69, *Cie. Française Commerciale* v. *Commission*, Rec. XVI 221, [1970] C.M.L.R. 369, is more difficult; there, the Court held that the regulatory nature of the act is not put in doubt by the possibility of ascertaining with some degree of precision the number or even the identity of the persons affected, as long as the criteria are objective. (See also 30/67, *Industria Molitoria Imolese* v. *Council*, Rec. XIV 171; 6/68, *Zuckerfabrik Watenstedt* v. *Council*, Rec. XIV 595, [1969] C.M.L.R. 26.)

13–09   The reason for restricting the right of appeal so as to exclude appeals against Regulations is perhaps that a Regulation is akin to a statute, in theory the outcome of an elaborate legislative progress which ought not to be impugned. This is in keeping with United Kingdom constitutional practice. This is the position only in theory, for Commission Regulations can be made with very little formality, although such Regulations will admittedly relate normally to matters of execution only. The Court declines, however, to distinguish between Council and Commission Regulations. This must also explain why directives may not be appealed against. Such acts cannot in any event affect individuals except at one remove (but see *e.g. Corveleyn* v. *État Belge*, [1969] C.D.E. 343). Directives may be attacked by way of municipal action, followed by a reference to the Court of Justice under Article 177, or else by way of an action under Article 178,* but neither process can achieve their annulment (see also *infra*, Chap. 16, plea of illegality).

It is clear that a State impugning any binding Community act need show no special interest or connection with the case. The right to bring an action is absolute, agreeably to the duty of Member States under Article 5 EEC (Art. 192 Euratom) to take all appropriate measures to ensure the fulfilment of the obligations arising out of the Treaty. It amounts to a form of control on constitutionality: *cf. SACE* v. *Ministry of Finance*, Rec. XVI 1213, [1971] C.M.L.R. 123.

Individuals, on the other hand, are much more restricted. A decision which is challenged need not, it is true, be one specifically addressed to the plaintiff but if not, it must nevertheless be of direct and individual concern to him (Art. 173,* second para.).

13-10   These requirements are not alternative, but must both be met if an individual is successfully to invoke Article 173,* first para., against a decision addressed to someone other than himself: *cf.* 38/64, *Getreide-Import Gesellschaft* v. *Commission*, Rec. XI 263, [1965] C.M.L.R. 276; 25/62, *Plaumann* v. *Commission*, Rec. IX 197, [1964] C.M.L.R. 29.

The Article speaks of decisions addressed "to another person." But the fact that the decision is addressed to a Member State, rather than to another person, does not in practice appear to affect the matter (see, however, 69/69, *Alcan* v. *Commission*, Rec. XVI 385, [1970] C.M.L.R. 337). Various unsuccessful actions against decisions addressed to Member States have failed for quite other reasons: 25/62, *Plaumann* v. *Commission*, *supra* (restrictions in Germany on imports of clementines); 1/64, *Glucoseries Réunies* v. *Commission*, Rec. X 811, [1964] C.M.L.R. 596 (restrictions in France on glucose imports); 38/64, *Getreide-Import Gesellschaft* v. *Commission*, *supra* (levy in Germany on sorghum imports); 106 and 107/63, *Toepfer* v. *Commission*, Rec. XI 525, [1966] C.M.L.R. 111 (restrictions in Germany on imports of maize); 63 and 64/69, *Cie. Française Commerciale* v. *Commission*, Rec. XVI 205 and 221, [1970] C.M.L.R. 369; 65/69, *Cie. d'Approvisionnement* v. *Commission*, Rec. XVI 229 [1970] C.M.L.R. 369 (compensatory amounts on exports of flour from France); and 41 and 44/70, *International Fruit Company* v. *Commission*, Rec. XVII 411. The fact that the decision is unpublished does not appear to affect the matter: *cf.* 73 and 74/63, *Internationale Crediet- en Handelsvereniging " Rotterdam " and Puttershoek* v. *Dutch Ministry of Agriculture and Fisheries*, Rec. X 1, [1964] C.M.L.R. 198.

It was indicated in *Plaumann* that it was necessary first to show that the plaintiff was individually concerned, the question of direct concern only arising thereafter. But this does not appear to have been an absolute statement, for the order of consideration was reversed in *Toepfer* and in 62/70, *Bock* v. *Commission*, Rec. XVII 897, [1972] C.M.L.R 160. This only serves to demonstrate, however, that the two criteria are distinct, and must both be fulfilled. If it is relatively easy to show direct concern (but see 69/69, *Alcan* v. *Commission*, *supra*, where the Court held that tariff quotas were facilities offered to States, and could not therefore confer rights on individuals), success in establishing individual concern has been rare. The plaintiffs got this far in *Toepfer*, *Fruit Company* and *Bock*, however, so that their actions were at least admissible if not necessarily successful.

13–11   The fact situations in these three cases are all fairly complicated and differ considerably, but they are alike in one respect; in each case the Commission took a decision restricting imports based upon information supplied by national authorities at a time when the persons who would be affected thereby were already identifiable. *Fruit Company* represents virtually no advance on *Toepfer* except, possibly, that the act in question in *Fruit Company* was a Regulation, which the Court held to be a bundle of individual decisions. *Bock* is perhaps an unusual case, in that the decision was designed specifically to deal with Bock's request for import licences. The *ratio* of each case thus varies somewhat, but they all turn on closely analogous fact-situations, and it is in consequence difficult to regard them as constituting a precedent of general validity except in so far as they represent the other face of the French *compensatory amount* cases (*supra*), which state clearly that a plaintiff is not individually and directly concerned by a general act having the character of a Regulation, so as to enable him to attack it.

13–12   Most Article 173 * actions at the instance of individuals have failed; the cases seem to have turned on the following points: *Plaumann*, who attacked a refusal to suspend the duty on imported clementines, failed because although he was one of thirty or so importers who would in fact be interested, nevertheless, the decision was addressed ultimately to clementine importers in general. *Glucoseries Réunies* failed because although they were the only Belgian exporters who could be affected by the safeguard provisions, nevertheless, there were others in the other Member States who might be affected. *Getreide-Import* is less straightforward at first sight; the company applied for an import licence on a certain day, as a result of which a particular levy was payable pursuant to a previous price-fixing decision. As a matter of fact, *Getreide-Import* was the only firm to apply that day. As a matter of abstraction, however, there might have been others, and it is on this, and on the fact that the decision also applied to exports, that the case must be taken to turn. It does not resemble the successful cases because there the number of persons affected was already finite. In the French *compensatory amount* cases the plaintiffs all failed to overcome the difficulty of showing that the Regulation attacked was not in fact a Regulation, but a bundle of individual decisions. The cases turned on much the same point as *Plaumann*. In the second of them (64/69) the plaintiffs were arguably very nearly individualised in the *Toepfer* sense, and the Court was therefore constrained to emphasise the general " *nature réglementaire* " of the act annulled rather than the lack of individualisation. This formula provides a more convincing basis for rejection.

The Court held in 25/62, *Plaumann* v. *Commission*, that:

"Persons other than those to whom the decision was addressed can justifiably claim to be concerned individually only if the decision affects them because of certain characteristics which are peculiar to them or by reason of a factual situation which is, as compared with all other persons, particularly relevant to them, and by reference to which they may be individually described in a way similar to that of the addressee of the decision." (Trans. [1964] C.M.L.R. 29 at p. 46.)

Conversely in 64/69, *Compagnie Française Commerciale et Financière* v. *Commission, supra*, the Court held that the *nature réglementaire* of an act is not put in question by the possibility that the number or even the identity of the persons to which it may apply may be determined at a given moment, as long as it is clear that the act is being applied to a legal or factual situation which, having regard to the purpose of the act, is assessed objectively.

A somewhat novel approach (the seeds of it may be seen *e.g.* in 5, 7 and 13–24/66, *Kampffmeyer* v. *Commission*, Rec. XIII 317 (*infra*, § 36–18) has been adopted in 96/71, *Haegeman* v. *Commission* (not yet reported) where the action is described (para. 3) as seeking in effect the annulment of a refusal to exempt the plaintiff from a compensatory tax, and the restitution of the disputed sums. The application was rejected on the short ground that the tax constituted Community "own resources" (as to which see *infra*, § 35–09), that own resources were collected by Member States in accordance with national rules, that the ascertainment and control of collection was in the first instance for the Member States, and that disputes concerning rules governing own resource taxes, etc., should in the first instance be brought before the national authorities or jurisdictions, the Article 177 procedure being available in the latter case.

This judgment would appear to remove at a stroke the possibility of action against any Community act involving own resources. Given that the elements of other grounds for rejection seem to have been present a more orthodox approach would have been preferable.

13–13   It is significant that the actions which were held to be admissible turned upon the fact that the names of those affected were already discoverable with complete certainty before the decision was taken. On the other hand, so in one sense were the names of those affected in the *Plaumann*, the *Glucoseries* and the *compensatory amount* situations; arguably, therefore, the whole potential class must actually be affected. The mere fact that the class *in abstracto* is affected is insufficient. 64/69, *Cie. Française Commerciale* v. *Commission* supports this line of reasoning in so far as that case held that a Regulation could only be considered to be a disguised decision when the criteria for fixing the price, levy, restriction, etc. ceased to be purely objective, but in effect became based upon specific actions or characteristics of those in fact affected, as was undoubtedly the case in 62/70, *Bock* v. *Commission,* Rec. XVII 897, [1972] C.M.L.R. 160.

13–14 The question whether the individuals were directly concerned also arose implicitly in the cases where the plea of illegality succeeded. In *Toepfer* the Court held that the plaintiff was so concerned, on the basis that the decision attacked was directly applicable. In *Fruit Company* the Court for some reason confined itself to saying that the applicant was individually concerned by the decision. In *Bock,* however, the Court had no difficulty in finding the plaintiff to be directly concerned, since the decision complained of was made with specific reference to him.

The meaning of the expression " of direct and individual concern " has fallen to be discussed exclusively in relation to acts addressed to Member States, although the Court's statements of law (*cf.* quotation from *Plaumann, supra*) appear to be designed to be of general application. If, however, the criterion is of a directly applicable decision addressed (through a Member State) to exactly defined individuals, then a decision addressed to another individual will *ex hypothesi* not concern the former directly and individually. It would seem, therefore, that the Court cannot avoid developing other criteria, should that fact situation arise.

The Court has avoided laying down any concrete criteria for ascertaining whether or not an individual is " concerned," which is in keeping with its flexible approach under the ECSC Treaty. It is unlikely, however, that the Court would uphold a future interest; the individual must be concerned at the time, not merely some time in the future.

13–15 Article 173 * is not the only Article concerned with review of legality of acts of Community bodies; Article 180 (*c*) gives Member States, the Commission and the Board of Directors of the European Investment Bank a right to bring Article 173 *-type proceedings against measures adopted by the Board of Governors of the Bank on the conditions laid down in Article 173.* A further limited right of action is given against measures adopted by the Board of Directors of the Bank. Actions may only be brought by Member States or the Commission under the conditions laid down in Article 173,* and solely on grounds of non-compliance with the procedure provided for in Article 21 (2), (5), (6) and (7) of the statute of the Bank.

REVIEW OF LEGALITY UNDER THE ECSC TREATY

13–16 Article 33 of the ECSC Treaty likewise provides for the review of legality of Community acts, and many of the rules developed under the

ECSC Treaty have been transferred in practice to the EEC. There are, however, certain specific differences between the two procedures.

In the first place, undertakings and associations may under the ECSC Treaty only attack decisions (*i.e.* Regulations) or recommendations (*i.e.* directives) on all four grounds if they are individual in character. The Court has developed an extensive jurisprudence on the notion of the general decision, which in its effects parallels the EEC Treaty provisions which exclude the attack of Regulations: 13/57, *Wirtschaftsvereinigung Eisen-und Stahlindustrie* v. *H.A.*, Rec. IV 261; 23, 24 and 52/63, *Henricot* v. *H.A.*, Rec. IX 439, [1964] C.M.L.R. 119; 3/64, *Chambre Syndicale de la Sidérurgie Française* v. *H.A.*, Rec. XI 567; 36–38, 40–41/58, *Società Industriale Metallurgica di Napoli* (*Simet*) v. *H.A.*, Rec. V. 331; 10/57, *Société Aubert et Duval* v. *H.A.*, Rec. IV 399; 42 and 49/59, *Société Nouvelle des Usines de Pontlieue - Aciéries du Temple S.A.* (*SNUPAT*) v. *H.A.*, Rec. VII 101, [1963] C.M.L.R. 60.

Secondly, the notion of " concerning " is rather more liberally interpreted: *cf.* 1/58, *Stork* v. *H.A.*, Rec. V 43, and 27–29/58, *Cie. des Hauts Fourneaux et Fonderies de Givors* v. *H.A.*, Rec. VI 501 (the Court did not even pronounce on the point in the latter case).

Thirdly, undertakings or associations may attack even a general decision where it is considered that it involves a misuse of powers affecting them, the Court holding that this is just a further aspect of the criterion of individual concern: 8/55, *Fédéchar* v. *H.A.*, Rec. II 199; 9/55, *Soc. Charbonnages de Beeringen* v. *H.A.*, Rec. II 323.

Fourthly, Article 33 only enables the Court of Justice to review economic facts or circumstances where the High Authority is alleged to have misused its powers or to have manifestly failed to observe the provisions of the Treaty, or any rule relating to its application. This rule is not taken up in Article 173,* and the Court appears to assess economic factors wherever required.

CHAPTER 14

ACTIONS AGAINST THE COUNCIL OR COMMISSION
FOR FAILURE TO ACT

14–01 CLEARLY, a right of action enabling parties to impugn administrative acts is only one form of control of administrative action by the judicial arm. One should be able to compel action, as well as to be able to attack allegedly illegal action. Accordingly, Article 175 * provides a remedy where the Council or Commission has, in infringement of the Treaty, failed to act. The judgment of the Court does not, however, compel action on the part of the Community, but only establishes the infringement of the Treaty. The notion of infringement of the Treaty is thought to be quite wide in this context, and could potentially include misuse of powers, presumably involving non-user of a discretion for wrong or illicit reasons (see generally, § 13–06, *supra*). The institution whose failure to act has been declared contrary to the Treaty is required to take the necessary measures to comply with the judgment of the Court (Art. 176 *).

Under Article 175,* as under Article 173,* the right of a Member State to bring an action is quite general. Thus the States need show no special interest, and the nature of the act which has not been done has no particular relevance to the right of action. The only restriction upon the action is that the institution concerned must have been called upon to act (*mise en demeure*). If, within two months of being so called upon, the institution has not defined its position, the action may be brought within a further period of two months (Art. 175,* second para.). The time-limit within which the action may be brought is the same as that under Article 173,* third para. (No Member State has yet brought such an action under the EEC Treaty.)

14–02 Individuals, on the other hand, have a right of action under the third paragraph of Article 175 * only if an institution has failed to address to them a binding act in the sense of Article 189 *; in fact only decisions can be addressed to individuals, and the rights of individuals are therefore limited to requesting a decision, which has an individual character at that. In 15/71, *Mackprang* v. *Commission*, Rec. XVII 797, [1972] C.M.L.R. 52, the Court rejected a request by an individual for a decision which would have been addressed to all the Member States, complementary to the DD4 Certificate Decision of July 17, 1962 (J.O. 1962, 2140).

" Such a decision could not, either in its form or its legal nature, be described as a measure which would have to be addressed to

the applicant firm within the meaning of Article 175, para. 3 "
(Trans. [1972] C.M.L.R. at p. 59.)

It is clear that the Court must have had in mind the undesirability
of enabling individual applicants to dictate Community legislation.

14-03   An essential prerequisite to an action under Article 175 * is that the
institution concerned should first have been called upon to act: *cf.* 24
and 34/58, *Chambre Syndicale de la Sidérurgie de l'Est de la France*
v. *H.A.*, Rec. VI 573, on the same point under Article 35 ECSC. The
request must further be sufficiently clear and precise for action to be
taken upon it, but there is no formal requirement, *e.g.* that the party
making the request put the institution on notice that the request constitutes the *mise en demeure* of Article 175 *; 17/57, *De Gezamenlijke
Steenkolenmijnen in Limburg* v. *H.A.*, Rec. V. 9; and 8/71, *Deutscher
Komponistenverband* v. *Commission*, Rec. XVII 705. Once the request
has been made the only party entitled to bring an action is the party
making the request (although an application to be allowed to intervene
is not excluded).

The practice of the Court under the ECSC Treaty indicates that the
issue of a binding act in the sense of Article 14 ECSC will alone
halt the running of time: 42 and 49/59, *SNUPAT* v. *H.A.*, Rec. VII
101, [1963] C.M.L.R. 60, and 5–11 and 13–15/62, *San Michele* v. *H.A.*,
Rec. VIII 859, [1963] C.M.L.R. 13. But Article 35 ECSC, the ECSC
counterpart to Article 175 EEC,* refers specifically to a failure to take
a binding decision.

14-04   Article 175 * refers only to a failure to act, and/or a failure to
define position. Admittedly the third paragraph of the Article, giving
individuals a right of action, requires the act called for to be an act
other than a recommendation or opinion, in other words a binding act,
but there is no guidance on what type of act is in question in the
first two paragraphs, dealing with actions brought by Member States
and by institutions. The Court held in 15/70, *Chevalley* v. *Commission*,
Rec. XVI 975, that the same types of act are in question under both
Article 173 * and 175,* and Article 173 * refers throughout to acts
other than recommendations and opinions, but this ruling cannot be
regarded as absolutely conclusive, since the Court was only ruling on
an individual application. 48/65, *Lütticke* v. *Commission*, Rec. XII 29,
[1966] C.M.L.R. 378, is not entirely helpful on the point, but would not
seem to exclude absolutely the possibility of requesting a non-binding
act (see also § 11–02).

14-05   The facts of the case were as follows. As from January 1, 1962,
the German Government began to levy a compensatory turnover tax
on dairy products imported from other Member States, instead of a
customs duty. The plaintiff (a natural or legal person within the meaning of Article 175,* third para.) complained that this tax was incompatible

with the provisions of Article 95 of the EEC Treaty, which permit such a substitution, but only on the basis that the new tax is not protective. He argued that the new tax was in fact protective; accordingly he asked the Commission to start proceedings against Germany under Article 169.* The Director-General for Competition (not the Commission as such) replied by letter that such a request was inadmissible. Lütticke therefore began an action before the Court, attacking the Commission for failure to act as requested under Article 175,* and attacking the letter for illegality under Article 173.* The plea of illegality failed because there was no binding act to attack. This is unexceptionable, but the decision in relation to the Article 175 * limb is less straightforward. The Court held that the fact that the Commission Directorate General for Competition had taken a position not to initiate Article 169 * proceedings, and had communicated this fact to the plaintiff, was sufficient to end the failure to act. This does not necessarily mean, however, that the Court decided that a party could not therefore demand the issue of a non-binding act; the act demanded was the opening of the Article 169 * procedure, not the reply. The Court did not have to decide whether there was a failure to act or to find a failure to issue an act of any particular kind, because the Commission had already taken a position ending any potential failure to act. On the question of what kind of act is demandable, the most that can be said is that *Lütticke* v. *Commission* decided that a simple definition of position ends the failure to act.

4–06   The reasoning of the Court in relation to Article 175 * seems dubious: Article 175 * was clearly designed to enable the parties (without prejudice to the question as to exactly which parties) to attack a failure to issue at least a binding act. To reduce this virtually to nothing by enabling the Commission or Council to confine itself to announcing its refusal to act is to deprive the article of its purpose. A much sounder approach would perhaps have been to hold that the act requested would have been addressed to a Member State and not to Lütticke, and furthermore would not have been a decision. Alternatively, it could have been argued that since the procedure in Article 169 * is non-binding and in some degree discretionary, a failure to act would not constitute an infringement of the Treaty. Both of these arguments appear to have been in the mind of the Advocate-General in the *Lütticke* case. The Court did in fact refer to the fact that the act requested was non-binding in 6/70, *Arese* v. *Commission*, Rec. XVI 961, [1970] C.M.L.R. 436, and in 15/70, *Chevalley* v. *Commission*, Rec. XVI 975, and in both cases this was the primary reason for rejecting the application.

4–07   A general conclusion to be drawn from the *Lütticke* case is that the failure ends with a simple statement of position (see further 8/71, *Deutscher Komponistenverband* v. *Commission*, Rec. XVII 705). It has been suggested that this rule would not apply where the act demanded would not be directed to the individual. If, however, the Court will permit at least the initiation of an action by an individual against a failure to issue an act directed to third parties, an authorisation apparently not sanctioned by the Treaty, there is no reason at all why the Court should not apply the same logic that it applies in such cases, namely that a simple statement of position will end the failure to act (8/71, *Deutscher Komponistenverband* v. *Commission*). There is probably, however, a final safeguard here, in that the definition of position must at least be in clear reasoned terms where the individual (or indeed any party) can demand a decision as of right. Thus, the Commission could not simply refuse to issue a decision one way or the other on a request for negative clearance, but it could reject the application as being incomplete.

In defence of *Lütticke* v. *Commission* it is said that it would be inadmissible to require an institution to work out a presumably complex act in a mere two months; but Lütticke only asked in effect for the Commission to invite Germany to submit its observations on the matter of taxes on powdered milk—hardly something that would take two months. If, on the other hand, it is right to argue that an individual could succeed if he requested a binding act addressed to himself, then that argument would go by the board, for such a decision might well take longer to produce than if, for instance, the act requested were a negative clearance.

14-08   Where an individual complains of a failure to address an act to himself, it is clear, quite apart from the issues described above, that at least some kind of interest must be demonstrable. Accordingly, the Court held in 5–11/62 and 13–15/62, *San Michele* v. *H.A.*, Rec. VIII 859, [1963] C.M.L.R. 13, that if the Commission acted even after the time-limit had elapsed, the action would not lie, for there would be no injury. This ruling must be contrasted with 7/61, *Commission* v. *Italy* (pig-meat imports case), Rec. VIII 633, [1962] C.M.L.R. 39, where the Court held that the Commission could still maintain an action under Article 169 * for failure to fulfil an obligation. The difference in that case was that the Commission had an interest as guardian of the Treaty in having the failure established. Although Article 173 * similarly speaks of an infringement, an individual does not have that same interest (*cf.* also 43/71, *Politi* v. *Italian Ministry of Finance*, Rec. XVII 1039).

The question can perhaps be raised whether the interest of the individual must be such that he is " directly and individually concerned " by the act requested. It is submitted that this cannot really arise; either the act is addressed to the individual, or it is not.

Lütticke v. *Commission* did not decide that an individual could attack an institution for failure to act. The Court was only concerned to say that there was no failure to act. There being no failure, there was no question of an action for failure. Nevertheless, it is probably true to say that an individual may, under Article 175,* third para., only request an act addressed to himself, although the contrary has been argued. An analogy with cases such as 25/62, *Plaumann* v. *Commission,* Rec. IX 197, [1964] C.M.L.R. 29, enabling individuals to request annulment of acts addressed to third parties does not seem permissible.

4–09 Attacks on a failure to act might conceivably succeed under Article 177, or under Article 215, but only for achieving their legitimate purposes (4/69, *Lütticke* v. *Commission,* Rec. XVII 325). In 21–26/61, *Meroni* v. *H.A.,* Rec. VIII 143, the Court rejected an attempt to avoid the expiry of the time-limit for bringing actions under Article 33 of the ECSC Treaty by means of an action for failure to annul the decisions in respect of which actions under Article 33 were no longer possible. A similar situation arose in 10 and 18/68, *Eridania* v. *Commission,* Rec. XV 459, where the plaintiffs attacked an implicit refusal to act with an action for illegality under Article 173 *; the Court of Justice rejected the application, since the Treaty provides specific procedures for actions for failure to act.

UNDER THE ECSC TREATY

4–10 As with Article 173 EEC,* and its relation to Article 33 ECSC, the differences between Article 175 EEC * and Article 35 ECSC are inherently differences in form. Where, however, the articles show similarities as between the two Treaties, the ECSC jurisprudence provides some guidance. Much of the practice under Article 33 ECSC turns on a fiction that the failure to act constitutes an implied decision not to act (7 and 9/54, *Groupement des Industries Sidérurgiques Luxembourgeoises* v. *H.A.,* Rec. II 53), which can be annulled; 42 and 49/59 *SNUPAT* v. *H.A.,* Rec. VII 101. There is no parallel in the EEC practice. The Court altered its position somewhat in 30/59, *Gezamenlijke Steenkolenmijnen in Limburg,* Rec. VII 1, however, holding that an action for failure to act lay only against an implied refusal to act; it could not lie against an actual decision of refusal to act, which would have to be annulled.

4–11 A significant difference in ECSC practice lies in the Court's holding that a binding act alone interrupts the failure to act; *SNUPAT* and 5–11 and 13–15/62, *Soc. Industriale Acciaierie San Michele* v. *H.A.,* Rec. VIII 859, [1962] C.M.L.R. 13. Unlike Article 175 EEC,* Article 35 ECSC itself distinguishes between acts which the Commission is obliged to take, and those in regard to which it has a discretion. In the former case, the right of appeal is quite general; in the latter, the Treaty itself limits the grounds of action to misuse of powers.

By contrast with Article 175 EEC,* which only permits attack on the basis of infringement of the Treaty, Article 35 ECSC is not so limited, but on the contrary is linked to Article 33 ECSC in so far as the action constitutes an attack on a decision. Thus all the grounds of attack there provided are admissible (7 and 9/54, *Groupement des Industries Sidérurgiques Luxembourgeoises* v. *H.A.*, Rec. II 53).

CHAPTER 15

PRELIMINARY RULINGS

TYPES OF JURISDICTION

5-01 ARTICLE 177 of the Treaty gives the Court of Justice jurisdiction to give preliminary rulings concerning:

(a) the interpretation of the Treaty;

(b) the validity and interpretation of acts of the institutions of the Community; and

(c) the interpretation of the statutes of bodies established by an act of the Council, where those statutes so provide.

The expression " preliminary rulings," which had currency before the definitive English text of the EEC Treaty was adopted, is not an entirely happy one, if only because it is rather opaque. The French *à titre préjudiciel* gives a much better idea of what is entailed; namely that the domestic court seised of a question should be able to stay proceedings before and pending an interpretative decision from the Court of Justice on the point on which the case turns. The reference to the Court of Justice is thus not chronologically prior to the municipal action, but only to the judgment in the case. The jurisdiction to give preliminary rulings gives the Court of Justice exclusive power to pass upon matters referred to it under any of the heads of Article 177 EEC, under the substantially identical provisions of Article 150 Euratom, and under Article 41 ECSC, which enables the Court to give such rulings on the validity of Council or High Authority (*i.e.* Commission) *délibérations*, but on a somewhat different basis.

5-02 Although Article 177 does not enable the Court of Justice to give a judgment binding on a party to the Treaties or on an institution, there can be no doubt that it has been of great importance in enabling the Court to discharge its duty under Article 164 * of ensuring that in the interpretation and application of the Treaty the law is observed. It is under Article 177 that some of its most important judgments have been delivered: *e.g.* 26/62, *Van Gend en Loos* v. *Nederlandse Administratie der Belastingen*; and 6/64, *Costa* v. *ENEL* (both discussed *infra*). It is thus through this Article that the Court has asserted the supremacy of Community law (*Costa*) and the need for a uniform application of the Treaty provisions: *e.g.* 39/70, *Fleischkontor* v. *HZA Hamburg St. Annen*, Rec. XVII 49, [1971] C.M.L.R. 281.

5-03 Article 177 EEC, Art. 150 Euratom and Article 41 ECSC between them confer jurisdiction on the Court to give preliminary rulings on matters falling into four categories. The practice in relation to each category nevertheless shows a considerable unity, so that it is not for instance particularly useful to examine the power of the Court to interpret the Treaty in isolation from its power to interpret acts of the institutions. Essentially the jurisdiction of the Court involves two powers: a power to give interpretations of Community law; and a power to rule on the validity of acts of the institutions. Before examining these two powers, however, it is necessary to analyse the categories of matters on which the Court may give preliminary rulings.

Interpretation of the Treaty

15–04　　In the first place the Court may interpret the Treaties by way of preliminary ruling. This power extends only to the EEC and Euratom Treaties, the power to act under Article 41 ECSC being limited to a power to rule on the validity of Council and Commission acts. The Court construes its power to interpret the Treaties strictly, and in its exercise will neither pronounce on the validity or otherwise of municipal acts or laws, nor take these into account in ascertaining the meaning of the Treaties. (6/60, *Humblet* v. *Belgium*, Rec. VI 1125; 100/63, *Van der Veen*, Rec. X 1105, [1964] C.M.L.R. 548; 24/64, *Dingemans* v. *Bestuur der Sociale Verzekeringsbank*, Rec. X 1259, [1965] C.M.L.R. 144; 34/67, *Lück* v. *HZA Köln-Rheinau*, Rec. XIV 359; 23/70, *Haselhorst* v. *Finanzamt Düsseldorf-Altstadt*, Rec. XVI 881, [1971] C.M.L.R. 1; 78/70, *DGG* v. *Metro Grossmärkte*, Rec. XVII 487, [1971] C.M.L.R. 631; and 10/71, *Ministère Public Luxembourgeois* v. *Muller-Hein*, Rec. XVII 723.)

15–05　　More generally indeed, the Court has held that the validity or effect of a Community instrument " cannot be affected by allegations that it strikes at either the fundamental rights as formulated in [a] State's constitution or the principles of a national constitutional structure," although " respect for fundamental rights has an integral part in the general principles of law of which the Court of Justice ensures respect. The protection of such rights, while inspired by the constitutional principles common to the Member States must be ensured within the framework of the Community's structure and objectives " (11/70, *Internationale Handelsgesellschaft* v. *EVSt*, Rec. XVI 1125, [1972] C.M.L.R. 225. Trans. [1972] C.M.L.R. at p. 283). The *Handelsgesellschaft* case produced something of a stir in Germany, and the court which referred the matter to the Court of Justice has now requested a ruling from the Federal Constitutional Court (see [1972] C.M.L.R. 177). While the Court of Justice will not apply national or Community law to municipal situations, but will only give an abstract interpretation of the applicable Community law, there are occasions when Community law may itself require a consideration of the applicable municipal rules, as in Article 215,* second para., of the EEC Treaty. In such cases the

Court will be obliged to give direct consideration to national law (*cf.* 24/71, *Meinhardt* v. *Commission*, Rec. XVIII 269). The point is well brought out in 49/71, *Hagen* v. *EVSt*, Rec. XVIII 23, and 50/71, *Wünsche* v. *EVSt*, Rec. XVIII 53, holding that in the absence of *renvoi*, whether explicit or implied, to national law, the legal concepts used by Community law must be interpreted and applied in a uniform fashion throughout the Community.

Validity and interpretation of acts of the institutions

5–06   Under sub-paragraph (*b*) of Article 177 EEC the Court of Justice has jurisdiction to give preliminary rulings on two related but separable categories of question, namely on

(1) the validity, and

(2) the interpretation of acts of the institutions.

Article 41 ECSC confers jurisdiction on the Court to give preliminary rulings on matters falling within the second of the above categories, but the jurisdiction so conferred is not on all fours with the jurisdiction under the Rome Treaties, in the first place because the ECSC provision extends only to acts of the Commission and the Council, and secondly because that provision does not in the sole authentic text (*i.e.* the French) refer to " acts " at all, but to " *délibérations*." Theory and indeed practice indicate, however, that these notions are more or less co-extensive (*cf.* 73 and 74/63, *Internationale Crediet- en Handels-vereniging " Rotterdam " and Puttershoek* v. *Dutch Ministry of Agriculture and Fisheries*, Rec X 1, [1964] C.M.L.R. 198). But the argument that only binding acts come in question in either case is less readily sustainable in relation to the expression " *délibérations*." There would, however, be at least an element of futility in the Court interpreting a non-binding act, let alone in ruling on its validity. The notion of a binding act must in any case be treated with caution; whether an act is binding depends upon content and intention rather than on form: 22/70, *Commission* v. *Council*, Rec. XVII 263, [1971] C.M.L.R. 335. Further, the notion is probably not to be limited to those types of acts listed in Article 189 *: Article 228 (2) states agreements concluded under the conditions of Article 228 (1) to be " binding on the institutions of the Community and on Member States."

5–07   Some difficulty arises over the term " institution " used in the Rome Treaties (Art. 41 ECSC refers expressly to the High Authority and the Council). The term must, it seems, be given its narrow meaning in Article 4 EEC (see *supra* § 3–03). But a request for a preliminary ruling could not be made in relation to a decision of the Court of Justice, if only because there is a special revision or interpretation procedure. The argument that a judgment of the Court is binding and cannot therefore be put in question is not convincing without more:

a Regulation cannot be attacked after the expiry of the two months, but it can certainly be interpreted.

Difficulties also arise over " acts " of the Parliament. As they are not binding, it is questionable whether they can be interpreted.

Finally, the question arises whether a Treaty concluded by the Communities is susceptible of Article 177 interpretation. The answer might at first sight be expected to be in the negative, since an international Treaty is not an act within Article 189,* but the reality is that all Community Treaties are concluded by a decision or Regulation, which annexes the Treaty itself, and interpretation could fasten upon the act concluding the agreement. This view appears to be confirmed by 21–24/72, *International Fruit Company* v. *Produktschap voor Groenten en Fruit,* not yet reported (Community concludes agreements of all kinds in the context of the GATT, and, in so far as the Community has assumed powers previously exercised by the Member States in relation to the GATT, the provisions of the GATT bind it).

The interpretation of statutes of bodies established by an act of the Council

15–08   The third sub-paragraph gives the Court jurisdiction to interpret the statutes of bodies established by an act of the Council, where those statutes so provide. The phrase " statutes of bodies established by an act of the Council " is itself open to difficulties of interpretation. The argument that the Treaty does not give the Council power to establish such bodies must be rejected; the residual powers in Article 235, if nothing else, enable the Council to set up such bodies. But since such a setting-up must inevitably be by an act of the Council, surely this is in itself subject to interpretation under the previous head. The restrictive phrase " where those statutes so provide " seems therefore to be without effect. It is in any case difficult to see how the matter could come before a domestic court in the first place so as to admit of an application to the Court of Justice, except perhaps in certain limited areas. For example the question might be raised whether, despite its subjection to the law of the State in which it resided, such a body enjoyed certain immunities. Article 150 Euratom gives jurisdiction to the Court under this head in any case in which the statutes of the body concerned do not otherwise provide. Here, therefore, jurisdiction is the rule rather than the exception.

THE CONCEPT OF INTERPRETATION

15–09   The first case to come before the Court of Justice under Article 177, 13/61, *De Geus* v. *Bosch,* Rec. VIII 89, [1962] C.M.L.R. 1, raised the question whether a territorially restricted agency agreement fell within the categories of agreements prohibited by Article 85 EEC, as of the entry into force of the Treaty. The defendants in the municipal action argued with some force that such a question involved not merely the interpretation of Article 85 but also its application. The Court held that the question of application was not one which it could decide under Article 177, and therefore confined itself to interpreting Article 85. There was, it held, no particular form in which questions had to be asked, and therefore it could sever those parts of the question over which it had jurisdiction, to give an interpretative ruling.

A further argument advanced in the *Bosch* case, though turning on the particular facts, has a more general relevance. It was argued that at the time of the application the interpretation of Article 85 was a matter for the Member States, because, under Article 88, it was for them to apply the rules of competition, not the Community, until the entry into force of Regulations implementing Article 87 (in the event, Reg. 17/62). The Court agreed that it was for the Member States to apply the Article, but rejected the corollary that it was therefore for them to interpret it, thus clarifying the distinction between interpretation and application. See also 26/62, *Van Gend en Loos* v. *Nederlandse Administratie der Belastingen*, Rec. IX 1, [1963] C.M.L.R. 125; 6/64, *Costa* v. *ENEL*, Rec. X 1141, [1964] C.M.L.R. 425 and 23/70, *Haselhorst* v. *FA Düsseldorf-Altstadt*, Rec. XVI 881, [1971] C.M.L.R. 1, where the Court refused to pronounce upon the compatibility of national measures with Community law under this Article, but was nevertheless prepared to spell out the applicable Community laws.

5–10   It is quite clear, then, that the Court will at least in theory distinguish questions of application and will give a general ruling on interpretation. But in practice it is extremely difficult to divorce the facts from the objective interpretation, and many of the decisions of the Court which are ostensibly interpretative in fact go some way towards deciding the case one way or the other, as is only to be expected. A classic example is 26/62, *Van Gend en Loos* v. *Nederlandse Administratie der Belastingen* (*supra*), where the Court held Article 12 of the EEC Treaty to be directly applicable in Member States. If, as the Court held, the Article creates rights for individuals, then an individual affected by a breach of that Article will have a very strong ground of action before domestic courts. There are now a dozen or so cases in which it has been held that Articles of the Treaty are directly applicable, *Van Gend en Loos* being only the earliest (see list, § 18–09).

Nevertheless, even though the questions of interpretation and application are inseparable, the Court will deliver its judgment in terms of general application. Though it may not discuss questions not asked of it, the Court will always reformulate the appropriate question even where the question is specific, and answer accordingly (*e.g.* 6/64, *Costa* v. *ENEL, supra*).

VALIDITY OF ACTS OF INSTITUTIONS

5–11   It is clear that where Article 177 EEC and Article 41 ECSC speak of validity, validity both as to form and as to content is referred to. It is less clear what is the effect of a ruling on the validity of an act under Article 177. Article 173 * enables an action to be brought for annulment of Community acts within certain narrowly defined limits. The Court has held that Article 175 * cannot be used to evade these limits—21–26/61, *Meroni* v. *H.A.*, Rec. VIII 143, and 10 and 18/68, *Eridania* v. *Commission*, Rec. XV 459—but on the other hand, the Court will not refuse to entertain an action under Article 215 where such an action stands on its own merits (4/69, *Lütticke* v. *Commission*, Rec. XVII 325) and it is likely that the same principle will operate in the case of a request for a preliminary ruling in such circumstances. (The situation in the *Meroni* case was somewhat different, in that the action under Article 35 ECSC was a colourable attempt to overturn the limitations of Article 33 ECSC.)

Further support for this view may be found in the wording of Article 177 itself as compared with Articles 173 * and 175.* The two latter Articles carry direct consequences; in particular, the act complained of will be annulled. Under Article 177, however, the Court is concerned only to give a ruling on whether the provision before it can be said to be valid. It does not thereby annul the act in question, and furthermore, the effect of its judgment is at least arguably limited to the parties to the case (although *cf.* § 10–14).

15–12   The Court of Justice has not as yet had to decide on what amounts to validity for these purposes, but the issue was at least raised in 73 and 74/63, *Internationale Crediet- en Handelsvereniging and Puttershoek* v. *Dutch Ministry of Agriculture and Fisheries*, Rec. X 1, [1964] C.M.L.R. 198. In 17/67, *Neumann* v. *HZA Hof/Saale*, Rec. XIII 571, the Court, in holding that the validity of a Regulation was not affected, implied that it could rule against its validity, had this been necessary. Similarly 37/70, *Rewe-Zentrale* v. *HZA Emmerich*, Rec. XVII 23, [1971] C.M.L.R. 238.

The Court of Justice made it quite clear in 31 and 33/62, *Milchfirma Wöhrmann* v. *Commission*, Rec. VIII 965, [1963] C.M.L.R. 152 (see also 44/65, *Hessische Knappschaft* v. *Singer*, Rec. XI 1191, [1966] C.M.L.R. 82) that the question whether or not to refer a matter to the Court of Justice was exclusively within the competence of the court of first instance, and that an individual could not coerce the national court or by-pass its procedures (see also *infra*, exception of illegality, Chap. 16).

What Bodies may Refer Questions

15–13 The last two paragraphs of Article 177 indicate that any court or tribunal (*juridiction*) may, if it considers that a decision on a question coming under any one of the heads listed is necessary to enable it to give judgment, request the Court to give a ruling thereon. The permissive facility becomes compulsory in the case of matters before courts " against whose decisions there is no judicial remedy under national law."

The translation " any court or tribunal " well reflects the content of *juridiction*, for it is clear that the latter term covers any body which has to decide questions by the application of law, and before which at least quasi-judicial procedures are observed. Nevertheless, there are certain difficulties.

In the first place, doubts have been expressed as to whether a court acting in interlocutory proceedings is entitled to refer a question to the Court (*e.g. KIM-Sieverding* case, [1960] S.E.W.(E.) 83, 323, Brinkhorst and Schermers, p. 203, and *Re Asbach-Uralt Brandy* [1969] C.M.L.R. 172). Doctrine is almost unanimous in thinking that such a right does exist, and *a fortiori* where a court of last instance is hearing an appeal in an interlocutory application. Whether in the course of such proceedings a reference is necessary or probable is another question.

Secondly, there is the question whether arbitrators have the right to refer questions. The answer must, subject to the views of the Court, be in the negative, since arbitral bodies are not constituted as standing tribunals, nor do their rulings constitute national jurisprudence. If these criteria are fulfilled, then questions would be admissible: 61/65, *Widow Vaassen-Göbbels* v. *Beambtenfonds*, Rec. XII 377, [1966] C.M.L.R. 508 (*Scheidsgerecht* was permanent, and in effect followed judicial procedures and applied law). Where these criteria were not fulfilled an arbitral tribunal in one case disqualified itself—*cf.* " *the Z. Contract* case," the Award of Arbitral Tribunal on Competition, Rotterdam, July 22, 1964, *Arbitrale Rechtspraak* 1964, No. 254, p. 240, Brinkhorst and Schermers p. 201.

Thirdly, some doubt has been expressed as to whether an individual can seise the Court of Justice under Article 177. The Court of Justice has made it quite clear that the decision to refer a question belongs to the municipal judge alone; individuals may no doubt press him to refer, but there is no way round his refusal to do so. There are no requirements of form as to how the question is referred, however.

Courts of last instance

5–14   The third paragraph of Article 177 states that where any question falling within one of the listed heads is raised in a case pending before a court or tribunal against whose decisions there is no judicial remedy under national law, that court or tribunal must bring the matter before the Court of Justice.

Rules have been laid down as to how references may be made by English courts.[1] Certain problems will have to be resolved in

---

[1] The Criminal Appeal (References to the European Court) Rules 1972, S.I. 1972 No. 1786 (L. 25) and The Crown Court (References to the European Court) Rules 1972, S.I. 1972 No. 1787 (L. 26) were to hand at the time of accession.

respect of the articulation between the Court of Appeal and the House of Lords; if the Court of Appeal refuses leave to appeal to the House of Lords, it will presumably be obliged to refer a question to the Court of Justice, since it will be acting as a final court of appeal. But the Court of Appeal would be in some dilemma in cases where it would be open for the House of Lords to give leave to appeal to itself, for the Court of Appeal would be unable to ascertain whether it was acting as a final court of appeal until after the event.

15-15   There has been some questioning in England as to what amounts to a court or tribunal against whose decisions there is " no judicial remedy." It is clear that the latter phrase refers not only to a full right of appeal, but also to rights of appeal to courts of cassation. Judicial review of administrative action under the prerogative writs would therefore prima facie come within the ambit of the phrase. It seems that courts whose decisions are not subject to review of any kind are obliged to refer questions, although they may only be courts equivalent to magistrates' courts, *cf.* first paragraph of judgment in 6/64, *Costa* v. *ENEL*, Rec. X 1141, [1964] C.M.L.R. 425.

The phrase " if it considers that a decision on the question is necessary to enable it to give judgment " has posed the problem of what constitutes the necessity. It is clear that the Court of Justice will not decide upon the question of necessity; this is for the national judge alone to assess : 13/61, *De Geus* v. *Bosch*, Rec. VIII 89, [1962] C.M.L.R. 1; 26/62, *Van Gend en Loos*, Rec. IX 1, [1963] C.M.L.R. 105; 28–30/62, *Da Costa en Schaake*, Rec. IX 56, [1963] C.M.L.R. 224; and 56/65, *La Technique Minière* (*LTM*) v. *Maschinenbau Ulm* (*MBU*), Rec. XII 337, [1966] C.M.L.R. 357. Certainly, however, the national judge cannot be expected to refer a question to the Court where the raising of a problem of Community law is no more than a side-wind, not affecting the outcome of the case before him.

15-16   A like question arises in connection with the obligation on courts of last instance (and of any court under Article 41 ECSC) to refer a question. How far are such courts obliged to refer any question of Community law which is raised? The absolute terms of the final paragraph of Article 177 would appear to suggest that even an irrelevant issue should be referred, but this is unlikely to be the intention, and is certainly not the practice. On the other hand, what amounts to a " question " of Community law, or in other words what amounts to a controverted aspect of Community law, on which the Court of Justice ought to give a ruling, is itself a question of interpretation. There has been a tendency at least in France for courts to take the matter into their own hands, and to decide whether or not there is a question for interpretation—*Shell-Berre*, [1964] C.M.L.R. 462 at p. 481; *French Republic* v. *Cornet*, [1967] C.M.L.R. 351 at p. 359; and see now *Administration des Contributions Indirectes* v. *Ramel*, [1971] C.M.L.R.

315—or in effect themselves to interpret the Treaty. These courts have tended to hold that the provision of Community law with which they were concerned was clear on the face of it. This is an application of the famous doctrine of the *acte claire*, first appearing in connection with Community law in *Shell-Berre*. The reference made to the Court of Justice by the Conseil d'Etat in 34/70, *SYNACOMEX* v. *ONIC*, Rec. XVI 1233, may nevertheless indicate a new readiness to refer questions to the Court.

5–17 Some commentators on Article 177 opine that a judge of last instance enjoys no freedom to decide whether or not a matter should be referred to the Court, the important thing being that there should be a dispute as to the interpretation of the matter, its relevance to the issue being apparently secondary. There is force in this view, but it is certainly not the practice, although the Court of Justice is prepared to accept a question even if it has already given an interpretation, so that from that point of view there arguably ought to be an *acte claire*: *Da Costa en Schaake*.

The better view would seem to be that the national judge should look to the relevance or " pertinence " of the question, and, having regard to the fact that he is administering a law applicable in all Member States, assess whether there is a question, not whether he has any doubt as to the matter. In this he ought at least to be guided by the jurisprudence of the Court of Justice. It is not, however, legitimate for a national judge to refuse to refer a question because he does not see any difficulty of interpretation; he may not himself decide on the " question " once found to be " pertinent."

5–18 If the Court has already ruled on the question in unequivocal terms, then there is no real need to refer the question a second time (*cf. Internatio and Puttershoek, supra*), but there is certainly no rule preventing a national judge from so doing: 28–30/62, *Da Costa en Schaake*. If, on the other hand, the apparently natural interpretation is different from that given previously by the Court, then there is almost certainly a " question " (25/67, *Milch- Fett- und Eierkontor* v. *HZA Saarbrücken*, Rec. XIV 305, [1968] C.M.L.R. 225, where the question substantially repeated that in 57/65, *Lütticke* as to Article 173,* in the hope that the Court would change its view).

Once the Court of Justice is seised of a question under Article 177, the reference can probably only be struck out, apart from mutual agreement on the point, if the reason for the question has disappeared. If the original decision to refer is overtaken by another decision on appeal, then the question no longer exists (*cf.* 13/61, *De Geus* v. *Bosch, supra*). In 31/68, *Chanel* v. *Cepeha*, Rec. XVI 403, [1971] C.M.L.R. 403, the Court of Justice stayed judgment (although not the other parts of the proceedings) upon being informed that a domestic appeal had been lodged, which had the consequence of suspending execution of the judgment pursuant to which the question had been referred to Luxembourg. Upon being informed that the decision appealed against had been quashed, the Court considered that the proceedings for interpretation had lost their substance, and accordingly ordered the case to be struck out.

15–19   There is always the possibility of a domestic appeal from a decision not to refer a question, the possibilities of appeal depending in large part upon national law. In the United Kingdom there would also be the possibility of control by prerogative order. Since, however, control by way of appeal or through the prerogative orders relates to findings of law, it is unlikely that a lower court would be ordered to make a reference to the Court of Justice, the decision whether or not to make a reference being primarily at the discretion of the former. It would of course be open to the higher court to make a reference itself, however. There is also the possibility of appeal against a decision of a lower court to make a reference: as already stated, the appeal may destroy the reason for the question; the granting of an appeal short of annulment of the judgment of the lower court is unlikely to result in an order that the lower court desist from its reference, but the lower court may be moved to reformulate its question of its own motion.

CHAPTER 16

THE PLEA (EXCEPTION) OF ILLEGALITY

6-01 ARTICLE 184 * EEC enables any party to invoke the inapplicability of a regulation, even after the expiry of the time-limit laid down in Article 173,* by pleading the grounds specified in Article 173,* first para. The grounds so specified all relate to a request for annulment on grounds of illegality, hence the name of plea (or exception—the French term) of illegality. The Article has been the subject of some misunderstanding, and it is therefore as well to set it out in full:

> "Notwithstanding the expiry of the period laid down in the third paragraph of Article 173, any party may, in proceedings in which a Regulation of the Council or of the Commission is in issue, plead the grounds specified in the first paragraph of Article 173, in order to invoke before the Court of Justice the inapplicability of that Regulation."

The leading case on the Article is 31 and 33/62, *Milchwerke Wöhrmann* v. *Commission*, Rec. VIII 965, [1963] C.M.L.R. 152 (see also 16 and 17/62, *Confédération Nationale des P.F.L.* v. *Council*, Rec. VIII 901, [1963] C.M.L.R. 160, in which the plaintiff brought an action under Article 184 * in respect of certain decisions of the Commission, which, he claimed, were disguised Regulations, thus coming within the Article. The Court of Justice did not have to decide whether or not the decisions complained of were in fact Regulations, or whether this was material, for it rejected the application on the logically prior ground that Article 184 * did not create a fresh cause of action parallel to Article 173,* but applied only in cases coming before the Court of Justice based on other grounds, and then only incidentally, and with limited effect (*cf. Dalmas* v. *H.A., infra*). The Court went on to indicate that Article 184 * could not be used to evade Article 177, under which reference may be made to the Court of Justice only at the instance of the national court (*cf.* also 44/65, *Hessische Knappschaft* v. *Singer*, Rec. XI 1191, [1966] C.M.L.R. 82).

6-02 Some guidance as to when the exception of illegality pleaded in an action based on other grounds may succeed is to be obtained from 9/56, *Meroni* v. *H.A.*, Rec. IV 9. The Court of Justice held that the somewhat similar exception under Article 36 ECSC was not limited (as its terms might seem to suggest) to cases in which the imposition of a fine or periodic penalty payment was appealed against, but was of general application. The Court of Justice further held that where the plea was admissible, any of the four grounds of illegality mentioned in Article 33

129

ECSC (equivalent to Article 173 EEC *) could be relied upon to establish the inapplicability of the general decision or recommendation (*i.e.* Regulation or directive in EEC terminology) but not so as to have that decision or recommendation annulled. According to later cases— 3/59, *Germany* v. *H.A.*, Rec. VI 117; 21/64, *Dalmas* v. *H.A.*, Rec. XI 227, [1966] C.M.L.R. 46—the plea is not available to enable the applicant to have an individual act annulled on the basis of Article 36 alone, but only so as to enable him to have it annulled under some other Treaty provision. These principles are clearly applicable to actions under the EEC Treaty, and it would seem that in their application they would work out as follows: in an action brought within the time-limit for the annulment of, for example, a decartelisation decision, under Article 173 EEC,* the exception of illegality could be raised against Regulation 17/62 (*cf.* facts of 32/65, *Italy* v. *Council and Commission*, Rec. XII 563, [1969] C.M.L.R. 39) assuming in the first place that the Regulation had some more or less direct bearing on the matter: *cf. Italy* v. *Council and Commission* and *Dalmas* v. *H.A.*, *supra*. Were the Court of Justice to find the Regulation invalid, it could not annul it, for the time to attack it under Article 173 * expired some little while ago. But it could annul the decartelisation decision, not so much under Article 184 * itself, but for illegality under Article 173.* Article 184 * is the door by which Article 173 * may be reached, but only if the matter complained of directly can still be attacked. If Article 184 * were not available, the intolerable result would ensue that it would be impossible to attack subsidiary acts which were illegal because the originating act was illegal, merely because time to attack the originating act had expired. If this were so, it would be only too easy to give far-reaching effect to illegal acts.

16–03   It has been suggested that since the Court of Justice has held that Article 36 ECSC applies generally to binding acts of general application, so Article 184 * EEC ought also to apply to directives as well as Regulations. The actual wording of the Article makes this interpretation very hard to accept, especially in view of the fact that directives are addressed to Member States (*cf.* Art. 189 *) and therefore by definition do not give rise to further Community acts in respect of which an action for illegality could be brought. If it be argued that such an action might be appropriate before a national court, it may be pointed out that the Court of Justice has exclusive jurisdiction to pronounce upon the validity and interpretation of acts of the institutions, under Article 177 (*b*). Indeed the Court of Justice has held on this basis that the exception applies only in actions before itself (31 and 33/62, *Wöhrmann*, *supra*). It reached this conclusion on an examination of the text of Article 184,* and such a result is the only one possible upon the French and especially the German texts, although the English text is arguably ambiguous. A reference to the Court under Article 177 could, however, achieve the same result as the exception of illegality, for the Court could point to the invalidity of a main Regulation and thus of an individual decision, and the national court would then apply the ruling.

Article 184 * states that " any party " may invoke the exception; but there are grounds for thinking that only private parties may do so. The matter is certainly not free from doubt, but it is noteworthy that if such an interpretation of " any party " conformed with the thinking of the Court of Justice, the Court could have rejected the application under Article 184 * in 32/65, *Italy* v. *Council and Commission (supra)* on that ground alone, or as a subsidiary ground.

CHAPTER 17

SUPREMACY OF COMMUNITY LAW

17–01 So far Community law has been discussed at the Community level, *i.e.* in relation to actions brought by or against the contracting parties to the Community Treaties, in relation to the institutions, and in relation to rights of action of individuals against institutions. Community law, nevertheless, obviously has a wider ambit than this; it applies within the Member States in as much as it binds those States, and it creates rights and obligations for individuals. The question then is to ascertain what the relationship is between Community law on the one hand, and the legal systems of the Member States on the other. The question breaks down into two rather more precise parts, themselves sub-divided:

1. (a) how can one explain the fact that Community law has effects in Member States?
    (b) how far does it do so?
2. (a) how can this intrusion of Community law be justified in national constitutional terms, and
    (b) in terms of its application by the courts of the Member States?

For the purposes of discussion the two parts may be described as the issue of the supremacy of Community law, and the issue of its reception as the law in the Member States.

THE CONCEPT OF SUPREMACY OF COMMUNITY LAW

17–02 It is probably misleading to attempt to construct a theoretical basis for the supremacy of Community law over national systems, although it has been variously argued that this is to be found in the so-called federal structure of the Communities; in the transfer of sovereign powers to the Communities; in the nature of the Treaties setting up the Communities as part of public international law, which as a matter of theory at least, prevails over internal law; or in the theory of *effet utile* of Community law, according to which Community law must prevail if its purpose is not to be nullified. These theories do not explain why Community law prevails, they merely justify the need for that prevalence. Accordingly, explanation for the supremacy of Community law should be sought in the statements of the Court of Justice and in the text of the Treaty, at the same time bearing in mind that the Community Treaties have been ratified and given the force of law in the Member States (although the scope of the concept "force of law" is a separate question: see Chap. 19).

7–03   The first case in which the Court of Justice was squarely faced with the question of the supremacy of Community law was 6/60, *Humblet* v. *Etat Belge*, Rec. VI 1125. There the Court said in relation to its own powers:

> " If the Court states in a judgment that a legislative or administrative act issuing from the authorities of a Member State is contrary to Community law, this State is obliged by virtue of Article 86 of the ECSC Treaty both to withdraw the act in question and to make amends for the unlawful effects which it may have produced. *This obligation is derived from the Treaty and from the Protocol, which have the force of law in the Member States as a result of their ratification thereof, and which overrule* [l'emportent sur] *domestic law.*"
>
> (Trans. Valentine II, 817 at p. 823, italics supplied.)

This statement seems a little bald, especially perhaps to the English lawyer, who is familiar with a dualist system which recognises individual rights under Treaties only where those rights have been transformed into domestic rights by legislative enactment. Nevertheless, the statement of the Court reflects constitutional theory in the six original Member States, the theory of the matter being that ratification itself creates rights. Express conversion of Treaty rights into domestic law is thus not an automatic requirement. The status to be accorded to a Treaty once ratified is a separate issue (considered Chap. 19, *infra*, as a matter of domestic law), but is clearly linked with the question of supremacy at the Community level.

The domestic enactment at issue in the *Humblet* case was the Belgian Income Tax Act of 1948, and the Court of Justice was not therefore faced with the problem of a later national law; an application of the rule *lex posterior derogat priori* would thus have sufficed for the purposes of national law, had the Court considered that the rule was in point.

7–04   In the next case, 26/62, *Van Gend en Loos* v. *Nederlandse Administratie der Belastingen*, Rec. IX 1, [1963] C.M.L.R. 105, the Court was faced with the question whether Community law was available in and prevailed over national law, for the Netherlands Tariefcommissie had asked whether Article 12 of the EEC Treaty had immediate effect in internal law, in the sense that nationals of the Member States could, on the basis of that Article, claim rights which national courts must safeguard.

The Court said that the spirit, organisation and wording of the Treaty must first be examined, and this it did in the following terms:

> " The purpose of the EEC Treaty—to create a Common Market, the functioning of which directly affects the citizens of the Community—implies that this Treaty is more than an agreement creating only mutual obligations between the contracting parties. This

interpretation is confirmed by the Preamble to the Treaty which, in addition to mentioning governments, affects individuals. The creation of organs institutionalising certain sovereign rights, the exercise of which affects both Member States and citizens is a particular example. In addition, the nationals of the States, united into the Community, are required to collaborate in the functioning of that Community, by means of the European Parliament and the Economic and Social Council. Furthermore, the role of the Court of Justice in the framework of Article 177, the aim of which is to ensure uniformity of interpretation of the Treaty by the national courts, confirms that the States recognised in Community law have an authority capable of being invoked by their nationals before those courts. *We must conclude from this that the Community constitutes a new legal order in international law, for whose benefit the States have limited their sovereign rights, albeit within limited fields, and the subjects of which comprise not only the Member States but also their nationals.* Community law, therefore, apart from legislation by the Member States, not only imposes obligations on individuals but also confers on them legal rights. The latter arise not only when an explicit grant is made by the Treaty, but also through obligations imposed, in a clearly defined manner, by the Treaty on individuals as well as on Member States and the Community institutions."

(Trans. [1963] C.M.L.R. 105 at p. 129, italics supplied.)

The crux of this decision lies in the italicised section. The Court describes the Community as constituting a new legal order for whose benefit the States have limited their sovereign rights. The Court does not, however, presume to apply the Community law at the Member State level, but leaves this to the courts of those Member States.

17–05   In the next case, 6/64, *Costa* v. *ENEL,* Rec. X 1141, [1964] C.M.L.R. 425, the Court further strengthened the line it had taken in *Van Gend en Loos,* holding that,

"As opposed to other international treaties, the Treaty instituting the EEC has created its own order which was integrated with the national order of the Member States the moment the Treaty came into force; as such, it is binding upon them. In fact, by creating a Community of unlimited duration, having its own institutions, its own personality and its own capacity in law, apart from having international standing and more particularly, real powers resulting from a limitation of competence or transfer of powers from the States to the Community, the Member States, albeit within limited spheres, have restricted their sovereign rights and created a body of laws applicable both to their nationals and to themselves."

(Trans. [1964] C.M.L.R. 425 at p. 455.)

This statement represents an advance on *Van Gend en Loos* in that the Court contemplates not merely a limitation of sovereign rights, but also possibly a transfer of powers to the Community. The real advance, however, is contained in the next sentence:

> " The reception, within the laws of each Member State, of provisions having a Community source, and more particularly of the terms and of the spirit of the Treaty, has as a corollary the impossibility, for the Member State, to give preference to a unilateral and subsequent measure against a legal order accepted by them on a basis of reciprocity."
>
> (*Ibid.*)

17–06   The Court thus rejected any attempt to make a later law prevail over the EEC Treaty, invoking its acceptance by the Member State on a basis of reciprocity.

This approach is further justified by the assertion that:

> " In truth the executive strength of Community laws cannot vary from one State to another in favour of later internal laws without endangering the realisation of the aims envisaged by the Treaty. . . . In any case the obligations undertaken under the Treaty creating the European Community would then not be unconditional, but merely potential if they could be affected by subsequent legislative acts of the signatories of the Treaty."
>
> (*Ibid.*)

This line of argument is based upon the requirement of uniformity, and also upon a need to give effect to the Treaty. Further, the Court pointed out that:

> " The pre-eminence of Community law is confirmed by Article 189 which prescribes that Community Regulations have an ' obligatory ' value and are ' directly applicable within each Member State.' Such a provision, which, it will be noticed, admits of no reservation, would be wholly ineffective if a Member State could unilaterally nullify its purpose by means of a law contrary to Community dictates."
>
> (*Ibid.* p. 456.)

Clearly, there is considerable strength in this argument; the Court reinforced it in referring to the " specific original nature " of the rights created by the Treaty and repeated its point that effect must be given to the Treaty.

Summing up its general statements, the Court said that:

> " The transfer, by Member States, from their national legal order, in favour of the Community order, of the rights and obligations arising from the Treaty, carries with it a clear limitation of their

sovereign right upon which a subsequent unilateral law, incompatible with the aims of the Treaty, cannot prevail."
(*Ibid.* p. 456.)

17–07   One of the next cases to come before the Court of Justice on this subject was 9/65, *San Michele* v. *H.A.*, Rec. XIII 1. In this application the Court was asked to suspend judgment pending a decision by the Italian Constitutional Court as to the constitutionality of law No. 766 of 1952, which gave effect to the ECSC Treaty. The Court, referring to its duty, mentioned in Article 31 ECSC, to ensure that the law is observed in the interpretation and application of the Treaty and of the rules laid down for the implementation thereof, refused to consider law No. 766, and would agree only to consider the instrument of ratification deposited by the Italian Government " which, together with the other instruments of ratification, has put the Treaty into effect," and went on to refer to the autonomous nature of the Community legal order and to the need for a uniform application of Community principles, holding that:

> " It follows from these acts of ratification, by which the Member States bound themselves in an identical way, that all the States adhered to the Treaty in the same circumstances, definitely and without any other reservations than those expressed in the additional Protocols and that therefore it would be contrary to the Community legal order for any citizen of any Member State to claim to put this adhesion in issue."

(Trans. Brinkhorst and Schermers, p. 105.)

Here the reciprocity argument appears to have been prevalent.

17–08   There can be no doubt as to the meaning of the passages cited above, but it is not entirely clear from these cases that the Court found any one argument totally persuasive. It has, after all, produced some half-dozen arguments:

(1) new, binding, legal order
(2) limitation of competence ⎫
                         ⎬ restriction of sovereign rights
(3) transfer of powers   ⎭
(4) reciprocity
(5) principle of uniformity, safeguarding Community aims
(6) specific original nature.

In view of this multiplicity of bases or reasons for the supremacy of Community law, it would be most dangerous to attempt to point to one or other as being decisive.

17–09   In 14/68, *Walt Wilhelm* v. *BKA*, Rec. XV 1, [1969] C.M.L.R. 100, the Court seems to have returned to the formula used in *Costa* v. *ENEL*. The holding of the Court in the *Walt Wilhelm* case is in the following terms:

" Article 87 (2) (*e*), in attributing to an institution of the Community the power to define the relations between the national laws and Community law on competition, confirms the pre-eminent character of Community law. The EEC Treaty instituted its own legal order, integrated into the legal systems of the Member States and which has priority before their courts. It would be contrary to the nature of such a system to accept that the Member States may take or maintain in force measures liable to compromise the useful effect of the Treaty. The imperative force of the Treaty and of the acts issued in implementation of it could not vary from state to state by the effect of internal acts, without the functioning of the Community system being obstructed and the attainment of the aim of the Treaty being placed in peril.

" Consequently, conflicts between the Community rule and the national rules on competition should be resolved by the application of the principle of the primacy of the Community rule."
(Trans. [1969] C.M.L.R. 100 at p. 119.)

In this case, the Court repeats the new legal order argument, and somewhat refines the argument that disparate measures would compromise the aims or " useful effect " of the Treaty. The latter term had not been used before in connection with supremacy of the EEC Treaty (although see 8/55, *Fédéchar* v. *H.A.*, Rec. II 199) but was already the name of one of the supremacy theories. Nevertheless, apart from the argument based on Article 87, the Court has reduced its grounds for requiring supremacy to two: the " new legal order " argument, and the " useful effect " argument.

17–10   In a more recent judgment of the Court relating directly to the supremacy of Community law, 11/70, *Internationale Handelsgesellschaft* v. *EVSt,* Rec. XVI 1125, [1972] C.M.L.R. 255, the Court, in referring to the protection of fundamental rights in the Community legal order, rejected the possibility of a reference to rules or legal concepts of national law as a means of determining the validity of Community acts, since this would have the effect of impairing the unity and effectiveness of Community law.

The Court went on to hold that:

" The validity of such instruments can only be judged in the light of Community law. In fact, the law born from the Treaty, the issue of an autonomous source, could not, by its very nature, have the courts opposing to it rules of national law of any nature whatever without losing its Community character and without the legal basis of the Community itself being put in question. Therefore the validity of a Community instrument or its effect within a Member State cannot be affected by allegations that it strikes at either the funda-

mental rights as formulated in that State's constitution or the principles of a national constitutional structure."
(Trans. [1972] C.M.L.R. 255 at p. 283.)

Interestingly, the headnote to the case in the *Recueil*, which sets out the three sentences above-quoted, makes specific reference to *Costa* v. *ENEL*, Rec. X 1141 at p. 1160: *i.e.* to the passages cited from the latter case above. The statement of the basis for supremacy of Community law, which is clearly a very strong one, refers only, however, to the " new legal order " and " useful effect " arguments, as indeed did *Walt Wilhelm.*

17–11 It has been considered useful to give a full survey of these cases, for they demonstrate that no one theory of the supremacy of Community law can be pointed to as being that which is decisive in the matter. There can be no doubt that the reasoning of the Court in requiring that Community law shall prevail is correct, but the justification for its supremacy must be found in a multiplicity of factors, and not in any particular one, despite the fact that *Wilhelm* and *Internationale Handelsgesellschaft* both rely on the same grounds. This fact cannot yet be considered to be conclusive in view of the earlier judgments of the Court, and of its decisions respecting the supremacy of Community law in specific fields, discussed below.

SUPREMACY IN SPECIFIC FIELDS

17–12 So far, the discussion of the supremacy of Community law has centred upon the abstract obligation of Member States to give effect to Community law in such a way that it prevails over contrary national law. The question arises when and in what circumstances there exists an obligation under Community law, and to whom that obligation applies. Clearly, there will generally be obligations laid on Member States, but there are also instances of the attribution of rights (and possibly obligations) to individuals.

OBLIGATIONS LAID ON MEMBER STATES

17–13 Article 5 EEC (Art. 86 ECSC, Art. 192 Euratom) requires Member States to take all appropriate measures to ensure fulfilment of the obligations arising out of the Treaty, or resulting from action taken by the institutions of the Community, and are to facilitate the achievement of the Community's tasks. They are also to abstain from any measure which could jeopardise the attainment of the objectives of the Treaty (see generally, Chap. 20, *infra*). Essentially, the Article obliges the Member States to give full faith and credit to the Treaty, but apart from a duty to abstain from prejudicial action, the only obligation is to take " all appropriate measures " to ensure fulfilment of *obligations* under the Treaty. Clearly, therefore, Article 5 does not turn Articles expressed in permissive terms into positive obligations, and it is difficult to say that this Article is itself " directly applicable " in the sense shortly to be discussed. Where, however, there is a positive duty under the Treaty to act (or not to act) then a Member State will be bound to fulfil that obligation, and if the Article is one which the Court considers to be directly applicable in the Member States, then an individual may rely upon that obligation in order to secure its fulfilment. A large proportion of the provisions imposing clear obligations on Member States are probably of a directly applicable nature, those provisions held not to be directly applicable not creating rights present or future for individuals. (See *e.g.* 69/69, *Alcan* v. *Commission*, Rec. XVI 385, [1970] C.M.L.R. 337 as to the borderline.)

17–14   Conversely, Member States are obliged to abstain from any measures which could jeopardise the attainment of the objectives of the Treaty (Art. 5, second para.). The Court has not held this obligation to be directly applicable, since the provision imposes a general obligation on Member States, the concrete content of which depends in a particular case on the provisions of the Treaty or the rules of law derived from the general system of the Treaty which are there in question : 78/70, *DGG* v. *Metro*, Rec. XVII 487, [1971] C.M.L.R. 631. But in a number of cases the existence of Community acts in given fields has been adduced as a basis for holding parallel or conflicting national action incompatible with a Community act. (See *e.g.* 22/70, *Commission* v. *Council*, Rec. XVII 263, [1971] C.M.L.R. 335, referring expressly to Art. 5.) The first clear statement to this effect is contained in 40/69, *Hauptzollamt Hamburg-Oberelbe* v. *Firma Paul. G. Bollmann*, Rec. XVI 69, [1970] C.M.L.R. 141, where the Court held that:

> " To the extent that the Member States have assigned legislative powers in tariff matters to the Community in order to ensure the proper operation of the common agricultural market, they no longer have the power to make legislative provisions in this field."
> (Trans. [1970] C.M.L.R. 141 at p. 153.)

(The holding in 74/69, *HZA Bremen-Freihafen* v. *Krohn*, Rec. XVI 451, [1970] C.M.L.R. 466 is almost identical, the word " autonomous " being substituted for " legislative ").

This was to be expected given the number of cases calling for a uniform application of Community law with priority over national law. (See *e.g.* 26/62, *Van Gend en Loos* v. *Nederlandse Administratie der Belastingen*, Rec. IX 1, [1963] C.M.L.R. 105; 6/64, *Costa* v. *ENEL*, Rec. X 1141, [1964] C.M.L.R. 425; 28/67, *Molkerei-Zentrale* v. *HZA Paderborn*, Rec. XIV 211, [1968] C.M.L.R. 187; 30/67, *Industria Molitoria Imolese* v. *Council*, Rec. XIV 171; 6/68, *Zuckerfabrik Watenstedt* v. *Council*, Rec. XIV 595, [1969] C.M.L.R. 26; 13/68, *Salgoil* v. *Ministry for Foreign Trade*, Rec. XIV 661, [1969] C.M.L.R. 181; and 14/68, *Walt Wilhelm* v. *BKA*, Rec. XIV 1, [1969] C.M.L.R. 100.

17–15   Since then the Court has given a number of judgments in the same sense (*e.g.* 34/70, *SYNACOMEX* v. *ONIC,* Rec. XVI 1233 [1]) but the clearest and perhaps most startling statement made by the Court is contained in the celebrated *AETR* case—22/70, *Commission* v. *Council,* Rec. XVII 263, [1971] C.M.L.R. 335—concerning the powers of the Council to conclude the European Road Transport Agreement. The Court held that as the ambit of the Common Transport Policy expanded with its elaboration, so the powers of Member States in this sector were reduced. The Court justifies this approach in the following terms:

> " In particular, each time the Community, with a view to implementing a common policy envisaged by the Treaty, lays down common rules, whatever form these may take, the Member States no longer have the right, acting individually or even collectively, to contract obligations towards non-Member States affecting these rules.
>
> To the extent that such common rules come into being, the Community alone is in a position to assume and carry out contractual obligations towards non-Member States affecting the whole sphere of application of the Community legal system.
>
> One cannot, therefore, in implementing the provisions of the Treaty, separate the category of measures internal to the Community from that of external relations.
>
> By the terms of Article 3 (*c*), the adoption of a common policy in the sphere of transport is specially mentioned among the aims of the Community.
>
> By the terms of Article 5, the Member States are required on the one hand to take all appropriate steps to ensure the carrying out of the obligations arising out of the Treaty or resulting from the acts of the institutions and, on the other hand, to abstain from any steps likely to jeopardise the attainment of the purposes of the Treaty.
>
> If these two provisions are read in conjunction, it follows that to the extent that Community rules are promulgated for the attainment of the purposes of the Treaty, the Member States cannot, outside the framework of the Community institutions, assume obligations to affect such rules or alter their scope."

(Trans. [1971] C.M.L.R. 335 at p. 355, paras. 17–22.)

17–16   This judgment has had a mixed reception, for although the submissions of the Commission that it should have been for the Community to conclude the *AETR* Agreement failed on the facts, there is no doubt that the Court laid down a principle of general application for future cases. A strong criticism of the judgment (" La Cour de Justice de Luxembourg a-t-elle outrepassé ses compéténces? " *Le Monde,* April

---

[1] See also 39/70, *Norddeutsches Vieh- und Fleischkontor* v. *HZA Hamburg-St. Annen,* Rec. XVII 49, [1971] C.M.L.R. 281.

1971) appears, however, to fail to appreciate that the judgment relates not merely to the conclusion of international agreements, but to the supremacy of Community law and Community powers in general. The Court does not limit the powers of the Community, but indicates that the ambit of those powers spreads with the growth of the various Community policies. For the purposes of this part of the discussion, therefore, it may be said that the obligations of the Member States are not static, but grow with the powers of the Community.

17–17   It appears, then, that what amounts to an obligation upon a Member State will not necessarily be immediately ascertainable. But even where there exist definite obligations upon Member States to follow certain courses of action, the effects of those obligations will not always entail identical consequences. Essentially there are two types of obligation upon Member States; those which create rights which may be enforced by individuals before national courts and those which do not. Of the latter type, one may cite as examples Article 102, which imposes an obligation on Member States to consult the Commission but nothing more, and Article 93 (3) which imposes a similar obligation (*cf.* 6/64, *Costa* v. *ENEL*, Rec. X 1141, [1964] C.M.L.R. 425). Article 12 provides an instance of the former type. This requires Member States to refrain from introducing between themselves any new customs duties on imports or exports, or any charges having equivalent effect, and from increasing those which already apply in their trade with each other. In 26/62, *Van Gend en Loos* v. *Nederlandse Administratie der Belastingen*, Rec. IX 1, [1963] C.M.L.R. 105, the Court was asked by the Netherlands *Tariefcommissie* whether this Article:

> " has an immediate effect in internal law, in that nationals of the Member States could, on the basis of the Article, enforce rights which the national court should protect."
> (Trans. [1963] C.M.L.R. 105 at p. 129.)

The Court held that:

> " Article 12 should be interpreted in such a sense as to produce direct effect and to create individual rights which internal courts should protect."
> (*Ibid.* pp. 130–131.)

and that:

> " Article 12 of the EEC Treaty has direct application within the territory of a Member State and enures to the benefit of citizens whose rights the internal courts should protect."
> (*Ibid.* p. 132.)

The Court of Justice thus enunciated a principle of direct applicability of Community law, which creates rights in individuals. Since the concept of direct applicability of Community law is undoubtedly one of the fundamental concepts of the Community, it is necessary to consider it in rather more detail.

CHAPTER 18

RIGHTS OF INDIVIDUALS: DIRECT APPLICABILITY
OF COMMUNITY LAW

18–01 THERE is only one reference to direct applicability of Community law in the Treaties themselves; Article 189 * refers to Regulations as being directly applicable in all Member States. The notion of the directly applicable Treaty Article is, however, a notion developed by the Court of Justice. Without prejudice to the question what are the criteria for a directly applicable Treaty Article (examined below) such an Article may be defined in terms of the question to the Court for a preliminary ruling under Article 177 EEC by the Netherlands Tariefcommissie in 26/62, *Van Gend en Loos* v. *Nederlandse Administratie der Belastingen,* Rec. IX 1, [1963] C.M.L.R. 105; the Tariefcommissie asked:

> "Whether Article 12 of the Treaty has an immediate effect in internal law, in that nationals of the Member States could, on the basis of the Article, enforce rights which the national court should protect."
>
> (Trans. [1963] C.M.L.R. at p. 129.)

In the event the Court held Article 12 to have such immediate effect, or to be directly applicable. An Article which is directly applicable thus gives rights which an individual may enforce by action before municipal courts. The importance of the descriptions " immediate " and " direct " lies in the fact that such an Article has the force of law in Member States without any need for the interposition of a domestic legislative act to give the force of law to the Article in question.

18–02 There is some ground for seeing in directly applicable provisions of Community law an analogy with so-called self-executing provisions of Treaties. There is little doubt, however, that the notion of directly applicable Community law is to be construed purely in relation to the structure of the European Communities. Most of the cases seem to suggest this, and indeed this view will seem more appropriate to the English lawyer, for Community Treaties are the only international Treaties, certain provisions of which may create direct internal effects in English law. For these reasons, it is better to speak of directly applicable Community law, as does the Court, rather than to refer to a notion drawn from monist theories of international law.

It is not, perhaps, wholly clear why any provisions of the Community Treaties should be regarded as being directly applicable in the Member States. It is asserted on the one hand that it is through the device of direct applicability alone that the supremacy of Community law can

142

be, and is in fact, assured. On the other hand it is argued that Community law is only directly applicable because it is superior to, or has supremacy over, national law, direct applicability being only a particular manifestation of this supremacy. On the whole, the best view would appear to be that supremacy of Community law and direct applicability are both children of the doctrine that Community law constitutes a new legal order in international law (26/62, *Van Gend en Loos, supra*); both are necessary appurtenances of the new legal order if it is to be effective.

18–03   If the Treaty itself refers to direct applicability of Community law only in relation to Regulations, how is the attribution of direct applicability to Treaty Articles to be justified? In the *Van Gend en Loos* case (*supra*), the first case in which the Court had been asked whether a Treaty Article was directly applicable, the Court referred to the need to look at its spirit, its arrangement and the terms used in order to ascertain whether the provisions of an international Treaty have such an effect. This it did in the following terms:

> " The purpose of the EEC Treaty—to create a Common Market, the functioning of which directly affects the citizens of the Community—implies that this Treaty is more than an agreement creating only mutual obligations between the contracting parties. This interpretation is confirmed by the Preamble to the Treaty which, in addition to mentioning governments, affects individuals. The creation of organs institutionalising certain sovereign rights, the exercise of which affects both Member States and citizens is a particular example. In addition, the nationals of the States, united into the Community, are required to collaborate in the functioning of that Community, by means of the European Parliament and the Economic and Social Council. Furthermore, the role of the Court of Justice in the framework of Article 177, the aim of which is to ensure uniformity of interpretation of the Treaty by the national courts, confirms that the States recognised in Community law have an authority capable of being invoked by their nationals before those courts. *We must conclude from this that the Community constitutes a new legal order in international law, for whose benefit the States have limited their sovereign rights, albeit within limited fields, and the subjects of which compromise not only the Member States but also their nationals.* Community law, therefore, apart from legislation by the Member States, not only imposes obligations on individuals but also confers on them legal rights. The latter arise not only when an explicit grant is made by the Treaty, but also through obligations imposed, in a clearly defined manner, by the Treaty on individuals as well as on Member States and the Community institutions.
> (Trans. [1963] C.M.L.R. at p. 129.)

18-04   The passage quoted is long and perhaps not entirely lucid, but perhaps one may take from it the one passage italicised, as distilling the thinking of the Court; given that the Member States have limited their sovereign rights in favour of a new legal order which also has individuals among its subjects, it is only natural that the same legal order should confer on individuals rights as well as obligations. The Court then goes on to say that:

> " To limit the sanctions against violation of Article 12 by Member States merely to the procedures laid down in Articles 169 and 170 would remove all direct judicial protection of the individual rights of their nationals. Reliance on these Articles would risk being ineffective if it had to be exercised after the enforcement of a national decision which misinterpreted the requirements of the Treaty. The vigilance of individuals interested in protecting their rights creates an effective control additional to that entrusted by Articles 169 and 170 to the diligence of the Commission and the Member States."
> (*Ibid.* at p. 130.)

Exactly similar views have been expressed in later cases where the very basis for direct applicability has been questioned, *e.g.* 28/67, *Molkerei-Zentrale* v. *HZA Paderborn*, Rec. XIV 211, [1968] C.M.L.R. 187.

A directly applicable provision of Community law thus confers rights on individuals which national courts must protect. Clearly, in cases of doubt, an interpretation of the provision of Community law in question is required. Under Article 177 of the Treaty, the Court of Justice has exclusive jurisdiction to give preliminary rulings—on questions of interpretation (see generally, Chap. 15) and thus the Court will decide whether or not the provision is directly applicable. It is through this Article that the Court has developed the concept of what constitutes a directly applicable provision.

THE CONDITIONS FOR DIRECT APPLICABILITY OF TREATY PROVISIONS

18-05 In the first place, the provisions of the Treaty must be " clear " (26/62, *Van Gend en Loos* [1963] C.M.L.R. 105) or " clear and precise " (*e.g.* 18/71, *Eunomia* v. *Ministry of Public Instruction*, Rec. XVII 811, [1972] C.M.L.R. 4) so as to be susceptible of direct application. The clarity required relates not merely to the straightforwardness of the wording, but in particular to an obligation which is identifiable and recognisable. Thus, an obligation not to increase existing customs duties under Article 12 (*Van Gend en Loos*) is readily recognisable, but the method for assessing the " total value " of global quotas under Article 33 (1) is not so clear (13/68, *Salgoil* v. *Ministry for Foreign Trade*, Rec. XIV 661, [1969] C.M.L.R. 181).

8–06   Secondly, the obligation imposed must be unconditional (*Van Gend en Loos*). The Court has not given any specific meaning to the term "unconditional," but it seems to mean at least an obligation not subject to, for example, any time factors. Thus the obligation contained in Article 13 (1) to abolish all customs duties on imports in force between Member States by the end of the transitional period only became directly applicable on January 1, 1970 (33/70, *SACE* v. *Italian Ministry of Finance*, Rec. XVI 1213, [1971] C.M.L.R. 123).

There is some suggestion that the rule that the obligation must be unconditional is only a particular aspect of the supposed rule that the obligation must consist not in a duty to act, but in a duty not to act. It cannot be said with any real certainty whether they are separate rules or not, but one may tentatively suggest that they are not the same. The answer to the question does not emerge from the *Van Gend en Loos* case, but later cases, notably 57/65, *Lütticke* v. *HZA Saarelouis*, Rec. XII 293, [1971] C.M.L.R. 674, and 13/68, *Salgoil* v. *Ministry for Foreign Trade, supra*, indicate that there may upon occasion be a duty to act. If this is so, then the rules are clearly separate. But on the other hand the Court laid some stress upon the fact that the obligation consisted in a duty not to act in a number of cases, although the decisions did not turn upon this point alone. (See *e.g.* 28/67, *Molkerei-Zentrale* v. *HZA Paderborn, supra*, and 27/67, *Fink-Frucht* v. *HZA München-Landsbergerstrasse*, Rec. **XIV** 327.)

8–07   In 57/65, *Lütticke* v. *HZA Saarelouis, supra*, the Court held a stipulation (Art. 95 (3)) requiring positive action to abolish provisions contrary to Article 95 (1) by a certain date to require no intervention by the Member States. This was based upon the view that Article 95 (1) would take effect as from the date specified, so that the duty to abolish under Article 95 (3) was to some extent immaterial. The interpretation of the Court was confirmed in the *Molkerei-Zentrale* case.

In 13/68, *Salgoil* v. *Italian Ministry for Foreign Trade*, Rec. XIV 661, [1969] C.M.L.R. 181, the Court appears implicitly to be reiterating its approach in *Lütticke* v. *HZA Saarelouis*; under Article 31, first para., Member States are under an obligation to refrain from introducing as between themselves any new quantitative restrictions or measures having equivalent effect. On its own, this Article would seem to be readily susceptible of being directly applicable, but, in fact, the obligation related only to products which had been notified to the Commission within a time-limit under the second paragraph. The Court nevertheless held the first paragraph to be directly applicable, even in the absence of notification.

18–08   The Court thus seems to hold Treaty provisions imposing duties to act to be directly applicable where the Member States have no latitude of action. This approach is considerably reinforced later in the judgment in *Salgoil*, where the Court discusses the nature of Article 33.

145

As already mentioned (§ 18–05, *supra*) the Court held that the uncertainty as to the concept of " total value " deprived the Article of the possibility of being directly applicable. Before reaching this conclusion, however, the Court said that:

> " as these are obligations to do something, we should consider whether, for their fulfilment, Member States enjoy any latitude of judgment of such a nature as to exclude totally or partially the aforementioned effects."
>
> (Trans. [1969] C.M.L.R. at p. 195.)

Finally, it is clear that if a provision is to be considered to be directly applicable, it must leave no discretion to the Member States or to the Community. If the criterion of there being not a duty to act, but a duty not to act, is an absolute criterion in case of direct applicability of Treaty provisions, then that criterion and the criterion of there being no discretion are clearly separate, but if the former criterion is not of an absolute nature, as appears may be the case, then the line between the two becomes blurred. The Court has relied upon the absence of discretion in a number of cases, notably in the *Molkerei-Zentrale* case and in the *Salgoil* case, and in 10/71, *Ministère Public luxembourgeois* v. *Muller-Hein,* Rec. XVI 723. It seems from *Lütticke* v. *HZA Saarelouis,* however, that an insignificant measure of discretion will not affect the direct applicability of the provision. If, then, these criteria are met, the Court will consider the provision to be complete and legally perfect (*Lütticke* v. *HZA Saarelouis*) and will hold it to be directly applicable.

18–09   Thus far the Court of Justice has held the following provisions of the Treaty of Rome to be directly applicable:

Article	Case No.	Name
9 and 13 (2)	33/70	*SACE* v. *Italian Ministry of Finance* Rec. XVI 1213, [1971] C.M.L.R. 123
12	26/62	*Van Gend en Loos* v. *Nederlandse Administratie der Belastingen* Rec. IX 1, [1963] C.M.L.R. 105
	28–30/62	*Da Costa en Schaake* v. *Nederlandse Administratie der Belastingen* Rec. IX 59, [1963] C.M.L.R. 224
16	18/71	*Eunomia* v. *Italian Ministry of Public Instruction* Rec. XVII 811, [1972] C.M.L.R. 4
31 and 32, 1st para.	13/68	*Salgoil* v. *Italian Ministry for Foreign Trade* Rec. XIV 661, [1969] C.M.L.R. 181
37 (2)	6/64	*Costa* v. *ENEL* Rec. X 1141, [1964] C.M.L.R. 425
53	6/64	*Costa* v. *ENEL* Rec. X 1141, [1964] C.M.L.R. 425

Article	Case No.	Name
95 (1)	28/67	*Molkerei-Zentrale* v. *HZA Paderborn* Rec. XIV 211, [1968] C.M.L.R. 187
	34/67	*Lück* v. *HZA Köln Rheinau* Rec. XIV 359
95 (2)	27/67	*Fink-Frucht* v. *HZA München-Landsbergerstrasse* Rec. XIV 327, [1968] C.M.L.R. 228
95 (1) and (3)	57/65	*Lütticke* v. *HZA Sarrelouis* Rec. XII 293, [1971] C.M.L.R. 674

18–10   It has been argued that 13/61, *De Geus* v. *Bosch*, Rec. **VIII** 89, [1962] C.M.L.R. 1 holds that Articles 85 and 86 are directly applicable. The Court did not, however, express itself in the language of direct applicability, although that language was not new to it—see *e.g.* 8/57, *Groupement des Hauts Fourneaux et Aciéries Belges* v. *H.A.*, Rec. **IV** 223, and 7 and 9/65, *Groupement des Industries Sidérurgiques Luxembourgeoises* v. *H.A.*, Rec. **II** 53—nor did it say that individuals derived rights from those Articles.

The Court was asked whether Article 85 was applicable from the entry into force of the Treaty, and it replied in the affirmative. By this it did not mean to say that the Article created rights, but only that Member States could apply it in addition within the framework of their own restrictive practices legislation. The Court made it quite clear that the Article was not fully effective until the entry into force of Regulation 17, and that the operative provision of the Article, paragraph 2, did not make prohibited agreements automatically void from the entry into force of Regulation 17. In these circumstances, it is difficult to see how Article 85 can, until after the date of entry into effect of Regulation 17, be said to create rights enabling an individual to invoke it, so as to have an agreement pronounced void, unless the question was submitted in the context of national legislation.

To put the matter another way, the Court did not hold that the Article was directly applicable, but only that it was applicable.

18–11   Article 8 (7) provides that save for the exceptions or derogations provided for in the EEC Treaty, " the expiry of the transitional period shall constitute the latest date by which all the rules laid down must enter into force and all the measures required for establishing the Common Market must be implemented."

On the face of it, the obligation to implement became an absolute or directly applicable obligation on January 1, 1970. Whether, however, all obligations which were due to be implemented by January 1, 1970, then became directly applicable in the sense understood above is less certain. The better view would seem to be that only those provisions in themselves susceptible of being directly applicable became directly applicable on that date. Certainly the judgments of the Court involving such cut-off dates seem to support such a conclusion: *e.g. Lütticke* v. *HZA Saarelouis, Eunomia.*

DIRECT APPLICABILITY OF COMMUNITY ACTS

Regulations

18–12   So far, direct applicability has been considered in relation only to provisions of the Treaty. There can be no doubt, however, that at least a part of the acts of the institutions of the Communities are also directly applicable. Of the acts that the Communities may make, Article 189 * states that

> "A Regulation shall have general application. It shall be binding in its entirety and directly applicable in all Member States.
>
> A directive shall be binding, as to the result to be achieved, upon each Member State to which it is addressed, but shall leave to the national authorities the choice of form and methods.
>
> A decision shall be binding in its entirety upon those to whom it is addressed."

From the wording of this Article alone it is clear that Regulations are directly applicable, subject only to the consideration that the Court will investigate the form and content of a so-called Regulation in order to ascertain whether it is in fact a Regulation, matters of form being largely immaterial: see *e.g.* 16 and 17/62, *Confédération Nationale des Producteurs de Fruits et Légumes,* Rec. VIII 901, [1963] C.M.L.R. 160. The finding that an act does not have the characteristics of a Regulation and is in reality a disguised individual decision will deprive it of its validity *erga omnes* and, apparently, of its directly applicable nature: *cf.* 8/55, *Fédéchar* v. *H.A.,* Rec. II 199. More difficult is the question whether all provisions of a given valid Regulation are directly applicable. The view that this may not invariably be the case receives support from 31/64, *La Prévoyance Sociale* v. *Bertholet,* Rec. XI 111, [1966] C.M.L.R. 191. In holding Article 52 of Regulation 3 to be directly applicable, the Court did so upon consideration of the merits, thereby suggesting that it could do the same for other Articles, without necessarily coming to the same conclusion. True, the Court admits *a contrario* arguments only as a last resort (8/55, *Fédéchar* v. *H.A., supra*) but it is difficult to deny the force of the argument, especially in view of the fact that a good many Regulations require Member States to take measures of execution which leave more discretion in the Member States than did Article 52 of Regulation 3, which was clear in its directions, but required Member States to conclude bilateral agreements with each other for its execution. Against this view is the statement in Article 189 * itself that regulations are binding *in their entirety.* In 20/72, *Belgium* v. *N. V. Cobelex* (not yet reported) the Court stated that " since they form part of a Community regulation the provisions of Article 19 [of Regulation 19] are, in virtue of Article 189 of the Treaty, directly applicable in all

Member States " (para. 12 : authors' translation). But this statement is made without analysis of the problem alluded to, and should not perhaps be considered conclusive.

Decisions and directives

8–13   The question of direct applicability of decisions and directives is somewhat controversial. The starting point for discussion must be the Belgian domestic decision of *Corveleyn* v. *Etat Belge* (Conseil d'Etat, October 7, 1968), [1969] C.D.E. 343 where the Conseil d'Etat held Article 3 of Directive 64/221, J.O. 1964, 850) on freedom of movement to be directly applicable. This Article provides that measures of public order are not to be based solely on the existence of a criminal conviction of an individual. The Belgian Court annulled an ostensibly illegal deportation order, which did not comply with this provision.

The decision is clearly open to criticism, for one is forced to ask in what the difference between a directive and a Regulation consists. Nevertheless, the Court of Justice has itself given support to the suggestion that parts at least of a directive may be considered to be directly applicable in a series of decisions given in October 1970: *e.g.* 9/70, *Grad* v. *Finanzamt Traunstein* (October 6, 1970) Rec. XVI 825, [1971] C.M.L.R. 1; 20/70, *Transports Lesage* v. *HZA Freiburg* (October 21, 1970) Rec. XVI 861, [1971] C.M.L.R. 1; 23/70, *Haselhorst* v. *Finanzamt Düsseldorf Altstadt* (October 21, 1970) Rec. XVI 881, [1971] C.M.L.R. 1.

8–14   In all three cases the Court began by saying that even though only Regulations are expressly stated to be directly applicable by virtue of Article 189,* this did not mean that the other categories of acts mentioned in that Article could never have similar effects. Turning first to decisions, the Court said that it would be incompatible with the binding effect attributed to decisions by Article 189 * to exclude on principle the possibility that the obligation imposed by a decision may be invoked by individuals. (*Cf.* also 106 & 107/63, *Toepfer* v. *Commission,* Rec. XI 525, [1966] C.M.L.R. 111, *sed quaere.*)

The Court then emphasised the need for individuals to be able to rely upon decisions where they obliged States to take action, and pointed out that whatever the difference between a Regulation and a decision, this did not prevent individuals from potentially being able to rely on them. On this basis, the Court, finding Article 4, paragraph 2 of Council Decision 65/271 (J.O. 1965, 1500)—prohibiting Member States from imposing both the common turnover tax system (VAT) and special taxes taking the place of a turnover tax on transport—" to be imperative and general . . . unconditional and sufficiently clear and precise," held it to be directly applicable.

In all three cases, the Court went on to acknowledge that the date upon which this obligation took effect was fixed by a directive (67/227 J.O. 1967, 1301), but concluded that the fact that the date was so fixed in no way detracted from the absolute nature of the obligation, which came into play once that date was passed.

It is true that none of these cases decided that an obligation of a generalised kind contained in a directive was directly applicable, but the Court does indicate in the context of Decision 65/271 that it might so hold in other circumstances. It is difficult to conclude that giving effect to a time-limit fixed by a directive amounts to calling a directive directly applicable, for the substantive obligation is contained elsewhere, and it is on the latter that an individual plaintiff will wish to rely; the directive, binding on the Member State, only activates the directly applicable substantive obligation.

18–15   The judgment in case 33/70, *SACE* v. *Ministry of Finance*, Rec. XVI 1213, [1971] C.M.L.R. 123, given on December 17, 1970, is at first sight on all fours with the three cases referred to, but it would appear that in fact, the Court may have gone further. In this case, the Court was asked whether following on the issue of Directive 68/31 (J.O. 1968, 12/8) the provisions of Article 13 (2) EEC, or else the provisions of the directive itself, became directly applicable in the Italian legal order. Under Article 13 (2) Member States were required to abolish charges having an effect equivalent to customs duties on imports, in force between Member States during the transition period, the timetable for such abolition to be fixed by directives. Pursuant to the acceleration decision of July 26, 1966 (Decision 66/532, J.O. 1966, 2971), the final cut-off date for removing all intra-Community charges was brought forward to July 1, 1968, and on the basis of this decision, the Commission issued a directive to the Italian Republic, requiring it to abolish certain administrative charges by that date.

The Court found the duty contained in Article 13 (2) EEC together with Article 9 to be directly applicable, and on that basis, considered the combined effect of the Treaty Articles, the decision and the directive to be directly applicable. The Court based its decision at least in part upon the fact that the directive did not apparently alter the obligations of the Member States in any way, but the Court does seem to indicate that the obligation only became directly applicable by virtue of the existence *inter alia* of the directive.

18–16   One of the chief arguments for contesting the view that the directives were directly applicable was that they are not required to be published in the *Official Journal* in accordance with Article 191,* but as the Court indicated in the *SACE* case, if the Member State was in fact informed of the directive, then its rights are safeguarded, and this is sufficient. The Court also rejected the argument that a directive addressed to a single Member State could not contain directly applicable obligations. This it did on the basis that the obligation imposed concerned not only relations between the issuing institution and the Member State addressed, but also had legal consequences upon which other Member

States might rely, and upon which individuals might rely where the provision setting out the obligation was by its very nature directly applicable.[1]

The obligation contained in the directive appears to be identical with that in the earlier cases, but it goes rather further than the earlier cases, for where there is an active duty to comply, a final date fixed amounts in practice to rather more than a terminal obligation, predicating dismantling obligations in the meantime. If this analysis is correct, then it is only a short step to the *Corveleyn* position; viewed in another way the obligation in that case was to have dismantled provisions contrary to that obligation by the date of entry into force of the directive.

It does, however, emerge from all four cases that the Court only finds a directive to be directly applicable where it focuses a pre-existing obligation. Whether it would be prepared to go further, and hold a directive to be directly applicable in the sense that it held Decision 65/271 Article 4 (2) to be directly applicable in *Grad*, etc., is less certain, but the way for it to do so would not appear to be closed.

DIRECT APPLICABILITY OF OTHER TYPES OF COMMUNITY ACT

18–17 There have been no express rulings holding other types of Community act to be directly applicable, but in 21–24/72, *International Fruit Co.* v. *Produktschap voor Groenten en Fruit*, not yet reported, the Court was asked to give a preliminary ruling on whether certain Community rules were compatible with Article XI of the GATT. In examining this question, the Court considered first whether the Community was bound by the GATT, and secondly whether the provision in question could be held to be directly applicable, so as to give individuals rights under it. Although the Community was held to be bound by the GATT in so far as the Community had assumed powers exercised previously by the Member States in the context of the GATT, Article XI was held not to be directly applicable. Conceivably, therefore, other international treaties may be held to be directly applicable in the Community context.

---

[1] This latter part of the judgment is also of interest in relation to decisions; decisions addressed to firms and individuals are not directly applicable in the sense under discussion although they do create direct obligations for their addressees, but a decision addressed to a single Member State might contain directly applicable provisions in much the same way as did the directive in *SACE*.

CHAPTER 19

RECEPTION OF COMMUNITY LAW AT THE NATIONAL LEVEL

19–01 IN the discussion of supremacy and direct applicability of Community law, virtually no mention was made of its application in Member States, and this for the very good reason that the Court of Justice cannot purport to apply Community law in the Member States, but can only declare that it applies, leaving the manner of its application to the Member States and their courts: cf. *Lück, Molkerei-Zentrale, Salgoil, supra.* This is a necessary situation if Community law constitutes a separate legal order (*Van Gend en Loos*) and thus is law *in* the Member States, but is not law *of* the Member States.

The question of the application of Community law in the Member States therefore needs to be examined separately. This application or reception is predicated in the first place by constitutional provisions, which shape the attitudes of the courts to Community law.

The questions involving the interpretation of Community law coming before national courts will generally relate to provisions which the Court of Justice may hold to be directly applicable. The national courts are of course able to refer to the Court of Justice in order to obtain a ruling on the nature of the disposition, but some courts have gone further and held dispositions which the Court would not have held to be directly applicable nevertheless to create rights: *Costa* v. *ENEL* [1968] C.M.L.R. 267 (judgment of *giudice conciliatore*, Milan, May 1 and 4, 1966, in relation to Article 102 of the EEC Treaty).

CONSTITUTIONAL PROVISIONS AND THE ACCEPTANCE OF COMMUNITY LAW BY THE COURTS

Belgium

19–02   Article 68 of the Belgian Constitution of 1831 requires Treaties such as the Community Treaties to be approved by Parliament. Criticisms of the constitutionality of the laws passed to give effect to the Community Treaties led to the Constitution being amended by the addition of Article 25 *bis*, which provides for the exercise of sovereign powers by institutions of public international law, these powers being conferred by Treaty or law. There is, however, no provision for the supremacy of Community law. The courts now clearly recognise the supremacy of Community law even over later internal law—*Minister for Economic Affairs* v. *Fromagerie Franco-Suisse " le Ski "* (Cour de

152

Cassation, May 27, 1971) [1971] J.T. 460, [1972] C.M.L.R. 330—on the principle that the two systems are separate legal orders.

Germany

9–03   According to Article 25 of the Basic Law, the general rules of international law form part of Federal law, and take precedence over that law and create rights and duties directly for the inhabitants of the Federal territory. This rule appears to apply only to customary international law, but Article 24 (1) provides for the transfer of sovereign powers to intergovernmental institutions by legislation.

The question whether Community law prevails over internal law is not without its difficulties; a number of cases have held that Community law will prevail even over subsequent national legislation: see *e.g. Re Import of Powdered Milk (No. 2)* [1967] C.M.L.R. 319; *Molkerei-Zentrale* v. *HZA Paderborn* [1969] C.M.L.R. 300 (Bundesfinanzhof, 1968); and *Neumann* v. *HZA Hof/Saale* [1969] C.M.L.R. 284, and the decision of October 18, 1967, of the Federal Constitutional Court ([1968] R.T.D.E. 203, [1967–68] C.M.L.Rev. 483). In the latter case the Constitutional Court held that the Community constituted a separate legal order, and that acts of its institutions were accordingly not acts of a German public authority for the purposes of constitutional review

Whether Community law prevails over fundamental or entrenched constitutional provisions was left open by the Constitutional Court in the decision of October 18, 1967. A number of cases before the Court of Justice have raised such questions, and it has been stated that fundamental rights have an integral part in the general principles of law, respect for which it assures (29/69, *Stauder* v. *Ulm-Sozialamt,* Rec. XV 419, [1970] C.M.L.R. 112; 25/70, *EVSt* v. *Köster, Berodt,* Rec. XVI 1161, [1972] C.M.L.R. 225; and 11/70, *Internationale Handelsgesellschaft* v. *EVSt,* Rec. XVI 1125, [1972] C.M.L.R. 255). The Constitutional Court appears in one case to have tacitly endorsed the view that Community law would prevail over such rights, presumably given that the Court of Justice normally assures their respect (see 47 N.J.W. (1971) 2122). Most recently, however, the Verwaltungsgericht in Frankfurt has referred the matter to the Constitutional Court for an explicit ruling (*Internationale Handelsgesellschaft* v. *EVSt* [1972] C.M.L.R. 177).

France

9–04   Article 55 of the French Constitution provides that duly ratified or approved Treaties have authority superior to that of laws (subject to the Treaty being applied by the other party or parties, *i.e.* on the basis of reciprocity).

There does not seem to be an authoritative decision of a French court clearly upholding the supremacy of Community law in the face of later inconsistent laws, but in *Administration des Contributions Indirectes* v. *Ramel* [1971] C.M.L.R. 315 (Cour de Cassation, Criminal Chamber, 1970) the Court refused to apply national rules as to the quality of wines which were inconsistent with EEC Regulation 24/62 on the subject. *Caisse Régionale* v. *Torrekens* [1971] C.M.L.R. 158 (Cour de Cassation, 1970) points in the same direction. Neither case concerned a later domestic law, but the tenor of Article 55 and of the judgment is such that it may be supposed that a French court might in suitable circumstances be prepared to refuse effect to such a law. Although the Conseil d'Etat did not hold a provision of Community law to prevail over a later national law the willingness of the same court in *Syndicat Général des Fabricants de Semoules* [1970] C.M.L.R. 395 to refer a question to the Court of Justice in another case (34/70, *SYNACOMEX* v. *ONIC,* Rec. XVI 1233) may possibly indicate a change of views.

Italy

19-05   Article 10, para. 1, of the Italian Constitution provides that " Italy's legal system conforms with the generally recognised principles of international law." Article 11 provides that " Italy . . . agrees, on conditions of equality with other states, to such limitation of sovereignty as may be necessary for a system calculated to ensure peace and justice between nations: it promotes and encourages international organisations having such ends in view." These constitutional provisions do not of themselves ensure the supremacy of Community law.

The Italian Constitutional Court held in *Costa* v. *ENEL* [1964] C.M.L.R. 425, that the EEC Treaty was given effect in Italy by an ordinary ratification law and had no greater status than an ordinary law. In such circumstances the Treaty could not prevail over later national law. The position of the Constitutional Court altered somewhat in the *San Michele* case [1967] C.M.L.R. 160. Taking the view that the Community constituted a separate legal order, it refused to treat the ECSC Treaty as having merely the effect of an ordinary law so as to make its provisions subject to the Italian Constitution. The Court did, however, indicate that certain constitutional rights might be inviolable (see also *Feram* v. *H.A.* [1966] C.M.L.R. 20).

Luxembourg

19-06   Subsequent to the ratification of the ECSC Treaty, the Luxembourg Constitution was altered so as to ensure that the delegations of power involved were in fact constitutional. Article 49 *bis* of 1956 provides for temporary delegation by Treaty to international institutions set up by international law of powers reserved to the legislature and to the executive and judicial powers.

The Luxembourg courts have from an early stage recognised that international Treaties take precedence over national legislation—

Chambre de Métiers v. *Pagani*, Pas.Lux. XVI 150, July 14, 1954—whether anterior or posterior to the Treaties.

The Netherlands

–07   The Netherlands Constitution lays it down both that the constitutionality of a Treaty is not to be challenged (Art. 60 (3)) and that a Treaty may override certain constitutional provisions (Art. 63); and further that any provision of municipal law is overriden by a prior or subsequent Treaty (Art. 66). These provisions naturally ensure the supremacy of Community law, and were indeed introduced with Community law in contemplation, being contained in the new constitution of 1953, as subsequently revised in 1956.

Part 4

FOUNDATIONS OF THE COMMUNITY: THE FOUR FREEDOMS

CHAPTER 20

THE SETTING UP OF THE
EUROPEAN ECONOMIC COMMUNITY

THE TREATY SETTING UP THE EEC

Preamble

20–01 The preamble to the EEC Treaty consists of a list of principles relating to the Economic Community. The list neither describes the principles exhaustively, nor lists all the applicable principles, and cannot as a result be said to contain clauses which have substantive legal effect. The preamble to any Treaty is nevertheless of some importance for its interpretation, and clearly constitutes an integral part of it. The preamble to the EEC Treaty is no different from others in this respect. The Court of Justice has indeed referred to the preamble in interpreting the Treaty. (See *e.g.* 26/62, *Van Gend en Loos* v. *Nederlandse Administratie der Belastingen*, Rec. IX 1, [1963] C.M.L.R. 105; in particular passages quoted at § 17–04 and § 18–03 *supra*.)

Perhaps the most notable feature of the preamble lies in its omissions. Apart from the expressed determination to lay the foundations of an ever closer union among the peoples of Europe, confirmed by the preambles to the Merger Treaty and the Treaty of Accession, there is no mention in the Treaty of Rome of European integration or of supranationality. It is clear, nevertheless, that the Treaty lays the foundations for progress towards at least some kind of political integration.

One of the most important aspects of the preamble is that it provides some guide to the interpretation and application of the substantive provisions of the Treaty. No real *travaux préparatoires* exist for the Treaty of Rome apart from the Spaak Report to the Foreign Ministers on the Unification of Europe (*Rapport des chefs de délégations aux ministres des affaires étrangères concernant l'unification de l'Europe dans le domaine économique*, Brussels, 1956), which formed the basis for the negotiations, and the reports of the national delegations to their respective parliaments. The preamble has apparently been relied upon to justify Community action under Article 235 of the Treaty (action necessary to achieve an objective of the Community, but where no power is provided in the Treaty), but cannot be considered to form a substantive basis for Community action.

There is some question as to whether the preamble can be said to have obligatory force. The better view would appear to be that the answer must be in the negative, but the point is of little importance in view of the vagueness of the dispositions of the preamble. They can at best be used to measure the *vires* of particular acts, and cannot easily be relied upon to support a line of legal argument except in the sense that they have evidentiary value. *Cf. Van Gend en Loos, supra.*

Part One of the EEC Treaty—" principles "—Articles 1 to 8

20–02   Article 1 gives substantive effect to the preamble, in setting up a European Economic Community between the High Contracting Parties, namely, Belgium, Germany, France, Italy, Luxembourg and the Netherlands. The Treaty of Accession of January 22, 1972, and the decision of the Council of the same date envisage the accession of Denmark, Ireland, Norway and the United Kingdom to all three European Communities. (See generally *supra,* § 2–08.) Following the negative result of a referendum, Norway will not now join the Community.

20–03   Article 2 sets out a number of objectives to be achieved by the Community: harmonious development of economic activities, continuous and balanced expansion, an increase in stability, an accelerated raising of the standard of living and closer relations between Member States. These objectives largely reiterate the preamble, and are, with the exception of the last, normal objectives of economic policy. They are to be achieved through the establishment of a common market and the approximation of national economic policies.

20–04   Article 3 sets out a non-exclusive list of the activities of the Community for the purposes of Article 2. The list must be considered non-exclusive since the activities " shall include " those listed, and since other, unlisted activities are provided for in the body of the Treaty— *e.g.* tax provisions, Articles 95 to 99. Article 235 would not, however, appear to be an instrument for licensing completely new activities not already provided for. The latter article provides for the Council, acting unanimously on a proposal from the Commission and after consulting the Assembly, to take the appropriate measures if action by the Community should prove necessary to attain, in the course of the operation of the Common Market, one of the objectives of the Community, and the Treaty has not provided the necessary powers. It emerges clearly from the enumeration of the Community activities in Article 3, and from their description elsewhere in the Treaty, that by " Common Market " is meant a single economic area in which conditions similar to those existing in a national market (" *Binnenmarktähnliche Verhältnisse* ") will prevail. This aim is a reflection of the neo-liberal economic theory inspiring the Treaty. As emerges from Article 3 and from the rest of the Treaty, the conditions referred to imply at least free movement of goods, and free movement of persons, services and capital (" the four freedoms "—Art. 3 (*a*) and (*c*) and Arts. 9 to 17 and 30 to 37, and 48 to 73), plus a common customs tariff and a common commercial policy towards third countries (Art. 3 (*b*) and Arts. 18 to 29 and 110 to 116), a common agricultural policy (Art. 3 (*d*) and Arts. 38 to 47) and a common transport policy (Art. 3 (*e*) and Arts. 74 to 84). In order to ensure that the conditions to be attained do not vary from one Member State to another, rules to ensure that competition is not distorted are required (Art. 3 (*f*) and Arts. 85 to 94); rules on economic policies (Art. 3 (*g*) and Arts. 103 to 116) rules on the approximation of laws (Art. 3 (*h*) and Arts. 100 to 102), and provisions on social and regional policies (Art. 3 (*i*) and (*j*) and Arts. 117 to 128 and 129 to 130). Finally Article 3 (*k*) makes mention of association of the overseas countries and territories, the purpose of which is " to increase trade and to promote jointly economic and social development." The substantive provisions on the association of those countries and territories are contained in Articles 131 to 136.

At first sight there would seem to be some conflict between the two tools provided in Article 2, the establishing of a common market and the approximation of economic policies, but it seems clear that the approximation of economic policies is only in question in matters outside the immediate ambit of the activities of the Common Market. To the extent that these activities may be expanded, opportunity for Member States to engage in their own distinctive economic policies may be affected (*cf.* 22/70, *Commission* v. *Council*, Rec. XVII 263, [1971] C.M.L.R. 335, discussed *supra*, § 17–15). Such expansion is clearly envisaged, for Article 3 (" in accordance with the timetable set out " in the Treaty) provides for the development of Community action in specific matters.

0–05   Article 4 relates back to Article 2, in that it stipulates that the tasks entrusted to the Community are to be carried out by an Assembly, a Council, a Commission and a Court of Justice. See generally *supra*, §§ 3–01 *et seq.* on the institutions of the Community. Here it is sufficient to note that the three Communities have shared a common Parliament and Court since the inception of the Rome Treaty Communities (Convention on certain institutions common to the European Communities, March 25, 1957, Cmnd. 4864, p. 144). The Communities now share a common Council and a common Commission (Merger Treaty of April 8, 1965, Cmnd. 4866). The Council and the Commission are assisted by a consultative organ, the Economic and Social Committee.

There are in addition a number of other subsidiary organs, notably the Monetary Committee (Art. 105) the Audit Board (Art. 206), and others, such as the management or advisory committees, set up by the institutions themselves. (See generally Chapter 7, *supra*, on committees, and § 22–09, *infra*.)

Apart from listing the institutions, it is to be noticed that Article 4 requires each institution to act within the limits of the powers conferred upon it by the Treaty. This phrase makes it clear that the powers of the institutions are powers of attribution; they extend only so far as the Treaty confers them, and no institution may arrogate powers or

161

competences to itself, although it may have certain implied powers. (See also § 4–15, *supra.*)

20–06   By Article 5, first para., the Member States are to "take all appropriate measures, whether general or particular, to ensure the fulfilment of the obligations arising out of this Treaty or resulting from action taken by the institutions," *i.e.* from secondary legislation in the sense of Article 189.* The obligation is one requiring action (or restraint) in execution of obligations. The second sentence of the first paragraph requires Member States to "facilitate the achievement of the Community's tasks." This is a more active obligation, requiring Member States to give the Community all assistance possible.

The duty laid down in the first paragraph of this Article is reinforced in negative form in the second paragraph, which requires the States to refrain from prejudicial behaviour.

In view of its general nature, it cannot readily be said that Article 5 is directly applicable, but it has been relied on in actions before the Court of Justice as a subsidiary ground of complaint that a Member State has failed to give full faith and credit to the Treaty obligations, and the Court has itself invoked it. (See generally § 17–13, *supra.*) The Member States can thus be said in some degree to be made agents of execution of the Treaty, and must facilitate positively the working of the EEC. This is largely reinforced by the judgment in the *AETR* case. (*Supra,* and see generally *supra* § 18–09.)

The Member States are required by Article 6 to co-ordinate their economic policies to the extent necessary to attain the objectives of the Treaty. This co-ordination is to take place in close co-operation with the institutions of the Community. These latter are required to take care not to prejudice the internal and external financial stability of the Member States (Art. 6 (2)).

20–07   Article 145, requiring the Council to ensure co-ordination of the general economic policies of the Member States, makes it clear that that institution bears a primary responsibility in economic matters. The various committees with economic responsibility are concerned here also, notably the Monetary Committee, Conjunctural Policy Committee, Medium-term Economic Policy Committee, Budgetary Policy Committee, and Committee of the Governors of the Central Banks (see generally Chapter 7, *supra*).

The Treaty contains additional provisions on economic policies in Article 103 (conjunctural policy) and Articles 104 to 109 (balance of payments). These dispositions are, however, much more specific, while the ambit of Article 6 (1) grows with the expansion of Community activities in general (see generally Chapter 33 on economic policies).

20–08   Article 7 prohibits discrimination between nationals of Member States on grounds of nationality (*cf.* Art. 40 (3), second sub-para., which excludes discrimination between producers and consumers of agricultural products). The article refers to discrimination exercised not only by the Member States, but also by individuals. In case 13/63, *Government of Italy* v. *Commission* (import tax on Italian refrigerators), Rec. IX 335, [1963] C.M.L.R. 289, the Court of Justice made it clear that different treatment of dissimilar situations did not amount to discrimination, but conversely that similar treatment of dissimilar situations might constitute such.

It is clear that the rule contained in Article 7 is one of the fundamental rules of the Community, but the Article is expressed to be without prejudice to other dispositions in the Treaty—*i.e.* it may be subject to derogation. It is not, however, clear in what this derogation might consist, although the Article is clearly not intended to affect the operation of the specific rules for the ending of discrimination, *e.g.* Articles 31, 40, 44, 45, 48, and 132, etc. *Cf.* also Articles 85 *et seq.* and Articles 92 *et seq. Cf.*, however, Article 233. It is to be noted that Article 7, second para., enables the Council, on a proposal from the Commission, to adopt rules designed to prohibit discrimination of the kind referred to in the first paragraph. (No such rules have been adopted.) Even in the absence of such rules, however, the first paragraph lays down a clear prohibition. It has been suggested on the basis of Article 8 (7), *infra*, and by analogy with 31/64 " *La Prévoyance Sociale*" v. *Bertholet*, Rec. XI 111, [1966] C.M.L.R. 191, that the first paragraph of Article 7 could be considered self-executing, being negative in form, and requiring no action by the Member States. (*Cf.* 26/62, *Van Gend en Loos* v. *Nederlandse Administratie der Belastingen*, Rec. IX 1, [1963] C.M.L.R. 105, and see generally § 18-03, *supra.*) It would seem, however, that a better analogy is to be drawn with 78/70, *Deutsche Grammophon Gesellschaft* v. *Metro-SB-Grossmärkte GmbH*, Rec. XVII 487, [1971] C.M.L.R. 631 (Art. 5, second para., not directly applicable because content varies) since the content of Article 7 will necessarily vary with the subject-matter.

20-09   For the most part the provisions of Article 8 are now spent, and are only of historical interest. The Article states the principle that the Community was to be progressively established during a transitional period of twelve years, divided into three equal stages of four years. It provided for modification of this timetable, but none of significance was in fact effected, although the setting up of the customs union was accelerated—see generally below, § 21-12.

Article 8 (7) states that the expiry of the transitional period which occurred on December 31, 1969, constituted the latest date by which all the rules laid down must enter into force. This is subject to any exceptions or derogations provided for in the Treaty (*e.g.* Art. 26; postponement of alignment with the CCT of specific items). The expiry of the period of transition clearly did not affect provisions intended to be of application throughout the existence of the Community, but as of that date certain provisions ceased to be of application (*e.g.* the transitional safeguards in Art. 226), while others came into operation for the first time (*e.g.* tariff negotiation provisions in Art. 113). A matter of greater uncertainty was whether these Treaty provisions, required to be carried out during the period of transition, and which had not been so carried out, became directly applicable on January 1, 1970. Where the obligations fulfil the normal requirements of a directly applicable provision (obligatory nature, clarity and susceptibility of immediate application etc.), the Court has held such provisions to have become directly applicable—*e.g.* 33/70, *SACE* v. *Italian Ministry of Finance,* Rec. XVI 1213, [1971] C.M.L.R. 123, as to Article 13 (2) EEC. It is thus clear that the fact that these obligations had not been implemented in time does not prevent their implementation thereafter.

CHAPTER 21

FREE MOVEMENT OF GOODS

FREE MOVEMENT OF GOODS—ARTICLES 9 TO 11

21–01 ARTICLES 9 to 11 of the Treaty set out the general principles of the customs union. Article 9 refers to the Community as being based upon a customs union covering all trade in goods. The notion of a customs union is more comprehensive than that of a free trade area; in addition to free trade between Member States ensured by prohibition of customs duties on imports and exports, and of equivalent charges, contained in Article 9—a customs union involves the adoption of a common customs tariff (CCT, sometimes referred to as common external tariff—CET) *vis-à-vis* non-Member States. Community action is not limited to this, for the customs union is only one element in the creation of a common market in goods and services (*i.e.* comprising the four freedoms and amounting to a "*Binnenmarkt*") and does not exhaust the potential of the Community: the plans for economic and monetary union are based upon the existing structure of the Community, and involve its amplification; they do not constitute a separate movement. (Werner Plan: Report to the Council and the Commission on the realisation by stages of Economic and Monetary Union in the Community: Bulletin, Supp. 11, 1970.) Economic and monetary union does not, however, involve integration to the degree obtaining in a federal state, and nor is it sought to go so far.

21–02 The EEC Treaty also calls for the suppression of quantitative restrictions under Articles 30 to 37. As the structuring of Title 1—"Free Movement of Goods"—of Part Two of the Treaty—"Foundations of the Community"—itself indicates, elimination of such restrictions was not apparently considered to be part and parcel of the customs union *stricto sensu*: Chapter 1 is entitled the "Customs Union," while the "Elimination of Quantitative Restrictions" forms a separate Chapter 2.

The abolition of customs duties between Member States does not eliminate all controls at frontiers at a stroke. In the first place, important restrictions are still permitted on grounds of public policy (*cf.* Art. 36, *infra*) and in the second place, customs controls are in many cases replaced by revenue controls operating as internal taxes. For although Member States may not tax goods imported from other Member States at a higher rate than the domestic product, they may nevertheless impose the same rate, and this will be done at the frontier (Arts. 95 and 96). Among the chief objects of the harmonisation of the national systems of turnover taxes and institution of a common value added tax system was the elimination on the one hand of instances of double taxation by enabling goods to be exported tax-free to other Member States, and on the other hand the securing of an even level of taxation (as yet still far from being achieved).

Controls are also required for the elimination of trade deflections; to this end safeguards may be applied with the sanction of the Commission by Article 115 of the Treaty, but the tendency is to reduce the number of authorisations granted.

21-03 The term "customs duty" is to be understood in its normal technical sense of a duty of customs fixed by a tariff list. An "equivalent charge" is a tax imposed solely on imports, and having the same effect on free circulation as a customs duty (2 & 3/62, *Commission* v. *Luxembourg and Belgium,* Rec. VIII 813, [1963] C.M.L.R. 199). This type of charge must be distinguished from one which is imposed both on national production and on imports, discriminating as a matter of fact against the latter: this latter type of tax is covered by Articles 95 and 96. (See *infra,* Chapter 30 on taxation aspects.) The Court has held that Articles 9 *et seq.* cannot be applied to the same situation: either the tax is an equivalent charge, or else it is an internal discriminatory tax: 10/65, *Deutschmann* v. *Germany,* Rec. XI 601, [1965] C.M.L.R. 259; 52 & 55/65, *Germany* v. *Commission,* Rec. XII 227, [1967] C.M.L.R. 22; 57/65, *Lütticke* v. *HZA Saarelouis,* Rec. XII 293, [1971] C.M.L.R. 674; 7/67, *Milchwerke Wöhrmann* v. *HZA Bad Reichenhall,* Rec. XIV 261, [1968] C.M.L.R. 234; 25/67, *Milch- Fett- und Eierkontor* v. *HZA Saarbrücken,* Rec. XIV 305, [1968] C.M.L.R. 225; and 2 & 3/69, *Sociaal Fonds voor de Diamantarbeiders* v. *Brachfeld and Chougol Diamond,* Rec. XV 211, [1969] C.M.L.R. 335. The test, therefore, for a tax falling within Articles 95 and 96 is to ask whether the tax is imposed both on home production and on imports, albeit at different rates. If the tax is imposed solely on imports as was necessarily the case in *Brachfeld,* then it falls within Article 9.

21-04 So-called statistical duties also come within the prohibition of Article 9—*e.g.* cases 24/68, *Commission* v. *Italy,* Rec. XV 193, [1971] C.M.L.R. 611; 8/70, *Commission* v. *Italy,* Rec. XVI 961; 43/71, *Politi* v. *Italian Ministry of Finance,* Rec. XVII 1039; and 84/71, *Marimex* v. *Italian Ministry of Finance,* Rec. XVIII 89, [1972] C.M.L.R. 907—unless for example the duty is of some benefit to the importer, or serves as a check on fraud—*e.g.* 52 & 55/65, *Germany* v. *Commission, supra.* Charges for health checks made on imported products only are not apparently within this exception: 29/72, *Marimex* v. *Italian Finance Administration,* not yet reported.

21-05 The provisions for free circulation of goods apply of course to all goods produced in the Community (Art. 9 (2)) but additionally they apply to goods obtained from outside the Community, and in free circulation in the Member States (same provision). Article 10 defines these latter as being goods which have complied with the import for-malities of the relevant Member State, and on which any customs duties or equivalent charges which are payable have been levied in that Member State, and which have not benefited from a total or partial drawback of such duties or charges. Regulation 802/68, J.O. 1968, L 148/1, provides a common definition of the concept of origin for general purposes, but may perhaps be referred to for the purpose of applying Article 10.

The Protocol to the Treaty of Rome on German Internal Trade (Cmnd. 4864, p. 125) makes it clear that goods originating in East Germany are to be considered as in free circulation, subject to limitations and to particular safeguards.

21–06   Article 10 (2) is the legal basis for decisions of the Commission determining the methods of administrative co-operation to be adopted for the purpose of applying Article 9 (2), *i.e.* for keeping a check on goods entitled to free movement. Control was at first largely effected through the use of movement certificates, but now that there is a unified régime for goods in transit in the Community (Regulation 542/69, J.O. 1969, L 77/1) the internal movement certificates have been suppressed, since goods in fact within the Community are by and large assumed to be entitled to benefit from the free movement pro-visions. (See also *inter alia* Regulations 2313/69, 2315/69, and 2662/70.) Personal luggage of a reasonable value is altogether exempt from customs duty upon import into the Community, and goods contained in personal luggage up to a value of 25 u.a. are likewise exempt (Regulation 1544/69, J.O. 1969, L. 191/1). They are, therefore, outside the ambit of the controls on free circulation altogether. Amendments to this particular régime are at present being considered. A bigger franchise is likely to be granted. A rather similar régime, set up by Directive 69/169, J.O. 1969, L. 133/6, as amended by Directive 72/230, J.O. 1972, L. 139/28, provides for exemptions from turnover tax and excise duty. The latter directive raised the franchise in respect of goods imported as part of personal luggage from 75 u.a. to 125 u.a. on journeys between Member States. Goods imported as part of personal luggage from third states still enjoy a franchise of only 25 u.a. This too is likely, however, to be increased in the near future. Certain other changes to the existing régime are envisaged by recent Commission proposals, notably involving suppression of intra-Community franchises (see J.O. 1972, C 113/15 and C 134/34).

At least one purpose of the Community rules on free circulation is to combat fraud, and to reinforce this the Member States concluded a Convention between themselves on Mutual Assistance between Customs Administrations (signed at Rome on September 7, 1967, B.G.Bl. 1969, 11, p. 65). This Convention relates largely to the exchange of information and to investigation of offences committed in the territory of another Member State.

21–07   The second sub-paragraph of paragraph 2 of Article 10 requires that rules be laid down for the control of inward processing trade between Member States, where customs duty has been paid on only a part of the material incorporated into a finished product. The principle to be aimed at here was clearly that all goods should comply with Article 10 (1) by the expiry of the period of transition, and Decision 68/284, J.O. 1968, L. 167/10, gave effect to this, replacing earlier partial solutions.

21–08   Article 11, requiring Member States to take all appropriate measures to enable governments to carry out, within the periods of time laid down, the obligations with regard to customs duties which devolve on them pursuant to the Treaty, applies the principles of Article 5 ("full faith and credit clause") to the specific case of Articles 9 to 17 on customs matters. But it has been suggested that the obligation is slightly wider than this, in that there is here in effect a duty on the Member States to see that legislation is passed or administrative measures are taken empowering the governments to act.

21–09   As already mentioned, Articles 9 to 11 set out the general principles of the customs union. The succeeding Articles are more specific; new duties and equivalent charges on imports and exports are prohibited (Art. 12); existing ones are abolished (Arts. 13 to 17); and the common customs tariff is set up (Arts. 18 to 29). All these provisions are of quite general application. In principle therefore, they apply equally to agriculture, save as otherwise provided in Articles 39 to 46 (*cf.* Art. 38 (2)).

In addition, however, quantitative restrictions or quotas, comparatively insignificant since the 90 per cent. abolition effectuated in the OEEC, must be abolished as between Member States if they are not to have a disproportionately distorting effect once customs duties are eliminated. Quantitative restrictions are therefore prohibited as a general rule (Art. 30); new ones are prohibited (Art. 31) and existing ones are not to be made more restrictive (Art. 32). Articles 32 to 36 then set out the schedule for abolition. It is to be noted that it was felt that export restrictions, in contrast to import restrictions, could be abolished at once, hence the specific dispositions in Articles 16 (customs) and 34 (quotas).

It will be noted that Articles 9 to 37 deal almost exclusively with intra-Community trade, except in so far as fixing an external tariff is concerned; other matters of external trade are dealt with in the Treaty chapter on Commercial Policy—Articles 110 to 116.

THE CUSTOMS UNION—ARTICLES 12 TO 29

1. The elimination of customs duties between Member States [1]

21–10   By Article 12 the Member States are bound to refrain from introducing between themselves any new customs duties on imports or exports,

---

[1] Arts. 12–17.

or any equivalent charges, and from increasing those already extant. Articles 9 and 12 together constitute a basic rule, and exceptions must be clearly provided for: 2 & 3/62, *Commission* v. *Belgium and Luxembourg*, Rec. VIII 813, [1963] C.M.L.R. 199. (See 73 & 74/63, *Internationale Crediet en Handelsvereniging " Rotterdam," and " Puttershoek "* v. *Dutch Ministry of Agriculture*, Rec. X 1, [1964] C.M.L.R. 198, as to Article 226, now spent; Article 115 could perhaps be said to create such an exception which is still in effect.) The rule applies to agriculture in the absence of contrary provisions—90 & 91/63, *Commission* v. *Belgium and Luxembourg*, Rec. X 1217, [1965] C.M.L.R. 58. Article 12, setting out a clear provision not requiring implementing legislation, has been held to be directly applicable: 26/62, *Van Gend En Loos* v. *Nederlandse Administratie der Belastingen*, Rec. IX 1, [1963] C.M.L.R. 105. (See generally Chapter 18, *supra*, as to the notion of directly applicable Community law.) Individuals may, therefore, rely on this article before national courts to resist a demand for payment of duty made under a municipal provision running counter to the prohibitions of Article 12, since the Article does not merely place an obligation on Member States, but creates rights for individuals. Whether an individual may recoup payments already made was a question decided affirmatively in Belgium: see *Belgian Minister for Economic Affairs* v. *" le Ski "* [1972] C.M.L.R. 330.

Where a derogation from Article 12 is expressly permitted, as under Article 115, *cf.* 73 & 74/63, *" Internatio,"* *supra*, no comparable individual right exists.

Article 12, in prohibiting increases in duties applied, is to be understood as referring to the duty actually applied (10/61, *Commission* v. *Italy*, Rec. VIII 1, [1962] C.M.L.R. 187). The notion of the duty actually applied would not, on the other hand, extend to a level of duty applied due to an isolated administrative error. The reclassification of a good in another tariff category is, if it produces a higher duty, equally illegal: *Van Gend en Loos*, *supra*. The provisions for the abolition of customs duties as between Member States are now largely of academic interest, since all such duties and equivalent charges were to be abolished by the end of the transitional period. It is sufficient to note that under Article 13 (1) customs duties on imports were to be abolished during the transitional period in accordance with the timetable laid down in Articles 14 and 15. In fact, however, the Member States abolished all duties on industrial goods as of July 1, 1968, by Decision 66/532, J.O. 1966, 2971.

21–11   Under Article 13 (2) equivalent charges were to be abolished during the transitional period on the basis of a timetable laid down by Commission directives. Despite the provision for directives, the paragraph has been interpreted as creating directly applicable obligations to abolish all equivalent charges by the end of the transitional period: 33/70, *SACE* v. *Italian Ministry of Finance*, Rec. XVI 1213, [1971]

C.M.L.R. 123. Nevertheless, some equivalent charges still survive—Fifth General Report (1971), p. 79.

21-12   Article 15 (1), providing for the suspension of collection of customs duties during the transitional period, is a very general provision, probably not giving rights to individuals. An interpretation that the Member States could, during the transitional period, cancel the suspension with impunity, would seem in line with 57/65, *Lütticke* v. *HZA Saarelouis*, Rec. XII 293, [1971] C.M.L.R. 674, where the directive on value added tax was in question. *Cf.* also the principles involved in 69/69, *Alcan* v. *Commission*, Rec. XVI 385, [1970] C.M.L.R. 337.

It was apparently on the basis of Article 15 (2), providing that " The Member States declare their readiness to reduce customs duties against the other Member States more rapidly than is provided for in Article 14 if their general economic situation and the situation of the economic sector concerned so permit," that the three so-called acceleration decisions were taken, abolishing customs duties in advance of the time-table. The final decision (referred to *supra*) was a normal decision of the Council, based on Article 235 of the Treaty, but the two earlier ones of May 12, 1960 (J.O. 1960, 1217) and May 15, 1962 (J.O. 1962, 1284) were decisions of the representatives of the Member States, a type of decision not provided for by Article 189* (see generally § 8–13, *supra*). It is considered, however, that the acceleration decisions are now irreversible.

21-13   The Court of Justice confirmed the direct applicability of the stipulations of Article 16, prohibiting export duties and equivalent charges as of the end of the first stage in 18/71, *Eunomia* v. *Italian Ministry of Public Instruction*, Rec. XVII 811, [1972] C.M.L.R. 4. This case in effect confirmed an earlier judgment of the Court (7/68, *Commission* v. *Italy*, Rec. XIV 617, [1969] C.M.L.R. 1), holding that Italian export taxes on art treasures were illegal, and being ineffective, could not benefit from the saving of Article 36 (savings *inter alia* in respect of national treasures possessing artistic, historic or archaeological value). Other examples of export duties, or, more likely, equivalent charges, may still exist—see Europe Bulletin No. 935, December 2, 1971, p. 7.

21-14   Article 17 deals specifically with the abolition of customs duties of a fiscal nature—*i.e.* those intended to produce revenue and not primarily designed to protect. These were to be abolished, since the difference between protective and revenue producing duties is not in practice entirely clear-cut. Article 17 (3) permits the replacement of fiscal duties by internal taxes complying with Article 95. (*Cf.* 2 & 3/69, *Sociaal Fonds voor de Diamantarbeiders* v. *Brachfeld and Chougol Diamond*, Rec. XV 211, [1969] C.M.L.R. 335—see *supra*, § 21–03.)

2. Setting up of the Common Customs Tariff (CCT) [2]

21–15   The section of the Treaty on the setting up of the CCT opens with a declaration that the Member States are ready to enter into agreements " designed . . . to reduce duties below the general level of which they could avail themselves as a result of the establishment of a customs union between them," for the purposes of contributing to the development of international trade and the lowering of barriers to trade (Art. 18). It may be questioned whether this provision imposes any obligation at all. The better view appears to be that it enunciates a principle to be acted upon, but not an obligation.

The most obvious example of action under this article was of course the Kennedy Round of tariff reductions.

The basic level of the CCT is fixed at the arithmetical average of the duties applied in the four customs territories (Benelux, France, Germany and Italy) comprised in the Community (Art. 19 (1)) on January 1, 1957 (Art. 19 (2)). This basic rule was, however, subject to a number of exceptions and restrictions, governed by Article 19 itself, and Article 20. Article 23 (3) provides that the CCT was to be applied in its entirety by the end of the transitional period at the latest. Article XXIV of the GATT places certain restrictions upon the fixing of a CCT, but the GATT never in fact gave a final ruling on the compatibilities of the EEC Treaty with its rules. This is not to say, however, that the Community is to be considered to exist in violation of GATT— cf. Written Question 456/71, J.O. 1972, C 23/11.

Article 21, now spent, provided for directives to take account of technical difficulties arising in applying Articles 19 and 20, and also provided for variations in the CCT.

Customs duties of a fiscal nature were to be adjusted under Article 22 of the Treaty. The level of such duties was set at the same time as the CCT.

21–16   The level of customs duties for any given year is now governed by an annual consolidating tariff regulation amending the annex to the first such Regulation, Regulation 950/68, J.O. 1968, L 172/1 and any subsequent amendments. The annual consolidating Regulation is usually number 1 in that year.

So far the discussion has confined itself to the determination of the CCT: Articles 23 to 29 are concerned with the implementation of the CCT. The implementation of the CCT did not follow the timetable set out in Article 23; rather it was speeded up by the same two acceleration decisions referred to in connection with elimination of duties between Member States (*supra*, § 21–10), and finally set in place for industrial products by the same final decision as for customs duties as of July 1, 1968, the tariff being set out in Regulation 950/68 and subsequent amendments to its annex. The legal basis for this alignment

---

[2] Arts. 18–29.

is to be found in Article 24, echoing Article 15 (2), and in Article 235. During the period 1966 to June 30, 1968, a number of duties were suspended at the level fixed by the second acceleration decision, and some upward alignments were deferred, and deferment still continues in a small number of cases—notably in the case of German wine alcohol imports. (See Fourth General Report (1970), p. 5.)

The common customs tariff sets out the tariff headings, divisions and sub-divisions, and beside them the applicable duties are set out, listed in two columns: autonomous duties in the sense of Article 28 (*i.e.* those fixed by the Community without particular reference to third states) in the first column, and duties arrived at under Article 113 (formerly 111) by international convention—*e.g.* the Kennedy Round, in the second. The tariff Regulation contains rules as to its interpretation. Most notable is the provision that the CCT is completely closed; no goods are outside it. The Commission, assisted by the nomenclature committee (set up by Regulation 97/69), issues explanatory notes on the sub-divisions of the CCT, themselves based upon the Brussels Convention on Customs Nomenclature of December 15, 1950, as amended (Cmnd. 4870, T.S. No. 11 (1972)) to which all Member States are party, and which is accepted by the Community.

Article 232 of the EEC Treaty states that the provisions of that Treaty " shall not affect the provisions of the [ECSC Treaty] " (para. 1) and " shall not derogate from those of the [Euratom Treaty]." The ECSC Treaty leaves matters of external policy in the hands of the Member States, and provides only for a maximum and minimum tariff level (Art. 72). There is a unified (but not *common*) ECSC Tariff. Import and export duties and quantitative restrictions are illegal (Art. 4). The Euratom Treaty provides for the elimination of the same measures (Art. 93). Where, however, there is no specific provision for dealing with a particular matter (*e.g.* harmonisation of legislation in the ECSC and Euratom Treaties) the EEC rules will be of application, since they apply to the other two Communities wherever there is no specific rule.

21–17   Up to Article 16 at least, the EEC Treaty provides parallel sets of provisions for customs duties on the one hand, and for equivalent charges on the other. But there is no provision as to equivalent charges in relation to the setting up of the CCT. While the imposition of such a charge is not therefore contrary to the Treaty *ipso facto*, nevertheless, a Member State imposing such a charge will be failing in its obligations under Article 5 in so far as the effect of such a charge may be deleterious, and Article 115 (safeguard provisions to counter trade deflections or economic difficulties caused by differences between national measures taken in execution of the common commercial policy) may be of application.

Article 25, which is an article of strict application since it is in derogation from the principles of the Common Market (24/62, *Germany*

v. *Commission*, Rec. IX 129, [1963] C.M.L.R. 347), provides for the granting of tariff quotas to Member States. Paragraph 1 directs that if the Commission finds that the Community production of particular products contained in list B, C and D falls short of the requirements of one of the Member States, and that such supply traditionally depends to a considerable extent on imports from third countries, the Council is to grant the Member State concerned tariff quotas at a reduced rate of duty or duty free, acting by a qualified majority on a proposal from the Commission. Under paragraph 2 the Commission is itself to grant such quotas for particular products contained in lists E and G where difficulties with supplies are such as to entail harmful consequences for the processing industries of a Member State. These quotas are granted on request from the Member State concerned. Under paragraph 3 the Commission may authorise a Member State to suspend collection of applicable duties on Annex II (*i.e.* agricultural) products or may grant tariff quotas. Action under any of the three paragraphs must be taken in such a way as to avoid harmful effects on other Member States or on the agricultural markets. The Commission had wished to abolish all tariff quotas in favour of individual Member States by the end of the transitional period, but this has not apparently proved possible (although none were given in 1971—Fifth General Report (1971), p. 79, nine authorisations were given in 1970—Fourth General Report (1970), p. 5). Part of the difficulty may lie in the fact that the Commission has little discretion in connection with the granting of a quota apart from fixing the rate, etc. Where the conditions for granting the quota exist, it must, under the first two of the three paragraphs, be granted. But the granting of a quota is never automatic, for all the elements must be taken into account, and in particular the Commission must have regard to the guiding principles set out in Article 29.

Under Article 26 suspensions in alignment with the CCT are permissible in case of special difficulty (see § 21–16, *supra*).

21–18   Clearly, there was a need to set up a mechanism for the harmonisation of national customs rules, and this is done by Article 27. This Article provides only for the issue of non-binding recommendations, however, and accordingly where possible other customs Articles and the power to issue directives under Article 100 have been resorted to. (See notably Directives 68/312, 69/73–76 and 69/354.) Where these powers have been insufficient, for lack of a strictly regulatory power, Article 235 has been used as the legal basis—Regulations 802 and 803/68, 1496/68 and 542/69.

Whether or not the power to make recommendations under Article 27 exists after the end of the first stage, the Commission has in fact continued to make them. But the view has been expressed that the power only extends to matters relating to external trade, since Articles 18 to 29 relate to the external tariff. This argument is not entirely convincing. The Commission appears, however, to avoid acting contrary to the view referred to, and where recommendations are required for intra-Community trade, they are made under Article 115 (recommendations on methods of co-operation to avoid trade deflection or economic difficulties). In practice, with the unification of the CCT on July 1, 1968 (see now Regulation 950/68, *supra*), recommendations have proved less useful than before, and Regulations are now the rule.

See Regulations 802/68 origin of goods
803/68 valuation of goods for customs purposes
1496/68 customs territory
97/69 customs nomenclature
542/69 Community transit
582/69 certificates of origin
1544/69 goods in personal luggage
1617/69 transit declaration forms
2313/69 Community transit documents
2315/69 transit document for checking use or purpose of goods
982/71 exchange rate for purposes of 803/68
1971/71 ditto.

(For directives in this area see 68/312, 69/73, 69/74, 69/75, 69/76, 71/235. And see the list of recommendations given by L. J. van der Berg, 7 C.M.L.Rev. 1970, 202.)

21–19   The Commission has not been satisfied with progress in the field of the approximation of customs legislation, and in April 1971 adopted a General Programme for the Approximation of Customs Legislation. This General Programme is primarily concerned to combat the distortions of competition arising from the discriminatory treatment of those required to pay duties, and is designed to ensure the correct administration of existing Community rules, to supervise the conditions under which the whole of customs legislation is to be applied, and to continue harmonisation. So far as harmonisation is concerned, the Commission proposes action on :

(a) national customs arrangements having a direct incidence on the amount of customs duties accruing as " own resources " and on the conditions of competition,
(b) measures to improve the functioning of the customs union,
(c) problems in connection with admission of new members to the Communities,
(d) codification of Community law.

(See generally Bulletin 6, 1971, pp. 46 *et seq.*)

21–20   Article 28 refers to " autonomous alteration or suspension of duties " in the CCT. An autonomous duty is a duty fixed by the Community, without particular reference to third States. Such a duty is to be contrasted with a duty fixed in the first place by international convention, and subsequently incorporated into the Community tariff. Conventional duties, so called, are arrived at under powers in Articles 111, now 113, and 114. The decision to alter or suspend duties under Article 28 is taken by the Council acting unanimously. No Commission proposal, of the type provided for in Article 149, is here in question, although the Council may in fact act at the instigation of the Commission. Temporary derogations from the CCT are fixed by the Council acting by a qualified majority on a proposal from the Commission. The alterations or suspensions carried out by way of derogation are not to exceed 20 per cent. of the rate in the case of any one duty, and may last for a period of six months maximum. A single extension for a further period of six months may subsequently be granted under the same conditions. It is in exercise of this latter power that tariff quotas (*i.e.* 100 tons of a given product at 5 per cent. or 0 per cent. instead of 10 per cent. import duty) are granted. Unlike the suspensions under Article 25, these are of general application, and do not concern one State alone. There were 119 authorisations in 1970, contained in Regulation 2635/70, J.O. 1970, L 283/5, and authorisations were given in respect of 141 products or groups of products in 1971 (Regulation 2780/71, J.O. 1971, L 287/22) (Fifth General Report (1971), p. 79).

21–21   In carrying out the tasks entrusted to it, the Commission is to be guided by a series of principles set out in Article 29, namely:

> " (*a*) the need to promote trade between Member States and third countries;
>
> (*b*) developments in conditions of competition within the Community in so far as they lead to an improvement in the competitive capacity of undertakings;
>
> (*c*) the requirements of the Community as regards the supply of raw materials and semi-finished goods; in this connection the Commission shall take care to avoid distorting conditions of competition between Member States in respect of finished goods;
>
> (*d*) the need to avoid serious disturbances in the economies of Member States and to ensure rational development of production and an expansion of consumption within the Community."

These principles are binding on the Commission only, but in so far as they must necessarily appear in Commission proposals, they affect the entire Community. The Court has referred to the necessity to have regard to these principles in granting tariff quotas under Article 25 (24/62, and 34/62, *Germany* v. *Commission*, **Rec. IX 129 and 269,** [1963] C.M.L.R. 347 and 369).

THE MEMBER STATES AND COMMUNITY CUSTOMS LEGISLATION

21–22 The Community system of customs legislation is not to be taken as being a complete system, entirely excluding national intervention in all cases, but where the Member States have given the Community power to legislate for the Community, they no longer have the power to legislate so as to modify or add to the Community provisions, and the latter are to be interpreted in the light of Community law alone. (See especially 40/69, *HZA Hamburg-Oberelbe* v. *Bollmann*, Rec. XVI 69, [1970] C.M.L.R. 141; 74/69, *HZA Bremen-Freihafen* v. *Krohn*, Rec. XVI 451, [1970] C.M.L.R. 466; 39/70, *Fleischkontor* v. *HZA Hamburg-St, Annen*, Rec. XVII 49, [1971] C.M.L.R. 281; 51–54/71, *International Fruit Company* v. *Produktschap voor Groenten en Fruit*, Rec. XVII 1107; and 94/71, *Schlüter & Maack* v. *HZA Hamburg-Jonas*, report not yet published. See also cases 14/70, 12, 13, 14/71, 21/71, 49, 50/71, and 77/71.)

This is not to say that national dispositions may not be applied in general areas where the Community has responsibility, but rather that national rules may not be applied where the Community has laid down rules for dealing with the specific problem in question—*e.g.* 40/69, *Bollmann*, and 74/69, *Krohn*, *supra*.

The rule that Member States may not legislate in areas in which they have given legislative powers to the Community applies of course to the whole range of Community law, and not merely to customs law, although most of the cases on the point relate to customs and agricultural matters.

THE ELIMINATION OF QUANTITATIVE RESTRICTIONS BETWEEN MEMBER STATES

21–23 " Quantitative restrictions on imports and all measures having equivalent effect [are], without prejudice to [Articles 31 to 37], prohibited between Member States " (Art. 30), and new restrictions of the same kinds are prohibited (Art. 31, first para.), but the latter obligation relates only to the degree of liberalisation attained in pursuance of the decisions of the Council of the OEEC of January 14, 1955 (Art. 31, second para.). The OEEC had achieved the suppression of quantitative restrictions on 90 per cent. of goods imported by OEEC Members from other OEEC Member States. Despite this liberalisation, however, it was considered that quantitative restrictions would, if not abolished, hinder the creation of the Common Market; hence the provisions for their elimination in the EEC Treaty. But even with their inclusion, EEC Member States were theoretically still at liberty to introduce quantitative restrictions or equivalent measures on goods not covered by the OEEC decisions.

Quantitative restrictions have the effect of limiting imports (or exports) of products by number, weight or value. These restrictions are more familiarly known as quotas, but the term "quantitative restriction" (of which quotas are but one type) is more accurate.

21-24   It may be asked what constitutes measures having equivalent effect; the notion is generally considered to include, for example, an obligation to include home-produced materials in products otherwise likely to be made entirely from imported materials. The notion is also considered to include price controls on imported or exported goods; an obligation to comply with special standards for imported goods; an obligation to export as a condition for permission to import; or a requirement that the importer himself fulfil certain requirements. (See also generally Written Question 118/66-67, J.O. 1967, 122 and 901.) There is some doubt, however, as to whether measures applying equally to nationally produced and to imported goods would be caught by Articles 30 *et seq.* The better view would seem to be that they are not so caught. The circumstance that the measure is not in fact restrictive does not appear to remove it from the prohibitions of Articles 30 *et seq.* But it has been held that the "all licences granted" (*toutes licences accordées*—TLA) system of controlling the movement of goods is not incompatible with existing Community rules: 51-54/71, *International Fruit Company* v. *Produktschap voor Groenten en Fruit*, Rec. XVII 1107. This case cannot be said to decide one way or the other whether or not the measure must in fact be restrictive in its effects. On the whole the view to be preferred is that any "measure" capable as a matter of abstraction of having such effects is incompatible with Articles 30 *et seq.*

21-25   The obligation imposed by Article 31 applies only to quantitative restrictions; thus new restrictions in other areas were theoretically permissible. The Court of Justice held the obligation contained in Article 31 to be directly applicable from the date when lists of liberalised products were notified pursuant to the second paragraph of Article 31, or, at latest, at the expiration of the time limit set for notifying such lists by the paragraph itself: 13/68, *Salgoil* v. *Italian Ministry for Foreign Trade*, Rec. XIV 661, [1969] C.M.L.R. 181. The standstill obligation set out in the first paragraph was held to be of an absolute character, admitting of no exceptions. Doubts have been expressed as to whether the *Salgoil* decision applies in respect of products which had been liberated under the OEEC decisions, but not consolidated under Article 31. Whatever the answer, new restrictions were prohibited in respect of such goods by the first acceleration decision, of May 12, 1960, J.O. 1960, 1217, confirmed by the third, Decision 66/532, J.O. 1966, 2971. It is considered that the decisions are now irreversible.

However this may be, the Court did not, in the *Salgoil* case, advert to the question already referred to, whether Member States are free to introduce quantitative restrictions between themselves on goods which were not affected by the OEEC liberalisation. The Court has not yet given a direct answer to this question, but it was stated in 51–54/71, *International Fruit Company, supra,* that

> "Quantitative restrictions and measures having equivalent effect are, in virtue of Articles 30 and 34, para. 1 of the Treaty, prohibited between Member States whether on imports or exports." (Rec. XVII 1107 at p. 1116. Author's translation.)

The view is generally accepted that Article 30 is intended to constitute an absolute bar on all quantitative restrictions or equivalent measures at least from the end of the original transitional period. Article 42 of the Act of Accession confirms this view—see *infra,* § 21–47. In conformity with this view of Article 30, the statement quoted above would seem to be wide enough to cover even those restrictions and measures not caught by the limited prohibition of Article 31, now that the transitional period has expired. Article 30 must be considered to have constituted an absolute bar before the expiry of the transitional period for such restrictions or measures as were not expected under Articles 31 to 37, for it is expressed to be without prejudice to those provisions, which are of a transitional character.

21–26   Article 32, first para., applying equally to products not consolidated under Article 31, requires Member States in their trade with one another to "refrain from making more restrictive quotas or measures having equivalent effect existing at the date of entry into force" of the Treaty. This requirement has been held to be directly applicable: 13/68, *Salgoil* v. *Italian Ministry for Foreign Trade,* Rec. XIV 661, [1969] C.M.L.R. 181, *supra.*

Article 32, second para., requires Member States to abolish the quotas referred to in the first paragraph by the end of the transitional period. The Court of Justice has not had cause to rule on whether this provision creates directly applicable obligations, but it seems likely that it would so rule if presented squarely with the question, on analogy with 33/70, *S.p.a. SACE* v. *Italian Ministry of Finance,* Rec. XVI 1213, [1971] C.M.L.R. 123, where the rather similar provisions of Article 13 (2) were held to be directly applicable.

21–27   Although the provisions on the movement of goods apply in principle to agricultural products, this is subject to specific exceptions (*cf.* Art. 38 (2)). Certain such exceptional arrangements had the effect of taking agricultural products out of the chapter on quantitative restrictions while the agricultural policy was being worked out. Most quantitative restrictions on such goods were abolished in the context of the setting up of market organisations (see generally Chapter 22), rather than under timetable provisions of Articles 30 *et seq.* As regards quotas, the time-table set out in Article 33 was not in fact followed for industrial goods either, the first acceleration decision of May 12, 1960, J.O. 1960, 1217 eliminating the last quotas on these goods on December 31, 1961. Quotas on agricultural goods not subject to market organisations followed

Article 33. Most types of agricultural produce are now covered by market organisations.

21–28   Article 33 (7) provided for directives for the abolition of equivalent measures, and five were issued during the period of transition—

    64/486, J.O. 1964, 2253,
    66/682, J.O. 1966, 3745,
    66/683, J.O. 1966, 3748,
    70/32, J.O. 1970, L 13/1,
    70/50, J.O. 1970, L 13/29.
    (And see Written Question 118/66–67, J.O. 1967, 122 and 901.)

Since the end of the period of transition, all quantitative restrictions have been prohibited, and thus the power to issue such directives is arguably at an end. The Commission in fact appears to confine its activities to ensuring that the prohibition is respected (*cf.* Fourth General Report (1970), p. 12, and Fifth General Report (1971), p. 188) but there is no conclusive ruling either way.

Article 34 prohibits quantitative restrictions and equivalent measures on exports; existing ones were to be abolished by the end of the first stage.

Article 35 constitutes the legal justification analogous to Articles 15 and 24 for the acceleration decisions of May 12, 1960, and May 15, 1962. The third decision of 1966 confirmed the existing situation (see § 21–12, *supra,* on these decisions).

Article 36

21–29   Article 36 reads as follows:

" The provisions of Articles 30 to 34 shall not preclude prohibitions or restrictions on imports, exports or goods in transit justified on grounds of public morality, public policy or public security; the protection of health and life of humans, animals or plants; the protection of national treasures possessing artistic, historic or archaeological value; or the protection of industrial and commercial property. Such prohibitions or restrictions shall not, however, constitute a means of arbitrary discrimination or a disguised restriction on trade between Member States."

21–30   This Article, which may be described as the public policy reservation clause, provides for the retention or reintroduction of prohibitions or restrictions on imports and exports, etc. This list of permissible grounds appears to be exhaustive in view of its *caractère dérogatoire,* and must be interpreted strictly (*cf.* 24/62, *Germany* v. *Commission,* Rec. IX 129, [1963] C.M.L.R. 347). National regulations amounting to a retention or reintroduction of prohibitions or restrictions not attributable to one or other of the permissible grounds cannot benefit from the derogation of Article 36, even though justified on public policy grounds;

thus the exclusion of imported goods on the basis that they do not conform, for example, to national packaging standards is probably contrary to the Treaty, despite any beneficial effect such regulations may have for public security. (See *e.g.* 7/61, *Commission* v. *Italy*, Rec. VII 633, [1962] C.M.L.R. 39.) Ultimately the only realistic test will be to ask whether the end justifies the means, bearing in mind that arbitrary discrimination and disguised restrictions on trade are expressly prohibited (Art. 36, second sentence). See 13/63, *Italy* v. *Commission*, Rec. IX 335, [1963] C.M.L.R. 289, the Italian refrigerators case; and 7/68, *Italy* v. *Commission*, Rec. XIV 617, [1969] C.M.L.R. 1 (export of Italian art treasures), where the Court held that the means must in fact have some effect in protecting art treasures. Similarly in 56 & 58/64, *Consten and Grundig* v. *Commission*, Rec. XII 429, [1966] C.M.L.R. 418, and 24/67, *Parke, Davis* v. *Probel*, Rec. XIV 81, [1968] C.M.L.R. 47, the Court held that protection of industrial property could not be permitted to clash with the provisions of Articles 85 and 86 (competition). See also 40/70, *Sirena* v. *Eda*, Rec. XVII 69, [1971] C.M.L.R. 260, and 78/70, *Deutsche Grammophon Gesellschaft* v. *Metro-SB-Grossmärkte*, Rec. XVII 487, [1971] C.M.L.R. 631, and *cf.* 22/71, *Béguelin Import Co.* v. *S.A.G.L. Import-Export*, Rec. XVII 949, [1972] C.M.L.R. 81.

Article 36 has been held to be of strict application (29/72, *Marimex* v. *Italian Finance Administration*, not yet reported) and is not to be understood as authorising measures other than those of the types envisaged by Articles 30 to 34. While Article 36 does not prohibit health controls, it is not to be interpreted as thereby permitting the levy of charges on imported goods subject to the controls and designed to cover the costs, the charge not being intrinsically necessary to the application of the controls, and thus likely to constitute an additional barrier to intra-Community trade.

21–31   A growing number of technical barriers to trade of the kind often justified by Article 36 have been or are to be harmonised under the Article 100 procedure, and the Council has adopted a non-binding action programme for the elimination of such barriers, J.O. 1969, C 76/1. (See generally Chapter 32, *infra.*)

Article 37: State commercial monopolies

21–32   Article 37, requiring Member States to adjust any state monopolies "of a commercial character so as to ensure that . . . no discrimination . . . exists between nationals of Member States," is located in the chapter on elimination of quantitative restrictions because it was considered that at least some such commercial monopolies exercised control on imports so as to amount to a quantitative restriction or equivalent measure, but were not caught by Articles 30 *et seq.*, since the control exercised would not be based upon the type of regulatory disposition prohibited by those Articles.

It is clear that there is a close relationship between Article 37 (1) first and second sub-paras., but there are widely divergent views as to the nature of this relationship. To some, the second sub-para. represents a definition, and to others an extension of the term " monopolies " used in the first sub-para. A third view is that the term " monopoly " is concerned with the economic reality, while the second sub-para. is concerned with the institutional organisation governing the monopolistic situation.

21-33 An English lawyer will usually define a monopoly in terms indicating less than complete control of the market, but it seems generally accepted that the term monopoly is here to be construed as describing a state of absolute control. Further support for this is drawn from Article 86, which defines what the common lawyer would otherwise describe as a monopoly as a dominant position. Use of the one term would seem to exclude the other. If, then, the term " monopoly " is to be understood in the absolute sense (and the *Concise Oxford Dictionary* would have it so), the second sub-para. must in fact represent an extension of the term " monopoly " (for a body which appreciably influences imports or exports can be in a dominant position, and need not have complete control—*cf.* the position of the British Steel Corporation in the United Kingdom, which, although not in complete control of the import market, nevertheless exerts influence by dint of its sheer size and economic power). The term monopoly must thus not be treated as having any technical meaning. This view appears to be the one adopted in 13/70, *Cinzano* v. *HZA Saarbrücken*, Rec. XVI 1089, [1971] C.M.L.R. 374.

Article 37 does not prohibit the existence of commercial monopolies after the end of the period of transition; Article 90 EEC presupposes their continued existence, and Article 37 (2) excludes new measures, and thus new monopolies, only to the extent that they violate *inter alia* Article 37 (1). This former provision was held to be directly applicable in 6/64, *Costa* v. *ENEL*, Rec. X 1141, [1964] C.M.L.R. 425. Adjustments were in principle, however, to be made progressively during the original period of transition, so as to ensure that thereafter no discrimination between nationals of Member States remains regarding the conditions under which goods are procured and marketed (Art. 37 (1)), in so far as this does not conflict with existing international agreements (Art. 37 (5)), such as the German-Swedish Treaty of 1926, conceding the German match monopoly to Svenska Tandstick A.B. in consideration of a loan, and the various international commodity agreements and the obligation to safeguard employment and the standard of living of agricultural producers supplying a monopoly dealing in agricultural products (Art. 37 (4)). Even subject to these provisions, however, it is doubtful how far the provision that adjustment was required to be complete by the end of the period of transition can be said to be directly applicable; the Commission may, under Article 37 (3), second sub-para., authorise the application of protective measures until the adjustment is complete, but the Commission even now continues to permit such measures, apparently on the ground that adjustment is not complete, and it would still appear to have power to make recommendations under Article 37 (6) for the necessary adjustments. It is uncertain whether the protection granted may protect industrial production against agricultural production, one view being that Article 46 is the appropriate provision for dealing with agricultural problems. It is arguable, however, that Article 46 may be invoked only to protect *agricultural* production against other agricultural products; but this interpretation would create an unintended loophole, since in some contexts it may be necessary to protect an industrial product from the effects of a state monopoly (in another Member State) of an agricultural product, or vice versa.

21–34   There is a definite link between Article 37 and Article 90, in that both relate to state enterprise; Article 90 makes it clear that (a) public undertakings, and (b) undertakings to which Member States grant special or exclusive rights, do not by virtue of their privileges escape the ambit of Article 7 (non-discrimination) or Articles 85 to 94 (competition, dumping and state aids) in particular, and the other Treaty rules in general. Clearly Article 37 commercial monopolies form one type of such undertaking. Commercial monopolies subject to Article 37 were not caught by the absolute prohibition of Article 37 (1) until the end of the period of transition, and therefore quota restrictions, restraints on competition and indiscriminate aids were to that extent permissible for such undertakings, notwithstanding Article 90.

A further qualification upon the clear prohibitions of Article 90 (1) lies in paragraph 2 of the same Article, providing that

" undertakings entrusted with the operation of services of general economic interest or having the character of a revenue-producing monopoly shall be subject to the rules of the Treaty, in particular to the rules on competition, in so far as the application of such rules does not obstruct the performance, in law or in fact, of the particular tasks assigned to them. The development of trade must not be affected to such an extent as would be contrary to the interests of the Community."

The term " particular tasks " relates of course to the task of *e.g.* operating a match monopoly, and protecting the revenue therefrom, and does not include *e.g.* any protective mission. This being so, it is generally agreed that such undertakings are subject to the adjustment procedures of Article 37.

21–35   In 6/64, *Costa* v. *ENEL*, Rec. X 1141, [1964] C.M.L.R. 425, the Court of Justice stressed that:

" To come within the terms of the prohibition of [Article 37], national monopolies and bodies must on the one hand have as objects transactions in commercial products capable of competition and exchanges between member-States; and on the other hand play a leading part in such exchanges." (Trans. [1964] C.M.L.R. 425 at p. 459.)

It was stated that the decision on these points in the concrete case was for the domestic judge. The subject-matter in the *Costa* case was electricity; it is clear that electricity can be bought and sold across frontiers, and at the same time its cost can have a considerable effect on the competitiveness of industry, and can have the effect of excluding imports. It would thus seem that an electricity monopoly would fall within the prohibition of Article 37.

21–36   There has been some suggestion that products which are not the subject of trade in the accepted sense are nevertheless subject to Article 37. In the first place, it is necessary to exclude services from this discussion; Article 37 (1), first sub-para., speaks in terms of imports and exports, and services are not goods susceptible of import and export. A national airline will not therefore be caught by the prohibitions of Article 37, although Article 90 may be relevant. On the other hand, there undoubtedly are goods which are in some sense *extra commercium*, and a monopoly of these could perhaps be said to fall within Article 37. So also might a monopoly exclusively concerned with manufacture if its products were the subject of trade. But before Article 37 can be said to apply, it will in any case be necessary to inquire whether the producer body has an effect on Community trade in the sense of Article 37.

THE TREATY OF ACCESSION AND CUSTOMS MATTERS

21–37   In principle, the provisions of the original Treaties and the acts adopted by the institutions of the Communities are binding on the new Member States and are to apply in those States under the conditions laid down in the Act of Accession (Art. 2 of the Act).

In order to facilitate the adjustment of the new Member States to the rules in force within the Communities, however, this principle is subject to the derogations contained in the Act of Accession (Art. 9 (1)). Except where differing dates, time limits or special rules provide otherwise, all transitional measures are to terminate at the end of 1977 (Art. 9 (2))—*i.e.* at the end of a five-year transitional period.

Derogations are perhaps most obviously required during the transitional period to permit the new Member States to align themselves with the provisions of the original Treaties relating to free movement of goods (Arts. 9 to 37 of the EEC Treaty), and these derogations are contained in Articles 31 to 49 of the Act of Accession. These provisions apply in principle to agriculture, but where the arrangement for agricultural products is different, it is set out in Articles 50 *et seq.* of the Act of Accession.

Customs duties

21–38   Article 32 (1) of the Act of Accession provides for the progressive abolition of customs duties between the new Member States and the Community as originally constituted. This is to take place in five " *tranches* " of 20 per cent., the first on April 1, 1973, the next three to take place on January 1, 1974, 1975 and 1976 respectively, the last on July 1, 1977. The basic duty to which successive reductions are to be applied is to be that which actually applied [3] on January 1, 1972 (Art. 31 (1), first sub-para.). If after January 1, 1972, any tariff reductions deriving from the Agreement supplementary to the Geneva Protocol to the GATT of 1967 relating principally to chemicals become applicable, the reduced duties will replace the basic duties referred to above (Art. 31 (3)). The provisions of Article 31 (3) are an oblique reference to the long-awaited abolition of the United States " American Selling Price " (ASP) for chemicals; multilateral tariff reductions on chemical products are dependent upon the abolition of ASP.

Article 32 contains a series of exceptions to the timetable set out in paragraph 1, namely (para. 2) that:

    (a) custom duties on imports of coal are to be abolished from the date of accession,

    (b) duties on imports of products listed in Annex III to the Act (essentially fissile materials and related equipment) are to be abolished on January 1, 1974,

    (c) duty-free entry is to apply as from the date of accession to imports benefiting from provisions relating to tax concessions applicable to persons travelling from one Member State to another. (Tax concessions, for there are now no duties as between the Six. The applicable provisions are Directive 69/169, J.O. 1969, L 133/6, as amended by Directive 72/230, J.O. 1972, L 139/28: see *supra*, § 21–06.)

Further exceptions are set out in paragraphs 3 and 4 of Article 32; paragraph 3 relates to a heterogeneous group of products listed in Annex IV, which are subject to contractual margins of preference between the United Kingdom and Commonwealth countries. The first " *tranche* " of reductions in duty in respect of these goods is to take place by July 1, 1973. Paragraph 4 makes it clear that the timetable set out in paragraph 1 does not preclude the possibility of opening tariff quotas for certain iron and steel products.

21–39   Article 32 is subject to the general rider that customs duties are in no case to be higher within the enlarged Community than those applied to third countries enjoying most-favoured-nation treatment (Art. 33). The Council is empowered to take the necessary measures for the maintenance of Community preference, acting by a qualified majority or

---

[3] The expression " duty actually applied " reflects the jurisprudence of the Court in interpreting Arts. 12 and 14 EEC, *supra* § 21–10.

a proposal from the Commission, if there is a danger that Community preference will evaporate because of the operation of amendments or suspensions to the CCT, or because new Member States align themselves more rapidly with the CCT than required by the timetable set out.

Article 34 permits the new Member States to suspend in whole or in part the levying of duties on products imported from other Member States, subject to informing the other Member States and the Commission. This does not, however, permit an acceleration in the application of the timetable, in the way that this was provided for in Article 15 (2) of the EEC Treaty. The only provision of this type in Article 41 of the Act of Accession relates to alignment with the external tariff only.

Charges having equivalent effect to a customs duty on imports

21–40 Article 35 of the Act of Accession permits only those charges having equivalent effect which were introduced before January 1, 1972, to subsist after January 1, 1973, and then only at the rate actually applied on the former date. It is not thought that any such charges exist in the United Kingdom, but the provision is there for completeness.

This is not to say, however, that equivalent charges are to be allowed to subsist in certain cases. Equivalent charges not caught by Article 35 are, under Article 36 (1), to be abolished in four " *tranches*," the first of 40 per cent. to take effect on January 1, 1974, the other three of 20 per cent. each, to take place on January 1, 1975 and 1976, and July 1, 1977 respectively, the basic rate being the rate actually applied on January 1, 1972. Article 36 (2) (*a*) and (*b*) embodies the same exception to the timetable contained in Article 32 (2) (*a*) and (*b*) in respect of coal and Euratom products.

Export duties and equivalent charges

21–41 Customs duties on exports and equivalent charges are to be abolished by January 1, 1974, at the latest (Art. 37). Here again it is not thought that any such duties exist in the United Kingdom.

Customs duties of a fiscal nature

21–42 Article 38, relating to the abolition of customs duties of a fiscal nature, resembles Article 17 of the EEC Treaty, but the instrument is more refined.

The basic principle is that such duties are to be abolished in accordance with the provisions for the abolition of ordinary customs duties (Art. 38 (1)). The new Member States do, however, retain the right to replace (a) such a duty, or (b) the revenue element, by an internal tax which is in conformity with Article 95 of the EEC Treaty (Art. 38 (2), first sentence).

Where the duty is so replaced, any element not represented by the internal tax is to constitute the basic duty within the meaning of Article 31, and is—

(a) to be abolished in accordance with Articles 32 *et seq.* in internal trade, and

(b) otherwise aligned with the CCT under the conditions laid down in Articles 32, 39 and 59.

Article 38 (3), first para., *mutatis mutandis* identical with Article 17 (4) of the EEC Treaty, requires the Commission (taking its decision before March 1, 1973) to authorise new Member States to retain the duty or the fiscal element up until January 1, 1976, at latest, if so requested before February 1, 1973, and if it finds that the new Member State is in serious difficulty over replacing it. The second sub-paragraph contains a new refinement, in that the protective element of the duty in respect of which an authorisation has been granted under Article 38 (3), first para., is to be fixed by the Commission as the basic duty provided for in Article 31 before March 1, 1972, and abolished in intra-Community trade and aligned with the CCT under the conditions laid down in Articles 32, 39 and 59.

Paragraph 4 permits the United Kingdom to retain customs duties of a fiscal nature or the fiscal element of such duties on tobacco for two additional years if by January 1, 1976, it has not proved possible to convert those duties into internal taxes on manufactured tobacco on the basis of proposals to be made under Article 99, either because there are no Community provisions applicable by January 1, 1975, or because the time limit set for the introduction of such provisions is later than January 1, 1976.

Directive 69/76 on deferred payment of customs dues, etc., is, by Article 38 (5) of the Act, made inapplicable to customs duties, etc., which a new Member State has been authorised to retain under Article 38 (3) and/or (4). Directive 69/73 on inward processing is likewise made inapplicable to the same situations, but only in the United Kingdom.

The Common Customs Tariff

21–43   Article 39 sets out the timetable for the alignment of the tariffs of the new Member States with the CCT, *i.e.* in respect of third countries. The basic duty to be used for this alignment is again that actually applied on January 1, 1972 (Art. 31 (1), second sub-para.). The alignment is to take place in four " *tranches*," the first, of 40 per cent., is to be applied from January 1, 1974, the other three, of 20 per cent. each, on January 1, 1975, January 1, 1976 and July 1, 1977 respectively, Where, however, the basic national duty varies from the CCT by not more than $\pm$ 15 per cent., the CCT is to be applied as from January 1, 1974. Where, after January 1, 1974, the CCT is altered or suspended, the new

Member States are to amend or suspend their tariffs proportionately in accordance with the rules just described (Art. 39 (2)). (It is inherent in Articles 32 and 39 that during the period in which transitional measures apply the Member States will be operating and applying *their own* tariffs (*cf.* use of " their " tariffs in Art. 39 (1)). For the new Member States there will therefore be *national* transitional tariffs until complete abolition of intra-Community duties and complete alignment with the CCT on July 1, 1977.)

The Annex III (*i.e.* Euratom) products are again excluded from the timetable provisions, the CCT applying *in integrum* as from January 1, 1974 (Art. 39 (3)).

Nomenclature etc.

–44   By Article 39 (4), only Ireland is to apply the CCT nomenclature as from accession; the other new States are to apply it as from January 1, 1974. All new Member States may retain existing national tariff nomenclature sub-divisions which are indispensable if, in effect, disturbances are to be avoided as they align themselves with the CCT.

Progressive introduction of the CCT

–45   Paragraph 5 of Article 39 enables the Commission to determine where necessary the provisions whereby new Member States alter their customs duties. This is intended in particular to empower the Commission to round up or round down the duties resulting from the operation of paragraph 1.

Acceleration

–46   Article 41 permits acceleration in respect of alignment with the CCT, but not in respect of abolition of duties in intra-Community trade.

Quantitative restrictions

–47   All quantitative restrictions are to be abolished in intra-Community trade as from the date of accession, but measures having equivalent effect are to be abolished by January 1, 1975 (Art. 42). Article 43 permits the retention of export restrictions on iron and steel waste and scrap on a most-favoured-nation basis.

State monopolies

1–48   Article 44 (1) requires the new Member States to adjust their State monopolies of a commercial character within the meaning of Article 37 (1) of the EEC Treaty so as to ensure that by December 31, 1977, no discrimination regarding the conditions under which goods are procured and marketed exists between nationals of Member States—in other words, the new Member States are required to place their State monopolies in the same situation as regards discrimination that the original Member States should have reached by the end of the transitional period under Article 37 EEC.

(The second paragraph of Article 44 (1) states that the original Member States shall have equivalent obligations in relation to the new Member States. This does not prejudge whether or not the original Member States are to be construed as already being in conformity with Article 37 of the EEC Treaty for the purposes of the Six.)

Article 44 (2) requires the Commission to make recommendations as to the manner in which and the timetable according to which the adjustment provided for in Article 44 (1), is to be carried out; the recommendations to be in the same terms for both new and original Member States. The Commission may make its recommendations as from the date of accession.

Administrative co-operation

21-49　　Article 45 (1), which is complementary to Article 10 (2) of the EEC Treaty, requires the Commission to determine the methods of administrative co-operation to ensure that the goods fulfilling the requisite conditions benefit from the abolition of customs duties, equivalent charges and quantitative restrictions and equivalent measures. These methods are specifically to have due regard for the provisions already in force, in particular those relating to the existing Community transit system.

Free circulation

21-50　　Article 45 (2) requires the Commission to lay down rules by April 1, 1973, for goods obtained within the Community but incorporating products which were not otherwise considered to be in free circulation (*cf.* Art. 10 (2), second sub-para., of the EEC Treaty). Similar provision is made in respect of agricultural products of the same type. These rules are to take into account the provisions of the Act of Accession relating to the integration of the new Member States and also to the CAP. Under the equivalent Article of the EEC Treaty, compensatory levies were charged on the extraneous element on a reducing basis.

Transition from national customs legislation

21-51　　Community customs legislation for trade with third countries will, by virtue of Article 46 (1), first para., continue to apply in intra-Community trade so long as customs duties are levied in that trade; once these duties have gone, the need to apply such legislation will have ceased. Article 46 (2), substantially repeating Article 39 (4), applies the rules therein laid down on CCT nomenclature to intra-Community trade under the same conditions.

Article 47

21-52   Article 47 provides for transitional measures in respect of products which are partly agricultural and partly industrial.

Article 48

21-53   Article 48 makes it clear that Article 1 of the Act of Accession is without prejudice to the Anglo-Irish Free Trade Agreement, although the Community administrative co-operation methods are to apply as from January 1, 1974.

Article 49

21-54   Paragraph 1 of Article 49 makes it clear that the duties fixed by Protocols 8 to 15 do not thereby lose their status as ordinary Community duties, and can still be altered under Article 28 of the EEC Treaty.

Paragraph 2, the only provision effectuating a tidying up of the earlier Treaties, revokes Protocols I to XVI annexed to the Agreement fixing the CCT for products in list G annexed to the EEC Treaty.

Other transitional tariff provisions

21-55   Articles 31 to 49 are not exhaustive of transitional tariff measures. *Cf.* Articles 59 and 60 which lay down special rules and a slightly differing timetable for certain agricultural products which are protected by customs duties.

CHAPTER 22

AGRICULTURE

22–01 ARTICLE 2 (*d*) of the EEC Treaty refers to the adoption of a common policy in the sphere of agriculture. Substantive provisions are contained in Articles 38 to 47.

OBJECTIVES OF THE AGRICULTURAL POLICY

22–02 The form of the Community in its agricultural sector is largely governed by Article 39, which sets out the objectives of the common agriculture policy. Given that Article 40 (3), second para. (subject to Art. 41) confines the objectives of the Common Market organisations to those set out in Article 39, that enumeration must be considered by and large to be exhaustive.

Article 39 states that the objectives of the common agricultural policy (or CAP) shall be to increase productivity, to ensure a fair standard of living for the agricultural community in particular by raising farm wages; to stabilise the markets; to ensure the availability of supplies, and reasonable prices for consumers.

The social, *i.e.* peasant structure of the sector is, however, to be taken into account, and is to be safeguarded, or at least not abruptly altered, and disparities between regions are not to be aggravated (Art. 39 (2)). In particular, account is to be taken of the fact that in the Member States agriculture constitutes a sector closely linked with the economy as a whole (Art. 39 (2) (*c*)). Clearly, therefore, an equilibrium has to be achieved between conflicting objectives (case 5/67, *Beus* v. *HZA München-Landsbergerstrasse,* Rec. XIV 125, [1968] C.M.L.R. 131).

CONTENT

22–03 Article 38 (1) states that "the common market shall extend to agriculture and agricultural products." This last term covers "products of the soil, of stockfarming and of fisheries and products of first-stage processing directly related to these products." Substance is given to these definitions by Annex II, which lists the products in question (*cf.* Art. 38 (3)). Article 38 (3) allows for additions to Annex II within two years of the entry into force of the Treaty. Additions were in fact made by Regulation 7 *bis*, J.O. 1961, 71. The list is now considered to be exclusive, in that the products falling outside it are not agricultural products for the purposes of the Common Market, *e.g.* timber (*cf.* 2 & 3/62, *Commission* v. *Luxembourg and Belgium,* Rec. VIII 813, [1963]

C.M.L.R. 199). It has been suggested that Article 235 (the general power clause) could be used to add to the list, and a proposal was in fact made on this basis by the Commission, but no action has been taken, and the view has been expressed that such action would clash with the clear intention of Article 38 (3), and the need for legal certainty.

Article 38 (4) specifically states that the development of internal free trade in agricultural goods is to be accompanied by the fashioning of a common agricultural policy under the powers established in Articles 40 *et seq.* Article 38 (2) provides that the rules laid down for the establishment of the Common Market are to apply to agricultural products, except where any of Articles 39 to 46 indicate a derogation from this principle, *e.g.* Article 42, suspending the competition rules. It is generally considered, however, that derogations from the principle of free movement of goods held good only for the transitional period (*cf.* 90 & 91/63, *Commission* v. *Luxembourg and Belgium*, Rec. X 1217, [1965] C.M.L.R. 58 as to Art. 12).

Establishment of the CAP

22-04 The CAP is established by Articles 40 *et seq.*, having regard to the objectives set out in Article 39. Article 40 (2) requires the establishment of a " common organisation of agricultural markets " in order to attain those objectives, and goes on to state that

" this organisation shall take one of the following forms, depending on the product concerned;
  (*a*) common rules on competition;
  (*b*) compulsory co-ordination of the various national market organisations;
  (*c*) a European market organisation."

Although the expression " common organisation of markets " is in the singular, it is clear from the phrase " depending on the product concerned," and its surrounding context, that individual market organisations for each product were envisaged. But it became immediately apparent that for most if not all agricultural sectors the only really practicable alternative specified was the third, since the first touches only one aspect of the agricultural markets, while the second would have been very difficult to introduce at the outset.

Article 40 (3) is the " powers " clause for the market organisations; providing that the market organisations may include all measures required to attain the objectives set out in Article 39, in particular, regulation of prices, aids for the production and marketing of the various products, storage and carry-over arrangements and common machinery for stabilising imports or exports. These powers are to be exercised in the light of Article 39, but with the additional condition of non-discrimination between producers or consumers within the Community (Art. 40 (3), second sub-para.). The fact that prices vary from Member State to Member State does not violate this principle, so long as the prices are " based on common criteria and uniform methods of calculation " (Art. 40 (3), third sub-para.) where a common price policy has been worked out, as it has for all products subject to market organisations. The principle of non-discrimination is to be contrasted with that contained in Article 7, which deals only with discrimination based on nationality.

Article 40 (1) requires in principle the setting-up of a CAP by the end of the transitional period, but Article 40 deals only with one aspect of it—the form that market organisations are to take (apart from Art. 40 (4), upon which the European Agricultural Guidance and Guarantee Fund is based—see further below).

Article 41 supplies limited additional powers to supplement those given in Article 40, providing notably for dispositions on training, research etc., in the context of a given market organisation. Article 42 suspends the application to the agricultural sector of the competition rules pending a decision of the Council. The rules of competition were in fact applied to agriculture by Regulation 26 of April 4, 1962, J.O. 1962, 993.

22–05   Article 43 provides the legal basis for the Regulations setting up the CAP and for subsequent rules governing it. The Council, acting on the basis of proposals from the Commission and after consulting the Assembly, has the power to make Regulations, issue directives and to take decisions without prejudice to any recommendation which it may make (para. 2, third sub-para.). The Council acts by a qualified majority vote—unanimity being required during the first two stages of the original transitional period. Most of the common organisations relating to agricultural products have now been set up, replacing the national organisations, subject to the safeguards of Article 43 (3) (*a*) and (*b*). As a source of new initiatives in setting up the CAP, the Article is still important, however, and the recent Mansholt plans (*cf.* proposals of April 29, 1970, as amended, on the reform of agriculture, *infra*, § 22–43) were, for instance, based on this Article.

22–06   In so far as Article 44 provided for the establishment of a system of minimum prices for the duration of the period of transition, it is largely spent. This system has been extended to later cut-off dates in respect of declining numbers of products, *e.g.* Decision 69/500, J.O. 1969, L 328/11, Decision 70/550, J.O. 1970, L 281/25, Decision 72/3, J.O. 1972, L 2/23 and Decision 72/71, J.O. 1972, L 26/1 on the basis of Article 44 (6), enabling the Council by a special voting system to " determine the system to be applied within the framework of the CAP after the end of the transitional period."

To the extent that the minimum price system was of fairly general application, Article 45 was of very little use. It provides for the conclusion of long-term importing contracts between the Member States where an import requirement exists, and until the substitution of a Common Market organisation for a national market organisation. This attempt to liberate trade within the Six by bilateral accord is an interesting step, but in fact only one contract was concluded under the Article— that concluded in 1959 between France and Germany for the supply of cereals.

Article 46 creates an automatic anti-dumping mechanism. Member States are, subject to the supervision of the Commission, to impose a countervailing charge against imports affecting "the competitive position" of home production. Since, however, the mechanism operates only where the imported product is subject to a national market organisation in the producer State it is now of limited application, since most of the national organisations of importance have now gone. The Article was at no time extensively used (but see decisions of March 15, 1961, J.O. 1961, 595—imports of powdered whole milk into Germany; and of April 28, 1961, J.O. 1961, 825—imports of malt into Germany). It may not in any case be used to protect agricultural production from similar industrial products—cf. Article 37, supra, § 21–32 and § 21–33.

The range of tools available for setting up the CAP is completed by special mention (Art. 47) of the agricultural section of the Economic and Social Committee, which is to hold itself at the disposal of the Commission to prepare the deliberations of the full Committee.

The Common Market organisations

22–07　　　The Common Market organisations have as their legal basis Article 40 (2) (c) coupled with the power of decision lato sensu contained in Article 43 (2), third sub-para. In accordance with Article 43 (1) a conference was held in 1958 at Stresa, Italy, with a view to ascertaining the requirements of the Common Agricultural Policy. It was not until the end of the first stage, however, that the first part of the CAP was set up by the issue by the Council of a series of Regulations after a marathon session in December 1961 and January 1962. The first such Regulations dealt with the grain sector, since the price of grains, a major input cost factor in food production, is of fundamental importance to the rest of the economy, and especially for other agricultural sectors.

Nearly all the Common Market organisations have now been set up, actual structures varying according to the product concerned and the strength of the production industry.

Some difficulty arose from the start over the definition of a Common Market organisation. Such an organisation must in some degree oversee the marketing of a particular product while guaranteeing a standard of living and employment to the producers (cf. Art. 39 and Art. 43 (3) (a) and (b)). These last objectives are achieved by controlling the movement of the goods in question—cf. answer to Written Question No.

71/59–60 as to the nature of market organisations, J.O. 1960, 608 and 1531.

The market organisations all aim to achieve all the objectives listed in Article 39, but in the first place they aim to protect home production, and ensure the economic survival of the producers.

To achieve this, the internal market is controlled and directed, while obstacles to free circulation of goods are removed. But in order to ensure that the control is not nullified, measures are taken to protect the market from influences from outside the EEC. The market organisations may be divided into two basic categories; (1) those establishing a watertight protective system; (2) those relying on the CCT for primary external protection, and lacking, to greater or lesser degree, the watertight characteristic of the first group.

Procedure

22–08   Under Article 43 of the Treaty the Council has a power of decision of the widest kind acting on proposals of the Commission and after consulting the Assembly. Under this power the basic principles of each market organisation are laid down by Regulation; they may of course subsequently be amended or varied. Power to legislate in detailed day-to-day matters is shared between Council and Commission, the Commission receiving delegated powers from the Council, which is the only institution here given decision-making powers directly—cf. Article 155, last hyphen. In practice, however, it was soon felt that there was a need for close co-operation between the Community and the Member States. In order to provide for this co-operation, management or advisory committees were set up for each product or group of products for the period of transition, it being left to be decided subsequently what permanent arrangement should be made. These committees are composed of representatives of each Member State, voting in accordance with the rules set out in Article 148 (2) * as amended by Article 14 of the Act of Accession, the required majority being forty-three votes. They are presided over by a representative of the Commission. The establishment of such bodies has no direct basis in the Treaty, but their legality was upheld by the Court in 25/70, *EVSt.* v. *Köster, Berodt*, Rec. XVI 1161, [1972] C.M.L.R. 255, and their importance is such that their existence has been maintained beyond the end of the transitional period (Regulation 2602/69, J.O. 1969, L 324/23).

22–09   The division of the power of decision is now as follows:—

(1) The Council sets up the market organisations and lays down other rules of the CAP under Article 43 (2). The Council also lays down the more important supplementary Regulations, including, for example, those fixing annually the price levels. Implementing Regulations made by the Council need not necessarily be made under Article 43 (2): 25/70, *EVSt.* v. *Köster, Berodt, supra.*

(2) The Commission acts on its own responsibility in minor or emergency matters, acting under delegated authority pursuant to Article 155, unless it has autonomous powers derived from other parts of the Treaty—*e.g.* Article 115.

(3) On other matters, the Commission consults the relevant management committee if there is one, and then takes its own decision. It is not obliged to take its decision in conformity with the opinion of the management committee, but if it does not do so, it must at once inform the Council. The Council may, generally within one month, amend the decision of the Commission; in the interim the Commission is not obliged to suspend application of its decision.

Mechanisms

22–10 For the purposes of directing the internal market a price is fixed at which it is intended that transactions take place within the Community. This price is usually called a target price (" *prix indicatif* "). The actual level of the target price is set having regard to the objectives of Article 39. To supplement this, a second price is fixed, generally expressed as a percentage of the first, at which the market organisation will intervene (by buying on the market) to maintain the price level. This is called the intervention price (" *prix d'intervention* "). (This system of market support is to be contrasted with the classic English system, which involves no support-buying system as such, but makes up the receipts of the producer " so as to ensure a fair standard of living " (deficiency payments system).)

Generally the target price in a sector, or part of a sector, will be fixed for a particular product of a standard type and quality, and prices for other products in the same sector will be derived from that price (derived price (" *prix dérivé* ")).

22–11 Full protection against imports is generally provided for by a system of variable levies on the commodity, the amount of the levy being expressed to be equal to the difference between the c.i.f. or the free-at-frontier price of the product on arrival in the importing State and the threshold price at a particular entry point fixed for the Community (or for the importing State—*cf.* Regulation 19/62—cereals). The threshold price is calculated so as to ensure that the selling price in the centre of greatest shortage is equal to the target price—*i.e.* the threshold price in that centre will equal the target price less the cost of transport from the point of entry for which the target price is fixed in relation to that centre. Thus the amount of levy payable in the centre of greatest shortage will in effect equal the target price, less the c.i.f. price at the point of entry, and less the cost of handling and transport to that centre from the point of entry.

In some cases the levy contains an additional element of protection, taking the price above the target price (*cf.* Regulation 120/67, Art. 14 (1) (B)).

The levy system is considered to be regulatory in character and not merely protective, and does not amount to a tax or a customs duty: 17/67, *Neumann* v. *Hauptzollamt Hof/Saale*, Rec. XIII 571.

22–12   Surpluses on the market, generally priced well above world-market prices because of the intervention system, are disposed of by export refunds (" *restitutions à l'exportation* "). These are fixed by the Community at a common level for each product for the whole territory of the Community, generally under a Regulation separate from that setting up the market organisation. A common system for exports is set up by Regulation 2603/69, J.O. 1969, L 324/25.

In addition to the refund system, there are mechanisms allowing for the denaturing of products (good butter into bad—good wheat into cattle fodder etc.), and for the distribution of products at reduced prices or, in the case of perishables, even free to certain organisations, including the armed forces, and to the indigent.

Although it has been maintained that intervention in any sector occurs only where necessary, support costs alone are estimated to run to 2,500 million u.a. for 1972–73 (Bulletin 7, 1972, p. 32). The cost of maintaining the olive oil market is said to be greater than Euratom's entire budget.

In many sectors quality standards have been established which effectively limit circulation of goods not complying with such standards and prevent both their export and import. These standards thus constitute a further protective element.

The protective and support mechanisms are reinforced by certification systems designed to keep track of transactions and movements, and to eliminate fraud.

Finally, the market structures are backed up by safeguard clauses, contained in the Regulations setting them up, generally of two kinds: Type (1) apply where serious disturbances (" *perturbations graves* ") are present or to be feared in the market and are liable to imperil the objectives of Article 39. The Commission has a power of decision here, subject to annulment or modification by the Council. Type (2) applies where it is necessary to annul price rises in the Community market.

Conditions of free movement of goods and free competition are stiffened generally by application of a régime of competition under the terms of Article 42, and application of Articles 92 to 94 on aids to the sector.

Clearly, the rules as to market organisations are to be interpreted at the Community level, and cannot be subject to national variations— *cf.* 74/69, *HZA Bremen-Freihafen* v. *Krohn*, Rec. XVI 451, [1970] C.M.L.R. 466, 40/69, *HZA Hamburg-Oberelbe* v. *Bollmann*, Rec. XVI 69, [1970] C.M.L.R. 141.

THE MARKET ORGANISATIONS EXAMINED

22-13 It is not possible to describe the minutiae of the individual market organisations in a book of this length, and indeed it is doubtful whether their description could serve any real purpose, given that the implementing Regulations of the Commission are varied or replaced with disconcerting frequency. The discussion which follows deals with the individual market organisations in broad terms, while giving particular attention to features which vary from the standard pattern described in outline above. The Regulation referred to at the head of each section sets up the relevant market organisation. Consolidating amendments are not generally issued and amending regulations must be sought in the *Official Journal. European Communities: Secondary Legislation,* published by H.M.S.O. in January 1972, contains amending regulations up to November 1971. It has since been supplemented with later Community acts. Reference is made where applicable to the particular transitional rules laid down in Articles 65 to 103 of the Act of Accession. The more general transitional rules are discussed *infra,* § 22–33. The relevant technical adaptations are contained or referred to in the Annexes to the Act.

Group 1: organisations controlled by the levy system

Cereals [1]

22-14 The market organisation for cereals covers most cereals, resulting flours etc., and certain closely connected products, the applicable rules varying according to the product.

The primary cereal products (common and durum wheat, barley, maize and rye) are governed by a single target price for a standard quality of each commodity fixed at the centre of greatest shortfall, Duisburg, set each year by Council procedure. A basic intervention price is also fixed for Duisburg, from which the prices for the other centres are derived. There is a guaranteed minimum price for durum wheat.

Protection is provided by the levy system, the amount of the levy being in most cases equal to the threshold price calculated for Rotterdam, less the c.i.f. price. To ensure that transactions are in fact carried out, and to eliminate the possibility of fraud, there is a deposit/ certification system on imports and exports.

Additional features are carry-over payments, available for common and durum wheat, rye and barley harvested within the Community, as well as for malt, still in hand at the end of the marketing season (Art. 9), and a minimum guarantee price paid to all producers of durum wheat where the intervention price in the area of greatest surplus falls below the minimum guarantee price fixed (Art. 10).

The Regulation provides for the setting up of an export refund system (Art. 16 and Regulation 139/67, J.O. 1967, 2453) and for

[1] Regulation 120/67, J.O. 1967, 2269, replacing Regulation 19/62.

denaturation (Art. 7 (4) and Regulation 172/67, J.O. 1967, 2602) and governs sale on world markets (Art. 7 (3)).

There are safeguard clauses for both standard types.

The import régime for manufactured cereal products (Regulation 1052/68, J.O. 1968, L 179/8) is rather different; there is no fixed threshold price, the levy being based on the amount of primary product contained in the manufactured goods. An additional feature for manu-factured goods is a refund on production payable on purchase, notably for use in the brewing industry, of certain cereal products (see Regulation 367/67, J.O. 1967, 174/36 and Regulation 3671/67, J.O. 1967, 174/40).

Articles 73 and 74 of the Act of Accession lay down particular transitional rules relating to the prices and the compensatory amounts applicable in respect of the products subject to this market organisation.

Pigmeat, eggs, and poultry meat [2]

22–15   Since the pigmeat, eggs and poultry meat sectors depend to a large extent upon the price of cereals, it is natural that they should be linked to some degree one to another and to the cereals market itself.

The markets are directed by measures aimed at achieving better organisation and by quality standards.

Intervention of a direct kind is provided for in the pigmeat sector by aids for private storage and by buying-in operations. This inter-vention is governed by a basic price (" *prix de base* ") for carcases, which includes protective features. A greater price fluctuation is permitted here than in the cereals market.

Imports are subject to the levy, which may be suspended in all three sectors in time of shortage. Pigmeat is subject to certification. The levy in all three sectors is founded upon a basic levy for the main product, plus derived levies for the others. The amount of the levy is arrived at by a complex calculation taking into account the amount of cereal required to produce a given amount of the basic product, and including an element of protection expressed as a percentage of the sluice-gate price (*infra*). There is, further, a levy on processed products in the pigmeat sector.

All three sectors are backed up by a sluice-gate price to ward off abnormally cheap imports. The mechanism ensures that where the free-at-frontier price falls below the relevant sluice-gate price, the levy is increased by an amount (" the additional amount ") equal to the difference between the two. The mechanism is not applied where the exporting country agrees to exercise voluntary limitation (see *e.g.* Regulation 1570/71).

There are the usual export refund arrangements (see Regulations 177, 175, & 176/67) and the two usual safeguard clauses.

---

[2] Regulations 121, 122 and 123/67, J.O. 1967, 2283, 2293, 2301 respectively, replacing Regulations 20, 21 & 22/62.

Articles 75 and 76, 77 and 78, and Article 79 of the Act of Accession lay down particular transitional rules in respect of these market organisations. They relate principally to the applicable compensatory amounts and to standards. A United Kingdom declaration on liquid milk, pigmeat and eggs (" the British breakfast ") together with a statement in reply on behalf of the Community is annexed to the Final Act (Cmnd. 4862–I, p. 122).

Rice [3]

22–16   The régime applicable to rice is very similar to that applicable to cereals. A target price for husked rice is fixed for Duisburg, and intervention prices for each of the two production centres (Arles and Vercelli) are fixed for paddy rice. Further support is provided by a refund on production and compensatory indemnity for stocks in hand. Exports and imports are subject to certification and to levy in much the same way as cereals. Export refunds are provided for (Art. 17). The two standard safeguard clauses are applicable.

Article 80 of the Act of Accession lays down the transitional rules relating to the fixing of the compensatory amounts applicable to the products subject to this market organisation.

Sugar [4]

22–17   Regulation 1009/67 sets up two régimes for the market organisation for sugar; a definitive régime to apply generally, and a régime in derogation from the latter, to apply until 1975. The regulation is chiefly concerned with European, *i.e.* sugar beet production, but its provisions apply also to the overseas, *i.e.* cane producers, so far as such production concerns the European market, and the financial provisions apply to them generally (*cf.* Art. 227 EEC).

The definitive régime fixes a target and intervention price for the area of greatest surplus in white sugar plus derived prices, backed up by a minimum price system for beet purchases.

The intervention procedure differs from that already described in that the manufacturers are required to pay at least the minimum price for beet. Intervention organisations then purchase processed sugar as offered.

Denaturation and export refund arrangements, reimbursement of storage charges and production refunds are all designed to meet the problem of structural surplus.

Imports, subject to the usual certification rules, pay an import levy. Import subsidies are provided for the case where the c.i.f. price of raw sugar is higher than the threshold price. Export rebates are provided for, and also export levies. The twin sets of provisions for subsidies and restrictions are necessary because of the fluctuating state of the sugar market. There is in addition a serious disturbance safeguard.

[3] Regulation 359/67, J.O. 1967, 174/1, replacing Regulation 16/64.
[4] Regulation 1009/67, J.O. 1967, 308/1.

At least until July 1, 1975, this régime is subject to considerable modifications, notably a quota régime allocating production amongst the Member States and the various Community producers. This unusual system was set up so as to avoid a crisis which would have arisen had the definitive régime been brought into operation at once, because of the regional disparities between producers.

This system is founded upon a basic quota, fixed by the Member States for each factory, followed by a maximum quota (fixed in Regulation 1060/71 at 135 per cent. of the basic quota for 1971/72). A guaranteed quantity is to equal foreseeable human consumption in white sugar for the year in question (Art. 26, Regulation 1009/67, as amended by Regulation 1067/71).

The whole of the basic quota is taken up by the intervention measures, but no excess over the maximum quota may be sold on the home market without penalty. The intermediate quantities benefit in theory from the intervention measures, but in fact pay a production contribution (" *cotisation à la production* ") designed to discourage excess production and to pay for a part of the intervention measures. The cost of the contribution can be passed on to the relevant growers.

The minimum price is payable for beet unless the beet is for manufacture of sugar beyond the maximum quota (Art. 29), but the whole purchasing system is subject to comprehensive controls and penalties. Derogations are, however, allowed for (Art. 31, Regulation 1009/67), chiefly where the grower and manufacturer is one and the same (as is often the case in Holland). The arrangements under the temporary and definitive régimes are both dependent on institutionalised inter-trade agreements, providing for purchase by the manufacturer of the raw material.

Articles 81 to 83 of the Act of Accession lay down particular transitional rules for determining the prices and the compensatory amounts applicable to the goods subject to this market organisation.

Protocol 17 deals with the import of Commonwealth sugar.

Milk and milk products[5]

22–18   The market organisation for milk and milk products extends to milk, cream, cheese and butter, and certain other products. The structure is based upon a target price for milk, and intervention prices for powdered skimmed milk, butter and certain Italian cheeses and certain other products.

Actual intervention in the butter and cream sector takes the form of buying-in and subsidies to private storage (Arts. 6 *et seq.*). Release of stocks must not disturb the market. Particular social groups and also industry are able to buy at reduced prices. Denaturation is also provided for. The powdered milk sector (Art. 7) is operated in much the same

---

[5] Regulation 804/68, J.O. 1968, L 148/10, replacing Regulation 13/64.

way. There are special rules of an appropriate kind for the Italian cheeses (Art. 8), and rules for other cheeses (Art. 9).

Imports of all groups of products are now subject to the usual certification and levy system (see Regulation 1410/71, J.O. 1971, L 148/3). Export refunds are available. There are the two usual safeguard clauses.

A basic feature of the whole sector is the peasant nature of milk production in the EEC, where the average size of a herd is about four cows. Attempts have been made to correct this, notably by offering " head-money " for cows destroyed and not replaced (Regulation 1975/69, J.O. 1969, L252/1) but these arrangements have now been terminated (Regulation 1290/71, J.O. 1971, L 137/1).

Articles 85 to 89 of the Act of Accession lay down particular transitional rules relating to this market organisation, notably rules on price fixing, compensatory amounts, subsidies and standards.

A United Kingdom declaration on liquid milk etc., together with a statement in reply on behalf of the Community is annexed to the Final Act (Cmnd. 4862–I, p. 122). The import of New Zealand dairy produce is covered by Protocol 18.

Fats and oils [6]

22–19   The rules on fats and oils vary with the type of oil etc. in question. For olive oil a production target price (" *prix indicatif à la production* ") is fixed, followed by a market target price. The intervention price is fixed close to the market target price, and thus the system provides virtually for a guaranteed price to producers. The system assumes that the production price may well be higher than the market price, and the difference is made up to the producer in the form of a subsidy or deficiency payment.

Imports are controlled by certification and levy. Export refunds are converted to export levies where the EEC price falls below the world price. Safeguards are of the serious-disturbance type, and there are additional safeguards where Community exports endanger the internal price structure.

For other oils, notably colza, rape and sunflower, target and intervention prices backed up by deficiency payments are fixed on much the same lines as for olive oil. Imports, however, are only subject to the CCT (Art. 2).

Residual types of oil etc. are outside this support system, and are subject only to the CCT unless brought within the system (Art. 21). For all substances in this sector there is a safeguard clause applying compensatory amounts to imports which have been subsidised abroad (Art. 3 (6)).

[6] Regulation 136/66, J.O. 1966, 3025.

Articles 70 to 73 of the Act of Accession lay down particular transitional rules on the prices and the compensatory amounts applicable in respect of this market organisation.

Beaf and veal, etc.[7]

22-20   The market organisation set up for beef and veal is designed in the first place to ensure that structural improvements are made in the sector. Article 2 encourages improvement in production methods etc. in this sector, while prices are directed by guide prices (" *prix d'orientation* "). Intervention takes the form of aids to private storage (Art. 5) and buying-in when the price falls below a fixed percentage of the guide price. In certain cases buying-in may take place over the whole of the Community territory, although only some prices in a certain area or areas have fallen below that percentage.

Outside protection is provided by the CCT, but a supplementary levy may be payable where the c.i.f. price plus the CCT is below the guide price (Art. 10).

There are special arrangements for chilled meat (*cf.* Art. 13), involving certification and a permanent levy in addition to the CCT.

There are the usual export refund and safeguard provisions.

Articles 90 to 93 of the Act of Accession lay down particular transitional rules *inter alia* on the prices and compensatory amount applicable in respect of this market organisation.

Group 2: Sectors not protected by the levy system

22-21   Where no market organisation has as yet been set up, the products in question are only subject to the CCT, and no additional intervention or protective machinery operates in relation to them. Free circulation for all products was supposedly achieved with the expiry of the period of transition, so national protection rules are now ostensibly illegal, but a special régime for residuary Annex II products for which an individual market organisation was not envisaged was set up by Regulation 827/68.

Residuary Annex II products [8]

22-22   Shortly before free circulation and CCT were established for industrial goods (on July 1, 1968) it was appreciated that at the end of the transitional period there would still be a certain number of agricultural products, largely of secondary importance, without a market organisation. Accordingly, Regulation 827/68, which entered into force on the same day as the final freeing of industrial products, set up a régime closely analogous to that provided for the residual agricultural categories. The sole measure of protection for these products is the CCT. The market is to some extent backed up by a safeguard clause

[7] Regulation 805/68, J.O. 1968, L 148/24, replacing Regulation 14/64.
[8] Regulation 827/68, J.O. 1968, L 151/16.

of the serious-disturbance type. There is provision for the addition to the list contained in the Regulation of further products.

Fruit and vegetables [9]

22–23   The market organisation for fruit and vegetables covers most types of fruit and vegetables with the notable exception of potatoes. It can be extended. Quality standards are of primary importance here (Arts. 2 et seq.)—only those goods conforming may be sold nationally or circulate freely, or be imported or exported freely (Arts. 3, 9 and 12). Derogations and additional categories are permissible in case of shortage (Art. 15).

Producer organisations operate a withdrawal price (" prix de retrait ") below which the product is not sold; compensation is payable to the grower (Art. 15). National intervention organisations operate from a basic price (" prix de base ") but the actual buying-in price may be as much as 60 per cent. lower (Art. 16). Additionally, there are facilities for paying compensation to producer organisations which intervene on the market (Art. 18). Given the perishable nature of the products in question, there is no realistic possibility of their storage. They may be sold at reduced prices for fodder or for processing or distributed free to certain classes of persons (Art. 21).

Imports are subject to the CCT and further, to a system of counter-vailing duties (Arts. 22 to 30) where their entry price falls below the so-called reference price (average of recorded producers' prices for a standard type in area of lowest prices: Art. 23).

Exports receive refunds in some circumstances (Art. 30) subject to the quality standards.

The safeguard clause is of the serious-disturbance type (Art. 29).

A particular feature connected with this market is the system of grubbing premiums offered to owners of apple, pear and peach orchards (Regulation 2517/69, J.O. 1969, L 318/15).

Articles 65 to 68 of the Act of Accession lay down particular transitional rules on the compensatory amounts and quality standards applicable in respect of the products subject to this market organisation. Certain technical adaptations to Regulation 1035/72 are embodied in Article 40 of the Regulation itself, in addition to those contained in Annex II to the Act of Accession, varying other acts governing this sector.

Processed products based on fruit and vegetables [9a]
Processed products not listed in Annex II

22–24   The market organisation (if such it can be called) for processed fruit and vegetables, complementing the fruit and vegetable market, has no interior structure, but, aside from the CCT, provides for refunds and supplementary levies based on sugar content, tied to Regulation 1009/

---

[9] Regulation 1035/72. J.O. 1972, L 118/1.   [9a] Regulation 865/68, J.O. 1968, L 153/8.

67. The applicable transitional compensatory amounts are to be fixed according to Article 94 of the Act of Accession.

22–25   Other processed products relate to the market organisation for the basic product; general rules on export refunds are laid down in Regulation 204/69, J.O. 1969, L 29/1. Regulation 1059/69, J.O. 1969, L 141/1 determines the system of trade applicable to certain of them (and see Article 97 of the Act of Accession on applicable transitional compensatory amounts).

Live plants and flowers [10]

22–26   The market organisation for live plants and flowers provides for the free circulation of goods (subject to certain derogations which are now spent), while aiming to improve quality, production methods and marketing of the products in question (although this is expressed to be without prejudice to other harmonisation measures—Art. 18).

Protection is provided in the first place by the CCT, but more important by quality standards, which must be complied with for the goods to move freely. These also have a protective effect (*cf.* the fruit and vegetables sector, *supra*).

A particular feature is the minimum export price system, persisting even after the transitional phase (Regulation 1767/68, J.O. 1968, L 271/7 as amended by Regulation 1946/70, J.O. 1970, L 215/15).

The main Regulation contains a " serious-disturbance " safeguard clause.

The United Kingdom is to apply the common quality standards to home marketed produce as from February 1, 1974, except in respect of cut flowers, where the relevant date is to be February 1, 1975 (Art. 84 of the Act of Accession).

Tobacco [11]

22–27   The Common Market organisation set up for tobacco is fairly similar to that in the cereals sector, with target (or norm) prices (" *prix d'objectif* ") and intervention prices and reference qualities. Imports are subject only to the CCT, however.

There is the additional feature of premiums payable to first purchasers of leaf tobacco, ensuring that the target price is reached. Intervention by national intervention organisations takes up such leaf tobacco as is not taken up under the premium system. Derived intervention prices may be fixed for baled tobacco which has undergone first processing.

There are the usual dispositions for export refunds and for safeguards in case of serious disturbance.

[10] Regulation 234/68, J.O. 1968, L 55/1.
[11] Regulation 727/70, J.O. 1970, L 94/1.

Wine [12]

22-28   Wine has been at least partially subject to Community rules from an early stage (Regulation 24/62, setting up a viticultural land register, and laying down basic rules on quality wines), but Regulation 816/70, setting out what are described as complementary dispositions in the vini-viticultural sector, is now the chief Regulation here, together with Regulation 817/70, J.O. 1970, L 99/20, on quality wines.

The market is governed by guide prices, followed by trigger prices ("*prix de déclenchement*") at which intervention starts. Aids (*i.e.* subsidies) to private storage are provided, and also aids for distilling if the storage aids do not suffice to restore the market. External protection is through the CCT, backed up where necessary by countervailing duties designed to guard against abnormally cheap imports, calculated on a reference price for red and for white wines. This is not levied where voluntary limitation is exercised. Export refunds are payable for " economically important " exports, and there are safeguards against price rises and serious disturbances.

The market is further controlled by the requirement of notification and licensing of new planting, aids for which are banned, and certification of imports and exports of wines. Additionally, there are rules on quality, blending etc. (Regulations 816 & 817/70).

The United Kingdom and Ireland are authorised to retain the use of " composite names including the word wine " for drinks such as apple wine etc. until December 31, 1975, in respect of sales other than to the original Member States (Article 69 of the Act of Accession).

Textile fibres—flax and hemp [13]

22-29   The regulation setting up a market organisation for flax and hemp provides first of all mechanisms designed to promote rational marketing of flax (production of which exceeds Community needs) and improvement in production techniques and quality, etc. Support is given in the form of standard aids, payable on each hectare of flax or hemp produced, fixed annually. Additionally, aids are payable for private storage, granted to holders of fibres concluding storage contracts with intervention agencies in time of surplus.

Safeguards are available in cases of severe disturbance of the market.

Article 95 of the Act of Accession lays down particular transitional rules on aid to flax growing.

Fisheries [14]

22-30   The market in fishery products set up under Regulation 2142/70 covers fresh, frozen and canned fish, and subjects them to common

[12] Regulation 816/70, J.O. 1970, L 99/1.
[13] Regulation 1308/70, J.O. 1970, L 146/1.
[14] Regulations 2141 & 2142/70, J.O. 1970, L 236/1 and 5.

marketing standards. Producer organisations play the leading role here, preventing most kinds of salt-water fish from reaching the market when prices fall below a withdrawal price. Ordinary support buying is effected on the basis of intervention prices expressed as a percentage of a guide price. Financial compensation is available to producer organisations operating the withdrawal system, but the latter organisations are also to be financed through levies, equalisation systems, etc. There are special provisions in respect of certain frozen products, and for tunny.

Protection is provided by the CCT, but additional protection is given by the operation of a reference price system; a countervailing duty is payable where the entry price falls below the reference price. It is not applicable where the exporting State practices self-limitation. These arrangements are backed up by a serious disturbance safeguard clause. For certain types of fish the CCT is suspended either totally or in part, and a compensatory indemnity (subsidy) is payable on tunny fish. Export refunds are payable in respect of economically important exports of all the products subject to the market organisation.

Articles 98 and 99 of the Act of Accession lay down particular transitional provisions on the prices and compensatory amounts applicable in respect of this market organisation.

22–31   The overall aim of the fisheries policy is to improve the structures in a fairly weak industry, and producer organisations will, it is hoped, assist in this aim. The structural policy itself (Regulation 2141/70) provides for equal access to national waters and for co-ordination of national structural policies. Significant derogations from Regulation 2141/70 are embodied in Article 100 of the Act of Accession authorising a six-mile limit restriction on equal access until at least December 31, 1982, supplemented by a twelve-mile limit restriction in respect of certain portions of the coastlines of Denmark, France, Ireland, Norway and the United Kingdom (Art. 101 of the Act). The whole situation is to be reviewed at a later date (Arts. 102 and 103 of the Act).

Hops [15]

22–32   The market organisation for hops, one of the last to be set up, is governed by certification of origin and by quality standards applicable to imports. Protection is provided by the CCT, backed up by a safeguard clause of the serious-disturbance type.

Intervention takes the form of aids per hectare of hops grown so as to enable all producers to achieve a fair income. There is a need for production rationalisation in this sector, and to this end aids are payable until December 31, 1975, for the creation of producer groups and for the restructuring and reconversion of hop-fields owned by members of such groups.

[15] Regulation 1696/71, J.O. 1971, L 175/1.

THE MARKET ORGANISATIONS AND THE ACT OF ACCESSION

22–33 Title II of the Act of Accession, entitled Agriculture, is concerned for the most part with the transition of the new Member States to the existing arrangements for the market organisations.

Title II is divided into four chapters, Chapter 1 (Arts. 50 to 64) dealing with general matters.

Articles 51 to 54 deal with price fixing in general. Articles 55 to 58 deal with the compensation of price differences during the transitional period. Articles 59 and 60 deal with customs aspects of the CAP.

Chapter 2 (Arts. 65 to 97) contains particular arrangements for the individual market organisations, many of the sections within that Chapter referring to the primary provisions in Articles 51 and 52.

Chapter 3 contains particular provisions relating to fisheries.

Chapter 4, other provisions, relates to adjustments to the Community directives on veterinary matters, and annexes a list of technical adaptations notably on seeds and plants, feeding stuffs and structural surveys.

Implementation

22–34 It is provided generally that the application to the new Member States of the Community rules established for production of and trade in agricultural products and certain processed agricultural products which are the subject of special arrangements is deferred until February 1, 1973 (Art. 151 (1) (*a*) of the Act of Accession), the only exception to this being amendments effected to the voting procedure in the management committee decision-making procedures which take effect according to the general rule, *i.e.* from accession, under Article 2 of the Act (para. 2). As in other areas the transitional period is to last until January 1, 1978 (Art. 9 (2)).

Article 50 states that save as otherwise provided in the title on agriculture, the rules provided for in the Act apply to agricultural products (*cf.* Art. 38 (2) EEC). The new Member States will therefore begin to apply the vast majority of the agricultural rules from February 1, 1973. This entails, for agricultural goods not covered by Community customs duties, but subject to customs duties in the new Member States, abolition of the latter duties on February 1, 1973, and application of the Community levy system.

Implementation of the levy system

Prices

22–35 Article 51 sets out a general rule for the fixing of prices which is to apply to the different market organisations where express reference is made to it in Chapters 2 and 3. The price fixed is to be what may be described as the base price from which moves towards the common price are to be made. The general rule is that this base price is to be fixed at " a level which allows producers in that sector to obtain returns equivalent to those obtained under the previous national system." Since the application of the general rule would produce unacceptable results in countries operating deficiency payments systems and guaranteed prices, the prices in respect of the United Kingdom are to be fixed at a level of market prices comparable to that prevailing during a representative period preceding the introduction of the Community rules on agriculture in these countries.

Where the price fixed pursuant to Article 51 is in fact different from the common price, the prices in respect of which Chapters 2 and 3 refer to Article 52 are to be aligned with the level of common prices in six stages (Art. 52 (1)). The moves up or down are to take place at the beginning of each marketing year (Art. 52 (2)) narrowing the gap between the base price as subsequently increased (or decreased) and the prevailing market price in such a way that the moves would each be of 20 per cent. of the difference between the base price and the Common Market price, if the Common Market price remained constant, *i.e.* the moves will successively be of a sixth, a fifth, a quarter, a third and a half of the difference between the two prices (Art. 52 (2) (*a*) and (*b*)). The Council may authorise in respect of one or more products for a given year a departure of not more than 10 per cent. from the prices which would result from the application of the alignment procedure. Subsequent departures are permitted. A return to the general system may not allow for any departures permitted, so that a departure of 10 per cent. permitted for the first year on a difference of 60 per cent. between the basic price and the Common Market price will necessitate a move of 11 per cent. of the base price for the second year, instead of only 10 per cent., assuming the Common Market price remains constant (Art. 52 (3)). The common prices must be applied in the new Member States by January 1, 1978, at the latest (Art. 52 (14)).

22–36　While differences remain between the prices obtained under the United Kingdom system of guaranteed prices and market prices resulting from the application of the mechanisms of the CAP and the provisions of Title II, the United Kingdom is authorised to retain production subsidies, *i.e.* deficiency payments (Art. 54 (1)) but they are to be abolished as soon as possible, and in any event by the end of the transitional period, and are not to raise returns above the common price level. The Council is to lay down rules to deal with the concession granted by this Article.

Compensation of price differences

22–37　Differences in prices between the new Member States themselves, and with the Community as originally constituted are to be made up through the levy by the importing State or grant by the exporting State of compensatory amounts (Art. 55 (1) (*a*)). Differences in price levels between the new Member States and third countries will be made up by the application of a similar system of compensatory amounts in addition to the normal levies etc. and export refunds applied by the new Member States as part of the CAP (Art. 55 (1) (*b*). In particular, where prices have been fixed according to the price-fixing rules described above, the compensatory amount applicable is to be equal to the difference between the base price as subsequently increased or decreased and the prevailing common price (Art. 55 (2)). Otherwise, the amount is to be arrived at in accordance with particular dispositions in Chapters 2 and 3.

Compensatory amounts between the new Member States themselves are to be determined by direct reference to the amount fixed in accordance with Article 55 (2) (Art. 55 (3)), but in no case are amounts to be fixed if they would be minimal, and GATT bindings are to be taken into account in fixing the CCT duty. Further the amount applicable in intra-Community trade is not to exceed that levied by Member States on imports from third States (Art. 55 (6)) although the Council may derogate from this, acting by qualified majority on a proposal from the Commission, in particular to avoid trade deflections, distortion of competition etc.

22–38   Article 56 provides for appropriate measures to be taken in various circumstances relating to external trade where Community prices rise above world prices, and in fixing the level of the various elements of the price and intervention system, except for the prices referred to in Articles 51 (base price fixing) and 70 (oilseeds), account is to be taken for the new Member States of the difference in prices expressed by the compensatory amount, to the extent necessary for the proper functioning of the Community rules (Art. 57).

The cost of the compensatory amounts granted is to be borne by the guarantee section of FEOGA (Art. 58). The sums collected by the new Member States under the provisions discussed above are in principle included as part of the Community's own resources (Art. 128 of the Act, and see generally Chapter 35).

Markets covered by the CCT duty

22–39   The Articles so far discussed relate primarily to market organisations governed by the levy system. For those governed by the CCT duty, duties between the Community as originally constituted and the new Member States and between the new Member States themselves are to be abolished in much the same way that customs duties are abolished on industrial products under Article 32 (1) (Art. 59) but the dates for the first cut of 20 per cent. differ (Art. 59 (*a*), (*b*) and (*c*)). (Customs duties on goods subject to market organisations are prohibited from February 1, 1973, by operation of Art. 151 and Art. 2 of the Act.)

Similarly the new Member States are to introduce the CCT by and large in accordance with Article 39 (1), the starting date for the moves in respect of the great majority of agricultural products being the same as that laid down in Article 39 (1) (Art. 59 (2)).

Paragraph 3 permits departures from the alignment procedures in substantially identical terms to Article 52 (3).

Where market organisations provide for the adoption of measures by management committee procedure the Commission may authorise new Member States to abolish or align duties more rapidly than provided for, or else to suspend them. No such authorisation is required in respect of other products (Art. 59 (4), first and second sub-paras.), but in neither case may this result in effective discrimination against other Member States. New Member States are to keep the other Member States and the Commission informed of the measures taken.

Free movement in general

22–40   The new Member States are, subject to Articles 55 and 59, to apply the rules laid down for each market organisation on customs duties and equivalent charges, and quantitative restrictions and equivalent measures (Art. 60 (1)). Most such bars to free movement were abolished in the context of these organisations. Where there is no Community market organisation, restrictions of the kind referred to are taken out of the provisions of Title 1 on equivalent charges and equivalent measures to the extent that the goods in question are subject to a national market organisation (Art. 60 (2)). This parallels the existing position with regard to such national market organisations as remain in the original Member States, and will allow retention of *e.g.* quotas on potatoes.

22–41   The new Member States are to apply the CCT nomenclature by February 1, 1973, at the latest in respect of goods covered by market organisations, but may be permitted to retain indispensable national sub-divisions (Art. 60 (3)).

Article 61 contains particular rules on inward processing.

The Council is empowered by Article 62 (1) to adopt the provisions necessary for implementing the agricultural title, acting by a qualified majority on a proposal from the Commission. Acting unanimously on a proposal from the Commission after consulting the Assembly it may make the necessary adaptations to the title, so far as this is necessitated by a change in Community rules. Special transitional arrangements may be made under the management committee procedure, to apply up until January 31, 1974, but the Council may extend this period by a further year, acting unanimously on a proposal from the Commission after consulting the Assembly (Art. 63).

Other safeguards are provided by the general provisions of Article 135 of the Act, permitting new Member States to seek authority to introduce, or to ask the Commission to take as a matter of urgency, measures to deal with a serious difficulty arising in any field of economic activity.

Protocol 16 annexed to the Act of Accession, on markets and trade in agricultural products, refers to the need to avoid problems concerning internal trade arising as a result of the enlargement of the Community, and calls on the Community institutions to ensure the guarantee of free circulation of all products—this in the context of the relevant market organisation. The Protocol also refers to potential problems for third countries in certain specific cases as a result of the application of the agricultural transitional arrangements. Where they do arise, the institutions are called upon to examine them and to overcome them so far as possible.

Finally, the title on agriculture is expressed not to affect the degree of freedom of trade in agricultural products resulting from the Anglo-Irish Free Trade Agreement (Art. 64).

Chapters 2 and 3 (Arts. 65 to 103) contain particular dispositions on individual market organisations. These have already been mentioned, *supra*, in the context of the discussion of each market organisation.

CAP—HARMONISATION OF LEGISLATION

–42 This topic is considered under the general heading of Harmonisation of Legislation—Chapter 32. The main subjects are animal health and animal feeding stuffs, food standards and seeds and propagating material and forestry.

CAP—STRUCTURAL POLICY

–43 A structural policy is an integral part of the CAP. Some of the market organisations are empowered to take steps to improve structures, but something of a more general nature was required. The emphasis has, however, been until recently on co-ordination of national policies.

So far, this co-ordination has been limited to a Council Decision (December 4, 1962, J.O. 1962, 2892) aimed at better documentation of national policies, and the setting up of an advisory committee on agricultural structures. The Commission now has its own agricultural consultative committee (Decision 64/488, J.O. 1964, 2256 and Decisions 65/371 and 71/79).

Other measures set up an agricultural information network (Regulation 79/65, J.O. 1965, 1859) and provide for collection of agricultural statistics, but have no positive effect.

The financial burden of national structural policies is relieved in part by the guidance section of the European Agricultural Guidance and Guarantee Fund, which pays a proportion of the cost of projects of value to the Community (projects for adaptation and improvement of conditions of production, for adaptation and guidance of production itself, for adaptation and improvement of marketing techniques etc., and for development of outlets—Arts. 11 and 12, Regulation 17/64, J.O. 1964, 586). The fact that the funds available were never fully drawn upon indicates that the scheme is not being used to the full, doubtless because the assistance it provides is in the form of partial reimbursement rather than by way of direct aid. Such funds as are available are nevertheless clearly inadequate for the tasks assigned to the guidance section; its level of expenditure was until recently limited to 285 million u.a. annually (Art. 9, Regulation 130/66, J.O. 1966, 2965, see now Regulation 2788/72, J.O. 1972, L 295/1, raising the ceiling to 325 million u.a.), while the guarantee outgoings have grown enormously each year.

Several plans for the reform of agriculture have been produced, concrete proposals being adopted only on April 17, 1972. The Commission proposed six draft directives on April 29, 1970. Following on the session of March 22 to 25, 1971, the Council passed a resolution (J.O. 1971, C. 52/1) on "new guidelines for the agricultural policy." Pursuant to this resolution the Commission submitted three proposals for directives on agricultural reform, and a proposal for a regulation, these being the original proposals recast. The proposal on the reduction of the surface area farmed was dropped, but there remained proposals on (1) modernisation; (2) retirement bonuses and re-allocation of land; (3) social and economic information and training; (4) producer groups and unions (regulation). The three directives were adopted on April 17, 1972. (Directives 72/159, 160 and 161, J.O. 1972, L. 96/1, 9 and 15. See generally Bulletin 4, 1972, p. 15, and also Bulletin 6, 1970, p. 21; Bulletin 3, 1971, p. 32; Bulletin 4, 1971, p. 62; and Bulletin 7, 1971, p. 30.)

CAP FINANCE: THE EUROPEAN AGRICULTURAL GUIDANCE AND
GUARANTEE FUND

22-44 Article 40 (4) of the Treaty provides for the setting up of one or more agricultural guidance and guarantee funds; in fact only one—known as FEOGA for the initials of the French *Fonds Européen d'Orientation et de Garantie Agricole*—was set up, covering all sectors subject to market organisation (Regulations 25/62, J.O. 1962, 991 and 17/64, J.O. 1964, 386). The Fund is not an organ or institution, but a part of the Community budget (Art. 1, Regulation 25/62 and 729/70, J.O. 1970, L 94/13). It was divided into a guarantee section (operating the support system) and a guidance system (operating the structural policy) by Regulation 17/64, J.O. 1964, 586, which sets out many of the functions. At first, the Fund paid one-sixth of the CAP costs, but it now bears the whole cost of the interventions on the market under its guarantee section, and up to 50 per cent. of approved structural programmes under the guidance section.

22-45 Common Market prices are expressed in terms of the unit of account, whose value was fixed by Regulation 129/62, J.O. 1962, 2553, and 653/68 (J.O. 1968, L 123/4) as being equivalent (in gold) to one United

States dollar. Elaborate rules have been laid down to allow for revaluation and devaluation (Regulation 129/62, J.O. 1962, 2553, Regulation 653/68, J.O. 1968, L 123/4 and Regulation 1134/68, J.O. 1968, L 188/1), but these were not observed during the monetary crises of 1969 and 1971. In 1969 measures were taken isolating the French franc and the German mark for more or less limited periods (see generally Third General Report (1969), p. 151). Following the monetary crisis beginning in May 1971, the Community continued to adhere to the principle of a unit of account, having set up by regulation of May 12, 1971, a system for isolating the individual currencies with countervailing charges (Regulation 974/71, J.O. 1971, L 106/1, of the Council, and Regulation 1013/71, J.O. 1971, L 110/8, of the Commission). A minimum movement in currency value of 2·5 per cent. in any one State brings the charge into operation automatically. The system, though not immediately useful, appeared to work during the monetary disturbances of 1972 (see Regulation 979/72, J.O. 1972, L 113/2, but see Regulation 1602/72, J.O. 1972, L 170/4, and see *infra*, § 33–14).

22–46   The funding of FEOGA raises the basic question of the Community's own resources; because of its difficulty it was left until the whole Community funding régime was worked out (see generally *infra*, Chapter 35). The definitive régime, set up by Decision 70/243, J.O. 1970, L 94/19 and Regulations 728 and 729/70, J.O. 1970, L 94/9 and 13, following on The Hague Conference of 1969 is as follows: from January 1975, the Community is to receive the levies (as defined in Article 2 (*a*) of Decision 70/243) in their entirety and an increasing proportion of the product of the CCT, subject to a 10 per cent. collection rebate, and up to 1 per cent. of the product of the common VAT system. Until then, the Community is to receive all the levies, a growing proportion of the CCT product, subject to Member States retaining 10 per cent. for collection expenses, and contributions from the Member States according to a special key (reference amount).

The arrangements before Decision 70/243, allowing for gradual assumption by FEOGA of all financial burdens, were very complex, and are now largely of historical interest; they are mainly contained in Regulations 25/62, 17/64, 130/66, and 741/67 (and see "The European Agricultural Guidance and Guarantee Fund since 1962," Bulletin 7, 1970, p. 22).

CHAPTER 23

THE WORKER AND THE COMMUNITY

23–01 THE Treaty of Rome deals with labour and related topics at two separate points: in Articles 48 to 51 in Part Two, Title III—" Free Movement of Persons, Services and Capital " under the chapter heading " Workers " and in Articles 117 to 128 in Part Three, Title III— " Social Policy." The division is somewhat arbitrary, but broadly Articles 48 to 51 lay down the principles of free movement of workers and provisions for the social security of Community migrant workers, while Articles 117 to 128 implement or list various social policy or labour law objectives and provide for the establishment of a European Social Fund, and a European policy of vocational training and guidance.

23–02 The chapter " Workers " relates only to persons who are employed by others and not to those who are self-employed, the latter being provided for under the chapter heading " Right of Establishment " (Arts. 52 to 58). The free movement of persons, more specifically, of workers, is one of the " four freedoms " of the European Economic Community. In an economic unit such as the Community and in an economically and technologically changing society, it is essential to maximise the use of labour, and thus workers must be able to move wherever they are most needed. The general scope of Articles 48 to 51 is more comprehensive than the isolated provisions of Article 69 of the ECSC Treaty and Article 96 of the Euratom Treaty which deal only with specialised categories of workers from the relevant industries.

Article 69 of the ECSC Treaty provides for free movement of workers with " recognised qualifications in a coalmining or steelmaking occupation." For its implementation, the Member States were to draw up common definitions of skilled trades and qualifications (Art. 69 (2)). The list which was eventually drawn up did not embrace the majority of workers in these industries. This narrow application of Article 69 was largely due to the economic situation within these two industries from the mid-fifties onwards, when, because of the substitution of other fuels for coal and because of technological innovation in the steel industry, a general surplus of labour prevailed.

Article 96 of the Euratom Treaty lays down that the Member States shall abolish all restrictions based on nationality which affect the right of nationals of any Member State to take skilled employment in the field of nuclear energy. Like Article 69 of the ECSC Treaty, this article is of narrow application. The directive of March 5, 1962, J.O. 1962, 1650, issued in application of Article 96, lists occupations requiring considerable qualifications as eligible for free movement. It would appear that for unqualified and unskilled workers in industries covered by the ECSC and Euratom Treaties, the general provisions of Articles 48 to 51 of the EEC Treaty apply. Article 232 of the EEC Treaty states that the provisions of that Treaty shall not affect those of the ECSC Treaty, nor shall they derogate from those of the Euratom Treaty; however, the EEC provisions regarding free movement of workers are supplementary to the other Treaties and deal with persons not otherwise covered by the sectoral Treaties (*cf.* Regulation 1612/68, J.O. 1968, L 257/2, Art. 42).

WORKERS AND THE EEC TREATY

Article 48

Article 48 (1) of the EEC Treaty provides that freedom of movement for workers was to be secured within the Community by the end of the original transitional period at the latest. As this is in absolute terms, the Article may perhaps be considered to have become directly applicable with the expiry of this period on December 31, 1969.

23–03 Article 48 (2) defines the freedom of movement as entailing the abolition of any kind of discrimination based on nationality between workers of the Member States as regards employment, remuneration and other conditions of employment.

No definition is given of the phrase " workers of the Member States," the beneficiaries of the abolition of discrimination under paragraph 2. Does this expression, therefore, include those stateless persons and nationals of third countries who were resident in the EEC countries prior to the establishment of the Community? The definitive régime of freedom of movement for workers instituted by Regulation 1612/68, J.O. 1968, L 257/2, describes the beneficiaries of the system as being nationals of Member States, but in practice stateless persons have been able to benefit from its provisions. Some discrimination exists in relation to migrant workers who have arrived from third countries since the establishment of the EEC. The Treaty does not deal with such categories and the Member States are left to make their own arrangements with the countries which supply the labour. These migrants do not always enjoy freedom of movement within the host country, let alone freedom to bring in their families, to change their job, or to join trade unions. Such treaty rights as accrue to them arise from bilateral agreements on social security and conditions concluded by some Member States with the supplier country. These agreements are not in standard form, nor do they cover all countries concerned. A degree of Community co-operation in relation to non-Community migrants would seem to be called for in order to counteract the worsening situation of " Europe's new lower class."

23–04 Article 48 (3) states that free movement is further to entail the right, subject to limitations justified on ground of public policy, public security or public health:

" (*a*) to accept offers of employment actually made;

" (*b*) to move freely within the territory of Member States for this purpose;

" (*c*) to stay in a Member State for the purpose of employment in accordance with the provisions governing the employment of nationals of that State laid down by law, regulation or administrative action; "

(this includes the right to stay during periods of sickness etc.)

" (*d*) to remain in the territory of a Member State after having been employed in that State, subject to conditions which shall be embodied in implementing regulations to be drawn up by the Commission."

(This right is apparently confined to the State in which the migrant was working at the time he ceased all work—*i.e.* on retirement.)

Article 48 (4) restricts the application of the prescribed freedom of movement by excluding from its ambit those employed in the public service. There is no definition of " public service " but practice suggests that free movement extends to nationalised industry, while workers in the higher echelons of public service or nationalised industry are less likely to move from country to country. It has been argued, however, that free movement does not extend to employment governed by public law.

Article 49

23–05 Article 49 makes it clear that the freeing of movement for workers was to be achieved by progressive stages:

(a) by ensuring close co-operation between national employment services;

(b) by abolishing administrative barriers in the shape of formalities and of qualifying periods for eligibility for available employment; or

(c) for free choice of employment; and

(d) by setting up a system for the communication of job opportunities and a balancing machinery to equalise supply and demand.

The Council is empowered to issue directives or Regulations to this end acting on a proposal from the Commission after consulting the Economic and Social Committee.

Free movement for workers was secured in three discernible stages, each stage being governed by a Regulation of general application. The first stage was inaugurated by the issue of Regulation 15 of August 16, 1961, J.O. 1961, 1073. This Regulation was superseded by Regulation

38/64 of March 25, 1964, J.O. 1964, 965 which inaugurated the second phase. This Regulation was itself superseded by Regulation 1612/68 of October 15, 1968, J.O. 1968, L 257/2. A directive on the abolition of restrictions on the movement and residence within the Community of workers of Member States and their families was adopted with each Regulation, the current one being Directive 68/360, J.O. 1968, L 257/15.

Regulation 15

23–06   Under Regulation 15 a migrant Community worker had first to obtain a permit from the State of destination, which allowed him to work only in the type of occupation for which he had been engaged. The permit was renewable after one year, and after four years of continuous employment the worker could obtain a permit for any kind of work. The Regulation maintained the preference of the national labour market for an initial period of three weeks; that is, job vacancies were only made available to nationals of Member States other than that in which the vacancy arose after the initial period had elapsed without the job being taken. An exception was made in respect of specific job offers made to named individuals who were nationals of other Member States; in such a case the named individual could accept the job offered at once. All quota restrictions on labour movements between Member States were abolished by this Regulation. It defined more explicitly than Article 48 EEC the rights of a migrant Community worker with regard to dismissal and trade union affiliation—both were to be on a non-discriminatory basis. Furthermore, it allowed other members of the migrant's family to join him in the host country in certain circumstances. It also established the mechanism whereby employment offers and relevant information could be diffused on a Community-wide basis. The bodies set up to deal with these matters were the European Co-ordination Office, an Advisory Committee and a Technical Committee. The accompanying directive, of August 16, 1961, J.O. 1961, 1513, effected a harmonisation of the rules on the documents to be carried by migrant workers, their issue and their validity.

Special groups of workers not covered by Regulation 15, notably frontier workers (*i.e.* those who travel across an internal Community frontier to and from their place of work each day or week), seasonal workers (*i.e.* those who move to another Community country, to work there for a specific period of the year only), and actors and musicians were included in later Regulations, which extended the benefits of Regulation 15 to them.

Regulation 38/64

23–07   The second stage of progress in freeing the labour market was reached with Regulation 38/64, J.O. 1964, 965, replacing Regulation 15, issued during a period of high economic activity, when labour was scarce throughout the Community except in Italy. This Regulation permitted migrants to change jobs after two years only, and "national priority" was completely suppressed, thus putting nationals of all Member States on an equal footing as regards job vacancies in any one Member State. A safeguard clause was, however, provided, allowing each Member State to reintroduce a national labour market priority of two weeks for periods of three months at a time, should there be an excess of labour in a particular region or profession (Art. 2). The safeguard did not affect frontier workers or offers of positions to individually-named workers. The rule of equality of treatment amongst Community workers was expanded by adding to the rights already given by Regulation 15 the right to be elected delegate or officer of a trade union branch, if the worker had been working at his job in the relevant country for at least three years. The right of workers to introduce their families was expanded to include not only spouses and minor children but also other dependent children and dependent ascendant relatives. The complementary Directive 64/240 on movement restrictions etc. (J.O. 1964, 981) required modification of national rules on residence permits so as to allow the holder of such a permit to move anywhere within the country for which it was issued. The validity of residence permits was also required to be co-extensive with that of work permits.

Regulation 1612/68

23-08   In practical terms the definitive régime was achieved more than twelve months before the end of the transitional period: Regulation 1612/68, J.O. 1968, L 257/2, came into force on November 9, 1968, replacing Regulation 38/64 in its entirety, and placing all Community nationals on an equal footing. Article 1 states that:

> " 1. Any national of a Member State, irrespective of his place of residence, shall have the right to take up an activity as an employed person, and to pursue such activity within the territory of another Member State in accordance with the provisions laid down by law, regulation or administrative action governing the employment of that State.
>
> 2. He shall, in particular be eligible for employment vacancies in the territory of another Member State with the same priority as nationals of that State."

There are no longer any exceptions to the basic principle. Article 3 makes inapplicable any quota restrictions or other practices which restrict employment offers to nationals of the State involved and Article 4 reiterates Regulation 15, declaring inapplicable to Community nationals quota restrictions in relation to the actual numbers of foreign nationals employed in any Member State. Articles 5 and 6 eliminate other forms of discrimination.

23–09   Article 7 ensures basic equality of treatment for Community workers in any Member State as regards terms and conditions of employment. Discrimination against Community nationals in social and tax matters, in eligibility for vocational training, and in the terms of collective or individual agreements on pay is prohibited. Article 8 gives Community nationals equal rights to become members of trade unions, and to exercise associated rights. The Community worker is to enjoy all rights afforded to national workers in matters of housing, including eligibility to be entered on housing lists on equal terms (Art. 9). Article 10 gives the worker the right to bring his spouse and children under twenty-one and dependent children and ascendant dependent relatives into the country in which he works, if he has obtained suitable accommodation for them (para. 3). Article 11 extends the right to work in the host State to his spouse and children, and Article 12 grants the children the right to be educated there.

Article 8 of Regulation 1612 provides that " a migrant Community national may be excluded from taking part in the administration of bodies governed by public law and from holding an appointment governed by public law." This provision relates specifically to the " Conseils des prud'hommes " or workers' tribunals in certain Member States, in which a lay worker may be called upon to act in a judicial capacity by virtue of his status as a worker. Exclusion of foreign nationals from such tribunals is paralleled by Article 48 (4) EEC which states that the provisions of Article 48 are not to apply to employment in the public service (and *cf.* Art. 55 EEC). There remain no other direct restrictions or safeguards on the free movement of workers, and other restraints may only be applied pursuant to safeguard clauses contained elsewhere in the Treaty—*cf.* Article 103 (2)—*sed quaere.*

23–10   Under Articles 13 and 14 of the Regulation the Member States are to co-operate through the Commission in dealing with employment questions and problems, and are, through the mechanisms established under Articles 15 to 18, to exchange information on employment vacancies. Measures are to be taken in conjunction with the Commission for controlling the balance of the labour market (Arts. 19 and 20). Overall responsibility for co-ordinating the balance of vacancies and applications for employment lies with the European Co-ordination Office, first set up under Regulation 15 (Arts. 21 to 23 of Regulation 1612). An Advisory Committee (Arts. 24 to 31) is responsible for assisting the Commission in the examination of problems regarding the free movement of workers, in the study of the effects of the Regulation, and in submitting proposals for revision of the Regulation (Arts. 24 and 25). The Committee, whose members are appointed by the Council (Art. 27) is composed of six members from each Member State, two representing the government, two the trade unions and two the employers' associations (Art. 26). It is chaired by a member of the Commission or his alternate (Art. 28). A Technical Committee has as its task the preparation and promotion and following up of technical aspects of implementing the regulation (Arts. 32 to 37); it is composed of representatives of the governments of the Member States (Art. 34) and is chaired by a member of the Commission or his alternate (Art. 35).

23–11   Directive 68/360, J.O. 1968, L 257/13, which accompanied Regulation 1612/68, provides for a document called " Residence Permit for a National of a Member State of the EEC " (Art. 4). The receiving State must, on production by the worker of a valid identity card or passport (Art. 3) and a declaration from the future employer, issue such a residence permit to the applicant, valid throughout the territory of that Member State for at least five years and automatically renewable (Art. 6). The permit may not be withdrawn merely because the holder is no longer working (Art. 7).

The only right mentioned in Article 48 (3) EEC which was not covered by Regulation 1612/68 is the right " (*d*) to remain in the territory of a Member State after having been employed in that State. . . ." Such a right is granted by Regulation 1251/70, J.O. 1970, L 142/24, to any migrant Community worker who

(a) has reached the qualifying age for an old age pension and has been employed in the host state for at least the last twelve months, and resided there continuously for more than three years; or

(b) ceases work because of a permanent incapacity to work, provided he has resided there for more than two years (no such residence qualification is imposed if the incapacity arose from an industrial accident or occupational disease); or

(c) been a frontier worker for at least three years.

The right to remain resident in the host country is extended to the worker's family originally qualifying for admission under Article 10 of Regulation 1612.

23–12   Regulations 1612/68 and 1251/70 both apply in the United Kingdom as from January 1, 1973; during the transitional period the United Kingdom may derogate in certain respects from the provisions of Regulation 1612/68 in relation to Northern Ireland, as may Ireland, in relation to the whole of its territory (Act of Accession, Annex VII, Cmnd. 4862–II, p. 147 at p. 154). A Joint Declaration annexed to the Final Act of the conference (Cmnd. 4862–I, p. 117) recognises that the enlargement of the Community " could give rise to certain difficulties for the social situation in one or more Member States as regards the application of the provisions relating to the free movement of workers." In consequence, Member States

" reserve the right, should difficulties of that nature arise, to bring the matter before the institutions of the Community in order to obtain a solution to this problem in accordance with the provisions of the Treaties establishing the European Communities and the provisions adopted in application thereof."

This declaration may be looked upon as introducing into the Act a safeguard clause against any possible disruption of national labour markets.

A further declaration, also annexed to the Act (p. 118), was made by the Government of the United Kingdom in respect of the definition of the term " nationals " stipulating that that term should, as to the United Kingdom, be understood as referring to:

> " (*a*) persons who are citizens of the United Kingdom and Colonies or British subjects not possessing that citizenship or the citizenship of any other Commonwealth country or territory, who, in either case, have the right of abode in the United Kingdom and are therefore exempt from United Kingdom immigration control;
>
> (*b*) persons who are citizens of the United Kingdom and Colonies by birth or by registration or naturalisation in Gibraltar, or whose father was so born, registered or naturalised."

The effect of part (*a*) of this declaration is to reflect the provisions of the United Kingdom Immigration Act 1971 (c. 77).

Although nationals of the Associated African States and Malagasy, and nationals of the Overseas Countries and Territories do not benefit from free movement of labour, by virtue of Decision 68/351, J.O. 1968, L 257/1, Articles 48 and 49 EEC and all subsequent measures were deemed to apply to the French overseas departments as now constituted.

Article 50

23–13   Article 50 EEC provides that Member States shall encourage the exchange of young workers within the framework of a joint programme. Member States had already made bilateral arrangements in this respect and a multilateral convention on the subject was drawn up in the context of the Brussels Treaty organisation (convention concerning student employees, of April 17, 1950, T.S. 8 (1952), Cmd. 8478). Responsibility for giving effect to Article 50 is largely left with the individual Member States. The Commission made proposals to the Council on linking the programme of exchange of young workers with the policy on vocational training. However, this plan was not adopted and a programme of exchanges was set up by a declaration of the representatives of the governments of the Member States of May 8, 1964 (64/307, J.O. 1964, 1226). This defines a young worker as being between eighteen and thirty years old. It governs the organisation of exchanges with regard to questions of duration, selection of workers, facilities available and conditions of work and study. (See Written Question 265/72, J.O. 1972, C 134/7, as to the implementation of the programme.)

SOCIAL SECURITY

23-14 Article 51 is of much greater import than Article 50, in that it forms the necessary complement to the principle of free movement of labour, providing for the adoption by the Council, acting unanimously on a proposal from the Commission of

> "such measures as are necessary to provide freedom of movement for workers; to this end, it shall make arrangements to secure for workers and their dependents:
>
> (a) aggregation, for the purpose of acquiring and retaining the right to benefit and of calculating the amount of benefit, of all periods taken into account under the laws of the several countries;
>
> (b) payment of benefits to persons resident in the territories of Member States."

The effect of this is to require that migrant workers be guaranteed in the country to which they migrate equivalent social security benefits, based on an aggregation (*i.e.* totalisation) of social security credits and qualifications earned or paid by them wheresoever within the Community. No worker would be tempted to move to another country if as a result he automatically lost his right to social security and pension benefits. Prior to the inception of the Community, bilateral treaties between Member States had secured a degree of reciprocal recognition of such benefits but their operation was not uniform. Article 51 EEC, requiring the adoption of positive measures goes further than the comparable Article in the Treaty of Paris, Article 69 (4), which merely states that the Member States "shall endeavour to settle among themselves any matters remaining to be dealt with in order to ensure that social security arrangements do not inhibit labour mobility."

It is considered, however, that Article 51 is not the means for laying down a completely uniform Community rule, since the rules laid down under it only effect a co-ordination of national rules—*cf.* 44/65, *Hessische Knappschaft* v. *Singer*, Rec. XI 1191, [1966] C.M.L.R. 82, 1/67, *Ciechelski* v. *Caisse Régionale*, Rec. XIII 235, [1967] C.M.L.R. 192, and 2/67, *De Moor* v. *Caisse de Pension*, Rec. XIII 255, [1967] C.M.L.R. 223.

23-15 Effect was given to Article 69 (4) ECSC and to Article 51 EEC by Regulation 3, J.O. 1958, 561, which took over the body of the European Convention on the Social Security of Migrants, signed at Rome on December 9, 1957, elaborated in the ECSC context, and itself based on ILO Convention No. 102 of 1952. The proposed implementing rules were taken over in large part in implementing Regulations 4, J.O. 1958, 597. These Regulations came into effect on January 1, 1959, more than two years before the first Regulation on the free movement of labour. Both Regulations were subject to constant modification from

1964 onwards. They are replaced respectively by consolidating Regulations 1408/71, J.O. 1971, L 149/2, and 574/72, J.O. 1972, L 74/1, which together entered into force on October 1, 1972. The original Regulations did not apply to all migrant Community workers, but Regulation 1408 specifically includes frontier workers, seasonal workers, seamen and civil servants. Certain multilateral accords are unaffected by it, notably the Agreement of July 27, 1950 concerning the social security of Rhine boatmen, and the European Convention of July 9, 1956 concerning the social security of workers engaged in international transport (Regulation 1408, Art. 7 (2)).

23–16   Article 51 of the Treaty does not define the scope of the notion of " social security " but Regulation 1408/71 covers all classical forms of social security benefits, namely sickness and maternity, disability, old-age, survivors', industrial accident and disease, death, unemployment and family benefits (Art. 4 (1)). But the Regulation excludes from its ambit social assistance and medical aid, war victims benefit schemes and special schemes for civil servants and assimilated persons (Art. 4 (4)).

Article 1 of the Regulation contains general definitions. Article 2 (1) states it to apply " to workers who are or have been subject to the legislation of one or more of the Member States and are nationals of a Member State or are stateless persons or refugees permanently resident in the territory of a Member State, as also to the members of their families and their survivors." Permanent residents, *e.g.* including aliens, are assimilated to nationals for the purposes of the Regulation (Art. 3). Article 12 provides that a migrant may not in general enjoy double social security benefits in respect of one and the same period of time by virtue of any double residence qualification.

Articles 13 to 17 set out rules on conflicts of national social security laws. The basic rule here is that a worker is to be subject to the legislation of the State in which he is employed, even if he is a permanent resident in another Member State, or his employer or the registered office of the undertaking which employs him is situated in another Member State (Art. 13 (2) (*a*)).

23–17   The structure of Regulation 1408 is such that there is, outside Articles 1 to 12, no general statement of the principles governing the benefits granted, the principles applicable to each type of benefit being set out with sole reference to that type. Nevertheless, apart from the principle of non-plurality of benefits already referred to, most types of benefit are governed by two basic rules; first, that of aggregation of all periods of social security insurance, wherever completed (*cf.* Art. 51 (*a*) EEC), which entails payment of benefits by the paying authority, in the State in which the Community worker is at the time residing, as though the worker had completed all the relevant aggregated periods in the host State; secondly, that the paying authority is entitled to reimbursement of benefits paid out in respect of periods completed by the worker in other Member States, the reimbursement to come from the States in which the worker was from time to time employed, in proportion to the time spent there.

Benefits payable to the migrant worker are thus the benefits which would be payable to a worker who had spent all his qualifying periods in the payer State. The migrant worker is assimilated to the local worker for all purposes, and cannot, for instance, claim to be entitled to a benefit which he would have had if he had continued to work in his home State.

Articles 18 to 79 deal with the various types of benefit available.

23-18   Articles 80 and 81 provide for an Administrative Commission for the Social Security of Workers, composed of representatives of the governments of the Member States, advised by a representative of the Commission, and empowered to call upon the ILO for further technical advice. A similar Commission had existed under Regulation 3. The prime duty of the Administrative Commission is to " settle all administrative questions and questions of interpretation arising under this Regulation and subsequent Regulations, or under any consequential agreement or arrangement, without prejudice to the right of the authorities, institutions and persons concerned to have recourse to the procedures and legal remedies prescribed under the legislation of Member States, in this Regulation or in the Treaty " (Art. 81 (*a*) of Regulation 1408). Some doubt arose as to whether the Administrative Commission could give definitive interpretative decisions under the identical Article 43 of Regulation 3. The Court of Justice held that these decisions have the value of opinions, and that any other interpretation of Article 43 (*a*) of Regulation 3 would conflict with Article 177, setting up a system for the interpretation of Community law (which confers exclusive jurisdiction on the Court of Justice): 19/67, *Bestuur der sociale verzekeringsbank* v. *van der Vecht*, Rec. XIII 445, [1968] C.M.L.R. 151, *cf.* 28/68, *Caisse Régionale* v. *Torrekens*, Rec. XV 125, [1969] C.M.L.R. 377.

The Administrative Commission's other tasks are essentially to foster and improve co-operation between Member States in the field of social security, in particular with a view to expediting payments of benefits (Art. 81).

In addition to the Administrative Commission, the Regulation provides for a Consultative (or Advisory) Committee for the Social Security of Migrant Workers (Arts. 82 and 83), which is made up in tripartite fashion, with two representatives each from government, trade unions and employers' organisations from each Member State, appointed by the Council, and chaired by a member of the Commission or his representative (Art. 82). The Committee is empowered:

" (*a*) to examine general questions or questions of principle and the problems arising from the implementation of the Regulations adopted within the framework of the provisions of Article 51 of the Treaty;

    (*b*) to draw up Opinions on the subject for the Administrative Commission and also Proposals for any revision of the Regulation " (Art. 83).

23–19 Effectively, however, responsibility for the operation of the Regulation rests with the national social security authorities and Article 84 recognises this by stating that:

    " 1. the competent authorities of Member States shall

        (*a*) communicate to each other all information regarding measures taken by them to implement this Regulation;

        (*b*) communicate to each other all information regarding changes in their legislation which are likely to affect the implementation of this Regulation.

    2. for the purpose of implementing this Regulation, the authorities and institutions of Member States shall lend their good offices and act as though implementing their own legislation."

Regulation 1408/71 is amended by a very comprehensive technical adaptation (Cmnd. 4862–II, p. 90). As is usual, the adaptation does not affect the substance of the Regulation.

CHAPTER 24

SOCIAL POLICY

24–01   THE provisions of the Treaty on social matters are contained in Articles 117 to 128, together forming Title III of Part Three of the Treaty—Policies of the Community—entitled " Social policy." The title is itself divided into two chapters—Chapter 1, " Social Provisions " and Chapter 2, " The European Investment Bank." The individual Articles in Chapter 1 do not, apart from Article 119, which relates to equal pay between male and female labour, contain any provisions imposing obligations either on the Community or Member States. The theory inherent in the chapter is that social progress will come about incidentally to progress in other spheres; this is indicated by the phrasing of Article 117, whereby " Member States agree upon the need to promote improved working conditions. . . . They believe that such a development will ensue not only from the functioning of the common market, . . . but also from the procedures provided for in this Treaty. . . ." These procedures are in particular those relating to the free movement and social security of workers (Arts. 48 to 51), the equal pay provision (Art. 119), the creation of the European Social Fund (Arts. 123 to 127), and the formulation of a common policy of vocational training (Art. 128). Tangentially involved are those provisions which erect common policies in specific areas, such as agriculture and transport, *e.g.* Articles 39 (1) (*b*) and 41 (*a*) and Article 75. The first Article of Chapter 1, Article 117, records the agreement of the Member States " upon the need to promote improved working conditions and an improved standard of living for workers, so as to make possible their harmonisation while the improvement is being maintained " (first para.). The second paragraph records the belief of the Member States that the development referred to in the first paragraph " will ensue not only from the functioning of the Common Market, which will favour the harmonisation of social systems, but also from the procedure provided for in this Treaty and from the approximation of provisions laid down by law, regulation or administrative action."

Article 118

24–02   Article 118 lists the particular fields (namely employment, labour law and working conditions, vocational training, social security, industrial safety, and hygiene, and the right of association and collective bargaining) in which the Commission is given the task of promoting close co-operation between the Member States so that the aspirations of Article 117 may be achieved. The Commission's powers cover other matters outside the list, but are without prejudice to other provisions of the Treaty, and are to be in conformity with its general objectives. Article 118 embodies no binding engagement or undertaking by Member States, but is a simple attribution of competence to the Commission in the matter of promotion, the ultimate responsibility in these affairs remaining with the Member States. The Commission is to act in close contact with the Member States by making studies, delivering opinions and arranging consultations both on problems arising at national level and those of concern to international organisations. Before delivering the opinions provided for, the Commission is to consult the Economic and Social Committee. Generally, the Commission has had recourse to the power under Article 155 to make recommendations. (These are nevertheless issued after consultation with the Economic and Social Committee.) Its achievements in the fields listed have been, amongst others, a recommendation of 1962 relating to the organisation of social services available to migrant workers (J.O. 1962, 2118), and a recommendation concerning the protection of young workers (J.O. 1967, 405). A recommendation was issued on vocational guidance, which aims at the development of schemes to benefit both young and adult workers through adaptation of their vocational guidance structures, and through a closer liaison between the employment services (J.O. 1966, 2815). The field of social security is dealt with by the Community primarily on the basis of Article 51, but the Commission has issued a number of recommendations concerning industrial accidents and diseases and occupational hygiene (J.O. 1962, 2181 and J.O. 1966, 2753). It adopted a list of occupational diseases on July 23, 1962 (J.O. 1962, 2188), which is primarily a listing of noxious agents without specifying the particular industry in which they shall be deemed occupational hazards. The Commission based a recommendation on occupational hygiene on ILO Convention No. 172 of June 24, 1955 (J.O. 1962, 2181); the recommendation sets out standards relating to health protection at work and the duties of factory doctors, although a subsequent report of the European Parliament established that but little progress had been made towards the implementation of the recommendation. The ECSC and Euratom, each with its own particular health and safety hazards, have achieved more progress. On the basis of Articles 31 *et seq.* of the Euratom Treaty, standards of health protection were established from the coming into force of that Treaty (directives of February 2, 1959, J.O. 1959, 221) and, in relation to the particular health and safety problems of coal mines, a separate Mines Safety and Health Commission was set up to study relevant problems (Decision of July 9, 1957, J.O. 1957, 487).

Possibly the most important achievement has been the setting up of the Standing Committee on Employment (Decision 70/532, J.O. 1970, L 273/25; based on Art. 145) composed of delegates from the Council, the Commission, employers' organisations and workers' organisations. The task of the Committee is:

> "to ensure . . . that there shall be continuous dialogue, joint action and consultation between the Council—or, where appropriate, the representatives of the Governments of the Member States— the Commission and the two sides of industry in order to facilitate coordination by the Member States of their employment policies while harmonising such policies with the objectives of the Community." (Art. 2 of the Decision.)

An Annex to the decision allocates the membership of the body between the various interested bodies; it gives eleven representatives to UNICE (the Union of Industries of the European Communities), nine representatives to the European Confederation of Free Trade Unions (ECFTU) and two to the Standing Committee of the CGT/CGIL (the French and Italian Communist dominated unions). In all, there are eighteen employers' and eighteen workers' representatives.

24–03   The Commission has, apart from measures enumerated above, published a document entitled *Preliminary Guidelines for a Community Social Policy Programme* (March 17, 1971: Sec. (71) 600 F, Bulletin, Supp. 2/71). The document consists of a statistical survey and analysis of current social conditions, and lists the social objectives to be achieved, especially in the context of the proposed economic and monetary union. The document states that:

> " The achievement of the economic and monetary union can contribute to [the fairer distribution of income], by eliminating to some extent the economic fluctuations which mainly affect long-term measures of reform. The harmonisation and approximation of legislative provisions for the establishment of the united market should be directed to this end." (Bulletin, Supp., p. 49.)

The Commission is of the opinion that the improvement of conditions of work should be achieved " more through agreements concluded between employers and workers at Community level than through regulations. The Commission therefore attaches the greatest importance to increasing the number of joint committees at Community level " (p. 52). The Commission also indicates the possible shape of a Community social policy programme and reviews the Community's powers under the Treaty in relation to progressive social improvement, specifically mentioning the possible use of Article 235, if the Treaty does not elsewhere empower the institutions of the Community to take necessary action. The document does not contain any radical new departure but indicates a continued awareness of the problems confronting the labour force inside an expanding Community.

Article 119

24-04   Article 119 of the EEC Treaty stands alone in the "Social Provisions" chapter in imposing a definite obligation on the Member States to conform to its provisions by a specific date—the end of the first stage of the period of transition on December 31, 1961. The first paragraph of Article 119 contains a clear statement of principle— Member States shall ensure and subsequently maintain the application of the principle that men and women should receive equal pay for equal work. For this purpose, the second paragraph defines "pay" as meaning " the ordinary basic or minimum wage or salary and any other consideration, whether in cash or in kind, which the worker receives, directly or indirectly, in respect of his employment from his employment." The third paragraph explains that pay without discrimination based on sex means:

> " (a) that pay for the same work at piece rates shall be calculated on the basis of the same unit of measurement;
> " (b) that pay for work at time rates shall be the same for the same job."

The first paragraph of the Article may perhaps now be considered directly applicable and indeed this was assumed to be so by Advocate-General Dutheillet de Lamothe in 80/70, *Defrenne* v. *Belgium*, Rec. XVII 445. Nevertheless, the statements contained in the Annual Report of the Commission indicate that the provisions of Article 119 have yet to be translated into effective national legislative provisions, and despite the definitions, the obligation is not entirely clear-cut, thus perhaps making it unlikely that the Court of Justice would in fact hold the Article to be directly applicable. Cases 20/71, *Sabbatini* v. *European Parliament* [1972] C.M.L.R. 947 and 32/71, *Chollet* v. *Commission* [1972] C.M.L.R. 947, which concerned the withdrawal of expatriation allowances consequent upon the marriage of female plaintiffs, take the matter no further. In both cases the plaintiffs attacked the decision of withdrawal, alleging violation of the general legal principle prohibiting sex discrimination, and in particular of Article 119 EEC. The impugned decisions were annulled in both cases, but upon grounds of creation of " an arbitrary difference of treatment between officials " rather than specifically upon grounds of sex discrimination.

24-05   The equal pay principle has an honourable international legal pedigree in that it was incorporated into the preamble to Part XIII of the 1919 Treaty of Versailles, which contains the original constitution of the ILO, and was reiterated in the 1944 Declaration of Philadelphia which renewed the mandate of the ILO. ILO Convention No. 100, of June 29, 1951 (T.S. 88 (1972), Cmnd. 5039), enunciates the principle in terms of equal pay for work of equal value. The European Social Charter, formulated under the guidance of the Council of Europe, states that " the contracting parties undertake . . . to recognise the right of men and women workers to equal pay for work of equal value " (Art. 4 (3)), although this Charter has had little legal effect to date. The principle in Article 119 is more concise, " equal pay for equal work," and the definition in the second paragraph is borrowed from the ILO Convention, but no clarification is given on the meaning of the phrase " directly or indirectly " used in the second paragraph in defining what constitutes pay received. It was thought that this referred to deferred payments of wages or salary, such as pensions, and this question was specifically posed in 80/70, *Defrenne* v. *Belgium*, Rec. XVII 445, where differential pension rights were given to staff of Sabena (the Belgian National Airline), dependent on their work and sex; air hostesses were compulsorily retired at 40 without having been able to accumulate pension privileges accorded to other staff. The Court of Justice decided that a pension is not wholly a payment by the employer, there also being contribution from the worker (but surely this is in reality payment he actually forgoes) and contributions from the relevant national authority, and that the worker's title to payment did not therefore depend upon the employer's contribution to the pension fund, but is merely based on the fulfilment by the worker of certain criteria, usually of age, and the payment of a certain number of contributions by the worker himself. Therefore, the principle of Article 119 did not apply to state pensions or other social security benefits, although it might apply to privately financed pension schemes.

The application of Article 119 nationally has progressed only with difficulty. The French Government recently announced that it was introducing a Bill designed to achieve the equalisation of female remuneration, especially in relation to the determination of differential wage scales, which disguise discrimination in wage payment between the sexes; this is one of the classic problems.

24–06 During the first stage of the period of transition, the Commission issued a recommendation (July 20, 1960, Bulletin 6/7, 1960, p. 46) on the subject, but by December 1961 it was admitted that the goal would not be achieved within the specified time limit, and therefore a resolution of the representatives of the Governments of the Member States was resorted to. This resolution of December 30, 1961 (Bulletin No. 1, 1962, p. 8) contained a timetable for the elimination of discrimination in pay by December 31, 1964. The elimination of such discrimination has nevertheless still to be achieved. In the United Kingdom, effect has already been given to the aims of Article 119 by the enactment of the Equal Pay Act 1970 (c. 41), although the actual scope of the Act is much wider than that of Article 119. The Act attempts to eliminate all discrimination between the sexes relating to the terms and conditions of employment, not simply pay. By section 1 (1) of the Act, employers must

" give equal treatment as regards terms and conditions of employment to men and to women, that is to say that . . . . :

> (*a*) for men and women employed on like work the terms and
> conditions of one sex are not in any respect less favourable
> than those of the other; and
>
> (*b*) for men and women employed on work rated as equivalent
> [by a job evaluation study] the terms and conditions of one
> sex are not less favourable than those of the other in any
> respect in which the terms and conditions of both are
> determined by the rating of their work."

The Act will not, however, come into operation until December 29,
1975.

Article 120

24-07   Although Article 120 stipulates that " Member States shall endeavour
to maintain the existing equivalence between paid holiday schemes," new
divergences in the systems of holidays with pay have appeared; in some
States workers may be paid double or even triple wages during their
holidays, while in others, single pay is the norm.   There has been a
general but unco-ordinated extension in the legal minimum allowance
of holidays throughout Member States.   The Commission has, however,
made a recommendation on the holiday allowances for young workers;
but otherwise execution of the article is in the hands of the Member
States, although they must of course have regard to Article 5 of the
Treaty (" full faith and credit clause ").

Articles 121 and 122

24-08   Article 121 enables the Council to assign to the Commission " tasks
in connection with the implementation of common measures, particularly
as regards social security for the migrant workers referred to in Articles
48 to 51."   The Article is self-explanatory as regards the delegation of
tasks to the Commission, but no definition is given of " implementation
of common measures."   It must be assumed that the expression covers
all general and particular objects of the Treaty in social affairs.

Article 122, first para., requiring the Commission to include a
separate chapter on social developments within the Community in its
annual report to the Assembly (now called the European Parliament),
reflects one aspect of the general duty of the Commission contained in
Article 156 * to publish an annual report, which by Article 143 * must be
discussed by the European Parliament.   The specific provision in Article
122, that the report should include a separate chapter on social developments, seems unique, as nowhere else does the Treaty list obligatory
chapter headings for the annual reports.   The Commission also publishes
a separate annual report on social questions, covering the same ground
in greater depth.   This too is stated to be published pursuant to Article

122. The second paragraph of Article 122 is in some sense the reciprocal of the first, for it empowers the Assembly to invite the Commission to draw up reports on any particular problems concerning social conditions; the two paragraphs thus institutionalise the dialogue which exists outside the Article.

THE EUROPEAN SOCIAL FUND [1]

24–09 The European Social Fund (ESF) was set up to make finance available to cope with changing social and employment situations within the Community. Article 123 of the EEC Treaty establishes the European Social Fund:

" in order to improve employment opportunities for workers in the common market and to contribute thereby to raising the standard of living; . . . it shall have the task of rendering the employment of workers easier and of increasing their geographical and occupational mobility within the Community."

Although the basic rules governing the Fund are outlined in the Treaty chapter entitled the " European Social Fund," the ESF was originally brought into full operation by Regulation 9 of August 25 1960, J.O. 1960, 1189, issued pursuant to Article 127 of the Treaty. The Fund is administered by the Commission, assisted in this task by a committee presided over by a member of the Commission and composed of representatives of governments, trade unions and employers' organisations (Art. 124 of the Treaty; see further below).

24–10 The principles of the ESF are still as set out in Article 123 although a substantial measure of reform was effected by Decision 71/66, J.O. 1971, L 28/15, but the purposes for which the Fund could provide assistance, originally set out in Article 125, have been radically altered by Decision 71/66 to fill the obvious lacunae preventing optimum use of the Fund. The terms of Article 125 did not enable the ESF to give assistance in the form of loans, but only in the form of grants. Further, funds were only payable to States or public agencies in respect of schemes dealing with an already existing crisis of employment. The ESF had no discretion not to approve a scheme, nor could it be used to combat deteriorating social or employment situations, since aid was only available in respect of those already out of work and even then it could only be granted *a posteriori*. Articles 46, 54 and 56 of the Treaty of Paris, on the other hand, confer far wider powers as regards the granting of financial aid in a social context. Article 46 (4) states that the High Authority shall " take part, at the request of the Governments concerned, in studying the possibilities for re-employing, in existing industries or through the creation of new activities, workers made redundant by

---

[1] Discussion of the ESF is also relevant to Regional Policy; see § 34–12 for these aspects.

market developments or technical changes " and the succeeding paragraph states that it shall " obtain the information it requires to assess the possibilities for improving working conditions and living standards for workers in the industries within its province, and the threats to those standards." Article 54 allows the High Authority to finance individual investment programmes, for both public and private undertakings either by loans or by guaranteeing loans made by other institutions.

24–11   By Article 56, the High Authority is given the power to finance programmes of investment for any industry whether coal or steel or otherwise, which aim at the reabsorption into gainful employment of the redundant workers. The High Authority is also authorised to grant non-repayable aids in the form of, for example, tide-over, resettlement or retraining allowances to workers who had either to suffer temporary unemployment while their employer was converting his establishment to a new type of production, or who became unemployed and were forced to move to find suitable employment elsewhere, or who, after becoming unemployed, found it necessary to undergo a period of retraining to learn a new trade or skill which would give them the opportunity of a job. Article 56 as originally formulated only envisaged the financing of new schemes in the context of technical innovations (in the context of the coal and steel industries) being responsible for causing widespread redundancies. After the coal crisis of the mid-1950s it became obvious that market forces other than technical advances were responsible for making workers in the coal and steel industries redundant. These forces were basically the increased use of alternative fuels and materials, so much so that it became necessary to amend Article 56 to take account of the situation. The amendment consists in the addition of a new paragraph 2 to the unamended provisions of the Article (now para. 1). (This is the only ECSC Article to be revised under the *petite révision* provisions of Article 95 ECSC. The other Community Treaties contain no such provision.) By paragraph 2 the High Authority is now empowered to finance investment programmes in situations where fundamental changes not directly connected with the establishment of the coal and steel Common Market may lead some undertakings permanently to discontinue, curtail or change their activities; the High Authority may also provide allowances for undertakings to enable them to continue paying such of their workers as may have to be temporarily laid off as a result of the undertaking's change of activity in addition to the types of allowance payable under paragraph 1. The relative freedom of action of the High Authority was to a certain extent due to the fact that unlike the ESF, the High Authority enjoys its own financial resources (see § 35–08) and because it deals with only two sectors of the economy. The ECSC also undertakes programmes of house-building to assist displaced workers or to ameliorate housing conditions generally, by virtue of the powers granted to it in Article 54.

24–12 By contrast, the scope of operation of the ESF was limited to the payment of 50 per cent. of vocational retraining expenses, resettlement and tide-over allowances. Assistance towards the cost of vocational retraining expenses could only be granted if the unemployed worker could not find another job in the trade he already knew, and if he had already been in productive employment for at least six months after retraining. Assistance towards resettlement allowances could only be granted if the unemployed worker had to move and had already been six months in his new employment. Assistance towards tide-over allowances was available only where the worker was once more working for the undertaking and had been doing so for six months. Even so, the grant of assistance was made conditional upon submission of a prior plan for approval of the Commission.

24–13 It became apparent that reform was necessary to adapt the Fund to an era of rapid technological change and mobility in employment (*cf.* Preamble, 1st and 2nd whereas of Decision 71/66, J.O. 1971, L 28/15). Proposals for reform were first made in 1965, but it was not until the Commission proposed action on the basis of Article 126 (*b*), which admits of a general revision of the ESF only after the end of the transitional period, that progress was achieved. Paragraph (*b*) states that the Council may, "when the transitional period has ended," abandon the previous grounds for granting assistance in whole or in part, and "unanimously determine what new tasks may be entrusted to the Fund within the framework of its terms of reference as laid down in Article 123," after receiving the opinion of the Commission, and after consulting the Parliament and the Economic and Social Committee. The Council adopted a decision reforming the ESF on February 1, 1971 (Decision 71/66, J.O. 1971, L 28/15). The decision specifically mentions that it is desirable to promote efforts designed to solve unemployment and structural underemployment in various areas, and that the need exists to intensify preventative action against unemployment and underemployment (Preamble, 4th and 5th whereas).

24–14 By Article 1 of Decision 71/66, the assistance provided under Article 125 of the Treaty is no longer to be granted. Articles 3 to 5 define the new tasks of the Fund. Article 3 extends the scope of application to persons apart from wage-earners, paragraph 2 stating that "in special cases to be decided by the Council, the assistance of the Fund may likewise be granted to persons who engage in a self-employed occupation." Article 4 lays down the field of intervention of the ESF; it

"may contribute when the situation in the labour market:
—is affected, or threatens so to be, either by special measures adopted by the Council within the framework of Community policies, or by measures agreed by common accord to further the objectives of the Community, or

234

—makes a specific common action appear necessary for better ensuring a balance of manpower supply and demand within the Community."

Council decisions granting aid are to be taken by a qualified majority on a proposal from the Commission, and are to be based in particular on the fact that

" the imbalance, observed or foreseeable, in the labour market:
—is of a scale justifying Community intervention,
—is of such a nature as to involve, or be capable of involving, for a considerable number of workers, the necessity either to change employment or to acquire new qualifications, or to move home within the Community."

Thus the Fund may act in a situation where unemployment would otherwise result. By Article 5 the Fund may also contribute

" when the situation in the labour market is affected, in certain regions, in certain branches of the economy or in certain groups of undertakings, by difficulties which do not arise from a special measure taken by the Council within the framework of Community policy, but which proceed indirectly from the operation of the common market or which impede the harmonious development of the Community."

Specific references are made to the eradication of long-term structural unemployment and underemployment. This Article reflects the provisions of Article 56 (2) of the ECSC Treaty, in that the Fund may act in situations where an employment problem has been created by forces completely outside any Community action, e.g. technological developments and the like. Article 8 maintains the level of assistance granted by the new ESF at 50 per cent. of the total cost of the project (cf. Art. 125 (1) of the Treaty), but it permits assistance to be granted to private corporations and other bodies, if they are guaranteed by the public authorities of the Member States on condition of an equal contribution from the public authority.

24–15 Assistance is to be granted on the basis of schemes submitted to the Commission (Art. 6). These schemes are to be submitted to the Economic and Social Committee for examination. The Commission is then to approve the schemes, within the scope of the credits available, if they comply with the conditions determined in the implementing Regulation. Implementing Regulations 2396/71, 2397/71 and 2398/71, J.O. 1971, L 249/54, 58 and 61, were issued on November 8, 1971, pursuant to Article 127, which provides for the issue of implementing provisions by the Council by a qualified majority on a proposal from the Commission and after consulting the Economic and Social Committee.

24–16 Regulation 2396 defines the type of operation which may qualify for financial assistance from the Fund; these are schemes which:

(a) aim at solving regional problems of slow development or decline;

(b) facilitate adaptation of employment to technical progress;

(c) counteract employment problems in declining industries.

Of the money which is available to the ESF, Article 2 of the regulation lays down that 60 per cent. of the credits shall be reserved for operations to eliminate long-term structural employment or underemployment in backward or declining regions.

Regulation 2397 lists the possible categories of ESF expenditure; these include the organisation of training courses and facilities, resettlement allowances, and aids for the employment and training of handicapped persons.

Article 9 of Regulation 2396 amplifies the role of the Committee of the ESF, provided for by Article 124 of the Treaty and originally constituted according to rules made on August 25 1960 (J.O. 1960, 1201). Two representatives each from the Government, trade unions and employers' associations, of each Member State form the membership of the Committee, whose original sole task was to help the Commission administer the Fund. Regulation 2396, Article 9, lays down that the Committee must now be consulted on any important question concerning the activity of the Fund, and it may, on its own initiative, submit opinions to the Commission. Article 10 obliges the Commission to consult the Committee on seven specific issues, including all proposals for the working of the Fund, all proposals directed at opening fields for intervention, applications for assistance submitted for approval and the possibility of amendment of the regulation. Thus the previously purely technical Committee has acquired a more active and innovatory role in the administration and forward planning of the Fund.

The entry into force of the decision and subsequent Regulations was scheduled for January 1, 1972, but this was subject to the necessary financial rules having been made. They were in fact made by Regulation 858/72, J.O. 1972, L 101/3, which did not come into force until May 1, 1972.

Article 128

24-17   Article 128 provides that the Council is to lay down general principles for the implementation of a common vocational training policy; however, this common policy cannot fairly be compared with the other common policies, such as agriculture, transport and the commercial policy. The obligation on the Council was to lay down only the general principles for such a common policy, and this was done by Decision 63/266, J.O. 1963, 1338. The decision lists ten such principles; the first principle contains a definition of a common vocational training policy as meaning " a coherent and progressive common action which entails that each Member State shall draw up programmes and ensure that these are put into effect in accordance with the General Principles " contained in the decision. Further, " it shall be the responsibility of the

Member States and the competent bodies of the Community to apply such General Principles within the framework of the Treaty." The second principle indicates the objectives of the policy as being generally to ensure the correct and adequate operation of training facilities and, *inter alia*, to promote basic and advanced vocational training and where appropriate, retraining, suitable to the various stages of working life. The third principle refers to the importance of training as well as to the forecasting and information services. The fourth, fifth and sixth principles indicate that the role of the Commission in this matter is to initiate measures, to carry out research, to encourage direct exchanges of information, and to collate information. The Commission is assisted in these tasks by a Tripartite Advisory Committee. The seventh principle indicates that the training of teachers and instructors should be developed, while the eighth principle envisages the eventual harmonisation of levels of vocational training, to facilitate the eventual interchange between Member States of qualified personnel. The tenth principle states that the financing of measures taken to implement the common vocational training policy may be jointly undertaken.

The principles have on the whole not been implemented, although the common programme for young workers of May 8, 1964, J.O. 1964, 1226, defines measures on training policies. The moves towards harmonisation of professional qualifications (§ 25–13, *infra*) taken especially in the field of freedom of establishment may be seen as an implementation of the eighth principle.

CHAPTER 25

RIGHT OF ESTABLISHMENT AND FREEDOM TO PROVIDE SERVICES

25–01 ALTHOUGH Title III of the Treaty of Rome is headed " The free movement of persons, services and capital," the title is in fact broken down into four individual chapters, between them covering the three freedoms involved, namely

(1) workers (Arts. 48 to 51);
(2) right of establishment (Arts. 52 to 58);
(3) services (Arts. 59 to 66);
(4) capital (Arts. 67 to 75).

The free movement of workers was discussed in the preceding chapter, the free movement of capital will be discussed in the next. It is with establishment and services, closely linked notions that this chapter is concerned.

25–02   The right of establishment (Arts. 52 to 58) is economically and legally speaking the right for a person or body, corporate or unincorporate, bearing the nationality of one State to cross into another State, and establish himself or itself there either by undertaking work from a permanent base, or by establishing an agency, branch, subsidiary etc.

The freedom to provide services (covered by Articles 59 to 66 of the Treaty) is the freedom to undertake a task for a person resident in one State from an established base in another State. This may be undertaken in one of three ways—

(a) the person who provides the service lives in State A, but travels to State B and performs the service there, *e.g.* a doctor travels from England to France to treat a sick patient;
(b) the person giving the service supplies it from State A, where he lives, across the border to State B, without, however, going there, *e.g.* a doctor established in England sends a diagnosis and prescription to a patient in France, both parties remaining in their respective countries;
(c) the recipient of the services travels from State B to State A where the person furnishing the service performs the necessary task, *e.g.* the sick Frenchman goes to see his doctor in England.

Case (a) in fact resembles the right of establishment in all but the degree of permanence of residence in the second State, and is the most important type of service treated by the chapter on services.

Case (b) may involve the transfer of processed goods and thus involve the dispositions on free movement of goods (Arts. 9 to 37) or on agriculture (Arts. 38 to 47) and the remuneration for the services provided involves the so-called fifth freedom, or freedom of payment outlined in Article 106 EEC Treaty.

Cases (a) and (b) are clearly catered for by the Treaty. The terms of Article 59 appear to cover case (c) also, and it is noteworthy that the General Programme on Services, (J.O. 1962, 32 (discussed *infra*)) refers to indirect restrictions on services which relate to the recipient of the services or the type of service (Title III: first para.). *Cf.* also Article 1 (1) of Directive 64/221, J.O. 1964, 850.

The difference between establishment and the provision of services is, in the context of the Treaty only slight, primarily involving questions of duration of residence in the receiving State. The similarity between the chapter on establishment and the chapter on services is emphasised by Article 66 in the latter chapter, which applies Articles 55 to 58 from the former to services.

RIGHT OF ESTABLISHMENT (ARTICLES 52 TO 58)

Article 52

25–03   Article 52, first para., states the basic principle that restrictions on the freedom of establishment of nationals of a Member State in the territory of another Member State were to be abolished by progressive stages in the course of the transitional period. This progressive abolition was also to apply to restrictions on the setting up of agencies, branches or subsidiaries in one Member State by nationals of another Member State.

The second paragraph of Article 52 makes it clear that freedom of establishment includes the right to take up self-employed occupations and to set up and manage undertakings, subject to applicable municipal laws of the host State, and to the provisions of the chapter relating to capital.

The persons who benefit from the freedom of establishment are, it is clear, totally different from those benefiting from the provisions on free movement of labour, for the former are essentially self-employed, while the latter are essentially employees. It is thought that the second paragraph of Article 52 goes much wider than the professions, although it has nowhere been defined. Article 52 evidently also includes employed management, for these persons are not regarded as labour by national legislation.

Beneficiaries

25–04   Prior to the drawing up of the Treaty of Rome most of the restrictions on establishment in force in the Member States were based on nationality. Thus only a Frenchman could practise at the French Bar. It was therefore natural that the right of establishment should be extended to *nationals* of other Member States. With respect to individuals, there is no difficulty in ascertaining nationality, but for legal persons it was deemed necessary to provide a rule for identification of potential beneficiaries. This is to be found in Article 58, which lays down a double criterion: undertakings which are incorporated in a Member State and have their " *siège social* " or administrative seat in a Member State are to be treated in the same way as natural persons who are nationals of Member States (see further *infra*).

Freedom of establishment involves for Community nationals various rights to take up and pursue activities under the same conditions as are laid down by domestic law for local subjects. But freedom of establishment differs from the freedom to provide services in that the person providing the services must not only be a Community national, but must also be established in one of the Member States.

The measures which restrict freedom of establishment and which are required to be abolished are those based on nationality, although a State may still maintain a nationalised monopoly for a particular industry or trade.

The principle of freedom of establishment is subjected by Article 52, second para., to the provisions relating to the free movement of capital, which is in theory an important restriction, since it is difficult to set up an establishment in another Member State without some transfer of capital. The restrictions on the movement of capital for investment purposes were, however, lifted before the adoption of measures to free establishment (by Directive of May 11, 1960, J.O. 1960, 921).

Article 52 required restrictions on establishment to be removed by the end of the transitional period. Progress has been slow because of the complexity of the subject, and much remains to be achieved. It is extremely doubtful whether the Article could now be considered to be directly applicable.

Article 53

25-05   Article 53 is a standstill clause, prohibiting the introduction of any new restrictions on the right of establishment of Community nationals, save as otherwise provided in the Treaty. In contrast to Article 52, Article 53 enunciates a clear and unconditional rule, which is complete and legally perfect. The latter Article was held to be directly applicable in 6/64, *Costa* v. *ENEL*, Rec. X 1141, [1964] C.M.L.R. 425.

Article 54

25-06   Article 54 lays down the timetable and the means of implementation of the general principle of the right of establishment, outlined in Article 52. By Article 54 (1) the Council, acting unanimously on a proposal from the Commission and after consulting the Economic and Social Committee and the Assembly, was to draw up a general programme for the abolition of restrictions on the freedom of establishment before the end of the first stage. This was done on December 18, 1961

(J.O. 1962, 36). A general programme is not one of the instruments mentioned in Article 189 * of the Treaty as having binding force, and cannot of itself create obligations binding on the Member States or on individuals. However, it is generally considered that the programme obliges the Community institutions to adhere to its provisions. The programme has not, however, been executed according to its own timetable, and much remains to be done.

Article 54 (1), second sub-para. requires the programme to set out the general conditions under which freedom of establishment was to be attained in the case of each type of activity and in particular the stages by which it was to be attained. The programme was drawn up having regard to those activities bearing most closely on the customs union— cf. Article 54 (3) (a)—the remaining part of transitional period was divided into portions of two years each, 1962–63, 1964–65, 1966–67, 1968 to the end of transition on December 31, 1969 (Title IV). During each of these periods certain activities were to be liberalised, the main ones in the first period being those activities relating to wholesaling and indus-try; in the second period, retailing and food; in the third and fourth periods, the liberal professions.

The Community is to implement the programme on the right of establishment by means of Council directives (Art. 54 (2) of the Treaty). Directives are the obvious tool here since the crux of the operation envisaged is a co-ordination of national rules on the particular subject, rather than the promulgation of directly applicable rules.

25–07   Article 54 (3) of the Treaty lists eight specific rules or priorities to be taken into account in adopting measures. The first three, (a) to (c), are mere elaborations upon the general principle in Article 52 of the elimination of restrictions on the freedom of establishment of Com-munity nationals requiring:

(a) priority examination and treatment of activities contributing to the development of Community trade;

(b) the achievement of close co-operation between competent authorities;

(c) the abolition of obstacles to freedom of establishment.

Article 54 (3) (d) requires the Community to ensure that provision is made enabling workers of one Member State employed in the territory of another Member State to remain in that territory for the purpose of taking up a self-employed occupation.

This principle is implemented in part by Directive 63/261, J.O. 1963, 1323, for agricultural workers who had lived and worked in another Member State for at least two years.

Article 54 (3 (e) calls for action to facilitate acquisition and use by nationals of one Member State of land or buildings situated in the territory of another Member State. Restrictions on land holding by aliens related particularly to agricultural holdings, and it is to this type of restriction that the sub-paragraph is primarily directed, but action taken under the sub-paragraph is not to conflict with Article 39 (2) which requires account to be taken of the nature and structure of agriculture in working out the CAP. Directive 67/530, J.O. 1967, 190/1 relating to the transfer of agricultural holdings, Directive 67/531, J.O. 1967, 190/3 relating to rural leases and Directive 67/532, J.O. 1967, 190/5 relating to access to co-operatives, were all issued in implementation of sub-paragraph (c).

In providing for the removal of restrictions in any given sector, the Council and the Commission are required by Article 54 (3) (f) to deal also with restrictions on the setting up of agencies etc., and with restrictions on the entry of personnel from the main establishment into managerial or supervisory posts in such agencies etc. This latter stipulation implicitly recognises that management does not fall to be considered under the heading of workers.

25–08 Article 54 (3) (g), relating to the co-ordination of safeguards built into corporate structures for the protection of members and others, is of wider application than its terms would suggest. This provision is the cornerstone of co-ordinating measures taken in the field of company law (see more generally Chapter 31, infra).

Article 54 (3) (h) requires the Council and the Commission to satisfy themselves that the conditions of establishment are not distorted by aids granted by Member States. A directive in the agricultural sector is so far the only legislative measure promulgated having regard to this provision (Directive 68/415, J.O. 1968, L 308/17).

Article 55

25–09 Article 55, first para. constitutes an exception to the general provisions on the liberalisation of restrictions on establishment, stating that those provisions are not to apply to activities which are, in any given state, connected even occasionally with the exercise of official authority.

Article 55, second para. enables the Council, acting by a qualified majority on a proposal from the Commission, to except other activities from the chapter. This facility has not so far been used.

The first paragraph of Article 55 is similar to Article 48 (4), excepting employment in the public service from the provisions on free movement of workers. But the former is much more broadly based, excepting as it does whole activities where their exercise has even an occasional official flavour. The provision could potentially lead to absurd results, and has in any case led to great difficulty in working out principles of freedom of establishment for lawyers. In practice the term " activity " has here been narrowly construed, however, and it is admitted in principle, for example, that lawyers have a right of establishment in other Member States, but cannot discharge particular functions which would constitute the exercise of " official authority." Thus Article 4 (2) of Directive 64/224, J.O. 1964, 869, excepts activities involving enforced auction of goods in France from the general freedom of establishment. Article 55 has not been referred to directly in such directives, however.

Article 56

5–10   Article 56 constitutes a permanent exception to the general principle of the right of establishment in Article 52, as does Article 55, first para., but whereas Article 55 acts to exclude specific categories from the general principles of freedom of establishment, Article 56 allows national rules providing for the special treatment of aliens on grounds of public policy, public security or public health to prevail over the general Community rule providing for freedom of establishment. It would appear that this exception has a double-edged application—it may be used against particular individuals, or it may be used to reserve certain activities to nationals of the Member State applying the Article; this would operate to exclude foreign nationals from, for example, activities concerning national defence. It may be argued that Article 223 (1) (*b*), enabling Member States to take measures considered necessary for the protection of the essential interests of their security connected with the production of ordnance, covers at least some of the ground, but would not cover, for example, certain aspects of nuclear energy production.

Article 56 (2) does not allow Member States to maintain their individual discriminatory rules regarding public policy untouched, but subjects them to a process of co-ordination by directive. Co-ordination of these measures was undertaken by Directive 64/221, J.O. 1964, 850, which applies to establishment and to free movement of workers and services (Art. 1). It applies to beneficiaries of the various types of liberalisation and to spouses and members of the family benefiting under any Regulations or directives adopted in these areas. The directive goes some way towards providing a limitative list of the situations in which Article 56 (1) may be invoked, and also places limitations on deportation and curtailment of stay.

5–11   No measures may be taken under the guise of public policy solely for economic ends (Art. 2 (2)) and Article 3 constitutes a condensed Community equivalent to the European Convention on Human Rights:

> " 1. Measures taken on grounds of public policy or of public security shall be based exclusively on the personal conduct of the individual concerned.

> " 2. Previous criminal convictions shall not in themselves constitute grounds for the taking of such measures."

(This latter provision was applied in *Corveleyn* v. *Etat Belge*, 1969 C.D.E., 343, to enable a convicted Frenchwoman to remain in Belgium (and see *infra*).)

" 3. Expiry of the identity card or passport used by the person concerned to enter the host country and to obtain a residence permit shall not justify expulsion from the territory.

" 4. The State which issued the identity card or passport shall allow the holder of such document to re-enter its territory without any formality even if the document is no longer valid or the nationality of the holder is in dispute."

Article 4 refers to an annexed list of diseases and disabilities which may be invoked for refusing entry to a Member State on health grounds. The list is expressed to be limitative. The diseases referred to are (a) diseases which might endanger public health, namely quarantinable diseases within the meaning of WHO Regulation 2 of May 25, 1951 and (b) diseases and disabilities which might threaten public policy or security, namely drug addiction and profound mental disturbance.

Articles 5 to 9 guarantee certain administrative and procedural safeguards to persons involved in a dispute regarding a refusal of entry etc. on one of the three grounds of public policy, security or health. A person must be notified of the result of his application for a first residence permit within six months (Art. 5); if his application is refused, he must be informed of the grounds on which the decision was taken (Art. 6); a person must be given at least fifteen days' notice of refusal to grant or to renew a permit, or of expulsion (Art. 7), and will have the local legal remedies against such a decision (Art. 8).

Article 57

25–12   Article 57 constitutes the second method of achieving freedom of establishment within the Community. It provides for the mutual recognition of qualifications, as opposed to the elimination of national restrictions on establishment as defined in Article 52. The two methods of attacking the problem are of course complementary, but it is generally considered that the more that can be achieved by co-ordination, the easier will be the task of eliminating national restrictions. Indeed this is recognised explicitly at least for the medical and allied and pharmaceutical professions, for Article 57 (3) states that for these professions " the progressive abolition of restrictions shall be dependent upon co-ordination of the conditions for their exercise in the various Member States." Article 57 envisages the issue of directives by the Council, acting now by a qualified majority on a proposal from the Commission and after consulting the Assembly, first to ensure " the mutual recognition of diplomas, certificates and other evidence of formal qualifications " (Art. 57 (1)), and secondly to co-ordinate the provisions in each Member State "concerning the taking up and pursuit of activities as self-employed persons" (Art. 57 (2)). The co-ordination referred to here is again to be effected by directives, issued by the Council acting on a proposal from the Commission and after consulting the Assembly. Where the subject-matter of the draft directive is the subject of legislation in at least one Member State, or relates to the protection of savings, in particular the granting of credit and the exercise of the banking profession, or to the medical and allied, and pharmaceutical profession, the Council is to act unanimously. In other cases the Council was to act unanimously during the first stage of the original period of transition, and now by qualified majority.

The two solutions for the problem of freeing establishment, that of Article 52 (elimination of restrictions) and Article 57 (co-ordination of measures regarding access to activities) are intermeshed by the General Programme, as well as by Article 57 (3) of the Treaty. Thus Title IV of the General Programme, which sets out the timetable for the elimination of restrictions, is in practice taken with the provisions of Title V, requiring the process of elimination of restrictions to be preceded, accompanied or followed by the co-ordination of qualifications for activities. Title V also makes provision for a transitional régime before full co-ordination of measures in order to facilitate access to activities. For some activities co-ordination alone, without simultaneous elimination of national restrictions, may hinder the freeing of establishment too greatly, so that a transitional period is desirable. The directives which have been issued on the freedom of establishment have normally been issued two at a time, one on the achievement of freedom of establishment and the other on a transitional period for the co-ordination of qualifications, e.g. Directives 68/363, J.O. 1968, L 260/1, and 68/364, J.O. 1968, L 260/6, concerning self-employed persons in the retail trade.

In relation to certain activities, and notably the liberal professions, no elimination of restrictions can usefully take place until the qualifications for entry to the profession concerned have been sufficiently co-ordinated. Since this latter task is extremely complex and requires a complete evaluation of the qualifications in a particular profession, progress towards the overall freedom of establishment for the liberal professions has been slow, notwithstanding that the Commission has since 1967 made a number of proposals in this field.

Article 58

25–13   Article 58 amplifies the definition of the beneficiaries of freedom of establishment in Article 52, providing that:

> "Companies or firms formed in accordance with the law of a Member State and having their registered office [*siège statutaire*],

central administration or principal place of business within the Community shall, for the purposes of [the chapter on establishment] be treated in the same way as natural persons who are nationals of Member States."

This definition employs all three of the tests by which the nationality of firms and companies may be determined, in addition to the basic test of incorporation. The definition was in effect revised and restricted both by the Convention on Mutual Recognition of Companies and Bodies Corporate of February 28, 1968 (supp. to Bulletin 2, 1969), and the General Programme on the Freedom of Establishment (J.O. 1962, 36). This latter states in Title I that where a company has only a registered office within the Community, its activities must have an effective and continuous link with the economy of the Member State if it is to benefit from the right of establishment. This provision is paralleled by similar provisions in various types of commercial treaties concluded by individual States, *e.g.* air services agreements and double taxation conventions.

SERVICES

Article 59

25–14 Article 59 provides for the progressive abolition of restrictions on freedom to provide services within the Community in respect of " nationals of Member States who are established in a State of the Community other than that of the person for whom the services are intended." This phrase makes clear the distinction between a right of establishment, which permits movement to the State where the service or activity is to be performed or carried out, and freedom to provide services, which generally involves retaining an establishment in one State, and effecting the service in another State (but see *supra,* § 25–02).

The second paragraph of Article 59 enables the Council, acting unanimously on a proposal from the Commission, to extend the provisions of the chapter on services to nationals of third countries established within the Community. There is no parallel provision in the chapter on establishment. This apparent lacuna is explained upon analysis by the fact that Article 59, second para., grants only a secondary right; the prerequisite for its exercise is establishment within the Community. The existence of this secondary right is thus dependent upon the prior acceptance by another Member State of the potential beneficiary as an established person in its territory. Admission of nationals of third States to establishment, without more, would eliminate any element of prior selection, such as is inherent in the provisions of Article 59. The distinction is nevertheless as yet academic, for the power has not yet been used.

Article 60

5–15   Article 60 provides that services shall be considered to be " services " within the meaning of the Treaty where they are normally provided for remuneration in so far as they are not governed by any of the other freedoms of the Treaty, *i.e.* goods, persons and capital; thus the provisions on services will apply to a particular situation only if the provisions on free movement of workers or on the right of establishment in particular are inapplicable.   Where the activity in question shows aspects of more than one freedom, however, the provisions of the Treaty relating to the predominant aspect will apply.

Article 61

5–16   Article 61 restricts the operation of the chapter on services in two distinct fields. Article 61 (1) excepts the provision of services in the field of transport from the chapter; these are dealt with in the chapter on transport (see generally § 27–01, *infra*). Article 61 (2) requires the freeing of banking and insurance services to be co-ordinated with the freeing of restrictions on capital, in so far as they relate to the movement of capital. The General Programme for services (J.O. 1962, 32, discussed below) envisaged elimination of restrictions on banking services not linked to the movement of capital by the end of 1965 (a target which was not met). Since the elimination of restrictions on the movement of capital has also been slow, the freeing of the related banking services has yet to be accomplished.

Capital movements are less likely to affect insurance except in the field of life assurance.   Community activity on insurance has been directed primarily to co-ordination of the laws governing it: this has yet to be accomplished.   The only directive adopted so far in the field of insurance is Directive 64/225, J.O. 1964, 878, relating to establishment and provision of services in the field of re-insurance and retrocession.   However, work has been continuing since 1960 with a view to providing for freedom of establishment and the provision of services for the insurance industry generally.   Particular problems of establishment are:

(a) the need to harmonise the national requirements for technical reserves (reserves held in the country where insurance liabilities are to be met); and

(b) the need to harmonise liquidity margins (assets required to be held free in a certain proportion to annual premium income, over and above technical reserves). The proposed figure has been around 17 per cent., higher than the 10 per cent. margin now required under English law.

The particular problems of insurance services are probably more fundamental than those of establishment in general, in that certain areas of contract law need to be harmonised before freedom can be achieved. A settled conflicts rule will be necessary for the solution of intra-Community insurance claims, in particular because of the wide range of fora now available under the Convention on Jurisdiction and Enforcement of Judgments (as to which see generally *infra*, § 32–23). Furthermore, taxes levied on insurance policies differ from State to State (running as high as 30 per cent. of the premium in France, unlike the United Kingdom, where no tax is imposed on the policy itself, brokerage fees and the income of insurance companies being taxed in the normal way).

Article 62

25–17   Article 62 is very similar to the standstill provisions of Article 53 in the chapter on establishment and is of the same legal effect.

Article 63

25–18   Article 63 is similar in import to Article 54 in the establishment chapter in that it indicates, for the field of services, the same series of Community measures to be taken for the freeing of the provision of services, and specifies some of the priorities to be taken into account. In common with Article 54, Article 63 makes provision for a general programme to be drawn up. This was done at the same time as the General Programme on establishment and its provisions are basically the same and, indeed, it refers to the timetable of abolition of restrictions contained in that Programme (see J.O. 1962, 32). The General Programme for services is similarly to be implemented by directives (Art. 63 (2) of the Treaty).

As regards the proposals envisaged, Article 63 (3) requires priority to be given as a general rule to those services which directly affect production costs or the liberalisation of which helps to promote trade in goods.

Article 64

25–19   By Article 64, the Member States declare their readiness to undertake the liberalisation of services beyond the extent required by the directives issued pursuant to Article 63 (2), if their general economic situation and the situation of the economic sector concerned so permit. To this end the Commission is to make recommendations to the Member States concerned. No such declaration is contained in the chapter on establishment, evidently because such liberalisation was not considered realistic in respect of that chapter. In common with the similar Article 71, second para. and Article 106 (1), second sub-para., however, Article 64 has never been used.

Article 65

25–20   Article 65 serves as an adjunct to the standstill provision of Article 62, providing as it does for non-discriminatory application of national restrictions until full freedom of services is established. Thus Member States may not apply more restrictive conditions to the provision of services by nationals or residents of one Member State than they do to those of another. Conversely the application of more favourable conditions to nationals or residents of one Member State than to those of the others is similarly prohibited.

It is generally considered that Article 65 does not require the extension to the other Member States of any liberalisation granted in the framework of Benelux or the BLEU which goes beyond that effected by the Treaty or in the context of the Treaty.

Article 66

5–21   Article 66 applies to services Articles 55 to 58 in the chapter on establishment, which are mainly concerned with the co-ordination of legislative measures relating to establishment. The application of Article 58 (companies) to services was revised and restricted in the General Programme on services, in the same way that this was done in the General Programme on establishment (*supra*).

The implementation of the Treaty provisions on establishment and services has proceeded in roughly the order stipulated in the General Programmes; wholesale and retail activities, industry, commerce and small crafts, agriculture, mining and prospecting, public service activities, film and catering have now been liberalised to a great extent. For the reasons given above, the greatest delay exists in legislation for freeing the so-called liberal professions.

5–22   A particular problem in the field of establishment and the provision of services is that of public works contracts. Since work to be performed on behalf of governments or governmental agencies now forms a very substantial part of the total capital expenditure in any country, the reservation of contracts for this work to nationals of the State in which the work is to be performed constitutes not only a non-tariff barrier to trade but also a discrimination against establishment and the free provision of services. The problem was recognised by the Community quite early; the first proposals on this subject were made in 1964 (Bulletin, Supp. 9/10, 1964, p. 12) but it was only in 1971 that two directives on the subject were issued. The first, 71/304, J.O. 1971, L 185/1, relates to the abolition of restrictions on freedom to provide services in the field of public works contracts and the award of public works contracts through the intermediary of agencies and subsidiaries. The directive was adopted on the legal basis of Articles 54 (2) and 63 (2)—the general implementing provisions of the establishment and services chapters. Article 1 states the aim of general abolition of discrimination against non-nationals and Article 3 (1) (c) particularly emphasises that discriminatory technical specifications in contracts, though applicable irrespective of nationality, shall be abolished. This would relate especially to the specification in a contract for the use of patented materials or devices.

The second directive, 71/305, J.O. 1971, L 185/5, aims at the co-ordination of procedures for the award of public contracts, and is based on Articles 57 (2), 66 and 100. It lays down elaborate provisions dependent on the size of the contract and the procedure to be adopted for publicising the contract, but the key provision is that any government contract worth more than 1 million u.a. must be publicised in the *Official Journal,* and that any firm registered in a Member State of the Community is eligible to tender for it. The directive entered into force on July 1, 1972.

25–23   The overall effect of the Treaty provisions on establishment and services and the subsequent legislation has been to establish the framework on which further measures for the elimination of restrictions and the co-ordination of professional qualifications can be based. The principles of establishment and services were amplified by the General Programmes which indicate priorities and timetables for implementing measures. Many specific directives have been and are still being drawn up on the basis of the General Programmes. The main work in co-ordination of the conditions of access to and exercise of professions is being carried out on the basis of Article 57, although as yet results are slight. Certain specific provisions of the Treaty envisaged special dispositions, *e.g.* Article 56 (2), which contemplates a co-ordination of provisions discriminating on grounds of public policy etc. This co-ordination was effected by Directive 64/221, J.O. 1964, 850. Restrictions on movement and residence within the Community were to be abolished on the basis of Directive 64/220, J.O. 1964, 845. It is similar in terms and operation to the directive of the same date for the benefit of workers, which was subsequently replaced by Directive 68/360, J.O. 1968, L 257/13 (see § 23–05). The directive on freedom of movement for establishment and services is a necessary administrative forerunner of any specific measures freeing establishment and services for a particular profession. It allows for entry for the purposes of establishment and the provision of services of beneficiaries, their spouses, minor children and dependent relatives on production of a valid identity card or passport (Arts. 1 and 2). Article 3 requires the issue of a residence permit to each such person, valid for at least five years and automatically renewable, the right of residence extending throughout the territory of the Member State concerned (Art. 4).

FREEDOM OF PAYMENTS

25–24 The other measures of general application relate to services alone and concern freedom of payments, without which the freedom to provide services would be worthless. The Article of the Treaty dealing with this question is Article 106, located in the chapter on balance of payments. The Article is somewhat misplaced in such a chapter, since, as the Article itself acknowledges, it effectively constitutes a freedom of its own, complementing the operation of the free movement of goods, services and capital. But the burden of implementing the Article is placed on the Member States themselves as it is in the other Articles concerned with economic policy, rather than upon the Community institutions, which share the task of implementing the four other freedoms. Paragraph 1, first sub-para., contains an undertaking on the part of Member States to authorise in the appropriate currencies, any payments connected with the movement of goods, services or capital and also any connected transfers of capital and earnings. This undertaking applies only, however, to the extent that the movement of goods, services or capital has been liberalised. The second sub-paragraph contains a declaration of intention to undertake further liberalisation than that required, if possible (*cf. supra*, § 25–19).

25–25   In so far as movements of goods, services and capital are hindered only by restrictions on related payments, paragraph 2 requires such restrictions to be abolished by application of the measures relating to goods, services and capital. Article 106 (2) contains no power to issue directives for this purpose, but such a measure was envisaged by the General Programme on services (Title V B). Directive 63/340, J.O. 1963, 1609 based on Article 63 and Article 106 (2), requires such restrictions to be abolished, and Member States are to grant all foreign exchange authorisations needed for the transfer of such payments (Art. 1).

The directive does not apply to transport services, nor does it apply to foreign exchange allowances for tourists (Art. 3 of the directive), but many of the restrictions had already been eliminated by Member States, so the effect of the directive was only of a residual nature.

Article 106 (3) of the Treaty requires Member States not to introduce any new restrictions on transfers connected with the invisible transactions listed in Annex III (Cmnd. 4864, p. 110) which includes freight charges, commission fees, subscriptions, claims for damages etc. Some of these are covered by the dispositions in paragraphs 1 and 2 and some by the chapter on the free movement of capital, but the others are to be abolished along the lines laid down in the chapter on services. Certain of these, notably bank charges, membership fees and fines, were dealt with by Directive 63/474, J.O. 1963, 2240, requiring Member States to enable the transfers relating to such transactions to be made at the exchange rates prevailing for payment relating to current transactions.

By 1964 an almost complete liberalisation of payments had been achieved by virtue of a combination of Article 67 (2), Directive 63/340 and Directive 63/474, except in the field of transport, and for tourist allowances.

CHAPTER 26

CAPITAL

26–01 THE free movement of capital, dealt with by Articles 67 to 73, together forming Chapter IV of Title III of Part Two of the Treaty, is the fourth of the four freedoms fundamental to the Community, but unlike the other three (free movement of goods, of persons and of services) this last freedom cannot be viewed in isolation, but rather must be considered as an adjunct to the other three, and as an aspect of Community economic policy which aims at the equalisation of opportunities and of competition throughout the territory of the Community.

26–02 The question of capital movements being closely connected with national economic policies, the obligation to liberalise those movements is primarily in the hands of the Member States, and probably creates no directly applicable rights for individuals. This is in line with the terms in which the stipulations of the title on Economic Policy (Arts. 103 to 116) are expressed. Part of that title, in particular the chapter on balance of payments (Arts. 104 to 109) relates also to free movement of capital. The powers relating specifically to capital movements contained in the Treaty as a whole are not sufficient to meet the needs of the Community and measures have been taken in this field under Article 100 (harmonisation of laws) to fill in some of the gaps (see generally Chap. 32, *infra*). The proposals for Economic and Monetary Union could, if implemented, lead to complete freedom of capital movement, and the responsibilities of the Community in this area would then be much greater than they are at present (see generally § 33–18, *infra*).

26–03 A two-fold approach is adopted for freeing capital movements; the first object of the chapter on capital is expressed to be the elimination of restrictions on movement of capital and discriminations based on nationality or residence or place of investment (Art. 67). This is complemented by a second object (set out in Art. 70) of co-ordinating the exchange policies of Member States *vis-à-vis* third countries with a view to avoiding the distortions and deflections of capital movements between the Community and third States, which would otherwise follow upon a simple dismantling of internal controls pursuant to Article 67.

Articles 67 to 73 do not define free movement of capital, nor do the implementing directives contain any such definition. But the lists, nomenclature and explanatory notes at the end of the First Directive for the implementation of Article 67 of May 11, 1960, J.O. 1960, 921, indicate what capital movements are covered by the directive and thus, indirectly, by the notion of free movement of capital.

It appears that the latter notion involves the abolition of exchange control restrictions, of any discriminatory laws and regulations regarding the nationality or residence of parties concerned and of any residual restrictions not necessarily discriminatory but which hinder capital flows. Capital includes both long-term direct investment capital, and short-term capital, invested in Treasury bills and other securities normally dealt in on the money market, and any capital falling in between these two extremes. The Community has, however, failed to free all types of capital movement, as will emerge below.

The obligation on Member States to abolish discrimination and restrictions affecting capital movement is limited under Article 67 " to the extent necessary to ensure the proper functioning of the Common Market." In practice, this has been accepted to mean that initiatives in this field will only follow progress in other fields. This is echoed by Article 5 (3) of the First Directive which states:

" The restrictions on capital movements under the rules for establishment in a Member State shall be abolished pursuant to this Directive *only in so far as it is incumbent upon the Member States to grant freedom of establishment in implementation of Articles 52 to 58 of the Treaty.*" (*Italics supplied.*)

Article 67

6–04   Article 67 (1) strikes at restrictions based on residence as well as on nationality. This is because national exchange control regulations are generally based on residence. The explanatory notes at the end of the First Directive leave to national exchange control regulations the definition of resident and non-resident status. The criterion of residence comprehends others besides " nationals," but nationals may of course be non-residents.

It is now generally accepted that besides residents of a State, all those persons established in that State, especially as defined by Article 58, benefit from the free movement of capital.

6–05   The First Directive implementing Article 67 (J.O. 1960, 921) issued under Article 69 is designed to secure the abolition of all restrictions on the movement of capital belonging to residents of Member States. A decision taken by the Council on the same day (J.O. 1960, 919) applies Articles 67 to 73 EEC to Algeria and the French overseas departments. The directive was modified slightly by Directive 63/21, J.O. 1963, 62.

In essence capital movements are divided into four groups. List A in the Annex to the directive comprehends capital movements such as direct investments, personal capital movements such as inheritances, short-term loans, sureties and transfers in performance of insurance contracts. Article 1 of the directive requires Member States to grant the foreign exchange authorisations necessary for such capital movements. An authorisation is still required to prevent fraudulent inclusion within this category of transactions properly outside it. Member States are required to authorise these capital movements at the normal exchange rates (Art. 1 (2)) and the Monetary Committee (set up under Art. 105 EEC) is entrusted with the task of following the parity movements so as to ensure that no disparities occur.

26–06   List B covers the acquisition of securities quoted on a stock exchange; Article 2 of the directive allows complete freedom in respect of such transactions and transfers, but without the monetary conversion safeguard incorporated in Article 1 (2). Member States have a duty merely " to endeavour to ensure that transfers are made at rates which do not show appreciable and lasting differences from those ruling for payments relating to current transactions."

List C relates to movements such as the issue of shares on a stock exchange, or the acquisition of securities not quoted on a stock exchange, and to the granting of long and medium-term commercial loans and to sureties in respect of long and medium-term credits. Article 3 affords some liberalisation to such movements, but with the reservation that:

> " Where such free movement of capital might form an obstacle to the achievement of the economic policy objectives of a Member State, the latter may maintain or re-introduce the exchange restrictions on capital movements which were operative on the date of entry into force of this Directive. It shall consult the Commission on the matter." (Art. 3 (2).)

In practice, the liberalisation under Article 3 has only applied to the Netherlands, Italy and France, the other three original members of the Community having already abolished all restrictions on capital movements included in List C. But in no country does there exist a guaranteed rate of exchange for such transactions, such as is stipulated for in respect of List A transactions.

List D covers the remaining types of capital movement, *e.g.* those in short-dated Treasury paper and short-term credits, bank deposits and the like, personal capital movements, loans and sureties, as well as the physical import and export of financial assets (which would include tourist allowances). For these movements no liberalisation is required, but Article 6 requires Member States to endeavour not to introduce within the Community any new exchange restrictions affecting capital movements which were free at the date of entry into force of the directive, nor to make existing provisions more restrictive. This standstill provision is not a simple repetition of the standstill clause in Article 71, first para. of the Treaty, relating only to new (*i.e.* post-1957) restrictions, for the operative date here is that of the entry into force of the directive.

Article 5 of the directive permits Member States to verify the nature and bona fides of transactions and transfers, so that capital frauds may be kept in check. Their ability so to do, is, however, already implicit in the maintenance of authorisations even for movements in List A.

The second directive, Directive 63/21, J.O. 1963, 623, deletes a safe-guard provision relating to List B. The only country which took advantage of this was Italy. The second directive also amends and expands the lists so as to include, for example, transfers of workers' savings and annual transfers of blocked funds within List A. No further measures in relation to the abolition of restrictions on the movement of capital have been promulgated.

26–07 Article 67 (1) EEC provides further for the abolition of discrimination based on the place of investment of capital. Progress here has been slight. In April 1964 the Commission made proposals on the elimination of such discriminations, but these were not adopted, nor were its revised proposals of 1967. Progress in this field, which was said to be of paramount importance in the Segré Report (*The Development of a European Capital Market*, Commission, Brussels, November 1966), has been negligible.

Article 67 (2) concerns current payments connected with the movement of capital; restrictions on these payments were required to be abolished by the end of the first stage. Since these payments had already been liberalised by all the Member States in the context of the Bretton Woods Agreement of 1944 (Article VIII) this paragraph has never been of any significance.

Article 68

26–08 Article 68 (1), requiring Member States to be as liberal as possible in granting " such exchange authorisations as are still necessary after the entry into force of this Treaty " was originally designed as a safeguard against delayed issue of a directive implementing Article 67. Even now that the directives have been issued, this paragraph must be regarded as encouraging further voluntary liberalisation of exchange authorisations, although the more general terms of Article 71, second para., cover the same ground and more (see *infra*). Neither Article prohibits the re-introduction of restrictions, but Article 67 and Article 71, first para. place considerable limits on this.

Article 68 (2) requires the domestic rules governing the operation of the capital market and the credit system to be applied in a non-discriminatory manner to the movements of capital liberalised in accordance with the provisions of the chapter. These rules do not necessarily relate directly to capital movements, but may have that effect. If operated in a discriminatory fashion, these rules may come within the prohibition of Article 67 (1). Like paragraph 1, paragraph 2 of Article 68 sets out a rule of general application, not requiring implementation by directive. The obligation of non-discrimination is probably directly applicable.

Article 68 (3) constitutes a derogation from the principles of free movement of capital outlined in Article 67; under its provisions neither the Member States nor their public authorities may obtain financing through loans placed in another Member State without prior agreement of that State. The exception is limited to the raising of loans, there being no bar to capital transactions and transfers for other purposes, such as currency swap agreements or the financing of the institutions of the Community under Articles 207 and 208. Article 68 (3) is expressed not to preclude the European Investment Bank from borrowing on the capital markets of Member States, as provided for by Article 22 of the Protocol on its statute.

Article 69

26–09　　　Article 69 sets out the procedure for the issue of directives implementing the provisions of Article 67. These are issued by the Council acting now by qualified majority on a proposal from the Commission, which must in this case consult the Monetary Committee provided for in Article 105. It may be doubted whether the limitation, apparently built into Article 69, that the Council may issue only the " necessary " directives, adds anything to its normal power of discretion.

Article 70

26–10　　　Article 70 forms the other side of the two-fold approach to free movement of capital, providing for proposals from the Commission to the Council for directives on the progressive co-ordination of all aspects of exchange policies *vis-à-vis* third States. The directives are to be issued by unanimous vote. Clearly, a common attitude to movements of capital between the Community and third States is necessary if the benefits of internal free movement are not to be lost, but there is now felt to be a need for something more than simple co-ordination, although, in issuing the directives the Council is required to endeavour to attain the highest possible degree of liberalisation (Art. 70 (1)).

Paragraph 2 of Article 70 contemplates the situation where differences remain in the exchange policies of Member States despite measures taken under paragraph 1. It permits a Member State to take appropriate safeguard measures after consulting with the other Member States and with the Commission, if the free circulation rules lead to capital movement deflection.

26–11　　　The question arises in connection with Article 70 (2) whether the capital deflection can be merely apprehended or has to be actual before a Member State may take appropriate safeguard measures. The phrase used in the English text, " could lead persons . . . to use," seems to suggest that there need only be a potential risk, as does the French " *inciteraient . . . à utiliser*," but the German " *Benutzen* " seems to require some concrete evidence of deflection. Nevertheless, the consultation requirement restricts the use of such safeguards, and should the Council find that the measures taken by a particular Member State restrict the free movement of capital within the Community to an extent greater than that required to meet the situation, it may, acting by a qualified majority on a proposal from the Commission, decide that the State concerned shall amend or abolish the measures.

Council Directive 72/156, J.O. 1972, L 91/13, based on Articles 70 and 103 (conjunctural policy), is designed to regulate international financial flows and to neutralise their undesirable effects on internal liquidity. The directive authorises Member States to take powers to control deposits and interest rates on the money market, and to control loans which Community residents contract in non-Community countries; the directive also permits measures to be taken to control the net external liability of credit institutions and to fix compulsory reserve margins, in particular for the assets of non-residents.

Article 71

26–12   Article 71 acts as a standstill provision in respect of restrictions dealt with by Article 67. Member States are required by this Article to endeavour to avoid introducing any new exchange restrictions on movement of capital and associated current payments, and are also to endeavour not to make existing rules more restrictive. As far as the Article deals with current payments, it is of minor significance, since all restrictions on such had been abolished prior to the entry into force of the Treaty. The phrasing of the Article reflects the general level of obligation within this chapter; it does not lay down an absolute rule— Member States are only to *endeavour to avoid* introducing any new restrictions. The ambit of the Article has been cut down by the subsequent standstill clause contained in the First Directive (*supra*).

The second paragraph of Article 71 is similar to provisions found elsewhere in the Treaty, affording Member States the possibility of going beyond the degree of liberalisation of capital provided for in the preceding articles, in so far as their economic situation, in particular their balance of payments, permits. The Commission may, after consulting the Monetary Committee, make recommendations to Member States on this subject.

Article 72

6–13   By Article 72, Member States are required to keep the Commission informed of any movements of capital to and from third countries which come to their knowledge. Article 72 was intended to provide the source material on the basis of which to establish measures to be taken under both Articles 70 and 105. But in practice the Article has not proved very useful. Only those capital movements which come to the attention of the Member States have to be reported to the Commission—an implicit acceptance of the principle of bankers' secrecy. In 1965 the Commission made proposals for the issue of a decision to be taken on the basis of Article 213, which enables the Commission to be given powers to collect information necessary for the performance of its tasks, so that a uniform and obligatory rule regarding disclosure of information on capital movements could be issued. The proposal has not been adopted. The Commission is also empowered by Article 72 to give opinions on the subject of capital movements. (*Cf.* the general power to deliver opinions under Article 155, second hyphen.)

Article 73

26–14   Article 73 (1) requires the Commission to authorise Member States to take safeguard measures should capital movements lead to disturbances on the national capital markets. The conditions and details of these measures are laid down by the Commission itself, after consulting the Monetary Committee, subject only to amendment or revocation by the Council, acting by qualified majority. It will be noted that the Article 73 (1) safeguards are not confined to combating the disturbances brought on as a result of measures of liberalisation.

Article 73 (2) enables a Member State in difficulties to take measures unilaterally where this is justified on grounds of secrecy or urgency. It must, however, inform the Commission and the other Member States of such measures by the date of their entry into force at the latest, and the Commission may, after consulting the Monetary Committee, require the amendment or abolition of the measures taken. It is somewhat surprising that the Commission has the last word over the presumably more important matters dealt with under Article 73 (2), but not under Article 73 (1). It would appear that such a result may not have been intended.

Articles 108 and 109, which relate to safeguards where the balance of payments is threatened, are fairly similar to the provisions of Article 73, and indeed would be applicable were the disturbances such as to affect the balance of payments of a Member State (see § 33–15, *infra* for a discussion of these provisions).

The Act of Accession

26–15   The Act of Accession contains special dispositions in relation to capital movements for the United Kingdom and the other new Members of the Community in Articles 120 to 126. These lay down the periods within which the new Member States must comply with the Council's directives on capital movements. Under Article 124, the United Kingdom may maintain restrictions for two years on direct investments in the Community by United Kingdom residents, for two-and-a-half years on transfers of capital by United Kingdom residents who have emigrated and on gifts and endowments etc., and for up to five years on List B operations (stock exchange operations in foreign shares) by United Kingdom residents. It was announced in May 1972 that restrictions on capital movements would be relaxed at once for those going to settle in Community countries.

CHAPTER 27

TRANSPORT

27–01 THE provisions relating specifically to transport in the EEC Treaty are Article 61, and Title IV of Part Two of the Treaty—Policy of the Community—entitled " Transport " (Arts. 74 to 84).

Article 61 (1) states that " freedom to provide services in the field of transport shall be governed by the provisions of the Title relating to transport." The question arises as to the applicability of the Treaty in general to the specific area of transport. Article 61 is in the chapter on services, and since, economically speaking, transport constitutes a service, a provision in that chapter is necessary, if transport is to be exempted from its general provisions. This in itself suggests that the general rules are of application in the absence of specific provisions to the contrary. The title on transport contains provisions in relation to aids (Arts. 77, 80, 82), a matter also covered by parallel provisions in the chapter " Rules on competition " (Arts. 92 to 94). But there is little doubt that the existence of special rules on aids to transport does not inhibit or restrict the operation of the general rules; they thus apply in addition to the specific rules. (See as to transport and competition rules *infra*, § 27–27.)

There is other evidence to indicate that the rest of the Treaty is considered to be applicable to the transport sector; freedom of establishment in the transport industries was allowed for in the General Programme on services of December 18, 1961, J.O. 1962, 36, and taxation features of transport policy are considered under both the transport title and the chapter on taxation (Directive 68/297, J.O. 1968, L 175/15, was issued on the legal basis of Arts. 75 and 99). There is, however, no conclusive statement one way or the other.

ARTICLES 74 TO 84

Types of transport covered

27–02 Article 84 (1) states that the provisions of the transport title apply to rail, road and inland waterway transport. Paragraph 2 stipulates that the Council may decide whether, to what extent and by what procedure provisions may be laid down for sea and air transport. The juxtaposition of the two paragraphs suggests that the matters referred to in paragraph 2 are not covered already by paragraph 1, but it is nowhere made clear whether this is so. Further, Article 84 appears to exclude from its ambit other forms of transport, such as transport by hovercraft, pipeline or vacuum tube, but again there is no clear statement to this effect.

The Community of Six had relatively little need for a coherent policy relating to air and sea transport, its geographical structure making it largely unnecessary and thus no comprehensive provision has been made. The operative provision of Regulation 141/62, Article 4, which exempted transport in general from the rules on competition is still in force for such types of transport, although rules on competition now apply to inland transport by virtue of Regulation 1017/68 (*infra*, § 27–28). The Commission has now submitted a draft decision relating to air transport, which would empower the Commission to undertake initial studies on air transport questions (Com. (72) 695, final, J.O. 1972, C 110/6).

It is thought that the other Treaty provisions still apply to the whole of sea and air transport, except of course for the transport title and the chapter on rules of competition.

No doubt with the enlargement of the Community a common policy in relation to air and sea transport will be necessary, especially as the United Kingdom is a major world maritime power, and two of the three new Member States are at present accessible to the rest of the Community only by sea or air.

Article 74

27–03 Article 74 provides that the objectives of the Treaty are, in matters governed by the transport title, to be pursued by Member States in the framework of a common transport policy.

Article 75

27–04 Article 75 provides powers for the elaboration of the common transport policy mentioned above, and gives some indication of the contents of that policy. The Council, now acting by a qualified majority on Commission proposals and after consulting the Economic and Social Committee and the Parliament, lays down the basic rules " taking into account the distinctive features of transport." Article 75 (3) provides that where the application of Community transport provisions would be liable to have serious effect on the standard of living and employment in certain areas, and on the operation of transport facilities, they are to be adopted by the Council acting unanimously.

Article 75 (1) indicates two specific areas to be covered by the transport policy before the end of the transitional period, namely:

" (*a*) common rules applicable to international transport to or from the territory of a Member State or passing across the territory of one or more Member States;

" (*b*) the conditions under which non-resident carriers may operate transport services within a Member State."

The Council has also to lay down:

" (*c*) any other appropriate provisions."

This last clause has enabled the Community to develop the notion of transport policy. The Commission also based its arguments that it was for the Community to negotiate international transport agreements upon this very clause; the Court endorsed this view in 22/70, *Commission* v. *Council (AETR)*, Rec. XVII 263, [1971] C.M.L.R. 335. Article 75 has been used as the legal basis for most of the subsidiary legislation issued in the transport field, except where a specific provision exists elsewhere in the transport title, but the work so far done has been piecemeal. Paragraphs 1 (*a*) and (*b*) of Article 75 quoted above have not yet been implemented completely.

Article 76

27–05   Article 76 prohibits Member States from making their national transport legislation more restrictive *vis-à-vis* carriers from other Member States pending the introduction of common rules unless such measures are unanimously approved by the Council. To assist with the implementation of this standstill clause, the Council instituted a procedure for prior examination and consultation in respect of legislative changes proposed by Member States in the transport sector: Decision of March 21, 1962, J.O. 1962, 720. Under this decision, Member States proposing legislation which may interfere with the establishment of the common transport policy must notify the Commission and at the same time inform the other Member States of such an intention (Art. 1). After the termination of the consultation procedure, the Commission is required to address an opinion or recommendation to the Member State concerned, indicating whether it considers the measure proposed compatible with the common transport policy (Art. 2). As both Article 76 EEC and this decision are operative in the context of the progressive implementation of a common transport policy, the need for both will be reduced as the policy is implemented.

Article 77

7–06   Article 77, stating aids to transport to be compatible with the Treaty if they meet the needs of co-ordination of transport or if they " represent reimbursement for the discharge of certain obligations inherent in the concept of a public service," stands as an exception to the general provisions on aids found in Articles 92 to 94 in the chapter on competition. Article 92 (1) specifically envisages such exceptions elsewhere in the Treaty, itself an additional indication that the Treaty in general and the transport title are not mutually exclusive. Aids to transport have been a consistent feature of governmental economic policies, since transport costs are a major input factor in the overall cost of goods, and thus it was felt necessary to allow at least certain types of aid to this sector. Article 77 gives a sidelight on the priorities envisaged for a common transport policy, in that although the second category of aids was the one most usually to be applied, the authors specifically included aids granted to co-ordinate transport, thus establishing co-ordination as a major objective of any efficient transport policy as early as 1957.

27–07   Regulation 1191/69, J.O. 1969, L 156/1, cuts down the scope of the Article particularly in relation to aids granted to cover public service obligations. Article 1 (1) of the Regulation requires Member States to terminate all obligations inherent in the concept of a public service as defined in the Regulation imposed on transport by rail, road or inland waterway. This is in accordance with the market economy philosophy of the EEC, since it was found that Member States were becoming over-liberal in giving aids on the pretext of meeting a public service obligation. The Regulation does permit aids to be given to ensure the provision of adequate transport services (Art. 1 (2)); this idea is clarified in Article 3 which states that the services should be the least costly mode to the community and the adequacy of such services is to be assessed having regard to the public interest and the possibilities of substitution and the rates and conditions. In practice the rewording of the criteria for according aids in the transport sector has had very little effect in reducing the granting of aid.

Regulation 1107/70, J.O. 1970, L 130/1, indicates when an aid for road, rail or inland waterway transport may be granted. It was designed to remove confusion regarding the scope of co-ordination measures and the public service obligations not covered by Regulation 1191/69. Article 3 specifies the possible circumstances where an aid may be granted. Compliance with the Regulation is ensured by the Commission, assisted in this task by an advisory committee (Arts. 5 and 6).

Article 78

27–08   Article 78 of the Treaty, which ordains that any measure taken in connection with transport " shall take account of the economic circumstances of carriers " is taken by those desirous of minimising the application of the rest of the Treaty rules to transport as acknowledging the special nature of the transport sector, which thus demands special treatment by the Community. The better view is that the Article is simply a statement that transport undertakings and particularly railway undertakings are in a special economic situation in view of their structure and infrastructure and obligations of public service. The Article is in fact of little practical importance.

Article 79

27–09   Article 79 is designed to eliminate discriminations which take the form of carriers charging different rates and imposing different conditions for the carriage of the same goods over the same transport links on grounds of the country of origin or of destination of the goods in question, and may be considered one of the special provisions mentioned by Article 7 (the general rule against discrimination); since Article 79 (1) only mentions carriage of goods, Article 7 must be held to apply to any discrimination relating to carriage of persons. These discriminations were to be eliminated by the end of the second stage; Article 79 (3) required the Council to lay down rules for the implementation of Article 79 (1) within two years of the entry into force of the Treaty. This was done by Regulation 11 of 1960, J.O. 1960, 1121, which obliges Member States to notify the Commission of any tariffs or agreements on transport rates or conditions which discriminate in terms of the country of origin or destination of the goods concerned (Art. 5). These discriminations are prohibited by Article 4 which reiterates Article 79. However, the Regulation excludes from its ambit private law contracts, *i.e.* individual agreements between carrier and trader; thus these may continue to be discriminatory in rates or conditions. As under Article 79 (4), the Commission is empowered by Article 14 of the Regulation to exercise a power of scrutiny and control over compliance with the Regulation, although it is in the first place the Member States who are responsible for ensuring such compliance. The scope of the Regulation is not perhaps very wide, for Article 79 (1) of the Treaty, re-enacted by Article 4 (1) of the Regulation, only proscribes discrimination in the carriage of "the same goods over the same transport links," which narrows the scope of the prohibition to exactly similar circumstances of transport.

Articles 80 and 82

–10 Article 80 prohibits the Member States from setting rates and conditions involving any elements of support or protection in the interest of one or more particular undertakings or industries, unless authorised by the Commission. The second paragraph of the Article goes on to require the Commission to examine such rates, taking into account " the requirements of an appropriate regional policy " (see generally § 34–16, *infra*, on this aspect), " the needs of under-developed areas and the problems of areas seriously affected by political circumstances." This last consideration relates to the problems of West Berlin, Upper Franconia and the Zonenrandgebiet. Article 82 provides in addition that the provisions of the transport title are not to prevent the application of German domestic measures to compensate for the economic disadvantages caused by the division of Germany, and thus the title provides two safeguards for Germany. Article 82 is probably slightly wider, however, and is not in any case logically identical: Article 80 (2) is directed to the Commission, whilst Article 82 is directed to the Federal Republic (*cf.* the similar provisions of Art. 92 (2) (*c*) in the general chapter on aids).

Taking into account the considerations mentioned in Article 80 (2), and after consulting the Member States concerned, the Commission is empowered to " take the necessary decisions " (Art. 80 (2), second sub-para.) to allow or suppress the subsidies and protective measures mentioned in Article 80 (1). The Commission cannot apparently take decisions on " tariffs fixed to meet competition," for these are excluded from the ambit of Article 80 (1) by Article 80 (3). Tariffs which subsidise one form of transport so as to enable it to compete with another are included within the term " tariffs fixed to meet competition."

Article 81

27-11 Article 81 requires Member States to endeavour to reduce the costs of charges or dues in respect of frontier crossings on a progressive basis. Although the Article refers only to a reduction of these dues, the ultimate aim is complete elimination of such charges, for with the elimination of internal customs duties these charges can become substantial barriers to trade, and yet have no economic value to the transporter. The transporters in turn are required to pass on no more than a reasonable charge, having regard to the cost actually incurred. The Commission is given a power to make recommendations for the application of these provisions, but none appear to have been issued.

Article 83

27-12 Article 83 sets up a Transport Advisory Committee, consisting of experts designated by the governments of Member States, to be attached to the Commission. The composition was made more specific by Article 1 of the Rules of Procedure of the Transport Committee of September 15, 1958, J.O. 1958, 509; each government designates one or two transport experts from among senior officials of the national administration. In addition governments may designate not more than one expert from road, rail and inland waterway transport. The Committee has an advisory role and its powers are expressed to be without prejudice to the powers of the transport section of the Economic and Social Committee (Art. 83 EEC). The very inclusion in the Treaty of Article 82 setting up the Advisory Committee is an indication that the transport sector was regarded as being of importance, since the Treaty contains few specific provisions for the establishment of advisory bodies (see generally Chapter 7).

THE COMMON TRANSPORT POLICY

27-13 Various attempts have been made at listing the objectives and targets of the common transport policy.[1] Although the details of the objectives

---

[1] See notably *Memorandum on the orientation to be given to the Common Transport Policy* (Schaus Memorandum) of April 10, 1961 (Doc. VII/Com. (61) 50, final); *Action Programme for the common transport policy* of May 23, 1962 (Doc. VII/Com. (62) 88, final); Decision 65/271, J.O. 1965, 1500, on the harmonisation of certain provisions affecting competition in transport by rail, road and inland waterway; the accord of the Council of Ministers of June 22, 1965 on the general principles of the transport market (Plan Jacquet: Bulletin No. 8 1965, p. 86); *Options in Tariff Policy* (Allais Report: EEC Transport Series, No. 1 1965); " *The*

and targets have been revised over the years, the heads of discussion of the Action Programme for the common transport policy of May 23, 1962 are still the topics of chief importance to the common transport policy, while the objective remains that set out in paragraph 59 of the Action Programme, namely the achievement of a common transport market organised according to Community rules, capable of meeting the envisaged transport needs of the Community, and ensuring the suppression of all discrimination based on nationality.

The Action Programme is divided into seven chapters. The most important questions—concerning access to the market, rates, and harmonisation of conditions of competition are discussed in the first three. The chapters are:

1. access to the market,
2. transport rates,
3. harmonisation in the taxation, social and technical fields,
4. co-ordination of investments,
5. approximation of operating conditions and structures as between the different types of transport,
6. the application of special provisions of the Treaty, particularly on discrimination, aids and ententes, and
7. studies on transport costs.

1. Access to the Market: licensing controls and quotas

27–14   Prior to the establishment of the EEC the Member States had bilateral agreements with each other providing for the reciprocal admission of predetermined numbers of commercial vehicles to each other's territories. These arrangements were uniform neither as to quantity nor as to their conditions of operation. The Commission pressed for the elimination of these bilateral agreements and the adoption of a Community licensing system whereby vehicles from Member States would be granted a licence to operate transport services on all routes between all Member States (the Community quota to be divided between all Member States). Such a system was adopted at the same time as the rate bracket publicity system.

A first Council directive of July 23, 1962, J.O. 1962, 2005, had already freed certain limited types of road transport from the bilateral quota system, e.g. frontier traffic up to a distance of 25 km. from a frontier internal to the Community; postal services; and carriage of goods by vehicles not exceeding six tons unloaded weight. Council Directive 65/269, J.O. 1965, 1469, had already provided standard types of form

common transport policy following the Council Resolution of 20 October, 1966 (Sec. (67) 346, final: Supp. to Bulletin No. 3, 1967 and Dictionnaire du Marché Commun); Decision 67/790, J.O. 1967, 322/4, concerning certain measures in connection with the common transport policy; Communication on the common organisation of the transport market, of September 16, 1971; and "Development of the Common Transport Policy" (Bulletin, Supp. 8/71). See also "What stage has the Common Transport Policy reached?" (Bulletin 6, 1971, p. 34).

authorising intra-Community carriage of goods by road on a vehicle-by-vehicle basis, either for single journeys or over a period of time.

27–15   The quota system, again applicable only to road transport, was instituted by Regulation 1018/68, J.O. 1968, L 175/13.   This Regulation enables the holders of Community quota licences or authorisations to effectuate the carriage of goods by road on all routes between Member States (Art. 2).   Cabotage traffic is excluded, but empty vehicles are given complete freedom of movement (*ibid*.).   The number of licences available to the Six was 1,200, divided thus:

Belgium	161
Germany	286
France	286
Italy	194
Luxembourg	33
Netherlands	240

The quotas have been fully taken up, and the Commission made proposals to expand them in May 1972 (*Europe* May 25, 1972, No. 1052, p. 3).   These proposals also aim at the complete elimination of a quota system by 1981.

Like the rate bracket Regulation, this Regulation was introduced only for an experimental period, but was automatically extended by one year (Art. 7 (3)) so that it will expire on the day before the accession of the new members on December 31, 1972 unless extended. The Act of Accession makes no provision for the revision of this Regulation because it is expressed to expire before the effective date of accession. A further Regulation renewing or extending the validity of the main Regulation would no doubt be based on the exigencies of a nine-member Community, and would perhaps take into account experience gained in the operation of the system so far.

27–16   Common rules regarding international carriage of passengers by coach and buses were laid down by Regulation 117/66, J.O. 1966, 2688 (thus prior to the introduction of similar provisions for goods vehicles) and a complete liberalisation was introduced for occasional services (Art. 5). The implementation of proposals on liberalisation of regular and shuttle services, envisaged by Articles 7 and 8, was achieved by Regulations 516 and 517/72, J.O. 1972, L 67/13 and 19.

2. Transport rates

27–17   It was clearly desirable for the Community to exercise some measure of control over transport rates; the institution of a fixed rate system was considered to be too violent a departure, given that the previous national systems had varied between the Dutch free rate and the German fixed rate systems. Therefore, as a compromise, the Commission proposed a system whereby rates were allowed to vary, but within certain defined limits, and these rate limits were to be effectively publicised. This system of a publicised band of transport rates within which operators may negotiate their actual rate is known as a forked-tariff or rate bracket system.

Regulation 1174/68, J.O. 1968, L 194/1, brought this system into operation in respect of the carriage of goods by road. It was not possible to include intra-Community waterway transport, since most of it is governed by the Act of Mannheim of 1868 [2] under the super-vision of the Central Commission for the Rhine, which maintains an absolute freedom to negotiate rates between parties. The structure of rail transport was felt to be sufficiently different for a rate bracket regulation to be unnecessary, rates being in the hands of nationalised concerns.

It was argued that the rate bracket system would be administratively unwieldy and that it was based on economic misconceptions, *i.e.* that on any given route there might be perpetual under-cutting of rates and inflation of rates by those in a dominant position. Thus the system was to have a set life-time—Article 17 states that the Regulation was to remain in force until December 31, 1971, although it was extended to the end of 1972. Proposals were made on July 20, 1972, to amend Article 17, so as to prolong the life of the Regulation to December 31, 1974 (J.O. 1972, C 94/25). The Regulation requires each Member State to provide for the publication of rates and conditions of transport through an agency (Arts. 6 and 8) and contemplates that each Member State should adopt appropriate provisions to safeguard the operation of the system, including sanctions for cases of infringement (Art. 12).

3. Harmonisation in the taxation, social and technical fields

7–18   A timetable for action on harmonisation in the taxation, social and technical fields was laid down by Decision 65/271 of May 13, 1965, J.O. 1965, 1500, on the harmonisation of certain provisions affecting competition in transport by rail, road and inland waterway. It deals in particular with taxation questions, certain kinds of State intervention and social questions.

(a) *Taxation*

7–19   Decision 65/271 called for the elimination of double taxation on international transport vehicles, the standardisation of duty-free franchise on motor spirit in commercial vehicles, the adoption of a uniform basis for the calculation of tax on goods vehicles and cargo-carrying inland waterway vessels. The taxation of carriage of goods was to be harmonised in step with the VAT system. So far the only action taken pursuant to Decision 65/271 is Directive 68/297, J.O. 1968, L 175/15, providing for a fifty-litre per vehicle per journey running fuel franchise, exempt

---

[2] Revised most recently by the Convention of Strasbourg of November 20, 1963, T.S. No. 66 (Cmnd. 3371).

from excise duty in other Member States. For the purposes of the operation of this directive in relation to vehicles travelling to the United Kingdom or Ireland a technical adaptation will be made to the directive, which will provide that commercial vehicles which cross the sea between two ports each situated in the territory of the Member States shall be regarded as crossing a common frontier between the Member States. Nevertheless, this directive is only a partial solution to wider problems which can only be solved by a general harmonisation of excise duties on hydrocarbon fuels.

(b) *State intervention*

27–20 Decision 65/271 calls for the termination of obligations inherent in the concept of a public service imposed on transport undertakings in so far as they are not essential in order to ensure the provision of adequate services, for the payment of compensation to transport undertakings in respect of " social " transport rates imposed by Member States, for the normalisation of railway accounts, for harmonisation of provisions governing financial relations between railway undertakings and States, and for proposals for the implementation of Article 77 of the Treaty.

Regulation 1191/69, J.O. 1969, L 156/1, on action by Member States concerning the obligations inherent in the concept of a public service in transport by rail, road and inland waterway, has already been discussed (*supra*, § 27–07).

Regulation 1192/69, J.O. 1969, L 156/8, institutes common rules for the " normalisation " of national railway accounts. This consists in assessing the financial benefits borne, or the benefits enjoyed, by railway undertakings, by reason of any provision laid down by law, regulation or administrative action, by comparison with their position if they were to operate under the same conditions as other transport undertakings. The deficit so revealed is required to be made up by the national authority concerned.

Certain types of infrastructure expenditure are excluded, *e.g.* those relating to minor railways, agricultural or forestry roads, waterways which can only carry vessels up to 250 metric tons, and waterways of a maritime character. As far as the United Kingdom is concerned, the only waterways of a maritime character which will be appended to the list provided for by Regulation 281/71 (J.O. 1971, L 33/11) are the Gloucester and Sharpness Canal and the Weaver Navigation. (The Manchester Ship Canal is thus excluded.)

The only other action taken in execution of the State intervention provisions of Decision 65/271 is Regulation 1107/70, J.O. 1970, L 130/1, on the granting of aids for transport by rail, road and inland waterway, implementing Article 77, and issued under Articles 75, 77 and 94 of the Treaty (see § 27–06, *supra*).

(c) *Social provisions*

7–21   Lastly, Decision 65/271 calls for harmonisation of laws, Regulations and administrative provisions relating to working conditions in the three surface modes of transport (excluding pay, etc.), of provisions on manning, and on working and rest periods.

Various committees have been set up to assist the Commission in its tasks relating to social questions in various transport fields; there are now a Joint Advisory Committee on social questions for road transport— Decision 65/362, J.O. 1965, 2184; a Joint Advisory Committee for inland navigation—Decision 67/745, J.O. 1967, 297/13; and a Joint Advisory Committee for the railway industry—Decision 71/122, J.O. 1971, L 57/22. The composition of the Committees is balanced between employers and transport employees; their function is to give opinions on topics referred to them by the Commission.

The major piece of legislation in the social field relating to transport is Regulation 543/69, J.O. 1969, L 77/49. This establishes various standards relating to the age of drivers, composition of crews, hours to be worked and rest periods, applicable to road transport anywhere within the Community. The Regulation does not apply to carriage by small vehicles, by vehicles of an essentially public character (police, military, fire, etc., but not refuse disposal), and by vehicles used for regular passenger services with a route of not more than 50 kilometres (Art. 4). A regulation of this kind was clearly required, and indeed one of the reasons why road transport is cheaper than other forms is that working conditions are primitive (although pay may be high) and drivers are encouraged to drive long, unbroken periods in order to make maximum use of the vehicle.

7–22   Article 3 of the Regulation empowered the Community to enter into negotiations with third countries with a view to implementing the Regulation. At the time the Regulation was drawn up the Member States were in the process of negotiating a wider agreement on working conditions in road transport, embracing most European countries, these negotiations taking place in the context of the Economic Commission for Europe (ECE) and the European Conference of Ministers of Transport (ECMT). The resulting agreement, known as the European Road Transport Agreement (ERTA or AETR) was concluded after the issue of Regulation 543/69, and proved to be rather less stringent. During the negotiations, the Commission objected that it was for the Community to conclude the Agreement, and not the Member States, since it now had competence in this sphere, following upon the adoption of Regulation 543/69. The Commission brought the matter before the Court (case 22/70, *Commission* v. *Council,* Rec. XVII 263, [1971] C.M.L.R. 335), which upheld the Commission on the principle, but rejected the case on the facts, on the grounds that the Member States had begun to negotiate before the issue of Regulation 543/69. Regulation 543/69 is amended by Regulation 515/72, J.O. 1972, L 67/11, which eliminates certain difficulties which had arisen in the application of the main Regulation. It excludes agricultural and forestry tractors from the ambit of Regulation 543/69, and allows each Member State to make certain derogations in respect notably of the length of driving period. Regulation 543/69 is also amended by Regulation 514/72, J.O. 1972, L 67/1, making the former Regulation accord with the provisions of ERTA.[3]

Regulation 1463/70, J.O. 1970, L 164/1, requires the installation of recording equipment (black boxes or tachygraphs) on passenger and goods vehicles, other than those referred to in Article 4 of Regulation 543/69 (*supra*), and vehicles used for regular passenger services with a route of more than 50 kilometres (Art. 3). All new vehicles must, after January 1, 1975, have these devices and from January 1, 1978, the installation and use of recording equipment will be compulsory for all vehicles (Art. 4); the Regulation has an elaborate annex containing technical specifications for the device.[3]

(d) *Harmonisation in technical fields*

27-23 A number of directives have now been issued under Article 100 relating to technical standards of road vehicles (see generally § 32-03, *infra*), but these do not form an integral part of the common transport policy as such. Technical standards relating to weight and dimension of road vehicles do, however, intimately concern the common transport policy, for national rules on the subject are clearly barriers to trade. Proposals currently before the Council involve a compromise standard of forty-two tons overall weight, with a maximum of eleven tons weight resting on each axle, and thus transmitted to the road surface.

4. The co-ordination of investments

27-24 In so far as co-ordination of investment entails the regulation of State aids, action already taken has been discussed *supra*, § 27-06. The decision of March 21, 1962, J.O. 1962, 720, instituting a procedure for prior examination and consultation in respect of certain laws, Regulations and administrative provisions concerning transport proposed in Member States, goes some way towards controlling unilateral action which might lead to diverging transport policies, but of greater importance here is Decision 66/161, J.O. 1966, 583, instituting a procedure for consultation in respect of transport infrastructure investment (see also *infra*, § 27-29). The decision calls for notification of all proposed infrastructure investment projects having as their object the construction of new railways, roads or inland waterways or a considerable increase in

---

[3] Regulation 543/69 and provisions identical to those of Article 4 (1) of Regulation 1463/70 are to apply in the acceding States as of January 1, 1976: Annex VII to the Act of Accession, Cmnd. 4862–II, p. 147.

the capacity of those already in existence. If necessary consultations are to be entered into.

5. The approximation of operating conditions and structures as between the different types of transport

27–25 To approximate the conditions under which the various types of transport operate, the Action Programme proposed that greater freedom in commercial matters be given to state railways that they may adapt themselves to the common transport market and policies. The Programme also proposed measures designed to improve the structure of transport undertakings. Outside the context of social measures and the provisions for normalisation of railway accounts, no action has been taken under this head.

6. The application of special provisions of the Treaty, particularly on discrimination, aids and ententes

27–26 Regulation 11 of June 27, 1960, J.O. 1960, 1121, concerning the abolition of discrimination in transport rates and conditions, has already been discussed (*supra*, § 27–09). Other measures designed in effect to create " *binnenmarktähnliche Verhältnisse*," authorise the movement of vehicles across frontiers internal to the Community (*supra*, § 27–14).

Rules relating to aids have already been discussed *supra*, § 27–06.

Competition

27–27 The title on transport contains no specific provisions on competition. It was originally considered, therefore, that the rules on competition set out in Articles 85 and 86 of the Treaty, and implemented under Regulation 17/62, J.O. 1962, 204, made under Article 87 of the Treaty, would apply to transport as well. Within ten months of the issue of Regulation 17/62, however, the Council issued a further Regulation on competition, Regulation 141/62, J.O. 1962, 2751, exempting transport from the application of Regulation 17. The preamble to Regulation 141 clearly indicates that transport was considered to be a special case; it reads in part as follows:

> " whereas in pursuance of the common transport policy, account being taken of the distinctive features of the transport sector, it may prove necessary to lay down rules governing competition different from those laid down or to be laid down for other sectors of the economy, and whereas Regulation 17 should not therefore apply to transport."

27–28 In fact, it appears from Article 12 of the Regulation that appropriate provisions for road, rail and inland waterway transport were to be adopted, and thus by Article 3, the Regulation was to expire on December 31, 1965, in so far as it applied to these three modes of transport. A Regulation to apply rules of competition to transport by rail, road and inland waterway was not in fact adopted until July 19, 1968 (Regulation 1017/68, J.O. 1968, L 175/1), but the latter Regulation does not derive its substance from the chapter on competition in the Treaty, although its preamble mentions Articles 75 (transport) and 87 (competition) as its juridical basis. The Regulation contains rewordings and adaptations of the basic rules of Articles 85 and 86 in its Articles 2 and 8, and Article 9 parallels Article 90 of the Treaty in that public undertakings are subjected to the general rules. It includes exemptions derived from Community practice: Articles 3 to 6 exempt from the general prohibition of Article 2 technical agreements, the grouping of small and medium-sized firms and specific agreements contributing to the improvement and increased productivity of transport services (*cf.* Commission Notice of July 29, 1968, J.O. 1968, C 75/3, [1968] C.M.L.R. D5) and also contains provisions similar to those contained in Regulation 17/62. The reason that Regulation 1017/68 includes its own redefinitions of Articles 85 and 86 is to be sought in the fact that the Community wished by this expedient to avoid juridical uncertainties as to the application of the rest of the Treaty to the transport sector.

7. Studies on transport costs

27–29   Studies on transport costs have related mainly to infrastructure costs. Decision 64/389, J.O. 1964, 1598, institutes mechanisms for the survey of infrastructure costs for transport by rail, road and inland waterways. The survey was instituted to ensure that adequate information would be available for planning future projects; the material for the survey was to relate to 1966 (Art. 2) and the provisions of the decision were amplified by a further decision (65/270, J.O. 1965, 1473), which indicates specific measures to be taken into account. Member States were authorised to carry out pilot studies concerning particular transport links (Art. 4 of the same decision).

An additional decision, Decision 70/108, J.O. 1970, L 23/24, instituted a study of urban road infrastructure costs, this not being covered by the first decision.

The material obtained from these surveys and studies has been used to assist the Commission in its task of co-ordinating Community infrastructure investment. This is carried out under Decision 66/161, J.O. 1966, 583, which set up procedures for consultation in respect of transport infrastructure investment (*supra,* § 27–24).

TRANSPORT AND THE ECSC TREATY

27–30   The Treaty of Paris treats transport as a complementary matter. It regards as a crucial problem the reflection in the retail price of goods of the additional cost factor of transport charges; thus, Article 70 of the Treaty enunciates the principle of non-discrimination in transport tariffs and, in keeping with the minimalist philosophy of the Treaty as a whole (see Art. 5 ECSC, last para.), implements this by prescribing publicity or notification to the High Authority of tariff rates. However, the fifth paragraph of Article 70 states that: " Subject to the provisions of this Article, and to the other provisions of this Treaty, transport policy . . . shall continue to be governed by the laws or regulations of the individual Member States." The other applicable portions of the Treaty are Article 4 (*b*) which prohibits measures or practices which discriminate between producers, between purchasers or between consumers, especially in prices and delivery terms or transport rates and conditions, and the provisions of Article 60 (1) regarding publication of prices and conditions. Paragraph 10 of the Convention on Transitional Provisions created a Commission of Experts to study the suppression of discriminations prohibited in Article 70, the establishment of through (or direct) international tariffs, and rates and conditions for carriage of coal and steel by the different modes of inland transport.

The arrangements for direct international tariffs, including those for transit by rail across the territories of Austria and Switzerland, were established gradually as from 1955 by the following agreements:

Agreement of March 21, 1955, on the establishment of through international railway tariffs, J.O. 1955, 701.

Supplementary Agreement of March 16, 1956, J.O. 1956, 130.

Agreement of July 28, 1956, on the drawing up of international railway tariffs for the transport of coal and steel in transit through Swiss territory, J.O. 1957, 223.

Agreement of July 26, 1957, on the introduction of direct international railway tariffs for the transportation of coal and steel through the territory of the Austrian republic, J.O. (ECSC) 1958, 78. (Amended: J.O. 1961, 1281; J.O. 1966, 3867. Supplemented: J.O. 1961, 1237.)

Agreement of February 1, 1958, on freight rates and conditions of carriage of coal and steel on the Rhine, J.O. 1958, 49.

Agreement of March 23, 1959, supplementing Agreement of March 21, 1955, J.O. 1959, 431.

The efforts of the High Authority to obtain publication of national tariff rates pursuant to the third paragraph of Article 70 ECSC received a setback in the decisions of the Court in 20/59, *Government of Italy* v. *High Authority,* Rec. VI 663, and 25/29, *Government of the Netherlands* v. *High Authority,* Rec. VI 723, holding that the High Authority had no implied power of execution in the matter of transport. Thus it might not challenge the Member States' failure to fulfil the obligation in question.

High Authority Recommendation 1/61, J.O. 1961, 419, concerning publication of transport rates, recognises that executive authority in the matter remains with the Member States, but nevertheless indicates what measures should be taken to comply with the Community obligation.

This approach was upheld by the Court of Justice when challenged in 9/61, *Government of the Netherlands* v. *High Authority*, Rec. VIII 413, [1962] C.M.L.R. 59. The Court held that Article 70, third para., was an obligatory rule to be observed by the Member States and thus the High Authority was entitled to issue recommendations to secure its observance.

Part 5

COMMUNITY POLICIES

CHAPTER 28

RULES ON COMPETITION

8–01 ARTICLES 85 and 86 are as follows:

"ARTICLE 85

" 1. The following shall be prohibited as incompatible with the common market: all agreements between undertakings, decisions by associations of undertakings and concerted practices which may affect trade between Member States and which have as their object or effect the prevention, restriction or distortion of competition within the common market, and in particular those which:

(*a*) directly or indirectly fix purchase or selling prices or any other trading conditions;

(*b*) limit or control production, markets, technical development, or investment;

(*c*) share markets or sources of supply;

(*d*) apply dissimilar conditions to equivalent transactions with other trading parties, thereby placing them at a competitive disadvantage;

(*e*) make the conclusion of contracts subject to acceptance by the other parties of supplementary obligations which, by their nature or according to commercial usage, have no connection with the subject of such contracts.

" 2. Any agreements or decisions prohibited pursuant to this Article shall be automatically void.

" 3. The provisions of paragraph 1 may, however, be declared inapplicable in the case of:

—any agreement or category of agreements between undertakings;

—any decision or category of decisions by associations of undertakings;

—any concerted practice or category of concerted practices; which contributes to improving the production or distribution of goods or to promoting technical or economic progress, while allowing consumers a fair share of the resulting benefit, and which does not:

(*a*) impose on the undertakings concerned restrictions which are not indispensable to the attainment of these objectives;

(*b*) afford such undertakings the possibility of eliminating competition in respect of a substantial part of the products in question.

"ARTICLE 86

" Any abuse by one or more undertakings of a dominant position within the common market or in a substantial part of it shall be prohibited as incompatible with the common market in so far as it may affect trade between Member States. Such abuse may, in particular, consist in:

    (*a*) directly or indirectly imposing unfair purchase or selling prices or other unfair trading conditions;

    (*b*) limiting production, markets or technical development to the prejudice of consumers;

    (*c*) applying dissimilar conditions to equivalent transactions with other trading parties, thereby placing them at a competitive disadvantage;

    (*d*) making the conclusion of contracts subject to acceptance by the other parties of supplementary obligations which, by their nature or according to commercial usage, have no connection with the subject of such contracts."

GENERAL OUTLINE OF THE RULES ON COMPETITION

28–02 Article 3 (f) of the EEC Treaty provides that the activities of the Community shall include " the institution of a system ensuring that competition in the common market is not distorted." Provision for such a system is made in Part Three of the Treaty—" Policy of the Community "—where Articles 85 to 94 are grouped together in Chapter 1, entitled " Rules on Competition." These Articles cover not only the Community rules on restrictive trade practices and monopolies (and, so current developments suggest, on mergers), but also on dumping and on aids granted by States to various sectors of the national economy. The application of rules on competition is indispensable if the tasks set out for the Community in Article 2 EEC are to be achieved: the so-called competition policy of the Community has been much enlarged upon by subsidiary legislation, and the case law on competition is highly developed.

The basic principles of the Community's competition policy are laid down in Articles 85 and 86 (reproduced in full above), which constitute a " *loi-cadre* " or basic framework on which to hang further rules of substance, exception and procedure. This reflects the general structure of the EEC Treaty, which, unlike the ECSC Treaty, does not generally establish definitive working rules in its articles, leaving such rules to be worked out in subsidiary legislation. This difference between the Rome and Paris Treaties is nowhere more apparent than in relation to competition; the Treaty of Paris deals with restrictive trade practices, mergers and monopolies at considerably greater length and in more detail than the EEC Treaty. Thus in any discussion of the EEC competition policy it must be remembered that Articles 85 and 86 form only the founding principles of that policy.

28–03   The EEC competition rules may be summarised as follows:

Article 85 (1) imposes a general ban on all restrictive trade agreements between firms. An agreement prohibited under paragraph 1 is automatically void (para. 2). But agreements may be exempted from Article 85 (1) where they are considered to be generally beneficial and to fulfil certain conditions (Art. 85 (3)). The rules for prohibiting and exempting agreements are set out in Regulation 17/62 (J.O. 1962, 204). The same Regulation provides for certification by the Commission that certain agreements or classes of agreements do not come within Article 85 (1) at all (negative clearance procedure). Agreements must be notified to the Commission under Regulation 17 if they are to qualify for exemption under Article 85 (3), and in practice firms will request a negative clearance, or failing that, an exemption, there being a single application form for both. Exemption is for classes of agreement which are prima facie void. Negative clearance is for classes of agreement about which there is some doubt. Classes of agreement which, under the terms of the Regulation, are prima facie valid, need not be brought to the attention of the Commission at all. There is an incentive to notify notifiable agreements, in that they enjoy a " provisional validity " prior to the Commission decision, irrespective of the outcome.

Article 86 imposes a general prohibition on any abuse of a dominant position held in a particular market. This refers to monopolies, and, possibly, to mergers.

Articles 87 to 89 contain provisions for the implementation of Articles 85 and 86, and provide for the definition of responsibilities as between national authorities and the Community.

Article 90 contains particular rules on public undertakings, and the applicability to them of the general rules on competition.

Article 91 contains transitional rules on dumping.

Articles 92 to 94 contain the Community rules on State aids to the national economy.

28–04   Agriculture was not subject to the Community rules initially (Art. 42 EEC), but was subjected to them by Regulation 26/62 (J.O. 1962, 993), which came into effect on July 1, 1962.

The chequered history of the application of the rules on competition to the transport industry has been reviewed above (§ 27–27); here it is sufficient to note that by Regulation 1017/68 (J.O. 1968, L 175/1) the general Community rules on competition are for the most part made applicable to transport, although notice is taken in the Regulation of the special position and structure of the transport industry in the Community.

Although the basic scheme set up by the Treaty involves a general prohibition on restrictive trade practices, with a limited provision for exemption, the Community now operates a complex system, which may be said to be aimed at the dual objectives of ensuring a balanced free market economic system, and establishing an industrial policy, adapted to all technological exigencies.

ARTICLE 85

28–05 Article 85 is divided into three paragraphs, setting out (1) a general prohibition of restrictive trade practices, (2) a statement of the legal consequences of such prohibition, and (3) provision for exemptions from the prohibition in certain cases. It is appropriate to discuss each paragraph separately.

Article 85 (1)

28–06 Article 85 (1) sets out the fundamental rule, from which all Community restrictive trade practice law has developed: it defines what is prohibited under Community law and then gives a non-exhaustive list of examples. The definition is not complete and the paragraph has been the subject of much controversy. It states that:

"all agreements between undertakings, decisions by associations of undertakings and concerted practices which may affect trade between Member States and which have as their object or effect the prevention, restriction or distortion of competition within the Common Market . . ."

are prohibited as being incompatible with the Common Market. Thus the restrictive practices barred by this paragraph must be examined under three distinct and separate heads:

(1) Is the agreement an agreement, *i.e.* involving a meeting of minds?

(2) Does the agreement affect trade *between* Member States, or only within one?

(3) Is the agreement designed to, or does it in fact prevent, restrict or distort competition within the Common Market?

1. *The agreement*

28–07 ". . . all agreements between undertakings, decisions by associations of undertakings and concerted practices. . . ."

These words describe the types of agreements prohibited, and also refer to the types of legal persons making such agreements, *i.e.* undertakings (French "*entreprises*," German "*Unternehmen*") and associations of undertakings. These concepts are no further defined in the Treaty. The word "*undertaking*" does not describe a specific type of legal person, and this suggests that it is to be given a very wide meaning. Within its scope must be included state and public enterprises, as they are included within the Community competition rules by Article 90

EEC, as well as companies and wholly-owned subsidiaries, which for
the purposes of the competition rules are usually treated as separate
firms. (*Christiani & Nielsen,* (negative clearance decision), J.O. 1969,
L 165/12, [1969] C.M.L.R. D36—but see judgments of the Court of
Justice in 48/69, *I.C.I.* v. *Commission* and related cases 49 & 51–57/69
discussed *infra,* § 28–89). It would not appear that the undertaking
need be a legal person according to national law (*cf.* Regulation 17/62,
Art. 11 (4)). The notion of "undertaking" is not limited to firms
incorporated in the Member States of the Community: several of the
Commission's decisions have involved companies incorporated in third
States:

> *Grosfillex-Fillistorf* (Fillistorf incorporated in Switzerland) J.O.
> 1964, 915, [1964] C.M.L.R. 237;
> *Bendix-Maertens & Straet* (Bendix incorporated in U.S.A.) J.O.
> 1964, 1426, [1964] C.M.L.R. 416;
> *Nicholas Frères-Vitapro* (Vitapro incorporated in England) J.O.
> 1964, 2287, [1964] C.M.L.R. 505;
> *Transocean Marine Paint Association* (included members
> incorporated in England) J.O. 1967, 163/10, [1967]
> C.M.L.R. D9.

28–08   In the *Aniline Dyes* or *Dyestuffs* decision, J.O. 1969, L 195/11,
[1969] C.M.L.R. D23 the Commission imposed fines totalling 485,000 u.a.
on firms found to have taken part in the "Aniline Trust," which
included three Swiss companies and I.C.I. (incorporated in England).
The Court of Justice has recently upheld the Commission's right to
fine firms from third States: 48/69, *I.C.I.* v. *Commission* and related
cases, discussed *infra,* § 28–89.

28–09   " *Associations of undertakings* " refers not only to *ad hoc* groupings
of various enterprises, but also to more formal combinations of firms
set up for the furtherance of group interests. Many of the Commission's
decisions have concerned the articles of membership or statutes of formal
associations.

28–10   " *Concerted practices* " covers what has not already been subsumed
under the headings " agreements " and " decisions of undertakings "
and thus it may safely be assumed that " agreements " in the context
of Article 85 may be taken as having a meaning akin to that of contracts
in normal civil law. The term " concerted practice " describes any
situation where parties act together without any semblance of overt
commitment but where elements of conscious co-operation can be
established: *Aniline Dyes* decision, J.O. 1969, L 195/11, [1969]
C.M.L.R. D23 and cases 48, 49/69 and 51–57/69, *infra,* § 28–89. It
must be borne in mind that if it is to be prohibited under Article 85, the
practice must also fall under heads (2) and (3) above, thus a concerted
practice can never exist *in vacuo* and must always be further evidenced
by concerted *conduct* in response to the concerted *practice.* This is a

relevant consideration when examining agreements and decisions as well, but because of the more clandestine nature of concerted practices, it is usually only the ensuing conduct which reveals the existence of such practices. (See especially *Pittsburgh Corning Europe–Formica Belgium–Hertel,* J.O. 1972, L 272/35, *infra* § 28–27, on simultaneous application of price lists.)

2. *Agreements etc. which " may affect trade between Member States "*

28-11   Agreements, decisions and practices must, if they are to be prohibited under Article 85 (1), be *capable* of affecting inter-State commerce having regard to the economic context. The condition has little legal significance, since it is not akin to the American concept of the *"rule of reason"* which allows a restrictive trade practice to be assessed in relation to its economic context, before a decision is reached on whether the practice is valid or not. It could be argued that " between Member States " adds a geographical criterion to conditions of application of Article 85, but this is actually irrelevant since the Treaty is designed to create a single economic area. This clause has nevertheless been the subject of a great deal of academic controversy, although the Community institutions do not appear to be troubled by it. The main arguments turn on the different renderings of the phrase in the four original Community languages: The German text reads ". . . *welche den Handel zwischen den Mitgliedstaaten zu beeinträchtigen geeignet. . . .*" The word " *beeinträchtigen* " imparts to the phrase the sense that the agreement must affect trade *adversely.* The Dutch ". . . *ongunstig . . . beinvloeden . . .*" and the Italian " *preguidicare* " have the same pejorative sense. The French ". . . *qui sont susceptibles d'affecter le commerce entre états membres . . .*" on the other hand, has no such pejorative sense. The authentic English text, using " affect " is assimilable to the French text, in that " affect " has of course no pejorative sense.

Even though it would thus appear that three of the four original Community languages express a narrower idea than that expressed in the French text, nevertheless the Commission appears to prefer the latter and thus to give the Article a wider scope than would obtain if the interpretation of the other three texts were applied. In its decision on *Grundig-Consten,* J.O. 1964, 2545, [1964] C.M.L.R. 489, the Commission said:

> ". . . for Article 85 (1) to apply, it is enough that a restriction of competition within the meaning of Article 85 (1) should cause the trade between Member States to develop under conditions other than they would have done without that restriction, and that its influence on the market conditions is of some importance."
> (Trans. [1964] C.M.L.R. 489 at p. 497.)

28-12   However, the Court of Justice was called upon to pronounce on the issue in 56/65, *La Technique Minière* v. *Maschinenbau Ulm (LTM*

v. *MBU*), Rec. XII 337, [1966] C.M.L.R. 357, which concerned an exclusive distribution contract between a German and a French company; a similar factual basis to that pertaining in the *Grundig-Consten* decision. The Court discussed the clause at some length, finding that:
" The agreement in question should, on the basis of a collection of objective legal or factual elements, allow one to expect, with a sufficient degree of probability, that it would exercise a direct or indirect, actual or potential, effect on the eddies of trade between member-States," so as " to render more difficult the economic inter-penetration desired by the Treaty " if the agreement under examination is to fall under the prohibition of Article 85 (1).

The same clause in Article 85 (1) was again discussed by the Court in 56 & 58/64, *Consten and Grundig* v. *Commission*, Rec. XII 429, [1966] C.M.L.R. 418, where the Court held that:

" it is necessary in particular to know whether the agreement is capable of endangering, either directly or indirectly, in fact or potentially, freedom of trade between Member States *in a direction which could harm the attainment of the objects of a single market between States.* So the fact that an agreement favours an increase, even a large one, in volume of trade between States is not sufficient to exclude the ability of the agreement to ' affect ' the trade in the above-mentioned direction."

(Trans. [1966] C.M.L.R. 418 at p. 472; italics supplied.)

The Court used very similar wording in 5/69, *Völk* v. *Vervaecke* (also known as the *Konstant* case), Rec. XV 295, [1969] C.M.L.R. 273.

28–13 It would seem, therefore, that the authentic English text and the French text of Article 85 (1) are both closer to the interpretation given by the Court than that suggested by the other original language versions. It would seem that the interpretation given by the Court is in any case the interpretation to be desired, for the criterion of affecting trade should not be that of "adverse effect," looking at trade only, but should rather be one looking at the Community objectives as a whole, to see whether their alignment is hindered. The agreement must, however, permit one to envisage, with a sufficient degree of probability, that it could affect intra-Community trade: 1/71, *Cadillon* v. *Höss*, Rec. XVII 351, [1971] C.M.L.R. 420.

A cartel limited to the territory of one Member State can nevertheless affect commerce between Member States, since it can restrict " economic interpenetration " by ensuring the protection of national production: 8/72, *Vereeniging van Cementhandelaren* v. *Commission* (not yet reported).

3. *Object or effect*

28–14 If an agreement or practice is to be prohibited under Article 85, it must also have as its:

" object or effect the prevention, restriction or distortion of competition within the Common Market."

This condition is postulated in very wide terms; whether the agreement is aimed at restraining competition and fails so to do, or is motivated by good intentions but unintentionally restrains competition, it is nevertheless prohibited.

The view that attempts come within Article 85 (1) was confirmed by the court in 56 & 58/64, *Consten and Grundig* v. *Commission*, Rec. XII 429, [1966] C.M.L.R. 418, where the Court, replying to the argument that the Commission should have taken into account the effects of the agreement in question, held that:

" for the purpose of applying Article 85 (1), it is superfluous to take account of the concrete effects of an agreement once it appears that it has the *object* of restraining, preventing or distorting competition."

(Trans. [1966] C.M.L.R. 418 at 473, italics supplied.)

28–15 Against this, however, is the slightly earlier judgment of the Court in 56/65, *La Technique Minière* v. *Maschinenbau Ulm*, Rec. XII 337, [1966] C.M.L.R. 357, where the " rule of reason " familiar to United States antitrust law appears to have been introduced. The Court held that:

" To be hit by the prohibition of Article 85 (1), the agreement in the proceedings should ' be designed to prevent, restrict or distort competition within the Common Market or have that effect.' The fact that these are not cumulative but alternative conditions, indicated by the conjunction ' or,' suggests first *the need to consider the very object of the agreement, in the light of the economic context in which it is to be applied.* The alterations in the play of competition envisaged by Article 85 (1) should result from all or part of the clauses of the agreement itself. Where, however, an analysis of the said clauses does not reveal a sufficient degree of harmfulness with regard to competition, examination should then be made of the effects of the agreement and, if it is to be subjected to the prohibition, the presence of those elements which establish that competition has in fact been prevented, restricted or distorted to a noticeable extent should be required. *The competition in question should be understood within the actual context in which it would occur in the absence of the agreement in question.*"

(Trans. [1966] C.M.L.R. 357 at p. 375; italics supplied.)

28–16 Thus in any examination of the question whether a particular agreement falls foul of Article 85 (1), the Court will take into consideration the entire economic circumstances of the agreement (unless presumably, *res ipsa loquitur*). This approach is to be welcomed. It was reiterated in 5/69, *Völk* v. *Vervaecke*, Rec. XV 295, [1969] C.M.L.R. 273, in the following terms:

" Furthermore, the prohibition in Article 85 (1) may apply only on condition that the agreement in question also has the object or effect of preventing, restricting or distorting competition in the Common Market. *These conditions should be understood by reference to the actual context in which the agreement exists.*"
(Trans. [1969] C.M.L.R. 273 at p. 282; italics supplied.)

The latter case concerned an exclusive distribution agreement with absolute territorial protection, similar to the *Grundig-Consten* agreement, though without a reference to trade marks. In contrast to the *Grundig-Consten* agreement, however, the two firms involved held only a very small proportion of the particular product market inside the EEC; thus, although the object of the agreement was to restrain competition inside the Common Market, the effect of it could be ignored, when set in its economic context.

28–17   In elaborating a definition of what is to be understood by the phrase " prevention, restriction or distortion of competition " a similar requirement that all the circumstances be examined seems to have been adopted. The listing of three different types of restraint on competition is considered to involve no differentiation of substance, but the entire phrase is to be understood as referring to a " noticeable restraint." The concept of " noticeable restraint " first appeared in the *Grosfillex-Fillistorf* negative clearance decision, J.O. 1964, 915 [1964] C.M.L.R. 237, where the Commission found that the circumstance that a double customs barrier would be present if goods the subject of the agreement were re-exported to the Common Market after having been exported to Switzerland, and that there were within the Common Market a large number of manufacturers and distributors of similar products:

" lead to the conclusion that the competition in the Common Market is neither prevented, restricted nor distorted *to any noticeable extent* as a result of the contract in question."
(Trans. [1964] C.M.L.R. 237 at p. 239; italics supplied.)

The additional test of noticeable effect obliges the Commission or the Court to assess the effect of the agreement, taking account of the surrounding economic circumstances. This test is inherent in Article 4 (2) (ii) and (iii) of Regulation 17/62, formally exempting agreements of minor importance from the notification requirement. This exception has subsequently been enlarged by the Commission's Notice concerning co-operation agreements between small and medium-sized undertakings, of July 29, 1968, J.O. 1968, C 75/3, [1968] C.M.L.R. D5 (see *infra*, § 28–36). The concept of " noticeable effect " was expressly referred to in the Commission's Notice Concerning Agreements of Minor Importance of May 27, 1970, J.O. 1970, C 64/1, [1970] C.M.L.R. D15 which exempts agreements between small and medium-sized firms which do not have " noticeable effects " on market conditions from the notification requirements of Regulation 17/62. Where the products covered by agreement account for less than 5 per cent. of the total common market turnover in identical products or their substitutes in the part of the Common Market covered by the agreement, or where the total annual turnover of the firms concerned does not exceed 15 million u.a. (20 million u.a. for firms engaged in distribution), the Commission considers Article 85 (1) to be of no application.

The notion of competition

28–18   The notion of " competition " is not defined by the Treaty, and has thus been subject to economic rather than legal interpretation. The degree of competition which this article aims to preserve is not the absolute *laissez-faire* ideal, and decisions would suggest that what is desired is " *workable* " or " *effective* " competition in a mixed economy. This does not mean, however, that competition is only safeguarded as between participant enterprises in any agreement; it follows from the Court's decision in 56 & 58/64, *Consten and Grundig* v. *Commission*, Rec. XII 429, [1966] C.M.L.R. 418, that Article 85 aims at protecting third parties' freedom of competition.

It is not clear whether Article 85 (1) prohibits agreements which affect potential competition, *i.e.* agreements between firms who do not at the time of their agreement compete with each other, but have the potential ability to compete.   The Commission granted a negative clearance to the *Alliance des constructeurs français de machines-outils*, J.O. 1968, L 201/1, [1968] C.M.L.R. D23, an export marketing and specialisation agreement between a number of French firms, who manufactured non-competing products, but amongst whom was one firm large enough to expand its range of production to compete with the other parties to the agreement.   The agreement prohibited firms from so doing, but the Commission nevertheless granted a negative clearance, apparently because the Alliance was set up on the basis that the firms were non-competing, and that members were free to leave the Alliance, and that the Alliance itself represents only a small part of total sales and production of machine tools in the Common Market.

28–19   The concept of competition envisaged by Article 85 (1) is not restricted to that between manufacturers or distributors situated at the same commercial stage, but covers restraints imposed between firms at different stages of production and distribution.   Indeed if it is accepted that there is a sufficient restraint on competition to fall foul of Article 85 (1) where a third party's freedom of competition is restrained, it is logically impossible to maintain that Article 85 does not prohibit so-called vertical restraints on competition, *i.e.* those where the agreement creating the restraint exists between two or more companies not directly engaged in the same stage of production or distribution (as opposed to " horizontal " restraints on competition which involve firms at the same stage of production).

The Court of Justice appeared to acknowledge this view in 13/61, *de Geus* v. *Bosch*, Rec. VIII 89, [1962] C.M.L.R. 1, in holding that restrictions imposed by a manufacturer on a purchasing wholesaler were not in principle outside the scope of Article 85 (1). The Italian Government argued in two later cases (56 & 58/64, *Consten and Grundig* v. *Commission*, Rec. XII 429, [1966] C.M.L.R. 418, and 32/65, *Italy* v. *Council and Commission*, Rec. XII 563, [1969] C.M.L.R. 39) that vertical agreements of this kind did not fall within the purview of Article 85 (1), but the Court rejected such arguments in fairly vigorous terms. It now appears to be generally accepted that Article 85 applies to all situations where competition is impaired by a restrictive practice of any kind.

The list of examples of restrictive trade practices given in Article 85 (1)

8–20   Article 85 (1) contains a list of practices deemed to be incompatible with the Common Market under the terms of the Article. The list is not apparently exhaustive and can only be used to provide illustrations of practices prohibited by Article 85 (1), since even agreements of the types described in the list (Article 85 (1) (*a*) to (*c*)) are only prohibited if they fulfil all the conditions set out in the first part of Article 85 (1). No restrictive trade practice is illegal *per se* under Article 85. It is instructive to examine what types of agreements and practices are included in the list.

(a) *Agreements which fix purchase or selling prices and trading conditions*

8–21   Sub-paragraph (*a*) refers to what are perhaps the most numerous of all restrictive trade practices; those whereby firms producing the same type of goods agree mutually on the price of such goods or the terms under which they are to be sold (horizontal agreement) or where a manufacturer and a distributor agree as to the terms and price on resale of any particular goods (vertical agreement). These are usually broadly called price-fixing agreements.

In 8/72, *Vereeniging van Cementhandelaren* v. *Commission* (not yet reported) the Court held that the " prix indicatifs " ("target prices " or suggested prices) affected competition because they enabled " all participants " to make reasonably accurate forecasts as to the pricing policy of their competitors.

(b) *Agreements which limit or control production, markets, technical development or investment*

8–22   Sub-paragraph (*b*) is extremely comprehensive in its scope and refers to all situations where parties to an agreement restrict their future freedom commercially, technically or financially. Of particular interest is the fact that specialisation and rationalisation agreements are mentioned. The Commission has announced that under certain conditions it would exempt such agreements from the application of Article 85 (1)

(Notice of July 29, 1968, concerning co-operation between small and medium sized Enterprises, J.O. 1968, C 75/3, [1968] C.M.L.R. D5). The Commission was empowered by Council Regulation 2821/71, J.O. 1971, L 285/46 to issue a Regulation granting block exemption in respect of specialisation agreements fulfilling certain criteria (*infra*, § 28–34). The Commission decision of exemption in *Bolloré-Braunstein*, J.O. 1972, L 182/24, [1972] C.M.L.R. D94, suggests that specialisation agreements will, in certain circumstances, be permitted even where the firms concerned account for a substantial part of the Community production of the products involved.

(c) *Market sharing agreements and agreements on sources of supply*

28-23 Sub-paragraph (*c*) covers cartels setting up horizontal division of markets between various producers, and it also applies to exclusive distributorship agreements. Commission Notice of December 24, 1962, concerning exclusive representation contracts with commercial agents, J.O. 1962, 2921, dealt specifically with this latter type of agreement, it being announced that the Commission would exempt even those agreements where the distributor was an independent agent as opposed to a mere extension of the producer. The Commission will, however, look to realities rather than form: *Pittsburgh Corning Europe–Formica Belgium–Hertel*, J.O. 1972, L 272/35.

Distributorship agreements usually give the distributor territorial protection: relative protection is provided if the supplier contracts to supply the goods in question to no other distributor in the area the subject of the agreement. This protection becomes absolute where the supplier contracts further to prohibit other distributors or first purchasers from exporting the goods into the protected territory.

28-24 The Court held in 56 & 58/64, *Consten and Grundig* v. *Commission*, Rec. XII 429, [1966] C.M.L.R. 418, that the mere fact that the agreement was in restraint of trade was enough to attract the prohibition of Article 85 (1). The Court did not appear to consider it necessary to decide whether there has been an abuse of the restraint.

With a view to dealing expeditiously with a large volume of the less serious restraints on competition, the Commission was empowered by Council Regulation 19/65, J.O. 1965, 533, to grant group or block exemptions from Article 85 (1) *inter alia* in respect of exclusive dealership agreements. Commission Regulation 67/67, J.O. 1967, 849, issued under this power exempts from the application of Article 85 (1) of the Treaty those agreements to which only two undertakings are party and whereby:

" (*a*) one party agrees with the other to supply only to that other certain goods for resale within a defined area of the common market; or

(*b*) one party agrees with the other to purchase only from that other certain goods for resale; or

(c) the two undertakings have entered into obligations as in (a) and (b) above, with each other in respect of exclusive supply and purchase for resale."

8–25 However, Article 3 of the Regulation states that this exemption shall not apply where:

" (a) manufacturers of competing goods entrust each other with exclusive dealings in those goods;

(b) the contracting parties make it difficult for intermediaries or consumers to obtain the goods to which the contract relates from other dealers within the Common Market, in particular where the contracting parties:

(1) exercise industrial property rights to prevent dealers or consumers from obtaining from other parts of the common market or from selling in the territory covered by the contract goods to which the contract relates which are properly marked or otherwise properly placed on the market;

(2) exercise other rights or take other measures to prevent dealers or consumers from obtaining from elsewhere goods to which the contract relates or from selling them in the territory covered by the contract."

The harmfulness of the practice mentioned in sub-paragraph (a) is self-evident, but there is more to sub-paragraph (b) than perhaps meets the eye: it amounts to a legislative conversion of the decision of the Court that:

" Article 36, which limits the scope of the rules on the liberalisation of trade contained in Title I, Chap. 2 [Quantitative Restrictions] of the Treaty, cannot limit the field of application of Article 85." (56 & 58/64, *Consten and Grundig* v. *Commission*, Rec. XII 429, [1966] C.M.L.R. 418: Trans. [1966] C.M.L.R. at p. 476. See generally § 21–29 as to Art. 36.)

8–26 Amongst the numerous exclusive dealing agreements notified to the Commission under Regulation 17/62 were many which, although made between firms which had their place of incorporation or headquarters inside the Common Market territories, concerned the export of goods to third countries. These agreements usually contained clauses ensuring absolute territorial protection for the distributor which would otherwise fall foul of Article 85 (1) as interpreted in the *Grundig-Consten* decision, J.O. 1964, 2545, [1964] C.M.L.R. 489, but the Commission considered that because these agreements were related only to trade with third countries, they were unlikely to affect inter-State commerce, so as to fall within Article 85 (1). The matter was settled by the Commission decision in *Rieckermann/AEG-Elotherm*, J.O. 1968, L 276/25, [1968] C.M.L.R. D78, which amounted to a test case.

28-27   The agreement in question gave Rieckermann the exclusive right to sell certain AEG products in Japan, and required it to purchase exclusively from AEG. Rieckermann was, however, permitted to sell AEG products in Korea as well, and was not for this purpose bound to purchase direct. AEG for its part agreed to supply the Japanese market exclusively through Rieckermann, and to prevent any of its other purchasers from reselling on the Japanese market. The Commission decided that the agreement could be given a negative clearance, but it would appear that the reasons for this were specific to the facts of the case. The Commission found that the equipment sold by AEG was usually made to order and would therefore be difficult to resell to any other than the original intended purchaser, and therefore Rieckermann would be unwilling to take on a dubious commercial risk in selling the equipment elsewhere than in Japan. Moreover, Rieckermann was set up as an exporter to the Far East and had no sales organisation through which he could resell the equipment inside the European Community. Thus, according to the Commission, this agreement did not affect trade inside the Common Market and could be accorded a negative clearance on the basis of this decision. Similar agreements, in substance exclusive dealing agreements between Community firms, but relating to sales to third countries were also given negative clearance, and it therefore became unnecessary to notify such agreements. The Commission's decision seems over-generalised in view of the particular facts of the case, and the reasoning is not entirely convincing, since a restraint on the freedom to compete inside the Common Market was certainly imposed by the obligation on Rieckermann not to purchase from other than AEG for its sales to Japan. The case is not comparable with the situation in *Grosfillex-Fillistorf*, J.O. 1964, 915, [1964] C.M.L.R. 237. The agreement the subject of the latter decision stipulated only that Fillistorf, Grosfillex's Swiss concessionary was not to re-export the French firm Grosfillex's products to the Common Market, but the Commission considered that such re-export was impractical because of the double customs duty the goods would have to bear, *i.e.* on import into Switzerland and on re-import into the Common Market. In *Rieckermann/AEG* the dealer was tied not only as to where he might sell the products he bought, but was also obliged to purchase from one Community producer exclusively, for a large part of his market; a much greater restriction.

The instrument used to divide up the market and thus to restrain parallel imports does not have to be an agreement as such; in *Pittsburgh Corning Europe–Formica Belgium–Hertel*, J.O. 1972, L 272/35, Pittsburgh Corning Europe (PCE) used its trading position to cause its Belgian (Formica Belgium) and Dutch (Hertel) distributors simultaneously to adopt price lists which would afford protection to PCE's own distribution subsidiary operating in Germany. The Commission found that the adoption of these price lists with PCE's approval amounted to a concerted practice.

(d) *Agreements which apply dissimilar conditions to equivalent transactions with other trading parties, thereby placing them at a competitive disadvantage*

28–28 Sub-paragraph (*d*) concerns agreements and the like which embody conditions which are discriminatory as between various trading parties, and is at the same time wider and narrower than the ban on discrimination on grounds of nationality contained in Article 7 of the EEC Treaty; wider, because it does not turn on the criterion of nationality, and narrower, since discrimination must occur in relation to a restrictive trade practice.

(e) *agreements which make the conclusion of contracts subject to acceptance by other parties of supplementary obligations, which, by their nature, or according to commercial usage, have no connection with the subject of such contracts*

28–29 Sub-paragraph (*e*) concerns tying-in transactions set in the framework of agreements between firms. It has been argued that this example refers only to an obligation to tie in subsequent third parties, but the example would appear to apply even more obviously to the simple situation whereby a distributor, for example, obliges a retailer to take a supply of non-essential material in order to obtain a supply of an essential commodity.

Article 85 (2)

28–30 Article 85 (2) sets out the effects of a prohibition under Article 85 (1); prohibited agreements and decisions are automatically void, and deprived of civil effects. (It was not necessary to stipulate this for concerted practices since they are not expressed in legally binding terms.) However, the effects of such nullity once declared by the Commission or the Court of Justice are to be regulated by domestic law, *i.e.* Restrictive Trade Practices Act 1956 for the United Kingdom. Before March 13, 1962, the date on which Regulation 17/62 came into effect, an agreement could only be *declared* void by a national authority acting under the powers granted to it by Article 88 of the Treaty, or by the Commission acting under the terms of Article 89 (see generally § 28–82 below). As from March 13, 1962, Regulation 17/62 displaced the powers granted by the above-mentioned Articles.

Article 85 (3)

28–31 Article 85 (3) provides for a declaration of inapplicability of Article 85 (1) in respect of agreements fulfilling the conditions set out. Agreements in respect of which such a declaration is made are not void according to Community law, but may still be subject to a declaration of illegality under any applicable provisions of national law. The Commission now has sole power, by virtue of Article 9 (1) of Regulation 17/62, to give the declaration of inapplicability referred to in Article 85 (3).

A conflict of legal opinion surrounded the status of Article 85 (3), since it was regarded by some authors as constituting a statutory exemption from the prohibition of paragraph 1, whereas others considered it to constitute a reservation of the power to declare inapplicable the said prohibition. The alternative possibilities may be phrased thus: " is an agreement invalid unless and until it is exempted under paragraph 3, or is such an agreement always valid if it fulfils the qualifying conditions set out in the paragraph? " Both the Commission and the Court regard paragraph 3 as forming a reservation of the power to declare paragraph 1 inapplicable and that such a declaration will alone exempt the agreement from paragraph 1.

Paragraph 3 provides for declarations of inapplicability to be made in respect of individual agreements etc., on a case-by-case basis and of categories of such agreements, but Regulation 17/62 makes no mention of the possibility of granting block or group exemptions. Article 9 of this Regulation simply empowers the Commission to grant exemptions pursuant to Article 85 (3) and the Commission considered that this was a sufficient basis on which to issue a Notice declaring its intention to establish mechanisms whereby it would exempt certain categories of exclusive dealership agreements from the Article 85 (1) prohibition (J.O. 1962, 2921). However, this action did not meet with the approval of the Council, and an empowering Regulation was issued (Regulation 19/65, J.O. 1965, 533), enabling the Commission to issue an implementing Regulation (*in casu* Regulation 67/67, J.O. 1967, 849 and see generally § 28–24) relating to certain types of exclusive dealership agreements.

Regulation 67/67

28–32 Regulation 67/67 specifically covers the exclusive dealing agreements mentioned in the Council Regulation 19/65 and builds on the accumulated Community jurisprudence to that date, especially 56/65, *La Technique Minière* v. *Maschinenbau Ulm*, Rec. XII 337, [1966] C.M.L.R. 357, 56 & 58/64, *Consten and Grundig* v. *Commission*, Rec. XII 429, [1966] C.M.L.R. 418 and 32/65, *Italy* v. *Council and Commission*, Rec. XII 563, [1969] C.M.L.R. 39, the cases decided by the Court concerning the interpretation of Article 85. The types of agreement in question have already been discussed. Article 6 of Regulation 67/67 is a safeguard against abuse of a group exemption, reserving to the Commission the power to examine an agreement individually and to withdraw the benefit of the exemption granted if:

" (a) the goods to which the contract relates are not subject, in the territory covered by the contract, to competition from goods considered by the consumer as similar goods in view of their properties, price and intended use;

(b) it is not possible for other manufacturers to sell, in the territory covered by the contract, similar goods at the same stage of distribution as that of the exclusive dealer;

(c) the exclusive dealer has abused the exemption:

(1) by refusing, without objectively valid reasons, to supply in the territory covered by the contract categories of purchasers who cannot obtain supplies elsewhere, on suitable terms, of the goods to which the contract relates;

(2) by selling the goods to which the contract relates at excessive prices."

Although this provision militates against legal certainty, an exempted restrictive trade practice nevertheless retains its legal validity under a group exemption until the Commission has established the conditions set out in this Article. The provision is necessary also to guard against the possibility of granting too wide a group exemption which would otherwise legitimate agreements not fulfilling the requirements of Article 85 (3).

Regulation 67/67 was expressed to expire on December 31, 1972. Its validity has now been extended to December 31, 1982, by Regulation 2591/72, J.O. 1972, L 276/15.

Regulation 2821/71 implementing Regulation 2779/72

28–33   An empowering Regulation similar to Regulation 19/65 is Regulation 2821/71 of December 20, 1971, J.O. 1971, L 285/46, by which the Council authorised the Commission to provide for block exemptions in respect of agreements relating to the application of standards and types, research and development, and specialisation. Implementing Regulation 2779/72, J.O. 1972, L 292/23 provides for exemption in respect of specialisation agreements not prohibiting other specialisation agreements, or requiring sale of the product in question to, or its purchase from, other parties to the agreements, although stipulations for minimum stocks and spares or after-sales service and guarantee are acceptable. The exemption would be applicable only in respect of agreements governing less than 10 per cent. of the " relevant market " in any one Member State, and where the undertakings involved have a total turnover of less than 150 million u.a. The Regulation entered into force on January 1, 1973, and is valid for five years. The effects of the Regulation are retroactive to the time at which its conditions were met, but in no case to a date prior to the date of notification where notification was, before January 18, 1972, required (Art. 6).

Commission Notices

28–34   In addition to the use of the block exemption, the Commission has made a practice of issuing Notices which outline the Commission's attitude and policy towards certain types of restrictive practices. The effect is rather similar to issuing a block exemption. To date the Commission has issued the following such Notices:

(i) Notice concerning exclusive representation contracts with commercial agents, of December 24, 1962, J.O. 1962, 2921.

(ii) Notice concerning patent licensing agreements, of December 24, 1962, J.O. 1962, 2922.

(iii) Notice concerning agreements on co-operation between enterprises, of July 29, 1968, J.O. 1968, C 75/3, [1968] C.M.L.R. D5.

(iv) Notice concerning agreements of minor importance, of May 27, 1970, J.O. 1970, C 64/1, [1970] C.M.L.R. D15.

(v) Notice concerning imports of Japanese products, of October 21, 1972, J.O. 1972, C 111/13.

These notices have no statutory force, and serve merely as statements of intent on dealing with certain matters, and as such do not bind the Court of Justice. It is unlikely that the Court would in fact ever be faced with the question of the interpretation of a Commission Notice, for they are in very broad terms.

28-35   The first of these Notices was discussed in the context of exclusive distribution agreements (*supra*, § 28-23); the second is designed to explain the role of Article 85 with regard to patent licensing agreements. The latter Notice states that restrictions placed on a licensee in respect of the use of the patent, its application, and the number of units produced under the patent are regarded as permissible. But such restrictions as are placed on the patent holder and the licensee must by and large be indispensable to the attainment of the objectives of the licence agreement. The Notice further states that obligations regarding an exchange of know-how and improvements are considered acceptable provided they are reciprocal and non-exclusive. The fourth Commission Notice, of May 27, 1970, concerning agreements of minor importance has been discussed *supra*, § 28-17. The fifth Commission Notice, of October 21, 1972, concerning imports of Japanese products, is discussed *infra*, § 28-91.

Notice of July 29, 1968

28-36   Substantively the most important of the Commission's Notices is that of July 29, 1968, concerning co-operation between small and medium-sized firms. It states that certain kinds of agreement will not be considered contrary to Article 85 (1) as between such firms adding that " co-operation among large enterprises, too, can be economically justifiable from the angle of competition policy." The Notice lists eight categories of restrictive trade agreements which the Commission considers not to restrict competition.

The Notice and its interpretation must be considered in the light of a number of Commission decisions on related matters which were given at about the time of the issue of the Notice, notably *Eurogypsum*, *ACF*, *Socemas*, and *ACEC-Berliet*.

28–37   *Category 1: Exchange of information and experience.*   Category 1 includes agreements having as their sole object:

    (a) an exchange of information or experience,

    (b) joint market research,

    (c) the joint execution of comparative studies of undertakings or industries, or

    (d) the joint preparation of statistics and calculation models.

As to the first of these, the Commission considers that such exchanges could cause difficulty where concrete recommendations are made, or where conclusions are given in a form likely to induce parallel action. Equally, such exchanges could cause difficulty where they relate solely to turnover or investment figures. As to joint market research agreements, cf. *Alliance des constructeurs français de machines-outils (ACF)*, J.O. 1968, L 201/1, [1968] C.M.L.R. D23, where the Alliance, although primarily a sales syndicate, also undertook export market research on behalf of its members (see also *supra*, § 28–18).

28–38   *Category 2: Co-operation in accounting and like matters; Category 3: Joint research and development.*   Category 2 concerns agreements having as their sole object co-operation in accounting matters, joint provision of credit guarantees, joint debt-collecting associations and joint business or tax consultancies.   Category 3 on research and development (R&D) is perhaps of particular significance in view of the generally inadequate levels of expenditure on R&D by European firms.   The Commission has for some time been in the process of promoting a progressive industrial policy, and is fully aware that an over-rigid application of the rules on competition might lead to a worsening of the Community's industrial position *vis-à-vis* the rest of the world, instead of improving it.   Hence the desire to promote R&D especially for relatively uncompetitive small and medium-sized firms.   Unnecessary restrictions on own account R&D or on access to or use of the results of research are, however, to be prohibited.   (In *Eurogypsum*, J.O. 1968, L 57/9, [1968] C.M.L.R. D1, there were no such restrictions.)

28–39   The Commission decision in *ACEC-Berliet*, J.O. 1968, L 201/17, [1968] C.M.L.R. D35, probably concerns " large " firms rather than small and medium-sized ones, but it is instructive on the permissible degree of restriction in research agreements.   ACEC, a Belgian electrical engineering firm, had devised a system of electrical transmission for use in heavy road vehicles, especially buses, and had made a co-operation agreement with Berliet, one of the major French manufacturers of such vehicles, with a view to exploiting the invention to best advantage.   Berliet was, however, to be the sole French purchaser of the invention, and ACEC was to be permitted to sell it to one manufacturer only in each of the other Community countries.   Berliet also agreed to buy electrical transmission systems only from ACEC.   The parties further agreed to fix in common the prices of the products resulting from their co-operation, and to share the results of any future research undertaken in common. The only trade mark restriction was that the jointly developed product was to bear the sole trade mark of Berliet for sale in France. The agreement had been notified to the Commission under Article 4 of Regulation 17/62 and was accorded exemption on the basis that, although the agreement did contain restrictions of a kind which would normally incur the prohibition of Article 85 (1), *i.e.* the sales restrictions on ACEC and the purchasing restriction on Berliet, the Commission nevertheless considered that in a research project of this nature such restrictions were essential if the innovation were to reach the stage of practical application.

It would appear that the Commission's Notice of July 29, 1968 was designed to enable such research agreements to proceed without interference, and that non-interference was to extend to industrial application of the fruits of the common research (Category 3 of the Notice). It was clearly the imposition of the additional sales restrictions that led the parties to the ACEC-Berliet agreement to seek an exemption under Article 85 (3). The basic research agreement here involved is illustrative of the type of agreement which was intended to benefit from the general exemption offered in the Notice.

28–40 A recent decision concerning joint R&D, *Henkel-Colgate*, J.O. 1972, L 14/14, related to an agreement between major manufacturers of detergents. The European market in such products is already considered to be oligopolistic, and the companies parties to the agreement could not be considered to be " small or medium-sized firms " within the meaning of the Notice of July 29, 1968, and were outside direct scope. Nonetheless the Commission granted an exemption under Article 85 (3). This decision is therefore of interest because it concerns firms of larger size than even ACEC or Berliet. The agreement set up a common research company, each of the founders, Henkel and Colgate, having equal access to the results of the research, and first option to exploit the results to actual production stage. The parties also bound themselves to grant licences to the research company in respect of any discoveries made individually. An exemption was nevertheless granted since neither firm was restricted by the agreement in their access to and use of the results of the research of the common company, and because the cost of jointly effected R&D would be less than R&D undertaken independently by the firms concerned.

28–41 *Category 4: Joint use of production and other facilities; Category 5: Temporary groupings.* Category 4 concerns the joint use of production and other facilities, and is of little importance. Category 5 allows agreements having as their sole object the setting up of working partnerships for the common execution of orders, where the participating undertakings do not compete with each other as regards the work to be done, or where each of them by itself is unable to execute the orders, or is directed to the supply of goods and services which the other party is not in a position to supply, and to consortium agreements between companies combining to carry out large-scale projects otherwise outside the capabilities of any one firm. The only real threat to workable competition that the Commission sees in this type of arrangement is the risk of the tie-up becoming permanent.

28–42   *Category 6: Joint sales and after-sales and repair agreements.* Category 6 indicates that joint sales agreements and joint after-sales and repair service arrangements will be deemed exempt from Article 85 (1) provided they do not form a noticeable restriction on competition, even though the firms involved may be in competition with each other. This exemption would seem rather wide, but the Notice leaves the criteria for evaluating the effects of the types of agreements to which it refers, deliberately vague, and the facts of the *Machines-Outils (ACF)* decision, J.O. 1968, L 201/1, [1968] C.M.L.R. D23 § 28–18, *supra,* seem well to illustrate the situation envisaged by this particular category, although the decision was given before the Notice was officially published, and the actual decision granted a negative clearance under Article 2, Regulation 17/62 in respect of a duly notified joint export sales agreement. Particularly important in the context of the present discussion is that the firms involved in the Alliance were all medium-sized (the Commission gives approximate market-share figures to support this assertion) and that they were each producing non-competing products before the Alliance was set up, but were left free to fix their own resale prices. It remains to be seen whether the Commission makes full use of the liberal wording in this category.

28–43   *Category 7: Joint advertising; Category 8: Common quality, etc., marks.* A general exception is accorded in respect of joint advertising agreements (Category 7) and in respect of agreements on quality marks, etc. (Category 8). Agreements falling into the two categories are probably not of any very great significance for the Community competition policy, but they are nevertheless of interest, in that they give some indication of types of co-operation which are of practical importance for industry. The marketing techniques coming within the two categories can be expected to result in better sales and a reduction in the cost of promotional activities generally. The Commission's sole concern in these matters appears to be that the participant enterprises should retain their freedom to act according to their own wishes and requirements. The negative clearance decision in respect of *Transocean Marine Paint Association,* J.O. 1967, 163/10, [1967] C.M.L.R. D9, is illustrative of the relevant considerations. The Association was formed between several small to medium-sized marine paint manufacturers, both inside and outside the Community, the main purpose of the Association being to provide for supply of a marine paint of a standard quality and name throughout all the countries in which the members of the Association operated, so that these manufacturers could compete effectively with the large marine paint manufacturers. Effective competition could only be provided if a common product were available in the widest possible market. Further, with a view to maximising market coverage, each member of the Association bound himself to keep his home territory supplied with stocks of the commonly marketed product. Finally a system of common advertising was necessary if potential consumers were to be informed that the standard paint was available in the territories covered by the members of the Association. The agreements provided for by the Association were favourably regarded by the Commission, since they were considered to improve the quality and availability of the products in question and on balance did more to increase competition than to restrict it.

28-44   Other decisions concerning common advertising and the use of common standards for products are *Vereniging van vernis en verffabrikanten in Nederland (VVVF)*, J.O. 1969, L 168/22, [1970] C.M.L.R. D1, and the *Association pour la promotion du tube d'acier soudé électriquement,* J.O. 1970, L 153/14, [1970] C.M.L.R. D31. Both of these were negative clearance decision, and were not as such based on the notice of July 29, 1968; they are, however, indicative of the Commission's likely attitude towards future applications for exemptions. In *VVVF*, the Commission allowed common quality standards to be set for members' exports after the restrictive parts of the Association agreement had been excised, although the Association did not stipulate resale export prices and conditions in sales to other Member States. The rules of the Association on sales to non-EEC countries were far more rigorous, fixing minimum prices, and requiring sample exports to be examined for compliance with the Association's quality standards; the Commission seems here to have taken the same view as that taken in *Grosfillex-Fillistorf,* J.O. 1964, 915, [1964] C.M.L.R. 237, assuming that a double customs duty barrier would in practice prevent re-import of minimum-priced goods back into the Common Market territory.

The Commission also gave a negative clearance in respect of the *Association pour la promotion du tube d'acier soudé électriquement,* which was set up to promote its members' sales and to maintain quality standards. Each of the four participant enterprises was allowed, however, to advertise on its own account, something which the Commission deems essential if there is to be no noticeable restraint on trade. The Association also used a trade mark to maintain its quality standards; the Commission considered that the end was more important than the means, and that since any manufacturer in that particular field could join the Association, there was no resultant restraint on trade.

28-45   The overall purpose of the Commission's Notice of July 29, 1968 has been to indicate the Commission's attitude towards co-operation agreements and the like between small and medium-sized firms; that was its intention, since it has no obligatory effect. Since the Notice acts as a block exemption, particular examples of operation of the Notice do not form the subject of Commission decisions, and one can only consider the Notice in comparison with extensions from it, *i.e.* in the *Henkel-Colgate* decision, J.O. 1972, L 14/14. It seems that the Commission has used this reasoning to give negative clearance under Regulation 17/62 (*viz. VVVF* and *Electrically-welded Tube Association*) rather than exemptions, although the Notice was intended to effect exemptions.

The fourth Commission Notice of May 27, 1970, J.O. 1970, C 64/1, [1970] C.M.L.R. D15, has been mentioned above (§ 28–17), but it is relevant to note that the criteria for exemption are statistical, thus revealing the Commission's awareness that a blind application of the Community competition rules could only lead to unsatisfactory results. The individual decisions taken since 1968 show an increasing willingness to accept a form of " rule of reason," based on economic facts such as market shares upon which to frame its pronouncements (*e.g. Machines-Outils (ACF)*, J.O. 1968, L 201/1, [1968] C.M.L.R. D23, *Socemas*, J.O. 1968, L 201/4, [1968] C.M.L.R. D28, and *Convention Chaufourniers* (*Limeburners'* or *Cement Makers' Agreement*), J.O. 1969, L 122/8, [1969] C.M.L.R. D15). The fourth Notice, of May 27, 1970, on agreements of minor importance is a logical extension of this thinking, besides reducing the number of notifications under Regulation 17/62 still remaining to be processed.

Conditions for exemption under Article 85 (3)

28–46   Examination of Article 85 (3) reveals that four conditions, two positive and two negative, must be fulfilled before an exemption may be granted under its provisions.

28–47   (1) " *Improving the production or distribution or . . . promoting technical or economic progress.*" Clearly it is in the Community interest to impugn only those agreements which are harmful to the best interests of a liberal market economy as envisaged by the Community Treaties. It follows that assessments of the compatibility with the Common Market of restrictive trade practices must take an overall view of the restraint in question, this in itself requiring an examination of the economic context of the agreement. The Treaty indicates that economic factors are to be taken into account, it being provided in Article 85 (3) that agreements which contribute to improving the production or distribution of goods or to promoting technical or economic progress may be exempted from Article 85 (1). Some indication of the type of examination required in respect of individual cartels was given by the Court of Justice in 56 & 58/64, *Consten and Grundig* v. *Commission*, Rec. XII, 429, [1966] C.M.L.R. 418.

The Court ruled that:

> " The undertakings are entitled to an adequate examination by
> the Commission of their requests for the application of Article 85
> (3). To that end, the Commission may not limit itself to requiring
> of the undertakings proof of the conditions required for the
> exemption, but should, as a matter of good administration, co-
> operate through its own resources in the establishment of the
> relevant facts and circumstances. Besides, the exercise of the Com-
> mission's powers necessarily implies complex economic judgments.
> Judicial control of these judgments should respect that character
> by limiting itself to an examination of the materiality of the facts and
> legal descriptions which the Commission deduces therefrom."
> (Trans. [1966] C.M.L.R. 418 at p. 477.)

28–48   Examples of restraints which may qualify under this condition are
exclusive dealing agreements, which may improve distribution and
supply by providing the manufacturer with a clearer idea of his
particular product market, and thus enable him the more easily to
adapt his products to the market demands; and specialisation agreements, since they may well have the effect of increasing the production
of each firm involved in the agreement. (See Commission's decisions of
exemption in *Clima-Chappée-Buderus,* J.O. 1969, L 195/1, [1970]
C.M.L.R. D7 and *Jaz-Peter,* J.O. 1969, L 195/5, [1970] C.M.L.R. 129.)
In the recent Article 85 (3) exemption decision on *Davidson Rubber
Co.,* J.O. 1972, L 143/31, [1972] C.M.L.R. D52, relating to Davidson's
patent licensing agreements with firms in Germany, Italy and France,
the Commission considered that the agreements fell under the Article
85 (1) prohibition, but was prepared to grant an exemption on the basis
that it considered all four conditions set out in Article 85 (3) to be fulfilled. In respect of the first condition, the Commission stated:

> " The patent licences and the know-how concessions granted by the
> Davidson Rubber Company to Happich GmbH, Maglum S.A., and
> Gallino S.p.A. [the Community firms benefiting from these agree-
> ments], contribute to promoting economic progress by permitting
> the exploitation in the countries which are at present part of the
> EEC of a modern process of moulding elbow-rests and cushions
> for motor cars, which consists, not as before in a group of assembled
> components, but in fitments padded in a single piece, without
> seams, which can be manufactured in large runs and under favour-
> able price conditions, in varied forms and designs and adapted to
> each car model.
> " These agreements also contribute to promoting technical pro-
> gress and improving the production of the articles made by the
> Davidson process in so far as by granting the exploitation of this
> process to European undertakings which have acquired a wide
> experience in the manufacture of accessories for the car industry

they permit a rational adaptation of the techniques introduced onto the European market to its tastes and requirements."
(Trans. [1972] C.M.L.R. D52 at p. D61.)

28–49   (2) *" Allowing consumers a fair share of the resulting benefit."* Although the second condition, that consumers be allowed a fair share of the resulting benefit, suggests that it might concern the man in the street as a consumer, it must be understood as referring generally to all users of a given product, that is, including any intermediate processor of the goods. The French word *" utilisateur "* used in this context expresses the idea more succinctly: "resulting benefit" can be taken to mean any advantage which enures to the user by virtue of the agreement; it should not be understood solely in pecuniary terms. It would appear from certain Commission decisions that the Commission is prepared to accept general assurances that this condition is fulfilled, *i.e.* that in a competitive market the parties to an agreement automatically extend to their consumers any benefit resulting from the agreement. (See Commission decision in *Clima-Chappée-Buderus.*)

In the *Davidson* decision, the Commission said of this condition:
" The users, namely the manufacturers of cars, derive a fair share of the profit resulting from the economic and technical progress examined above because, thanks to these licences they can have available in the Common Market fitments for car interiors manufactured by a new technique and even perfected since its creation, adapted to their particular needs and offering increased security and greater comfort. Most of them, thanks to the presence on their territory and close to their assembly plant of a Davidson licensee, can count on a more regularised and more continuous supply of car interior fitments of this type."
(*Ibid.*)

28–50   (3) *" [Do] not: impose on the undertakings concerned restrictions which are not indispensable to the attainment of these objectives."* The third condition that the agreement should not impose indispensable restrictions in effect merely underlines further the exemption idea of Article 85 (3) as a whole, since no restrictions will be tolerated which do not fulfil the two positive criteria. Application of this condition often results in the deletion of any clauses which the Commission deems superfluous to the "attainment of these objectives," before it grants exemption. Such was the situation in the *Davidson* decision. The Commission explained that in the initial versions of the licence agreements, there was an obligation on licensees not to contest the validity of the Davidson patent: after representations by the Commission, the parties excised this clause and the Commission was then able to state there were no superfluous restrictions in the agreements. The Commission has nevertheless been not ungenerous in its interpretation of the third condition, as for example in the decision in *ACEC-Berliet,* J.O.

1968, L 201/17, [1968] C.M.L.R. D35 (and see §28–39, *supra*). Here the Commission was of the opinion that the clauses of the agreement which restricted the commercial freedom of both parties were indispensable if commercial exploitation of the electrical transmission was to be realised.

28–51   (4) " [*Do not*] *afford such undertakings the possibility of eliminating competition in respect of a substantial part of the products in question.*" The fourth condition, that the agreement should not eliminate substantially all competition, demands an assessment of the effects of the agreement as a whole on the market for the particular goods in question. Thus one must take into account whether the agreement eliminates competition in products of substitution; in other words a determination of " the relevant market " for the goods in question is necessary. ("Relevant market " is the term commonly used in United States antitrust law to denote those goods which in practice compete with the goods, the subject of the agreement in question.)   The fourth condition also excludes from Article 85 (3) exemption agreements which offer the *possibility* of an elimination of competition in an agreement. However, the condition will only operate if the possibility of such elimination arises in respect of a *substantial* part of the products in question : the Commission usually finds that such is not the case.

In the *Davidson* decision, J.O. 1972, L 143/31, [1972] C.M.L.R. D52, the Commission said, concerning the fourth condition, that although the position held by the licensee inside the EEC was an important one, the agreements did not lay open the possibility of elimination of competition, since there were other ways of making the interior parts for cars and moreover many car manufacturers made their own. In the *ACEC-Berliet* decision, the Commission stated that there was no such possibility because of the competition provided by buses equipped with conventional transmisssions, as opposed to the electrical transmission system, the subject of the agreement.

ARTICLE 86

28–52 Article 86 is considered to provide the Community with powers to control what are described in the Article as dominant positions, or, more familiarly, monopolies. However, Article 86 strikes not only at monopolies *stricto sensu* but provides also for the control of oligopolistic market situations. But Article 86 operates only against the *abuse* of a dominant position held in a particular market by one or more enterprises. The abuse must also potentially affect trade between Member States (*cf.* use of the latter expression in Art. 85 (1)). The Treaty does not therefore prohibit dominant positions as being illegal *per se* (in contrast to the strict approach adopted by the Monopolies and Mergers Act 1965, C. 50, the comparable United Kingdom statute).

Article 86 thus envisages the fulfilment of three separate conditions before the prohibition in the Article may be invoked. These are that:

(a) a dominant position must exist;

(b) such a position must be abused;

(c) there must be a possibility that trade between Member States may be affected by the abuse.

These three conditions were indicated as necessary before Article 86 could operate in 24/67, *Parke, Davis* v. *Probel,* Rec. XIV 81, [1968] C.M.L.R. 47. There the question was whether the enforcement of national patent rights for the purposes of prohibiting parallel imports from another Member State as well as for enforcing a retail price in the State protected by a patent higher than that pertaining in the exporting State, where patents on the type of goods in question—pharmaceuticals—were not permitted, could be regarded as a violation of Article 86. The Court held that the legitimate application of acquired national patent rights to prevent the circumvention of the protection afforded by that patent did not of itself constitute an abuse of a dominant position, if it only incidentally prevented parallel imports. *Cf.* also 78/70, *DGG* v. *Metro,* Rec. XVII 487, [1971] C.M.L.R. 631. Further, the Court did not consider that the simple fact that a patentee charged more for his product than the importer of a comparable product not the subject of a national patent *ipso facto* indicated an abuse of a dominant position. In 40/70, *Sirena* v. *Eda,* Rec. XVII 69, [1971] C.M.L.R. 260, the Court nevertheless indicated that a large price differential might be regarded as an abuse of dominant position if it did not seem objectively justified. See also 78/70, *DGG* v. *Metro.*

(a) A dominant position must exist

28–53   The Treaty provides no definition of " dominant position " but in economic terms it is considered to exist where a firm wields sufficient economic power to influence its particular market in a substantial and predictable manner. The Commission does not favour a mathematical calculation of market shares as a means of defining the dominant position, a means used by some systems of municipal monopolies law, although it would appear to have adopted this method of assessment for ECSC purposes (*cf. infra,* § 28–55 and Proposal Regarding the Restructuring of the Steel Industry, J.O. 1970, C 12/5).

The EEC Treaty contains no specific provision on the control of mergers, and it remains controversial whether, and if so to what extent, Article 86 can be employed for this purpose (see below). ECSC practice seems to indicate that the Commission may in fact evolve statistical criteria in assessing what constitutes a dominant position for EEC purposes, especially if it is moving, as the *Continental Can* (or *Europemballage*) decision, J.O. 1972, L 7/25, [1972] C.M.L.R. D11, would suggest, towards using Article 86 to control what are in its view dangerous mergers. Indeed, much of the ongoing argument between the Commission and Continental Can has centred on their opposing calculations of Continental's market share before and after the proposed merger, and on the question of the market to be considered in assessing whether a dominant position already exists.

The use of statistical criteria assumes an assessment of the dominant position in relation to a given market, since a dominant position cannot be said to exist of itself, and must be related to the economic context in which it operates. The narrower the definition of the economic context, the easier it becomes to establish the existence of a dominant position. The economic inquiry involved is customarily referred to as the assessment of the "relevant market." As already mentioned this is held to include not only the products directly equivalent to the product which is claimed to enjoy a dominant position, but also products of substitution.

(b) Abuse of a dominant position

28–54   As already stated it is only the *abuse* of the dominant position that is illegal under Article 86. For example a merger between companies which results in the newly-formed company holding a dominant position in a particular market will not be considered contrary to Article 86. However, use of its predominance in that market to impose unfair conditions on customers, or attempts in the short term to undercut remaining rivals to a degree inconsistent with sound economic principles, in the hope of driving these rivals out of the market, would be considered to constitute an abuse of the dominant position, to which the Article 86 prohibition would apply. It would appear also that such an abuse exists where a firm in a dominant position attempts further to increase its control of the particular market by taking over further rival firms —*Continental Can* decision.

28–55   Unlike the EEC Treaty, the ECSC Treaty has express provisions on mergers. Article 66 provides that all concentrations in the field covered by the ECSC Treaty must have the prior authorisation of the High Authority, and that this authorisation will be granted only if the criteria set out in paragraph 2 of the Article are fulfilled, *i.e.* if the concentration does not give the undertaking concerned the power to determine prices, or to control production, or to evade the rules on competition in the Treaty, particularly by creating an artificially privileged position on the market, giving substantial advantage in access to supplies or markets. Article 66 (3) ECSC provides for general exemption from this authorisation procedure, implemented in very liberal terms by Decision 54/25, J.O. 1954, 346, now replaced by Decision 67/25, J.O. 1967, 154/11. The basis for exemption from Article 66 (2) is statistical; if the combined annual output of the firms involved in the concentration is below the upper output limit (10 million metric tons for coal production firms) a concentration will be allowed without any prior authorisation. Decision 67/25 also applies criteria of total annual turnover, thus concentrations between steel distribution firms having a combined annual turnover of less than 60 million u.a. may proceed without prior authorisation.

Under the ECSC Treaty the Commission may thus control the formation of larger groupings between firms and there is consequently no need to use the powers contained in Article 66 (7), which parallel those contained in Article 86 of the EEC Treaty, to control dominant positions where the abuse consists in further concentration or merger.

28–56   The Commission has in the absence of express powers attempted to deal with concentrations in the field of the EEC Treaty through Article 86. In a study published in 1966 (*Le problème de la concentration dans le marché commun*, Série concurrence no. 3, Brussels 1966) the Commission reviewed its powers. It considered that although Article 85 could be used in certain instances, *e.g.* where a merger was by agreement, Article 86 would be more apposite if the Commission were first able to establish that a firm or group held a dominant position, and that it used this position to take over similar firms. Such an extension of the scope of Article 86 was hotly contested in academic and industrial circles; the Commission nevertheless applied it in practice in its decision on *Continental Can*, J.O. 1972, L 7/25, [1972] C.M.L.R. D11.

The Commission took exception to the acquisition by Continental Can through Europemballage S.A., its Belgian operational subsidiary, of a majority shareholding in Thomassen & Drijver-Verblifa NV (TDV), the most important packaging firm in Benelux when it already controlled Schmalbach-Lubeca-Werke AG, the largest producer of metal packaging and containers in Germany. The Commission considered that Europemballage had, with the take-over of Schmalbach, acquired a dominant position in the metal containers market and packaging, taking into account the interests it already held, and the tie-up with Continental Can, by virtue of which Europemballage had access to considerable technical know-how and patents. The abuse of dominant position was considered to consist in the take-over of one of its principal rivals, TDV, with the result that in certain specific fields the competition that had previously existed despite Europemballage's market dominance was to all intents and purposes eliminated. The interpretation of the notion of abuse as applied in this decision needs no evidence of actual abuse on the market; it assumes such abuse from statistical data evidencing market shares. It is considered desirable to apply such an interpretation of abuse, for prevention is better than cure; a conventional application of Article 86 would require subsequent de-cartelisation rather than prior prohibition. In practice it is obvious that this is the only way in which the Commission could acquire any real form of control over concentrations and mergers, but nevertheless it is considered in some quarters that the abuse must be of a more practical and concrete nature to attract Article 86. It was argued in defence by Continental Can that TDV freely agreed to the take-over by Europemballage. While it would always be difficult to establish coercion by any party, except in a publicly-contested take-over bid, any take-over involves an assertion of economic power by the acquiring party. The Commission ruled against Continental Can in its decision, and ordered Continental Can to divest itself of some of its European interests. Continental Can denied that it held any dominant position, and argued that the Commission had not considered the correct relevant market. Continental Can has applied to the Court of Justice for annulment of the decision under Article 173 EEC (case 6/72, J.O. 1972, C 24/1).

28–57   The only other Commission decision so far taken under Article 86 is that in respect of *Gesellschaft für musikalische Aufführungs- und mechanische Vervielfältigungsrechte (GEMA)*, J.O. 1971, L 134/15, [1971] C.M.L.R. D35. GEMA is the body which protects German musical copyrights, and parallels similar semi-public bodies operating in other Member States of the EEC. (The Commission was at pains to point out, however, that GEMA could not benefit from any kind of exemption under Article 90 (as to which, see *infra,* § 29–01), since it was in no real sense a public undertaking.) The Commission had considered that since GEMA and the comparable organisations in the other Member States each held a national monopoly over affairs relating to musical copyright in their own country, each organisation was therefore in a dominant position within a substantial part of the Common Market. It had made representations to each of these bodies, with a view to obtaining the voluntary abandonment of certain discriminatory practices. All the other organisations agreed to drop such practices, with the exception of GEMA. The Commission then took proceedings against GEMA under Article 86, since it considered that the maintenance of the discriminatory practices constituted an abuse of dominant position.

GEMA was considered to be exploiting the dominant position in an improper manner by:

(1) discriminating against nationals of other Member States;
(2) binding its members to unnecessary obligations, in particular by unfairly complicating the movement of members to other authors' rights societies;
(3) preventing, through its system, the establishment of a single market in the supply of services of music publishers;
(4) extending copyright, through contractual means, to non-copyright works;
(5) discriminating against independent importers of gramophone records as compared with manufacturers of records and by levying the whole licence fee for imports from other Member States, although the licence fee had already been paid for the records;

(6) discriminating against the importers of tape recorders and optical sound recorders as compared with the German manufacturers of such recorders.

An application to the Court for the annulment of the Commission's decision in *GEMA* has been lodged as case 45/71, J.O. 1971, C 84/11. Pending its final decision, the Court has suspended execution of the Commission decision for six months (45/71R, *GEMA* v. *Commission,* Rec. XVII 791, [1972] C.M.L.R. 694). The Commission has slightly amended its own decision, allowing a technical objection by *GEMA,* J.O. 1972, L 166/22, [1972] C.M.L.R. D115.

(c) There must be a possibility that trade between Member States may be affected by the abuse of the dominant position

28–58   This condition parallels a condition in almost exactly the same words in Article 85 (1). The considerations which apply to Article 85 (1) in this respect apply here too (see *supra,* § 28–11).

List of examples of abuse

28–59   Article 86 gives four examples of abuse of dominant position; these examples are directly comparable with examples (*a*) (*b*) (*d*) and (*e*) in Article 85 (1). There is no illustration comparable to Article 85 (1) (*c*), although the restrictive trade practices there referred to, namely market sharing, may constitute manifestations of an abuse of a dominant position held by a group of firms acting in concert. However, the examples given in both Articles are prefaced by the phrase " in particular," so neither of the lists is to be regarded as being exhaustive.

So far as unfair purchase or selling prices are concerned, it should be remembered that the Court of Justice does not consider price differentials *per se* illegal, although high prices which do not seem objectively justified may constitute conclusive evidence of an abuse: 24/67, *Parke, Davis* v. *Probel*, Rec. XIV 81, [1968] C.M.L.R. 47; 40/70, *Sirena* v. *Eda*, Rec. XVII 69, [1971] C.M.L.R. 260, and 78/70, *DGG* v. *Metro*, Rec. XVII 487, [1971] C.M.L.R. 631. Similarly the exercise of national patent rights so as incidentally to protect one national market from another is not *per se* illegal: *Parke, Davis*; *DGG* v. *Metro*.

The other examples given in Article 86 are practices which operate in exactly the same way as the examples given in Article 85, except that the practices arise not out of an agreement, decision or concerted practice between enterprises, but out of the exploitation of a dominant position within a substantial part of the Common Market. However, the examples given stand more obviously as examples of the action of a dominant enterprise rather than as that of a group of enterprises acting pursuant to an agreement with each other.

Effect of prohibition

28–60   Article 86 states that any abuse of dominant position within the Common Market or a substantial part of it is prohibited. If the abuse fulfils the three criteria set out in *Parke, Davis* (see § 28–52, *supra*) it is automatically prohibited without the need for any prior decision by any Community body. Unlike Article 85 (2), however, Article 86 did not indicate what civil consequences are to flow from the Community prohibition. The respective national authorities must therefore make domestic provision in respect of violations of the prohibition of Article 86. The Commission has power by virtue of Article 3 of Regulation 17/62 to require undertakings involved to end the infringement. The Commission may, in respect of violations of Article 86, impose fines of up to 10 per cent. of the turnover for the previous year of the firm or firms involved (Art. 15, Regulation 17/62). By Article 16 of the same Regulation the Commission may enforce observance of the prohibition by imposing periodic penalty payments.

Regulation 17/62 [1]

28–61 Regulation 17/62 was the first Regulation to be issued implementing Articles 85 and 86 of the Treaty. Power to lay down implementing rules is conferred by Article 87 (1) EEC, which in its first paragraph provides that within three years of the entry into force of the Treaty the Council was, acting unanimously on a proposal from the Commission and after consulting the Assembly, to adopt any appropriate Regulations or directives to give effect in Community law to the principles set out in Articles 85 and 86. It was evidently not considered appropriate to issue instruments requiring municipal legislative action for the purposes of establishing uniform rules on competition, and thus no directives implementing Articles 85 and 86 have been issued, only Regulations. Regulation 17 itself was not adopted until shortly after the expiry of the three-year period already referred to and it may therefore be supposed to have been made by virtue of Article 87 (1), second sub-para., which permits such provisions to be laid down thereafter by qualified majority vote.

28–62   Article 87 (2) states that the Regulations and directives referred to in paragraph 1 are to be designed in particular to fulfil certain aims. The preamble to Regulation 17 suggests that these aims were in practice to be tempered by measures of expediency. Thus it refers to the necessity of providing for a balanced application of Articles 85 and 86 in a uniform manner (first whereas); this implies a divergence of views as to the effect and applicability of the basic Treaty rules on competition. The Regulation attempts to resolve some of the differences. Accordingly Article 1 declares that:

[1] J.O. 1962, 204.

" . . . agreements, decisions and concerted practices of the kind described in Article 85 (1) of the Treaty and the abuse of a dominant position in the market, within the meaning of Article 86 of the Treaty, shall be prohibited, *no prior decision to that effect being required.*"

In case 13/61, *de Geus* v. *Bosch*, Rec. VIII 89, [1962] C.M.L.R. 1, the Court stated:

"Articles 88 and 89 are, however, not of such a nature as to ensure complete and consistent application of Article 85 so that their mere presence would permit the assumption that Article 85 would have been fully effective from the date of the entry into force of the Treaty. . . .

"It follows [from the effect of Article 6 (2) and Article 5 (1) of Regulation 17] that the authors of the Regulation seem to have envisaged also that at the date of its entry into force there would be subsisting agreements caught by Article 85 (1) but in respect of which decisions under Article 85 (3) had not been taken; without such agreements thereby being null and void.

"The opposite interpretation would lead to the inadmissible result that some agreements would have been null and void already for several years without having been so declared by any authority, and even though they might ultimately be validated subsequently with retroactive effect."

(Trans. [1962] C.M.L.R. 1 at pp. 27–28.)

The Court thus held that Articles 85 and 86 did not begin to bite until after the entry into force of Regulation 17. In strict terms, therefore, it is the Regulation which is to be considered immediately applicable, not the Treaty provisions. (See also § 18–10 on direct applicability of these Articles.)

Regulation 17: implementation of aims set out in Article 87 (2)

–63 As already mentioned, Article 87 (2) sets out a number of aims which the Regulations or directives referred to in paragraph 1 are to be designed to achieve namely:

"(*a*) to ensure compliance with the prohibitions laid down in Article 85 (1) and Article 86 by making provision for fines and periodic penalty payments;

(*b*) to lay down detailed rules for the application of Article 85 (3), taking into account the need to ensure effective supervision on the one hand, and to simplify administration to the greatest possible extent on the other;

(*c*) to define, if need be, in the various branches of the economy, the scope of the provisions of Articles 85 and 86;

(*d*) to define the respective functions of the Commission and of the Court of Justice in applying the provisions laid down in this paragraph;

(*e*) to determine the relationship between national laws and the provisions contained in this Section or adopted pursuant to this Article."

(a) *Fines and periodic penalty payments*

28–64   Provision is made in respect of fines in Article 15 of the Regulation, in Article 16 in respect of periodic penalty payments. The general system of control is set up by Articles 1 to 11 inclusive.

(b) *The application of Article 85 (3)*

28–65   Detailed rules for application of Article 85 (3) are laid down in Articles 4 to 10 of the Regulation. It is to be noted that one of the arguments used against the immediate applicability of Article 85 was that Article 85 (3) (on exemptions) lacked effective implementing provisions. This was contended on the basis that the Article formed an integral whole, and the Court accepted this view. It is true that the Court has in some later cases considered individual paragraphs of certain Articles to be directly applicable—*e.g.* 6/64, *Costa* v. *ENEL,* Rec. X 1141, [1964] C.M.L.R. 425, but equally it was subsequently held that in certain contexts individual articles or groups of articles must be considered as a whole—*e.g.* 13/68, *Salgoil* v. *Italian Ministry for Foreign Trade,* Rec. XIV 661, [1969] C.M.L.R. 181. The ground for rejection has thus not been superseded.

The need to ensure effective supervision and to simplify administration to the greatest possible extent is emphasised especially in this sub-paragraph: and Regulation 17 attempts to reconcile these requirements, the substantive provisions being contained in Articles 1 to 11 and Articles 15 and 16. The Commission is the prime executive power in this, as in most areas.

(c) *Definition of scope of Articles 85 and 86 in the various branches of the economy*

28–66   The definition of the scope of application of Articles 85 and 86 to the various branches of the economy was clearly not considered to be an important function, and it was in any case considered in some quarters that such definitions would derogate from the desired uniformity of rules. Article 12 of the Regulation nevertheless provides for the carrying out of inquiries to determine whether there is a breach of Articles 85 and 86 in the sector as a whole. But this does not seem to be directed to the same problem.

(d) *Division of powers*

28–67   Articles 11 to 14 of the Regulation set out the general investigative process of the Commission, Article 17 providing for review of penalties by the Court of Justice. Decisions as to the inapplicability of Article 85 (3) are subject to revision by the Court (Art. 9 of the regulation). These provisions are of course without prejudice to the Court's other powers of review contained in the Treaty, notably Articles 173 * and 175.*

(e) *Relationship of Community and national rules*

68   So far as the relationship between Community and national rules is concerned, Article 9 (3) of the Regulation provides that the Member States remain competent to apply Articles 85 (1) and 86 so long as the Commission has not initiated any procedure under the Regulation. Only the Commission may grant exemptions under Article 85 (3), however: Article 9 (1). Articles 10, 11, 13 and 14 provide for liaison with national authorities and for Commission investigative powers.

Regulation 17: detailed examination

Article 2

69   Article 2 empowers the Commission to certify that agreements do not come within the ambit of either Article 85 (1) or Article 86 of the EEC Treaty. This procedure was not envisaged by the Treaty, but forms part of the Community strategy for dealing expeditiously with the huge number of agreements potentially subject to Articles 85 and 86. Other devices are the use of block exemptions, test cases and Notices.

The procedure laid down in Article 2 of the Regulation is generally referred to as " negative clearance "—the English title of the Article. It has also been referred to as " negative attestation "—a direct translation of the French " *attestation négative.*"

Undertakings or associations must apply for clearance to the Commission. Clearance will be given only if, on the basis of the facts known to it, the Commission finds no grounds for action under Article 85 (1) or 86. This does not amount to a finding that the agreement does not infringe these Articles but only that there is no present evidence that it does. Originally the Commission required firms to submit separate forms, depending on whether they sought a negative clearance or an exemption under Article 85 (3) (Form A for negative clearance, Form B for exemption applications: Art. 4, Regulation 27/62, J.O. 1962, 1118). It emerged in practice that firms wished their agreements to be considered for both types of exoneration, *i.e.* for negative clearance first and then, if unsuccessful, for exemption. It was thus considered administratively more efficient to combine the two forms into a Form A/B, since both applications concerned exactly the same facts. (See now Regulation 1133/68, J.O. 1968, L 189/1.) (It is noteworthy that the Commission in its First Report on Competition Policy (Brussels— Luxembourg, 1972) does not make any real attempt to differentiate between negative clearance and exemption decisions.)

28–70   According to Article 2, application for negative clearance must be by "the undertakings or associations of undertakings concerned." Article 1 of Regulation 27/62 makes it clear that notification can be effected by any undertaking party to the agreement.

Once notified to the Commission on Form A/B, the agreement is first examined with a view to certifying that there are no grounds for action under Articles 85 (1) and 86. The clearance is valid only in respect of the facts on which it was granted and will lapse if the facts change or new evidence comes to light. A new interpretation of the law will not, however, cause a clearance to lapse.

A negative clearance has no civil legal consequences, but once the Commission has initiated a procedure under Articles 2, 3 or 6 of Regulation 17, the authorities of the Member States are no longer competent to apply Articles 85 (1) and Article 86 (Art. 9 (1)). The latter authorities may, however, adjudicate upon agreements in accordance with national law even after the Commission has given a final decision.

28–71   The negative clearances so far granted are as follows:

Grosfillex-Fillistorf	J.O. 1964, 915	[1964] C.M.L.R. 237
Bendix-Maertens & Straet	J.O. 1964, 1426	[1964] C.M.L.R. 416
Nicholas Frères-Vitapro	J.O. 1964, 2287	[1964] C.M.L.R. 505
DECA (Dutch Engineers' and Contractors' Association)	J.O. 1964, 2761	[1965] C.M.L.R. 50
Eurogypsum	J.O. 1968, L 57/9	[1968] C.M.L.R. D1
ACF (Alliance des constructeurs français de machines-outils)	J.O. 1968, L 201/1	[1968] C.M.L.R. D23
Socemas	J.O. 1968, L 201/4	[1968] C.M.L.R. D28
Cobelaz-Usines de synthèse	J.O. 1968, L 276/13	[1968] C.M.L.R. D45
Cobelaz-Cokeries	J.O. 1968, L 276/19	[1968] C.M.L.R. D68
Rieckermann-AEG Elotherm	J.O. 1968, L 276/25	[1968] C.M.L.R. D78
CFA (Comptoir français de l'azote)	J.O. 1968, L 276/29	[1968] C.M.L.R. D57
CECIMO (EEMO)	J.O. 1969, L 69/13	[1969] C.M.L.R. D1
Convention Chaufourniers (Cement-Makers' or Limeburners' Agreement)	J.O. 1969, L 122/8	[1969] C.M.L.R. D15
Christiani & Nielsen	J.O. 1969, L 165/12	[1969] C.M.L.R. D36
VVVF (Vereniging van vernis en verffabrikanten in Nederland)	J.O. 1969, L 168/22	[1970] C.M.L.R. D1
SEIFA	J.O. 1969, L 173/8	
Pirelli-Dunlop	J.O. 1969, L 323/21	

Kodak	J.O. 1970, L 147/24	[1970] C.M.L.R. D19
ASPA (Association syndi-cale belge de la par-fumerie)	J.O. 1970, L 148/9	[1970] C.M.L.R. D25
Electrically-welded tube association (Alliance pour la promotion du tube d'acier soudé elec-triquement)	J.O. 1970, L 153/14	[1970] C.M.L.R. D31
Supexie	J.O. 1971, L 10/12	[1971] C.M.L.R. D1
SAFCO	J.O. 1972, L 13/44	[1972] C.M.L.R. D83
Burroughs-Delpanque	J.O. 1972, L 13/50	[1972] C.M.L.R. D67
Burroughs-Geha	J.O. 1972, L 13/53	[1972] C.M.L.R. D72
Wild Paris-Leitz	J.O. 1972, L 61/27	[1972] C.M.L.R. D36
Raymond-Nagoya	J.O. 1972, L 143/31	[1972] C.M.L.R. D45

Article 3

8–72　　*Paragraph 1.* Article 3 (1) empowers the Commission to take a legally binding decision requiring termination of infringements of Articles 85 and 86 EEC. It appears from 56 & 58/64, *Grundig and Consten* v. *Commission,* Rec. XII 429, [1966] C.M.L.R. 418, that the Commission decision can only strike at the whole agreement where it violates Articles 85 or 86 in its entirety. Where this is not the case the decision should only strike at the parts which are incompatible with the Treaty. The Commission may itself set in motion the procedures for investigating whether there is an infringement, or it may be requested to do so. A decision under Article 3 (1) will also be taken in conse-quence of a refusal of a negative clearance or a refusal of an exemption under Article 85 (3), where the agreement is not voluntarily abandoned.

8–73　　*Paragraph 2.* Article 3 (2) states that Member States and natural or legal persons may apply to the Commission to start proceedings under paragraph 1. Member States do not have to assert a particular interest, but natural and legal persons must claim a legitimate interest, meaning that they must be able to justify that claim. A legitimate interest will be constituted by evidence that the complainant is in some measure affected by the practice complained of. Form C has space for declara-tion of legitimate interest.

8–74　　*Paragraph 3.* Article 3 (3) empowers the Commission to make recommendations to undertakings or associations involved in practices which infringe Article 85 or 86 with a view to bringing about a voluntary modification of the practices in question so that they no longer infringe the Community rules. If a modification is satisfactory a negative clearance or exemption may be given; otherwise the Commission will take a decision under Article 3 (1) of the Regulation.

Article 4

28–75   Article 4 (1) states that:

> "Agreements, decisions and concerted practices of the kind described in Article 85 (1) of the Treaty which come into existence after the entry into force of this Regulation and in respect of which the parties seek application of Article 85 (3) must be notified to the Commission. Until they have been notified, no decision in application of Article 85 (3) may be taken."

The terms of the paragraph are self-explanatory. There is no duty to notify, but there is a clear incentive to do so, for no exemption can be granted without notification.

The only agreements which need not be notified are those listed in paragraph 2 of the Article, although they may in fact be notified if desired, with the same legal consequences (see further below).

As already stated, notification for the purposes of Article 4 follows the same procedure as that for the applications for negative clearances. The agreement once notified enjoys "provisional validity," in that even if the Commission eventually takes an adverse decision on it, no fine for violation of Article 85 (1) may be imposed in respect of the period between notification and decision (Article 15 (5) (*a*) of Regulation 17/62). It was held in 13/61, *De Geus* v. *Bosch,* Rec. VIII 89, [1962] C.M.L.R. 1, that a duly notified agreement enjoys full legal validity during the period between notification to and decision by the Commission. Thus the parties to it may during this period enforce it through the domestic courts, etc.

The concept of provisional validity relates both to those agreements in existence prior to the entry into force of the Regulation ("old agreements") and those which entered into force only subsequently ("new agreements"), though it was at first feared that since the *Bosch* case concerned the validity of an old agreement, different considerations might apply in respect of new agreements. In 10/69, *Portelange* v. *SCM International,* Rec. XV 309, the Court referred to provisional validity as applying to all agreements. It said:

> "The question of knowing whether a notified agreement is in fact prohibited rests on the evaluation of economic and legal considerations which cannot be taken as having been established until it has been explicitly determined that the particular agreement not only combines all the elements condemned in [Article 85 (1)] but also does not qualify for exemption under [Article 85 (3)]. Until these matters have been determined, any agreement which is properly notified must be regarded as valid."
>
> (Rec. XV 316, Authors' translation.)

The "operative part of the judgment" ("*dispositif*") refers to agreements being "fully valid" ("*Reçoivent leur plein effet*") between notification and decision.

3-76   The situation is thus that an agreement is invalid under Article 85 (1) if it is in existence and not notified; on notification it becomes provisionally valid and therefore legally enforceable, even though after consideration the Commission may decline to grant an exemption, and the agreement will then revert to a status of illegality.

8-77   Article 4 (2) exempts certain agreements (whether new or old: see also Art. 5 (2)) from notification. These agreements are deemed to have "special features which may make them less prejudicial to the development of the Common Market" (Preamble, fourth whereas). The exempted agreements are:

(1) so-called national agreements, which concern firms from one Member State only, and relate neither to imports nor to exports;

(2) agreements between two undertakings only, which do no more than:

    (a) impose restrictive conditions on the resale of goods the subject of the agreement. This may include restrictions on fixing resale prices;

    (b) impose restrictions on the exercise of industrial property rights, methods of manufacture or know-how, grant of such rights being the subject of the agreement;

(3) agreements having as their sole object:

    (a) the development or uniform application of standards or types; or

    (b) joint research agreements, provided the results are available to all the parties.

The above exemptions apply only where the agreement in question otherwise falls under Article 85 (1). Article 4 (2) was subsequently expanded by Regulation 2822/71, J.O. 1971, L 284/49, substituting for category (3) (b) above agreements having as their sole object:

"(b) joint research and development;

(c) specialisation in the manufacture of products, including agreements necessary for the achievement thereof;

    —where the products which are the subject of specialisation do not, in a substantial part of the Common Market, represent more than 15% of the volume of business done in identical products or those considered by the consumers to be similar by reason of their characteristics, price and use, and

    —where the total annual turnover of the participating undertakings does not exceed 200 million units of account."

This new provision is of particular interest in that it adopts a statistical criterion in order to establish an exemption, and points towards the merging of the objectives of competition and industrial policy, in that the precepts of the former should not hinder the attainment of the objectives of the latter.

Article 5

28–78   Article 5 states that agreements, etc., which were in existence at the entry into force of Regulation 17/62, and which are not covered by Article 4 (2) of the Regulation and thus exempt from notification (Art. 5 (2)), and for which participants seek exemption under Article 85 (3), must be notified to the Commission within the specified time limit. This limit was originally set at August 1, 1962, but by Regulation 59/62, J.O. 1962, 1655, was extended to November 1, 1962, except for agreements in which only two enterprises participate, which were to be notified by February 1, 1963. The value of notification for old agreements is the same as that for new cartels (see above, discussion of Article 4) if it is effected within the time limits prescribed. The agreement enjoys provisional validity: 13/61, *De Geus* v. *Bosch*, Rec. VIII 89, [1962] C.M.L.R. 1 (see *supra*). The Court held that old agreements and decisions falling under the Article 85 (1) prohibition could not be considered null and void if they had been properly notified within the time limits set by Regulation 17 as amended by Regulation 59/62. Nullity could only arise where the Commission had established that the agreement did not qualify for exemption, or the national cartel authorities had used the powers given them under Article 88 to declare the agreement void under Article 85 (2).

Article 6

28–79   Agreements, whether old or new, notified out of time, can only benefit from provisional validity from the date of notification, and are prima facie void prior to that date: Article 6 (1) of the Regulation provides that Commission decisions exempting agreements under Article 85 (3) shall not take effect from an earlier date (although the decision may have retroactive effect to that date or a later date).

Article 6 (2) states that the Commission may make exceptions to the rule in paragraph 1 in respect of agreements which do not formally require notification under Regulation 17/62, and old agreements which have been notified within the time limits set. These exceptions are logical. For in the first place an agreement not needing to be notified might be unduly affected if it were subsequently notified and the Commission exempted it only in respect of the period since notification. Secondly, application of Article 6 (1) would mean that old agreements could not be exempted definitively since there is necessarily a period between conclusion of those agreements and their notification. In 13/61, *De Geus* v. *Bosch*, Rec. VIII 89, [1962] C.M.L.R. 1, the Court of Justice held that old agreements were in any case valid prior to entry into force of Regulation 17. The Commission decision thus needs to cover retroactively the period between entry into force of Regulation 17 and notification.

Article 7

3–80   Article 7 is a special provision designed to cater for old agreements which were notified in time but which cannot be exempted under the terms of Article 85 (3) in their present form. The enterprises party to such agreements must either desist from operating them or alter them in such a way that they no longer conflict with Article 85 (1), or else can be exempted under Article 85 (3).

Article 8

3–81   Article 8, para. 1, states that an exemption may be given for a specific time period only and may be subject to conditions and obligations. The Commission frequently requires to be kept informed of relevant matters occurring in the context of the agreement as a condition of granting the exemption, and may thus keep the circumstances under review. The exemption may be renewed on application if the conditions of Article 83 (3) are still satisfied. The Commission may revoke or amend the decision of exemption where (a) there has been a fundamental change in the factual situation underlying the agreement, (b) in case of breach of any obligation imposed on the parties by the Commission's decision, (c) where the decision is based on incorrect information or was induced by deceit, or (d) the exemption is abused by the parties to the agreement.

Article 9

8–82   Prior to the entry into force of the rules to give effect to Articles 85 and 86 (*in casu* Regulation 17/62) the Member States were themselves to rule on the admissibility of restrictive trade practices and monopolies in accordance with national law and with Article 85, in particular paragraph 3, and Article 86 (Art. 89 EEC). During this period the Commission was to co-operate with Member States and was to investigate suspected infringements, but could not itself terminate infringements (Art. 89).

The jurisdiction of the Member States was, under Article 88, specifically limited to the period before the appropriate implementing rules had been laid down, and it appears that the Commission's powers under Article 89 may be similarly limited, for Article 87, providing for the drawing up of implementing rules, requires the respective functions of the Commission and of the Court of Justice to be defined for the purposes of the implementing provisions (Art. 87 (2) (*d*)).

This requirement is fulfilled by Article 9 of Regulation 17, giving the Commission sole power to grant exemptions from Article 85 (1) and 86, subject to review by the Court of Justice. The Member States are thus correspondingly left without powers in this area.

Article 9 defines the respective areas of competence of the national authorities and of the Commission. So long as the Commission has not initiated any procedure under Article 2, 3 or 6 of Regulation 17, the national authorities remain competent to apply Articles 85 (1) and 86. They are free to apply the repressive provisions of Community law up to the time when the Commission begins to act in the matter, but the grant of exemption is in the hands of the Commission exclusively (Art. 9 (1)).

The Member States may of course continue to apply their own cartel laws. Agreements which infringe both community and national competition rules may therefore be attacked and punished twice, but national enforcement action must not impinge upon the uniform application of Community law, and national authorities are not to nullify the effects of the Community decision: 14/68, *Walt Wilhelm* v. *Bundeskartellamt*, Rec. XV 1, [1969] C.M.L.R. 100.

28–83   In the *Wilhelm* case the Court was asked in particular whether there were objections to a double penalty, as opposed to a double prohibition, so as to exclude the possibility of two sets of proceedings. The Court held that:

" The possibility of a cumulation of sanctions would not be of a nature to exclude the admissibility of two parallel proceedings pursuing different ends "
(Trans. [1969] C.M.L.R. 100 at p. 120)

but that there is a general equitable requirement which implies that any previous decision imposing sanctions should be taken into account in determining further sanctions.

Relying in part upon this case, Boehringer, one of the firms fined by the Commission in its *Quinine Cartel* decision (J.O. 1969, L 192/5, [1969] C.M.L.R. D41, discussed *infra*, § 28–87) applied to the Commission requesting reduction in the fine of 190,000 u.a. by the amount of the fine of $80,000 imposed on it by the United States Federal District Court for the Southern District of New York, for its participation in the Quinine Cartel. In its decision refusing the request (J.O. 1971, L 282/46), the Commission stated that the equitable principles applied only in the context of sanctions imposed by authorities of the Member States of the Community in respect of matters which violated both national and Community law. The Commission went on to say that there was no general principle of law common to the Member States requiring that a fine imposed in a third State be taken into acount in imposing a Community fine; further, the principle *non bis in idem* applied to proceedings in respect of the same violation, rather than of the same facts; the United States proceedings had been in respect of restraints on competition making themselves felt in the United States rather than in the Common Market, while the Community proceedings were in respect of similar restraints obtaining within the Community.

Boehringer raised the same argument in its action before the Court of Justice in 45/69, *Boehringer* v. *Commission,* Rec. XVI 769 (discussed *infra*), but the Court rejected it on the basis that the fine imposed in the United States was in respect of restraints on competition outside the Common Market.[2] This must be taken to cast doubt on the Commission's interpretation of *Wilhelm*.

Of the original Member States, only Germany, Belgium and the Netherlands in fact require agreements to conform with national as well as Community rules although it will be open to the United Kingdom authorities to apply this system (see *infra*, § 38–21). But where such a system is operated, the question arises as to which types of Community decision the national authorities must respect—and therefore may not nullify. There is some doubt, for instance, as to whether national authorities may order the dissolution of an agreement in respect of which an exemption under Article 85 (3) was validly given. Similarly, there is some doubt as to whether the same authorities may take proceedings against an agreement in respect of which a negative clearance has been issued. The better view appears to be that an excepted agreement may not be impugned. There is more doubt about negative clearances, but they are issued at the end of similar procedures, and the same rule ought therefore to apply.

Article 9 (2) is a transitional provision empowering the Commission to apply the Community competition rules even though the time limits set in this Regulation and in Regulation 59/62 had not then expired.

Article 10

28–84   Article 10 provides for liaison between the Community and the national authorities. The Commission is without delay to furnish the national authorities with copies of all applications and notifications made to the Commission in respect of Articles 85 and 86, together with the main supporting documents (para. 1).

Paragraphs 2 to 6 provide for the establishment of a special committee to assist the Commission in competition matters. Called the Advisory Committee on Restrictive Practices and Monopolies, it is more usually referred to as the Consultative Committee. It is composed of officials from each Member State competent in competition matters, and thus ensures the continuing interest of the Member States in any investigation carried out by the Community.

Articles 11 to 14

28–85   Articles 11 to 14 contain all the investigative powers granted to the Commission by the Regulation. Such powers are obviously necessary if the Community competition policy is to work.

Article 11 (1) is quite wide in its purview:

[2] The Court confirmed its judgment on this point in a later case, 7/72, *Boehringer* v. *Commission* (not yet reported).

"In carrying out the duties assigned to it by Article 89 and by provisions adopted under Article 87 of the Treaty, the Commission may obtain all necessary information from the Governments and competent authorities of the Member States and from undertakings and associations of undertakings."

It represents little more than a particular application of the general power contained in Article 213. The Article also contains provisions to compel firms to supply the required information. If a firm does not comply with a formal request for information within a time limit set, the Commission can proceed to a formal decision requiring the information. This decision specifies a further time limit for reply, and must state that under Article 16 (1) (c) the Commission has the power to impose periodic penalty payments to compel production of complete and correct information. (There is no exact equivalent of the French legal term "astreinte" in English, but it connotes a financial penalty fixed at a certain sum per day, imposed to enforce compliance with a Court order or judgment. The penalty continues to mount up daily until the wrongdoer complies with the directions of the Court.) The decision must also mention that the furnishing of incorrect information may be penalised.

The Commission's use of information received is limited by the provisions of Article 20 of Regulation 17, which lays down that any information given to the Commission, whether under Article 11, 12, 13 or 14, shall be used only for purposes relevant to the investigation in hand. In addition the Community and the national authorities involved are under an obligation not to infringe the code of professional secrecy by making public information disclosed to them under the above-mentioned Articles (Art. 20 (2)). But general information may be made public (Art. 20 (3)).

28-86   Article 11 is designed to empower the Commission to make specific requests for particular information from States and firms; Article 12 gives the Commission general authority to investigate the situation in any part of the economy where it fears a breach of Articles 85 and 86 of the EEC Treaty, while Article 14 permits the Commission to carry out on-the-spot investigations at any firm, in pursuance of its duties under this Regulation. Article 13 allows the Commission to authorise the national cartel bodies to perform this function on its behalf. The investigations of the Commission under Articles 11 and 14 must be carried out only for the purposes of provisions adopted under Article 87, in carrying out duties assigned to it by Article 89, but this is not a real limitation.

Article 15: The Quinine Cartel: the I.C.I. case

28-87   Under Article 15 the Commission may by decision impose fines on undertakings or associations of undertakings for supplying incorrect, incomplete or misleading information pursuant to various articles of the Regulation, calling for the supply of information.

Article 15 (2) empowers the Commission to impose fines of between 1,000 to 1 million u.a., or of up to 10 per cent. of the turnover in the previous year, if that is greater, for infringement of Article 85 (1) or 86 or a breach of the conditions subject to which an Article 85 (3) exemption is granted. The infringement or breach may be intentional or negligent. The Commission has imposed fines in three cases concerning non- or late-notified restrictive trade practices banned under Article 85 (1). In the first case the fines were imposed in respect of a series of gentlemen's agreements between Community manufacturers of quinine and quinidine (*Quinine Cartel* decision, J.O. 1969, L192/5, [1969] C.M.L.R. D41). The heaviest fine imposed was that of 210,000 u.a., on Nedchem (now ACF Chemiefarma), the Dutch member of the agreement. The three firms most heavily fined each instituted proceedings before the Court of Justice, for review of legality under Article 173 EEC * (cases 41, 44 and 45/69, *ACF Chemiefarma, Buchler,* and *Boehringer* v. *Commission,* Rec. XVI 661, 733 and 769). The Court held that the purpose of the power to fine was not only to put an end to existing infringements, but also to prevent their recrudescence, so that the fact that the agreement had already been terminated did not invalidate the decision. The Court reduced the fines somewhat, in exercise of its unlimited jurisdiction in regard to the penalties provided for in the Regulation, under Article 172 EEC (see generally Chapter 12) and Article 17 of the Regulation itself.

28-88 It was argued incidentally in these cases that Community law must or should contain a rule on limitation or prescription of actions, to be derived from national law or from the general principles of law of the Member States. The Court confined itself to holding that the texts empowering the Commission to impose fines for violation of the rules of competition did not provide for prescription, and that legal certainty required a period of prescription to be fixed in advance, something which was for the Community legislature alone. Following these judgments the Commission has drawn up a draft regulation on limitation of actions in cases of prosecution and execution of judgment in the field of transport and competition law (J.O. 1972, C43/1 and [1972] C.M.L.R. D40 (translating European Parliament Session Doc. 245/71)). The draft, which has yet to be approved by the Council, provides for a limitation period in respect of the Commission's power to impose sanctions under Regulation 11/60, Regulation 17/62 and Regulation 1017/68. For infringement of the provisions relating to requests for information and investigations (Art. 15 (1) of Regulation 17/62), the period is to be three years; for all other infringements, five years. The Commission's power of execution in respect of fines and penalties is also to be made subject to a limitation period of three years.

28–89   The Commission next imposed fines for a contravention of Article 85 (1) in the *Aniline Dyes* or *Dyestuffs* decision (J.O. 1970, L195/11, [1969] C.M.L.R. D23). There a cartel had been discovered between six Community firms and four from outside the Community, designed to keep up prices and to maintain each company's share of the market. The firms fined, I.C.I., BASF, Bayer, Geigy, Ciba (now Ciba-Geigy), Sandoz, Francolor, Cassella, Hoechst, and ACNA, each instituted proceedings under Article 173 EEC*—cases 48/69, 49/69, and 51–57/69, [1972] C.M.L.R. 557, repeating many of the arguments used in the *Quinine Cartel* cases, notably that a rule of limitation ought to be applied, since the cases concerned uniform price increases taking place as long ago as 1964, and that in any case no concerted practice existed, the uniform price increases being attributable to " price leadership." In the *I.C.I.* case, the Court stated the general principle that:

> " Although a parallelism of behaviour cannot by itself be identified with a concerted practice, it is nevertheless liable to constitute a strong indication of such a practice when it leads to conditions of competition which do not correspond to the normal conditions of the market, having regard to the nature of the products, the importance and number of the undertakings and the volume of the said market. Such is the case especially where the parallel behaviour is such as to permit the parties to seek price equilibrium at a different level from that which would have resulted from competition."
>
> (48/69, *I.C.I.* v. *Commission* [1972] C.M.L.R. 557 at pp. 622 and 623. Identical statements in the other eight cases.)

The Court then went on to examine the facts of the cases and found that:

> " Having regard to the characteristics of the market in these products, the behaviour of the applicant, in conjunction with other undertakings against whom proceedings have been taken [in particular in co-ordinating price rises], was designed to substitute for the risks of competition, and the hazards of their spontaneous reactions, a co-operation which amounts to a concerted practice prohibited by Article 85 (1) of the Treaty." (*Ibid.* at p. 628. Identical findings in the other eight cases.)

28–90 Of particular interest are the contentions of the three non-Community firms that the Commission had no power to impose fines upon them by reason merely of the effects produced in the Common Market by acts they might have committed outside the Community.

The Court considered nevertheless that the price rises, although fixed outside the Community, took effect in the Community, and constituted practices carried on directly within the Common Market. It was argued that the price rises were not the acts of the firms themselves because they were carried out by subsidiaries with separate legal personality incorporated in Member States. The Court rejected this argument on the basis that the subsidiaries enjoyed no real autonomy in the matter, and that the parent companies could therefore be considered to have taken action within the Common Market. This ground for finding an undertaking based outside the Community in breach of the competition rules is to be contrasted with the finding in 22/71, *Béguelin Import v. G.L. Import-Export S.A.*, Rec. XVII 949, [1972] C.M.L.R. 81, where the Court considered that the provisions of Article 85 (1) could apply to actions of an undertaking established in a third country having " effects " within the Community. It is not perhaps entirely clear whether the Court was avoiding applying the " effects " doctrine in *I.C.I.*, but *Béguelin* indicates that the doctrine is not considered to be inappropriate to the Community system.

Arguments put forward for a period of limitation in *I.C.I.* and related cases were rejected on the same grounds as in the *Quinine Cartel* cases (*supra*).

The Commission also fined Pittsburgh Corning Europe 100,000 u.a. (*Pittsburgh Corning Europe–Formica Belgium–Hertel*, J.O. 1972, L 272/ 35, *supra* § 28–27).

28–91   Since the judgments in *Béguelin* and *I.C.I.* the Commission has published a Notice concerning the Import of Japanese Products (October 21, 1972, J.O. 1972, C111/13) in which the Commission recommends notification under Regulation 17 of agreements with or between Japanese undertakings limiting the export of Japanese goods to the Community. The Notice in effect reminds interested parties of the terms of Article 85 (1) of the Treaty, and states that " the fact that several or all participant undertakings are established outside the Community is not incompatible with the application of this disposition, in so far as the effects of the agreements, decisions or concerted practices extend to the territory of the common market " (Authors' translation). The Commission is to examine agreements of the type in question for compatibility with the competition rules, and warns that it may find it necessary to propose measures of commercial policy in order to counter the problems in question.

Article 16

28–92   Article 16 empowers the Commission to impose periodic penalty payments (see also *supra*, § 28–85). These penalties are fixed by formal decision at so much per day, and are designed to enforce compliance with an obligation imposed by a formal act under Regulation 17. Once the obligation is complied with, the Commission may in fact fix a lower total penalty than would otherwise be payable.

Article 17

28–93   Pursuant to Article 173 * of the EEC Treaty, Article 17 of the Regulation gives the Court of Justice unlimited jurisdiction over Commission decisions imposing fines or periodic penalties (see generally *supra*, Chapter 12 on actions relating to penalties).

Articles 18 to the end

28-94 The rest of Regulation 17/62 deals mainly with administrative matters. Safeguards are provided for the observance of natural justice, Article 19 giving undertakings or associations of undertakings concerned by Commission action the right to be heard before a final decision is taken. Article 21 obliges the Commission to publish most of the decisions it takes pursuant to the Regulation. Article 20 on professional secrecy has been mentioned above (see § 28-85).

ENLARGEMENT OF THE COMMUNITY

28-95 Annex II to the Act of Accession contains a technical adaptation to Regulation 17, to take account of the enlargement of the Community (Cmnd. 4862-II, p. 74). The adaptation consists in the addition of a new Article 25 to the Regulation. Agreements coming under Regulation 17 for the first time are considered to be affected by the Regulation from the date of accession, that date being substituted throughout the Regulation for the date of its entry into force for such purposes (para. 1). Agreements existing at the date of accession must be notified under Article 5 (1) or 7 of the Regulation within six months of accession (para. 2). New Member States are, within six months of accession, to arrange for assisting Commission officials where investigation proves necessary in the face of opposition by an undertaking (para. 3). The original Member States were to make such arrangements under Article 14 (4) of the Regulation by October 1, 1962.

CHAPTER 29

ADDITIONAL RULES ON COMPETITION

ARTICLE 90

9–01 ARTICLE 90 is a general provision for the application of the Treaty rules to public undertakings and undertakings to which Member States grant special or exclusive rights. It underlines that such undertakings are subject to the rules of the Treaty, and especially to the competition rules.

Article 90 (1) requires Member States neither to enact nor maintain in force any measure in favour of public undertakings to which they grant special or exclusive rights which run counter to the rules of the Treaty. No further definitions are given. In respect of undertakings, this is hardly necessary, since the paragraph makes them subject to the Treaty on an equal footing with all other firms. But it has been suggested that the word " measure " is to be interpreted as widely as possible, and that it embraces not merely legislative enactments but also tangible steps taken by the Member State; for example, a loan from a subsidiary statutory body to a public enterprise.

9–02 Article 90 (2) makes a small but significant exception to the general rule above: " Undertakings entrusted with the operation of services of general economic interest or having the character of a revenue-producing monopoly " are to be subject to the Treaty rules only in so far as " the application of such rules does not obstruct the performance in law or in fact, of the particular tasks assigned to them." It is in fact with the latter type of undertaking that the Community has been mainly concerned here, although Commission action has been based primarily on Article 37 of the Treaty, which aims at the progressive adjustment of State commercial monopolies (see generally § 21–32, *supra*). Although the monopolies mentioned in Article 37 are wider in scope than those covered by Article 90 (2), nevertheless the Commission has attempted to encourage Member States to adjust their State trading monopolies so as not to conflict with the general equilibrium in trading conditions existing inside the Community. The monopolies covered incidentally by Article 90 (2), which the Commission is attempting under Article 37 to eliminate, include tobacco in France and Italy, and matches in Italy. The main class of undertaking coming specifically within the Article 90 (2) exemption are the national issuing banks, although a recent case before the Court, 10/71, *Ministère public luxembourgeois* v. *Muller-Hein*, Rec. XVII 723, suggests that a port authority enjoying certain statutory privileges and operating in close concert with the national authorities may constitute an undertaking which is entrusted with a service of general economic interest. Article 90 (2) was held not to be directly applicable.

DUMPING

29–03 Dumping may be defined broadly as the delivery for sale of goods on an export market at a price at least lower than the selling price in the home market. Goods so exported enjoy an unnatural competitive advantage over any similar goods produced in the importing State. Where a manufacturer is able to recoup his investment and production costs from his home market sales the economic motive for charging a realistic price on the export market vanishes altogether, and the price actually charged may be below the real cost of production. A situation of this sort is encouraged where the manufacturer is protected by a high tariff wall.

Intra-Community dumping

29–04 It is clear that practices of the kind described are unacceptable within a Community based upon a customs union. It was argued that dumping in trade between Member States would disappear as the customs union developed, since the country suffering from dumping would be able to re-export the goods dumped back to the country whence they came at a price below the elevated, but now unprotected, price demanded in the home market. The dumping provisions of the EEC Treaty (Art. 91) were therefore made applicable only for the transitional period, the latest date for the establishment of the customs union. The customs union was in fact fully inaugurated on July 1, 1968 by the third acceleration decision (*supra*, § 21–12). Similar anti-dumping rules are, however, necessary during the transitional period following the accession of the new Member States to the Community. These are provided by Article 136 of the Act of Accession.

Article 136 (1) (with which Article 91 (1) EEC is substantially identical) provides that if during the transitional period the Commission, on application of a Member State or of any other interested party, finds that dumping is being practised between the Community as originally constituted and the new Member States, or between the new Member States themselves, it is to address recommendations to the person or persons with whom such practices originate for the purpose of putting an end to them. Should the practices continue, the Commission is to authorise the injured Member State or States to take protective measures, the conditions and details of which are to be fixed by the Commission.

29–05 Neither Article 136 nor Article 91 EEC provide a definition of "dumping." The Community therefore employs that given in Article

VI of the GATT. During the original transitional period Article 91 EEC was resorted to upon three occasions for the issue of recommendations. In twelve other cases the practices objected to were terminated voluntarily without the need for recommendations. No protective measures were authorised. (Commission's *Premier Rapport sur la politique de concurrence*, Brussels-Luxembourg, April 1972, p. 92.)

Article 91 (2) permitted firms to use a " boomerang " method of retaliation against dumping; goods exported at dumping prices could be re-exported to the originating States free of all customs duties, quantitative restrictions or equivalent measures. (Implementing measures were provided by Regulation 8 of March 11, 1960, J.O. 1960, 597, as amended by Regulation 13 of March 15, 1961, J.O. 1961, 585.)

Article 91 (2) has no counterpart in Article 136 of the Act of Accession, perhaps because the former was not in practice very workable, although it had deterrent effect. Article 136 (2) of the Act of Accession requires the Commission to evaluate all the relevant factors in applying Article 136 (1) to agricultural products, in particular the level of prices at which these products are imported into the market in question from elsewhere, account being taken of the provisions of the EEC Treaty relating to agriculture, in particular Article 39.

Dumping by third states

9–06   The provisions discussed above relate of course only to intra-Community dumping. Community protection against dumping by third States is provided by Regulation 459/68, J.O. 1968, L93/1, which was issued as part of the panoply of instruments implementing the commercial policy. The Regulation sets out a procedure for examining whether damaging practices exist (" the anti-dumping procedure "), involving discussions with the interested parties. The system is based upon the imposition of an anti-dumping duty on the dumped product if its introduction causes or threatens to cause substantial prejudice to an established Community producing industry, or causes considerable delay in the setting up of a Community producing industry which is envisaged in the near future (Art. 2). An elaborate definition of dumping is provided by Article 3. The Community system is considered to be in complete accordance with the GATT anti-dumping code.

No anti-dumping duties have to date been applied, although procedures have been opened in about a dozen cases since 1970.

Where the products concerned do not immediately appear to fall into the " dumped " category, they may be kept under surveillance under the supervisory procedure provided by Articles 7 *et seq.* of Regulation 1025/70, J.O. 1970, L124/6, establishing a common system to be applied to imports from third countries (see generally § 37–32).

AIDS: ARTICLES 92 TO 94 [1]

29–07 A Community rule on aids is necessary in order to avoid the distortions of Community competition rules which might result from grants of assistance to certain areas or industries without reference to Community requirements as a whole. The Community rule established by Articles 92 to 94 making up Section 3 of the Chapter on competition consists of a general provision that aids which distort competition are incompatible with the Common Market (Art. 92 (1)). This prohibition is subject to exceptions, by which certain defined aids are recognised as compatible with the Common Market (Art. 92 (2)), certain defined aids can be considered compatible (Art. 92 (3)), and, exceptionally, other aids can be considered compatible if approved unanimously by the Council (Art. 93 (2), third sub-para.).

General supervision of aids is in the hands of the Commission.

Article 92

29–08 Article 92 lays down the basic Community rule on the subject of aids. However, this rule is not expressed in absolute terms, for in the first place it applies only " save as otherwise provided in this Treaty." Other Treaty provisions on aids are found in Articles 42, 77, 82 and 223. Article 42 allows the Council to authorise special agricultural aids, while Articles 77 and 82 envisage certain aids to the transport sector (see generally *supra*, § 27–06). Article 223 makes it clear that the Treaty is without prejudice to the right of a Member State to take necessary measures for " the protection of the essential interests of its security which are connected with the production of or trade in arms, munitions and war material." This permits Member States to subsidise ordnance factories and the like, Articles 92 to 94 notwithstanding.

Secondly, unlike Articles 85 and 86, which deem incompatible with and *prohibited* in the Common Market restrictive trade practices and the abuse of dominant positions, Article 92 merely states that aids " shall . . . be incompatible with the Common Market." There is no general interdiction under the rule of the Treaty; the Commission must take a decision ordering the State to abolish the aid under Article 93 (2) and (3) (below) before the aid can be said to contravene Community law.

29–09 The notion of " aids " is not defined by the Treaty, although Article 92 indicates that aids are " granted by a Member State *or through State resources in any form whatsoever.*" An aid which distorts or threatens to distort competition by favouring certain undertakings or the production of certain goods, in so far as it affects trade between Member States, is incompatible with the Common Market. The italicised phrase aims at catching aids granted by semi-public agencies or local authorities,

---

[1] See also Chapter 34, " Regional Policy," with which this Section is closely connected.

deriving their funds for this particular purpose from the central government. Aids are only incompatible if they are selective in any particular
economic sector—if they distort competition by "favouring certain undertakings or the production of certain goods." On the other hand it is
clear that aids are not to be granted as a general subsidy to all industry
and all areas of national territory: cf. first resolution of October 20, 1971
concerning the general arrangements for regional aid, J.O. 1971, C111/1.
In 1972 the Commission objected to just such a scheme for Belgium (J.O.
1972, L105/13, and 106/26).

Though the Treaty does not indicate what form aid may take, in
response to a written question in the European Parliament (Question 48
of 1963), the Commission indicated that it considered that aid could
manifest itself in the form of subsidies, tax exemptions, interest rate
reductions, loan guarantees on favourable terms, preferential conditions
of sale, loss indemnities, or any other measure having equivalent effect
(J.O. 1963, 2235).

Aids can also take the form of reductions in the selling price of a
finished article to the consumer; such was the case in France where,
prior to Community objection, such a system was operated for French-
manufactured gliders. The reduction in price acted as a stimulus to
sales and indirectly to production. In 6 & 11/69, *Commission* v. *France*,
Rec. XV 523, [1970] C.M.L.R. 43, the Court considered that a preferential discount rate available for exports constituted an aid incompatible with the Common Market.

Derogations from the principle of incompatibility

29–10 *Aids which are compatible with the Common Market.* Article 92 (2)
sets out a list of aids which " shall be compatible [definitively] with the
Common Market." Sub-paragraph (*a*) concerns " aids having a social
character "; this does not relate to social security and welfare payments
by the national authorities to individuals, but rather to aids granted
to firms in order that they may perform necessary social functions, *e.g.*
keeping down the price of bread.

Under sub-paragraph (*b*) aids which compensate for natural disasters
and " *other exceptional occurrences* " are compatible with the Common
Market. Although this clause would seem to cover only the " Act of
God " type of circumstance, it appeared that in the initial stages the
Commission was willing to give a wide interpretation to the italicised
phrase, and approved a German plan for assistance to be given to the
lead and zinc mines, which had suffered considerable financial losses.
The Commission supported its argument by referring to the peculiar
distortions in the world market for these base metals. However, in a
more recent decision relating to Belgian aids to firms whose chances of
showing a profit are very seriously in jeopardy, the Commission emphasised the requirements that such aids be designed to produce lasting

improvements, and be directed to regional or sectoral problems (J.O. 1972, L10/22).

Sub-paragraph (c) relates to the general agreement amongst the Member States on the signing of the EEC Treaty that special provision should be made to assist those areas of Germany known as the *" Zonenrand-gebiet,"* which border on East Germany and Czechoslovakia. Provision was made in Article 82 of the Treaty for the application of measures in the transport sector to compensate for the economic disadvantages of this area, and the clause here merely amplifies this, permitting aids of any kind to assist the economy of these districts.

It is to be noted that all the aids listed in paragraph 2, although definitively compatible with the Common Market, must nevertheless be notified to the Commission in accordance with the provisions of Article 93 (1) and (3) (see § 29–16, *infra*).

29-11   *Aids which may be considered to be compatible with the Common Market.* Paragraph 3 of the Article provides that certain aids " may be considered to be compatible with the Common Market." The procedure for approval involved here must be deduced from the provisions of Article 93. There is no actual provision stating that the Commission shall take a positive decision if it approves an aid as coming within the categories set out in this paragraph. It would appear that if after consideration of the aid in question, the Commission is of the opinion that it qualifies under Article 92 (3), then it informs the Member State concerned in unofficial fashion, but reserves to itself (Art. 93 (1)) the power to review its decision at any time. (*Cf.* the Commission decision that a German investment grant scheme for coal-producing areas in North Rhine Westphalia, begun in 1968, should no longer be deemed compatible with the Common Market, because the conditions under which the aid was authorised were no longer fulfilled (J.O. 1971, L 57/19).)

It thus seems that the granting of Community approval under Article 92 (3) is similar to the granting of an exemption under Article 85 (3).

29-12   The various types of aid set out in Article 92 (3) are as follows: Category (*a*) comprises aids for regions where there is an abnormally low standard of living or serious underemployment. The category is self-explanatory, but no satisfactory criteria for determining what is an abnormally low standard of living have been evolved. This category is, however, seldom used to justify aids, since category (*c*) embodies a much more generous definition, under which it is possible to subsume most regional problems, whether social, economic or industrial. Category (*b*) allows aids to be used for a project of common European interest, *i.e.* which involve more than one Member State directly or indirectly. This would include a road tunnel under the Alps, a hydro-electric scheme in Luxembourg, whose power serves Germany, France and/or Belgium, and presumably the Channel Tunnel. The category also permits aids where a serious disturbance in the economy of a Member State has occurred, although it is difficult to see how this can be utilised, except in the case of a certain industry undergoing some kind of short-term yet fundamental economic setback. It might, however, have been applicable during the French crises of 1968. Category (c) is the most important category in that it is wider in scope than either of the two categories already mentioned. It is around this category that the Community aid policy hinges. It permits aids to be granted " to facilitate the development of certain economic activities or of certain economic areas, where such aid does not adversely affect trading conditions to an extent contrary to the common interest." It is at once apparent that the category includes not only regional but also sectoral aids, *i.e.* aids which benefit a particular industry or branch of it.

29–13   The particular industries which generally benefit from aids are: shipbuilding, the textile industry, the film industry, and aircraft manufacture. For the first-mentioned of these, the Council has issued a directive (69/262, J.O. 1969, L 206/25) designed to harmonise the aids granted by Member States at a ceiling of 10 per cent. of the contract price of a vessel (Art. 2). Although this directive expired at the end of 1971, the Commission proposed that these aids be continued but at a lower and more exactly determined level. Aids to shipbuilding are now governed by Directive 72/273, J.O. 1972, L 169/28. In July 1971 the Commission issued guidelines for the textile industry, stating what aids in this sector would be considered compatible with the Common Market.

29–14   The Commission is currently engaged in attempting to rationalise the system of national subsidies to the film industry. It is possible that the British Eady fund, which is used to subsidise British productions, may have to be reorganised, since it operates on a levy on all box-office receipts. This type of taxation, in which receipts are used to fund systems of national aid, was condemned by the Court of Justice in a case concerning a somewhat similar French scheme, under which retail sales of textiles were taxed to subsidise textile production (47/69, *France* v. *Commission,* Rec. XVI 487, [1970] C.M.L.R. 351). The Court held that even though the form of taxation was not discriminatory in terms of Article 95 of the EEC Treaty, since it applied to all textiles equally, whether French or imported from the other Member States, the fact that the product of this taxation was used to subsidise the French textile industry alone meant that the conditions of competition within the Common Market were being distorted. Some widening of the Eady scheme is effected by the European Communities Act 1972, however (see *infra,* § 38–19).

29–15   The Commission is anxious to achieve some co-ordination of aid systems, and a first step towards this was the resolution of October 20, 1971 on general arrangements for regional aids, J.O. 1971, C111/1 (see

§ 34–06). It hopes that this will lead eventually to the Community taking over all responsibility for co-ordination and surveillance of aids, whether regional or sectoral.

Paragraph 3 of Article 92 provides a final category (*d*) of aids which may be considered to be compatible with the Common Market, namely " such other categories of aid as may be specified by decision of the Council acting by a qualified majority on a proposal from the Commission." No such proposals have been made.

Article 93

29–16   Article 93 lays down procedures for dealing with both old and new systems of aid. By paragraph 1, the Commission has the task of co-operating with the Member States to " keep under constant review " all existing forms of aid. It has power to propose amendments required by changing economic circumstances, so that aids remain compatible with the Common Market and do not distort competition to any degree. By paragraph 3 Member States are required to submit plans to grant or alter aids before their implementation so that the Commission may comment. If the Commission considers a proposed aid to be incompatible with the Common Market having regard to Article 92, in that it distorts competition, the Commission is to initiate the procedure provided for in paragraph 2. The Member State concerned may not put its proposed measures into effect until this procedure has resulted in a final decision.

Following the submission of schemes to the Commission under paragraph 3, there is usually discussion between the latter and the Member State concerned. As a result the Member State either modifies its aid or its proposal to the satisfaction of the Commission, or refuses to do so. If, after giving notice to the parties concerned to submit their comments, the Commission finds that aids granted or to be granted are not compatible with the Common Market having regard to Article 92, or is being abused, it takes a decision requiring the State either to abolish, alter, or refrain from implementing the aid (para. 2, first sub-para.). If the State fails to comply with this decision within the prescribed time, the Commission may, in derogation from the provisions of Article 169 * and 170,* refer the matter to the Court of Justice direct (para. 2, second sub-para.).

The Commission procedures may, however, be suspended: Article 93 (2), third sub-para., enables a Member State to apply to the Council for a decision, taken unanimously, that the aid which that State is granting or intends to grant shall be considered compatible with the Common Market in derogation from the provisions of Article 92 or any implementing Regulations, if such a decision is justified by exceptional circumstances.

" If, as regards the aid in question, the Commission has already initiated the procedure provided for in the first sub-paragraph of this paragraph, the fact that the State concerned has made its application to the Council shall have the effect of suspending that procedure until the Council has made its attitude known."

The only occasion on which this procedure has been used was to approve a French aid for wood pulp (J.O. 1960, 1972).

Article 93 was held not to be directly applicable in 6/64, *Costa* v. *ENEL*, Rec. X 1141, [1964] C.M.L.R. 425.

Article 94

29–17   Article 94 empowers the Council to make all necessary regulations to put into effect Articles 92 and 93. Although in 1966 the Commission made certain proposals for a Regulation exempting certain categories of aid from the requirement of prior examination, and laying down detailed rules for the purposes of Article 93 (3) for the submission of all necessary information with regard to plans for aids, no generalised rules have as yet been issued on the basis of this Article. It would appear that in practice the Community and the Commission in particular is still able to perform its tasks sufficiently well under the rules the Treaty provisions themselves contain.

CHAPTER 30

TAXATION

30–01 CHAPTER 2 in Title I, " Common Rules," in Part Three of the Treaty, " Policy of the Community," entitled " Tax Provisions," is the basis for the greater part of Community action on taxation. Harmonisation of direct taxation is, however, carried out under Article 100 (see generally § 32–03 *et seq., infra*). The title " Tax Provisions " given to this chapter by the authentic English text of the Treaty is somewhat misleading, for, as emerges from the French title, " *Dispositions Fiscales,*" the chapter is intended to cover all types of taxation, while " Tax Provisions " is more limitative.

The chapter is included in the " Common Rules," indicating that the purpose of the Community taxation rules is to ensure that disparities in national tax structures do not distort the balance of competition or hinder the operation of the customs union. The maintenance of discrimination in taxation systems has a similar effect to the retention of customs barriers, and therefore taxation of goods and services inside the Common Market is to be on a basis of non-discrimination as between Member States.

30–02 Article 95 sets out the basic Community rule of non-discrimination in the matter of internal taxation against imports from other Member States. Nor are Member States to apply protective taxation in the same respect. Article 96 prohibits refunds on exports exceeding the actual taxation imposed on the goods. This complements the rule in Article 95. Article 97 is a transitional provision, providing for the establishment of average rates of tax, to be imposed in execution of Articles 95 and 96, where Member States still operate a cumulative multi-stage or cascade turnover tax system. Article 98, unlike the three preceding Articles, operates in respect of direct as distinct from indirect taxation. It prohibits Member States from operating systems of compensation for the effects of direct taxation on intra-Community trade, in the absence of express and limited authorisation. Article 99 is the basis for Community action designed to harmonise national systems of indirect taxation.

INDIRECT TAXATION

Article 95

30–03 Article 95, first para., provides that:

> " No Member State shall impose, directly or indirectly, on the products of other Member States any internal taxation of any kind in excess of that imposed directly or indirectly on similar domestic products."

" Furthermore, no Member State shall impose on the products of other Member States any internal taxation of such a nature as to afford indirect protection to other products." (Second para.)

The third paragraph provides for repeal or amendment of any provisions of national legislation which conflict with the principles set out in the first two paragraphs by January 1, 1962, the start of the second stage.

The effect of the Article has been somewhat clarified by a number of decisions of the Court of Justice; the real starting point for this line of cases was 57/65, *Lütticke* v. *Hauptzollamt Saarelouis*, Rec. XII 293, [1971] C.M.L.R. 674, which came before the Court by way of reference under Article 177 from the Finanzgericht (local taxation court) for the Saar. The plaintiff in the domestic action claimed that a demand for payment of a compensatory tax in place of turnover tax on the import of powdered milk from Luxembourg was invalid, since domestic powdered milk was exempt from turnover tax. This being so, the compensatory tax was, so the plaintiff argued, illegal under Article 95. The Finanzgericht referred the matter to the Court of Justice, asking whether Article 95, first para. had direct effects and created rights for the individual to which national courts should give effect. The Court stated that:

" Article 95 (1) provides, as a general and permanent Community rule, that the burden of internal taxes borne by the products of the other Member States should not be greater than that borne by similar national products.

" Such a system, often adopted by the Treaty to ensure equality between citizens of the Community with regard to the national laws, constitutes in fiscal law the indispensable basis of the Common Market."

(Trans. [1971] C.M.L.R. 674 at p. 684.)

Furthermore the Court found that Article 95, first para., fulfilled the requirements for direct applicability, the time condition in the third paragraph of the Article being a simple suspensive condition, which in no way detracted from the directly applicable character of the first paragraph, after the time for the fulfilment of that condition had elapsed.

30–04   As a result of this decision there ensued a flood of domestic actions in Germany, all contesting the imposition of compensatory taxes on imports at a level higher than that applied to similar domestic products. In 28/67, *Molkerei-Zentrale* v. *Hauptzollamt Paderborn*, Rec. XIV 211, [1968] C.M.L.R. 187, the Bundesfinanzhof, the highest German taxation court, asked the Court of Justice for a preliminary ruling on whether it still held to the opinion given in the *Lütticke* case, pointing out that if this was so, individuals had a more extensive right of enforcement in respect of this provision than the Community had itself, since the *Lütticke* decision obliges national courts to treat the individuals concerned in a taxation dispute as if the Member State had already performed its duties under Article 95, whereas the Community could only require the State to proceed to fulfil those obligations.

The Court of Justice affirmed the directly applicable character of Article 95 and stated that:

> " the interpretation of Article 95 in case 57/65 cannot be invalidated by a comparison of the rights conferred on individuals by that Article with the powers granted to the Community's institutions. . . . The purpose of an action brought by an individual is to protect his individual rights in a particular case, whereas intervention by an EEC institution is intended to ensure general and uniform observation of a rule of Community law."
> (Trans. [1968] C.M.L.R. 187 at p. 218.)

The Court went on in this case to clarify the meaning of the phrase " internal taxation . . . imposed directly or indirectly on similar domestic products."

" Directly or indirectly " imposed refers to taxation actually imposed. In particular, indirect imposition refers to the taxes charged on the domestic product at all stages of manufacture and distribution, but not, it would seem, where the imposition becomes insignificant through remoteness, *e.g.* taxes imposed on production facilities or distribution transport.

30–05 The Court held in 31/67, *August Stier* v. *Hauptzollamt Hamburg-Ericus*, Rec. XIV 347, [1968] C.M.L.R. 222, that Article 95 did not prohibit the internal taxation of imported goods where there were no similar domestic products nor domestic products which might thus be protected against imports. This is because internal taxes are fiscal in purpose and there is no reason why certain imported goods should hold a privileged position, exempt from internal taxation, merely because there are no competing domestic products.

30–06 In 27/67, *Fink-Frucht GmbH* v. *Hauptzollamt München*, Rec. XIV 327, [1968] C.M.L.R. 228, the Court of Justice was asked whether Articles 95 and 30 were applicable where goods are imported from other Member States when there are no similar domestic products or products of substitution (a similar question to that in *Stier*); while in respect of Article 95, the Court reiterated what it had said previously, it indicated that a charge could not be both a measure of equivalent effect to a quantitative restriction under Article 30, and an internal tax under Article 95. In addition the Court stated that Article 95, second para., contained straightforward prohibition against protection and could, along the lines of the first paragraph, have immediate effects and confer specific rights on individuals which the national courts are bound to uphold. However, the decision went further into the meaning of the second paragraph, pointing out that unlike the first paragraph, the second did not contain any specific criteria for assessing whether a tax was illegal in its rate or not (the first paragraph states that such a tax is illegal if it exceeds the rate of tax imposed on similar domestic goods). The Court stated that it would consider a protective tax illegal if it was imposed at a rate which is capable of having the effect of protecting domestic products of substitution.

30–07   In 25/67, *Milch- Fett- und Eierkontor GmbH* v. *Hauptzollamt Saarbrücken*, Rec. XIV 305, [1968] C.M.L.R. 225, the Court of Justice decided that despite any similarity in subject-matter between internal taxes in the context of Article 95 and charges having equivalent effect to customs duties in the context of Articles 12 and 13, a tax could never be both at the same time. Moreover the Court stated that Articles 12 and 13 on the one hand and Article 95 on the other could never be applied to the same set of facts. The difference between the charges subject to Articles 12 *et seq.* and to Articles 95 *et seq.* was briefly discussed by the Court of Justice in 10/65, *Deutschmann* v. *Aussenhandelsstelle für Erzeugnisse der Ernährung und Landwirtschaft*, Rec. XI 601, [1965] C.M.L.R. 259, where the Court stated that an import licence charge, necessary for any import to be made, was not a tax within the scope of Article 95. Articles 12 and 95 did not cover the same subject-matter because each had separate and different timetables for the elimination of their respective taxes. (For definition of the notion of charges having equivalent effect to customs duties see 24/68, *Commission* v. *Italy* (*Re Statistical Levy*), Rec. XV 193, [1971] C.M.L.R. 611 and § 21–03, *supra.*)

30–08   In 2 & 3/62, *Commission* v. *Luxembourg and Belgium* (*Re Import duties on gingerbread*), Rec. VIII 813, [1963] C.M.L.R. 199, the Court distinguished between internal taxes subject to Articles 95 *et seq.* and charges having equivalent effect to customs duties, emphasising that unlike customs duties and equivalent charges, internal taxes are imposed on imports and domestic products alike. The Court elaborated upon this somewhat in 7/67, *Wöhrmann* v. *HZA Bad Reichenhall*, Rec. XIV 261, [1968] C.M.L.R. 234, holding that turnover taxes imposed on all products, whether domestic or imported:

> " are, by their nature, mainly fiscal, and when they are imposed on imports, their purpose is to put all types of goods, whatever their origin, into one and the same fiscal situation."
> (Trans. [1968] C.M.L.R. 234 at p. 235.)

30–09   The Court again went into the differences between charges having equivalent effect to customs duties and internal taxation in 2 & 3/69, *Sociaal Fonds voor de Diamantarbeiders* v. *Brachfeld and Chougol Diamond*, Rec. XV 211, [1969] C.M.L.R. 335, where it was held that contributions to the social fund levied solely on the value of diamonds imported from other Member States amounted to equivalent charges.

It was here emphasised that equivalent charges were levied on imports alone, whereas internal taxation (which might incidentally be discriminatory) is levied on all goods of whatsoever origin.

30-10   As far the technical interpretation of Article 95 is concerned, the Court of Justice held in 16/69, *Commission* v. *Italy*, Rec. XV 377, [1970] C.M.L.R. 161 that a contravention of Article 95 existed where an internal tax was imposed on imports of " *eaux de vie* " on the basis of a presumed alcohol content, while the tax was imposed on domestic " *eaux de vie* " on the basis of actual alcohol content. In 77/69, *Commission* v. *Belgium*, Rec. XVI 237, the Court ruled that a tax applied at the same rate for imported and domestically-produced timber nevertheless contravened the principles of Article 95 in that it was applied at different stages of their processing; Belgian wood was taxed on its value on sale standing or on felling, while imported wood was taxed on delivery to the user, taking into account any processing already effected, and thus bore a greater tax burden.

In 28/69, *Commission* v. *Italy* (*Re tax on imported cocoa beans*), Rec. XVI 187, [1970] C.M.L.R. 448, Italy had imposed a tax on cocoa beans and products at rates which differentiated between imported processed products and domestically-processed products. In response to allegations that this tax was contrary to Article 95 Italy argued that the differential rate was imposed to compensate for higher domestic processing costs. This argument was rejected and the Commission allegations upheld, the principle of non-discrimination being valid independently of the incidence of factors other than fiscal.

Article 96
30-11   Article 96 provides the complement to Article 95 in the aim of achieving an indirect taxation system in the Community which does not discriminate between home-produced and imported goods. Article 95 forbids the taxing of imports at a higher rate than that imposed on domestic goods, while Article 96 prohibits refunds on exports to other Member States in excess of the internal taxes actually imposed. The Court of Justice examined the role of Article 96 in 45/64, *Commission* v. *Italy* (*Re drawback on Italian machine parts*), Rec. XI 1057, [1966] C.M.L.R. 97; the Italian system of drawback (export refunds) permitted compensation for tax levied on the firms in addition to tax levied on the goods exported. The Court held drawbacks in respect of taxes not levied on the goods themselves (whether directly or indirectly) to be contrary to Article 96. It considered that " indirectly " referred to those charges which were borne by the goods during their various manufacturing stages. The Court was, however, prepared to accept a system of flat-rate rebates on exports, since it is difficult to calculate the exact tax burden incurred by a particular product under the cascade system of taxation (for the difficulties created by this in the operation of Article 95, see the discussion of Art. 97 below).

The Court of Justice has been concerned not to rule on the effect to be given to a judgment finding a tax to be contrary to Article 95, holding that it is for domestic courts to decide on the effects: 34/67, *Lück* v. *HZA Köln-Rheinau,* Rec. XIV 359.

Article 97

30-12   Article 97 permits Member States operating a cascade system of indirect taxation (turnover tax) to establish average rates of taxation for products, to be used in taxing imports and granting refunds on exports. The average rates applied must conform to the non-discriminatory principles laid down in Articles 95 and 96. The administration of these systems of compensation is in the hands of the Member States but is subject to the supervision and guidance of the Commission.

Such a scheme was necessary since the Member States operated and still do operate different systems of turnover taxes with different bases for assessment and different rates; the obvious long-term solution in the context of an economic union is to have a common system of turnover taxes with common rates, such as will be progressively implemented by the application of value added tax (VAT) throughout the Community.

Article 97 therefore operates in a subsidiary role and works towards the implementation of Articles 95 and 96. The Court of Justice in 57/65, *Lütticke* v. *HZA Saarelouis,* Rec. XII 293, [1971] C.M.L.R. 674, recognised this in saying that Article 97 operates as a special rule for the adaptation of Article 95 and could not, unlike Article 95, first para., give rise to direct effects in the relations between Member States and their subjects. See also 28/67, *Molkerei-Zentrale* v. *HZA Paderborn,* Rec. XIV 211, [1968] C.M.L.R. 187.

The fact that the Court decided that Article 97 is not directly applicable did not prevent uncertainty arising over the interpretation of the Article, particularly over the meaning of the phrase " average rates." The Article does not define the phrase, nor does it give any indication as to how such rates should be established. Thus it was for each Member State to set an average rate for a particular product if it so desired. The compensatory taxes which implemented the average rates were frequently challenged on the grounds that the tax was not based on average rates of internal taxation then prevailing, or that the average rate was incorrectly assessed. In a case before the German Federal Taxation Court, *Lütticke* v. *Hauptzollamt Saarelouis* [1969] C.M.L.R. 221, it was decided that a rate of taxation for the purposes of compensation introduced before the entry into force of the EEC Treaty may nevertheless be an average rate for the purposes of Article 97, and in 29/68, *Milch- Fett- und Eierkontor GmbH* v. *Hauptzollamt Saarbrücken,* Rec. XV 165, [1969] C.M.L.R. 390, the Court of Justice reached a similar conclusion, affirming that a declaration that an existing tax rate was an average rate is sufficient for the purposes of Article 97. The Court also considered that individualisation of the average rate for each product or type of product was not necessary and that the State was free to group products into categories and to allot to them the general rate of taxation.

Article 98

30–13   Article 98 is discussed in relation to direct taxation; see *infra*, § 30–27.

Article 99

30–14   Article 99, requiring the Commission to " consider how the legislation of the various Member States concerning turnover taxes, excise duties and other forms of indirect taxation . . . can be harmonised in the interest of the Common Market " is the basis for all harmonisation work on indirect taxation.   Any harmonisation of direct taxation must be carried out under Article 100 (general provision on approximation of laws —see generally § 32–03 *et seq.*).

Article 99, second para., requires the Commission to submit proposals to the Council on the harmonisation of indirect taxation.   The Council is to act unanimously, without prejudice to the power to issue directives contained in Articles 100 and 101.   Under Article 99, the Council may use any type of instrument, although it has in fact only used directives (notably Directives 67/227 and 228, J.O. 1967, 1301 and 1303 on VAT).

Value added tax

30–15   Disparities between the Member States' systems of indirect taxation were considered to be a much greater hindrance to the creation of the Common Market than were the differing systems of direct taxation; hence the singling out of indirect taxation in Article 99.   The Commission deemed the harmonisation of indirect taxation so important that it set up three working groups to establish the requirements of a non-discriminatory system of indirect taxation as early as 1962; as a result of these inquiries it was concluded that a non-cumulative multi-stage tax would be the best for operations inside a common market.   This form of taxation, already in existence in France, is referred to as the value added system.   Amongst its advantages may be mentioned the fact that it is economically neutral, *i.e.* it does not differentiate between goods produced by a vertically integrated firm and goods produced by the combined efforts of a line of specialist firms.

In response to this report, the Commission published a draft directive relating to the general modalities of VAT (Supp. to Bulletin 12, 1962, Doc. IV, Com. (62), 217).   This draft was revised and refined (Supp. to Bulletin 7, 1964, Doc. IV, Com. (64), 144).   To this a draft second directive was added, setting out detailed rules of application of the tax (Supp. to Bulletin 5, 1965, Doc. IV, Com. (65), 144).   The two directives in their final form were issued as Directives 67/227 and 228, J.O. 1967, 1301 and 1303.   It was originally hoped that the VAT system would be fully operative throughout the Community by January 1, 1970 (Art. 1 of

Directive 67/227) but economic and political difficulties necessitated the postponement of the operation of VAT in both Belgium and Italy. A third directive, 69/463, J.O. 1969, L 320/34, was issued to postpone the date for the implementation of the entire system to January 1, 1972. The Belgian VAT entered into force on January 1, 1971, and Italy introduced the tax on January 1, 1973, having obtained a further stay until that date: Directive 72/250, J.O. 1972, L162/18.

0–16   *The VAT directives.* The two directives, (67/227 and 228, J.O. 1967, 1301 and 1303) lay down the basic principles and the fundamental mechanics for the operation of the system of value added tax. The tax system is defined by Article 2 of the First Directive in the following terms:

> " The principle of the common system of value added tax involves the application to goods and services of a general tax on consumption exactly proportional to the price of the goods and services, whatever the number of transactions which take place in the production and distribution process before the stage at which tax is charged.
>
> " On each transaction, value added tax, calculated on the price of the goods or services at the rate applicable to such goods or services, shall be chargeable after deduction of the amount of value added tax borne directly by the various cost components.
>
> " The common system of value added tax shall be applied up to and including the retail trade stage."

VAT is therefore a " general tax on consumption," applicable up to and including the retail stage (although many national systems in fact make exceptions for small retailers whose gross annual turnover is less than a specified sum). It is also a tax which, unlike the cascade system of taxation, is economically neutral, in that it is applied in respect of the price of goods and services, irrespective of whether they have passed through several hands before reaching the consumer, or have emerged from a completely integrated producer.

0–17   The First Directive does not lay down any aim of establishing common rates for the tax, common classification of goods and services for taxation purposes, or common exemptions from the tax, and neither are these provided for in the Second Directive, which was envisaged by Article 3 of the First Directive as concerning " the structure of, and the procedure for applying, the common system of value added tax."

The Second Directive defines those concepts necessary in the application of any taxation régime; Article 2 states that:

> " The following shall be subject to the value added tax:
> > (*a*) the supply of goods and the provision of services within the territory of the country by a taxable person against payment;
> > (*b*) the importation of goods."

The notions of " territory of the country," " taxable person," " supply of goods," " provision of services " and " importation of goods " are defined by Articles 3, 4, 5, 6 and 7 respectively. Successive Articles set out a definition of the basis of assessment, the manner of fixing the applicable rate, exemptions, deductions, accounts, administrative procedures, special régimes for small firms. Articles 15 to 19 make provision for further implementation, consultation and transitional arrangements.

Annex A to the directive contains a list of twenty-eight points, which comment on and amplify the substantive Articles of the directive.

30–18   Article 5 defines " supply of goods " as meaning " the transfer of the right to dispose of tangible property as owner." Tangible property means both movable and immovable tangible property (Annex A, point 3). The Articles also give a list of examples of operations which are to be considered as the supply of goods, including compulsory purchase, and the handing over of a new construction. Annex A, point 3, adds to the definition by stating, *inter alia*, that the " supply of electric current, gas, heat, refrigeration and the like " are to be considered as the supply of goods rather than services.

Article 6 defines provision of services in a negative way, as meaning any transaction which does not constitute a supply of goods within the meaning of Article 5. The directive therefore covers all possible consumer transactions. Article 9, which defines the manner of fixing the rates of tax, permits Member States to apply reduced rates to certain goods and services, the goods and services in question to be determined by the Member States concerned (second para.). Article 7 defines the idea of importation of goods as meaning the entry of such goods into the " territory of the country " defined in Article 3, the " chargeable event " occurring at the time of entry. Member States may lay down special mechanisms for the collection of the tax on imports at the same time as those goods are charged with import duties, *i.e.* on import from third countries. Articles 5 and 6 define the occurrence of " the chargeable event " as being, respectively, the moment when delivery is effected and the moment when the service is provided.

30–19   Article 3 defines the territory of the Member States in which VAT shall be applied as being the whole of the national territory including the territorial waters, although Annex A, point 1, permits the Member States to apply VAT over less than the whole of the national territory, subject to consultations. Article 4 defines the concept of the taxable person, the person subject to VAT legislation, as " any person who independently and habitually engages in transactions pertaining to the activities of producers, traders or persons providing services whether or not for gain." Annex A, point 2, further defines the scope of the taxable person under any national VAT legislation. In particular it clarifies the idea behind the word " independently," which " is intended to exclude from taxation " all persons who are employees and therefore not in business on their own account. It also points out that public organs and enterprises when pursuing their "official capacity as official authorities" are not to be considered as taxable persons.

30–20 Article 8 defines the basis for assessment of value of the imposable goods or services ("*assiette*"). The Community VAT system is not that known as the tax-on-tax system, whereby tax is payable not only on the value of the goods or services but also on the tax already paid prior to this taxable event, for the VAT itself is excluded from the basis. (The tax-on-tax system of assessment was in fact rejected by the working groups of 1962 in favour of the base-on-base method, here adopted, where the tax is paid, in the case of goods, solely on the difference between the price on acquisition and the price on resale.) Article 9, as mentioned above, defines the way that rates of tax may be established. Although it does not contain any direction concerning the actual rate or number of such rates that may be imposed by the Member States, Member States are free to provide for increased or reduced rates of tax (second para.). The third paragraph is of interest in that it reiterates in the context of a common system of indirect taxation inside the Common Market the idea expressed in Article 95 of the Treaty; it states that: "The rate applicable to importation of goods shall be that which is applied in the territory of the country to the supply of like goods." The notions in Article 95 of "similar" and "other" products have here been synthesised in the expression "like goods."

30–21 Articles 11 and 12 are the heart of the VAT system in that they lay down the basis for a common régime for the calculation and payment of the actual tax. Articles 14, 15 and 17 envisage that exceptions may be made in the implementation of the VAT system for small undertakings (Arts. 14 and 17) and for agricultural products (Art. 15). Implementation of the VAT system, though in the hands of the Member States, is subject to the obligation placed on the Member States by Article 16 to consult with the Commission on specific matters; this consultation is envisaged in Article 10 (the general granting of exemptions to the VAT régime), Articles 14 and 15 and Article 17 (transitional measures).

Article 13 envisages that co-operation between the Member States, the Commission and the Council may be necessary to avoid fraud or abuse of the VAT system. Article 18 prescribes that the Commission shall consult with the Member States in order to be able to submit a report to the Council on the working of the tax. This complex schema of consultations provided for in the directive aims to avoid the situation whereby the national systems of VAT diverge and conflict, as well as to provide for the speedy introduction of such new Community legislation on the operation of the tax as may prove necessary.

30–22 The system of VAT now operates in all the original Members of the Community, and also in Denmark (although the latter country will have to adapt her tax to conform with the Second Directive).

The first proposals on VAT for the United Kingdom were outlined in a Green Paper on the tax entitled *Value Added Tax* (Cmnd. 4621) and. after being deliberated on for a year, were presented to Parliament in March 1972 in Cmnd. 4929. Statutory effect is given to these proposals by Part I of the Finance Act 1972. The provisions of Part I of the Act follow closely those of the Second Directive.

Article 6 (2) of the Second Directive makes the rules laid down therein on the taxation of services compulsorily applicable only to the services listed in Annex B to the directive. Most States have, in application of the directive, made most services subject to the tax with only specific exceptions; the Finance Act exemptions include insurance, postal, financial, educational and health services.

30–23   The Finance Act envisages a two-rate system of application of the tax, as is employed in the Netherlands and Germany, but with the difference that while the standard rate of tax in the United Kingdom will be 10 per cent., the other rate will be zero. (Section 9 of the Act reserves to the Treasury the right to alter the standard rate of tax to between $7\frac{1}{2}$ per cent. and $12\frac{1}{2}$ per cent. before the implementation of the tax on April 1, 1973, and thereafter to alter the rate by 20 per cent. of the rate in force, both these alterations being effected by order.)

In the normal application of the tax at the standard rate, a purchaser of goods will be liable to pay VAT at 10 per cent. of the price of the goods supplied to him, but he will be able to deduct from the sum due all the VAT which has been already paid by all persons in the production chain down to and including the vendor. With a zero-rated good (which may include materials which are subject to the standard rate) the purchaser still pays VAT, but at the notional rate of 0 per cent., and the tax is zero. But the deduction rule mentioned above still applies to zero-rated goods and services, and thus the purchaser will be able to recover the tax previously paid on that particular good. Zero-rating constitutes a considerable tax saving on the goods and services affected. Zero-rated goods and services (listed in Sched. 4) must be distinguished from exempted goods and services (listed in Sched. 5). Where goods and services are exempted from the tax, the vendor does not charge VAT on the sale he makes, but the purchaser cannot recoup the tax which has already been paid in previous transactions involving the goods; consequently an exempted good will very often bear an undefined burden of VAT. Zero-rating on a good or service is thus more valuable to its purchaser than its exemption.

The Finance Act institutes special procedures for collection and for appeal against a taxing decision and also deals with special cases such as local authorities, the Crown, partnerships and trading stamp schemes. These are not specifically provided for in the directive since it is only a guideline for the implementation of a common system.

–24   The Community has allowed the Member States to introduce VAT at the rates which differ between the various States; it will be necessary to harmonise the rates imposed as well as their number and scope if the distorting effects of taxation are to be totally neutralised. The Commission has already undertaken a study of the budgetary, economic and social consequences of the harmonisation of rates of taxes (*Collection Etudes Série Concurrence* No. 16, 1970). The probability is that the Community will evolve two rate brackets within which each State can operate its VAT, and that these brackets will be progressively reduced to arrive at two rates, one standard and one reduced, to apply throughout the Community.

Excise duties

–25   Article 99 provides for the harmonisation of not only turnover taxes, but also of excise duties and other forms of indirect taxation. Excise duties are significant revenue-producers in the Community and in particular the United Kingdom. In 1972 the Commission produced draft directives (one general and four specific) and a draft decision on such duties. (See Supp. to Bulletin 3, 1972 and J.O. 1972, C 43/23 *et seq.*) The draft general directive would establish five excise duties, on tobacco, mineral oil, alcohol, wine and beer, which would be applied on a system to be proposed in specific directives. All other forms of excise duty and indirect taxation would have to disappear or be subsumed within VAT. These proposals appear to supersede all previous Commission proposals in this field.

Residual forms of indirect taxation

0–26   Certain measures have been taken to harmonise residual forms of indirect taxation. Directive 69/335, J.O. 1969, L 249/25, provides for the harmonisation of charges " on contributions of capital to capital companies," referred to as " capital duty "; under this directive capital duty is not to exceed 2 per cent. and is not to be less than 1 per cent. (Art. 7 (1) (*a*)), but is subject to certain exceptions. The Commission has since proposed a common rate of 1 per cent., but this would still be significantly higher than the present stamp duty on capital, the comparable United Kingdom imposition. (See also § 31–11 for company law aspects.)

The Community has adopted a directive (69/169, J.O. 1969, L 133/6 as amended by Directive 72/230, J.O. 1972 L 139/28) which allows individuals to import goods free of turnover taxes and excise duties to the value of 25 u.a. in respect of journeys made from third countries into the Community, and to the value of 125 u.a. for journeys from one Member country to another. This directive is complemented by Regulation 1544/69 (J.O. 1969, L 191/1), which sets a standard *ad valorem* customs duty of 10 per cent. for goods contained in personal luggage over a basic franchise of 25 u.a. Concessions as between Member States will, however, become redundant when indirect taxation is harmonised between all the Member States, and may well be phased out fairly rapidly (see also § 21–06, *supra*).

A similar type of tax concession on individual travel between Member States is that given by Directive 68/297, J.O. 1968, L 175/15, which lays down that Member States shall admit free of duty 50 litres of fuel in the fuel tanks of commercial motor vehicles when the vehicles cross common frontiers of Member States (see generally § 27–19, *supra*).

DIRECT TAXES

30–27 The EEC Treaty does not by and large deal with direct taxation in specific terms. It would appear that in 1957 they were not viewed as factors which would inhibit the formation of a common market and they did not therefore receive special treatment in the Treaty. Articles 95 to 97 and 99 deal solely with indirect taxation, and only Article 98 concerns itself with direct taxes, the Article defining such taxes negatively as " charges other than turnover taxes, excise duties and other forms of indirect taxation." The Article prohibits the granting of remissions and repayments of these other charges in respect of exports to other Member States, and the imposition of countervailing charges in respect of imports from other Member States, in the absence of prior approval granted for a limited period by the Council acting by a qualified majority on a proposal from the Commission. It is clear that such drawbacks and countervailing charges are unacceptable within a common market for they constitute a patent subsidy to exporting industries and protect domestic industry. The Article was apparently inserted to take account of the difficulties experienced by France following the devaluation of the franc in 1958. The approval mechanism to gain a derogation from the Article has never been used.

30–28   In the absence of specific provisions, harmonisation of direct taxes must be based on Article 100, providing for the approximation of laws by means of directives. It was made apparent by the Segré Report (*The Development of a European Capital Market,* EEC Commission, Brussels, November 1966) that unequal fiscal conditions whereby each Member State maintained its own different taxes and rates of tax on income prohibited the emergence of a European capital market. The specific obstacles were stated to be:

  (a) the double taxation of investments placed abroad;
  (b) the preferential treatment of investments made in the country where the taxpayer is domiciled and conversely the discriminatory taxation by the taxing State of investments made by a non-resident;
  (c) the discriminatory taxation of institutional investors; and

(d) the discrepancies between the national tax collection systems, which consequently favoured certain types of investment as opposed to others.

The ideas in the Report were taken up and reworked by the Commission into a Programme for the harmonisation of direct taxes (Supp. to Bulletin 8, 1967), which contained a five-point plan to ensure fair competition, free movement of capital and investment, and industrial reorganisation and to co-ordinate national fiscal policies. The plan aimed to:

(1) harmonise the system of corporation tax throughout the Community;

(2) approximate the bases of assessment for taxes on company profits (*i.e.* establish common accounting principles);

(3) approximate the tax arrangements applicable to parent companies and subsidiaries, to company mergers and winding-up operations;

(4) harmonise the system of withholding taxes on dividends and interest payments; and

(5) organise a multilateral convention to avoid double taxation phenomena which remained despite the measures mentioned above.

0–29 On the basis of the programme, the Community has begun to work towards a harmonised system of company taxation in order to eliminate economic double taxation, which involves taxation of company dividends not only in the hands of the company but also in the hands of the individual shareholder. This often results in a greater tax burden falling on distributed profits than on retained profits. The situation is made more difficult inside the EEC since three different systems of company profit taxation are in existence. The problems were examined in detail in a report made on behalf of the Commission by Prof. A. J. van den Tempel (*Impôt sur les sociétés et impôt sur le revenu dans les Communautés européennes, Etudes Série Concurrence* No. 15, Brussels, 1970). The Report favoured the adoption throughout the Community of the system known as the classical system (the system instituted in the United Kingdom by the Finance Act 1965). However, it would now appear that the so-called imputation system, at present operating in Belgium and France, is being favoured as the system to operate in the Community; a White Paper published in 1972, entitled *The Reform of Corporation Tax* (Cmnd. 4955), proposes the introduction (or to be exact, re-introduction) of such a system for the United Kingdom.

0–30 The Commission has prepared a draft directive relating to the annual accounts of limited liability companies (Supp. to Bulletin 12, 1971), to be issued on the legal basis of Article 54 (3) (*g*). The principle expressed in the proposal is that all legislative requirements for publication should be the same in order to protect the public. It is perhaps unlikely that the directive will be approved in its present form since it differs radically from United Kingdom accountancy law and practice.

The Commission submitted two draft directives to the Council in January 1969, one relating to the taxation on mergers and similar transactions and the other to the taxation of parent and subsidiary companies (J.O. 1969, C 39/1 and 7). It would not appear likely that either of these directives will be adopted in their present form, especially as both are intimately connected with the proposals for a European company statute, and measures in application of Community principles in these particular fields will probably follow approval of a European company statute (as to which see §§ 31–17 *et seq.*).

The problem of withholding taxes and the consequent international double taxation was seen as acute by the Segré Report. The Commission issued two memoranda on the subject (1967, Supp. to Bulletin 8, 1967, and 1969, Doc. Com. (69), 201), ultimately recommending that no withholding tax should be imposed on the payment of bond interest, with a view to countering the attraction of the tax-free Eurobond market. No substantive action has been taken. In respect of taxation of company dividends remitted to another Member State the Commission advocated a system of taxation in the country of the recipient rather than a simple harmonisation of rates of withholding tax. No positive measures have been taken in this particular sphere, and the removal of fiscal barriers within the Common Market involving direct taxation does not in general appear to enjoy a very high priority.

CHAPTER 31

THE COMMUNITIES AND COMPANY LAW

INTRODUCTORY

1-01 FREEDOM of establishment in the context of the EEC Treaty (Arts. 52 to 58) relates to all Community nationals, whether these be natural or legal persons; thus a definition is included in the second paragraph of Article 52, of " freedom of establishment " as embracing " the right to set up and manage undertakings, in particular companies or firms within the meaning of the second paragraph of Article 58," upon the same terms as nationals of the country of establishment, subject, however, to the provisions of the chapter relating to capital.

By Article 58, second para., " companies or firms " are defined to mean companies or firms " constituted under civil or commercial law, including co-operative societies, and other legal persons governed by public or private law, save for those which are non-profit-making."

By Article 58, first para., companies and firms formed in accordance with the law of any Member State and having their " registered office, central administration or principal place of business within the Community " are to be treated " in the same way as natural persons who are nationals of Member States " (non-profit-making entities excepted).

1-02 The Treaty thus avoids the adoption of any single determinant of the national character of companies, as perhaps it was bound to do since within the Six the tests adopted vary from the place of registration or principal place of business in Italy, to place of registration exclusively in the Netherlands, location of the actual or real head office in France, Germany and Luxembourg. But instead of simply referring the whole question to national law, Article 58 so far combines the tests of the place of registration and of actual or real head office as to provide for treatment on an equal footing with nationals of Member States of companies registered under the law of any Member State and having their registered offices or central administrations or principal places of business wheresoever within the Community.

It has been suggested that the apparent breadth of this provision is cut down so as to include within it only those companies having an effective link with the Community, for Article 52 confines freedom of establishment to the right to set up and manage undertakings " under the conditions laid down for its own nationals by the law of the country where such establishment is effected." But this limitation would appear to relate exclusively to the capacity of nationals of one Member State to incorporate companies under the law of another.

31–03 Article 54 provides for the progressive abolition of existing restrictions upon freedom of establishment through action of the Council and Commission *inter alia* under paragraph 3 (*g*),

" by co-ordinating to the necessary extent the safeguards which, for the protection of the interests of members and others, are required by Member States of companies or firms within the meaning of the second paragraph of Article 58 with a view to making such safeguards equivalent throughout the Community."

In addition, Article 220 stipulates that

"Member States shall, so far as is necessary, enter into negotiations with each other with a view to securing for the benefit of their nationals . . . the mutual recognition of companies or firms within the meaning of the second paragraph of Article 58, the retention of legal personality in the event of transfer of their seat from one country to another, and the possibility of mergers between companies or firms governed by the laws of different countries."

DIRECTIVES

31–04 Directive 68/151, J.O. 1968, L 65/8, issued pursuant to Article 54 (3) (*g*) of the Treaty, applies only to companies and partnerships limited by shares (Article 1: see also technical adaptation, Cmnd. 4862–II, p. 67) and thus not to every type of concern within Article 58 (2). The directive is designed not only to effect the co-ordination of safeguards for third persons dealing with companies, but also to afford uniform protection to persons belonging to one Member State becoming members or shareholders of companies in other Member States, as they have tended increasingly to do as a result of the freeing of the movement of capital within the Community and of the achievement of national treatment for investors under Article 221 of the Treaty.

31–05 This directive lays down what information concerning its affairs a company must be required to disclose (Art. 2), and how this is to be made available to the public (Art. 3). The information required includes the memorandum and articles, the names of directors, the amount of paid-up capital, the balance sheet and profit and loss account, and any details of transfer of domicile, winding-up or liquidation.

The disclosure of financial information is in general required only of limited companies. A separate directive is envisaged by Article 2 (1) (*f*) and by the technical adaptation replacing it (Cmnd. 4862–II, p. 67) in respect of private companies such as the *Gesellschaft mit beschränkter Haftung* (GmbH) or *Société à Responsabilité Limitée* (SARL) and like forms of company, which do not exist in English law or Scots law (but *cf.* private company under law of Northern Ireland).

The making of uniform provisions in relation to the disclosure of financial information concerning all types of public companies is to be desired because of the very large differences in the national laws applicable, Italy requiring the publication of the accounts of all bodies corporate and Germany only the publication of those of public companies (*Aktiengesellschaft* (AG)), as distinct from private companies (GmbH) notwithstanding that there are very many large private companies.

Article 3 (5) of the directive operates as a sanction by providing that documents or particulars required to be disclosed may be relied upon by the company against a third party, in the absence of proof that the latter had knowledge thereof, only after publication in the appropriate national gazette as required under Article 3 (4). The non-publication of financial provisions is left to be penalised expressly (Art. 6).

31–06   By Article 7 promoters of a company are to be made jointly and severally liable for any act performed during the promotion of a company, for which responsibility is not subsequently accepted by the company. Article 8 provides that where the formalities of disclosure of the names of persons authorised to represent the company have been completed, any actual irregularity in the appointment of those persons may not be relied upon by the company against third parties unless actual notice is proved. Article 9 follows German law in dispensing with the notion of *ultra vires* altogether. By this Article companies are to be made liable for acts going beyond the scope of their objects but which are within their capacity under local statute. Member States may, however, legislate so as to negate liability to third parties having actual notice of the *ultra vires* quality of any act (Art. 9 (1)).

31–07   The third part of the directive employs techniques of " nullity " or " invalidation " of corporate acts largely unknown to English company law. In Article 11 (2) are listed six grounds upon which nullity may be ordered, including the illegal purpose of the act in question and the omission in any written instrument of the corporate style. Article 12 (3) lays down, consistently with the general aim of protection of persons dealing with companies, that notwithstanding that the annulment of an act may result in the termination of a company's existence it shall not affect the validity of earlier transactions. The consequences of an order of nullity are not dealt with by the directive save in so far as they are remitted to the sphere of national law (Art. 12 (4)).

The directive does not require Member States to introduce rules on nullity of companies where none existed before, and the United Kingdom has not adopted such a course in the European Communities Act.

In so far as the provisions of the directive are not already law in the United Kingdom, effect is given to them by section 9 of the European Communities Act (*infra*, § 38–20).

31–08   A further directive, so far merely proposed, and not yet adopted (J.O. 1970, C 48/8) is designed to co-ordinate safeguards respecting the initial constitution, and the conservation and increase or reduction of capital of joint stock companies. It deals only with joint stock companies, as opposed to private companies and partnerships, since it is the former which attract the unwary investor. But the protection of creditors is no less within its purview. Companies are, in order that their credit-worthiness may be established, to be required to disclose details of their capital structure (Art. 2). The minimum prescribed paid-up capital would be fixed at 25,000 u.a. (Art. 6). By Article 12 companies are to be restrained from declaring dividends if at any time their assets, including reserves, fall below the amount of their paid-up capital. Article 18 would seek to impose restrictions upon purchase of their own shares by companies more stringent than those prevailing under the municipal legislation of the Six, though less severe than those applying in English law. Articles 27 and 28 would permit capital reductions only by resolution in general meeting and of meetings of each class of shareholders affected. Article 29 would institute a system for securing debts contracted before any reduction of capital.

31–09   A third directive, likewise only at the stage of a proposal so far (J.O. 1970, C 89/20) relates to mergers of companies in a single Member State. Those Member States where mergers have hitherto been unknown will be required to make legal provision for them. Adequate information must be furnished to all interested parties on all the main features of the merger, *inter alia* by publication of the draft of the terms of merger and of the final terms themselves. The shareholders' rights are to be safeguarded by notification to them of the opinion to be obtained from outside experts as to whether the proposed ratio of share exchange is a fair one. The employees of the firms concerned must be informed of the merger's implications for them, and creditors are to be afforded special guarantees safeguarding them against any infringement of their rights.

31–10   Proposals for a fourth directive on the basis of Article 54 (3) (*g*) call for the co-ordination of guarantees which are required in the Member States from companies to protect the interests both of shareholders and outsiders as regards the structure and the contents of the annual accounts and the business report, the method of evaluation and the publication of these documents (Supp. to Bulletin 12, 1971; J.O. 1972, C 7/11). The directive would introduce common forms of layout for accounts, together with harmonised rules on the way accounts should be drawn up. Less stringent rules would be applied to limited liability companies than to public companies. It is unlikely, however, that the draft directive will be issued in its present form.

Proposals for a fifth directive have been made (Bull. Supp. 10/1972; J.O. 1972, C 131/49), which call for the institution of a supervisory board as well as a board of directors and the general meeting in all limited companies. Worker participation would be obligatory in the case of companies with more than 500 employees. Member States would be free to choose between a system similar to the German type, whereby one-third of the supervisory board would be appointed by the employees, and a system similar to that prevailing in the Netherlands whereby the members of the supervisory board would be co-opted subject to opposition to a candidate by the employees or the shareholders. Company boards would be required to report quarterly to their supervisory board on the affairs of the company. The board would be empowered to demand special reports at any time on any matter. Other powers would include the power to appoint and remove the directors, and a veto over most important decisions. The proposals also cover actions against members of either board, and lay down rules on the rights and obligations of shareholders' meetings, especially regarding the calling and conduct of meetings and of information to be supplied, the agenda, proxies and voting trusts, the alteration of articles, class rights, minutes, accounts and audit.

Proposals for a further directive on the basis of Article 54 (3) (*g*) (unnumbered) (Bull. Supp. 8/1972; J.O. 1972, C 131/61) call for the harmonisation of national rules regarding the publicity to be given prior to the admission of securities on to the stock exchanges, i.e. prospectuses. This proposal would seek to facilitate an openness in cross-national investment not at present possible.

31–11   A directive has been issued by the Council (69/335, J.O. 1969, L 249/25) on the bases of Articles 99 and 100 to harmonise rates of indirect taxes applied by Member States to the raising of capital, akin to the United Kingdom's stamp duty on capital. The capital duty falls due on contributions of capital to capital companies (Art. 1) and is payable in the Member State where the " effective centre of management " is situated (Art. 2 (1)) (however, if the centre of management is outside the Community although the registered office of the company is situated in a Member State, any transactions relating to capital duty will be taxable in that Member State). Article 4 of the directive lists the transactions subject to capital duty: these include the formation of a capital company, the increase of its capital, and its transfer to a Member State from outside the Community. Article 5 indicates the method of assessment of duty, while Article 7 lays down that the rate of capital duty is not to be more than 2 per cent. nor less than 1 per cent. (para. (1) (*a*)), reduced by 50 per cent. or more upon a transfer of all assets and liabilities or a portion of the business (para. (1) (*b*)). Holding and investment companies may be charged a special 1 per cent. rate as from January 1, 1973—0·5 per cent. until that date (para. (1) (*c*)). Proposals have been made (J.O. 1971, C 34/1) for a harmonised 1 per cent. rate under paragraph (1) (*a*), and a 50 per cent. reduction rate under paragraph (1) (*b*). In view of the fact that there is no tax in the United Kingdom on operations coming under paragraph (1) (*b*), the proposal is unlikely to be adopted in its present form. Point V (2) of Annex VII to the Act of Accession (Cmnd. 4862–II, p. 149) nevertheless requires Ireland and the United Kingdom to implement the measures necessary in order to comply, by January 1, 1974, at the latest, with paragraph (1) of the directive as it now stands if the work " concerning the extension of the field of application of Article 7 (1) (*b*) " has not been completed before accession. Extension is envisaged by Commission proposals of September 21, 1972, J.O. 1972, C 113/9.

Article 3 (1) (*a*) of the directive is replaced by a technical adaptation (Cmnd. 4864–II, p. 76) defining " capital company " as including what is known in the United Kingdom as the company incorporated with limited liability.

31–12   A further proposed directive (J.O. 1969, C 39/1), which would introduce a common tax régime for mergers and for the international transfer of assets, is of interest here also, as is another (J.O. 1969, C 39/7) respecting the taxation of companies and their subsidiaries where parent company and subsidiary are situate in the territories of different Member States. Article 5 of this proposal would do away with withholding tax upon dividends remitted to parent companies holding not less than 20 per cent. of the share capital of the subsidiary. Article 7 would permit the presentation of consolidated accounts in the case of a participation of at least 50 per cent.

CONVENTIONS

31–13 The Hague Convention on Mutual Recognition of the Legal Personality of Foreign Corporations of June 1, 1956, is inadequate for the purposes of the Community, being not yet in force nor of absolute obligation as respects a company to which nationality is attributed on the basis of the location of its actual or real head office. But Article 58 EEC, although it in effect extends " national treatment " to corporations, neither defines the requisites for recognition of foreign companies nor indicates with any precision the consequences of such recognition. Accordingly, recourse was had to Article 220 (negotiations with a view *inter alia* to securing mutual recognition of companies: *infra*, § 32–19), pursuant to which the Convention on the Mutual Recognition of Companies and Bodies Corporate was drawn up (February 29, 1968: Supp. to Bulletin 2, 1969).

By Article 1 of the latter Convention:

" Companies under civil or commercial law, including co-operative societies, established in accordance with the law of a Contracting State which grants them the capacity of persons having rights and duties, and having their statutory registered office in the territories to which the present Convention applies, shall be recognised as of right."

Article 2 of the Convention provides:

" Bodies corporate under public or private law, other than the companies specified in Article 1, which fulfil the conditions stipulated in the said Article, which have as their main or accessory object an economic activity normally exercised for reward, and which, without infringing the law under which they were established, do in fact continuously exercise such activity, shall also be recognised as of right."

The Convention thus applies to companies established with capacity under civil or commercial law of a Member State and having their statutory registered office in the territories to which the Convention applies (Art. 1), and to legal persons of public or private law, established under the same conditions, having as their aim or necessary object an economic activity normally exercised for reward (Art. 2). Article 8 of the Convention provides that recognition is not to be denied or restricted merely because the law in accordance with which an entity is established does not grant it the legal status of a body corporate; thus for example the *Offene Handelsgesellschaft* (OHG) of German law qualifies. But contracting States may declare that they will not apply the Convention to entities having their real registered office outside the Convention territories, and having no genuine link with the economy of one of the territories. Exceptionally, a contracting State may in addition require certain special requirements of its own legislation to be complied with where the entity to be recognised has its real registered office on its own territory (Art. 4). " Real registered office " is defined by Article 5 as meaning the place where the entity's central administration is established.

31-14   The effect of recognition is such that the recognised entity is to have in the recognising State the capacity accorded to it by the law under which it is established (Art. 6), but the recognising State may refuse certain rights and powers which it does not grant to similar entities governed by its own law, but this is not to result in the withdrawal of the capacity to contract, or to accomplish other legal acts or to sue or to be sued (Art. 7, first para.). The limitations arising from restrictions thus imposed may not be invoked by the recognised entity (Art. 7, second para.). The application of the Convention, moreover, is, by Article 9, made subject to accepted principles of public policy (" *ordre public* ").

31–15   A convention is proposed respecting the bankruptcy of individuals and of companies (*i.e.* involving compulsory winding-up of insolvent companies), supplementary to the Convention of Jurisdiction and the Enforcement of Civil and Commercial Judgments (September 27, 1968, Supp. to Bulletin 2, 1969), to be drawn up with a view to securing uniform effect throughout the Community of adjudications in bankruptcy etc. (*Avant-Projet de convention relative à la faillite, aux concordats et aux procédures analogues,* CEE Doc. 3, 327/XIV/70–F).

31–16   A Common Market Patent Convention is also envisaged. The preliminary draft proposals, dated 1971 (R/1307/71: *Second advance draft agreement on a European patent for the Common Market,* 1971, European Communities, Luxembourg), provide that the Convention shall be a " special agreement " within the meaning of Article 8 of the Draft European Patent Convention, which embraces twenty countries, including all the Nine. Article 8 provides that: " any group of Contracting States may provide by special agreement that a European Patent granted for all those States has a unitary character throughout their territories and is subject to the provisions of that special agreement; and that a European Patent may not be granted in respect of some only of those States." The draft Common Market Convention will inaugurate a single system of patent law for the Community.

THE DEVICE OF THE EUROPEAN COMPANY

31–17 It is of course theoretically possible to set up by treaty a legal entity or corporation not possessing the nationality of any State, though in practice at least in the past it has usually been thought more convenient to incorporate such essentially international institutions as the Bank for International Settlements under a system of municipal law—in this case Swiss law. But even the theoretical possibility of establishing a non-national company does not exist for private enterprise, as opposed to States. The creation of the Common Market has not so far altered this situation.

In 1966, however, the Commission responded to a French proposal for the adoption of a uniform company law by each of the Six with a suggestion for the establishment by convention of a system of European company law under which European companies might be incorporated (Supp. to Bulletin 9/10, 1966). The Sanders Committee, appointed to consider this suggestion, reported in favour of the plan whereby European companies might be brought into existence by the merger of companies incorporated under different systems of national law; as holding companies associated with such companies, or by direct registration as

European companies. This plan envisaged a body of European company law under the aegis of the Court of Justice of the Communities (*Etudes Concurrence* 6, 1967, Brussels). A feature of it was a somewhat ill-defined scheme for employee participation in European companies. It was rejected, however, by the Commission in favour of the latter body's own proposal made under Article 235 of the EEC Treaty (Supp. to Bulletin 8, 1970; J.O. 1970, C 124/1).

31–18   This proposal does not allow of the establishment of European companies by direct registration, but contemplates rather that they shall come into existence exclusively through the merger of companies incorporated under the laws of two or more Member States. It would provide, however, for a system of employee participation through works councils and supervisory boards. Though no tax advantages such as would prejudice the revenue of any Member State are envisaged for the European company, it is clear that these entities would benefit from the proposed directive on the taxation of mergers (*supra*), and that they would be free to adopt a system of consolidated accounting allowing a loss made in one country of the Community to be set off against a profit made elsewhere before submission of a tax return to the country of domicile. This would be subject to adequate safeguards for the shareholders. Another feature of the proposal is the reservation to shareholders of concerns merged into European companies of an option to be bought out at a fair price.

The proposals for the European Company are presently under active discussion by the institutions of the Community. It seems unlikely that the proposals will be adopted in their present form, or even in the immediate future, but the need for such an entity is clear, so the necessary provision will undoubtedly be made in due course.

31–19   The Commission has made a proposal (J.O. 1971, C 107/15) regarding what are described as Joint Undertakings (*cf.* Euratom Joint Undertakings—Arts. 45 *et seq.* Euratom). The Joint Undertaking would operate in two specific areas:
(a) as the legal framework for the transnational pooling of public service operations, and
(b) as the legal basis for the establishment of undertakings comprising bodies from at least two Member States, whose aim would be the execution of a project of Community interest in the field of technical development or the supply of primary goods.

The Joint Undertaking is therefore envisaged as serving a purpose which the European Company could never fulfil, since the latter would operate in the sphere of civil rather than public law. The opinion of the Economic and Social Committee (J.O. 1972, C 131/15) indicates that the legal form of the undertaking will need to be further defined before the Joint Undertaking becomes a reality.

CHAPTER 32

APPROXIMATION AND HARMONISATION OF LAWS

INTRODUCTORY

32–01 PARAGRAPH (*h*) of Article 3 of the EEC Treaty specifies " The approximation of the laws of Member States to the extent required for the proper functioning of the Common Market " as an activity to be undertaken by the Community for the sake of the general purpose of establishing the Common Market, set out in Article 2. " Approximation of Laws " is further the heading and subject-matter of the third and last chapter in Title I, " Common Rules," of Part Three of the Treaty, which deals with the policy of the Community. An identical or similar process in specific contexts is envisaged by numerous other Articles throughout the Treaty. Thus Article 27 requires the Member States before the end of the first stage of the original transitional period to take all steps necessary " to approximate their provisions laid down by law, regulation or administrative action in respect of customs matters," acting on recommendations of the Commission. Article 56 likewise contemplates " the co-ordination of . . . provisions laid down by law " providing for special treatment for foreign nationals on grounds of public policy, and Article 57 " the co-ordination of . . . provisions . . . concerning the taking up . . . of activities as self-employed persons." Equally, Article 99 provides that " the Commission shall consider how the legislation of the various Member States concerning . . . indirect taxation . . . can be harmonised. . . ." Article 117 similarly recites the belief of the parties to the Treaty that the improvement of working conditions and standards of living will follow " from the approximation of provisions laid down by law," etc. Similar processes of approximation or harmonisation of laws are to be found in or are implied by Articles 43, 49, 54, 67, 69, 75, 87, 111 to 114, 118 and 119.

32–02 The different expressions " approximation," " harmonisation," " co-ordination," etc. are not particularly happy, especially in their English versions. It is not thought, however, that their variety implies, as has been suggested, any particular order of things, or that " co-ordination " involves, for instance, something less than " harmonisation " or " approximation." Nor is it considered that the draftsman has, by ringing the changes upon these expressions, meant to distinguish between the case where Member States are called upon, for instance, to adopt identical laws, and that in which it is sufficient that their laws do not conflict.

Perhaps the only distinction that may validly be drawn is this: that where a completely uniform Community rule is envisaged, terminology implying harmonisation, etc. is not used, and a power to issue directly applicable instruments (Regulations) is generally conferred. Where, conversely, it is intended to leave to Member States liberty to legislate in a given area, but where a greater or less degree of adjustment is nevertheless necessary if the objectives of the Treaty are to be met, the Treaty speaks in terms of harmonisation, co-ordination, etc., and generally confers a lesser power of Community action, usually by directive, *i.e.* laying down the ends to be achieved, but leaving the choice of means to the Member States. The scope left to national action may, however, be quite limited where the directive is very detailed. The Treaty in fact rarely gives a specific power to issue Regulations, that power being more usually subsumed under a general power to take any type of action. Two other provisions already referred to as relating to harmonisation do in fact confer a power to issue directives or Regulations (Arts. 49 and 87). But neither is a true exception to the suggested distinction, since these Articles contemplate a common rule on certain matters, while on others harmonisation is all that is necessary. Nevertheless, no directives have been issued pursuant to Article 87, whereas both Regulations and directives have been issued on the legal basis of Article 49, generally in complementary pairs (see currently Regulation 1612/68, J.O. 1968, L 257/2, on the freedom of movement for workers within the Community, complemented by Directive 68/360, J.O. 1968, L 257/13, on the abolition of restrictions on movement and residence within the Community of workers of Member States and their families).

The Chapter on Approximation of Laws (Articles 100 to 102)

32–03 It is perhaps slightly anomalous that the chapter heading " Approximation of Laws " should come within the Title " Common Rules," since what it aims at is the reconciliation in one way or another of existing national laws rather than the adoption of a new and uniform law throughout the Community. It is not only laws which, by virtue of Article 100, are to be subjected by directive to the process of approximation, but all " such provisions laid down by law, regulation or administrative action in Member States as directly affect the establishment or functioning of the Common Market," the Assembly and Economic and Social Committee being consulted if any directive promulgated involves for its implementation the amendment of the legislation of one or more Member States.

Possibly this wording, wide though it be, does not embrace unwritten administrative practice, as does Article 49; no doubt, however, Article 235 could be prayed in aid to justify a directive aimed at the approximation of any such practices.

Presumably where a matter is not the subject of any provision " laid down by law, regulation or administrative action " in any of the Member

States, Article 100 cannot be relied upon and used, as it were, to establish a rule where none existed before. On the other hand, a Member State desirous of introducing a new rule which may cause distortion of the conditions of competition in the Common Market is under an obligation, under Article 102 (*infra*), to consult the Commission.

32–04   Article 100, though not of infinite scope, is nevertheless wider than Article 101, which deals not with the approximation generally of national provisions directly affecting the establishment or functioning of the Common Market, but merely with differences between such provisions which the Commission finds to be causing a distortion of conditions of competition requiring elimination. Where this situation arises the Commission has a duty to consult the Member States concerned. If such consultation does not result in an agreement putting an end to the distortion in question, the Council is, on the proposal of the Commission, to issue any necessary directives, and Commission and Council may take any other appropriate measures for which the Treaty provides.

As the Common Market develops, however, the possible scope of Article 100 must contract. For, where the Community has assumed legislative competence, that of the Member States is displaced. See for example 40/69, *HZA Hamburg-Oberelbe* v. *Bollmann*, Rec. XVI 69, [1970] C.M.L.R. 141. See also *supra*, § 17–16. The need for the approximation of national provisions is in consequence diminished.

32–05   Article 100 has commonly been invoked in conjunction with other provisions of the Treaty, for instance with Article 43, for purposes of agricultural standardisation and harmonisation (see § 32–10 for examples) the latter Article making no specific mention of approximation of national provisions. It has similarly been used together with Article 99 in connection with the VAT directives (67/227 and 228, J.O. 1967, 1301 and 1303), harmonisation in this context being deemed essential to the Community and best achieved with the assistance of the Economic and Social Committee and the European Parliament in their consultative capacity such as Article 100 enables, but Article 99 alone does not in terms enable, to be invoked.

Action for material purposes taken under Article 100 alone has related notably to preservatives etc. and colouring matter in food (food standards) (Directive of October 23, 1962, Directives 65/54, 65/469, 66/722, 67/427, 67/653, 68/419, 68/420, 70/357, 70/358, 70/359, 71/160 . . .); standardisation in motor vehicle construction, and noise and pollution levels in motor vehicles (Directives 70/156, 70/157, 70/220, 70/221, 70/222, 70/311, 70/387, 70/388, 71/127, 71/320 . . .); certain customs matters, notably warehousing and free zones (Directives 68/312, 69/74–76 . . .); classification, packaging and labelling of dangerous substances (Directives 67/548, 69/81, 70/189, 71/144 . . .); crystal glass (Directive 69/493, J.O. 1969, L 326/36); classification of wood in the rough (Directive 68/89, J.O. 1968, L 32/12); measuring and measuring instruments (Directives 71/316, 71/317, 71/318, 71/319, 71/347, 71/348, 71/349, 71/354 . . .); textile appellations (Directive 71/307, J.O. 1971, L 185/16); and proprietary medicinal products (Directive 65/65). And see the General Programme of May 28, 1969, J.O. 1969, C 76/1, on the elimination of technical barriers to trade.

32–06 The stipulations of Article 101 respecting the remedying of distortion of conditions of competition arising through differences between existing national provisions are reinforced by those of Article 102, to which allusion has already been made. By this article a Member State wishing to introduce a new legislative etc. provision must consult the Commission if there is reason to fear that the result will be distortion within the meaning of Article 101. The Commission is then, after consultation with the Member States, to recommend appropriate preventive measures. Should the State making the innovation fail to comply with the Commission's recommendations, the other Member States are relieved of any obligation to amend their own provisions under Article 101. If, further, the Member State ignoring the Commission's recommendation causes distortion detrimental to itself alone, that Article is expressed not to apply.

32–07 In 6/64, *Costa* v. *ENEL,* Rec. X 1141, [1964] C.M.L.R. 425, a preliminary ruling on the interpretation of Article 102 was requested from the Court of Justice. The Court held that the Article was not directly applicable, so that the question whether Italy had any obligation thereunder to consult the Commission in relation to legislation nationalising electricity undertakings was not examinable at the suit of an individual.

OTHER PROVISIONS

32–08 The existence in the Treaty, outside the Articles of the chapter specifically headed "Approximation of Laws," of provisions expressly or impliedly stipulating in particular contexts for the same or for similar processes has been referred to already. Those provisions of this sort in the chapter on the customs union have been discussed already (*supra,* § 21–18), and there is no need to advert to them here.

32–09 Article 43 has been relied on (together in most cases with Article 100) for the issue of directives relating to agricultural matters such as plant health (Directives 69/464–466); sylvicultural propagation material (Directives 66/404, 69/64 and 71/161); sampling and analysis of, and control of additives in, animal feeding stuffs (Directives 70/373 and 70/524); general census of agricultural holdings (Directive 69/400); inquiries relating to pig-breeding (Directive 68/161); production potential of orchards of certain species of fruit trees (Directive 71/286); public health problems relating to livestock and fresh meat (animal health)

(Directives 64/432 and 433, 65/276 and 277, 66/600 and 601, 69/349, 70/360, 70/486, 71/118, 71/285); and marketing of seeds and propagating material (Directives 66/400–403, 68/193, 69/60–63, 69/208, 70/457 and 458, 71/140, 71/162).

Article 49, however, is of some interest. This makes specific mention of national legislation as one of the sources of obstacles to the free movement of workers which are to be progressively removed by directive or Regulation. What is here in contemplation is, as it were, a species of negative approximation of national laws. The current dispositions under this article are Decision 68/359, Directive 68/360 and Regulation 1612/68 (see *supra*, § 23–08).

32-10   Article 54 similarly provides for the progressive abolition of restrictions on freedom of establishment by means of directives for, *inter alia*, the elimination of " administrative procedures and practices, whether resulting from national legislation " or from prior agreements between Member States, the maintenance of which would fetter such freedom (para. (3) (*c*)).

The same Article (paragraph (3) (*g*)) calls for co-ordination " to the necessary extent [of] the safeguards which, for the protection of the interests of members and others, are required by Member States of companies or firms . . . with a view to making such safeguards equivalent throughout the Community." This provision is generally thought to endow the organs of the Community with capacity to bring about co-ordination in the entire field of company law. A possible view is, however, that, having regard to the place of the paragraph in an Article of the chapter dealing primarily with the right of establishment, Article 100 (*supra*, § 32–03) or Articles 220 or 235 (*infra*, §§ 32–19 and 32–18) would provide a more satisfactory basis for any comprehensive process of harmonisation in this field. See further, § 31–04, *supra*, and see European Communities Secondary Legislation, H.M.S.O. 1972, Part 9, " Right of Establishment " for directives issued under Article 54.

32-11   Article 56, in the same context of the right of establishment, calls for the co-ordination before the end of the transitional period of " provisions laid down by law, regulation or administrative action " for " special treatment for foreign nationals on grounds of public policy, public security or public health." The directive issued pursuant to this stipulation (64/221, J.O. 1964, 850) defines the concept of " public policy [*ordre public*] public security or public health " (Arts. 2 to 4) and sets time limits upon adverse determinations made upon any of these grounds (Arts. 5 to 7). In *Corveleyn* v. *Belgium* (1969, C.D.E. 343) Article 3 of this directive was held by the Belgian Conseil d'Etat to be directly applicable in Belgian law, so that a ministerial decision ordering deportation which failed to comply therewith, was quashed.

32-12   Article 57 (1) provides for the issue of directives for the mutual recognition of diplomas and other evidence of formal qualifications, and

Article 57 (2) for directives " for the co-ordination of the provisions laid down by law, Regulation or administrative action in Member States concerning the taking up and pursuit of activities as self-employed persons."

(For directives issued *inter alia* under Article 57, see 64/222 (wholesale trade and intermediaries in commerce, industry and small crafts); 64/427 (manufacturing and processing industries); 68/364 (retail trade); 68/366 (food manufacturing and beverage industries); 68/368 (personal services—restaurants, hotels etc.); 69/77 (amending 64/427); 69/82 (oil prospecting and drilling); 70/523 (wholesale coal trade and intermediaries).)

32–13   The effect of Article 66 is to apply the provisions of Articles 56 and 57 *mutatis mutandis* in relation to freedom to provide services within the Community. The directives issued *inter alia* under Article 57 (*supra*) have indeed all been issued under Article 66 as well, and thus apply to freedom of establishment and the freedom to provide services in the sectors affected. As respects Article 57, moreover, no very general action thereunder is as yet apparently possible owing to the wide differences in professional qualifications prevailing in the several Member States. See generally *supra*, Chapter 25.

32–14   Article 75 (1) (*a*) provides for the laying down by the Council of the proposal of the Commission of " common rules applicable to international transport to or from the territory of a Member State or passing across the territory of one or more Member States." Regulations, decisions and directives have been employed for the implementation of this provision—for example a decision respecting competition in road, river and rail transport (65/271, J.O. 1965, 1500) and a directive regarding the international road transport of goods (July 23, 1962, J.O. 1962, 2005). Road transport being dependent on fuels still dutiable within the territory of each Member State, the process of harmonisation of indirect taxes under Article 99 has on occasion been associated with that of the formulation of common rules under Article 75. Thus Directive 68/297, J.O. 1968 L 175/15, " on the standardisation of provisions regarding the duty-free admission of fuel contained in the fuel tanks of commercial motor vehicles," was issued on the legal basis of both Articles 75 and 99. See generally §§ 27–19 and 30–26. (See European Communities Secondary Legislation, H.M.S.O. 1972, Part 13, " Transport," for other instruments issued under Art. 75.)

32–15   As respects commercial policy, Articles 111 and 113 may be construed to call for the harmonisation or co-ordination of national legislation in so far as tariff rates and the like, with which those Articles deal, depend upon domestic legislation. Equally Article 112 contemplates the harmonisation of the legislative bases of aids to exports to third countries. This article applies only to aids to exports outside the Community, otherwise Articles 92 to 94 apply. However, in practice it would appear that Article 112 applies only to indirect financial assistance to exports (see generally Chapter 37, *infra*, on commercial policy).

32-16   Equally, in so far as concerns social policy, Article 117, as has been mentioned already, contemplates " the approximation of provisions laid down by law " etc., though of itself it imposes no obligation in this regard. Article 118, too, though it specifies as among the tasks of the Commission those of promoting close co-operation between Member States *inter alia* in matters relating to labour law and working conditions and the right of association, to name but two areas obviously ruled by law, confines the role of the Commission to making studies, delivering opinions, and arranging consultations. Article 119, however, which deals with the principle of equal pay for equal work, purports to impose an obligation upon Member States to see that this principle is applied within their respective territories. Thus far the Article has not been implemented and itself specifies no method for its enforcement. See generally on these Articles, *supra*, § § 24–01 *et seq.*

32-17   The foregoing tabulation does not exhaust the list of provisions of the Treaty which expressly or by implication call for or envisage the approximation, harmonisation or co-ordination of the laws of Member States. Certain others were drawn attention to in the Weinkamm Report on the harmonisation of legislation (P.E. session doc. 54/65), notably Article 84 (2), which empowers the Council to " decide whether, to what extent, and by what procedure appropriate provisions may be laid down for sea and air transport."

32-18   Article 235, moreover, is at least in theory capable of invocation in order to bring about the approximation of legislation, providing as it does that " if action by the Community should prove necessary to attain . . . one of [its. objectives] and this Treaty has not provided the necessary powers, the Council shall . . . take the appropriate measures." Resort to this residual provision was in fact proposed to overcome the difficulty caused by the omission of fruit juices from the list of products within the scope of the agricultural provisions of the Treaty (Art. 38 and Annex II), but the proposal was not proceeded with (proposal of February 7, 1969, J.O. 1969, C 39/19).

Upon a consideration of the Weinkamm Report on progress in legislative approximation up to 1965, the European Parliament adopted a resolution (J.O. 1965, 2035) advocating a general programme of harmonisation, the transfer of certain responsibilities therefor from Council to Commission, the extension of the process of harmonisation to the realm of penal law, the establishment of arrangements for reciprocal recognition and execution of judgments, and the necessity of taking into account the evolution of Community law in revising municipal law. This resolution did not fail to emphasise the importance of utilising the Parliament itself as a legislative body.

APPROXIMATION UNDER TREATY OR CONVENTION: ARTICLE 220

32–19 Article 220 of the Treaty provides that the Member States shall, so far as is necessary, negotiate with each other with a view to securing for their respective nationals four particular types of benefit, namely: national treatment generally, relief from double taxation, mutual recognition and like advantages for companies, and reciprocal recognition of judgments and arbitral awards. Though the negotiations which this Article contemplates need not be negotiations for a Treaty or convention, but might equally well be productive, for instance, of parallel legislation, the Article has been resorted to for the conclusion of two conventions, each having associated with it a supplementary protocol, concluded later (June 3, 1971), conferring jurisdiction in relation to it upon the Court of Justice of the Community (Supp. to Bulletin 4, 1971). The first convention, which was signed on February 29, 1968, is on the Mutual Recognition of Companies and Bodies Corporate (Supp. to Bulletin 2, 1969); and the second, signed on September 27, 1968, deals with Jurisdiction and the Enforcement of Civil and Commercial Judgments (Supp. to Bulletin 2, 1969). A further convention on recognition of arbitral awards has been proposed but has not been proceeded with. The elaboration of a preliminary draft of a double taxation convention has also been begun.

32–20 It must be clear that the two conventions which have been concluded, as well as other possible conventions falling within the ambit of Article 220, may call for significant modifications in the law both of the six original States and of the acceding States.

For instance, the Convention on Jurisdiction purports within its sphere of operations (which does not include questions of personal status and capacity, bankruptcy, social security or arbitration (Art. 1)) to exclude bare presence of the defendant as a basis of jurisdiction, which is grounded in general on domicile or residence. In such contexts therefore, the implementation of the convention must call for a special process of " approximation " or " harmonisation " of law. This follows, however, not from the EEC Treaty itself but from the ordinary obligations of public international law which the Member States have accepted by their interpretation of Article 220 as requiring or enabling them to becoming contracting parties to what are independent instruments, though of course linked to the Community and its objectives, such instruments relating to matters of municipal law.

32–21 As respects the new members of the Community it is to be noted that, by Article 3 (2) of the Act of Accession, these States undertake to accede to the conventions provided for in Article 220, and to the protocols on their interpretation by the Court of Justice, and to this end to enter into negotiations with the original Member States in order to make the necessary adjustments thereto.

Convention on the Mutual Recognition of Companies and Bodies Corporate

32–22   The Convention on the Mutual Recognition of Companies and Bodies Corporate is discussed in relation to company law (see *supra*, § 31–13).

Convention on Jurisdiction and the Enforcement of Civil and Commercial Judgments

32–23   As stated above the Convention on Jurisdiction and the Enforcement of Civil and Commercial Judgments excludes from its ambit matters of personal status and capacity, bankruptcies etc., matters of social security, and arbitration (Art. 1). For other matters, Articles 2 to 6 lay down general rules on jurisdiction, providing that persons " domiciled " in a Contracting State shall be answerable to the courts of that State whatever their nationality (Art. 2),[1] and that otherwise (Art. 5) they may be sued in the courts of the country of:

(1) the contractual obligation,
(2) the " domicile " or usual place of residence of the claimant for compulsory maintenance,
(3) the *locus delicti*,
(4) the " court of prosecution," in claims for damages or restitution arising from a tort,
(5) the location of a subsidiary establishment, where a dispute concerns the way that establishment's affairs have been conducted.

There are particular provisions on insurance matters in amplification of the general rules (Arts. 7 to 12). There are similar provisions in relation to hire-purchase etc. (Arts. 13 to 15). Only the courts of the country where the subject-matter is located or arose have jurisdiction in questions involving:

(1) rights *in rem*;
(2) winding-up etc. of companies;
(3) validity of entries in public registers;
(4) patent, trade and design mark matters;
(5) enforcement of judgments (Art. 16).

Subject to limited provisions of Articles 12 and 15, permitting waiver of the special rules on insurance matters and hire-purchase, and to Article 16, parties may by agreement in writing or by oral agreement subsequently confirmed in writing, designate the courts of a Member State as being solely competent, provided at least one of the parties is domiciled in the Community (Art. 17).

---

[1] An immediate problem of translation or interpretation arises here: the French concept of " *domicile* " does not carry with it all the technical connotations of the English concept of " domicile," but is more nearly equivalent to what is to be understood by " habitual residence " in English practice.

Articles 19 *et seq*. deal with questions of judicial competence (Arts. 19 and 20), the problem of concurrent hearings in different countries (" *lis pendens* ") (Arts. 21 to 23), interlocutory measures (Art. 24), recognition and enforcement of foreign judgments (Arts. 25–45), subject to a public policy clause (Art. 27), and proof of documents etc. (Arts. 46 to 51). There then follow general and final provisions, notably substituting the present convention for certain earlier bilateral ones (Art. 55), and providing for extension to the various overseas territories (Art. 60). The convention is concluded for an indefinite period but is open to revision (Arts. 66 and 67). The Convention entered into force on February 1, 1973.

32–24   The protocols referred to above (§ 32–19), link the two conventions jurisdictionally with the Community (Supp. to Bulletin 4, 1971) by conferring jurisdiction on the Court of Justice. Rather surprisingly the two protocols are not in identical terms; the Protocol to the first Convention confers jurisdiction on the Court to give preliminary rulings. The wording used to confer the right (or duty) to refer to the Court is substantially that of Article 177 EEC. By contrast to the first Protocol, the second Protocol, in conferring jurisdiction on the Court to give preliminary interpretations, states specifically which courts may, and which courts must, refer matters to the Court (Arts. 2 and 3). Article 4 provides for references to the Court by the " competent authorities " where the decisions of the courts of one State conflict with those of another State or those of the Court of Justice itself.

Both protocols were to come into force at earliest at the same time as the relevant main convention, and being very closely linked to these latter have no real autonomous existence.

367

CHAPTER 33

ECONOMIC POLICY

ARTICLES 103 TO 109

33–01 TITLE II of Part Three of the Treaty, "Policy of the Community," is entitled "Economic policy." It contains three chapters, Chapter 1: Conjunctural policy (Art. 103), Chapter 2: Balance of payments (Arts. 104 to 109), and Chapter 3: Commercial policy (Arts. 110 to 116). In the strict sense of the term, "economic policy" embraces only the first two chapters, and Chapter 3 is considered in connection with the foreign relations of the Community in general (§§ 37–13 *et seq. infra*).

33–02 In the context of a customs union, where individual States are not permitted to apply the usual methods of economic control unilaterally (*e.g.* increase or introduction of duties or quotas, subsidies and the like), and where free movement of goods, labour and capital in any case lessens the effect of applying permissible restrictive controls, basic economic problems seem both more difficult to control at a national level, and more likely to spread to the other members of the customs union. Therefore it was deemed necessary to insert provisions into the Treaty tending towards the co-ordination of national economic policies and providing some form of mutual co-operation between Member States in case of economic difficulty. However, in inserting such provisions, it was necessary to strike a balance between the need to leave the basic powers of the Member States over their economic policies unimpaired, and the necessity for Community action and control. Chapters 1 and 2 of this title contain phrases such as:

"Member States shall regard their conjunctural policies as a matter of common concern" (Art. 103 (1));

". . . Member States shall co-ordinate their economic policies" (Art. 105 (1));

"Each Member State shall treat its policy with regard to rates of exchange as a matter of common concern" (Art. 107 (1)).

These indicate that the balance of initiative of action rests with the Member States, subject to their general duty to ensure fulfilment of their obligations arising out of the Treaty—Article 5 EEC; see generally § 20–06, *supra*. But Article 103 (2) and (3) provide, with regard to measures to be taken on conjunctural policies, for Council decisions (*lato sensu*) and for directives.

33–03 Moreover, Article 105 (2) sets up a Monetary Committee to promote the co-ordination of Member States' economic policies, and

368

Article 107 (2) empowers the Commission to authorise other Member States to take necessary action in response to a unilateral parity change. Articles 108 and 109 permit special measures (" mutual assistance," " protective measures ") to be taken by a Member State in balance of payments difficulties, but these are only permissible under the strict control of the Community institutions.

The Community also exercises general powers, conferred on it by the Treaty; in particular, Article 145 states that:

" To ensure that the objectives set out in this Treaty are attained, the Council shall, in accordance with the provisions of this Treaty:

—ensure co-ordination of the general economic policies of the Member States . . ."

and Article 155 requires the Commission to ensure that the Treaty is applied, and to formulate recommendations on any matter where it thinks them necessary or where the Treaty so provides.

In implementation of its general decision-making powers, the Council has set up various committees with economic responsibilities, notably: Conjunctural Policy Committee (Decision of March 9, 1960, J.O. 1960, 764), Medium-Term Economic Policy Committee (Decision 64/247, J.O. 1964, 1031), Budgetary Policy Committee (Decision 64/299, J.O. 1964, 1205), Committee of the Governors of the Central Banks (Decision 64/300, J.O. 1964, 1206). Recommendations have been made with regard to specific national measures, *e.g.* the German revaluation in 1961 (written questions 3 and 4/61, J.O. 1961, 649 and 661).

However the later development of the Community has pointed to the need for more institutionalised Community powers in relation to Member States' economic policies. The Final Communiqué of the 1969 Hague Summit Conference, issued on December 2, 1969 (text in J.O. 1970 C 94/9 and in Third General Report (1969), p. 486), indicated agreement that an economic and monetary union should be created for the continued progress of the European Communities. Paragraph 1 of the Paris Summit Communiqué of October 21, 1972 [1] reaffirms the determination of the Member States of the enlarged Community to achieve the economic and monetary union, and calls for action with a view to completing it by December 31, 1980 (see further *infra*).

Chapter 1—Conjunctural policy [2]—Article 103

33–04   There is little in the subject-matter of Article 103 to distinguish it from the chapter it precedes, but it is generally considered that Article

---

[1] Cmnd. 5109.

[2] Some confusion has existed over the title given to this chapter of the Treaty. In the H.M.S.O. translation of the EEC Treaty published in 1967, this Article was headed " Policy on Current Trends," and elsewhere the French idea of " *politique de conjoncture* " and the German " *Konjunkturpolitik* " (which have exact parallels in the Italian and Dutch texts) have been translated as " short-term economic policy " and " cyclical policy." It would appear that although these latter two

103 was given a separate chapter heading in order to emphasise the importance of its aims, especially in the context of a customs union. Since the subject-matter of the two chapters is so similar, discussion of the one necessarily involves examination of aspects of the other.

Article 103 (1) requires Member States to regard their conjunctural policies (*i.e.* their short-term economic policies) as a matter of common concern. They are to consult each other and the Commission as to measures to be taken in the light of prevailing circumstances. Paragraph 2 gives the Council a general power, acting unanimously on a proposal from the Commission, to decide upon the measures appropriate to the situation. This power of decision is expressed to be without prejudice to any other procedures provided for in the Treaty. Acting by a qualified majority on a proposal from the Commission, the Council may under paragraph 3 issue any directives needed to give effect to the measures decided upon under paragraph 2. These powers can be used to meet sudden emergencies (*e.g.* Regulation 974/71, J.O. 1971, L 106/1, on short-term policy measures to be taken as a result of the temporary widening of currency margins, but see also powers contained in Arts. 108 and 109). They can also be used to encourage co-operation and co-ordination between Community and Member States; Decision 69/227, J.O. 1969, L 183/41, on the co-ordination of short-term economic policies of Member States (prior consultation on economic measures to be organised between Member States in the context of the Monetary, Conjunctural Policy and Budgetary Policy Committees) and Decision 71/141, J.O. 1971, L 73/12, on the strengthening of this co-ordination (three Council meetings per annum to examine the economic situation in the Community, and to lay down obligatory guidelines for the Member States to follow including ones concerning national budgetary matters) were both adopted on the basis of Article 103.

33–05 Since no particular type of act in the sense of Article 189 * is mentioned in paragraph 2 as constituting " the measures appropriate to the situation," it must be taken that the paragraph permits the Council to take any measures provided for in the Treaty. This is in contrast to paragraph 3 which provides for the issue of directives to implement paragraph 2 on a qualified majority vote.

The Council has tended to implement this Article by using the following techniques:

(a) the strengthening of the means of co-ordination within the Community by the formation of committees (see above);

(b) the issue of recommendations to Member States when it became apprised of various national economic problems (*e.g.* J.O. 1964, 1029, on the re-establishment of economic equilibrium in the

phrases express the idea conveyed in the original Community languages reasonably well, it was felt necessary to anglicise the term used in them for the Community appears to draw some distinction between conjunctural and short-term policies.

Community, especially in Italy and France; see also J.O. 1965, 985, J.O. 1966, 4059, J.O. 1967, 159/6). And, more recently, recommendations laying down short-term economic guidelines;
(c) the issue of Regulations to deal with currency fluctuations (*e.g.* Regulations 1586/69, 677/70 and 974/71) and flows of "hot money," Regulation 156/72, J.O. 1972, L 91/13.

In addition, the Community has of late expanded the role of Article 103 as the basis for legal action; the directive on stocks of crude oil of December 20, 1968, J.O. 1968, 416, was issued under this power, as was Decision 71/143, J.O. 1971, L 73/15, on medium-term financial aid. The directive may be considered to have been issued under Article 103 (4) which provides for application of the decision-making powers when there are supply difficulties for certain products (see also Decision 69/227 and Decision 71/141, *supra*).

33–06   The objectives of short-term economic policy are not to be found in Article 103, but in Article 104, which requires each Member State to pursue the economic policy needed to ensure the equilibrium of its overall balance of payments and to maintain confidence in its currency while taking care to ensure a high level of employment and a stable level of prices. It must be considered that this Article is of general application, and its objectives are to be borne in mind not only in the context of the chapter on balance of payments, but in all contexts.

If this interpretation of Article 104 is correct, Article 105 (1), which calls for co-ordination of economic policies in order to facilitate attainment of the objectives set out in Article 104, is of application in the context of short-term economic policy, and the Monetary Committee set up in paragraph 2 can also be used to assist in the co-ordination of this policy.

The original Werner Plan for Economic Monetary Union (*Report to the Council and the Commission on the realisation by stages of Economic and Monetary Union in the Community*, Supp. to Bulletin 11, 1970) made concrete proposals for the monetary aspects of such union but contained less specific plans for its economic aspects. However, Decision 71/141, J.O. 1971, L 73/12, *supra*, is based at least in part on ideas set out in the Werner Plan (see generally below).

Articles 104 to 109—balance of payments

33–07   It has been explained above why balance of payments questions are dealt with in a chapter separate from that on short-term economic policy, and that the former is not entirely separable from the latter. Chapter 2 does specifically envisage monetary policy amongst its concerns, although recent international events underline that this can never be divorced from short-term cyclical economic problems.

As already stated, Article 105 is the Community operational key to the achievement of the aims enumerated in Article 104. On the basis of paragraph 1 and of the general powers given to the institutions by the Treaty, the Medium-Term Economic Policy Committee, the Budgetary Policy Committee, and the Committee of the Governors of the Central Banks were set up to assist in co-ordination of economic policies.

33–08   The Medium-Term Economic Policy Committee (set up by Decision 64/247, J.O. 1964, 1031) has as its aim the preparation of medium-term economic policy programmes of about five years' duration. To enable it to perform its tasks, the Committee draws in particular on the forecasts prepared by the economic policy experts of the Community (*Groupe d'Etude des Perspectives Economiques à Moyen Terme*). In practice, the Committee co-ordinates Member States' medium-term economic policies. The Council has since adopted three Medium-Term Economic Policy Programmes, the third of which (Decision 71/107, J.O. 1971, L 49/1), for the period of 1971 to 1975, is more ambitious and precise in statistical terms than either of its predecessors. In order to make this policy effective, and also to provide for procedures for mutual assistance, the Council set up a fund of medium-term credits, available to Member States as mutual assistance on a qualified majority decision of the Council (Decision 71/143, J.O. 1971, L 73/15, issued on the legal basis of Arts. 103 and 108).

33–09   The Budgetary Committee (set up by Decision 64/299, J.O. 1964, 1205) and the Committee of Governors of the Central Banks (Decision 64/300, J.O. 1964, 1206) were both set up on the legal basis of Article 105 (1). The former seeks to study and compare the broad lines of budgetary policies of the Member States, so that their economic and financial policies can be more easily co-ordinated. The Committee of Governors of the Central Banks seeks to co-ordinate national credit and exchange rate policies, with a view to ensuring stability in exchange rates in the Community.

33–10   Article 105 (2) itself provides for the establishment of the Monetary Committee. This Committee is to promote co-ordination of Member States' monetary policies to the extent needed for the functioning of the Common Market. The rules governing the Committee were established by a Council decision of March 18, 1958, J.O. 1958, 390. These rules elaborate upon the tasks of the Committee as set out in Article 105 (2). The Committee must be consulted on matters falling within Articles 69, 71, 73 (1) and (2), 107 (2), 108 (1) and 109 (3). The Council and the Commission may request the opinion of the Monetary Committee in any other cases, and the Committee has in any event " the power and the obligation " to draw up opinions on its own initiative wherever it considers such necessary.

Article 105 is therefore the key to current Community action on co-ordination of economic policy, although when the Economic and Monetary Union is realised, an amplification of the Community's powers of initiative, decision and implementation may be necessary.

33–11   Article 106 concerns the authorisation of the freedom of payments for transactions between Member States, and is discussed *supra*, § 25–23.

33–12   Article 107 states that the Member States shall treat their exchange rate policy as a matter of common concern, and that if any Member State revalues or devalues its currency when such action is inconsistent with the objectives set out in Article 104, and which seriously distorts conditions of competition, the Commission may, after consulting the Monetary Committee, authorise other Member States to take for a strictly limited period the necessary measures, the conditions and details of which it will determine, in order to counter the consequences of such action.

This mechanism has not operated in the way intended, for each Member State has been inclined to act without reference to the Commission when effecting parity changes. However, the changing of parity does affect the delicate balance on which the financing of the CAP is based; producers are paid and prices are set in units of account (u.a.), which are fixed by reference to the gold standard of a United States dollar. In practice, since the unit of account does not change, any alteration in national currency parities automatically reduces or increases that currency's value *vis-à-vis* the Community's unit of account. Following the German and French currency movements of 1969, the cash returns on German farm produce expressed in DM fell, and French agricultural products became more competitive in the rest of the Community. In order to redress this imbalance, the Community had to institute complex systems of compensatory taxes to enable the CAP to function properly. The problem of tying agricultural finance to a fixed unit was made all the more difficult when the world monetary crisis occurred in May 1971, and the Council responded with a Regulation of general application (974/71, J.O. 1971, L 106/1) to meet all future difficulties caused by changing national parities. (See also § 22–45, *supra*.)

33–13   Articles 108 and 109 form the Community machinery for alleviating any balance of payments difficulties experienced or apprehended by a Member State, " where such difficulties are liable in particular to jeopardise the functioning of the Common Market or the progressive implementation of the common commercial policy " (Art. 108 (1)). This condition has legal validity but economically it is devoid of substance, since a State's balance of payments difficulties will on all occasions " jeopardise the functioning of the Common Market."

33–14   Article 108 sets out three distinct phases of action.

(1) Action by the Member State itself within the aims of Article 104, together with investigation by and consultation with the Commission,

which may state what measures it recommends the State concerned to take.

33–15   (2) If these measures prove inadequate, Article 108 (2) provides for the granting of " mutual assistance." The Commission recommends to the Council the granting of mutual assistance and the appropriate methods therefor after consulting the Monetary Committee, and is to keep the Council regularly informed of the situation and how it is developing (para. 1, second and third sub-paras.). The Council is to grant mutual assistance acting by a qualified majority; it is to adopt directives or decisions laying down the conditions and details of such assistance (para. 2) which may take such forms as:

(a) recourse to international organisations such as the IMF or the Bank for International Settlements (at Basle) for credit arrangements;

(b) measures to avoid trade deflection where the State which is in difficulties maintains or reintroduces quantitative restrictions against third countries;

(c) the granting of limited credits by other Member States, subject to their agreement.

Mutual assistance granted to France in 1968 (Directive 68/310 of July 20, 1968, J.O. 1968, L 189/13) consisted in exhortations to the other Member States to aim at a high growth rate, combined with a policy of steady interest rates, while permitting issue of French loans on their markets. The Member States were to take a common attitude in the OECD and in GATT. During the transitional period it was possible for mutual assistance to comprise reductions in customs duties or enlargements of quotas. It does not appear that such arrangements will again operate in the transitional period following the new accessions.

33–16   (3) If mutual assistance is not granted, and the measures taken are insufficient, the Commission is to authorise the Member State in difficulties to take such " protective measures " as the Commission defines and determines (para. 3) subject to veto or variation by the Council (para. 3, second sub-para.). This must be interpreted as permitting the Member State to derogate from the Treaty and the implementation of measures taken thereunder, and this means that special duties or quotas are imposable under this paragraph, even when the Community has entered the definitive period.

Three days after the granting of mutual assistance to France on July 20, 1968, the Commission was constrained to act under Article 108 (3). In an elaborately reasoned decision (Decision 68/301, J.O. 1968, L 178/15) it authorised retention of exchange controls, application of aids to exports to other Member States, and import controls on goods from other Member States, in particular on motor vehicles, household goods, textiles and steel products. This decision was amended by Decision

68/406, of December 4, 1968, J.O. 1968, L 295/10, which permitted retention of certain controls on capital movements.

Article 109

3–17   Article 109 is an exception provision which permits Member States on their own initiative to take necessary protective measures in the face of a sudden balance of payments crisis. The Community, and the Commission in particular, keeps a watching brief over these exceptional measures and paragraph 2 of the Article permits the Commission to recommend Article 108 (2) measures of mutual assistance. Under paragraph 3, the Council may, after the Commission has delivered an opinion and the Monetary Committee has been consulted, decide that the State concerned should amend, suspend or abolish the protective measures.

Although the Member States would appear relatively free to carry out their own economic policies, albeit under the obligation to observe a certain modicum of co-operation and co-ordination between each other and the Community, they are only free to operate within the scope of the institutionalised Common Market, and measures which are outside this latter (such as those envisaged in Articles 108 (3) and 109 (1)) can only be taken by Member States when special permission has been granted and special controls imposed by the Community. They are ultimately subject to Council control.

ECONOMIC AND MONETARY UNION

3–18 Economic and Monetary Union is an idea much discussed elsewhere and referred to at various points in this book.

The Commission, in its role as initiator of Community policy, has been calling for a unified monetary policy for many years, even during the " fat years " of the early 1960s. However, the onset of monetary and economic difficulties towards the end of that decade convinced the Commission that Community action in this field would prove essential to development in the 1970s, especially once the customs union had been fully completed on July 1, 1968.

The Commission presented a memorandum to the Council on February 12, 1969 on the co-ordination of economic policies and on monetary co-operation (*Memorandum of the Commission to the Council on the Co-ordination of Economic Policies and on Monetary Co-operation within the Community,* Supp. to Bulletin 3, 1970) and this was accepted as the starting point for the expressions in the Hague Summit Communiqué of December 2, 1969 (see J.O. 1970, L 94/9 and Third General Report (1969), p. 486 for text) of the need to work out plans to establish an economic and monetary union. By Council decision of March 6, 1970, the so-called Werner Committee was set up to investigate the possibilities of such plans and its report was submitted on October 8,

1970 (*Report to the Council and the Commission on the realisation by stages of economic and monetary union*, Supp. to Bulletin 11, 1970). On October 30, 1970 the Commission submitted to the Council a memorandum and proposals on the establishment by stages of an economic and monetary union in the light of the Werner Report (*Commission Memorandum and proposals to the Council on the establishment by stages of economic and monetary union*, Off-print to Bulletin 11, 1970). These were mainly adopted in the Council's resolution of March 22, 1971, J.O. 1971, L 28/1, and Bulletin 4, 1971, p. 19.

33–19   The general aim of the resolution is the creation of an economic and monetary union, so that the main economic policy decisions will be taken at Community level. A consequence may be the adoption of a single currency for the Community. The resolution spells out a ten-year period for the achievement of various aims explained in fairly extensive detail. By the end of this period the Community would:

" 1. constitute a zone within which persons, goods, services and capital will move freely and without distortion of competition, without, however, giving rise to structural or regional imbalances, and in conditions which will allow persons exercising economic activity to operate on a Community scale;

2. form an individual monetary unit within the international system, characterised by the total and irreversible convertibility of currencies, the elimination of fluctuation margins of rates of exchange, and the irrevocable fixing of parity rates—all of which are indispensable conditions for the creation of a single currency— and including a Community organisation of the Central Banks;

3. hold the powers and responsibilities in the economic and monetary field enabling its Institutions to organise the administration of the union. To this end, the required economic policy decisions shall be taken at Community level and the necessary powers shall be given to the Institutions of the Community."

33–20   The resolution sets out in fairly specific terms the action deemed necessary in order to attain these aims in the first phase (January 1, 1971 to December 31, 1973), while leaving the period from then to the finalisation of the Economic and Monetary Union vague and uncharted; it calls initially for:

(1) reinforcement of co-ordination of short-term economic policies;

(2) greater harmonisation in taxation structures, tending towards the alignment of VAT and excise duty rates throughout the Community;

(3) greater movement of capital and co-ordination of financial market policies;

(4) greater efforts to solve regional and structural problems;

(5) reinforcement of co-ordination in monetary and credit policies, by means of consultation at the level of the Committee of the Governors of the Central Banks and the Monetary Committee;

(6) adoption of common Community attitudes in monetary relations with third countries;

(7) narrowing of margins of fluctuation in parities between the Member States' currencies; and

(8) drawing up of a report on the role and organisation of a European Monetary Co-operation Fund.

33–21   However, because of the problems of the past two years, it has proved difficult to implement much of the first phase. Decisions 71/141, J.O. 1971, L 73/12 and 71/142, J.O. 1971, L 73/14, taken at the same time as the resolution, relate to co-ordination and co-operation in short-term economic policies, and between the Central Banks.

The first of these decisions requires an examination by the Council of the Community economy three times yearly. The Council is to adopt guidelines for policy and budgets to be followed by the Member States. The second decision encourages greater co-operation between Central Banks, especially in the fields of bank liquidity, credit supply and interest rate levels.

Outside the direct scope of the Werner Plan, Decision 71/143, J.O. 1971, L 73/15, set up a credit fund available for medium-term use by the Member States.

33–22   The movement towards economic and monetary union which ran into difficulties during the 1971 monetary crisis, was relaunched by the Council resolution of March 21, 1972 (J.O. 1972, C 38/3, Bulletin 4, 1972, p. 41). In the first place the resolution is designed to reinforce the co-ordination provided for in Decision 71/141, J.O. 1971, L 73/12, in the field of Member States' short-term economic policies. Secondly, it marks the Council's agreement in principle to the use of FEOGA for regional development purposes, and to the setting up of a Regional Development Fund or a similar fund with a view to promoting regional development. Thirdly the resolution provides for the establishment of the so-called Community currency snake, which allows a maximum spread of 2·25 per cent. between the strongest and the weakest Community currencies, enforced by an organised intervention and repayment system operated by the Community Central Banks. This is by far the most important element in the resolution and the only one on which positive progress has so far been achieved. It came into operation on April 24, 1972, but although the applicant countries voluntarily adhered to the system from May 1, 1972, the United Kingdom, Ireland and Denmark withdrew on June 23, 1972, leaving the present Community countries to continue the mutual support of their currencies. Lastly, the resolution marks the readiness of the Council to consider the Commission's proposals on tax harmonisation and the development of a European capital market as a matter of high priority.

33–23   The importance of the economic and monetary union was fully recognised at the Paris Summit. Paragraph 1 of the Final Communiqué of October 21, 1972 (Cmnd. 5109) states that:

> " The heads of state or of government reaffirm the determination of the Member States of the enlarged European Communities irreversibly to achieve the economic and monetary union, confirming all the elements of the instruments adopted by the Council and by the representatives of Member States on March 22, 1971, and March 21, 1972.
>
> " The necessary decisions should be taken in the course of 1973 so as to allow the transition to the second stage of the economic and monetary union on January 1, 1974, and with a view to its completion not later than December 31, 1980."

The Communiqué affirms that the Member States consider fixed but adjustable parities to constitute an essential basis for the achievement of the union, and records the determination to set up mechanisms for defence and mutual support in currency matters. The corner-stone of these mechanisms would be a European Monetary Co-operation Fund, to be administered by the Committee of Governors of Central Banks, within the context of general guidelines on economic policy laid down by the Council of Ministers. The fund is to be set up before April 1, 1973, and is to be created " by solemn instrument," based on the EEC Treaty itself.

In the initial phase the fund is to facilitate concerted action among the central banks for the purposes of narrowing the margins of fluctuations between the Community currencies, and multilateralisation of support intervention and settlements. It is to use for these purposes a European unit of account, and is to administer short-term monetary support among the Central Banks.

In Paragraph 3 of the Communiqué it is recorded that the need for closer co-ordination of national economic policies and for more effective Community procedures were stressed at the Conference. Priority is to be given to anti-inflation measures, which were to be adopted by the Council on October 30 and 31, 1972.

Paragraph 4 of the Communiqué records the determination that the Member States of the enlarged Community " should contribute by a common attitude to directing the reform of the international monetary system towards the introduction of an equitable and durable order." The system envisaged, which would involve fixed but adjustable parities, general convertibility, reduction in the role of reserve currencies, " effective and equitable functioning of the adjustment process," equal rights and duties for all participants, the need to lessen the hazards of " hot money " movements, and the need to take into account the interests of the developing countries, is considered to be fully compatible with the economic and monetary union.

33–24　At the Council meeting referred to above a resolution was duly adopted on action against inflation (October 31, 1972: Europe Documents No. 702, November 6, 1972, annexed to *Europe,* No. 1155, November 6/7, 1972 [2]). The resolution lays down guidelines for combating short-term inflationary problems, being related to the period up to the end of 1973. It was adopted with the concurrence of the acceding States (para. XI). Essentially the resolution calls for a reduction in the rate of increase in consumer prices to 4 per cent. over the period, together with wage restraint, a cutting back in the expansion of the money supply to the rate of growth of GNP, strict budgetary control, and anti-inflationary commercial policy action, possibly involving tariff cuts (duties on beef and veal were to be cut at once).

Paragraphs VIII and IX relate essentially to harmonisation in the conditions of competition: the Council takes note of the Commission's desire to accelerate action in respect of price-fixing agreements, and to introduce proposals on merger control. Besides this, domestic rules governing trade practices ultimately having an inflationary effect are to be applied strictly (para. VIII). Action is to be taken on technical barriers to trade in foodstuffs and medicinal products, and close supervision of the existing rules on public works contracts and " concessions to competition " is called for. Immediate action on the proposal for a directive on the award of public supply contracts is stipulated (para. IX).

[2] Since published in J.O. 1972, C 133/12 as Council Resolution of December 5, 1972.

CHAPTER 34

REGIONAL POLICY

34–01 THE preamble to the Treaty of Rome states that the High Contracting Parties were "anxious to strengthen the unity of their economies and to ensure their harmonious development by reducing the differences existing between the various regions and the backwardness of the less favoured regions."

The body of the Treaty does not itself, however, contain the elements of a coherent regional policy; such provisions as there are for dealing with regional problems are scattered at various points throughout the EEC and ECSC Treaties (discussed *infra*). The Commission has proposed the elaboration of what is described as a fully integrated regional policy. (See generally *A Regional Policy for the Community*, Commission, 1969, and "Memorandum on Regional Policy in the Community," Supp. to Bulletin 12, 1969, and J.O. 1969, C 152/6; and see further below.) But as yet such action as has been taken has been somewhat limited in scope.

The lack of specific powers contained in the Treaty for dealing with regional problems as a whole is emphasised by the fact that the Commission's proposals are based upon the general power contained in Article 235.

34–02 The aim of the Community in regional matters is not to pre-empt national action, but rather to co-ordinate and direct such action so as to make it more effective. Thus the territorial definitions of regions adopted by the Community are the same as those adopted at the national level for the purpose of national regional policies. It is doubtful whether what constitutes a region can be defined with any degree of precision, but it seems to be generally agreed that national regional policy is aimed at particular geographical areas forming socio-economic unities of national territory, and consists in measures designed to correct local difficulties and to place all areas on a more equal footing. The European Communities clearly have an interest in such policies, for if regional disparities are to persist, the aim to create a single economic area will be jeopardised by the distortions in economic conditions and in competition inherent in the regional imbalances.

34–03 The Commission has since 1969 submitted several sets of proposals to the Council on regional matters, the proposals of October 1969 forming the foundation for the later ones. The 1969 proposals were accompanied by a fairly comprehensive study (since brought up to date by *L'évolution régionale dans la Communauté Bilan Analytique*, Commission, December 1971) of national regional policies, and of

380

regional problems from a Community viewpoint. The study also set out the need for a Community regional policy, whose objectives are in general terms expressed to be the establishment, development and operation of the facilities needed for the location of economic activities and people, in the light of technical and economic requirements, human needs and aspirations and the characteristics of the areas in question. More specifically a Community regional policy would aim to counter-act regional disparities, and guide production towards more pro-ductive sectors with the infrastructure improvements needed for these sectors, the aims varying according to whether the region in question is industrialised, semi-industrialised or agricultural.

The proposals of October 1969 take the form of a draft decision. Article 1 of the proposals provides that the Commission should carry out a regular examination with each Member State of the situation of the regions for which development plans should be drawn up as a matter of urgency. Such urgency is presumed in :

(a) regions lagging behind in development, mainly because of the predominance of agricultural activities;

(b) regions which are declining because of the trend of the predomi-nant economic activities (*e.g.* coal);

(c) frontier regions, where the need for co-ordination between Member States is felt particularly strongly;

(d) regions where there is structural unemployment.

Such examinations would be carried out *ad hoc,* and otherwise annually.

A new departure in the otherwise straightforward powers to be contained in the proposed decision would be to give the Commission the power to recommend that development plans be drawn up or amplified and discussed, where the examinations provided for in Article 1 fail to produce joint conclusions. Plans submitted for discussion would have to contain a minimum of information (Art. 2).

34-04   On the basis of the discussions, which could also take place in the context of a standing Regional Development Committee, set up by Article 8 of the proposals, and which would have to do so if financial aid is to be given (Art. 4), the Commission would be empowered to address

" any Opinions or Recommendations regarding development plans the main purpose of which is that account should be taken, from the economic and social angles of [1] :

(a) the need for better co-ordination of measures adopted by the Member States, especially in frontier areas;

---

[1] The French text of this part of the passage quoted, having " *relatifs aux plans de développement régional* " between commas, suggests that the opinions or recom-mendations are to point up the factors listed, but the English text suggests that the opinions or recommendations will only apply to regional development plans taking the factors into account. The interpretation indicated by the French must surely be the correct one.

> (b) Community needs where improvements are made to infra-
> structure, in particular communications, oil or gas pipe-
> lines, ports, airports, and where natural sites and resources
> are developed;
> (c) the implications of policy on agricultural structure;
> (d) the demands of industrial policy in the Common Market
> and the need to avoid uneconomic production;
> (e) vocational training and guidance needs.

The Commission's Opinion may take the form of approval pure
and simple of the regional development plan submitted " (Art. 5).

The standing Regional Development Committee, to be set up by
Article 8, would be composed of representatives of Member States,
chaired by a member of the Commission or his alternate and having
an EIB observer. The Committee would have as its task the examination of " national regional policy forecasts and general programmes,
and more generally the regional problems arising out of the common
market," with a view to reaching " converging regional policy solutions which contribute to the accomplishment of the task set out
in Article 2 of the Treaty." It would for these purposes have a power
to formulate opinions.

Article 9 would require the Commission to examine national
medium-term forecasts of allocations of credits for regional development, with a view to assessing the amount of Community contributions which would prove necessary.

Finally, Article 10 would provide for an information system designed
to keep private and public investors better informed of regional development plans, with a view to eliciting a practical contribution to regional
development.

34–05   As this examination indicates, the proposals are primarily concerned with regional developments of an essentially *ad hoc* and local
character. They do not really answer the need for a global regional
policy, setting out a general line on given types of regional problems.
No action has been taken on these proposals, but the Commission has
since made additional proposals on regional matters which indicate
a more generalised or Community approach. It is questionable how
far the Community can be expected to deal with all regional problems
in view of the immense cost of such an undertaking, and indeed the
Council, in its deliberations of October 26, 1970 discussing the 1969
proposals, while calling for closer consultation on regional problems
and aids and better use of Community financial mechanisms for regional
purposes, considered that Community action should be concentrated on
a limited number of priority areas, such as the peripheral areas, the
frontier regions, and the declining regions. Later proposals are, therefore, more specific, with more limited aims, but are designed to deal
with the problems of particular types of regions as a whole.

4-06 Although no positive action has been taken on the 1969 proposals the Commission has made further proposals for regulations on Community regional policy action in priority agricultural areas (J.O. 1971, C 90/14). The first of two proposals in this context is designed to facilitate development operations in priority agricultural regions by FEOGA, consisting primarily in the financing of jobs for displaced agricultural workers. This creation of new jobs should act as an incentive to persons to give up agricultural activity voluntarily (see generally § 22–43, *supra*, as to structural proposals for agriculture). The second proposal provides the specific rules for the Interest Rebate Fund envisaged in the 1969 proposals; this would ensure a coherent body of productive investment and infrastructure projects. The rebates are to be limited to loans made by the European Investment Bank (as to which see generally *infra*, § 34–14).

By way of positive action, the Member States agreed in the First Resolution on Regional Aids of October 20, 1971 (J.O. 1971, C 111/1) to respect an aid-ceiling of 20 per cent. in the central areas of the Community and to eliminate aids which are not "transparent," *i.e.* quantifiable in cash terms. These aids may not in principle extend to the whole territory of the Member States, and should by and large cover only specific regions. The Commission is to be the watch-dog of the scheme, which came into effect on January 1, 1972. The scope of the resolution is limited to the so-called central areas of the Communities, where the need for co-ordination is considered to be greatest. It is hoped that adherence to the principles of the resolution will eliminate the situation where Member States were in some sense bidding for new industry by competing with each other in the level of aids to industry they offered. Proposals for the peripheral areas—*e.g.* western and south-western France and southern Italy and Scotland— are already envisaged. Admittedly the resolution is of a non-binding character, but in this field of closely-guarded national interests a binding instrument is not a realistic possibility at present.

4-07 The principles of the resolution of October 20, 1971 and the Commission communication upon which it was based are to apply in the new Member States from July 1, 1973 at latest, Article 3 (3) of the Act of Accession notwithstanding (Art. 154 of the Act). "These texts will be supplemented to take account of the new situation of the Community after accession, so that all the Member States are in the same situation in regard to them" (second para.).

4-08 In its as yet unimplemented proposals of 1971, the Commission cites the resolution on Economic and Monetary Union of March 22, 1971 (J.O. 1971, C 28/1) and the Third Programme on Medium-Term Economic Policy (J.O. 1971, L 49/1) both of which make regional questions a matter of priority, stressing that common action and co-ordination of regional matters is part and parcel of the progress towards economic union. On March 21, 1972 (J.O. 1972, C 38/3) the Council undertook to act on the basis of Commission proposals on a Community regional policy before October 1, 1972; in the meantime it gave its agreement in principle that FEOGA should be used on regional development from 1972 and that either a Regional Development Fund should be set up or that there should be some other Community financing system capable of being earmarked for regional development. The Commission issued a communication on May 31 (Com. (72), 530, Final) in response to a request for proposals contained in the Council resolution of March 21, 1971, stating that it considered its three earlier sets of proposals to constitute a coherent whole, and going on to press for the necessary powers to be given to FEOGA, and for the Regional Development Fund, originally suggested in the 1969 proposals, Article 7 (2) of which refers to the setting up of a guarantee system for regional development, and making subsidiary proposals for a Regional Development Corporation (after the fashion of the now-abolished United Kingdom Industrial Redevelopment Corporation and the Italian IRI).

The date for taking decisions on regional policy was postponed to December 1972 at a Council meeting in October, but this date is to some extent overtaken by paragraph 5 of the Paris Summit Communiqué of October 21, 1972, inviting Community institutions to set up a Regional Development Fund by December 31, 1973. The Communiqué calls for a further analysis of regional problems and records an undertaking to co-ordinate national regional policies from now on. Priority is to be given to the aim of correcting structural and regional imbalances which might affect the realisation of the economic and monetary union, in particular to those resulting from the preponderance of agriculture and from industrial change and structural unemployment. It will be noted that these priorities differ somewhat from those suggested in the 1969 proposals (*supra,* § 34–03).

SPECIFIC PROVISIONS RELATING TO REGIONAL MATTERS

34–09 As indicated, the Community does not as yet possess a generalised regional policy, but the Treaty itself contains a number of Articles providing more or less incidentally for action on regional matters. The provisions of the Treaty of Rome relating to regional questions are scattered throughout the Treaty in Articles 92 to 94, 123 to 128, and 129 and 130; other provisions more or less bearing upon regional matters are contained in Articles 39, 42, 49, 80 and 226.

Aids granted by states [2]

34–10 Article 92 (1) lays down the general proposition that, save as otherwise provided, aids which distort or threaten to distort competition

---

[2] See also generally § 29–07 on " Aids."

are incompatible with the Common Market. Article 92 (2) sets out the types of aid which are in a general way incontestably compatible with the Common Market ("shall be compatible"). These aids are rather limited in kind, namely aids having a social character, granted to individual consumers, aids to make good damage caused by natural disaster and the like, and aids to "the economy of certain areas of the Federal Republic of Germany affected by the division of Germany." Clearly none of these is the basis for generalised action.

34–11   Article 92 (3) sets out the aids which *may* be considered compatible with the Common Market. It is these aids which are the primary instruments of regional policy; they are:

(a) aid to promote economic development of areas where the standard of living is abnormally low or where there is serious under-employment;

(b) aid to promote the execution of an important project of common European interest or to remedy a serious disturbance in the economy of a Member State;

(c) aid to facilitate the development of certain economic activities or of certain economic areas . . .;

(d) such other categories of aid as may be specified by decision of the Council acting by a qualified majority on a proposal from the Commission.

The Commission is to review national aid systems (Art. 93 (1)), and if it finds that a national aid is not compatible with the Common Market having regard to Article 92, it is to order its abolition or adjustment (Art. 93 (2)). If the Member State does not comply, the matter may be referred to the Court of Justice direct, in derogation from Articles 169 * and 170,* by the Commission or any other interested State.

There is, however, a special "exceptional circumstances" provision, enabling the Council to permit an otherwise incompatible aid in derogation from Article 92 or any Regulations of application under Article 94 (Art. 93 (2), third sub-para.). A request for such permission has a suspensory effect on Commission action already initiated for a maximum period of three months. If, however, the Council has not acted by the end of this period, the Commission is to act.

Clearly, the powers here are fairly general, and the Commission must be informed of any national proposals in advance, but the powers are nevertheless essentially negative, and do not enable any positive measures to be outlined by the Communities.

European Social Fund [3]

34–12   The European Social Fund (ESF) (provided for in Article 3 of the Treaty) is set up by Article 123 to improve employment opportunities

---

[3] See also § 24–09 for social policy aspects.

for workers, and to contribute thereby to raising the standard of living. To this end, it has the task of "rendering employment of workers easier, and of increasing their . . . mobility."

The Fund, administered by the Commission, assisted by a special committee (Art. 124) has, on request, to meet up to 50 per cent. of certain expenditures complying with the objectives of Article 123, and mentioned in Article 125. By Article 126, the Council was empowered to decide that assistance provided for in Article 125 should no longer be granted or to determine new tasks for the Fund. This was in fact done by Decision 71/66, J.O. 1971, L 28/15, fixing new tasks for the Fund.

Under the new arrangements, the assistance of the Fund may be granted for the benefit of persons who belong to the active population and who engage in a wage-earning occupation after having benefited from a measure within the competence of the Fund.

By Article 4 of the Decision, the Fund may contribute where the labour market is affected by Community action or where specific common action appears necessary for better ensuring a balance of manpower supply and demand. These contributions are founded upon specific decisions of the Council acting by qualified majority on a proposal from the Commission.

The Fund may also contribute where the situation in the labour market is affected by difficulties which do not arise from a special measure taken by the Council within the framework of Community policy, but proceed indirectly from the operation of the Common Market or which impede the harmonious development of the Community (Art. 5). Here the Fund is to aim in particular at eliminating structural unemployment and underemployment. Special account is to be taken of the handicapped, older workers, women and young people. The Council takes decisions here in accordance with Article 127 of the Treaty —*i.e.* by qualified majority on proposals from the Commission and after consulting the Economic and Social Committee.

The amount of the assistance remains at 50 per cent., but is available to public departments, bodies under public law, and other social agencies of like standing entrusted with tasks in the public interest. If a Member State guarantees the implementation of the measures, funds equal to those contributed by the Member State or States may be granted on measures taken by private corporations or other bodies.

34–13   Three Regulations of application were made on November 8, 1971 (2396–2398/71, J.O. 1971, L 249/54, 58 and 61).

Regulation 2396/71 lists the operations covered by Article 5 of Decision 71/66, namely:

(a) aids to backward and declining regions with employment problems;

(b) aids to retraining of manpower to new skills;

(c) aids to sectors forced to terminate, reduce or transform their activities in a permanent way (*e.g.* the coal industry).

Aids aimed at eliminating unemployment and underemployment, and which benefit the unemployed or the redundant and the like, will all qualify.

Additionally, Article 3 of the Regulation provides for the establishment of a list of eligible aids, which is to include:

(a) acquisition of new skills (retraining);

(b) removal grants;

(c) income supplements to those awaiting retraining or employment;

(d) information and guidance;

(e) assistance to the handicapped in finding work;

(f) promotion of better conditions of employment in less-developed regions.

(The list is set out in Regulation 2397/71, J.O. 1971, L 249/58.)

Applications for assistance to the Fund may be channelled only through the Member States, and they must be *a priori* requests (Art. 5 of Regulation 2396/71).

Article 7 provides for the Commission to carry out preparatory studies and pilot schemes.

Clearly, the powers granted to the Community under the ESF provisions are fairly wide, but they are limited essentially to employment problems, and it is the Council which has the primary authority here.

The European Investment Bank

34–14 The European Investment Bank (EIB) is set up by Article 129 of the Treaty of Rome. It is a separate organ of the Community, having legal personality, and governed by a statute annexed by protocol to the Treaty (Cmnd. 4864, p. 114). Under Article 130 of the Treaty it is the task of the EIB to contribute to the balanced and steady development of the Common Market in the interest of the Community. To this end it makes loans at market rates, and gives guarantees to regional development projects; to projects for the modernisation and reconversion of industry and for the development of fresh activities, if they are of such a size or nature that they cannot otherwise be entirely financed by the various measures available in the individual Member States; and, on the same conditions, to large projects of interest to several Member States.

Loans may be granted to Member States or to private or public undertakings for investment projects to be carried out in the European territories of Member States (Art. 18 of the EIB Protocol). Projects elsewhere may, exceptionally, be authorised (*ibid.*). Guarantees are available to public or private undertakings or other bodies for the purpose of carrying out projects provided for in Article 130 (*ibid.*).

Loans and guarantees may only be made where, in the case of projects carried out by undertakings in the production sector, interest and amortisation payments are covered out of operating profits, or, in other cases, where the viability of the enterprise is in some way guaranteed

(Art. 20 (1) (*a*) of the Protocol). The project must in addition contribute to an increase in economic productivity in general and promote the attainment of the Common Market (Art. 20 (1) (*b*)).

Proposals were presented on July 18, 1972 (COM (72) 710, Final) for the implementation of Community development contracts. The three main aims of the contracts, which would be under the supervision of the EIB would be:

1. To encourage the development by Community industries of new products or processes of substantial importance for the Community's economic and social development.
2. To encourage cross-frontier technical and industrial co-operation.
3. To meet public needs still inadequately satisfied in the Community.

Provided in the first place that they are presented and implemented in co-operation by undertakings established in more than one Member State, projects fulfilling the following criteria would qualify:

(a) Projects whose aim is the creation or initial use of a new product or process.

(b) Projects of sufficient general importance from an economic or social standpoint.

(c) Projects offering reasonable likelihood of technical success and good prospects of medium-term exploitation.

(d) Projects involving a technical and financial risk, such that in the absence of public aid they would be deferred.

(e) Projects carried out as to a significant part in the Community (the aim of this provision being to enable co-operation also to be set up between Community and non-Community undertakings, particularly when the non-Community undertakings are supported for this purpose by their governments).

Community contracts would be concluded in the form of loans at the low interest rate of 3 per cent. per annum. This could be modified in the light of economic trends. Community participation would normally be limited to a ceiling of 70 per cent. (exceptionally 100 per cent. in cases of " public interest ").

ADDITIONAL PROVISIONS

Agriculture

34–15   Article 39 sets out the objectives of the Common Agricultural Policy. These include aims:

" (*a*) to increase agricultural productivity by promoting technical progress and by ensuring the rational development of agricultural production and the optimum utilisation of the factors of production, in particular labour;

" (*b*) thus to ensure a fair standard of living for the agricultural community, in particular by increasing the individual earnings of persons engaged in agriculture."

In addition Article 42, second para., provides that the Council may authorise the granting of aid:

> " (*a*) for the protection of enterprises handicapped by structural or natural conditions;
> (*b*) within the framework of economic development programmes."

These objectives and powers are implemented in part by the actions of the guidance section of FEOGA on structural policy (as to which see *supra*, § 22–43). The recent proposals on priority agricultural regions (*supra*) are based upon the power of decision contained in Article 43.

Transport

4–16   Article 80 (1) of the Treaty of Rome prohibits the imposition by a Member State of transport rates and conditions involving any element of support or protection in the interest of one or more particular undertakings or industries, save in so far as authorised by the Commission.

Article 80 (2) requires the Commission, in examining the rates and conditions referred to, to take into account the requirements of an appropriate regional policy, the needs of underdeveloped areas (*e.g.* the Mezzogiorno of Italy) and the problems of areas seriously affected by political circumstances (*e.g.* that part of Niederbayern (Upper Franconia) screened from the northern part of the Federal Republic of Germany by the dead angle created by the southern part of the German Democratic Republic).

This Article of the Treaty cannot be said to contain a general measure of Regional Policy, but is of importance in so far as it can be used to bring distant parts of the Community nearer the centre in competitive terms. Distance can, however, also help to limit competition, as Article 80 (1) recognises; the needs of fair competition have to be balanced with the need to protect the weak economy of *e.g.* the Mezzogiorno. Measures may therefore take the form of favourable rail tariffs for production coming from the Mezzogiorno, with no reciprocal measure enabling northern production to penetrate to the south where it competes with southern production.

Article 226

4–17   Article 226, containing a safeguard provision permitting protective measures where difficulties arise which are serious and liable to persist in any sector of the economy or which could bring about severe deterioration in the economic situation of a given area, was only valid for the period of transition, and is no longer of application, although it is re-enacted *mutatis mutandis* by the Act of Accession, Article 135.

ECSC Treaty

4–18   Article 2 of the ECSC Treaty, in aiming at a raising of the standard of living in the Member States and at ensuring the most rational distribution of products at the highest possible level of productivity, while safe-guarding continuity of employment and avoiding the provoking of fundamental and persistent disturbances in the economies of Member States, is of course concerned first and foremost with coal and steel pro-duction, but in so far as difficulties were foreseeable in these sectors, this Article has as a background an intention to attempt to deal with any regional problems which might arise in the context of the Treaty.

For the initial period of the existence of this Community a system of equalisation between the coal mines and the market was applied in accordance with the provisions of Article 24 of the Transitional Conven-tion. The system was designed to eliminate harmful price increases in individual regions, or in other words, the efficient, rich regions were to pay for the inefficient, poor ones. The system ended with the ECSC period of transition. It does not appear to have been very effective.

In the permanent provisions of the Treaty, Article 46 provides, *inter alia* (third para., sub-para. 4), for studies of the possibility of re-employing, in existing industries or through the creation of new activities, workers made redundant by reason of the development of the market or technical changes.

34–19   Substantive powers of regional activity are contained in the first place in Article 54, providing for assistance in the form of loans and guarantees to the financing of works and installations which contribute directly and primarily to increasing production, or facilitating the market-ing of products over which the High Authority has jurisdiction, in other words contributing to the costs of rationalisation and modernisa-tion, thus improving structures of the regions concerned. The funds here provided for are raised on the one hand from the levy imposed by the High Authority on the coal and steel industries and on the other by loans floated on national financial markets (Art. 49).

The real powers for regional action, however, are contained in Article 56, enabling the High Authority, on application by the govern-ments concerned, to finance new projects and to provide re-adaptation subsidies where regional problems appear as a result of unemployment.

The Article is in two parts: paragraphs 1 and 2. Paragraph 1 pro-vides only for finance on the terms of Article 54 of industrial projects (whether within the scope of the ECSC or not—in practice no loans have been made to collieries) which will create " new and economically sound activities capable of re-absorbing the redundant workers into pro-ductive employment " as a result of exceptionally large reductions in labour requirements in the coal and steel industries caused by the intro-duction of new technical processes or equipment. Non-repayable aid is also available towards tide-over allowances, resettlement allowances, and retraining costs. The Member State concerned is required to meet 50 per cent. of these allowances and costs, unless an exception is authorised by the Council, acting by a two-thirds majority.

As originally drawn up, this was the only paragraph of the Article, but it was realised from 1958 onwards that the provisions of this first paragraph were totally inadequate to meet the needs of the coal and steel sectors in matters of regional assistance, confined as it was to the exigencies of technical advance, since the industries were by then in a state of structural crisis.

34–20 The Article was, therefore, revised, in accordance with the " *petite révision* " provisions of Article 95 of the ECSC Treaty. After the transitional period amendments may be made to the Treaty under this Article on joint proposal of the High Authority and the Council, the latter acting by vote of a five-sixths majority of its members (nine-tenths under Art. 13 of the Act of Accession). The proposal must be submitted to the Court, which is here fully competent to review all matters of fact and of law. If, as a result of such consideration, the Court finds that the proposals are in accordance with the provisions of Article 95, third para. (limiting revisions under Article 95 to those made necessary by the emergence of unforeseen difficulties arising in the light of experience in the application of the Treaty, or a profound change in economic or technical conditions directly affecting the common market for coal and steel, and only permitting revisions which do not affect the provisions of Articles 2, 3 and 4 of the Treaty, or the relationship between the powers of the High Authority and those of the other institutions of the Community respectively), the proposals are forwarded to the Assembly. They come into force if they are approved by a majority of three-quarters of the votes cast and two-thirds of the total membership of the Assembly.

If the Court does not so find, the amendment is rejected, but it could of course be made under Article 96, providing for amendments of any type by multilateral agreement of the Member States. Such an amendment was made to Article 56 ECSC by the Decision of January 26, 1960, J.O. 1960, 781.

The amendment of Article 56 under Article 95 was the only revision of the kind to survive the critical appraisal of the Court (see J.O. 1960, 781).

34–21 The amendment takes the form of the present paragraph 2 to the Article, providing for the financing of industrial projects capable of providing productive re-employment for workers made redundant as a result of fundamental changes in the coal and steel industries marketing conditions not directly connected with the setting up of the Common Market in coal and steel, forcing certain undertakings permanently to discontinue, curtail or change their activities. The type of project which may benefit from Community finance is the same as that in paragraph 1 with the addition of programmes for the remodelling or reconversion of existing undertakings. There are also provisions for non-repayable aid of the same three categories and on the same terms as in paragraph 1, but aid is now also available towards payments of allowances to undertakings to enable them to continue paying such of their workers as may have to be temporarily laid off as a result of the undertaking's change of activities.

COMMUNITY POLICY ON THE ENVIRONMENT

34–22 The problems of the environment are today very topical, and the Community has been quick to recognise the need for a Community policy on the environment. The Commission issued a first communication on environmental policy on July 22, 1971 (SEC (71) 2616, Final) designed primarily to promote discussion of the relevant problems by the Community institutions, and by the appropriate authorities and in economic and professional circles of what was then the Ten.

On the basis of the ensuing dialogue the Commission issued a communication to the Council on March 24, 1972, on a "European Communities' Programme concerning the Environment" (SEC (72) 666, Final; Bulletin, Supp. 5, 1972; J.O. 1972, C 52/1).

The latter communication outlines the environmental problems as viewed by the Commission, and sets out a programme on environmental matters, including a programme to reduce pollution and nuisances and to safeguard the natural environment. It is envisaged that the programme should be implemented in successive phases, the first phase to run for 1972 and 1973, and set out in more detail in the annexed draft Council resolution on the programme.

The programme further advocates the establishment of a system designed to keep the Commission informed of national environmental action with a view to eventual harmonisation of such action. A draft accord of the representatives of the governments of the Member States is annexed.

There would be an attempt to arrive at a common attitude in international organisations involved with environmental questions. As a first step the Commission has put forward a draft recommendation from the Council to the Member States signatories to the Berne Convention setting up the International Commission for the Protection of the Rhine against Pollution. Account would also be taken of relations with developing countries.

Action is proposed to improve working conditions in factories, and also to improve the diffusion of information on environmental questions.

No action has as yet been taken on these proposals, although the Community institutions are called upon by paragraph 8 of the Paris Summit Communiqué of October 21, 1972, to establish an action programme accompanied by a precise timetable before July 31, 1973.

Initial guidelines are contained in the Communiqué of the Bonn Conference on the Environment, held on October 31, 1972 (Europe Documents No. 705, November 14, 1972).

Part 6

ADDITIONAL INSTITUTIONAL QUESTIONS

CHAPTER 35

THE FINANCES OF THE COMMUNITIES

35–01 THE rules governing the finances of the Communities in relation to income, expenditure and attendant administrative procedures are laid down by the following provisions of the Treaties:

Articles 199 to 209 EEC;

Articles 49 to 53, and 78 ECSC;

Articles 171 to 183 Euratom;

Articles 20 to 23 Merger Treaty (Cmnd. 4866);

Budget Treaty *passim* (Cmnd. 4867);

Articles 127 to 132 Act of Accession (Cmnd. 4862–I),

as supplemented from time to time by various Regulations and decisions.

Although the ECSC had its own financial resources through a levy on coal and steel production (Art. 49 ECSC) the other two Communities were not initially self-financing, but were financed by means of a system of keyed contributions from each Member State (Art. 200 EEC, Art. 172 Euratom). However, the needs and responsibilities of the evolving Communities made it imperative that they should be given financial autonomy and basic provision for this was made by the Budget Treaty; but the mechanisms are not all fully operative as yet.

EXPENSES OF THE COMMUNITIES

35–02 The Treaty rules for drawing up the budget were originally laid down by the Articles of the ECSC, EEC and Euratom Treaties referred to above. These were subsequently revised in certain respects by the Budget Treaty of April 22, 1970 (Cmnd. 4867).

The expenses of the Communities are divided into two broad categories: administrative and operational. The administrative expenses are similar for all three Communities, being the expenses consequent on running the Community institutions, such as salaries, rent, business equipment, printing and general administrative overheads.

The operational expenses, however, vary from Community to Community according to their several roles.

ECSC

35–03 Article 50 (1) ECSC indicates what expenses are to be covered out of the production levies, namely:

(1) administrative expenses,

(2) readaptation and resettlement aid under Article 56,

(3) loans and loan guarantees for investment projects undertaken within the scope of Articles 54 and 56,

(4) expenditure in the form of grants or joint financing with the undertakings engaged in technical and economic research as provided for in Article 55 (2).

EEC

35–04   The EEC Treaty sets up a single budget fund through which all expenditure is channelled. Various subsidiary funds have been subsequently established. They all form part of the Community Budget. The European Social Fund, established by Article 125 and reformed by Decision 71/66, J.O. 1971, L 28/15, is to meet up to 50 per cent. of the expenditure incurred by the Member States in providing assistance in situations where Community measures have affected or will affect the labour market, and where there is long-term structural unemployment (Arts. 4 and 5 of Decision 71/66) (see *supra*, § 24–09).

35–05   The European Development Fund was set up originally by Article 1 of the Implementing Convention on the Association of the Overseas Countries and Territories with the Community (Cmnd. 4864, p. 134) to facilitate development projects in the social and economic spheres in those countries associated with the Community by way of loans and aids.   When the Implementing Convention was revised by the First Yaoundé Convention, the European Development Fund was reconstituted by an internal agreement between the Member States of the Community (J.O. 1964, p. 1493), though its aims remain the same. See now internal agreement of July 29, 1969, J.O. 1970, L 282/47.

35–06   The European Agricultural Guidance and Guarantee Fund,[1] envisaged by Article 40 (4), was set up by Regulation 25/62, J.O. 1962, 991, to finance the Common Agricultural Policy. This it does by means of market interventions, and export subsidies (Guarantee) and by loans and grants to assist modernisation and improvements in agricultural facilities (Guidance), although the participation of the Guidance part of the fund is confined to 25 per cent. of the total investment cost, and is at present limited to quite low overall ceilings (see *supra*, § 22–43).

Future development of the Community may well require the setting up of further funds, *e.g.* a Regional Development Fund, agreed upon at the Paris Summit (Final Communiqué of October 21, 1972 (Cmnd. 5109), para. 5: see generally § 34–08).

Euratom

35–07   The expenditure of Euratom, although divisible into administrative and operational expenditure, is divided by Article 172 into two budgets —operating, and research and investment. This division is further clarified

---

[1] EAGGF or FEOGA.

by Article 174, which lays down what heads of expenditure should be included in each of these budgets.

The operating budget is to show:

(a) administrative expenditure; and

(b) expenditure relating to safeguards and to health and safety;

while the research and investment budget relates in particular to

(a) expenditure on the Community research programme;

(b) any participation in the capital, and investment expenditure, of the special agency set up by Article 52 Euratom as the supply agency for atomic source materials;

(c) expenditure on the equipping of training centres;

(d) costs of participation in joint undertakings and joint operations.

RESOURCES OF THE COMMUNITIES

35–08 As indicated above, the ECSC Treaty is the only Treaty granting to one of the Communities the right to raise its own income. This income is raised primarily by means of production levies (Arts. 49 and 50 ECSC). The ECSC was further given the facility of raising loans and the right to receive gifts (Art. 49). The funds raised from loans are, however, only to be used for the purpose of granting loans (Art. 51).

Euratom also has the right to raise loans in order to finance the expenses of research and investments (Art. 172 (4)).

For the rest of Euratom's expenditure, and for the entirety of the expenditure of the EEC, the Rome Treaty Communities originally relied on contributions by Member States according to certain contribution "keys." Article 172 Euratom and Article 200 EEC laid down the percentage contributions to the respective budgets to be made by each Member State. These contribution keys varied for Euratom according to whether the contributions were to the operating budget or to the research and investment budget. Article 200 EEC laid down different contribution scales for the general budget and for the European Social Fund; the assessment in each case was based on the use made by, and resources available to, each Member State.

The agricultural policy is financed through FEOGA under a series of regulations relating specifically to agriculture. (These are discussed *supra,* § 22–46.)

On the merging of the Councils and the Commissions by the Merger Treaty (Cmnd. 4866), it was found appropriate to provide for a single budget for all of the Communities (Art. 20 of the Merger Treaty). The resources of the ECSC were pooled with the financial contributions of the Member States under the EEC and the Euratom Treaties. To this end Article 20 (2) of the Merger Treaty fixes the portion of the expenditure covered by the ECSC production levies at 18 million u.a., although this may if necessary be revised to take account of any increase of expenditure in the application of the ECSC Treaty.

35–09   The EEC and the Euratom Treaties both envisaged (Arts. 201 and 173 respectively) the elaboration of a scheme whereby the financial contributions of Member States could be replaced by furnishing each Community with its own resources. Proposals were made and implemented by the decision on the replacement of financial contributions from Member States by the Communities' own resources of April 21, 1970 (Decision 70/243, J.O. 1970, L 94/19; Cmnd. 4867, p. 19) whereby the keyed financing system originally prevailing is to be progressively replaced with three different types of resources, ultimately accruing automatically to the Communities.

Article 2 of this decision provides that as from January 1, 1971, the revenue from all types of agricultural levies imposed in execution of the CAP together with the income from the Common Customs Tariff duties (less 10 per cent. refunded to Member States to cover the administrative expenses of collection) are to constitute the Communities' own resources to be entered into their budget as such. The income from the customs duties is not to be appropriated to the Communities in its entirety at once, but is to be attributed in increasing proportions between 1971 to 1975 according to a scale laid down in Article 3 (1) of the decision, so that the Communities receive 100 per cent. of this revenue as from January 1, 1975.

As income from the agricultural levies and customs duties may not be sufficient to cover expenditure the Community income is to be supplemented from 1971 to the end of 1974 by a keyed contribution from each Member State, on a scale similar to that originally prevailing in the EEC and Euratom Treaties. The scale is established by Article 3 (2) of the decision and is based on each Member State's share in the Community gross domestic product (GDP). The actual sums required from each Member State by way of keyed contribution are, however, much less than were required under the Treaties as they originally stood, since the levies and the duties form the major proportion of the Community income under this decision.

35–10   The definitive system of Community financing is laid down in Article 4 of the decision. From January 1, 1975, the budget is to be financed entirely from the Communities' own resources. The resources are to be those already indicated above (agricultural levies and customs duties) and also the product of up to 1 per cent. of the value added tax applied throughout the Community on a uniform assessment basis. This may require some harmonisation of the assessment bases before January 1, 1975.

A safeguard has been incorporated for the years 1975 to 1977. During this period the yearly variation in each Member State's share of the budget is limited to 2 per cent. of the previous year's contributions, which means that by 1977 the contributions due from any one State in respect of VAT can only exceed by 6 per cent. the percentage contribution due according to the scale laid down in Article 3 (2). By

January 1, 1978, the financing of the Community from its resources under this decision will become automatic.

Article 6 of the decision provides for the collection of the three types of resources to be made by the Member States who shall then make these resources available to the Community. (See 96/71, *Haegeman* v. *Commission*, not yet reported (*supra*, § 13–12), as to jurisdiction in respect of disputes concerning own resources.)

TRANSITIONAL ARRANGEMENTS RELATING TO FINANCING

35–11 The accession of new members to the Community has presented certain difficulties relating to financing, since the transitional period of accession cuts across the period laid down by Decision 70/243 for the progressive provision of the Communities' own resources. Special transitional arrangements are therefore provided for by Articles 127 to 132 of the Act of Accession. Article 128 makes the products of the compensatory amounts and internal customs duties fixed by the Act of Accession part of the Communities' own resources within the meaning of Article 2 of Decision 70/243. Article 129 sets out the "key" of direct financial contributions to be required from the new Member States under Article 3 (2) of the decision for the period up to December 31, 1974. These percentages are again fixed on the basis of each new Member State's projected share of the Community GDP. The contributions of the original Member States are due in unchanged proportions, but the assessment basis is to be arrived at having subtracted from the total budget figure the percentage due from the acceding States. The new Member States will, however, be required to pay only a rising proportion of the sums otherwise due under Article 129 of the Act, being liable for the full amount as from January 1, 1978 (Arts. 130 and 131 (1)). Article 131 (1) (*a*) and (*b*) of the Act of Accession provide a safeguard limiting the increase in the relative share to be contributed by each new Member State after the expiry of the transitional period up to December 31, 1979. Up to this date, therefore, the amounts due from the new Member States under a combination of Articles 129 to 131 are to be established, and then the balance of the Community's financial requirements is to be worked out, and added to the amount to be apportioned for the original Member States in accordance with Article 129. The total amount thus determined is then to be apportioned among the original Member States in accordance with Decision 70/243 (Art. 132).

CHAPTER 36

PARTICULAR LEGAL QUESTIONS RELATING TO THE COMMUNITIES

(1) THE LEGAL PERSONALITY OF THE COMMUNITY

36–01 THE problem of the legal personality of the Community has two distinct yet interrelated aspects; one concerns the Community as an international legal person and the other concerns the Community's status in the Member States of the Community. Although in law the aspects of international and internal legal personality may be distinguished, such a differentiation is not made in the texts of the European Treaties. The relevant texts are:

Article 6 ECSC

Articles 210 and 211 EEC

Articles 184 and 185 Euratom

Although the EEC and the Euratom Articles are identical, they differ from the ECSC Article mentioned above; the latter is more complete, reading as follows:

" The Community shall have legal personality.

" In international relations, the Community shall enjoy the legal capacity it requires to perform its functions and attain its objectives.

" In each of the Member States, the Community shall enjoy the most extensive legal capacity accorded to legal persons constituted in that State; it may, in particular, acquire or dispose of movable and immovable property and may be a party to legal proceedings.

" The Community shall be represented by its institutions, each within the limits of its powers."

The Rome Treaties make no mention of the capacity enjoyed by the EEC and by Euratom in international relations. In practice there is little difference between the Treaties since the ECSC Treaty contains few dispositions (Arts. 93, 94) which allow the Community to exercise its international capacity, Article 71 (1) reserving to the Member States matters of commercial policy. The EEC and Euratom Treaties on the other hand attribute to the Community the competence to act in international relations in individual Articles: Articles 3 (*b*), 113, 114, 228, 229, 230, 231 and 238 EEC, and Articles 2 (*h*), 101, 102 and 106 Euratom (concerning commercial policy, relations with other States and with international organisations).

36–02 The capacity accorded to the EEC and Euratom has been used in the conclusion of commercial and association agreements with other States and State organisations, although on occasions the Community has entered into these agreements jointly with the Member States. In 6/64, *Costa* v. *ENEL*, Rec. X 1141, [1964] C.M.L.R. 425, the Court of Justice clarified the notion of legal capacity when it stated that in creating a Community (the EEC) which amongst other things had its own legal personality, legal capacity and the capacity of representation at an international level, the Member States had limited their sovereign rights, albeit in a restricted area.

36–03   Furthermore, in 22/70, *Commission* v. *Council*, Rec. XVII 263, [1971] C.M.L.R. 335, the Court made it clear in discussing Article 75 (1) (*c*) on transport that an express attribution to the Community was not necessary for it to have the power to negotiate and conclude agreements with other States and international organisations. This power could be implied from other dispositions of the Treaty, especially in the context of establishing a common policy in a particular field. Therefore despite the fact that the EEC and Euratom Treaties say nothing in general terms about the Communities' capacity to act in international relations, nevertheless the current jurisprudence of the Court indicates this capacity and the international legal personality it reflects is a positive and growing concept.

36–04   In the international sphere, no distinction has been made between the Community and the institutions which it comprises; it is the Community alone which is endowed with legal personality, as follows from Articles 6 ECSC, 210 EEC and 184 Euratom. It is clear from the above-mentioned Articles that the respective Communities also enjoy ordinary legal personality at the national level, but the Treaties grant personality to certain Community bodies: the European Investment Bank (Art. 129 EEC), the Euratom Joint Undertakings (Art. 49 Euratom) and the Supply Agency (Art. 54 Euratom). These three form a distinct group in that they all have a commercial purpose and have autonomous powers.

36–05   The Court of Justice underlined in 7/56, *Algera* v. *Common Assembly*, Rec. III 81, that personality was granted by the ECSC Treaty only to the Community and not to the institutions. In 43, 45 & 48/59, *von Lachmüller* v. *Commission*, Rec. VI 933 and 44/59, *Fiddelaar* v. *Commission*, Rec. VI 1077, the Court stated that the Community (the report says " Commisssion," but this is a patent error) when acting within the limits of the attributions conferred on it by the Treaty, enjoys the legal personality conferred by Article 210 EEC.

36–06   The provision in all three Treaties that " the Community shall enjoy the most extensive legal capacity accorded to legal persons under [the laws of the Member States] " contrasts with that used in the corresponding clause in the United Nations Charter (Art. 104), where the United Nations is accorded only that capacity necessary for it to fulfil its functions. Confusion is created by the provisions in the Treaties, in so far as they may be interpreted as suggesting that the capacity of the Community differs from Member State to Member State, there being no uniform rule on the capacity of legal persons. It is clear, however, that what is intended is that the Community should not be subject to limitative rules on the capacity of certain legal persons, *e.g.* non-profit-making bodies. The Articles give examples of aspects of this capacity, mentioning acquisition and disposal of movable and immovable property and the ability to be a party to legal proceedings. The list is not exhaustive. Article 49 of the Treaty of Paris extends the capacity of the ECSC to include the ability to receive gifts; although this is not mentioned by the EEC and Euratom Treaties, the Communities concerned have this ability, since legal persons in Member States may also receive gifts.

36–07   The last sentences of Articles 6 ECSC, 211 EEC and 185 Euratom deal with the representation of the Community, but the Treaties differ on this point. Under the ECSC Treaty the institutions (High Authority, Assembly, Council and the Court) represent the Community, each within the scope of its own powers. No other subsidiary institution can therefore bind the Community or be sued in national courts. For the EEC and Euratom, the role of representing the Community in all questions involving its legal personality is reserved solely to the Commission.

The successive financial regulations on the drawing up and execution of the budgets of the EEC and Euratom (now of the Communities) nevertheless recognise that the powers necessary to execute the sections of the budget referring to the Parliament, the Council or the Court are conferred on the Presidents for the time being of these institutions; these powers can of course be delegated. Thus each institution in practice has the power to contract and to act on its own behalf, having been granted the necessary financial powers for the implementation of such action.

These institutions are, however, represented by the Commission where litigation becomes necessary or is instituted against them before national courts. (See *supra,* § 9–16 as to representation of the institutions before the Court of Justice. See *supra,* § 3–03 as to the notion of institution.)

(2) PRIVILEGES AND IMMUNITIES

36–08   Article 28, first para., of the Merger Treaty, repealing and re-enacting Articles 76 ECSC, 218 EEC and 191 Euratom, states that the Communities shall enjoy in the territories of the Member States such privileges and immunities as are necessary for the performance of their tasks, under the conditions laid down in the Protocol annexed to the Merger Treaty. The annexed Protocol on the Privileges and Immunities of the European Communities (Cmnd. 4866, p. 15) likewise replaces the

Protocol on the same subject annexed to the Treaties setting up the three Communities.[1]

The new Protocol annexed to the Merger Treaty specifies broadly speaking the usual privileges and immunities which are traditionally accorded to States and which now attach to international organisations. Article 1 states that the premises and buildings of the Communities shall be inviolable and that the property and assets of the Communities shall not be subject to any measure of constraint *without the authorisation of the Court of Justice* (*cf.* Art. 22 of the Vienna Convention on Diplomatic Relations of 1961). Requests for permission to exercise a measure of constraint forms a particular type of jurisdiction of the Court (see *e.g.* 4/62, *Demande d'autorisation de pratiquer saisie-arrêt entre les mains de la Haute Autorité*, Rec. VIII 79).

The archives of the Communities are to be inviolable (Art. 2). The Communities are to be exempt from direct taxes and indirect taxes are to be rebated where possible (Art. 3). They are further to be exempt from customs duties and other import and export restrictions, in particular on Community publications (Art. 4). With regard to communications and the transmission of documents, the Community institutions are to enjoy in the territory of each Member State the treatment accorded by that State to diplomatic missions. In particular official correspondence and communications are not to be subject to censorship (Art. 6).

Article 7 provides for the use of *laissez-passer* as travel documents to be issued to members and servants of the institutions of the Communities by the presidents of these institutions. These documents are automatically valid within the Member States. The Commission may negotiate for the recognition of these *laissez-passer* by third countries.

Articles 8 to 16 are concerned with the privileges and immunities granted to different categories of persons concerned with the functioning of the Community. Articles 8 to 10 set out the privileges and immunities of members of the European Parliament who do not benefit under the privileges granted to the employees of the Community. Article 8 provides for unrestricted movement on official journeys to or from the Assembly, and for customs and exchange control exemptions. Articles 9 and 10 provide for the normal parliamentary privileges granted to the members of the parliaments of most States, exemption from arrest, legal proceedings etc. Article 11 gives " the customary privileges, immunities and facilities " to representatives of Member States participating in the work of the Communities.

36-09   Articles 12 to 16 concern officials and servants of the Communities. Article 12 (*a*) gives these persons immunity " *from legal proceedings in respect of acts performed by them in their official capacity,*" although this is subject to the jurisdiction granted to the Court of Justice in such

[1] The European Investment Bank has its own particular disposition on privileges and immunities: " The property of the Bank shall be exempt from all forms of requisition or expropriation " (Art. 28 (2), Statute of the EIB).

matters by the Treaties. The meaning of the italicised phrase was raised in 5/68, *Sayag* v. *Leduc* (Rec. XIV 575; [1969] C.M.L.R. 12) where a Euratom official, Sayag, having been asked to take two guests of the Commission to a plant at Mol, took them in his own car. He was involved in a collision, for which he was responsible, and in which he and his two passengers were injured. One of his passengers, Leduc, brought domestic legal proceedings against Sayag, who pleaded immunity under Article 11 (*a*) of the Protocol on Privileges and Immunities annexed to the Euratom Treaty (now Article 12 (*a*) of the Protocol annexed to the Merger Treaty). Although the Commission waived Sayag's immunity, the case was fought up to the Cour de Cassation. The latter Court asked the Court of Justice for a preliminary ruling (under Art. 150 Euratom) on whether immunity arises in connection with acts performed by officials in the exercise of their duties or merely in connection with those acts which are to be carried out in the actual exercise of their official duties.

The Court was of the opinion that the immunity extends only to:

" those acts which, by their nature, represent a participation of the person covered by the immunity in the carrying out of the tasks of the institution to which he is responsible."
(Trans. [1969] C.M.L.R. 12 at p. 22.)

On the facts, Sayag, not being a Commission chauffeur, was not performing his official duties when driving guests to a plant and therefore could not benefit from the Community immunity.

36–10   Article 12 (*b*) to (*e*) lay down privileges and immunities with respect to immigration restrictions on families, exchange regulations and duty free imports. Article 13 provides that the Community employees shall be exempt from any national personal taxation on salaries paid by the Communities (see 6/60, *Humblet* v. *Belgium*, Rec. VI 1125), but that they shall be liable to pay a similar tax to the Communities. Article 14 is a special provision to alleviate any problems arising from transfer of " domicile " consequent on Community employment, with regard to income tax, wealth tax or death duties. The employee of the Community is for these purposes to be regarded as having maintained his original tax domicile if that is within the Community.[2]

Article 15 requires the Council to lay down a special scheme of social security benefits for Community employees and their dependants.

Article 16 permits the Council to establish categories of employees to whom Articles 12 to 14 shall apply. The Community is under an obligation to inform the governments of Member States of the names and addresses of the employees contained in such categories.

The general provisions regarding the application of the privileges and immunities (Arts. 18 to 21) recite that the privileges granted are

---

[2] *Cf.* footnote 1, § 32–23, *supra.*

solely in the interests of the Communities (Art. 18, first para.), and provide that the institutions are to waive any immunity given to personnel when the interests of the Community demand it (Art. 18, second para. : as in *Sayag*). To ensure efficient application of the Protocol, the institutions of the Communities are to co-operate with the relevant bodies in the Member States (Art. 19). Article 22 extends the privileges of the European Investment Bank as laid down in its own Protocol (and in the rest of the Protocol), to include exemption from taxation on the increase of its capital or on its dissolution or liquidation. The Bank's activities are not to be subject to any kind of turnover tax.

By Article 20, Articles 12 to 15 and Article 18 of the Protocol apply to members of the Commission.

Privileges and immunities and the Court of Justice

36–11 By Article 21 of the Protocol on Privileges and Immunities, " Articles 12 to 15 and Article 18 shall apply to the Judges, the Advocates-General, the Registrar and the Assistant Rapporteurs of the Court of Justice, without prejudice to the provisions of Article 3 of the Protocols on the Statute of the Court of Justice concerning immunity from legal proceedings of Judges and Advocates-General." Article 3 of the Protocols on the Statute of the Court of Justice are identical in their first three paragraphs. They provide that:

> " The Judges shall be immune from legal proceedings. After they have ceased to hold office, they shall continue to enjoy immunity in respect of acts performed by them in their official capacity, including words spoken or written.
> " The Court sitting in plenary session, may waive the immunity.
> " Where immunity has been waived and criminal proceedings are instituted against a Judge, he shall be tried, in any of the Member States, only by the Court competent to judge members of the highest national judiciary."

Article 3 of the ECSC Statute has a fourth paragraph, granting to the Judges the privileges set out in Article 11 (*b*), (*c*) and (*d*) of the ECSC Protocol on Privileges and Immunities. The latter privileges are now contained in Articles 13, 12 (*b*) and 12 (*d*) respectively of the current Protocol on Privileges and Immunities. As such the fourth paragraph of Article 3 of the ECSC Statute adds nothing to Article 21 of the Current Protocol on Privileges and Immunities.

Persons appearing before the Court of Justice also enjoy certain privileges and immunities : by the third paragraph of Article 17 of the EEC Statute * (*cf.* Article 20 of the ECSC Statute) " such agents, advisers and lawyers shall, when they appear before the Court, enjoy the rights and immunities necessary to the independent exercise of their duties under conditions laid down in the rules of procedure." Article 32 of the Rules of Procedure, J.O. 1960, p. 17, grants exemption from search and confiscation in respect of papers and documents relating to the proceedings, entitlement to currency allocations, and the necessary freedom of movement. The persons enjoying these privileges are required to give proof of status (Art. 33) and the privileges are granted solely in the interest of the proceedings, and may be waived by the Court when it considers such waiver not against the interests of the proceedings (Art. 34).

(3) LOCATION OF THE INSTITUTIONS OF THE COMMUNITY

36–12 No definitive assignment of locations for the various institutions has ever taken place. This is due partly to political and partly to practical considerations. Article 77 ECSC, Article 216 EEC and Article 189 Euratom state: "The seat of the institutions of the Community shall [will: ECSC] be determined by common accord of the Governments of the Member States." In fact, no seats have ever been fixed definitely, and thus the Community has enjoyed only "provisional locations" for its institutions.

When the ECSC was set up it was simply declared that the High Authority and the Court would start work at Luxembourg, and that the Assembly would meet at Strasbourg. The ECSC Council Secretariat was set up at Luxembourg in 1952.

With the setting up of the EEC and of Euratom it was recommended that the Commission meet at Val-Duchesse (near Brussels) or at Luxembourg, while it was stated that the Council and the Bank would meet at the residence of their presidents, and that the Assembly would meet in Strasbourg. The Court of course remained in Luxembourg. The Assembly Secretariat and services were also set up in Luxembourg.

Certain changes were made in these arrangements by the decision of April 8, 1965 (Cmnd. 4866, p. 23) which was required to enter into force on the same day as the Merger Treaty. Article 1 of the decision states that Luxembourg, Brussels and Strasbourg are to remain the provisional places of work of the Community institutions. In particular, however, to compensate Luxembourg for the fact that the ECSC institutions were merged into those of the EEC and Euratom, the Council sessions of April, June and October are to be in Luxembourg, while the Court of Justice remains in Luxembourg. Other Community departments were moved to Luxembourg.

(4) LEGAL LIABILITY OF THE COMMUNITY

1. Non-contractual liability of the Community

36–13 Non-contractual liability of the Community is governed primarily by Article 215 EEC, second para., which provides that:

"In the case of non-contractual liability, the Community shall, in accordance with the general principles common to the laws of the

Member States, make good any damage caused by its institutions or by its servants in the performance of their duties."

The Court of Justice itself has jurisdiction in disputes relating to the compensation for damage provided for in Article 215, second para. (Art. 178 EEC *).

Article 40 ECSC, first para., provides that:

"Without prejudice to the first paragraph of Article 34, the Court shall have jurisdiction to order pecuniary reparation from the Community, on application by the injured party, to make good any injury caused in carrying out [the ECSC] Treaty by a wrongful act or omission on the part of the Community in the performance of its functions."

Further, Article 40, second para., first sentence, as amended by Article 26 of the Merger Treaty (Cmnd. 4866), stipulates: "The Court shall also have jurisdiction to order the Community to make good any injury caused by a personal wrong by a servant of the Community in the performance of his duties."

None of the Treaties now gives any direct action against a Community servant. Such actions as will be possible against a Community servant must thus be brought in a national court.

The provisions of the EEC and ECSC set out above are broadly similar in effect. But Article 40 ECSC is expressed to be without prejudice to Article 34, first para., which requires the High Authority to make good any direct and special harm suffered by reason of a decision or recommendation held by the Court to be void and to involve a fault of such a nature as to render the Community liable. Failure to do so opens the way for proceedings for damages (second para.).

36–14 All other disputes to which the Community is a party (except staff disputes: Article 179 EEC *) are left to the national courts by Article 40 ECSC and Article 183 EEC.* It would appear, however, that all possible causes of action other than contractual come within Article 178 EEC * and Article 40 ECSC, and as such may be entertained only before the Court of Justice.

36–15 Although the effect of the Rome Treaty provisions as to non-contractual damage is broadly similar to those of the Paris Treaty as amended, the translation of Article 40 ECSC, first and second paras., offered in Cmnd. 4863 is somewhat deceptive, for it emerges from the French text that the injury for which reparation may be had must have been caused in the execution of the ECSC Treaty by a "*faute de service de la Communauté,*" or by a "*faute personnelle*" on the part of a Community servant in the performance of his duties, while the equivalent phrase in Article 215 EEC, second para., is "*dommages causés* par ses institutions ou par ses agents *dans l'exercice de leurs fonctions*" (italics supplied). Nevertheless, it would seem that similar principles are applicable, and that fault is required under all three Treaties. Even under the EEC Treaty where there is no reference to "*faute de service,*" there is a tendency for the parties to use that phrase, and indeed in 5, 7 & 13–24/66, *Kampffmeyer* v. *Commission,* Rec. XIII 317, the Court established a "*faute de service*" ("*Amtsfehler*" in the original German) under the EEC Treaty on the part of the Commission in so many words (Rec. XIII 339). There are similar references in *e.g.* 23/69, *Fiehn* v. *Commission,* Rec. XVI 547 and 30/66, *Becher* v. *Commission,* Rec. XIII 369, [1968] C.M.L.R. 169. In two more recent cases, however, 4/69, *Lütticke* v. *Commission,* Rec. XVII 325, and 5/71, *Aktien-Zuckerfabrik Schöppenstedt* v. *Council,* Rec. XVII 975, the term seems to have been avoided. It cannot therefore be said with absolute certainty that the provisions of the Rome Treaties and the Paris Treaty are precisely similar in effect, particularly in view of the fact that Article 40 ECSC, in which there is no mention of the general principles common to the laws of the Member States, as in Article 215 EEC, is arguably describing a creature of Community law alone. This cannot be conclusive, however, for the Court may in any case refer to those general principles even in the absence of an express requirement to do so.

With these reservations, it is nevertheless permissible to treat the provisions of the Rome and Paris Treaties together, for there has been no indication so far that the Court considers clearly different principles to be applicable, although differences in specific aspects may later emerge.

The fault

36-16   "*Faute de service*" and "*faute personnelle,*" referred to in Article 40 ECSC, are both notions derived from French administrative law, but as with all elements of national law adopted by Community law, they must now be considered as notions of Community law alone.

Article 215 EEC, second para., speaks of liability for damage caused in the performance of duties. It is generally thought that this provision subsumes the notion of "*faute de service,*" but is potentially wider if only in so far as it omits mention of "fault" and speaks only of damage. This opens the way for an application of the principle of strict liability, but it is doubtful whether the Community would be held liable on such a basis. *Kampffmeyer* and 5/71, *Aktien-Zucker-fabrik Schöppenstedt* v. *Council* (*supra*) are not suggestive of a strict liability (see similarly 30/66, *Becher* v. *Commission,* Rec. XIII 369, [1968] C.M.L.R. 169).

Whether or not the "*faute*" complained of is "*de service*" or "*personnelle,*" the Court of Justice has jurisdiction to order compensation from the Community. The position is now the same under both the Paris and Rome Treaties, Article 40 ECSC, second para., being aligned with the provision of Article 215 EEC in this respect by Article 26 of the Merger Treaty (Cmnd. 4866). Prior to the Merger Treaty the second paragraph gave the Court jurisdiction to order

a servant of the Community to make good any injury caused by a
" *faute personnelle.*"

36–17   *What constitutes a "faute de service."* Laferrière, cited by Vedel
and quoted by Dumon in "La responsabilité extracontractuelle des
Communautés," 1969, *Cahiers de Droit Européen,* 1 at p. 14, differentiates "*faute de service*" from "*faute personnelle*" in the following
terms :

> "il y a faute de service si l'acte dommageable administratif est
> impersonnel et révèle l'administrateur plus ou moins sujet à erreur.
> La faute personnelle, au contraire, est celle qui révèle l'homme avec
> ses faiblesses, ses passions, son imprudence."

A "*faute de service,*" or an act attracting the liability of the Community (*cf.* 4/69, *Lütticke* v. *Commission,* Rec. XVII 325 at p. 337)
was perhaps best defined in that case where the Court held that in
virtue of Article 215, second para., and the general principles referred
to in that provision, the liability of the Community presupposes the
combination of a number of conditions relating to the reality of damage,
the existence of a causal link between the injury relied upon and the
behaviour of the institutions complained of, and the illegality of this
behaviour.

36–18   (a) REALITY OF THE DAMAGE. The requirement that damage be real
is another expression of the principle set out in various cases that the
damage must be certain, or actual and certain, and not merely potential
(*cf.* 10/55, *Mirossevich* v. *H.A.,* Rec. II 365; 19, 21/60 and 2, 3/61,
Fives Lille Cail v. *H.A.,* Rec. VII 559, [1962] C.M.L.R. 251; 14, 16, 17,
20, 24, 26 & 27/60 and 1/61, *Meroni* v. *H.A.,* Rec. VII 319; 55–59,
61–63/63, *Acciaierie Fonderie Ferriere di Modena* v. *H.A.,* Rec. X 413,
[1964] C.M.L.R. 401; and 9 & 25/64, *Feram* v. *H.A.,* Rec. XI 401, [1965]
C.M.L.R. 298). Rather similar views were expressed in 5, 7 & 13–24/66,
Kampffmeyer v. *Commission,* Rec. XIII 317, where the Court had to
consider the admissibility of alleged damage to three groups of persons.
The facts of the case were that the Commission had in error
authorised the importation of grain at a zero levy rate. Upon receiving
a number of applications for import licences at the zero rate the Commission became aware of its mistake, and re-imposed a levy. Three
groups of importers were affected :

(1) those who in fact imported grain, paying the levy demanded;
(2) those who resiled on their contracts to resell the grain imported
    at the zero rate;
(3) those who had made no contracts at the time the levy was
    re-imposed.

The Court held that the first group might in principle recover the amount
of the levy paid upon proof that they had exhausted domestic administrative remedies. The second group were also in principle permitted to

recover to the extent of their liability to their buyers, but the Court refused to concede that they should recover the whole amount of what would have been their profit, since this was of an essentially speculative nature, and further because they had avoided any commercial risk by resiling. The Court accordingly assessed the loss of expected profit (*lucrum cessans*) recoverable at a maximum of 10 per cent. of the levy which they would have had to pay. But the actual liability of the Community under these two heads was left undetermined pending the outcome of domestic actions for reparations, so that damages could be assessed fairly. The Court rejected the third group of actions, since compensation for loss of profit presupposed at least some concrete preliminary steps.

36–19   The *Kampffmeyer* case on this point covers much of the ground already covered in ECSC cases, and indeed goes further in relation to loss of expected profit. Although the damage must be certain and actual, it seems that it need not be liquidated; mental suffering and loss of reputation have both been accepted as valid heads: 7/56 and 3–7/57, *Algera* v. *Assembly*, Rec. III 81; 35/62 and 16/63, *Leroy* v. *H.A.*, Rec. IX 399, [1964] C.M.L.R. 562; 44/59, *Fiddelaar* v. *Commission*, Rec. VI 1077.

The reparation available under Article 40 ECSC is quite explicitly described as pecuniary. Article 215 EEC,* second para., merely refers to making good the damage, but the reparation ordered will normally be pecuniary—*cf.* 110/63, *Willame* v. *H.A.*, Rec. XI 803, [1966] C.M.L.R. 231. Actual repair of the damage will generally, however, remove at least part of the damage in respect of which damages are claimable.

36–20   (b) THE BEHAVIOUR OF THE INSTITUTION COMPLAINED OF. Clearly the behaviour of the institution complained of can be an act illegal in itself —see, *e.g.* 7/56, 3–7/57, *Algera* v. *Assembly*, Rec. III 81, and 5, 7 & 13–24/66, *Kampffmeyer* v. *Commission*, Rec. XIII 317, but as already indicated, the fact that an act is illegal does not *per se* attract Community liability—5/71, *Aktien-Zuckerfabrik Schöppenstedt* v. *Council*, Rec. XVII 975. There can be little doubt that an act which is not attacked for illegality (*e.g.* because time has expired) can nevertheless be the subject of an action for indemnity, *cf.* 4/69, *Lütticke* v. *Commission*, Rec. XVII 325, and 9 & 12/60, *Vloeberghs* v. *H.A.*, Rec. VII 391, [1963] C.M.L.R. 44, where the Court was not asked to annul an act (for the High Authority had taken no decision) and indeed considered the nature of the two proceedings to be quite separate. But such a situation has to be carefully distinguished from that where annulment is requested and refused; in such a case damages clearly cannot be awarded—25/62, *Plaumann* v. *Commission*, Rec. IX 197, [1964] C.M.L.R. 29 (plaintiff not directly and individually concerned in the sense of Art. 173, second para.*).

Secondly, acts of maladministration will attract liability; 7/56, 3–7/57, *Algera* v. *Assembly*, Rec. III 81 (irregular dismissal); 36/62, *Société des Aciéries du Temple* v. *H.A.*, Rec. IX 583, [1964] C.M.L.R. 49 (" attitude " of High Authority, leading to error on the part of the plaintiff).

A somewhat similar category of acts, including incompetent or negligent behaviour on the part of the Community, or a breakdown in the system, will also attract liability; 9 & 12/60, *Vloeberghs* v. *H.A.*, Rec. VII 391 (failure to take decision); 19, 21/60, 2, 3/61, *Fives Lille Cail* v. *H.A.*, Rec. VII 559, [1962] C.M.L.R. 251 (gross negligence in duties of supervision which normal diligence would have imposed); 19/69, *Richez-Parise* v. *Commission*, Rec. XVI 325; 23/69, *Fiehn* v. *Commission*, Rec. XVI 547 (failure to rectify mistaken interpretation or information). On the other hand the act complained of must be due to fault or error on the part of the Community itself; 23/59, *Feram* v. *H.A.*, Rec. V 501, where the acts complained of had been committed by a fraudulent official in the Dutch Civil Service; the Court held that the reliance of the High Authority on those acts was wholly justifiable.

36-21   (c) DEGREE OF FAULT. Whether or not the notion of fault is to be derived from Community law alone under the ECSC Treaty, or from the general principles under the EEC Treaty is probably immaterial (*supra*, § 36–15). But there is some question as to the degree of fault required. The Court referred to " *dol* " or " *negligence coupable* " in 7/56 and 3–7/57, *Algera* v. *Assembly*, Rec. III 81, and said in 19, 21/60 and 2, 3/61, *Fives Lille Cail* v. *H.A.*, Rec. VII 559, [1962] C.M.L.R. 251 that the High Authority had " *gravement negligé* " its duty. On this basis it was argued in 5, 7, 13–24/66, *Kampffmeyer* v. *Commission*, Rec. XIII 317 and similarly in 30/66, *Becher* v. *Commission*, Rec. XIII 369, [1968] C.M.L.R. 169 that " *faute lourde*," or something more than simple negligence, was the required standard. This was, however, rejected, the Court finding that in this case a violation of the applicable Community law was enough on the facts (although it may not be in all cases—see below).

The Court did not fix any minimum standard. Clearly negligence and recklessness are included, but it is more doubtful whether there can be liability without fault even under the EEC Treaty, which does not use the word " *faute*." The fact that *Kampffmeyer* and 5/71, *Aktien-Zuckerfabrik Schöppenstedt* v. *Council*, Rec. XVII 975, require that the individual bringing an action show some interest is suggestive of a rather selective approach to Community liability, perhaps inimical to the notion of strict liability (see similarly 19/69, *Richez-Parise* v. *Commission*, Rec. XVI 325).

The question next arises how a fault may be attributed to the Community; in the first place it is clear that the fault of an institution is that of the Community (*cf. Fives Lille Cail*, *supra*) and secondly, the notion of fault of a Community servant (which notion is very wide) is likewise attributable. There is a certain overlap here of the notions " *faute de service* " and " *faute personnelle* " (see *infra*, § 36–25 on this notion in general).

36–22   (d) ILLEGALITY OF THE BEHAVIOUR. The criterion of illegality of behaviour must, it seems, be understood extremely broadly. As 4/69, *Lütticke*, itself makes clear, the Court did not mean to suggest that the act complained of need be illegal in the sense that it could be attacked under any one of the four heads of Article 173 *; the case concerned a failure to act, as did 9 & 12/60, *Vloeberghs* v. *H.A.*, Rec. VII 391, [1963] C.M.L.R. 44, where the Court said much the same thing. On the other hand, the sole fact that the act is illegal will not necessarily give rise to liability to make compensation—5/71, *Aktien-Zuckerfabrik Schöppen-stedt* v. *Council*, Rec. XVII 975. The argument that bare illegality was not enough on the facts of *Kampffmeyer* was raised by the Commission and rejected by the Court, apparently on the grounds that the interests violated were the very ones that the act violated was designed to protect. This is not stated as a general principle, but becomes one in *Schöppenstedt* v. *Council*.

36–23   (e) THE PERSON INJURED. Some question has arisen as to whether the damage alleged must be special—*i.e.* characterising the person injured separately from all others; 14, 16, 17, 20, 24, 26, 27/60 and 1/61, *Meroni* v. *H.A.*, Rec. VII 319, points in this direction, but this view appears to have been refined in *Kampffmeyer*, where the Court held that although the disposition of Community law in question was not directly applicable, nevertheless it was intended to protect individual rights, and the individuals affected did not have to be directly and individually concerned in the technical sense of Article 173 EEC.* This approach was further developed in 5/71, *Aktien-Zuckerfabrik Schöppenstedt* v. *Council*, Rec. XVII 975, where the Court said that the liability of the Community would be attracted " *en présence d'une violation suffisamment caracterisée d'une règle supérieure de droit protegeant les particuliers* " (para. 17), the act in question being one of a general legislative character.

The matter was raised in particular in 9 & 11/71, *Compagnie d'Approvisionnement* v. *Commission*—report not yet published—where the plaintiffs pointed to the practice of French Conseil d'Etat as holding a public authority liable even in the absence of illegality where " *préjudice anormal et spécial* " existed. The Court rejected the argument on the ground that liability for a legal act could not exist in a case of the kind in question, apparently because the act of the Commission was a general act. This being so, damage will only be " special " if the act complained of is directed to the plaintiff.

Speciality of damage nevertheless merges into the problem of the applicability of the " *Schutznormtheorie.*" The principle of the *Schutz-*

normtheorie is applied in English law in relation to breach of statutory duty; English courts will not uphold claims for damages in actions for breach of statutory duty if the damage complained of is not that which the statute was designed to guard against: *Gorris* v. *Scott* (1874) L.R. 9 Ex. 125; the *Schutznormtheorie* looks to the other side of the rule in *Gorris* v. *Scott*. The upshot of it is that courts will not entertain actions alleging violation of a rule of law which was not designed to protect the interests of persons such as the plaintiff. Whether this principle applies in Community law is somewhat uncertain. The holding of the Court of Justice in *Kampffmeyer* would seem to suggest that such a theory had been rejected (although there was some suggestion of it in *Vloeberghs*) but *Schöppenstedt* casts doubt on this. It is difficult to ascertain what would be the practical application of the principle enunciated by the Court in the passage quoted above, but it does seem to be more restrictive than *Kampffmeyer*. Whether, however, the Court can be said to be applying the principles of the *Schutznormtheorie* is not entirely clear. It would seem to have adopted its own rule, namely to ask whether individuals at large are protected, and not whether those individuals bringing the action are protected. (This latter criterion, amounting almost to a requirement that the plaintiff be directly and individually concerned, would amount to a true application of the *Schutznormtheorie*; see 30/66, *Becher* v. *Commission*, Rec. XIII 369, [1968] C.M.L.R. 169.)

The final point of doubt here is whether Article 40 ECSC enables an individual (as opposed to an enterprise or association) to bring an action; it is clear that this must be so—*Vloeberghs*.

6-24　　(f) THE CAUSAL LINK. The Court requires that there be a causal link between the injury and the act complained of. Community rules on causation are not perhaps as complex as those of English law, but the normal basic requirement is there, namely that there be a direct link (*cf.* 36/62, *Société des Aciéries du Temple* v. *H.A.*, Rec. IX 583, [1964] C.M.L.R. 49) and that the result should not have been impossibly remote (*ibid.*) and 5, 7, 13–24/66, *Kampffmeyer* v. *Commission*, Rec. XIII 317, discussed (*supra*).

6-25　　*Faute personnelle.* Laferrière defines " *faute personnelle* " as being " *celle qui révèle l'homme avec ses faiblesses, ses passions, son imprudence* " (see *supra*, § 36–17). The same definition differentiates " *faute de service* " as being essentially anonymous. Nevertheless, a " *faute de service* " of the Community probably need not be actually anonymous. The difference must probably be sought in the fact that the " *faute de service* " is essentially an act which results from corporate behaviour, from the system, whereas the " *faute personnelle* " is of a clearly individual nature not unconnected with official functions. If this is so, a " *faute personnelle* " will be more readily identifiable than a " *faute de service*," although sometimes it will be difficult to separate the two. The difference is no longer as material as it was prior to the amendment of Article 40 ECSC by Article 26 of the Merger Treaty, for all three Communities are now liable for all acts committed by the institutions or by its servants in the performance of their duties, and actions based upon such acts can only be brought before the Court of Justice. Whether the Court may hear actions against individuals guilty of " *faute personnelle* " is not undisputed. The better view would appear to be that it may not, and indeed the texts of the Paris and Rome Treaties point this way. The Community institution must thus be the defendant in place of the servant.

36–26   The division between Community liability and individual liability not attributable to the Community must thus be sought in the meaning to be attached to the phrase " in the performance of their duties." The only case that has really dealt with the problem is 5/68, *Sayag* v. *Leduc*, Rec. XIV 575, [1969] C.M.L.R. 12. That arose out of a road accident caused by a Community official using his own car on official duty. The question coming before the Court for a preliminary ruling under Article 150 Euratom (Art. 177 EEC) was whether the official could be said to be performing an act in his official capacity within the meaning of Article 12 (*a*) of the Protocol on Privileges and Immunities annexed to the Merger Treaty (Cmnd. 4866, p. 15). For the Protocol to apply, the act complained of must have been done, the Court held, " within the framework of the task entrusted to the Community " (Trans. [1969] C.M.L.R. 12 at p. 22). Since the ambit of Community privileges and immunities was considered to be quite narrow, the test was applied to the *faute* in the following terms:

> " driving a motor car is not in the nature of an act performed in one's official capacity, save in the exceptional cases where this activity cannot be carried out otherwise than under the authority of the Community and by its very own employees."
> (*Ibid.*)

This is undoubtedly a very narrow application of the principle; whether the Court would necessarily apply it to a situation where the question of a Community liability was directly raised before it is unclear; the test is certainly capable of being applied to such a situation, and it would seem advisable to apply the same test in both situations, for they are in some sense alternate, but such an interpretation perhaps limits Community liability unduly.

Where a " *faute personnelle* " of a servant in the performance of his duties is shown to exist, his personal liability towards the Community is governed by the provisions laid down in the Staff Regulations (Art. 215 EEC, third para., and Art. 40 ECSC, second para., as amended by the Merger Treaty). The applicable provisions are Articles 86 *et seq.*, Regulation 31 of December 18, 1961, J.O. 1962, 1385.

Where there is no " *faute personnelle*," *i.e.* where the act is merely done during office hours, but is otherwise unconnected with official functions, an action against the individual will lie in a municipal court, and not in the Court of Justice at all; nor will a plea of immunity succeed.

Compensation under the ECSC Treaty

6–27   Article 34 ECSC provides that:

> " If the Court declares a decision or recommendation void, it shall refer the matter back to the High Authority. The High Authority shall take the necessary steps to comply with the judgment. If direct and special harm is suffered by an undertaking or group of undertakings by reason of a decision or recommendation held by the Court to involve a fault of such a nature as to render the Community liable, the High Authority shall, using the powers conferred upon it by this Treaty, take steps to ensure equitable redress for the harm resulting directly from the decision or recommendation declared void and, where necessary, pay appropriate damages.
>
> " If the High Authority fails to take within a reasonable time the necessary steps to comply with the judgment, proceedings for damages may be instituted before the Court."

The first requirement is the annulment of the decision. Fault rendering the Community liable is a very general notion, probably different from, and potentially wider than " *faute de service*," but here again " *faute de service* " must probably be considered to be subsumed. Damage must here, however, be special, probably in contrast to Article 40 ECSC and Article 215 EEC. Equitable redress is here not confined to pecuniary compensation, but there is some doubt as to the extent of " equitable "—namely whether the duty of the Commission is limited to repairing the damage, or whether it extends to putting the undertaking in the position it would have been but for the act annulled.

Prescription

6–28   Article 43 * of the EEC Statute on the Court of Justice, with which Article 40 of the ECSC Statute is, *mutatis mutandis,* identical, provides that proceedings against the Community in matters arising from non-contractual liability (*i.e.* under Art. 215 EEC, second para., and Art. 40 ECSC, but not Art. 34 ECSC) shall be barred after a period of five years from the occurrence of the event giving rise thereto. The second sentence of these articles provides for the " interruption " of time running by introducing an action before the Court, or by application to the relevant institution, followed by introduction of an action within two months (one month ECSC), the provisions of the second paragraph of Article 17 of the EEC and Euratom Statutes (Art. 35 ECSC) applying " where appropriate."

This is a decidedly obscure provision but it is clear that the application made to the relevant institution does not turn the action into something other than an action for indemnity under Article 215 EEC, second para., or Article 40 ECSC; *cf.* 42, 49/59, *SNUPAT* v. *H.A.*, Rec. **VII** 101. *SNUPAT* does not provide much more assistance but 5, 7, 13–24/ 66, *Kampffmeyer* v. *Commission*, Rec. XIII 317 suggest that:

(1) an action brought on the last day of the five years from the date of the injury (not of the wrongful act—*cf.* 46 & 47/59, *Meroni* v. *H.A.*, Rec. VIII 783 at 803 and *Kampffmeyer*) will be in time whenever the judgment is given, and

(2) a preliminary application made within five years, followed by an action, will be in time if the action is brought within two months if the act complained of is an illegal act, or within four months if a failure to act was complained of, for the institutions are normally given no time to remedy the illegal act, but two months to fill a lacuna. In either case the plaintiff has two months for his own benefit.

General provision as to limitation of actions

36-29   It is to be noted that Article 43 * of the EEC Statute on the Court of Justice and Article 40 of the ECSC Statute are the only provisions on limitation of actions contained in the Treaties. In the *Quinine Cartel* and *Dyestuffs* cases: 41/69, *ACF Chemiefarma* v. *Commission*, Rec. XVI 661; 44/69, *Buchler* v. *Commission*, Rec. XVI 733; and 45/69, *Boehringer* v. *Commission*, Rec. XVI 769; and 48/69, *I.C.I.* v. *Commission* and related cases [1972] C.M.L.R. 557, the Court refused to refer to general principles of law in order to fix a general period of prescription, leaving it to the Community legislator to do so. The Commission has now produced proposals for limitation of actions appealing against fines imposed under Regulations 11/60, 17/62 and 1017/68. (See generally *supra*, § 28–90.)

It appears, however, that the Court may be developing a rule of limitation for more general purposes, notably to prevent Community institutions bringing actions long after the event complained of having occurred, see *e.g.* 59/70, *Netherlands* v. *Commission*, Rec. XVII 639, and 48/69, *I.C.I.* v. *Commission*, *supra*.

2. Contractual liability of the Community: actions brought by Community servants, and other contractual actions

36-30   Article 181 EEC,* with which Article 42 ECSC is identical, gives the Court of Justice—

"... jurisdiction to give judgment pursuant to any arbitration clause contained in a contract concluded by or on behalf of the Community, whether that contract be governed by public or private law."

Article 179 EEC * gives the Court of Justice—

"... jurisdiction in any dispute between the Community and its servants within the limits and under the conditions laid down in the Staff Regulations or the Conditions of Employment."

Article 215, first para., amplifies the above-mentioned provisions, stating that: " The contractual liability of the Community shall be governed by the law applicable to the contract in question."

Article 179 * is a specific application of Article 181,* at least in so far as contractual matters are concerned. There is no equivalent in the ECSC Treaty, such actions being brought pursuant to Article 42 ECSC, which is identical with Article 181 EEC.*

So far as Community employees are concerned, their contracts of employment have been held to be contracts under public law: 1/55, *Kergall* v. *Assembly*, Rec. II 9; 43, 45 & 48/59, *Lachmüller* v. *Commission*, Rec. VI 933; 44/59, *Fiddelaar* v. *Commission*, Rec. VI 1077. As such they are subject to the general rules of administrative law relating to rights of defence, etc.

The conditions of employment of Community servants are governed by Regulation 31 of 1962, J.O. 1962, 1385 and Regulation 258/68, J.O. 1968, L 56/1, as amended (see J.O. 1972, C 100/1 for consolidated amendments). Article 91 (1), which picks up Article 179 EEC,* provides that the Court of Justice is to have jurisdiction over disputes between the Community and its servants regarding the legality of any act complained of by such person. It is accepted that this jurisdiction embraces the four grounds of illegality provided for in Article 173 * (see generally § 13–02, *supra*), and also failure to act (*cf.* Art. 175,* § 14–01, *supra*).

The second limb of Article 91 (1) provides for unlimited jurisdiction (*cf.* Art. 172 * as to this notion; § 12–03, *supra*) (a) in the cases mentioned in Regulation 31 itself, and (b) in disputes of a financial character.

Article 91 (2) lays down a three-month time-limit from publication or notification for actions against acts, and a two-month time-limit from the expiry of a two-month period of silence in the case of failure to react to a complaint. There appear to be no grounds for thinking that the " unlimited jurisdiction " provision of Article 99 (1) would enable the Court to hear a case time-barred by Article 91 (2).

36–31   As already mentioned above, Article 215, first para., leaves the contractual liability of the Community to be governed by the law applicable to the contract in question. In relation to service contracts with Community servants the applicable law is Regulation 31 itself, although the Regulation will not necessarily provide all the answers.

More problematic are ordinary contracts with the Community; even if such a contract confers jurisdiction on the Court of Justice under Article 181,* as is frequently the practice, it does not follow that the applicable law will be some form of " Community " contract law; rather contractual liability must be governed by the proper law of the contract, as determined by municipal law. This provides a relatively simple solution where the matter comes before a national court even though such

417

courts may produce divergent solutions, but if the matter were to come before the Court of Justice under Article 181,* the Court would itself be obliged to determine the proper law of the contract (as it would under Article 177). Normally the Court of Justice rejects the possibility of applying national law itself, but it would under Article 181 * be obliged to apply it. It may be asked how the Court could justify applying national law, given that its decision was pursuant to an " arbitration clause "; it would seem, however, that use of the expression " arbitration clause " is misleading, for application of the " arbitration clause " results in a binding judgment, not subject to appeal before domestic courts.

(5) Territorial Application

36–32 Article 227 EEC as originally formulated provides that the Treaty applies to the Six original Member States (para. 1). The definition of " Member State " for these purposes is probably to be taken as that used by the Member State in question. Paragraph 2 provided that with regard to Algeria and the French overseas departments, the general and particular provisions of the Treaty relating to free movement of goods, agriculture (save for Art. 40 (4), the juridical basis for the setting up of FEOGA), services, competition, the protective measures provided for in Articles 108, 109 and 226, and the institutions, should apply as soon as the Treaty entered into force. The manner of application of the rest of the Treaty to these same territories was to be determined within a further two years. The Treaty ceased to apply to Algeria when the latter achieved independence on July 1, 1962, and Algeria is now treated as a third State, although some Member States continue to maintain the status quo (see Written Question 298/68, J.O. 1969, C 73/1, and *Syndicat général de fabricants de semoules de France* (Conseil d'Etat) [1970] C.M.L.R. 395). So far as the overseas departments are concerned, limited parts of the Treaty were made applicable (Decision of May 11, 1960, J.O. 1960, 919: capital; Decision 64/350, J.O. 1964, 1484: establishment and payments; Directive 68/359, J.O. 1968, L 257/1 [2]: Arts. 48 and 49—free movement of labour; Decision 71/238, J.O. 1971, L 149/1: Art. 51—social security; Decision 71/364, J.O. 1971, L 249/73: Arts. 123 to 127—ESF). A small number of other instruments, relating mainly to agricultural matters and to customs, are expressed to be based in part upon Article 227 (2).

Paragraph 3 annexes the list of overseas countries and territories to whom the special arrangements for association set out in Part Four were to apply. (As to these arraangements see § 37–21.) Paragraph 4 states

---

[2] Notwithstanding Decision 68/359, point VII (2) of Annex VII to the Act of Accession permits retention of provisions requiring prior authorisation for immigration to the Republic of Ireland and to Northern Ireland for workers from the overseas departments up until December 31, 1977.

that the Treaty applies to the European territories for whose external relations a Member State is responsible. (This category would appear to include Monaco and San Marino, but not Andorra.)

36–33   The stipulations of Article 227 EEC are added to by Article 26 of the Act of Accession, so as to take account of particular territorial questions relating to the acceding States.

Article 26 (1) of the Act of Accession effects amendments to Article 227 (1) so as to include the four States which were to accede to the Community.[3]

Article 26 (2) of the Act of Accession makes it clear that the EEC Treaty (in particular the special arrangements for association set out in Part Four) is not to apply to those overseas countries and territories " having special relations with the United Kingdom of Great Britain and Northern Ireland " which are not included in the list contained in Annex IV, by adding a further sub-paragraph to this effect to Article 227 (3) EEC. Annex IV itself is extended by Article 24 (2) of the Act of Accession so as to include most of the remaining non-European territories " having special relations with the United Kingdom of Great Britain and Northern Ireland." The principal omissions are Hong Kong and Rhodesia. Special provision is made in respect of the Sovereign Base Areas in Cyprus and the Channel Islands and the Isle of Man in Article 26 (3) of the Act of Accession, which adds a new paragraph 5 to Article 227 EEC. Paragraph 5 (*b*) states that the Treaty shall not apply to the Sovereign Base Areas.[4] Paragraph 5 (*c*) provides that the Treaty is to apply to the Channel Islands and the Isle of Man " only to the extent necessary to ensure the implementation of the arrangements for those islands set out in the Treaty " of Accession (see Protocol 3 to the Treaty of Accession, Cmnd. 4862–I, p. 82). They are thus taken out of Article 227 (4) EEC, providing that the Treaty is to apply to the European territories for whose external relations a Member State is responsible. They are, however, within the customs territory of the Community under Article 1 of Regulation 1496/68, J.O. 1968, L 238/1 (see further *infra*). Paragraph 5 (*a*) states that the ECC Treaty is not in principle to apply to the Faroe Islands, but the Government of Denmark may give notice by December 31, 1975 at the latest that it shall so apply. (Guidelines for the arrangements for the Faroes are set out in Protocol 2, Cmnd. 4862–I, p. 81.)

Articles 25 and 27 of the Act of Accession add clauses to the ECSC and Euratom Treaties which are substantially similar in effect to those added to Article 227 EEC.

---

[3] Following the negative result of a consultative referendum held in October 1972, Norway announced that she would not in fact accede. The express references to Norway in Art. 26 of the Act of Accession are therefore left out of account (see generally *supra*, § 1–10).

[4] The arrangements applicable to the Sovereign Base areas are to be defined in the context of the projected association agreement with Cyprus: Joint declaration on the Sovereign Base areas, annexed to the Final Act: Cmnd. 4862–I, p. 116.

It is clear that Gibraltar falls within Article 227 (4) EEC in much the same way as would the Channel Islands and Isle of Man, but Article 28 of the Act of Accession expressly provides that the Community rules on agriculture and on value added tax are not to apply in Gibraltar unless the Council, acting unanimously on a proposal from the Commission, decides otherwise. Gibraltar, being a free port, is also excluded from the customs territory of the Community, for Article 1 of Regulation 1496/ 68, J.O. 1968, L 238/1 as amended by point 4 of Annex I of the Treaty of Accession (Cmnd. 4862–II, p. 5) in referring to the territories comprising the customs territory of the Community, refers only to the territory of the United Kingdom of Great Britain and Northern Ireland and the Channel Islands and the Isle of Man. Gibraltarians will, however, benefit from the free movement provisions of the Community Treaties, for they are included within the declaration of the United Kingdom on the term " nationals " contained in a declaration annexed to the Final Act (Cmnd. 4862–I, p. 118; see § 23–12, *supra*).

36–34 The Act of Accession and its Protocols contain a number of other territorial clauses; the United Kingdom is added to the Member States specified in Article 131 EEC, first sentence by Article 24 (1), the States so specified all having non-European dependencies not considered to be part of the metropolitan territory. Article 24 (2), besides adding to Annex IV EEC the territories with purely British connections, also adds the Anglo-French condominium of the New Hebrides. Protocol 4 provides for arrangements to be made for Greenland.

36–35 As already mentioned, Regulation 1496/68, J.O. 1968, L 238/1 (as amended by point 4 of Annex I to the Treaty of Accession and Council Decision—Cmnd. 4862–II, p. 5) defines the customs territory of the Community, the definition not corresponding exactly with that to be expected from an examination of the Treaty texts. The territories included in the definition of the customs territory are the territories of all the Member States, with the express exclusion of the island of Heligoland and the territory of Büsingen (Germany), the French overseas territories, the Italian communes of Livigno and Campione d'Italia and " the national waters of Lake Lugano which are between the bank and the political frontier of the area between Ponte Tresa and Porto Ceresio." The Austrian territories of Jungholz and Mittelberg, the Principality of Monaco and San Marino are expressly included within the customs territory (Annex 1 of the Regulation). This leaves the Republic of Andorra, which is tacitly excluded. Gibraltar is also excluded.

36–36 So far as other areas of Europe are concerned, the Protocol on German Internal Trade and Connected Problems (Cmnd. 4864, p. 125), and the Declaration on the definition of the expression " German National " (*ibid.*, p. 163) are of particular interest. The Protocol confirms that since trade with East Germany is part of German internal trade, no special measures were needed. This is, however, subject to Member States being permitted to take appropriate measures to prevent any consequential difficulties arising (para. 3). The effect of the Declaration on German Nationals is to assimilate persons from East Germany to nationals of the Federal Republic.[5] By the declaration by the Government of the Federal Republic on the application of the Treaties to Berlin, Germany reserved the right to declare, when depositing its instruments of ratification, that the EEC and Euratom Treaties should apply equally to Berlin (and see *Re Levy Assessment in Berlin* [1971] C.M.L.R. 713). Such a declaration was duly made. Note was taken of a similar declaration to the Final Act of the Conference at which the instruments of accession were signed (Cmnd. 4862–I, p. 118). The latter declaration relates to all three Communities.

36–37   The question of the application of the Treaties to the continental shelf is somewhat uncertain. The Commission issued a Memorandum on the subject on September 18, 1970 (*Memorandum concernant l'application du Traité de la Communauté Economique Européenne au plateau continental*, SEC (70) 3095 final) which maintained that the EEC Treaty, and in particular the directives on establishment and services relating to mining and quarrying (64/428, J.O. 1964, 1871) and to prospecting and drilling for oil and natural gas (69/82, J.O. 1969, L 68/4) was so applicable. The Commission cites no basis in the EEC Treaty for this proposition and it is noteworthy that the Council has in no sense confirmed it.

---

[5] See *supra* § 23–12 on Declaration by the Government of the United Kingdom on the Definition of the Term " Nationals," annexed to the Final Act of the Conference at which the instruments of accession were signed.

Part 7

CHAPTER 37

EXTERNAL RELATIONS

INTRODUCTORY

37–01 ALL the Communities are in some measure empowered by their constituent Treaties to conduct relations with third States or with other international organisations (*cf.* notably Art. 6 (2) ECSC, Art. 228 EEC, Art. 101 Euratom). The *AETR* case (22/70, *Commission* v. *Council*, Rec. XVII 263, [1971] C.M.L.R. 335), suggests, moreover, that the Communities may possess a degree of agreement-making power which is to be implied from their internal powers (§ 37–26, *infra*). Furthermore, note must be taken of Article 228 EEC, to the effect that, should an opinion be obtained from the Court of Justice adverse to the compatibility with the Treaty of a proposed international agreement, such may enter into force only in accordance with Article 236, *i.e.* by way of a proposed amendment of the Treaty.[1]

The provisions of the three constituent Treaties respecting the conduct of external relations are somewhat various. In the practice of the Communities also, resort has been had to the device of the so-called mixed agreement, negotiated and concluded not by the Community institutions alone, but by the Member States as well. This manner of proceeding has been resorted to where it has been considered that the subject-matter of the proposed agreement exceeded the competence of the Community and impinged upon that of the Member States. In these cases (*infra*) amendment of the Treaty in accordance with Article 236 to give the Community competence does not seem to have been contemplated.

EXTERNAL RELATIONS OF THE ECSC

37–02 Though Article 6 of the ECSC Treaty provides that in " international relations, the Community shall enjoy the legal capacity it requires to perform its functions and attain its objectives," Article 71 stipulates that " the powers of the Governments of the Member States in matters of commercial policy shall not be affected by this Treaty, save as otherwise provided therein." It has accordingly been contended that the power of the Community to enter into relations with third States con-

---

[1] The view that Art. 228, in referring to Art. 236, relates only to the third paragraph of Art. 236, *i.e.* calling for ratification only of the proposed agreement, does not appear to enjoy general acceptance—see J. Rey in *Droit des Communautés européennes*, ed. Ganshof van der Meersch, Larcier, Brussels 1969, p. 653, Kovar in *Les relations extérieures de la Communauté européenne unifiée*, Liège, 1969, p. 143 and J. Raux, *Les relations extérieures de la Communauté Economique Européenne*, Cujas, Paris, 1969, pp. 90 *et seq.*

formably to Article 6 is restricted to the cases where the Treaty in other articles may specifically so provide.

Article 6, fourth para., provides that the Community " shall be represented by its institutions, each within the limits of its powers." Article 8, however, invests the High Authority with the duty of ensuring " that the objectives set out in this Treaty are attained in accordance with the provisions thereof." This indicates an allocation to the High Authority of a major store of executive power, including power in the sphere of external relations. The role of the Council under the ECSC Treaty is apparently much more limited than under the EEC Treaty (see generally, *supra*, § 3–05). The High Authority, under Article 49, is empowered in order to procure the funds required for its tasks to impose levies on production and also to contract loans. And in addition to floating bond issues within the Community the High Authority in 1954 entered into an agreement with the United States for a loan repayable over twenty-five years (April 23, 1954 : J.O. 1954, 325).

37–03   Articles 93 and 94, the forerunners of Articles 229 to 231 EEC and Articles 199 to 201 Euratom, provide for the maintenance of " all appropriate relations " with the United Nations and OEEC (now OECD), and equally for the maintenance of relations between " the institutions of the Community " (which institutions are unspecified) and the Council of Europe, pursuant to the Protocol annexed to the Treaty. The Protocol (Cmnd. 4863, p. 142), drafted on the basis of recommendations of the Assembly of the Council of Europe, invites (Art. 1) Governments of Member States to recommend to their respective Parliaments that the members of the ECSC Assembly (now the European Parliament) they are to designate be chosen preferably from among the representatives to the Consultative Assembly of the Council of Europe. It provides further (Arts. 2, 3) for the annual reporting of the Community's Assembly to the Council of Europe's Assembly and for the communication to the latter, and also to the Committee of Ministers, of the High Authority's annual general report (*cf.* Art. 17 of the Treaty). The High Authority is also to inform the Council of Europe of any action taken on any recommendations of the latter (Art. 5) and further that other agreements between the organisations may provide *inter alia* for any other type of mutual assistance and co-operation (Art. 6).

Article 93 makes no mention of relations with the specialised agencies of the United Nations, in contrast to Article 229 EEC. But the first international agreement entered into by the High Authority was that of August 14, 1953, with the International Labour Organisation, J.O. 1953, 167, which is expressed to be between the latter organisation and the ECSC " represented by the High Authority." It has to do with methods of co-operation in matters of mutual interest and provides *inter alia* for the representation of the High Authority by an observer at meetings of the ILO Coal Industry and Iron and Steel Committees.

37-04   The Convention on Transitional Provisions (Cmnd. 4863, p. 146), drawn up in accordance with Article 88 of the Treaty to enable the provisions of the latter to be brought into full force, provides in Article 1 (3) (*b*) (2) for the conduct by the High Authority during the preparatory period (*i.e.* from date of entry into force to that of establishment of the Common Market) of " negotiations with third countries " for the purpose of laying " the foundations for co-operation between the Community and these countries," and " to obtain, before the elimination of customs duties and quantitative restrictions within the Community, the necessary derogation from: most-favoured-nation treatment under the General Agreement on Tariffs and Trade and under bilateral agreements; [and] the principle of non-discrimination in liberalisation of trade within the Organisation for European Economic Co-operation." Pursuant to this provision the Community did obtain the necessary waivers from GATT and OEEC, and in addition undertook negotiations with Japan in 1955 on methods of co-operation, with Austria in 1956 with particular reference to steel prices, and with Sweden in 1957. Negotiations with Switzerland in 1956, which, however, went beyond the scope of the provisions of the Convention quoted, resulted in an agreement, dated May 7, in that year (J.O. 1957, 85), stipulating for consultations between the High Authority and the Swiss Federal Council respecting any shortfall within the Community of ECSC products normally exported to Switzerland.

Article 10 of the Convention, which provided for the immediate convening of a Committee of Experts to study arrangements to be proposed for the transport of coal and steel, envisaged the obtaining of the consent of the Governments of Member States to these arrangements through " negotiations " to be initiated by the High Authority, which organ should likewise initiate " any necessary negotiations with third countries concerned." Agreeably to this provision, agreements respecting direct international railway tariffs have been concluded with Switzerland (July 28, 1956, J.O. 1957, 223) and Austria (July 26, 1957, J.O. (ECSC) 1958,78, as supplemented by the agreement of November 29, 1960, J.O. 1961, 1237 and 1281). These agreements were framed as mixed agreements, the Member States also being expressed to be parties, the view being taken, evidently, that the Treaty did not contemplate or authorise their conclusion by the High Authority acting alone. They provide for acceptance by the High Authority on signature, no procedure for ratification or like process by the Community existing. By contrast, the Member States are enabled to become party by signature followed by acceptance (Switzerland, Art. 10; Austria, Art. 9). On the other hand, the High Authority, if so authorised by the Member States, is at liberty to denounce the agreements unilaterally, as the Member States individually are not (Switzerland, Article 11, second para.; Austria, Art. 10, second para.).

37–05   Article 14 of the Convention, which is the opening Article both of Part Two, headed " Relations between the Community and Third Countries," and of Chapter 1 of that Part, itself headed " Negotiations with Third Countries," provides :

> " Once the High Authority has taken office, Member States shall open negotiations with the Governments of third countries, and in particular with the British Government, on the whole range of economic and commercial relations concerning coal and steel between the Community and these countries. In these negotiations the High Authority shall act, upon instructions unanimously agreed by the Council, for the Member States jointly. Representatives of the Member States may be present at the negotiations."

Pursuant to this Article there was negotiated the Agreement of December 21, 1954 (Cmd. 13), whereby there was established an " Association " between the United Kingdom and the Community, and the further Agreement respecting commercial relations of November 25, 1957 (Cmnd. 695). Though no express provision for the abrogation of these Agreements is made by the Act of Accession, they will lose all *raison d'être* with the entry of the United Kingdom into the Community.

Upon the replacement in 1963 of the Implementing Convention on the Association of the Overseas Countries and Territories with the EEC (Cmnd. 4864, p. 134) by the so-called Yaoundé Convention I, an additional agreement relating to ECSC products was concluded. A similar additional agreement was entered into on July 29, 1969 (J.O. 1970, L 282/31) with the replacement of Yaoundé I by Yaoundé II. Both additional agreements were cast in the form of agreements between the Member States of the Coal and Steel Community and the Associated States, their subject-matter lying outside the powers of the Community in the sense of Article 71 of the Treaty (*supra*).

37–06   Despite that, as will be seen, ECSC's powers in the sphere of external relations are more limited than those of either the EEC or Euratom, the Treaty of Paris does, it may be noted in conclusion, contain a provision conducing to the effective co-ordination of the commercial arrangements of Member States with third States. For by Article 75 the Member States undertake to keep the High Authority informed of proposed agreements or arrangements. Should any such contain any clause hindering the implementation of the Treaty the High Authority may make to the State concerned " the necessary recommendations." Though this provision was introduced in amplified form into the Euratom Treaty (Art. 103), it was lacking in the EEC Treaty, its absence being in due course compensated for by a decision dated October 9, 1961 (J.O. 1961, 1273) establishing a more elaborate limitation upon the freedom of Member States to contract with third States (see § 37–34, *infra*).

EXTERNAL RELATIONS OF EURATOM

37–07 The Euratom Treaty, by reason of the special nature of the substances falling within its scope and the need for co-operation between States to achieve advances in the peaceful uses of atomic energy, contains rather more provisions than the EEC and ECSC Treaties respecting external relations. Article 2 thus lays it down that in order to perform its task the Community shall *inter alia*:

> "(*h*) establish with other countries and international organisations such relations as will foster progress in the peaceful uses of nuclear energy."

Article 10 further provides that the Commission:

> "may, by contract, entrust the carrying out of certain parts of the Community research programme to Member States, persons or undertakings, or to third countries, international organisations or nationals of third countries";

and, under Article 29:

> "Where an agreement or contract for the exchange of scientific or industrial information in the nuclear field between a Member State, a person or an undertaking on the one hand, and a third State, an international organisation or a national of a third State on the other, requires, on either part, the signature of a State acting in its sovereign capacity, it shall be concluded by the Commission."

By means of the provision last quoted the Community is able to keep itself informed of licensing arangements entered into by individual Member States for their own benefit.

The Treaty provides (Art. 45) that undertakings "which are of fundamental importance to the development of the nuclear industry in the Community may be established as Joint Undertakings," having legal personality and "the most extensive legal capacity accorded to legal persons under [the] respective national laws" (Art. 49). Proposals for the creation of a Joint Undertaking may (Art. 46 (2) (*e*)) envisage:

> "participation by a third State, an international organisation or a national of a third State in the financing or management of the Joint Undertaking."

By Article 52 there is established a Supply Agency to ensure a common policy for the supply of nuclear materials, which is invested with the "exclusive right to conclude contracts relating to the supply of ores, source materials and special fissile materials coming from inside the Community or from outside"; and endowed (Art. 54) with "legal personality and financial autonomy" under (Art. 53) the supervision of the Commission. The exclusive right of the Agency "to enter into agreements and contracts whose principal aim is the supply of ores, source materials and special fissile materials coming from outside the

Community" is reiterated in Article 64. And by Article 73 the prior consent of the Commission is required, so far as delivery of the products is concerned, to the conclusion or renewal of an "agreement or contract between a Member State, a person or an undertaking on the one hand, and a third State, an international organisation or a national of a third State on the other, [which] provides *inter alia* for delivery of products which come within the province of the Agency."

Under Article 77 the Commission must "satisfy itself that, in the territories of Member States, . . . (*b*) the provisions relating to supply and any particular safeguarding obligations assumed by the Community under an agreement concluded with a third State or an international organisation are complied with."

37–08   In addition to these provisions, the Euratom Treaty, unlike either the EEC and ECSC Treaties, contains further a distinct chapter—Chapter X (Arts. 101–106) entitled "External Relations." Article 101 provides that the agreements or contracts which the Community may make with third States, international organisations or nationals of third States shall be negotiated by the Commission in accordance with the "directives" of the Council and concluded by the former with the latter's approval, accorded by qualified majority, save that agreements or contracts not calling for any action by the Council and capable of being effected within the limits of the relevant budget may be negotiated and concluded by the Commission acting alone, keeping the Council informed. This provision stands in some contrast to Article 228 EEC (see *infra*).

Article 102 stipulates that agreements or contracts with a third State, international organisation or national of a third State to which one or more Member States are parties in addition to the Community shall not enter into force until the Commission shall have been notified by each Member State concerned that such agreements etc. have become applicable in terms of their respective national laws.

Under Article 103 draft agreements or contracts of this category, to the extent that they concern matters within the purview of the Treaty, are to be communicated to the Commission which shall within one month make known to the State concerned its comments in the case that any such draft contains clauses impeding the application of the Treaty. Such State shall not proceed to the conclusion of the agreement etc. until it has satisfied the Commission's objections "or complied with a ruling of the Court of Justice, adjudicating urgently upon an application from the State, on the compatibility of the proposed clauses with [the] Treaty."

37–09   Article 104 prohibits the invocation of any agreement etc. concluded after the entry into force of the Treaty for the evasion of its terms. But by Article 105 it is laid down that the Treaty shall not be invoked to prevent the implementation of any earlier agreement etc.

notified to the Commission within thirty days of the entry into force of the Treaty. This Article contains in addition provisions with respect to agreements etc. entered into before the signature and entry into force of the Treaty. Article 104 further provides for the communication to the Commission of information on agreements concluded by persons or undertakings with third parties, for the purpose of verifying that such agreements do not contain clauses impeding the implementation of the Treaty. The Court is given jurisdiction on application by the Commission to rule on compatibility questions.

By Article 106 Member States concluding agreements for co-operation on the uses of nuclear energy with third States before the entry into force of the Treaty are required to undertake, jointly with the Commission, negotiations for the assumption as far as possible by the Community of the rights and obligations of such agreements.

Finally, it may be noted that, by Article 182 (5) of the Treaty, the Commission " may freely make use of any amounts in the currency of third countries derived from loans it has raised in such countries "; by Articles 199 to 201 the Community is to maintain appropriate relations with the organs of the United Nations, the specialised agencies, GATT, " all international organisations," the Council of Europe and OEEC (now OECD); and that under Article 206 (identical with Art. 238 EEC, *infra*), the Community may conclude association agreements with any third State, union of States or international organisations. No such agreements have been concluded under the Euratom Treaty.

Euratom agreements with third States and with nationals of third States

37–10   An agreement between Euratom and the United States providing for co-operation in programmes for the advancement of the peaceful applications of atomic energy, signed by all five Commissioners, was entered into on May 29 and June 19, 1958: J.O. 1959, 309. A further agreement of November 8, 1958, J.O. 1959, 312, between the same parties, established a joint programme of development and research based on particular types of reactors, approximately 60 per cent. of the necessary funds being furnished from European sources and 40 per cent. being provided by the United States Government in the form of long-term credit. This agreement also provided for the sale to the Community by the United States Atomic Energy Commission of enriched uranium (Art. III) and for the patenting and use of discoveries made in the course of execution of the joint programme (Arts. VI, VII).

An agreement expressed to be concluded *inter alia* to " reinforce European solidarity " was entered into with the United Kingdom on February 4, 1959.[1a] Thereunder each party is to make available to the other relevant unclassified research material (Art. I) and the United Kingdom Atomic Energy Authority is to deal with the Supply Agency on commercial terms (Arts. X, XI). This agreement was extended

[1a] Cmnd. 702.

for the period up to December 31, 1972 (Exchange of Notes of February 3, 1972).

A co-operation agreement with Canada signed on October 6, 1959 (J.O. 1959, 1165) provides for the exchange of information and for a joint programme of research etc. in relation to a particular type of reactor. Following this agreement the Community entered into a further technical agreement with Atomic Energy of Canada Ltd. (a national of a third country) for the detailed conduct of the joint programme.

An additional agreement with the United States for the sale to the Community of certain nuclear fuels was concluded on June 11, 1960, J.O. 1961, 668. Amending agreements with the United States were entered into on May 21 and 22, 1962, J.O. 1962, 2038, 2048, August 22 and 27, 1963, J.O. 1964, 2586. An exchange of letters was effected between the Commission and the United States Atomic Energy Commission on May 27, 1964, J.O. 1966, 2481, relating to fast reactors.

The co-operation agreements with the United States, the United Kingdom and Canada were concluded primarily in order to benefit the Community, which was less advanced in nuclear technology than the three States concerned. But in the agreement with Brazil of June 9, 1961, J.O. 1969, L79/7, the emphasis is upon enabling the Brazilian National Atomic Energy Commission to benefit from the Community's research and experience. A similar agreement was concluded with the Argentine Republic on September 6, 1962, J.O. 1963, 2966.

Agreements with international organisations

37–11　　　　Euratom entered into a co-operation agreement with the ILO on January 26, 1961, providing for consultation whenever necessary on matters of common interest for the purpose of realising the objectives of the two organisations in the social field and in order to eliminate unnecessary duplication of effort (J.O. 1961, 473). On December 9–14, 1961 an exchange of letters was effected between the President of the Euratom Commission and the Director-General of the FAO on the subject of co-operation in relation to the use of radio isotopes and radiations in research, processing and production in the field of food and agriculture and to the study of radionuclides (J.O. 1962, 1356). On November 18, 1965, an exchange of letters in regard to co-operation and the exchange of information was effected between the Director-General of External Relations of the Euratom Commission and the Director of the International Bureau of Weights and Measures (J.O. 1966, 614).

EXTERNAL RELATIONS OF THE EEC

37–12　　The dispositions of the EEC Treaty respecting external affairs are to be found in Chapter 3—Commercial Policy (Arts. 110 to 116), within Title II, " Economic Policy," of Part Three; in Part Four—Association of the Overseas Countries and Territories (Arts. 131 to 136); and in various Articles within Part Six—General and Final Provisions—that is to say Articles 227 to 231, 237, 238. The dispositions referred to cover the four main areas of external relations: commercial and trade relations; association with other States; co-operation with international organisations; and admission of third States to membership of the Community. But because of the essentially limited scope of the organisation, the external relations are in all cases no more than aspects of its common commercial policy.

The common commercial policy—Articles 110 to 116 EEC

37–13   The necessity for a common commercial policy derives from the fact that unlike the ECSC, the EEC is founded on a full customs union and therefore presents a common face to exporters from third countries. It is natural that this should be translated into a common policy for the Community in respect of both imports and exports. Similar considerations lie behind the concept of association with the Community, described in Article 238 as involving *vis-à-vis* a third State, a union of States or an international organisation, reciprocal rights and obligations, common action and special procedures (see generally *infra*, § 37–21).

Although the terms of the chapter on commercial policy appear to link the content of the common commercial policy with the customs union and the movement of goods, it has been cogently argued that there is no reason why the definition of commercial policy should be so limited. The chapter is to be found in a title of general import: " Economic Policy," and nowhere else in the Treaty is there any express attribution of powers for the conduct of external relations with reference to general economic affairs. Therefore, this chapter is considered to be of general relevance to Parts One, Two and Three of the Treaty. Emphasis is placed on the expressed aim of the Member States, by establishing the customs union between themselves, " to contribute, in the common interest, to the harmonious development of world trade, the progressive abolition of restrictions on international trade and the lowering of customs barriers " (Art. 110). They are to do this according to the guidelines laid down in the succeeding articles.

37–14   Article 110 itself is a general policy statement, outlining the aim of a common Community trade policy. It has no distinct legal force, but it gives some indication of the intended scope of the common commercial policy outlined in the succeeding Articles, and required by the second paragraph to " take into account the favourable effect which the abolition of customs duties between Member States may have on the increase in the competitive strength of undertakings in those States." Further indications of the potential scope of the commercial policy may be derived from Articles 111 and 113, referring respectively to tariff negotiations and the achievement of uniformity in measures of commercial policy and in liberalisation lists and to the abolition of quantitative restrictions during the transitional period and, in the long term, in particular to "the conclusion of tariff and trade agreements, the achievement of uniformity in measures of liberalisation, export policy and measures to protect trade such as those taken in cases of dumping or subsidies." But despite attempts to clarify the notion, the content of the common commercial policy remains controversial. In practice its application has been, as the Articles referred to imply, to trade in goods.

Co-ordination

37–15   By Article 111 (1), Member States were to "co-ordinate their trade relations with third countries so as to bring about, by the end of the transitional period, the conditions needed for implementing a common policy in the field of external trade." During the transitional period the Commission was to submit proposals to the Council regarding the procedure for common action during that period and regarding the achievement of uniformity in the commercial policies of the Member States, the Council acting unanimously during the first two stages, and by qualified majority thereafter (para. 3). Responsibility for co-ordination is thus imposed equally on the Member States and on the institutions of the Community. A similar dual responsibility was imposed by paragraphs 4 and 5 of Article 111. By paragraph 4 Member States were required in consultation with the Commission to:

> "take all necessary measures, particularly those designed to bring about an adjustment of tariff agreements in force with third countries, in order that the entry into force of the common customs tariff shall not be delayed."

By paragraph 5, first sub-para., Member States were to:

> "aim at securing as high a level of uniformity as possible between themselves as regards their liberalisation lists in relation to third countries or groups of third countries. To this end, the Commission shall make all appropriate recommendations to Member States."

By the second sub-paragraph Member States abolishing or reducing quantitative restrictions in relation to third countries were required to inform the Commission beforehand and to accord the same treatment to other Member States.

Article 113 is silent upon co-ordination of the policies of the Member States, if only because most of the matters dealt with by Article 111 related to the customs union which was only to be established at the end of the transitional period. The transitional period being ended, the commercial policy is required to be—

> "based on uniform principles, particularly in regard to changes in tariff rates, the conclusion of tariff and trade agreements, the

achievement of uniformity in measures of liberalisation, export policy and measures to protect trade such as those to be taken in case of dumping or subsidies " (para. 1).

By paragraph 2 " The Commission shall submit proposals to the Council for implementing the common commercial policy," the latter acting by qualified majority (para. 4). It therefore appears that while many matters will be governed by a Community rule, there may be areas in which harmonisation may still be appropriate. In either case it is clear that the Commission has sole responsibility for initiating action. The powers of the Commission under paragraph 2 are apparently not confined merely to making proposals for giving effect to the commercial policy already established during the transitional period, but may also be used to propose adoption of the uniform principles themselves.

The negotiation of Community commercial agreements

37–16   During the transitional period the Commission was, by Article 111 (2) to " submit to the Council recommendations for tariff negotiations with third countries in respect of the common customs tariff." The Council (acting in accordance with para. 3, *supra*) was to authorise the Commission to open negotiations which were to be conducted in consultation with a special committee (" the Article 111 Committee ") appointed by the Council to assist the Commission in this task and within the framework of such directives as the Council might issue to it, again acting in accordance with paragraph 3.

Now that the transitional period has expired:

" Where agreements with third countries need to be negotiated, the Commission shall make recommendations to the Council, which shall authorise the Commission to open the necessary negotiations.

" The Commission shall conduct these negotiations in consultation with a special committee appointed by the Council to assist the Commission in this task and within the framework of such directives as the Council may issue to it."

(Art. 113 (3)).

Thus the powers of the Commission to negotiate agreements with third countries are now much wider than they were, but it is still to act in consultation with a special committee (" the Article 113 Committee," the successor to the Article 111 Committee) appointed by the Council to assist it in this task, and within the framework of such directives as the Council may issue to it.

Under both Artices 111 and 113 the Commission is responsible only for negotiations. By Article 114:

" The agreements referred to in Article 111 (2) and in Article 113 shall be concluded by the Council on behalf of the Community, acting unanimously during the first two stages and by a qualified majority thereafter."

Conclusion is effected usually by a decision in the sense of Article 189.*

Article 112

37–17   Article 112 is concerned with the harmonisation by Member States of their systems of aids for exports to third countries. Under paragraph 1 this was to be effected by the end of the transitional period, the Council issuing any necessary directives, acting unanimously until the end of the second stage and by a qualified majority thereafter, on a proposal from the Commission. Such harmonisation was clearly necessary, for the incidence of export aids is reflected in export prices, and differences between national systems of aids would result in an imbalance in export prices and would affect the relative competitiveness of the exports.

Article 112 (2) exempts drawbacks of customs duties and equivalent charges, and repayments of internal indirect taxation (*cf.* Art. 96 for intra-Community trade) from the incidence of paragraph 1 in so far as they do not exceed the actual amount imposed, directly or indirectly, on the products exported. Matters falling within Article 112 are now governed by Article 113.

Article 115

37–18   Article 115 provides for safeguards both during and after the transitional period. The operative paragraph of the Article reads:

> " In order to ensure that the execution of measures of commercial policy taken in accordance with this Treaty by any Member State is not obstructed by deflection of trade, or where differences between such measures lead to economic difficulties in one or more of the Member States, the Commission shall recommend the methods for the requisite cooperation between Member States. Failing this, the Commission shall authorise Member States to take the necessary protective measures, the conditions and details of which it shall determine." (first para.)

Priority is to be given to measures which cause the least disturbance to the functioning of the common market (third para.). Now that the transitional period has expired Member States may no longer take unilateral action even in case of urgency, as was permitted under the second paragraph. The obligation to take into account the need to expedite the introduction of the CCT (third paragraph) has lost its force now that the CCT is fully in force.

Action under Article 115 may be taken to protect the Community or a Member State against imports of particular products from a particular country.

In theory, when a complete commercial policy is instituted, a safeguard clause benefiting individual Member States will become obsolete. The prime importance of the Article at present is in relation to commerce with state-trading countries, where market considerations do not always control prices. It is also relevant *vis-à-vis* countries with low labour costs. (See further below on particular measures taken to counteract these problems.)

Article 116

37–19   Article 116 provides for co-ordination of action " within the framework of international organisations of an economic character." During the transitional period Member States were merely to consult each other with a view to concerting action to be taken and adopting uniform attitudes " as far as possible." Now that the transitional period has ended, they are required, in respect of all matters of particular interest to the common market, to proceed only by common action. To this end the Commission is empowered to submit proposals to the Council, which is to act by a qualified majority, concerning the scope and implementation of such action.

Article 116 would appear to be of general application and not to be restricted to the scope of the common commercial policy, the common action within the framework of economic organisations being called for " in respect of *all* matters of particular interest to the Common Market." The Article assumes that Member States will retain their membership of these international organisations as individual states; this is because the Community is unlikely to be recognised as an entity or state for the purposes of membership of such organisations, although some organisations, GATT in particular, have made constitutional amendments for the recognition of the Community not only as spokesman for the Six but also as competent to sign in respect of those matters over which the Member States have accorded powers to the Community. Article 116 would appear to be subject to Articles 229 and 231 in so far as these relate to maintenance of appropriate relations or co-operation with specialised agencies having an economic character, and with GATT and with the OEEC (now the OECD).

Association with the EEC

1. *Part Four of the Treaty*

37–20   When the EEC was set up its members still maintained special relations with colonial or ex-colonial territories, mainly in Africa (listed in Annex IV to the EEC Treaty, Cmnd. 4864, p. 113). Part Four of the Treaty (Arts. 131 to 136) set out the guidelines for an association of these territories with the EEC, elaborated upon in an implementing convention (Cmnd. 4864, p. 134) annexed to the Treaty. The purpose of this association is expressed to be to promote the economic and social development of the countries and territories concerned and to establish close economic relations between them and the Community as a whole (Art. 131, second para.).

" In accordance with the principles set out in the Preamble to this Treaty, association shall serve primarily to further the interests and prosperity of the inhabitants of these countries and territories in order to lead them to the economic, social and cultural development to which they aspire " (third para.).

The objectives of association are:

1. Community treatment for trade with the countries and territories concerned;
2. equality of treatment for the rest of the EEC with that accorded to the former metropolitan territory;
3. aid to development from the EEC;
4. for investments financed by the Community, participation in tenders and supplies to be open on equal terms to all natural and legal persons who are nationals of a Member State or of one of the countries and territories; and,
5. in principle, freedom of establishment between the Member States and the countries and territories (Art. 132).

The association was founded on a series of customs unions between each of the associated countries and the Six (Art. 133). The Implementing Convention created a Development Fund (Art. 1) (succeeded later by the European Development Fund), financed by annual contributions from Member States to assist social and economic projects in the associated countries (Arts. 2 and 3). The Convention was concluded by the six Member States of the Community acting alone, the countries to be associated not being fully independent at the time.

Article 227, on the territorial application of the EEC Treaty, confirms the application of Articles 131 to 136 to the overseas countries and territories, paragraph 3 stating the special arrangements set out in Part Four of the Treaty to apply to the overseas countries and territories listed in Annex IV.

2. *Article 238*

37-21   The Treaty contains in Article 238 a quite general disposition on association providing for the conclusion of association agreements with a third State, a union of States or an international organisation, involving reciprocal rights and obligations, common action and special procedures.

This Article was used when new association arrangements were negotiated with the countries previously associated under Part Four of the Treaty which had become independent during the period of validity of the latter association arrangements.

Article 238 has led to difficulties of interpretation; basically it is an empowering article. It has to be inferred that the Community has power to conclude such agreements only within the scope of its competence, and that therefore outside that scope the Member States retain their own powers to conclude such agreements. The Article itself contemplates that " where such agreements call for amendments to this Treaty," *e.g.* where their potential scope goes wider than the existing powers of the Community, " these amendments shall first be adopted in accordance with the procedure laid down in Article 236 " (revision of the EEC Treaty: see *supra*, § 37–01). In practice this latter procedure has never been used, but rather where the Community lacked powers in respect of certain aspects of the projected agreement the Member States have joined with the Community, sometimes at the negotiation stage, and always at the conclusion stage, to create a so-called mixed agreement (*supra*, § 37–01).

The procedure for the conclusion of an association agreement is as follows: negotiations may be conducted on the Community side by representatives of the Community, or by both Community and Member States. Where the Community alone is involved the agreement is concluded by the Council acting unanimously after consulting the Assembly (Article 238, second para.). Thus the Parliament is involved only after the agreement has been negotiated. This is, however, more than is provided for in the chapter on commercial policy, where no participation of the Parliament is specified at all. The Commission keeps the Parliament informed of developments, however, and it is able to exert some indirect influence on the conduct of negotiations, notably by means of Parliamentary Questions.

Co-operation with international organisations

37-22   Relations with international organisations of a particular type are mentioned in Article 116 (*supra*, § 37–19) and Article 238 permits the Community to establish association agreements with international organisations as well as with third States. Specific provisions regarding relations with international organisations are to be found in addition in Articles 229 to 231.

By Article 229:

" It shall be for the Commission to ensure the maintenance of all appropriate relations with the organs of the United Nations, of its specialised agencies and of the General Agreement on Tariffs and Trade.

" The Commission shall also maintain such relations as are appropriate with all international organisations."

Clearly, the residuary provision of the second paragraph gives the Commission a very wide margin of discretion in determining what relations shall be established or maintained.

Articles 230 and 231 concern the establishment respectively of all appropriate forms of co-operation by the Community with the Council of Europe, and of close co-operation with the OEEC (now OECD), the details of the latter to be determined by common accord.

The procedure for the conclusion of agreements with international organisations, with the exception of association agreements, is laid down in Article 228 (see below).

The admission of third States to membership of the Communities

37–23   Article 237 EEC, with which Article 206 Euratom is identical, lays down the conditions and procedure for the admission of a third country to membership of the Community. The prior conditions are:

(a) the applicant must be a European State (although what constitutes a European State is not uncontroverted);

(b) the applicant must apply to the Council;

(c) the Council must agree unanimously on the application after obtaining the opinion of the Commission
(first para.).

Conduct of the negotiations is not mentioned specifically by this article, and although the Commission argued that it should be for it to negotiate on behalf of the Community and the Member States, the negotiations relating to the applications of Denmark, Ireland, Norway and the United Kingdom made in 1970, were conducted neither by the Commission nor the original Member States, but by the Council. Prior to each of the negotiation sessions with the applicant countries, the Council met to agree on common positions to present to such countries.

By the first sentence of the second paragraph of Article 237 " the conditions of admission and the adjustments to this Treaty necessitated thereby shall be the subject of an agreement between the Member States and the applicant State." In respect of the applications just referred to this agreement is constituted by the Treaty and Act of Accession of January 22, 1972 (Cmnd. 4862—see generally *supra*, § 2–10) concerning the accession of the above-mentioned States to both the EEC and Euratom.

37–24   As respects accession to the ECSC Treaty, the opening sentences of Article 98 ECSC are substantially similar to the first paragraph of Article 237 EEC, but the former Article goes on to provide that " the Council shall also determine the terms of accession, likewise acting unanimously." Provision for the accession of the applicant States to the ECSC was therefore made by a decision of the Council of the Communities, taken on the same day as the Treaty of Accession was signed and expressed in substantially similar terms. The Act of Accession is expressed to be annexed to this decision as well as to the Treaty of Accession.

Article 237 EEC, second para. requires " the agreement " (*i.e.* the Treaty of Accession), to be submitted for ratificaton by all the contracting States in accordance with their respective constitutional requirements. Article 98 ECSC does not call for ratification of the Council decision, since thereunder accession is effected by a Community act rather than by a wholly international agreement.

Other provisions relating specifically to external relations

37–25   Where the EEC Treaty provides for the conclusion of agreements between the Community and one or more States or an international organisation, Article 228 lays down a general rule, requiring such agreements to be negotiated by the Commission and, subject to the powers vested in the Commission in this field, to be concluded by the Council, after consulting the Assembly where required by the Treaty.

In each of the major areas involving external relations, however (agreements, association agreements, and relations with international organisations), the Treaty contains specific provisions, which would appear in practice to override Article 228 (see below).

The procedure prescribed by Art. 228 (1) is more complete than that laid down in Articles 111, 113, 237 or 238, in that the second paragraph establishes a means for determining whether the content of a proposed agreement is compatible with the provisions of the Treaty. The Council, Commission or a Member State may, prior to the conclusion of an agreement, obtain the opinion of the Court of Justice on the question. Where the opinion of the Court is adverse the agreement may enter into force only in accordance with Article 236 (see *supra*, § 37–01 as to the nature of this procedure). This procedure has not so far been used. (See *supra* § 37–01 as to " mixed agreements," which are resorted to instead.)

Of greater significance is Article 228 (2), to the effect that " Agreements concluded under these conditions shall be binding on the institutions of the Community and on Member States." This paragraph is generally considered to apply to all " Community alone " agreements; Article 228 (1) being considered merely to reiterate *mutatis mutandis* the other provisions of the Treaty relating to the conclusion of agreements, differences of detail being allowed for by the words " subject to the powers vested in the Commission in this field " and " where required by this Treaty." But the other Articles authorising the negotiation and conclusion of agreements contain nothing comparable to Article 228 (2). But such a provision is appropriate since international agreements do not constitute a category of binding acts within Article 189 EEC.* This circumstance is partly offset by the practice of issuing a Community act in the sense of Article 189,* concluding the agreement, and in effect ratifying the agreement, which is annexed. In 21–24/72, *International Fruit Co.* v. *Produktschap voor Groenten en Fruit,* not yet reported, the Court pointed out that the Community concluded all kinds of agreements in the context of the GATT and held that in so far as it has assumed powers previously exercised by the Member States in connection with the GATT, the Community is bound by the provisions of the GATT itself. Article 228 (2) is also useful in making it clear that the Community is to be regarded as having international responsibility through its institutions (*cf. supra,* § 36–04) for its acts, and that the Member States enjoy no species of limited liability in respect of " Community alone " agreements which will enable them to repudiate them at will. Furthermore, States not recognising the international personality of the Communities are safeguarded by this provision.

Indirect attribution of powers in respect of external relations

37–26   The arguments for an extensive interpretation of the ambit of the commercial policy referred to above have not gained full acceptance. Be that as it may, the Court of Justice appears, in its judgment in 22/70, *Commission* v. *Council* (the *AETR* or *ERTA* case), Rec. XVII 263, [1971] C.M.L.R. 335, to favour a broad interpretation of the powers of the Community to negotiate and conclude international agreements. The facts of the case, as far as they are relevant, have already been set out *supra*, § 27–22. The Court decided:

" [12] In the absence of specific provisions of the Treaty relating to the negotiation and conclusion of international agreements in the sphere of transport policy—a category into which the ERTA falls by its very nature—one must turn to the general system of Community law relating to agreements with non-member States.

" [13] Article 210 provides that ' the Community shall have legal personality.'

" [14] This provision, placed at the head of Part Six of the Treaty, devoted to ' General and Final Provisions,' means that in its external relations the Community enjoys the capacity to establish contractual links with non-member States over the whole extent of the field of objectives defined in Part One of the Treaty, with which Part Six must be read together.

" [15] To determine in a particular case the Community's authority to enter into international agreements, one must have regard to the whole scheme of the Treaty no less than to its specific provisions.

" [16] Such authority may arise not only from an explicit grant by the Treaty—as is the case with Articles 113 and 114 for tariff and commercial agreements and with Article 238 for Association agreements—but may equally flow from other provisions of the Treaty and from steps taken, within the framework of these provisions, by the Community institutions.

" [17] In particular, each time the Community, with a view to implementing a common policy envisaged by the Treaty, lays down common rules, whatever form these may take, the member-States no longer have the right, acting individually or even collectively, to contract obligations towards non-member States affecting these rules.

" [18] To the extent that such common rules come into being, the Community alone is in a position to assume and carry out contractual obligations towards non-member States affecting the whole sphere of application of the Community legal system.

" [19] One cannot, therefore, in implementing the provisions of the Treaty, separate the category of measures internal to the Community from that of external relations.

" [20] By the terms of Article 3 (c), the adoption of a common policy in the sphere of transport is specially mentioned among the aims of the Community.

" [21] By the terms of Article 5, the member-States are required on the one hand to take all appropriate steps to ensure the carrying out of the obligations arising out of the Treaty or resulting from the acts of the institutions and, on the other hand, to abstain from any steps likely to jeopardise the attainment of the purposes of the Treaty.

" [22] If these two provisions are read in conjunction, it follows that to the extent that Community rules are promulgated for the attainment of the purposes of the Treaty, the member-States cannot, outside the framework of the Community institutions, assume obligations likely to affect such rules or alter their scope."
(Trans. [1971] C.M.L.R. 335 at pp. 354–355.)

Although the Court rejected the application on the facts, the *AETR* case establishes the clear principle that where the Community has laid down rules in implementation of a common policy, Member States no longer have the right to contract conflicting international obligations. (See also *supra*, § 17–15 for other aspects of this case, and *infra*, p. 492, bibliography, for literature thereon.)

Measures internal to the Community taken in execution of the common commercial policy

37–27   The original transitional period for the implementation of the EEC Treaty having expired, the common commercial policy should now be based on uniform principles with regard to both import and export policy (Art. 113). Although complete uniformity has yet to be achieved, substantial progress has been made. It was relatively easy for the Community to establish its policy with regard to tariffs, since the setting up of the common customs tariff enabled it to present one face to the rest of the world in tariff matters. It must thus be remembered that Articles 18 to 29 of the Treaty, on the setting up of the CCT, are closely related to the common commercial policy, the establishment of the former being a fundamental prerequisite to that policy. The implementation of the common agricultural policy, and the consequent setting up of individual market organisations also contribute to the common commercial policy, each Regulation setting up a market organisation containing dispositions relating to external trade in the products subject to it.

The following are the principal Community acts currently in force, specifically governing internal aspects of the common commercial policy.

1. *Regulation 459/68,*[2] *on protection against dumping actions or subsidies practised by non-member countries of the EEC*

37–28   Regulation 459/68 is discussed in connection with dumping generally (*supra,* § 29–06).

2. *Regulation 2603/69,*[3] *establishing a common system for exports*

37–29   Article 1 of Regulation 2603/69 lays down the basic principle that exports from the EEC to third countries shall be free, *i.e.* not subject to any quantitative restrictions. Article 10, however, exempts from this principle an annexed list of products (subsequently cut down by Regulations 234/71, J.O. 1971, L 28/2 and 2182/71, J.O. 1971, L 231/4). The basic principle is subject to derogations where difficulties arise in the Member States, because of an overall Community deficit in a particular product, Articles 6 to 8 providing for the imposition of export controls after consultations under Articles 2 to 5.

3. *Regulation 109/70,*[4] *establishing a common system applicable to imports from State trading countries*

37–30   Regulation 109/70 is designed to deal with difficulties arising in trade with State trading countries, particularised by the current Annex as meaning Bulgaria, Hungary, Poland, Romania, Czechoslovakia, U.S.S.R., Albania, the People's Republic of China, North Vietnam, North Korea, and Mongolia. These States do not recognise the EEC as an international legal person competent to conduct tariff negotiations, and therefore, despite the fact that a common commercial policy should have been instituted, relations with them remain on a strictly bilateral State-to-State basis. Effectively, therefore, the CCT does not apply with respect to these States and this regulation represents the Community's attempt to deal with the commercial aspects of the situation. Annexed to it is a list frequently amended (see Decision 72/322, J.O. 1972, L 208/11 for consolidated amendments in force as from August 15, 1972) of products whose import into each Member State is completely free of quantitative restrictions. The Regulation provides for a system of Community information and consultation (Arts. 3 to 5) and for supervision procedures (Art. 6). These are supplemented by Articles 7 to 10, permitting protective measures to be taken on an emergency basis by the Member States, subject to control by the Commission and the Council, or by the Commission, in either case subject to definitive arrangements being laid down by the Council on proposals from the Commission.

4. *Regulation 1023/70,*[5] *establishing a common administrative procedure for quantitative quotas*

37–31   Regulation 1023/70 sets up a Community system for the allocation between Member States of quantitative import and export quotas on

---

2 J.O. 1968, L 93/1.   3 J.O. 1969, L 324/25.
4 J.O. 1970, L 19/1.   5 J.O. 1970, L 124/1.

products other than agricultural products subject to a market organisation (Art. 13), which the Community has fixed independently or by agreement (Art. 1). The quota for the whole Community is fixed by the Council (Art. 2) but the individual Member State allocations are made by the Commission and the Administrative Committee for Quotas acting as a normal management committee—*cf. supra*, § 22–09—upon principles laid down by the Council (Art. 11). Although it is nowhere stated, it would appear that this Regulation applies to products covered by Regulation 2603/69 (*supra*) instituting a common system for exports and under which exports from the Community are to be free (that is to say they shall not be subject to quantitative restrictions with the exception of those which are applied in accordance with provisions of this Regulation: Article 1 of the latter Regulation). It appears to apply under similar conditions also to the liberalised products imported under Regulation 109/70 (*supra*—imports from State trading countries) and under Regulation 1025/70 (*infra*) establishing a common system to be applied to imports from third countries. Quotas fixed by the Member States themselves, whether unilaterally or by agreement, are not covered by the Regulation. Such quotas may still exist for products not covered by Regulation 1025: see below.

5. *Regulation 1025/70,*[6] *establishing a common system to be applied to imports from third countries*

37-32   Regulation 1025/70 is the reciprocal of Regulation 2603/69 on the common system for exports. It provides in Article 1 that "Imports into the Community of the products set out in Annex I shall be liberalised in relation to the third countries shown in Annex II, that is to say, not subject to quantitative restrictions." As in the case of imports from State trading countries, however, a system of Community information and consultation is provided for (Arts. 3 to 6) and supervisory procedures are established (Arts. 7 to 9). In the last resort protective measures may be applied (Arts. 10 to 13). Annex I has been amended on a number of occasions: see Decision 72/309, J.O. 1972, L 197/9, for consolidated amendments in force as from July 8, 1972. Annex II is to be replaced by a new Annex II, set out as a technical adaptation in Cmnd. 4862–II, p. 78 covering more than 150 main countries or territories.

6. *Regulation 1471/70,*[7] *establishing a common procedure for the autonomous increase of imports into the Community of products subject to measures of voluntary restraint by exporting countries*

37-33   Regulation 1471/70 provides that where the Community decides to propose or to accept that a third country practising voluntary restraint

---

[6] J.O. 1970, L 124/6.   [7] J.O. 1970, L 164/41.

in respect of exports to the Community may increase its exports to the Community the decision is to be taken in accordance with the management committee procedure laid down in Article 11 of Regulation 1023/70 (*supra*), establishing the common procedure for administering quantitative quotas, and having due regard to certain listed factors.

The above Regulations are the bases for the internal operation of the common commercial policy. Other measures operating internally concern the co-ordination of export aids in the form of credit insurance and guarantees under Article 112. A decision of the Council of September 27, 1960, J.O. 1960, 1339, set up a policy co-ordination group in this connection. Under the action programme for the Community in matters of common commercial policy, established by Council decision of September 25, 1962, J.O. 1962, 2353, the Commission established a list of all existing export aids. Council Decision 65/53, J.O. 1965, 255, revised the consultation procedure previously applicable in the field of credit insurance etc. to facilitate harmonisation of the systems throughout the Community. On the basis of this preparatory work, the Community has now issued instruments respecting the adoption of common credit insurance techniques for various types of operations, and rules on export guarantees: Directive 70/509, J.O. 1970, L 254/1, respecting the adoption of a common credit insurance policy for medium and long-term operations involving public buyers; Directive 70/510, J.O. 1970, L 254/26, respecting the adoption of a common credit insurance policy for medium and long-term operations involving private buyers; Decision 70/552, J.O. 1970, L 284/59, on the rules applicable, in the matter of export guarantees and finance, to certain sub-contracts for supply from other Member States or non-Member States of the European Communities; and Directive 71/86, J.O. 1971, L 36/14, concerning the harmonisation of essential provisions for the guaranteeing of short-term transactions (political risks) involving public buyers and private buyers.

Co-ordination of relations with third countries

37–34   As was pointed out in connection with the ECSC and Euratom (*supra*, § 37–06) the EEC Treaty lacks any provision by which the agreements of Member States with third countries can be co-ordinated. This lacuna was filled by the Council Decision of October 9, 1961, J.O. 1961, 1273, obliging Member States to communicate details of all negotiations concerning commercial relations to the other Members and to the Commission, and instituting a system of prior consultation between the Member States and the Commission. This is reinforced by another decision of the same date, J.O. 1961, 1274, aimed at standardising the duration of trade agreements with third countries. No new trade agreement was to be extended in duration beyond the end of the original transitional period (Art. 1) pending the establishment of the common commercial policy. The Council had already laid it down by decision of July 20, 1960 (see Written Question 78, J.O. 1960, 1965), that Member States should insist on the insertion of a clause guaranteeing the benefits of any bilateral agreement to all Member States of the Community, so avoiding potential conflicts with the progressive implementation of the common commercial policy. By Article 2 of the second decision of October 9, 1961 agreements not containing an " EEC clause " nor a clause providing for annual notice were not, subject to Article 1 (*supra*), to be valid for more than one year.

During the transitional period, this system operated well. For the definitive period Article 113 requires that trade agreements shall be negotiated by the Commission on behalf of the Community. Provisions needed for the transition from the old to new procedure were laid down by Decision 69/494, J.O. 1969, L 326/39. Difficulties arise here because as mentioned above, certain countries do not recognise the Community as an international legal person and will not therefore undertake trade negotiations with it.

The decision establishes a system of notification (Art. 1) and consultation between States and the Commission prior to the re-negotiation or extension, express or tacit, of any trade agreements (Art. 2). Article 3 permits the express or tacit extension of such agreements for up to one year where they do not hinder the implementation of the common commercial policy. Where the agreement has a reservation clause or a clause providing for annual notice of termination, extension may be authorised for a longer period. If the agreement seems likely to hinder the common commercial policy, the re-negotiation of the agreement is to be governed by Title II (Art. 4). Title II sets out the system of Community negotiations, which is merely the Article 113 procedure in expanded form. However, Title III makes provision for the situation where such negotiating procedure is not appropriate, notably in respect of State trading countries. In the latter case negotiations may, after consultations, be conducted by Member States (Art. 12) but they must follow the recommendations put forward by a special committee of representatives of the Member States, set up by the decision of October 9, 1961, J.O. 1961, 1273. The result of the negotiations must be reported to the Commission and the other Member States; if no objections are lodged by Member States and if the Commission approves, the agreement may be concluded; otherwise, it may be concluded only after authorisation by the Council, acting by qualified majority on a proposal from the Commission (Art. 13).

The Council has authorised the tacit extension of a number of trade agreements acting under Article 3 of Decision 69/494 (see *e.g.* Decision 72/113, J.O. 1972, L 56/10).

Principal commercial or trade agreements concluded with third States on the basis of Articles 111 and 113 [7a]

Iran

37–35   The first trade agreement to be concluded by the Community as such, on the basis of Article 111, was that between the Council and Iran of October 14, 1963, J.O. 1963, 2554. The negotiations for it were conducted in mixed fashion, by Member States and the Community jointly. It is a preferential agreement for the suspension of CCT duties at prescribed levels on certain of Iran's exports, notably wool or fine hair carpets, dried grapes, dried apricots and caviar. The agreement also sets up a mixed committee for the development of trade between Iran and the Community. It was concluded for an initial period of three years (Art. V) and is renewable for one year at a time (see most recently J.O. 1972, L 269/34). The agreement was modified by an exchange of letters of October 3, 1967, J.O. 1967, 309/6.

Israel

37–36   The Community entered into a preferential trade agreement with Israel, valid for five years from signature on June 4, 1964, J.O. 1964, 1517. This agreement expired and its effects were largely revived by an agreement of June 29, 1970, J.O. 1970, L 183/1, also for five years, concluded on the basis of Article 113. It is entirely commercial in nature and involves reciprocal tariff reductions for certain products, although the only real reductions of importance are those conceded by the Community (cf. agreement with Spain infra). A Joint Commission is responsible for the supervision of the agreement (Art. 14).

The Lebanon

37–37   A non-preferential trade agreement was signed with the Lebanon by the Council and the Member States on May 21, 1965, J.O. 1968, L 146/1. The mixed form was used since the agreement provided also for certain measures of technical co-operation not within the competence of the Community (Arts. V to VIII), involving inter alia the sending of experts and teachers to the Lebanon and the training of Lebanese in commercial, educational and industrial establishments in the Member States, and the setting up of a joint technical co-operation group with a Commission observer. So far as the trade aspects of the agreement are concerned, each party is to grant most-favoured-nation treatment to the goods of the other party on a reciprocal basis. This agreement is likely to be replaced by a preferential type of trade agreement. It was extended to July 1, 1973, by Decision 72/310, J.O. 1972, L 201/12.

Switzerland

37–38   The Community has in the light of recent membership negotiations negotiated free trade agreements with the non-candidate EFTA countries, Switzerland included (see infra, § 37–56). The Community

---

[7a] Expired and/or short-term agreements are not discussed.

has already had indirect trade agreement contacts with the latter country. Letters were exchanged between Switzerland and the Community, represented by the Council, on the reduction of customs duties on woven silk fabrics (J.O. 1968, L 266/2) over and above the tariff cuts agreed under the 1967 Geneva GATT Protocol (Kennedy Round of tariff cuts).

A further trade agreement with Switzerland was signed on August 1, 1969, by the Council, adopting for Community purposes the agreements relating to " the reciprocal finishing trade in textiles " between Switzerland and Germany, France and Italy, J.O. 1969, L 240/5. The agreement allows products resulting from these operations to be admitted free of customs duties up to a certain limit, a mixed administrative Commission being set up to supervise the system and to propose any necessary changes.

India

37-39   The Community has concluded trade agreements with India, relating in particular to textiles. Several agreements in the form of exchanges of letters have been made in relation to sensitive Indian exports: coconut products, J.O. 1969, L 240/1, handicraft products,[8] J.O. 1970, L 170/1, jute products,[9] J.O. 1969, L 287/32.

Of wider importance are the agreements between the Community and India, amongst other countries, regarding trade in cotton textiles. (See the agreements with India, United Arab Republic, Pakistan, of March 12, 1971, J.O. 1971, L 43/2, 43/12 and 43/22, that with the Republic of China of April 20, 1971, J.O. 1971, L 43/32, that with South Korea, of April 29, 1971, J.O. 1971, L 55/12, that with Hong Kong, of July 22, 1971, J.O. 1971, L 220/23, and that with Japan, dated February 7, 1972, J.O. 1972, L 134/32.) These agreements set a maximum quota for import into the Community of cotton textiles emanating from the countries concerned. There are no concessions by the Community and the agreements are stated to be in accordance with the GATT long-term arrangement regarding international trade in cotton textiles. The GATT arrangement has been adopted by the Community as a party thereto by Decision 70/461, J.O. 1970, L 225/28.

Yugoslavia

37-40   The agreement with Yugoslavia of March 6, 1970, J.O. 1970, L 58/1, described as a Trade Agreement, is the first bilateral agreement between the Community and an eastern European country. It implements in part the Community policy of forging links with the countries surrounding the Mediterranean basin (see Bulletin 4, 1971, p. 30). It is non-preferential in form, each party granting to the other most-favoured-

---

[8] A similar agreement was reached with Pakistan, December 19, 1969, J.O. 1970, L 175/3.

[9] A similar agreement was reached with Pakistan, January 19, 1970, J.O. 1970, L 170/4.

nation treatment. The agreement contains special provisions regarding Community levies on the most important Yugoslav export to the Community, beef (Art. VI and Protocol No. 1). A Joint Committee is responsible for the supervision of the Agreement (Art. VII), which is concluded for three years.

Spain

37-41 A preferential trade agreement with Spain was signed on June 29, 1970, J.O. 1970, L 182/1; it provides for tariff reductions by both contracting parties and prohibits discrimination. It contains also rules for determining origin of goods (Art. 8 and Protocol), provisions for consultations in the case of dumping (Art. 9), freedom of payment provisions (Art. 10), a " serious disturbance " clause (Art. 11) and an " *ordre public* " clause (Art. 12). A Joint Committee is responsible for the supervision of the agreement (Art. 13).

A further agreement with Spain is envisaged in the light of experience under this agreement.

Austria

37-42 An agreement between Austria and the Community, relating to the export of cattle for manufacturing processes was signed on July 22, 1970, J.O. 1970, L 140/1. It provides for reductions in the rate of levies on imports, and embodies on Austria's part an obligation to help stabilise the internal market of the Community by providing effective control procedures for its exports of cattle (Art. 4), and to inform the Community of export prices and related factors (Art. 5). The agreement was extended for three years to run from April 1, 1971, by an exchange of letters of March 31, 1971, J.O. 1971, L 99/1. The principal agreement is expressed to be linked to that with Denmark on the same subject (June 30, 1967, and March 31, 1971, J.O. 1971, L 99/4).

The Argentine

37-43 The second so-called Trade Agreement to be signed by the Community was with the Argentine, J.O. 1971, L 249/19. It is of the non-preferential type, each side granting the other most-favoured nation treatment. It provides in addition for the suspension of levies and duties on certain agricultural products, notably beef (Art. 4 (1)). The agreement also institutes a system of mutual co-operation in agriculture (Art. 3) and establishes a mixed commission to assist in its implementation (Art. 5).

Association agreements

1. *Association Agreements with non-European States*

37-44 (a) *Association with the African States and Malagasy.* The association of eighteen independent African States with the Community was forecast by Part Four of the EEC Treaty. Part Four set up an association between the then colonial territories of the Member States listed in

Annex IV to the Treaty. This was superseded for the most part (Guinea opted out of the new system shortly after gaining independence) by the First Yaoundé Convention (Yaoundé I) signed on July 20, 1963, J.O. 1964, 1430, and in force until May 31, 1969. This Convention was replaced by Yaoundé II of July 29, 1969, J.O. 1970, L 282/2. Both Yaoundé Conventions were concluded in mixed form. Neither was based expressly on a particular Article of the Treaty.

Yaoundé II reflects the progress achieved inside the EEC and current thinking in world trade circles on preferential treatment given by developed to developing countries. Provision is made for reciprocal import of goods free of duty or quantitative restrictions (Arts. 2 and 3, and 6 and 7), although as in the original Implementing Convention annexed to the EEC Treaty, the Associated States may maintain duties to protect their developing industries. The Convention contains the usual non-discrimination clause (Art. 5), "*ordre public*" clause (Art. 9), definition of origin clause (Art. 10)—the rules are those of Yaoundé I— and "serious disturbance" clause (Art. 16).

The trade provisions are little more than the Community has agreed with other third countries in its commercial agreements. The real significance of this association lies in the provisions on financial and technical co-operation (Arts. 17 to 30) and the institutional aspects. By Article 18 of the Convention, funds are provided for development aid in the Associated States, to be administered by the European Development Fund and the European Investment Bank; this follows previous grants of financial assistance in the two earlier conventions. The uses to which the funds may be put are outlined in Article 19. A special reserve fund to deal with natural or economic emergencies is established by Article 20.

The Convention also provides for non-discrimination between or against Member States in respect of establishment, services, payments and capital (Title III—Arts. 31 to 40).

37-45   Articles 41 to 55 set out the institutional arrangements governing the Association. By Article 41 the institutions of the Association are to be the Association Council assisted by the Association Committee, the Parliamentary Conference of the Association, and the Court of Arbitration of the Association. The Association Council is composed of members of the Council of the European Communities, of the Commission and of a member of the governments of each of the Associated States. It meets at least once annually, and otherwise *ad hoc*, and can take binding decisions within the scope of the Convention; it is assisted by the Association Committee, composed of representatives of each of the contracting parties, to ensure continuity. The latter acts in a similar way to COREPER (see above, § 7-01) but has a power to formulate recommendations, resolutions or opinions, and may be delegated a real power of decision.

The Parliamentary Conference, composed of equal numbers of

members of the European Parliament and of members of the parliaments of the Associated States, meets once a year. Each year the Association Council must submit a report on its activities to the Conference. The agenda of the Conference is prepared by a Joint Committee.

The Court of Arbitration acts to settle any dispute concerning the interpretation or application of the Convention arising between the two sides party to the Convention, if the Council has failed previously to arrange an amicable settlement. The Court is composed of five members, two being nominated by the Council of the European Communities, two by the Associated States, and the President by the Association Council. Alternates are appointed by the Association Council for each judge. The decisions of the Court are binding on the parties to the dispute, who are required to take all necessary measures to carry them out. The Statute of the Court is contained in Protocol No. 8 to the Convention.

The structure of the institutions is comparatively simple, affording elements of democratic control. It cannot be said, however, that the association arrangement has been a complete success. It is criticised by GATT and by other countries for its selective preferential treatment and for its tendency towards a form of neo-colonialism. The Convention will expire on January 31, 1975 at the latest and will then require revision.

37–46 The remaining overseas territories and countries mentioned in Annex IV of the Treaty are covered by a decision similar in content to the tariff, financial and technical co-operation, and freedom of establishment and services parts of Yaoundé II, and coterminous with it: Decision 70/549, J.O. 1970, L 282/83. Special arrangements were made by the Community to accommodate the Netherlands Antilles and Surinam with the Annex IV territories (Decision 64/532, J.O. 1964, 2413) at the time of Yaoundé I. The remaining " Annex IV " countries and territories are listed in Annex VIII to Decision 70/549.

37–47 (b) *Nigeria.* Certain other African States approached the Community with a view to forming links similar to those created by the Yaoundé Convention. The Community and the Member States in fact signed an association agreement with Nigeria on July 16, 1966, timed to expire with Yaoundé I, but it never came into force. It was based on Yaoundé I but lacked any provisions for financial assistance.

37–48 (c) *Kenya, Uganda and Tanzania.* The Member States of the Community and the Council signed an association agreement with Kenya, Uganda and Tanzania, the partner States of the East African Community, on July 26, 1968. The agreement (known as Arusha I) was superseded by a second agreement, Arusha II, signed on September 24, 1969, J.O. 1970, L 282/54. This follows closely the provisions of Yaoundé II with regard to trade, but it lacks any provisions on financial and technical co-operation, and its institutional provisions are less developed than those of Yaoundé II. It provides for a Parliamentary

Conference and an Association Council, but not for a Court of Arbitration. The agreement expires on the same date as Yaoundé II.

37–49   (d) *Tunisia and Morocco* (*Maghreb States*). The Community has concluded association agreements with two Maghreb States, Tunisia and Morocco. Although these agreements were negotiated on the basis of Article 238 EEC, and have the status of association agreements, they are " Community alone " agreements, not involving the Member States in their conclusion, and are in effect little more than preferential trade agreements with a slightly more sophisticated institutional system than usual. The agreement with Tunisia was signed on March 28, 1969, J.O. 1969, L 198/1; that with Morocco on March 31, 1969, J.O. 1969, L 197/1 (amended by two exchanges of letters of December 15, 1970, J.O. 1971, L 53/1). They provide principally for reduction and elimination of customs duties on the part of the Community and quota concessions on the part of the Associated States. Tunisia also grants the Community certain additional tariff concessions. The agreements themselves are identical, the differences arising in the annexes.

Article 10 of each agreement sets up a Council of Association composed of members of the Council of the European Community, of the Commission and of members of the respective governments of Tunisia and Morocco (Art. 11). The agreements expire on September 1, 1974.

2. Association agreements with European States

37–50   (a) *Greece.* As has been indicated above, associations may serve one of several purposes, including that of providing a framework for relations with European States which are not yet in a position to become full members of the Community, but which, it is hoped, may become such eventually.   Indeed it has been stated that this was originally the sole purpose of Article 238. The first association agreement entered into by the Community was that signed with Greece on July 9, 1961, J.O. 1963, 294.   This provides for the establishment of a customs union between the Community and Greece over a transitional period of twelve years. Provision is made for the free movement of goods along the lines of Title I of Part Two of the EEC Treaty—Articles 6 to 11 provide for free movement of goods in general. Articles 12 to 19 provide for the elimination of customs duties as between the contracting parties, Articles 20 and 21 provide for the adoption by Greece of the CCT and Articles 22 to 31 provide for the elimination of quantitative restrictions as between the parties. The agreement also contains special provisions relating to agriculture, in effect obliging Greece to adopt the Community's common agriculture policy, which must itself take account of Greek interests and problems (Arts. 32 to 43). The Agreement further provides for free movement of persons and services (Arts. 44 to 50) as well as laying down rules relating to competition, taxation and the approximation of laws (Arts. 51 to 57). Articles 58 to 64 require the co-ordination of aims in the field of economic policy and call for freedom for payments and capital movements. From this survey it may be seen that the agreement is largely based on the EEC Treaty itself, this being indicative of the fact that the eventual aim of the association is admission of Greece to full membership of the Community.

The agreement provides for a Council of Association, composed of members of the governments of Member States, of members of the Council and Commission, and of members of the Greek Government. No other institutions are mentioned although Article 67 (2) provides for the establishment of an *ad hoc* Court of Arbitration to settle disputes unresolved by the Council of Association. However, in addition to the above, a joint parliamentary committee was set up to assist in co-operation between the European Parliament and the Greek Parliament.

Protocol No. 19 annexed to the Agreement, the Financial Protocol, provides for Community loans to the Greek Government up to $125 million, to be used for investment in Greece, particularly in infrastructure.

However, since the Greek *coup d'état* in April 1967 the Association has been limited to current affairs only (Fifth General Report (1971), p. 309).

37–51 (b) *Turkey.* Turkey followed Greece's example in concluding an association agreement with the Community. This was signed by the Member States, the Council and Turkey on September 12, 1963, J.O. 1964, 3687. It aims at the progressive establishment of a customs union, but the timetable envisaged is slower than that for Greece; three phases of association are provided for: a preparatory phase lasting five to nine years, a transitional phase lasting twelve to twenty-two years depending on the products involved, and a final phase. The conditions for the implementation of the transitional period were detailed in an Additional Protocol of November 23, 1970. An Interim Agreement of July 27, 1971, J.O. 1971, L 130/2 implements certain of its provisions from the date of the Protocol. The Interim Agreement was by agreement extended in validity to December 31, 1972 (Decision 72/1568, J.O. 1972, L 167/7. See also generally Regulations 2055–2058/71, J.O. 1972, L 222/1, 4, 8 and 12).

As in the Greek Agreement, the provisions regarding the implementation of the customs union, and elimination of quantitative restrictions, are based on the principles of the EEC Treaty. Financial Protocols to the original Agreement and to the Additional Protocol provide for financial aid to Turkey.

The Agreement sets up a Council of Association, composed as under the Greek agreement and with the same duties, but there is no provision for an *ad hoc* arbitration court.

37–52   (c) *Malta.* The Council signed an association agreement with Malta on December 5, 1970, J.O. 1971, L 61/2. It is similar in content to the agreement with the Maghreb countries, and consequently no Member State participation was required in its negotiation, signing or ratification.

A second agreement is envisaged which will establish a customs union between Malta and the Community. The present agreement, in force until March 31, 1976, involves primarily tariff concessions in both the agricultural and industrial sectors. It contains the standard clauses prohibiting discrimination and dumping, and providing safeguards. A Council of Association is set up, responsible for the administration and supervision of the association.

Arrangements with international organisations

37–53   The EEC early on established relations with the ILO (as did the ECSC) by means of an Agreement of July 7, 1958, under Article 229, signed by the President of the Commission and the Director General of the ILO, J.O. 1959, 521. It provides for co-operation in the form of consultation, exchange of information and technical assistance, but it establishes no new organs through which to channel this co-operation.

Co-operation with the Central Commission for the Navigation of the Rhine was established by an exchange of letters between the President of the EEC Commission and the President of the Central Commission, dated June 6, 1961, J.O. 1961, 1027, under which the Director General for transport of the EEC Commission as it then was, is to take part in meetings of the Central Committee.

Less formally the Community is represented at GATT meetings, and participated actively in the Dillon Round of tariff negotiations in the early 1960s, and in the Kennedy Round. The Community participated in the GATT Protocol resulting from the latter, J.O. 1968, L 305/1. Within the GATT framework the Community has entered into a number of bilateral trade agreements. The Community participates in or observes the workings of various other international organisations, or engages in exchanges of views and information with them—*e.g.* the United Nations Conference on Trade and Development, the Organisation for Economic Co-operation and Development, the Western European Union, the European Free Trade Association and the United Nations Economic Commission for Europe, and a large number of specialised agencies of the United Nations.

The Community participates in various food aid programmes, and was a signatory to the First and Second Food Aid Conventions. It has entered into various agreements providing help to the World Food Programme, the International Red Cross Committee and the United Nations Relief and Works Agency (UNRWA).

The Community also participates in the workings of the various international commodity agreements, to which it is party (*e.g.* Fourth

International Tin Agreement of January 27, 1971, Decision 72/155, J.O. 1972, L 90/1).

37-54   A particular result of the Community's participation in and co-operation with various international organisations, notably GATT, UNCTAD and OECD has been the offer of generalised tariff preferences to developing countries. As a result of various pressures, especially UNCTAD II, held in New Delhi in 1968, the Community decided from July 1, 1971, to forgo customs duties on a large range of manufactured and semi-finished products on their import into the Community from developing countries. The applicable Community texts were initially Regulations 1308 to 1313/71, and Decisions 71/231 to 233 (for ECSC products), J.O. 1971, L 142, now Regulations 2794 to 2800/71, and Decisions 71/403 and 404, J.O. 1971, L 287.

By Protocol 23 to the Act of Accession the new Member States are authorised to defer application of the scheme until January 1, 1974. Ireland is authorised to apply customs duties on products coming within Regulations 2796 to 2799/71 equal to those applied *vis-à-vis* Member States other than the United Kingdom until December 31, 1975 (para. 2 of Protocol No. 23).

Development co-operation

37-55   The " Commission Memorandum on a Community development co-operation policy " of July 27, 1971, Bulletin, Supp. 5, 1971, described as a summary document (" *document de synthèse* "), to some extent draws together the threads of the present external relations policy of the Community, pointing to Community action adapting " the Mediterranean agreements to an enlarged Community, the renewal of the agreements with the Maghreb countries on a broader basis, the negotiation of the association with the AASM [African Associated States and Malagasy] and with some Commonwealth countries under the enlarged Community, the measures relating to commodities, to generalised preferences, etc." (p. 4). But the Memorandum also calls for a coherent policy. First concrete steps were considered to be the adaptation of the agreements in the Mediterranean Basin to take account of the enlargement of the Community; renewal on a broader basis of the agreements with Morocco and Tunisia, and the development and reinforcement of the Community's policy towards the Mediterranean in general; negotiations for the extension of Yaoundé II and Arusha II; developments in the context of generalised preferences, food aid, participation in UNCTAD III, and participation in work under the second Development Decade; and finally, implementation of measures decided on by the Council following study of the Commission's Memorandum on Latin American problems (Council Document 5/913/2/70 (COMER 211), Rev 2). Further, the Commission advocated various generalised measures designed to facilitate exports from developing countries and to provide the latter with development aid and technical assistance.

In the " Memorandum from the Commission on a Community Policy on Development Co-operation," of February 2, 1972, Bulletin, Supp. 2, 1972, described as a programme for initial action, reference is made to " Measures to benefit exports from developing countries," involving action on commodities, notably coffee, cocoa and sugar; action to promote the export trade of developing countries with the Community; gradual abolition of excise duties on tropical produce; and protection of the guarantee of origin of foodstuffs. The programme also refers to " other measures favouring economic development of developing countries," which should be taken especially in order to intensify public aid and ensure its regularity, to ease the financial conditions attached to aid, to institute Community untying of public aid, to harmonise aid action, and to encourage regional co-operation between developing countries.

Proposals for a global policy towards trade with Mediterranean countries were made in a Commission communication to the Council of September 22, 1972 (" *Les relations entre la Communauté et les pays du bassin méditerranéan* ").

Agreements with EFTA non-candidate countries, consequential upon the Accession arrangements of January 22, 1972

37-56   Agreements between the EFTA non-candidate countries and the Community were signed on July 22, 1972, setting up free trade areas between the Community and Austria, Iceland, Portugal, Sweden, Switzerland [9a] and Finland (initialled only). These agreements are purely bilateral, dealing with specific issues and problems concerning the particular EFTA country. Those with Portugal and Iceland contemplate the longest delay before institution of a free trade area. The agreement with Austria will create such an area more rapidly than the others.

An Interim Agreement (J.O. 1972, L 223/3) was signed with Austria at the same time as the principal agreement and is to expire with the entry into force of the latter and in any case by July 1, 1974 (Art. 31). This makes provision for the first steps towards a free trade area and contains dispositions on restraints on competition (Art. 19). The Interim Agreement as a whole is under the supervision of a mixed committee (Art. 25).

Regulation 2042/72, J.O. 1972, L 223/1, formally concluding the Interim Agreement, came into force on October 1, 1972, the date on which the agreement itself came into force (J.O. 1972, L 223/84). See also Regulation 2047/72, J.O. 1972, L 223/81, on safeguard measures,

---

[9a] The signed agreements are published in the United Kingdom as Misc. Nos. 49 to 53 (1972), Cmnd. 5159, 5182, 5164, 5180 and 5181 respectively. ECSC agreements, entered into at the same time, are published as Misc. Nos. 43 to 47 (1972), Cmnd. 5131, 5150, 5151, 5155 and 5152 respectively.

and Decision 72/333, J.O. 1972, L 223/83, of the representatives of the Member States, on ECSC tariff preferences.

THE ACT OF ACCESSION AND EXTERNAL RELATIONS

37–57　Articles 4 and 5 of the Act of Accession contain general provisions on the application of the " *acquis* " (*i.e.* that which has already been achieved) in external relations by the new Member States.[10]

Community-alone agreements or conventions with a third State or States, an international organisation or with a national of a third State are to be binding on the new Member States under the conditions laid down in the original Treaties and in the Act (Art. 4 (1) of the Act). New Member States are thus bound at once in most cases.

By contrast new Member States only " undertake to accede " to mixed agreements and to related agreements concluded by the original Member States (Art. 4 (2) of the Act). The Community and the original Member States are to assist the new Member States in this respect. The formula covering the internal agreements concluded by the original Member States for the purpose of implementing the agreements or conventions referred to in paragraph (2) is different again : new Member States " accede [to them] by this Act and under the conditions laid down therein."

By Article 4 (4) of the Act of Accession new Member States are to take " appropriate measures, where necessary, to adjust their positions in relation to international organisations and international agreements to which one of the Communities or to which other Member States are also parties, to the rights and obligations arising from their accession to the Communities." This is without prejudice, however, to Article 5 of the Act of Accession, which provides that :

" Article 234 of the EEC Treaty and Articles 105 and 106 of the Euratom Treaty shall apply, for the new Member States, to agreements or conventions concluded before accession."

Article 234 EEC, first para., provides :

" The rights and obligations from agreements concluded before the entry into force of this Treaty between one or more Member States on the one hand, and one or more third countries on the other, shall not be affected by the provisions of this Treaty."

But the second paragraph calls for elimination of incompatible aspects of such agreements. Member States are, where necessary, to assist each other to this end and are, where appropriate, to adopt a common attitude.

37–58　　In applying agreements entered into prior to joining the Community, Member States are required to take into account the third paragraph of Article 234, by which :

[10] See also *supra*, § 2–12.

" [. . .] Member States shall take into account the fact that the advantages accorded under this Treaty by each Member State form an integral part of the establishment of the Community and are thereby inseparably linked with the creation of common institutions, the conferring of powers upon them and the granting of the same advantages by all the other Member States."

This somewhat roundabout formulation in effect calls for preferential treatment to be granted to the Community, in view of its special status *vis-à-vis* individual Member States. This is necessary in order, apparently, to avoid the implication that third States enjoying most-favoured-nation status are entitled to avail themselves of the advantages accorded to each other by the Member States.

Articles 105 and 106 Euratom have already been discussed, *supra*, § 37-09.

37-59   Part Four of the Act of Accession, on transitional measures, contains a separate Title III on external relations, itself divided in three chapters, relating (1) to agreements of the Communities with certain third countries; (2) to relations with the Associated African and Malagasy States and with certain developing Commonwealth countries, and (3) to relations with Papua-New Guinea.

Agreements of the Communities with certain third countries

37-60   The single Article of Chapter 1 on agreements of the Communities with certain third countries (Art. 108) relates solely to the Mediterranean agreements—those with Greece, Turkey, Tunisia, Morocco, Israel, Spain and Malta. It requires new Member States to apply the provisions of the existing agreements, taking into account transitional measures and adjustments to be negotiated (para. (1)). These transitional measures are to take into account the existing Community measures and are to be coterminous with them. They are also to be designed to ensure a progressive application by the Community of a single system for its relations with the contracting third countries, as well as the indentity of the rights and obligations of the Member States (para. (2): this foreshadows the elaboration of a global Mediterranean policy). Paragraphs (1) and (2) apply to any Mediterranean agreements concluded before the entry into force of the Act (para. (3), second sub-para.). This covers agreements with Egypt, the Lebanon and Cyprus signed on December 18 and 19, 1972.

Relations with the Associated African and Malagasy States and with certain developing Commonwealth countries

37-61   Article 109 of the Act exempts new Member States from " the arrangements resulting from " Yaoundé II or Arusha II, and also from any obligation to accede to the Yaoundé ECSC protocol (para. (1)). By paragraph (2) of the same Article imports into the new Member States from the Associated States are, subject to Articles 110 and 111, to be subject to the arrangements applied to these imports before accession, as are products from the independent Commonwealth countries listed in Annex VI (para. (3)),[11] *i.e.* the status quo is to be maintained. Articles 110 and 111, to which paragraphs (2) and (3) of Article 109 are stated to be subject, relate to agricultural products. Products listed in Annex II EEC (*i.e.* agricultural products), subject to a market organisation or to import rules, originating in the Associated States or in the Annex VI Commonwealth countries, are to be subject in the new Member States to the rules laid down in the Act of Accession. But where customs duties are applicable, the new Member States will, subject to Article 111, apply the tariff arrangements previously applicable, and special adaptations are to be decided on as regards other protective components, so as to preserve the status quo (Art. 110). Article 111 provides that where alignment with the CCT leads to a reduction of a customs duty in a new Member State, the reduced customs duty shall apply to imports covered by Articles 109 and 110.

37–62   Article 112 effects a transitional " *cloisonement du marché* " by providing that products from Annex VI countries are not to enjoy free movement in the Six, and products originating in Yaoundé and Arusha countries are not to enjoy free movement in the acceding States. The Commission may, however, depart from this where there is no risk of trade deflection and in particular in the event of minimal disparities in import arrangements.   The date on which " *cloisonement* " is to terminate is to be fixed according to Article 115 (*infra*).

Article 113 provides for reciprocal communication by the Three to the Six and the Commission, and by the Commission to the Three, of information on import régimes relating to products from Yaoundé and Arusha and from Annex VI countries.

By Article 114, only the votes of the original Member States are to count in Council decisions in the context of the internal agreements for the implementation of Yaoundé and Arusha, and in EDF Committee opinions, in the context of the Yaoundé internal agreement on financing.

37–63   Article 115 (1) states that Articles 109 to 114 are to apply until January 31, 1975. This is the date upon which both Yaoundé II and Arusha II expire. The basic principle of paragraph (1) is subject to two derogations :

(1) Annex VI countries not electing for association (see *infra* as to this) are to enjoy in respect of matters not covered by such agreements as they conclude with the Community the third country arrangements applicable to products of the type they export to the Community, taking into account the transitional provisions of the Act.

---

[11] The Annex VI countries are Barbados, Botswana, Fiji, The Gambia, Ghana, Guyana, Jamaica, Kenya, Lesotho, Malawi, Mauritius, Nigeria, Sierra Leone, Swaziland, Tanzania, Tonga, Trinidad and Tobago, Uganda, Western Samoa and Zambia.

(2) The date fixed by Article 115 (1) may be deferred for the period during which the transitional measures provided for by Yaoundé II and Arusha II are being implemented. Article 62 of Yaoundé II and Article 36 of Arusha II provide in identical terms that:

> "Eighteen months before the expiry of this Convention, the Contracting States shall examine the provisions that might be made for a further period.
> "The Association Council shall take any transitional measures required until the new Convention comes into force."

Relations with Papua-New Guinea

37–64   Articles 109 (3) and 110 to 113 are to apply until December 31, 1977, to products originating in or coming from Papua-New Guinea imported into the United Kingdom (Art. 116 (1)). But these arrangements may be reviewed, in particular if Papua-New Guinea becomes independent in the meantime.

Association of overseas countries and territories

37–65   Title IV of Part Four of the Act of Accession, entitled " Association of Overseas Countries and Territories," makes provision for the association of the non-European territories maintaining special relations with the acceding States, listed in Article 24 (2) of the Act of Accession (see further, *supra*, § 36–33). These include most of the remaining territories having such special relations with the United Kingdom, including the Anglo-French condominium of the New Hebrides. Association of these territories is to take effect on February 1, 1975, at the earliest, upon a decision of the Council taken under Article 136 of the Treaty (Art. 117 of the Act of Accession).[12]

By Article 118 the provisions of the third part of Protocol No. 22 on relations between the EEC and the Associated African and Malagasy States (AASM) and the independent developing Commonwealth countries are to apply to all Annex IV countries and territories, new and original.

By Article 119 (1) the Decision of September 29, 1970 (70/549, J.O. 1970, L 282/83) is not to apply in relations between the AASM and the new Member States. Paragraph 2 is comparable to Article 112, providing that products from the (original) AASM are to be subject to the pre-Accession arrangements on import into the new Member States and that products from the non-European territories listed in Article 24 (2) (*i.e.* new Annex IV countries and territories) are similarly to be subject to pre-Accession arrangements on import into the Six. Articles 110 and 114 are to apply.

---

12 These territories will thus be assimilated to the remaining " Annex IV " territories (*supra*, §§ 37–21 and 37–46). The present arrangements for Annex IV territories are governed by Decision 70/549, J.O. 1970, L 282/83 (as to which see further *infra*) which expires with Yaoundé II. New Member States are not required to accede to the parallel decision, 70/541, J.O. 1970, L 282/31, on ECSC products (Art. 117 (2)).

Article 119 as a whole is stated to apply until January 31, 1975, but if Article 115 (3) is applied, the date may be deferred in accordance with the procedure laid down in that article. This linkage is necessary since Decision 70/549 is linked with Yaoundé II.

Protocol No. 22 on relations between the EEC and the AASM and also the independent developing Commonwealth countries in Africa, the Indian Ocean, the Pacific and the Caribbean

37–66   Protocol No. 22 is divided into three parts. Part I relates to general provisions for ordering relations with Annex VI States [13] (listed *supra*). Part II relates specifically to Yaoundé-type association arrangements, and Part III to exporters of primary products.

37–67   *Part I of Protocol No. 22.* Under Paragraph 1 of Part I of Protocol No. 22, Annex VI countries are offered:

(1) association with the Community in the context of the agreement which will replace Yaoundé II;

(2) a special association agreement on the basis of Article 238 EEC (which involves reciprocal obligations);

(3) the conclusion of trade agreements with a view to facilitating and developing trade.

The Community invites immediate response to this offer, and in particular offers immediate participation in Yaoundé II for those opting for alternative (1) (para. 2). Mauritius signed an agreement with this end in view on May 28, 1972. The internal agreement on Yaoundé finance was amended at the same time. The arrangements were put into immediate effect by means of temporary measures, pending ratification.

It is recognised in paragraph 3 that special arrangements will be needed in the event that Botswana, Lesotho or Swaziland choose one of the first two alternatives, in view of the fact that they form part of a customs union with South Africa (first indent). The Community will require most-favoured-nation treatment, and rules on origin designed to avoid trade deflection (second and third indents).

37–68   *Part II of Protocol No. 22.* Part II of the Protocol lists certain factors to be taken into account on extending Yaoundé. Essentially, the widening of the arrangements should not lead to any weakening of Community relations with the existing AASM. The special nature of the existing arrangements is recognised, and the "*acquis*" is not to be impaired, while at the same time account will need to be taken of "the special economic conditions common to the independent developing Commonwealth countries" and of the existing AASM, "the experience acquired within the framework of association, the wishes of the Associated States and the consequences for those States of the introduction of the generalised preference scheme."

[13] Protocol No. 22, as printed in Cmnd. 4862–I, p. 98 refers to Annex V: this is clearly an error.

37–69   *Part III of Protocol No. 22.* It is stated in Part III of the Protocol that:

> " The Community will have as its firm purpose the safeguarding of the interests of all the countries referred to in this Protocol whose economies depend to a considerable extent on the export of primary products, and particularly of sugar.
>
> " The question of sugar will be settled within this framework, bearing in mind with regard to exports of sugar the importance of this product for the economies of several of these countries and of the Commonwealth countries in particular."

THE PARIS COMMUNIQUÉ

37–70   Paragraphs 10 to 14 of the Final Communiqué of the Paris Summit, of October 21, 1972 (Cmnd. 5109), set out a number of guidelines for Community action in foreign relations. Essential importance is attached to the association policy as confirmed in the Act of Accession, and to the commitments to the Mediterranean agreements, which should be the subject of an overall and balanced approach (para. 11). In the same perspective an overall policy on development co-operation is called for, involving in particular " trade promotion " efforts in the sense of the Commission Memorandum of February 2, 1972 (*supra,* § 37–55), improvement of the generalised preference scheme, increase in the volume of aid, and improvement in the terms of the aid (same para.).

With regard to industrial countries, the Community is determined to promote progressive trade liberalisation and to maintain constructive dialogue in particular with the United States, Japan and Canada. Major importance is attached to multilateral negotiations in the context of GATT. The Community institutions are invited to decide not later than July 1, 1973, on a global approach covering all aspects affecting trade (para. 12). The Community declares its readiness to seek a speedy solution to the problems facing Norway in its relations with the Community (same para.).

A common commercial policy is to be followed towards the countries of Eastern Europe from January 1, 1973. Co-operation founded on reciprocity is to be the key. The policy is expressed to be linked with the preparation and progress of the Conference on Security and Co-operation in Europe, to be held in 1973 (para. 13).

In paragraph 14 it is agreed that co-operation on foreign policy matters has gone well, and the Davignon Committee should meet four times a year in future rather than biannually.

Part 8

Part 5

CHAPTER 38

THE EUROPEAN COMMUNITIES ACT 1972

38–01 IT is not appropriate in a book of this kind to examine the legislation implementing Community law in the United Kingdom with a view to analysing its relationship to existing English law.[1] Rather it is the intention to examine the European Communities Act 1972 in order to see how it gives effect to Community law.

Section 1

38–02 Section 1 of the Act provides for its citation as the European Communities Act 1972, and goes on to lay down definitions and rules of interpretation. For the purpose of the 1972 Act and any future Act (whether of the United Kingdom or of Northern Ireland) " the Communities " is to mean the three existing Communities, and " the Treaties " or " the Community Treaties " is, subject to subsection (3) to mean the so-called pre-accession Treaties (defined in Part 1 of Sched. 1 [2]) taken with the Treaty of Accession and the Decision on Accession to the ECSC, together with " any other treaty entered into by any of the Communities, with or without any of the Member States, or entered into, as a treaty ancillary to any of the Treaties, by the United Kingdom " (subs. (2)). This latter part of the definition ensures that Community Treaties will all have a close link with the existing structure, for on the one hand the powers (express or implied) of the Communities to enter into treaties are based on the existing Community Treaties, and on the other, any other treaties entered into must be " ancillary " to some other Community Treaty. (See generally Chap. 37 on Community treaty-making powers.)

38–03 Section 1 (3) makes provision for procedures facilitating the identification of " Community Treaties." It provides for declarations by

---

[1] For this type of commentary the reader is referred to the annotations to the Act in Sweet and Maxwell's *Current Law Statutes,* and to " Constitutional Aspects of the Treaty and Legislation Relating to British Membership," by J. D. B. Mitchell, S. A. Kuipers and B. Gall, 9 C.M.L.Rev. 1972, 134 and " Parliamentary Sovereignty and the Primacy of European Community Law," by F. A. Trindade (1972) 35 M.L.R. 375.

[2] Part 1 of Sched. 1 to the Act lists the pre-accession treaties as being the EEC, ECSC and Euratom Treaties, the Convention on Certain Institutions Common to the Communities, the Merger and Budget Treaties, and " any treaty entered into before January 22, 1972 by any of the Communities (with or without any of the Member States) or, as a treaty ancillary to any treaty included in this Part of this Schedule, by the Member States (with or without any other country)." A more accurate description of the Treaties described in the Schedule might be " pre-signature Treaties," but " pre-accession Treaties " is the usual term applied. This latter category of treaties includes treaties listed in Cmnd. 4862–I, p. 137, and accepted by the new Member States under Arts. 3 and 4 of the Act of Accession—*cf.* § 2–12, *supra.*

Order in Council that a given treaty is to be regarded as a Community Treaty as defined in subsection (2). The Order is to be conclusive as to whether or not a treaty is a Community Treaty, and no treaty entered into by the United Kingdom after January 22, 1972, other than a pre-accession treaty to which the United Kingdom acceded on terms settled on or before that date may be regarded as a Community Treaty unless an Order is made in relation to it. Any Order made in respect of a treaty entered into by the United Kingdom after January 22, 1972, other than a pre-accession treaty to which the United Kingdom accedes on terms settled on or before that date, is to be subject to affirmative resolution of each House of Parliament. It is noteworthy that the affirmative resolution procedure is not made to apply to treaties concluded by the Community alone with third States, for such treaties are not " entered into by the United Kingdom." Such treaties are directly binding on Member States by virtue of Article 228 EEC (as to which see § 37–25) so that a requirement for an affirmative resolution would be inappropriate. ECSC and Euratom " Community alone " Treaties are likewise excluded from the approval procedure, but these Treaties do not contain a provision equivalent to Article 228 EEC, and do not therefore impose obligations on Member States in the absence of some domestic enactment giving them force as municipal law, and do not therefore affect the scope of Community law as received into English law under section 2 of the Act.

38–04   Subsection (4) provides that the term " treaty " used in the two preceding subsections " includes any international agreement, and any protocol or annex to a treaty or international agreement." Decisions of the representatives of the Member States are thus potentially within subsections (2) and (3) to the extent that they constitute international agreements. (See *supra*, § 8–13 on decisions of the representatives.)

Section 2

38–05   Article 2 of the Act of Accession provides that " the provisions of the original Treaties and the acts adopted by the institutions of the Communities shall be binding on the new Member States and shall apply in those States under the conditions laid down in those Treaties and in this Act." In so far as Article 2 of the Act of Accession creates rights and obligations at the domestic level, it is clear that legislative action is necessary. Section 2 (1) of the Act relates to such rights, etc., under Community law " as . . . are without further enactment to be given legal effect or used in the United Kingdom " (*i.e.* Regulations) while section 2 (2) provides for implementation of Community obligations imposed on, and enjoyment of rights of, the United Kingdom—*i.e.* under treaties, directives, etc. Certain specific obligations are dealt with by particular provisions of the Act.

Section 2 (1) provides that:

"All such rights, powers, liabilities, obligations and restrictions from time to time created or arising by or under the Treaties, and all such remedies and procedures from time to time provided for by or under the Treaties, as in accordance with the Treaties are without further enactment to be given legal effect or used in the United Kingdom shall be recognised and available in law, and be enforced, allowed and followed accordingly; and the expression ' enforceable Community right ' and similar expressions shall be read as referring to one to which this subsection applies."

Section 2 (1) provides for the reception of directly applicable Community law: it refers to "rights . . . liabilities, obligations and restrictions " which may be directly enjoyed by or imposed on Member States or private parties, and provides also for the recognition of, for example, Commission " powers " of control over cartels, and appears to allow for references by domestic courts to the Court of Justice under Article 177 ("remedies and procedures ").

38–06   Subsection (1) does not make Community law part of the law *of* the United Kingdom, but provides only that it is to be law *in* the United Kingdom. This recognises that Community law is a separate legal order. Thus, when United Kingdom courts have to consider a provision of directly applicable Community law, they will be considering not a provision having the character of a United Kingdom enactment, but a provision of a separate system of law which, by virtue of the European Communities Act, has become a new source of law in the United Kingdom. This applies as much to the provisions of instruments made under the Treaties as to the provisions of the Treaties themselves ("rights . . . created or arising by or under the Treaties, and . . . remedies . . . provided for by or under the Treaties "). It is clear that English courts will under subsection (1) be obliged to take account of Community law as interpreted by the Court of Justice, for the formula " as in accordance with the Treaties are without further enactment to be given legal effect or used in the United Kingdom shall be recognised and available in law, and be enforced, allowed and followed accordingly," carries the implication that the Treaties are to be received as interpreted in accordance with the Treaties themselves. This is amplified by section 3 (1) of the Act—*infra.*

Section 2 (2)

38–07   Certain specific provisions of Community law which are not directly applicable but which are nevertheless to be given effect to in municipal law are dealt with elsewhere in the Act, or in other Acts (Finance Act 1972 for VAT). Section 2 (2) confers a quite general power to give effect to present and future Community law which is not directly applicable, and to deal with matters supplementary to such rights and obligations or to directly applicable Community law, present and future. Under this subsection,

> "Subject to Schedule 2 to this Act, at any time after its passing Her Majesty may by Order in Council, and any designated Minister or department may by regulations, make provision—
>
> (a) for the purpose of implementing any Community obligation of the United Kingdom, or enabling any such obligation to be implemented, or of enabling any rights enjoyed or to be enjoyed by the United Kingdom under or by virtue of the Treaties to be exercised; or
>
> (b) for the purpose of dealing with matters arising out of or related to any such obligation or rights or the coming into force, or the operation from time to time, of subsection (1) above; . . ."

Broadly, Schedule 2 to the Act excludes from the ambit of subsection (2) power (a) to impose or increase taxation, (b) to take retroactive measures, (c) to sub-delegate powers to legislate (with minor exceptions), (d) to create new serious criminal offences.

An Order in Council or Regulation, when contained in a statutory instrument, made under section 2 (2) otherwise than by modification or extension of an existing power is subject to disallowance if made without prior affirmative resolution (paras. 2 and 3 of Sched. 2). The choice in the matter lies with the executive.

38-08 Orders and Regulations may be made under subsection (2) at any time after the Royal Assent, and thus before accession.

Orders or Regulations made under subsection 2 may include Orders or Regulations for the purpose of implementing any Community obligation of the United Kingdom, defined by Part II of Schedule 1 as meaning "any obligation created or arising by or under the Treaties, whether an enforceable Community obligation or not" (*i.e.* including directives). The phrase "enabling any such obligation to be implemented" contemplates *inter alia* the amendment of existing United Kingdom law. Section 2 (4) *infra*, and also Schedule 2, para. 1 (2), make it quite clear that Orders or Regulations made under section 2 (2) can modify existing legislation, or the common law.

38-09 Section 2 (2) (b) is designed to enable the United Kingdom to take all necessary residual action and make any necessary adjustments. It also provides for the making of subsidiary rules for supplementing directly applicable law where this is required or appears necessary.

All action taken under subsection (2) (b) must, however, show some link with matters falling within subsection (2) (a) or section 2 (1).

The last phrase of section 2 (2) of the Act provides that:

> "in the exercise of any statutory power or duty, including any power to give directions or to legislate by means of orders, rules,

regulations or other subordinate instrument, the person entrusted with the power or duty may have regard to the objects of the Communities and to any such obligation or rights as aforesaid."

This is at first sight a rather curious formulation: a discretion is given rather than a duty imposed to have regard to the objects of the Community (*cf.* Arts. 2 and 3 EEC) or to the Community obligations imposed or rights to be enjoyed (*cf.* working of section 2 (2) (*a*)). The phrase is designed to enable persons entrusted with a power or duty to have regard to Community obligations where this would not otherwise be permitted under the empowering statute. The duty to comply with Community law is imposed by the international obligations arising from membership of the Communities.

38–10 Section 2 (4) of the Act reads as follows [3]:

[1] " The provision that may be made under subsection (2) above includes, subject to Schedule 2 to this Act, any such provision (of any such extent) as might be made by Act of Parliament,

[2] and any enactment passed or to be passed, other than one contained in this Part of this Act, shall be construed and have effect subject to the foregoing provisions of this section;

[3] but, except as may be provided by any Act passed after this Act, Schedule 2 shall have effect in connection with the powers conferred by this and the following sections of this Act to make Orders in Council and regulations."

It follows from phrase [1] of the subsection that Orders or Regulations made under section 2 (2) may amend the common law and repeal or amend Acts of Parliament, subject to the limitation laid down in Schedule 2, already referred to. Phrase [1] is designed also to ensure that where the power of legislation by statute is wider than that inherent in subordinate powers, the Orders or Regulations made under this Act may be considered to have equal scope—thus the Orders or Regulations may have extraterritorial effect.

It is already provided that Schedule 2 applies at least to provisions made under subsection (2); phrase [3] reiterates this in part, providing that Schedule 2 applies to powers to make Orders or Regulations conferred by section 2 and subsequent sections, and that while Schedule 2 is not amendable by Order or Regulation, it may be amended, or its application suspended, by statute. Phase [3] also avoids the implication that phrase [2] prevents the amendment of Schedule 2, for phrase [2] requires " any enactment passed or to be passed " other than Part I of the Act is to be " construed and have effect subject to the foregoing provisions of this section."

---

[3] As set out in the statute, the subsection is in fact printed as a continuous un-paragraphed block of print: it is set out here in three numbered phrases so as to make it more readily apparent that the subsection contains three separate themes.

38–11   Phrase [2] is clearly designed to ensure supremacy of Community law over domestic law in so far as this is possible. It certainly assures supremacy over earlier domestic law (as would the normal rules of statutory interpretation). Its effect upon later domestic law is less clear-cut. The phrase must be taken as a rule of construction and interpretation in cases of doubt, thus limiting scope for potential conflicts, but where there is a clear conflict between a later domestic law and this statute, commentators consider that the later domestic law must prevail. This is in keeping with traditional constitutional theory (Mitchell *et al.*, *op. cit.*; Trindade *op. cit.*, speech of Sir Geoffrey Howe (the Solicitor-General) to Chatham House Conference on Community law on October 5, 1972).

Section 2 (3), (5) and (6)

38–12   Section 2 (3) is largely self-explanatory:

" There shall be charged on and issued out of the Consolidated Fund or, if so determined by the Treasury, the National Loans Fund the amounts required to meet any Community obligation to make payments to any of the Communities or Member States, or any Community obligation in respect of contributions to the capital or reserves of the European Investment Bank or in respect of loans to the Bank, or to redeem any notes or obligations issued or created in respect of any such Community obligation; and, except as otherwise provided by or under any enactment,—

(*a*) any other expenses incurred under or by virtue of the Treaties or this Act by any Minister of the Crown or government department may be paid out of moneys provided by Parliament; and

(*b*) any sums received under or by virtue of the Treaties or this Act by any Minister of the Crown or government department, save for such sums as may be required for disbursements permitted by any other enactment, shall be paid into the Consolidated Fund or, if so determined by the Treasury, the National Loans Fund."

Subsections (5) and (6) relate to legislation for Northern Ireland, and for the British Islands and Gibraltar respectively.

Section 3

38–13   Section 3 (1) provides:

" For the purposes of all legal proceedings any question as to the meaning or effect of any of the Treaties, or as to the validity, meaning or effect of any Community instrument, shall be treated as a question of law (and, if not referred to the European Court, be for determination as such in accordance with the principles laid down by and any relevant decision of the European Court)."

The requirement that questions as to the interpretation of Community law be treated as a question of law ousts the normal United Kingdom requirement that foreign law be treated as a question of fact, and thus be proved like any other fact in issue. Particularly important, avenues of appeal and judicial review applicable to questions of law will be available on questions of Community law. The phrase in brackets makes it clear that decisions of the Court of Justice have authority before United Kingdom courts (see also subs. (2) *infra*). Procedural provision for reference to the Court of Justice of questions of interpretation is to be made by Order in Council under section 2 (2). The obligations of Article 177 of the Treaty of Rome are already imported by section 2 (1).

The two parts of subsection (1) do not of course make Community law a part of United Kingdom law, but only law in the United Kingdom (see also comments on section 2).

Section 3 (2)

Subsection (2) provides:

" Judicial notice shall be taken of the Treaties, of the Official Journal of the Communities and of any decision of, or expression of opinion by, the European Court on any such question as aforesaid; and the Official Journal shall be admissible as evidence of any instrument or other act thereby communicated of any of the Communities or of any Community institution."

It is thought that this subsection is largely self-explanatory, but it should be pointed out that the inclusion of " expression of opinion " is intended to make it clear that judicial notice is to be taken of all parts of the " *motifs* " of a judgment of the Court of Justice. This is important since the distinction between *ratio decidendi* and *obiter dictum* is not formally observed in continental jurisprudence. " Expression of opinion " covers the whole " *motifs*," and " decision " covers the " operative part of the judgment " (" *dispositif* ").

Section 3 (3)

38–14   Subsection (3) concerned with proof of Community instruments and other documents provides:

"Evidence of any instrument issued by a Community institution, including any judgment or order of the European Court, or of any other document in the custody of a Community institution, or any entry in or extract from such a document, may be given in any legal proceedings by production of a copy certified as a true copy by an official of that institution; and any document purporting to be such a copy shall be received in evidence without proof of the official position or handwriting of the person signing the certificate."

Such provision is necessary since not all Community instruments are published in the Official Journal; Regulations only are required to be so published (see *supra*, § 8–08).

Section 3 (4)

38–15   Subsection (4) provides for proof of Community instruments by means of copies printed by the Queen's Printer or, in the case of instruments in the custody of a government department, copies certified by an official.

Under subsection (5):

> " In any legal proceedings in Scotland evidence of any matter given in a manner authorised by this section shall be sufficient evidence of it."

PART II OF THE ACT

Section 4

38–16   Section 4 of the Act provides for various amendments to and repeals of, existing legislation consequential upon acceptance by the United Kingdom of Community obligations. The necessary repeals are listed in Schedule 3 (including repeals of provisions in the coal and steel statutes), and the amendments in Schedule 4. The repeals and amendments are in many cases to take effect from days to be appointed. The enactments affected include statutes dealing with customs matters, import duties, sugar, seeds, food and drugs, horticultural produce, fertilisers and feeding stuffs, animal health, plant health and road vehicles and road transport.

Section 5

38–17   Section 5 of the Act, in conjunction with Part I of Schedule 3 and Part A of Schedule 4 deals with import duties and customs matters, consequential upon acceptance by the United Kingdom of Community obligations. The structure of the section is as follows: subsections (1) and (2) deal with automatic application of Community customs duty after the end of the transitional period laid down in the Act of Accession. Subsections (3) and (4) make mechanical adaptations to existing United Kingdom law. Subsection (5) provides for transitional powers under the Import Duties Act 1958. Subsection (6) provides generally for reliefs, while subsections (7) and (8) provide for the application of Community control procedures.

Subsection (1) provides that after the expiry of the transitional period set out in the Act of Accession (on July 1, 1977) " there shall be charged, levied, collected and paid on goods imported into the United Kingdom such Community customs duty, if any, as is for the time being applicable in accordance with the Treaties." The further provision for such other duty, if any, as may be fixed where the CCT does not apply is directed primarily to the ECSC tariff which is separate from the CCT. The CCT is supposedly a complete system, which admits of no tariffs outside its scope other than the ECSC tariff.

Subsection (2) provides for exceptional levy or exemption of customs duty even after the transitional period where so permitted or required by Community law—*e.g.* under safeguard mechanisms (*supra*, § 21–17), tariff quotas (*supra*, § 21–17), or suspension provisions (*supra*, § 21–20).

Subsections (3) and (4) make mechanical provision in relation to domestic legislation. Subsection (5) provides that so long as section 1 of the Import Duties Act 1958 remains in force (that Act is, under Schedule 3, to be repealed as from a date to be appointed: this is likely to coincide with the end of the transitional period) the Import Duties Act is to have effect subject to certain modifications, notably the power under section 1 to impose duties is to include the power to impose duties with a view to securing compliance with any Community obligation.

Subsection (6) provides for reliefs from import duties " having regard to the practices adopted or to be adopted in other member States, whether by law or administrative action and whether or not in conformity with Community obligations."

Subsection (7) provides for co-operation with other customs services on matters of mutual concern for the purpose of implementing Community obligations, notably in relation to control of Community transit (Regulation 542/69: *supra*, § 21–06), including the compensatory amount system (*supra*, § 22–37), and for the control of fraud, etc. (*supra*, § 21–06), notably in the context of the Rome Customs Convention (*supra*, § 21–06).

Subsection (8) provides for verification of certificates of origin and of movement certificates, required in connection with exports to third countries and with Community movement (*supra*, §§ 37–29 and 21–06).

Under subsection (9) " subsections (7) and (8) shall have effect as if contained in the Customs and Excise Act 1952."

Agriculture: sections 6 and 7

38–18   Section 6 (1) of the Act sets up an Intervention Board for Agricultural Produce to implement the CAP; the Board is to be " in charge of a government department " and is to be subject to the direction and control of the agricultural Ministers. The section makes provision for the collection of agricultural levies, and for commodities to be removed from the scope of the present agricultural guarantee system as the Community system replaces it (subs. (7)).

Most notably, the levies are, under subsection (5) to be dealt with " as if they were Community customs duties "; and the Commissioners of Customs and Excise are thus to be responsible for the collection and administration of the levy system. Levy is defined as including a measure having an equivalent effect to a customs duty (subs. (8)).

Section 7 makes the necessary changes to existing legislation to enable compliance with the Community sugar rules (*supra*, § 22–17).

Our existing arrangements turn upon the Commonwealth Sugar Agreement which expires at the end of 1974.

Section 8

38–19   Section 8 ensures compliance with the Council directive on the removal of restraints on the right of establishment and the freedom to provide services in the film industry (Directive 63/607, J.O. 1963, 2661). Notably it amends the British Quota System. In effect Community films become quota films. In compliance with the directive, section 8 (4) provides for exemption in respect of " foreign language " cinemas from the quota requirements. Such cinemas do not appear to be at all usual in this country.

The section does not cover payments from the Eady Levy. It is not yet clear whether any changes in the system will be required or not. The registration of Community films as quota films effects some broadening of the system.

Section 9

38–20   Section 9 implements Directive 68/151, J.O. 1968, L. 65/8 (*supra*, § 31–04) in so far as it is not already implemented in English law. The references to the measurement of time in section 9 (4) reflect Regulation 1182/71, J.O. 1971, L 124/1, determining the rules applicable to periods, dates and time limits laid down in Acts of the Council and the Commission.

Section 10

38–21   Section 10 gives effect to the United Kingdom obligations in respect to competition law. Primarily subsection (1) is designed to delineate the division of functions between the Restrictive Practices Court and the Community, having regard on the one hand to regulations on competition and on the other to exemption decisions. Essentially the fact that one agreement is void or exempted does not take it out of the Restrictive Practices Court's jurisdiction, but the Court may decline or postpone exercise of its jurisdiction, having regard to exemptions or authorisations (whether individual or general) and the Registrar may refrain from taking proceedings. The United Kingdom Restrictive Practices authorities may therefore operate the " *double barrière* " (*supra*, § 28–82) if they wish.

Section 10 (2) provides for establishing a system for collecting information on Community action taken against or in respect of an individual firm, and for the recording of such information in the Restrictive Practices Register. Agreements authorised under Article 65 ECSC are exempted from this registration requirement.

Section 10 (3) provides for the disclosure of information obtained under the Act pursuant to a Community obligation—*i.e.* pursuant to a request from the Commission under Article 11 of Regulation 17 (*supra*, § 28–85).

Section 11

38–22 Section 11 (1) deals with perjury before the Court of Justice. Provision for hearing witnesses is made by Article 25 of the EEC Protocol on the Court of Justice (Art. 26 Euratom, Art. 28 ECSC) and Articles 47 and 49 of the Rules of Procedure. Article 27 of the EEC Statute (Art. 28 Euratom, *cf.* Art. 28 ECSC) provides:

> "A Member State shall treat any violation of an oath by a witness or expert in the same manner as if the offence has been committed before one of its courts with jurisdiction in civil proceedings. At the instance of the Court, the Member State concerned shall prosecute the offender before its competent court."

Notification of witnesses' misconduct is governed by Article 109 of the Rules of Procedure and Articles 6 and 7 of the Supplementary Rules of February 5, 1962.

Section 11 (2) provides penalties for the disclosure of Euratom classified information to unauthorised persons, pursuant to Article 194 (1), second sub-para. Euratom, which states:

> "Each Member State shall treat any infringement of this obligation as an act prejudicial to its rules on secrecy and as one falling, both as to merits and jurisdiction, within the scope of its laws relating to acts prejudicial to the security of the State or to disclosure of professional secrets. Such Member States shall, at the request of any Member State concerned or of the Commission, prosecute anyone within its jurisdiction who commits such an infringement."

Although this subsection is to be construed with the Official Secrets Act 1911, and although the Official Secrets Acts are to have effect as though this subsection were incorporated in those Acts, the effect is not such as to make an offence under subsection (2) an offence under the 1911 Act, although subsidiary offences and penalties are attracted, notably section 2 (2) on receiving information communicated in contravention of the Act.

Section 12

38–23 Section 12 provides for the disclosure to a Community institution of estimates, returns and information which may be disclosed to a government department or to a Minister in charge, pursuant to section 9 of the Statistics of Trade Act 1947 or section 80 of the Agriculture Act 1947.

BIBLIOGRAPHY

General Bibliographies

Cosgrove, C. A. *A reader's guide to Britain and the European Communities.* London: Chatham House/PEP, 1970.

Publications juridiques concernant l'intégration Européenne. 1966 and annual supplements. Luxembourg, Service de Documentation de la Cour de Justice des Communautés Européennes.

Bibliographie de jurisprudence européenne concernant les décisions judiciaires relatives aux traités instituant les Communautés européennes. 1965 and annual supplements. Luxembourg, Service de Documentation de la Cour de Justice des Communautés Européennes.

Catalogue des publications 1952–1971. Communautés Européennes, Brussels/Luxembourg, 1972.

Where to find your Community law. London: British Institute of International and Comparative Law, 1972.

A brief Bibliography of European Integration. London: European Communities Information Office, ISEC/B3/72, January 1972.

Selected Bibliography of European law. Strasbourg: Council of Europe, April 1971.

Periodicals

The following are the main specialist periodicals:

Cahiers de Droit Européen (Brussels: Larcier)
Common Market Law Review (London: Stevens)
Europarecht (Munich: Verlag C. H. Beck)
Journal of Common Market Studies (Oxford: Basil Blackwell)
Revue du Marché Commun (Paris: Revue du Marché Commun)
Revue Trimestrielle de Droit Européen (Paris: Editions Sirey)
Rivista di Diritto Europeo (Rome: Rivista di Diritto Europeo)

Useful articles on Community topics also appear in:

Journal of World Trade Law (Twickenham, Middlesex: Journal of World Trade Law)
Neue juristische Wochenschrift (Munich: Beck'sche Verlagsbuch-Handlung)
Sociaal-economische wetgeving (Zwolle: Pjeemk-Willink)

Many of the journals on international law, and many of the more general legal and economic journals carry occasional articles on Community topics. The following news journals are also useful:

Agence Europe (Brussels/Luxembourg: Agence Europe)
Communauté européenne—Informations (Paris: Bureau d'information des CE)
European Community (London: European Community Press and Information Service)
30 jours d'Europe (Paris: Bureau d'information des CE)

General

Britain and the EEC: the economic background, 1967 (H.M.S.O.).

Legal and constitutional implications of United Kingdom membership of the European Communities. Cmnd. 3301, 1967.

Membership of the European Communities. Cmnd. 3269, 1967.

Britain and the European Communities: an economic assessment. Cmnd. 4289, 1970.

The United Kingdom and the European Communities. Cmnd. 4715, 1971.

479

Britain and the European Communities. Background to the Negotiations. London, H.M.S.O., 1962.

BRUGMANS   *L'idée européenne 1920–1970.* Bruges: de Tempel, 1970.

CAMPS, M.   *Britain and The European Community 1955–1963.* London: Oxford University Press, 1964.

CAMPS, M.   *European Unification in the Sixties.* New York: McGraw-Hill, 1966.

CAMPS, M.   *What kind of Europe?* London, 1965.

CARTOU, LOUIS   *Organisations européennes* (2nd ed.). Paris: Dalloz, 1967.

DE ROUGEMONT   *The idea of Europe.* London: Macmillan, 1966.

KITZINGER, UWE   *The Challenge of the Common Market.* Oxford: Blackwells, 1966.

LINDBERG, L. N. and SCHEINGOLD, S. A.   *Europe's would be polity.* New York: Prentice Hall, 1970.

MAYNE, RICHARD   *The Institutions of the European Community.* London: PEP European series No. 8, 1968.

MAYNE, RICHARD   *The Recovery of Europe.* London: Weidenfeld & Nicolson, 1970.

MEADE, JAMES E.   *U.K. Commonwealth and Common Market: A Reappraisal.* London: Institute of Economic Affairs, 1962.

MITCHELL, J. D. B.   " What do you want to be inscrutable for, Marcia?" or The White Paper on the Legal and Constitutional Implications of United Kingdom Membership of the European Communities, 5 C.M.L.Rev. 1967, 112–132.

PALMER, MICHAEL and LAMBERT, JOHN   *European Unity. A survey of the European Organisations.* London: Unwin/PEP, 1968.

PINTO, ROGER   *Cours d'organisations européennes.* Paris: Les Cours de Droit, 1960–1961.

PINTO, ROGER   *Les organisations européennes* (3rd ed.). Paris: Payot, 1965.

REUTER, PAUL   *Organisations européennes.* Paris: Presses Universitaires de France, 1965, Collection " Themis."

ROBERTSON, A. H.   *European Institutions* (3rd ed.). London: Stevens, 1973.

SERVAN-SCHREIBER, J.-J.   *The American Challenge.* London: Pelican, 1969.

SPAAK, P.-H.   *Combats inachevés.* Paris: Fayard, 1969.

STEIN, E. and HAY, P.   *Law and Institutions in the Atlantic Area.* New York: Bobbs Merrill, 1967. 2 vols.

SWANN, D.   *The Economics of the Common Market.* Penguin modern economics (2nd ed.). 1971.

TRINDADE, F. A.   " Parliamentary Sovereignty and the Primacy of European Community Law " (1972) 34 Mod.L.Rev. 375.

URI, P. (Ed.)   *From Commonwealth to Common Market.* London: Penguin, 1968.

WEIL, GORDON L.   *A Handbook of the European Economic Community.* New York/Washington/London: Praeger, 1965.

WORKS ON COMMUNITY LAW

Works covering several or all aspects [1]

BATHURST, M., SIMMONDS, K., MARCH HUNNINGS, N. and WELCH, J. (eds.)   *Legal Problems of an enlarged European Community.* London: Stevens, 1972.

BRINKHORST, L. J. and SCHERMERS, H. G.   *Judicial Remedies in the European Communities: A Case Book.* Deventer: Kluwer, London: Stevens, South Hackensack, N.Y.: Rothman, 1969.

CAMPBELL, ALAN   *Common Market Law.* London/New York: Longmans/Oceana, 1969. Two vols. and annual supplements.

CATALANO, NICOLA   *Manuel de droit des Communautés Européennes,* 2nd edition. Collection Eurolibri. T.9. Paris: Dalloz et Sirey, 1965.

Droit des Communautés européennes; sous la direction de W. J. Ganshof van der Meersch. Bruxelles: Larcier, 1969, Les Novelles.

GIDE, LOYRETTE J. and NOUEL, P. H.   *Dictionnaire du Marché Commun* (mise à jour). Paris: Dictionnaires Joly, 1968.

---

[1] *N.B.* Works referred to under this head are not referred to under the specialised heads.

GROEBEN, HANS VON DER and BOECKH, HANS VON *Kommentar zum EWG-Vertrag.* Bd. I, II. Baden/Bonn/Frankfurt: Lutzeyer, 1958.

KAPTEYN, P. J. G. and VERLOREN, VAN THEMAAT, P. *Inleiding tot het recht van de Europese Gemeenschappen.* Handboek voor de Europese Gemeenschappen, Deventer: Kluwer, Alphen a/d/Rijn/Brussels: Samson, 1970.

MEGRET, J., LOUIS, J. V., VIGNES, D. and WAELBROECK, M. *Le droit de la Communauté économique européenne. Vol. I—Préambule—principes—libre circulation des marchandises. Vol. II—Agriculture. Vol. III—Libre circulation des travailleurs—établissements et services—capitaux—transports. Vol. IV— Concurrence.* Brussels: Presses Universitaires de Bruxelles, 1970. (Institut d'Etudes Européennes de l'Université de Bruxelles).

Zur Integration Europas.—Festschrift Ophüls.

QUADRI, ROLANDO, MONACO, RICCARDO and TRABUCCHI, ALBERTO *Trattato istitutivo della Communita Economica Europea—Commentario.* Vol. I: Art. 1–84, Vol. II: Art. 85–136, Vol. III: Art. 137–248, Vol. IV: Appendice—Indice. Milan: Giuffrè, 1965.

SCHRANS, GUY *Inleiding tot het europees economisch recht.* Ghent/Louvain: E Story-Scientia, 1969.

WOHLFARTH, ERNST, EVERLING, ULRICH, GLAESNER, HANS JOACHIM and SPRUNG, RUDOLF *Die Europäische Wirtschaftsgemeinschaft. Kommentar zum Vertrag.* Berlin/Frankfurt: Vahlen, 1960.

General aspects

Communication de la Commission sur les reflections d'ordre juridique et les indications d'ordre technique susceptibles d'éclairer la portée du paragraphe 7 de l'article 8 du traité instituant la Communauté Economique Européenne. Brussels: Commission des Communautés Européennes, 1969.

Document du parlement européen: Rapport fait au nom de la commission juridique sur la portée juridique et politique de l'article 8, paragraphes 5, 6 et 7, du traité de la CEE. Rap. DEHOUSSE, FERNAND: Doc. No. 185, January, 1969.

DUMON, FREDERIC "La responsabilité extracontractuelle des Communautés Européennes et de leurs agents. (Art 40 CECA, 215 CEE et 188 CEEA)," C.D.E. 1969, 3–48.

GORI, PAOLO "Les clauses de sauvegarde des Traités CECA et CEE," Heule (Belgium): U.G.A., 1967.

LESGUILLONS, HENRY *L'application d'un traité-fondation: le traité instituant la CEE.* Paris: L.G.D.J., 1968.

MARENCO, GIULIANO "Les conditions d'application de l'article 235 du Traité CEE," R.M.C. 1970, 147–157.

MUCH, WALTER *Die Haftung der Europäischen Gemeinschaften für das rechtswidrige Verhalten ihrer Organe.* Cologne: Carl Heymanns Verlag, 1967.

MUELLER-HEIDELBERG, TILL *Schutzklauseln im Europäischen Gemeinschaften. (mit Ausnahme des Agarrechts).* Hamburg: Fundament-Verlag Dr. Sasse & Co., 1970, Schriftenreihe zum Europäischen Integration, No. 4.

SALMON, J. A. and TORRELLI, MAURICE "La représentation juridique des Communautés Européennes," R.M.C., 1968, No. 114, 815–822.

SETTEN, G. VAN *Ontsnappingsclausules en het recht van de lid-staten der EEG. De bescherming van publieke en private belangen.* Deventer: Kluwer, 1966, Europese Monographieen, no. 6: *De rechtsorde der Europese Gemeenschappen tussen het internationale en het nationale recht,* pp. 135–159.

TORRELLI, MAURICE *L'individu et le droit de la Communauté économique européenne.* Montreal: Les Presses de l'Université de Montréal, 1970.

THE JURISDICTION OF THE COURT OF JUSTICE

ALEXANDER, WILLY *Questions et réponses préjudicielles dans la procédure de la Cour de Justice des Communautés Européennes.* Brussels: Institut d'Etudes Européennes, 1964 Publications de l'Institut d'Etudes Européennes, No. 8.

ALEXANDER, WILLY "Questions préjudicielles: l'application récente de l'article 177 C.E.E. par la Cour de Justice et par les juridictions nationales," C.D.E. 1965, No. 1, 47–58.

ANGULO, MANUEL P. and DAWSON, FRANK G. "Access by natural and legal persons to the Court of Justice of the European Communities," 5 C.M.L.Rev. 1967, 583–649.

BEBR, G. *Judicial Control of the European Communities.* London: Stevens, 1962.

BEBR, G. "Judicial Remedy of Private Parties against Normative Acts of the European Communities: The Role of the Exception of Illegality," 4 C.M.L.Rev. 1966, 7–31.

CAHIER, PHILIPPE "Le recours en constatation de manquements des Etats membres devant la Cour des Communautés Européennes," C.D.E., 1967, 123–162.

CATALANO, NICOLA "Les voies de recours ouvertes aux personnes physiques ou morales contre les actes non réglementaires de la Commission C.E.E.," S.E.W., 1965, 526–566.

COLIN, JEAN-PIERRE *Le Gouvernement des Juges dans les Communautés Européennes. T. I: Les fonctions de la Cour de Justice des Communautés Européennes. T. II: La politique jurisprudentielle de la Cour de Justice des Communautés Européennes.* Nancy: Faculté de Droit et des Sciences Economiques, Université de Nancy, 1963.

DAIG, HANS-WOLFRAM *Zum Klagerecht von Privatpersonen nach Art. 173 Abs. 2 EWG-, 146 Abs. 2 EAG-Vertrag.* Festschrift für Otto Riese. Karlsruhe: Verlag C. F. Muller, 1964, 187–219.

DELVAUX, LOUIS *La Cour de Justice de la Communauté Européenne du Charbon et de l'Acier. Exposé sommaire des principes.* Paris: L.G.D.J., 1956.

Document du parlement européen: Rapport fait au nom de la commission juridique sur la protection juridique des personnes privées dans les Communautés européennes. Rap. DERINGER, A.: Doc. No. 39, May 1967.

DUMON, F. *Le renvoi préjudiciel.* Bruges: de Tempel, 1965. Cahiers de Bruges, N.S. 14. *Droit communautaire et droit national*, 197–278.

EYNARD, SERGIO F. "L'article 169 du traité de Rome: douze ans d'application de la procédure d'infraction à l'égard des Etats membres de la C.E.E.," R.D.E., 1970, 99–125.

FERRIERE, GEORGES "Le contrôle de la légalité des actes étatiques par la Cour de Justice des Communautés européennes," R.G.D.P., 1967, 879–1008.

FROMONT, MICHEL "L'influence du droit français et du droit allemand sur les conditions de recevabilité du recours en annulation devant la Cour de Justice des Communautés européennes," R.T.D.E. 1966, 47–65.

GOFFIN, LEON "Quelles sont les juridictions belges qui sont tenues au renvoi préjudiciel devant la Cour de Justice?" J.T. 1968, No. 4629, 541–543.

GREEN, ANDREW WILSON *Political integration by jurisprudence. The work of the Court of Justice of the European Communities in European political integration.* Leyden: Sijthoff, 1969.

GREMENTIERI, VALERIO *texte français* "Le statut des juges de la Cour de Justice des Communautés européennes." R.T.D.E. 1967, 817–830.

KNAUB, GILBERT "La procédure devant la Cour de Justice des Communautés européennes," R.T.D.E. 1967, 269.

KOVAR, ROBERT "Le droit des personnes privées à obtenir devant la Cour des Communautés le respect du droit communautaire par les Etats membres," A.F.D.I. 1966, 509–543.

MASHAW, J. L. "Ensuring the observance of law in the interpretation and application of the EEC Treaty: the role and functioning of the renvoi d'interpretation under Article 177," 7 C.M.L.Rev. 1970, 258–285.

MERCHIERS, LAURENT "Rapport fait, au nom de la commission juridique du parlement européen sur les problèmes posés par l'application de l'article 177 du traité C.E.E.," *Parlement européen*, 1969/70, Doc. No. 94.

MERTENS DE WILMERS, J. and VEROUGSTRAET "Proceedings against Member States for failure to fulfil their obligations," 5 C.M.L.Rev. 1970, 385–406.

NERI, SERGIO "Le recours en annulation dans les Communautés Européennes: rôle et limites," R.M.C. 1967, 452–465.

PEPY, ANDRÉ "Le rôle des juridictions nationales dans l'application de l'article 177 et la jurisprudence de la Cour de Justice," C.D.E. 1966, 21–39.

RASQUIN, GERARD and CHEVALLIER, ROGER-MICHEL "l'article 173, alinéa 2 du traité C.E.E.," R.T.D.E. 1966, 31–46.

REEPINGHEN and ORIANNE *La Procédure devant la Cour de Justice des Communautés Européennes.* Brussels/Paris: Larcier/Dalloz, 1961.

REUTER, E. "Le recours en carence de l'article 175 du traité de la C.E.E. dans la jurisprudence de la Cour de Justice des Communautés Européennes," C.D.E. 1972, 159.

RICHEMONT, JEAN DE *Communauté Européenne du Charbon et de l'Acier. La Cour de Justice, Code annoté.* Paris: Librairie du Journal des Notaires et des Avocats, 1954.

"Le rôle de la Cour de Justice des Communautés économiques dans l'application de l'article 177 du Traité de Rome," C.D.E. 1966, 459–489.

SOLDATOS, PANAYOTIS "L'introuvable recours en carence devant la Cour de Justice des Communautés Européennes," C.D.E. 1969, 313–334.

VALENTINE, D. G. *The Court of Justice of the European Coal and Steel Community.* The Hague: Nijhoff, 1955.

VALENTINE, D. G. *The Court of Justice of the European Communities.* Vols. I, II. London: Stevens, 1965.

VANDERSANDEN, GEORGES "Le recours en intervention devant la Cour de Justice des Communautés européennes," R.T.D.E. 1969, 1–27.

VERPRAET, GEORGES and LECERF, JEAN *L'Europe judiciaire.* Brussels: Communautés Européennes, Presse et Information, 1970.

WAELBROECK, MICHEL "La notion d'acte susceptible de recours dans la jurisprudence de la Cour de Justice des Communautés Européennes," C.D.E. 1965, 225–236.

WALL, EDWARD H. *The Court of Justice of the European Communities. Jurisdiction and Procedure.* London: Butterworths, 1966.

WEBER, YVES "La preuve du détournement de pouvoir devant la Cour de Justice des Communautés Européennes," R.T.D.E. 1967, 507–552.

COMMUNITY LAW AND NATIONAL LAW: DIRECT APPLICABILITY: SUPREMACY

BEBR, GERHARD "Directly applicable provisions of Community law: the development of a Community concept" [1970] I.C.L.Q. 257.

BEBR, GERHARD "Law of the European Communities and Municipal Law" (1971) 33 Mod.L.Rev. 481.

CONSTANTINESCO, LÉONTIN-JEAN *Die unmittelbare Anwendbarkeit von Gemeinschaftsnormen und der Rechtsschutz von Einzelpersonen im Recht der EWG.* Baden-Baden: Nomos Verlagsgesellschaft, 1969, Schriftenreihe zum Handbuch für Europäische Wirtschaft, Bd. 40.

CONSTANTINIDES-MEGRET, COLETTE *Le droit de la Communauté Economique Européenne et l'ordre juridique des Etats membres.* Paris: L.G.D.J., 1967.

Document du parlement européen: Rapport fait au nom de la commission juridique sur l'application du droit communautaire par les Etats membres. Rap. DEHOUSSE, F.: Doc. No. 38, May 1967.

Document du parlement européen: Rapport fait au nom de la commission juridique sur la primauté du droit communautaire sur droit des Etats membres. Rap. DEHOUSSE, F.: Doc. No. 43, May 1965. Rap. comp. WEINKAMM, OTTO: Doc. No. 95, October 1965.

DONNER, ANDRÉ "Les rapports entre la compétence de la Cour de Justice des Communautés Européennes et les tribunaux internes," R.C.A.D.I. 1965, 5–58.

Droit communautaire de droit national. Bruges: de Tempel, 1965.

DUMON, F. "La notion de 'disposition directement applicable' en droit européen," C.D.E. 1968, 369.

"Gemeinschaftsrecht und nationale Rechte," K.S.E. Vol. 13, Cologne: Carl Heymann, 1971.

LAGRANGE, M. "The European Court of Justice and National Courts. The Theory of the Acte Claire: a bone of contention or a source of unity?" 8 1971, C.M.L.Rev. 313–324.

LECOURT, ROBERT *Le juge devant le marché commun.* Geneva: Institut Universitaire de Hautes Etudes Internationales, 1970 (Etudes et Travaux No. 10).

Le juge national et le droit communautaire. Leyden/Brussels: Sijthoff/Larcier, 1966.

MERTENS DE WILMERS, JOSSE "De directe werking van het europese recht," S.E.W. 1969, No. 2, 62–81.

PESCATORE, PIERRE "Les droits de l'homme et l'intégration européenne," C.D.E. 1968, 629–657.

PESCATORE, PIERRE "Fundamental Rights and Freedoms in the system of the European Communities," A.J.C.L. 1970, 343–351.

PRASCH, GERHARD *Die unmittelbare Wirkung des EWG-Vertrages auf die Wirtschaftsunternehmen.* Baden-Baden: Nomos Verlag, 1967.

RUPP, HANS HEINRICH "Die Grundrechte und das Europäische Gemeinschaftsrecht," N.J.W. 1970, 353–359.

WALL, EDWARD *Europe, Unification and Law.* London: Penguin, 1969.

ZIEGER, GOTTFRIED *Das Grundrechtsproblem in den Europäischen Gemeinschaften.* Tübingen: Mohr, 1970, Recht und Staat, Heft 384/385.

ZULEEG, MANFRED "Das Recht der Europäischen Gemeinschaften im innerstatlichen Bereich," K.S.E. Vol. 9. Cologne: Carl Heymann, 1969.

ACTS OF THE COMMUNITY INSTITUTIONS

BEBR, GERHARD "Acts of Representatives of the Governments of the Member States taken within the Council of Ministers of the European Communities," S.E.W. 1966, 529–545.

BERTRAM, C. "Decision-Making in the EEC: the Management Committee Procedure," 5 C.M.L.Rev. 1967–68, 246–264.

BOERNER, BODO *Die Entscheidung der Hohen Behörde.* Tübingen: Mohr (Paul Siebeck), 1965.

Document du parlement européen: Rapport fait au nom de la commission juridique sur les actes de la collectivité des Etats membres de la Communauté ainsi que sur les actes du Conseil non prévus par les traités. Rap. BURGER: Doc. No. 215, March 1969.

La décision dans les Communautés européennes. Grands Colloques Européens, No. 2: Publications de l'Institut d'Etudes Européennes de l'Université Libre de Bruxelles.

DUMON, F. "La formation de la règle de droit dans les Communautés européennes." R.I.D.C. 1960, 75–107.

ECONOMIDES, CONSTANTIN P. *Le pouvoir de décision des organisations internationales européennes.* Leyden: Sijthoff, 1964, Aspects Européens—Série E: Droit—No. 3.

FOIS, PAOLA *Gli accordi degli Stati membri delle Communita Europee.* Milan: Giuffrè, 1968.

KAISER, JOSEPH H. "Die im Rat vereinigten Vertreter der Regierungen der Mitgliedstaaten." *Zur Integration Europas.* Karlsruhe: Verlag C. F. Muller, 1965.

KOVAR, R., LAGARDE, P. and TALLON, D. "L'exécution des directives de la CEE en France," C.D.E. 1970, 274–302.

Document du parlement européen: Rapport fait au nom de la commission juridique sur les procédures communautaires d'exécution du droit communautaire derivé. Rap. JOZEAU-MARIGNE: Doc. No. 115, September 1968.

LAGRANGE, MAURICE "Le pouvoir de décision dans les Communautés Européennes: théorie et réalité," R.T.D.E. 1967, 1–29.

LAGRANGE, MAURICE *Le processus d'élaboration des décisions dans les Communautés Européennes: théorie et réalité.* Deventer: Kluwer, 1968, Europese Monographieen, no. 10: Besluitvorming in de europese Gemeenschappen, pp. 11–42.

LASSALLE, CLAUDE "Aspects communautaires de certains actes du droit international," R.G.D.I.P. 1969, 987–1017.

LOUIS, J.-V. "Applicabilité directe du règlement," C.D.E. 1972, 325.

LOUIS, J.-V. "Competence des Etats dans la mise en oeuvre du règlement. C.D.E. 1971, 627–640.

LOUIS, J.-V. *La décision dans la CEE.* Brussels: Presses Universitaires de Bruxelles, 1969.

LOUIS, J.-V. *Les règlements de la Communauté Economique Européenne.* Brussels: Presses Universitaires de Bruxelles, 1969, Publications de l'Institut d'Etudes Européennes de l'Université Libre de Bruxelles—theses et travaux juridiques, No. 3.

MORAND, C.-A. *La législation dans les communautés européennes.* Paris: L.G.D.J., 1968, Bibliothèque de Droit International.

MORAND, C.-A. "Les recommendations, les résolutions et les avis du droit communautaire," C.D.E. 1970, 623.

OPHUELS, C. F. "Die Mehrheitsbeschlüsse der Räte in den Europäischen Gemeinschaften," Eur. 1966, 193–586.

OPHUELS, C. F. "Les règlements et les directives dans les traités de Rome," C.D.E. 1966, 3–20.

PESCATORE, P. "Remarques sur la nature juridique des décisions des représentants des Etats membres réunis au sein du conseil," S.E.W. 1966, 579.

RAMBOW, GERHARD "L'exécution des directives de la Communauté Economique Européenne en République Fédérale d'Allemagne," C.D.E. 1970, 379–411.

ROUTER-HAMERAY, BERNARD *Les compétences implicites des organisations internationales.* Paris: L.G.D.J., 1962, Bibliothèque de droit international, T. XXV.

SCHERMERS, H. G. "Besluiten van de vertegenwoordigers der lid-staten; Gemeenschapsrecht," S.E.W. 1966, 545–579.

INTERNATIONAL LAW AND COMMUNITY LAW

PANHUYS, H. F. VAN "Conflicts between the Law of the European Communities and other Rules of International Law," 3 C.M.L.Rev. 1965–1966, 420–449.

PESCATORE, P. "L'apport du droit communautaire au droit international public," C.D.E. 1970, 501–525.

PESCATORE, P. *Droit international et droit communautaire. Essai de reflexion comparative.* Nancy: Centre Européen Universitaire, 1969, Publications du Centre Européen Universitaire de l'Université de Nancy—Collection des Conférences Européennes, No. 5.

PESCATORE, P. "International Law and Community Law," 7 C.M.L.Rev. 1970, 167–183.

VAN DER MENSBRUGGHE, Y. "La mer et les Communautés européennes," R.B.D.I. 1969, 87–145.

WAELBROECK, MICHEL *Traités internationaux et juridictions internes dans les pays du Marché commun.* Brussels: C.I.D.C.; Paris: Pedone, 1969.

INSTITUTIONS

BUERSTEDDE, SIGISMUND *Der Ministerrat im konstitutionelles System der Europäischen Gemeinschaften.* Bruges: De Tempel, 1964, Cahiers de Bruges, N.S. 9.

COOMBES, DAVID *Politics and Bureaucracy in the European Community. A portrait of the Commission of the EEC.* London: George Allen and Unwin, 1970.

HOUBEN, P.-H. J. M. *Les Conseils de Ministres des Communautés Européennes.* Leyden: Sijthoff, 1964, Aspects Européens, Série C: Politique, No. 17.

Document du parlement européen. Rapport fait au nom de la commission des affaires politiques et des questions institutionnelles sur le siège des institutions des Communautés Européennes. Rap. KOPF, HERMANN: Doc. No. 33, May 1959.

NOEL EMILE *Le Comité des représentants permanents*—Publications de l'Institut d'Etudes Européennes de l'Université Libre de Bruxelles, 1968, No. 1: *Institutions communautaires et institutions nationales dans le développement des Communautés,* pp. 9–48.

NOEL, EMILE "The Committee of Permanent Representatives," J.C.M.S. 1966–1967, 219–251.

NOEL, EMILE *Comment fonctionnent les institutions de la Communauté Econo-mique Européenne.* Paris: Bureau d'Information des Communautés Euro-péennes, 1966, Les Documents, No. 3. Also in English as *How the European Economic Community's Institutions work.* London: European Community Information Office. 1972, Community Topics No. 38.

Merger of the institutions

GLAESNER, HANS-JOACHIM *Perspectives d'avenir des organes executifs (Conseil et Commission des Communautés Européennes).* Liege: Faculté de Droit; The Hague: Martinus Nijhoff, 1967, La fusion des Communautés Européennes au lendemain des accords de Luxembourg, pp. 51–59.

HOUBEN, P.-H. J. M. "The Merger of the Executives of the European Communities," 3 C.M.L.Rev. 1965, 37–74.

LOUIS, J. V. "La fusion des institutions des Communautés Européennes," R.M.C. 1966, 834–856.

NOEL, EMILE *La fusion des Institutions et la fusion des Communautés Européennes.* Nancy: Imprimerie Idoux, 1966.

WEIL, GORDON "The Merger of the Institutions of the European Communities," A.J.I.L., 1967, 57–65.

European parliament

BIRKE, WOLFGANG *European elections by direct suffrage: a comparative study of the electoral systems used in western Europe and their utility for the direct election of a European parliament.* Leyden: Sijthoff, 1971.

Document du parlement européen. Rapport fait au nom de la commission politique sur l'élection du Parlement européen au suffrage universel direct ainsi que sur la proposition de résolution du Groupe socialiste. (Doc. 185/69.) Rap. DEHOUSSE, FERNAND: Doc. No. 210, January 1970.

Elections européennes au suffrage universel direct. Colloque des 14 et 15 avril 1960. Brussels: Edition de l'Institut de Sociologie Solvay, 1960. Centre national d'étude des problèmes de sociologie et d'économie européennes.

Document du parlement européen.

Rapport fait au nom de la commission juridique sur les problèmes juridiques de la consultation du Parlement européen. Rap. JOZEAU-MARIGNE: Doc. No. 110, August 1967.

WIGNY, PIERRE *L'Assembiée Parlementaire dans l'Europe des Six.* Luxembourg: Service des Publications des C. E.

COMMUNITY OFFICIALS

BLOCH, ROGER and LEFEVRE, JACQUELINE *La fonction publique internationale et européenne.* Paris: L.G.D.J., 1963, Collection Economie et Législation Européennes, No. 1.

CLEMENS, ADRIAN *Der Europäische Beamte und sein Disziplinarrecht.* Leyden: Sijthoff, 1962, Europäische Aspekte, Reihe E: Recht No. 1.

EULER, AUGUST MARTIN *Europäisches Beamtenstatut: Kommentar zum Beam-tenstatut der EWG und EAG.* Erster Teilband, Zweiter Teilband, Dritter Teilband, Cologne: Carl Heymanns Verlag KG, 1966–, K.S.E. Bd. 4a, 4b, 4c.

HOLTZ, THEODOR *Handbuch des Europäischen Dienstrechts.* Baden-Baden: Verlag August Lutzeyer, 1964– (Mise à jour).

TEKUELVE, EWALD "Das Beamtenrecht der Europäischen Gemeinschaften," *Bayerische Beamtenzeitung,* 1968, No. 10, 146–148, 1968, No. 11, 172–173, 1968, No. 12, 184–185, 1969, No. 1, 8–12.

FREE MOVEMENT OF GOODS: THE CUSTOMS UNION

AMPHOUX, JEAN "Customs legislation in the EEC," J.W.T.L. 1972, 133.

BERAUD, CHRISTIEN "Les mesures d'effet équivalent au sens des articles 30 et suivants du Traité de Rome," R.T.D.E. 1969, 293.

Colliard, Claude-Albert "L'obscure clarté de l'article 37 du Traité de Communauté Economique Européenne. *Recueil Dalloz*, 1964, No. 40, Chronique—XXXVII, 263–272.

Dallier, P. *L'harmonisation des législations douanières des états-membres de la CEE.* Paris: L.G.D.J., 1972.

Ehle and Meier *EWG Warenverkehr. Aussenhandel-Zöllen-Subventionen.* Cologne: Schmidt KG, 1971.

Franceschelli, Remo "Les monopoles nationaux de caractère commercial visés dans l'article 37 du Traité CEE et leur aménagement," R.M.C. 1968, 855–876.

Les monopoles dans le marché commun. L'article 37 du Traité de Rome. Travaux d'un groupe d'étude 1965–1967. Milan: Giuffrè, 1968, Ligue Internationale contre la concurrence déloyale.

Pescatore, P. "La notion du marché commun dans les traités instituant l'union économique belgo-luxembourgeoise, le Benelux et les Communautés européennes." In *Homage à Victor Gothot,* Faculté de droit de Liège, 1962, 497–546.

Rapport au Conseil et à la Commission concernant la réalisation par étapes de l'Union économique et monétaire dans la Communauté "Rapport Werner" (texte final). Supplément au Bulletin 11/1790 des Communautés Européennes, 3–72. *Le Droit et les Affaires,* 1970, No. 185, Doc. 27/70, 1–13.

Van Der Burg, L. J. "The Customs Tariff and Customs Legislation in the European Communities (some juridical problems)," C.M.L.Rev. 1970, 184–204.

Agriculture

Agarrecht der EWG. K.S.E., Vol. 10, Cologne: Carl Heymann, 1969.

The Common Agricultural Policy of the European Economic Community. London: H.M.S.O., 1967.

Melchior, Michel "Les organisations communes de marchés agricoles de la CEE," C.D.E. 1967, 247–289.

Melchior, Michel "L'organisation des marchés agricoles de la CEE au stade du marché unique," C.D.E. 1970, 127–153.

Olmi, Giancarlo "Agriculture and Fisheries in the Treaty of Brussels of January 22, 1972," 9 C.M.L.Rev. 1972, 293.

Free Movement of Workers, Establishment and Services, Social Policy

European Social Security Systems—A comparative Analysis of Programs in England, Sweden, and the Common Market Countries, together with a description of the U.S. system. Washington: U.S. Government Printing Office, 1965.

Everling, Ulrich *Das Niederlassungsrecht im Gemeinsamen Markt.* Berlin/Frankfurt: Verlag Franz Vahlen, 1963. *English text: The Right of Establishment in the Common Market.* New York/Chicago/Washington: CCH, 1964.

Kiss, Alexandre Charles "Entrée en vigueur de la Convention Européenne d'Etablissement et de la Charte Sociale Européenne. A.F.D.I. 1965, 686–691.

Lyon-Caen, Gerard *Droit Social Européen.* Paris: Précis Dalloz (2nd ed.), 1972.

Maestripiere, C. *La libre circulation des personnes et des services dans la CEE.* Heule (Belgium): UGA, 1972.

Mazzeotti, Manlio, and others *La liberté d'établissement et la libre prestation des services dans les Pays de la CEE.* Milan: Giuffrè, 1970.

O'Grada, Cormac "The Vocational Training Policy of the EEC and the Free Movement of Skilled Labour," J.C.M.S. 1969, 79–109.

Platz, Klaus Wilhelm "EWG-Niederlassungsrecht und individuelle Rechtspositionen." *Beiträge zum ausländischen öffentlichen Recht and Völkerrecht.* Bd. 45. Cologne: Carl Heymanns Verlag, 1966.

Ribas, Jacques-Jean *La politique sociale des Communautés européennes.* Paris: Dalloz et Sirey, 1969.

RIGAUX, FRANCOIS " Le critère de nationalité et la notion de personne morale dans l'article 58 du traité CEE et dans les dispositions d'application." Antwerp: Standard Wetenschappenlijke Uitgeverij, 1968. In Europees Vennootschapsrecht, 9–20.

TRANSPORT

BABUDIERI, F. " Les transports maritimes dans le cadre de l'intégration européenne." Antwerp: E.T.L., 1969, Gemeinsamer Markt & Verkehr, pp. 221–238, D.E.T. 1969, 405–422.

COLLINSON, W. S. " Economic regulation of transport under the Common Transport Policy of the European Communities," 24 Stan.L.Rev. 1972, 221–346.

DE FERRON, OLIVIER Le problème des transports et le Marché Commun. Geneva: Droz, 1965, Etudes d'histoire économique, politique et sociale, Vol. XLVIII.

DESPICHT, NIGEL S. Policies for Transport in the Common Market. Sidcup, Kent: Lambarde Press, 1964.

DESPICHT, NIGEL The Transport Policy of the European Communities. London: PEP, 1969, European Series, No. 12.

FISCHER, A. L'Organisation des transports dans le cadre de l'Europe des Six. Leyden: Sijthoff, 1968.

GAUDET, M. and BAEYENS, R. " Aperçu de quelques problèmes juridiques communautaires concernant les transports dans la CECA et la CEE," E.T.L. 1969, 205.

KLAER, WERNER Der Verkehr im Gemeinsamen Markt für Kohle und Stahl. Beiträge zur europäischen Verkehrspolitik. Baden-Bonn: Lutzeyer, 1961.

MICHELET, PIERRE Les transports au sol et l'organisation de l'Europe. Paris: Payot, 1962.

Etudes CEE. Série transports—No. 1/1966—Options de la politique tarifaire dans les transports. Brussels: Services des Publications des Communautés Européennes, 1966.

SOHIER, MARC " Apercu du développement actuel de la politique commune des transports," C.D.E. 1970, 154–184.

STABENOW, W. Les transports aériens dans le cadre de l'intégration européenne (1). Antwerp: E.T.L., 1969, Gemeinsamer Markt & Verkehr, pp. 239–261. D.E.T. 1969, 423–445.

STABENOW, WOLFGANG " Opportunities for an External Policy of the EEC in the Field of Transport," 4 C.M.L.Rev., 1966, 32–50.

TAXATION

ANSCHUTZ, ULRICH " Harmonization of direct taxes in the EEC," 13 H.I.L.J. 1972, 1–58.

Conséquences budgétaires économiques et sociales de l'harmonisation des taux de la TVA dans la CEE. Collection Etudes—Série Concurrence No. 16, Brussels, 1970.

COURTOIS, PIERRE " La concentration d'entreprises, aspects fiscaux," Bulletin des juristes Européens, 1970, Nos. 31–32, 47–70.

DALE, ARTHUR Tax Harmonization in Europe. London: Taxation Publishing Co., 1963.

Fiscale harmonisatie in de EEG, Deventer: Kluwer, 1966, Europese Monografieen, No. 7.

FONTANEAU, PIERRE Fiscalité européene (2 vols.) (feuilles mobiles). Paris: Les Cahiers Fiscaux Européens, 1969.

L'imposizione dei redditi di capitali mobiliari nei sei paesi della C.E.E. Roma: Istituto per l'Economia Europea, 1965, Quaderno, No. 12.

L'imposta sul valore aggiunto nei paesi della C.E.E. Roma: Camera dei Deputati, Segretariato Generale, Servizio Studi Legislazione e Inchieste Parlamentari, 1970.

JACQUEMIN, ALEX and PARMENTIER, CLAUDE *La double imposition économique des bénéfices de sociétes et les mesures d'allègement*, Louvain: Librairie Universitaire, 1968.

Rapport général des sous-groupes A, B et C créés par la réunion plenière du 23.2.1960 de la Commission C.E.E. avec les experts gouvernementaux pour les questions fiscales pour examiner differentes possibilités en vue d'une harmonisation des taxes sur le chiffre d'affaires. Brussels: Services des Publications des Communautés Européennes, 1962.

SCHOUP, CARL S. (ed.) *Fiscal Harmonization in Common Markets.* Vols. I, II. New York/London: Columbia University Press, 1967.

Tax harmonization programme.

Programme for the harmonization of direct taxes. Supp. to Bull. No. 8–1967.

COMPETITION

ALEXANDER, W. *Brevets d'invention et règles de concurrence du Traité CEE.* Brussels: Bruylant, 1971.

BRAUN, ANTOINE, GLEISS, ALFRED and HIRSCH, MARTIN *Droit des ententes de la Communauté Européenne.* Brussels: Larcier; Paris: Dalloz, 1967.

CEREXHE, E. " L'interpretation de l'article 86 du traité de Rome et les premiers décisions de la Commission," C.D.E. 1972, 272.

CONSTANTINESCO, LEONTIN " Les positions dominantes: aspects juridiques." In *Les ententes à l'échelle européenne*, pp. 79–100, Paris: Dunod, 1967.

DERINGER, A. *Competition law of the EEC.* Chicago: C.C.H., 1968.

DUBOIS, JEAN-PIERRE *La position dominante et son abus dans l'article 86 du Traité de la CEE.* Paris: Librairies Techniques, 1968.

L'entreprise publique et la concurrence. Les articles 90 et 37 du Traité CEE et leurs relations avec la concurrence. Bruges: De Tempel, 1969, Cahiers de Bruges, N.S. 22.

GERVEN, WALTER VAN *Principles du droit des ententes de la Communauté Economique Européenne.* Brussels: Bruylant, 1966.

GIDE-LOYRETTE-NOUEL *Le droit de la concurrence des communautés européennes. Traité pratique—Recueil de textes.* Paris: Joly, 1969.

GRAUPNER, R. *The Rules of Competition in the European Economic Community.* The Hague: Nijhoff, 1965.

Guide Pratique concernant les articles 85 et 86 du Traité instituant la C.E.E. et leurs règlements d'application. Brussels: Service de presses et d'information, 1962.

HONIG, FREDERICK, BROWN, WILLIAM J., GLEISS, ALFRED and HIRSCH, MARTIN *Cartel Law of the European Economic Community.* London: Butterworths, 1963.

MCCLACHLAN, D. L. and SWANN, D. *Competition Policy in the European Community.* London/New York/Toronto: Oxford University Press, 1967.

MANN, F. A. " The English Approach to the Extra-Territorial Effect of Foreign Anti-Trust Legislation (with special reference to the EEC)." Cahiers de Bruges, N.S. 14. In *Droit Communautaire et droit national*, pp. 381–387.

Mémorandum de la Commission de la CEE du 1.12.1965: le problème de la concentration dans le Marché Commun. R.T.D.E. 1966, 651–677. Also Brussels: Commission, 1965.

MOK, M. R. " The Cartel Policy of the EEC Commission, 1962–1967," C.M.L. Rev., 1968, 67–103.

OBERDORFER, C. W., GLEISS, ALFRED and HIRSCH, MARTIN *Common Market Cartel Law.* Chicago: CCH (2nd ed.) 1971.

PLAISANT, R., FRANCESCHELLI, R. and LASSIER, J. *Droit Européen de la Concurrence, Articles 85 à 89 du Traité CEE.* Paris: Delmas, 1966.

La réparation des conséquences dommageables d'une violation des articles 85 et 86 du traité instituant la CEE. Brussels: Service des Publications des Communautés Européennes, 1966, Série Concurrence, No. 1.

COMMERCIAL LAW: COMPANY LAW: INDUSTRIAL POLICY

Les entreprises publiques dans la Communauté Economique Européenne. Paris: Dunod, 1967.

GOLDMANN, B. *Droit commercial européen.* Paris: Dalloz, 1971 (2nd ed.).

HAERTEL, KURT "The Draft Conventions for a European System for the Grant of Patents and for the European Patent for the Common Market," *International Review of Industrial Property and Copyright Law,* Vol. 1/1970, No. 3, 289–306.

MANN, F. A. "The European company" [1970] I.C.L.Q., 468–482.

Memorandum de la Commission de la Communauté Economique Européene sur la création d'une sociéte commerciale européenne. R.T.D.E. 1966, No. 3, and Brussels: Commission, April 22, 1966.

Objectives and instruments of a common policy for scientific research and technological development. Bull. supp. 6/72.

La politique industrielle de la Communauté. Brussels: Commission des Communautés Européennes, 1970.

RENAULD, J. *Droit européen des sociétés.* Brussels: Bruylant; Louvain: Vander, 1969.

STEIN, E. *Harmonisation of European Company Laws—National Reform and Transitional Coordination.* New York: Bobbs Merrill, 1971.

THOMPSON, DENNIS *The proposal for a European Company.* London: PEP, 1969, European Series, No. 13.

Vers une politique industrielle européenne. Brussels: Presses Universitaires de Bruxelles, 1970, Publications de l'Institut d'Etudes Européennes de l'Université Libre de Bruxelles, Colloques Européens, No. 4.

HARMONISATION OF LAW

" Angleichung des Rechts der Wirtschaft in Europa: Le Rapprochement du Droit de l'économie en Europe," K.S.E. 11, Cologne: Carl Heymann, 1971.

Document du parlement européen: Rapport fait au nom de la commission juridique sur la proposition de la Commission des Communautés européennes au Conseil (doc. 15/68) concernant un programme general pour l'élimination des entraves techniques aux échanges resultant de disparités entre législations nationales. Rap. ARGMENGAUD, A.: Doc. No. 114, September 1968.

L'harmonisation dans les Communautés. Brussels: Editions de l'Institut de Sociologie, 1968, Publications de l'Institut d'Etudes des Européennes de l'Université Libre de Bruxelles—Enseignement complémentaire—Nouvelle serie, No. 2.

LOCHNER, NORBERT "Was bedeuten die Begriffe Harmonisierung, Koordinierung und Gemeinsame Politik in den europäischen Vertragen? " *Zeitschrift für die gesamte Staatswissenschaft,* 1962, No. 1, 35–61.

SEMINI, A. *La CEE: Harmonisation des législations,* Paris: Delmas, 1971.

VON DER GROEBEN, HANS *La politique de la Commission européenne dans le domaine du rapprochement des législations.* Brussels: Service des Publications des Communautés Européennes, 1969.

Document du parlement européen: Rapport fait au nom de la commission juridique sur l'harmonisation des législations européennes. Rap. WEINKAMM, OTTO: Doc. No. 54, June 1965.

PENAL LAW

Droit pénal européen: Congrès organisé les 7, 8 et 9 novembre 1968 par l'Institut d'Etudes Européennes. Brussels: Presses Universitaires de Bruxelles, 1970, Publications de l'Institut d'Etudes Européennes de l'Université Libre de Bruxelles, No. 5.

JOHANNES, HARTMUT " Das Strafrecht im Bereich der Europäischen Gemeinschaftein," Eur. 1968, 63–126.

ECONOMIC POLICY

EVERLING, ULRICH " L'aspect juridique de la coordination de la politique économique au sein de la Communauté Economique Européenne," A.F.D.I. 1964, 576–604.

MORISSENS, LUCIEN *La politique économique de la Communauté Economique Européenne.* Brussels: Institut d'Etudes Européennes, 1965, Thèses et Travaux Economiques, No. 1.

" Politique économique de la CEE et du Comecon " (colloque). C.E.B. 1972, 158–276.

" Le rapprochement du droit de l'économie en Europe," K.S.E. Vol. II, Cologne: Carl Heymann, 1971.

REGIONAL POLICY

FLOCKTON, CHRISTOPHER *Community Regional Policy.* London: PEP, 1970, European Series, No. 15, pp. 19–54.

LIND, HAROLD *Regional Policy in Britain and The Six.* London: PEP, 1970, European Series, No. 15, pp. 5–18, 55–75.

La politique régionale dans la Communauté Economique Européenne. Rapports des groupes d'experts (German, French, Italian, Dutch). Brussels: Services des Publications des Communautés Européennes, 1964.

La politique régionale du Marché Commun. Université Catholique de Louvain. Centre d'études européennes. Louvain: Vander, 1971.

Une politique régionale pour la Communauté. Brussels: Commission des Communautés Européennes, 1969.

Les régions frontalières à l'heure du marché commun. Brussels: Presse Universitaire de Bruxelles, 1970. Publications de l'Institut d'Etudes Européennes de l'Université Libre de Bruxelles, Grands Colloques européens, No. 6.

VON DER GROEBEN, HANS " La politique régionale de la Communauté Economique Européenne." *Les problemes de L'Europe,* XIIème annee/1969, No. 45, 7–23.

FINANCE AND CAPITAL

CARREAU, DOMINIQUE " Les unités de compte des Communautés européennes," R.T.D.E. 1966, pp. 228–241.

CARTOU, L. *La politique monétaire de la C.E.E.* Paris: Colin, 1970.

Documents—La coordination des politiques économiques et la coopération monétaire au sein de la Communauté. Mémorandum de la Commission des CE du 5.12.1968. *Bulletin Europe,* 1969, *Europe Documents,* No. 515, February 27, 1969.

A description of certain European Capital Markets. Economic Policies and Practices: Paper No. 3, Joint Economic Committee, 88th Congress, 2nd Session. Washington: U.S. Government Printing Office 1964.

Le développement d'un marché européen des capitaux. Rapport d'une groupe d'experts constitué par la Commission de la CEE. Brussels: Services des Publications des Communautés Européennes, 1966.

Les émissions de titres de sociétés en Europe et aux Etats-Unis. Brussels: Presses Universitaires de Bruxelles, 1970. Publications de l'Institut d'Etudes Européennes de l'Université Libre de Bruxelles, Série thèses et travaux juridiques, No. 6.

Institutions et mécanismes bancaires dans les pays de la Communauté Economique Européenne. Paris: Dunod, 1969.

MENAIS, G.-P. *Le marché européen des capitaux.* Paris: Les Editions de l'Epargne, 1969.

Mesures d'aménagement en matière d'impôts directs en vue de faciliter le développement et l'interpénetration des marchés de capitaux dans la Communauté économique européenne (Mémorandum de la Commission au Conseil)—COM (69) 201, Brussels, March 5, 1969.

Necessité et modalités d'une action dans le domaine des capitaux (Mémorandum de la Commission au Conseil)—COM (69) 200, Brussels, March 5, 1969.

La politique du marché obligatoire dans les pays de la C.E.E. Instruments existants et leurs applications de 1966 à 1969. Brussels: Communautés Européennes, Comité Monétaire, 1970.

Document du parlement européen: Rapport fait au nom de la commission des finances et des budgets sur la proposition de la Commission de la CEE au Conseil (doc. 63) d'un règlement relatif à la définition de l'unité de compte en matière de politique agricole commune. Rap. WESTERTERP: Doc. No. 115, July 1967.

EXTERNAL RELATIONS

L'association à la Communauté Economique Européenne: Aspects juridiques. Brussels: Presses universitaires de Bruxelles, 1970.

BETTE, AUGUSTO G. *Les relations extérieures de l'Euratom.* Paris: Centre Français de droit comparé, 1965.

Colloque sur les relations entre la Communauté Economique Européenne et les pays en voie de développement (Renouvellement de la Convention de Yaoundé). Berlin. September/October 1968. Paris: EDIAFRIC, La documentation africaine, 1970.

COSTONIS, JOHN J. "The Treaty-Making Power of the European Economic Community: the Perspectives of a Decade," 5 C.M.L.Rev. 1968, 421–457.

EVERLING, ULRICH "Legal Problems of the Common Commercial Policy in the European Economic Community," 4 C.M.L.Rev. 1966, 141–165.

EVERTS, PHILIP P. (ed.) *The European Community in the World: the external relations of the enlarged European Community.* Rotterdam: University Press, 1972.

FELD, WERNER "The Competences of the European Communities for the Conduct of External Relations," Tex.L.Rev. 1965, 891–926.

FELD, WERNER *The European Common Market and the World.* New Jersey: Prentice-Hall, 1967.

GANSHOF VAN DER MEERSCH, W. J. "Les relations extérieures de la CEE dans le domaine des politiques communés et l'arrêt de la Cour de Justice du 31 mars 1971," C.D.E. 1972, 129.

GARRETSON, ALBERT H. "Some Aspects of the Foreign Relations Power of the European Communities," Wash.L.Rev. 1966, 411–422.

JAEGER, FRANZ *GATT, EWG und EFTA. Die Vereinbarkeit von EWG- und EFTA-Recht mit dem GATT-Statut.* Bern: Verlag Stämpfli & Cie, 1970, Schweizerische Beitrage zum Europarecht, No. 4.

KIM, CAE-ONE "The Common Commercial Policy of the EEC," J.W.T.L. 1970, 20.

KIM, CAE-ONE *La Communauté Européenne dans les relations commerciales internationales.* Institut d'Etudes Européennes del'Université Libre de Bruxelles. Brussels: Presses Universitaires de Bruxelles, 1971.

KIM, CAE-ONE "Developments in the Commercial Policy of the European Economic Community," 7 C.M.L.Rev. 1970, 148–167.

KOVAR, ROBERT "La mise en place d'une politique commerciale commune et les compétences des Etats membres de la communauté économique européenne en matière de relations internationales et de conclusion des traités," A.F.D.I. 1971, 783.

Document du parlement européen: Rapport fait au nom de la commission des relations économiques extérieures sur les résultats des négociations Kennedy et les conclusions à en tirer. Rap. KRIEDEMANN, H.: Doc. No. 176, January 1968.

LE TALLEC, GEORGES "The Common Commercial Policy of the EEC" [1971] I.C.L.Q. 732.

MELCHIOR, MICHEL "La procédure de conclusion des accords externes de la Communauté Economique Européenne," R.B.D.I. 1966, 187–215.

PESCATORE, P. "Les relations extérieures des Communautés Européennes," R.C.A.D.I. 1961, 1–244.

PLESSOW, UTTA "Neutralität und Assoziation mit der EWG," K.S.E. Vol. 8. Cologne: Carl Heymann, 1967.

Document du parlement européen: Rapport fait au nom de la commission politique sur les relations extérieures de la Communauté Européenne de l'énergie atomique. Rap. PROBST, MME.: Doc. No. 124, January 1964.

RAUX, JEAN "La Cour de Justice des Communautés et les relations extérieures de la C.E.E.," R.G.D.I.P. 1972, 36.

RAUX, JEAN "La procédure de conclusion des accords externes de la Communauté Européenne de l'Energie Atomique," R.G.D.I.P. 1965, No. 4, 1019–1050.

RAUX, JEAN *Les relations extérieures de la Communauté Economique Européenne.* Paris: Editions Cujas, 1966.

REICHLING, CHARLES *Le droit de légation des Communautés Européennes.* Heule (Belgium): Editions UGA, 1964. Centre International d'Etudes et de Recherches Européennes—Cours.

Les relations extérieures de la Communauté Européenne unifiée. Institut d'études juridiques européennes de la faculté de droit de l'université de Liège, 1969.

SIMMONDS, K. R. "The Community and the neutral states," 2 C.M.L.Rev. 1964, 5–20.

TESTA, GAETANO "L'intervention des Etats membres dans la procédure de conclusion des accords d'association de la Communauté Economique Européenne," C.D.E. 1966, 492–513.

TOMUSCHAT, CHRISTIAN "EWG und DDR. Völkerrechtliche Überlegungen zum Sonder-status des Aussenseiters einer Wirtschaftsunion," Eur. 1969, 298–332.

WAELBROECK, MICHEL "L'arrêt AETR et les compétences externes de la Communauté économique européenne" (1971) *Integration* 78–89.

WOHLFARTH, E. *Fondements juridiques des relations entre les Communautés européennes et les Etat-tiers.* Brussels: Institut d'Etudes Européennes, 1964. Publications de l'Institut d'Etudes Européennes, No. 6.

ECSC AND EURATOM: GENERAL

BEBR, GERHARD "The European Coal and Steel Community. A political and legal innovation," Y.L.J. 1953, 1–43.

ERRERA, J. E. SYMON, VAN DER MEULEN, J. and VERNAEVE, L. *Euratom: Analyse et commentaires du Traité.* Brussels: Librairie Encyclopédique, 1958.

MATHIJSEN, P. R. S. F. *Le droit de la Communauté Européenne du Charbon et de l'Acier.* Une étude des sources. 's-Gravenhage: Nijhoff, 1957.

REUTER, PAUL *La Communauté Européenne du Charbon et de l'Acier.* Paris: L.G.D.J., 1953.

VISSCHER, PAUL DE *Le droit public de la Communauté Européenne du Charbon et de l'Acier.* Liège: Les Presses Universitaires de Liège, 1956–1957.

INDEX

Accession
Act of. *See* Act of Accession.
Final Act of. *See* Final Act of Accession.
instruments of, 2-08 *et seq.*
Treaty of. *See* Treaty of Accession.
Accords of Luxembourg, 5-06 *et seq.*
Council, effects on voting procedure, 5-06
legal status of, 5-07
Act of Accession, 2-09 *et seq.*
adaptations under, 2-14
capital, free movement of, 26-15
common customs tariff, provisions for, 21-43
Community budget, provisions concerning, 35-11
Community preference, maintenance of, provision for, 21-39
competition, rules of, effect on, 28-95
customs duties,
abolition of, 21-38, 21-49
fiscal nature, of, abolition of, 21-42
customs matters, provisions for, 21-37 *et seq.*
transitional period, 21-38
existing treaties, adaptations to, 2-13
external relations, provision for, 37-57 *et seq.*
implementation of, 2-16
imports, charges on, provisions for, 21-40
market organisations, application to. *See* market organisations.
new Member States, effect on, 2-11 *et seq.*
principles of, 2-11 *et seq.*
quantitative restrictions, provision for abolition of, 21-47, 21-49
Regulation 17 adapted by, 28-95
state commercial monopolies, provisions concerning, 21-48
transitional measures, 2-15
Actions against Commission,
failure to act, for, 14-01 *et seq.*
ECSC Treaty, under, 14-10 *et seq.*
EEC Treaty, under, 14-01 *et seq.*
individuals, *locus standi,* of, 14-02 *et seq.*
Member States, *locus standi* of, 14-01
penalties, regulations providing for, 12-01 *et seq.*
Actions against Council,
failure to act, for, 14-01 *et seq.*
ECSC Treaty, under, 14-10 *et seq.*
EEC Treaty, under, 14-01 *et seq.*
individuals, *locus standi* of, 14-02 *et seq.*
Member States, *locus standi* of, 14-01

Actions against Council—*cont.*
penalties, regulations providing for, 12-01 *et seq.*
Actions against Member States,
obligations, failure to fulfil, 10-10, 11-01 *et seq.*
Commission, role of, 11-02 *et seq.*
Court of Justice, jurisdiction under Article 182, 11-12 *et seq.*
Member States, *locus standi* of, 11-02
procedure, 11-01 *et seq.*
Article 170, under, 11-10
ECSC Treaty, under, 11-11
opinions of Commission, issue of, 11-06
reference to Court by Commission, 11-08 *et seq.*
penalties, regulations providing for, 12-01 *et seq.*
Acts of Institutions, 8-01 *et seq.*
decisions. *See* Decisions.
direct applicability of, 18-01 *et seq.*, 18-12 *et seq.*
directives. *See* Directives.
illegality of. *See* Illegality, plea of.
new members, effect on, 8-03
opinions. *See* Opinions.
preliminary rulings on, 15-06 *et seq.*
limitation of, 15-07
publication and citation of, 1-05
reasons, requirement for, 8-12
recommendations. *See* Recommendations.
regulations. *See* Regulations.
Administrative Commission for the
Social Security of Workers, 23-18
Admission of new Members, 37-23 *et seq.*
Act of Accession, 37-23
conditions, 37-23
Advisory Committee for the Social Security of Migrant Workers, 23-18
Advisory Committee on Restrictive Practices and Monopolies, 28-84
Agriculture. *See* Common Agricultural Policy.
Aid to Development, 37-55
Aids, 29-07 *et seq.*
British Eady fund, 29-14
Commission decisions on, 29-08
compatible with Common Market, 29-10
approval required, 29-11 *et seq.*
Co-ordination of systems, 29-15 *et seq.*
Council, role of in controlling, 29-16 *et seq.*
exports to third countries, for, harmonisation of, 32-15, 37-17
film industry to, rationalisation of, 29-14

Aids—*cont.*
 forms of, 29-09
 industries generally benefiting, 29-13
 prohibition on, 29-07
 review by Commission, of, 29-16
 scope of prohibition on, 29-09
 textile industry, guidelines on, 29-13
Anglo-Irish Free Trade Agreement,
 Act of Accession effect on, 21-53
 agriculture, transitional measures,
  effect on, 22-41
Annual General Report of Communities, 1-08
Annulment, action for. *See* Court of
 Justice.
Approximation of laws, 20-04, 32-01 *et
 seq.*
 agricultural standardisation, 32-05
 agriculture, directives concerning,
  32-10
 Assembly, function in, 32-03
 Commission, role of in, 32-01, 32-03
  et seq., 32-06 *et seq.*
 company law, 32-10
 competition, distortion of, in absence
  of, 32-04, 32-06
 co-ordination distinguished, 32-02
 crystal glass, 32-05
 customs matters, 21-18 *et seq.*, 32-05
 dangerous substances, provisions on,
  32-05
 Economic and Social Committee, consultation of, 32-03, 32-05
 food standards, 32-05
 free movement of workers. *See*
  Workers.
 freedom of establishment. *See* **Free-**
  dom of establishment.
 harmonisation distinguished, 32-02
 measuring instruments, 32-05
 medicinal products, 32-05
 motor vehicle standards, 32-05
 scope, 32-03
 textile appellations, 32-05
 value added tax, 32-05
 Weinkamm Report, 32-17 *et seq.*
 wood, 32-05
Arbitral awards, recognition of, 32-19
Article 111 Committee, 37-16
Article 113 Committee, 37-16
Assembly, 6-01 *et seq.*
 advisory powers, 6-08 *et seq.*
 approximation of laws, function in,
  32-03
 delegates, 6-02 *et seq.*
 EEC Treaty, provision for, by, 20-05
 members, 6-02 *et seq.*
  election of, 6-03
  immunity of, 36-08
  mandate, length of, 6-04
  qualification as, 6-04
 motion of censure, 4-20, 6-12
 officers,
  election of, 6-06
  function of, 6-06
 opinion of, 6-08 *et seq.*
 political groupings, 6-07
 powers, 3-07, 6-02, 6-08 *et seq.*
 President, 6-06

Assembly—*cont.*
 procedure, 6-05 *et seq.*
 representatives, 6-02 *et seq.*
 sessions,
  duration of, 6-05
  location of, 6-05
 supervisory powers, 6-11 *et seq.*
Association agreements, 37-20 *et seq.*,
 37-44 *et seq.*
 African States, with, 37-44
 Arusha Conventions, 37-48, 37-55
 East African Community, with, 37-48,
  37-55
 future provisions, 37-66 *et seq.*
 Greece, with, 37-50
 institutions for, 37-45 *et seq.*
 Malta, with, 37-52
 new Member States, with, 37-65
 Nigeria, with, 37-47
 procedure for, 37-21
 Tunisia and Morocco, with, 37-49,
  37-55
 Turkey, with, 37-51
 Yaoundé Convention, 37-44, 37-46
  et seq.
  new Member States, exemption
   from, 37-61 *et seq.*
Association Committee, 37-45
Association Council, 37-45
Audit Board, 20-05

Balance of payments,
 control of, 33-06 *et seq.*
 stabilisation of, measures for, 33-17
Bank for International Settlements,
 31-17
Bankruptcy, 31-15
Banks, co-operation between, 33-21
Beef. *See* Market organisations.
British Eady fund. *See* Aids.
Brussels Convention on Customs No-
 menclature, 21-16
Budget Treaty, 35-01 *et seq.*
 expenses of Communities,
  administrative, 35-02
  operational, 35-02 *et seq.*
Budgetary Policy Committee, 20-07,
 33-03, 33-07, 33-09
Bulletin of European Communities, 1-08

Capital. *See* Free movement of capital.
Cartel Law. *See* Competition.
Central Banks,
 committee of governors of, 33-03,
  33-07, 33-09, 33-23
 co-operation between, 33-21
Cereals. *See* Market organisations.
Cheese. *See* Market organisations.
Colonial territories, former, 37-20
Commission,
 action against Member States, role in
  11-02 *et seq.*
 acts of,
  illegality, plea of. *See* Illegality,
   plea of.
 agricultural consultative committee,
  22-43

Convention on Jurisdiction and the Enforcement of Civil and Commercial Judgments—*cont.*
interlocutory measures, 32-23
judicial competence, 32-23
location of subject matter, limitation of, 32-23
new Member States, accession of, to, 32-21
proof of documents, 32-23
recognition and enforcement of foreign judgments, 32-23
scope of, 32-20, 32-23
Convention on Mutual Assistance between Customs Administrations, 21-06
Convention on the Mutual Recognition of Companies and Bodies Corporate, 31-13, 32-19 *et seq.*
Court of Justice, jurisdiction under, 32-24
Convention on Transitional Provisions, external relations of ECSC, provision for, 37-04 *et seq.*
Council, 5-01 *et seq.*
acts of,
illegality, plea of. *See* Illegality, plea of.
agenda, division of, 5-07
aids, control of, 29-16 *et seq.*
bodies established by acts of,
statutes of, interpretation of, 15-08
Commission, influence on decisions of, 5-08
common agricultural policy, role with regard to, 22-05, 22-08 *et seq.*
common vocational training policy, implementation of, 24-17
composition, 5-02
decision-making machinery, 5-09
economic policies of Member States, co-ordination of, 20-07, 33-03 *et seq.*
EEC Treaty, provision for, by, 20-05
Euratom, external relations, role in, 37-08
failure to act, actions against, for, 14-01 *et seq. See also* Actions against Council.
legality of acts of, review of, 13-01 *et seq.*
powers, 5-10 *et seq.*
President, 5-03
procedure, 5-04 *et seq.*
reasoning of acts, necessity for, 8-12
relationship with other institutions, 3-05, 5-08
role, 5-01
suspension, power of,
Merger Treaty, effect of, on, 3-05
tariff quotas, granting of, 21-17
voting procedure, 5-05
Accords of Luxembourg, effect of, 5-06 *et seq.*
written procedure, use of, 5-07
Council of Europe, relations of ECSC with, 37-03
Court of Arbitration of the Association, 37-45

Court of Justice, 9-01 *et seq.*
Advocates-General,
appointment of, 9-03 *et seq.*
disqualification of, 9-13
function of, 9-07
submissions of, 9-07
annulment, action for, 13-01 *et seq.*
competence, lack of, ground for, 13-03
grounds of, 13-03 *et seq.*
powers, misuse of, ground for, 13-06
procedural requirement, infringement of, ground for, 13-04
Treaty, infringement of, ground for, 13-05
chambers,
division into, 9-09
functions of, 9-10 *et seq.*, 9-25
Commission, actions against. *See* Actions against Commission.
Community servants, proceedings by, 9-33, 36-30
composition, 9-02 *et seq.*
costs, orders for, 9-24
Council, actions against. *See* Actions against Council.
EEC Treaty, provision for, by, 20-05
"instruction." *See* procedure of inquiry.
judges,
appointment of, 9-03 *et seq.*
disqualification of, 9-13
judgments,
effect in actions for failure to act, 14-01
enforceability, 10-08
legality of Community Acts, review of, 10-11, 13-01 *et seq.*
nature of, 10-10 *et seq.*
non-enforceable, effects where, 10-09
provisions for, 9-23
publication and citation of, 1-06
jurisdiction,
action for non-contractual liability, 36-14
Article 182, under, 11-12 *et seq.*
ECSC Treaty, derived from, 10-03
EEC Treaty, derived from, 10-02
Euratom Treaty, derived from, 10-04
penalties, imposition of, 12-01 *et seq.*
scope of, 10-01 *et seq.*
language, selection of, 9-15
legal aid, 9-25
location, 9-14
opinions of, 9-36
oral procedure, 9-17, 9-22
preliminary rulings, 10-13 *et seq. See also* Preliminary rulings.
preparatory inquiries, 9-10, 9-21
President, 9-06
privileges and immunities of, 36-11
procedure, 9-12 *et seq.*
oral, 9-17, 9-22
preliminary points of, 9-31
rules of, 9-18
service of documents, 9-27

Regional policy—*cont.*
financing of, 34-08
national action, coordination of, 34-02
new Member States, application to, 34-07
positive action on, 34-06
powers, specific, lack of, 34-01
Regional Development Committee, 34-04
transitional difficulties, 34-17
transport, 34-16
Treaty provisions relating to, 34-09
Regulations,
application, 13-08
character of, 13-08 *et seq.*
consolidating tariff regulation, 21-16
direct applicability of, 18-12
EEC, of, 8-06 *et seq.*
applicability to Member States, 8-07
requirements 8-08
effect, 8-01
Regulation 17. *See* Competition.
Residence Permit. *See* Workers.
Restrictive Trade Agreements. *See* Competition.
Revenue controls, 21-02
Review of Legality, action for. *See* Court of Justice.
Rice. *See* Market organisations.
Right of Establishment. *See* Establishment, right of.

Sanders Committee, 31-17
Segré Report, 30-28, 30-30
Services, free movement of. *See* Free movement of services.
Session documents, 1-08
Social policy, 20-04, 24-01 *et seq.*
Commission, annual report of, social developments, inclusion of, 24-08
Commission, role of, 24-02
equal pay,
interpretation of, 24-05
origins of principle of, 24-05
provision for, 24-04 *et seq.*
U.K. legislation, 24-06
European Social Fund. *See* European Social Fund.
fields of co-operation, 24-02
harmonisation of, 32-16
holidays, 24-07
obligations of Member States, 24-04
paid holiday schemes, 24-07
Social security, 23-14 *et seq.*
Administrative Commission, 23-18
Advisory Committee for Social Security of Migrant Workers, 23-18
basic rules governing, 23-17
Community employees, for, 36-10
conflicts in national laws, rules for, 23-16
definition of, 23-16
national authorities, responsibility for, 23-19
reciprocal arrangements, 23-14

Sources of Law,
Community Treaties, outside of, 8-15 *et seq.*
general principles. *See* General principles of law.
International law. *See* International law.
Standing Committee on Employment. *See* Employment, Standing Committee on.
State commercial monopolies,
adjustment of, 21-34 *et seq.*
definition of, 21-33
new Member States, adjustment of, 21-48
services, non-applicability of provisions to, 21-36
Treaty provisions, application to, 21-34 *et seq.*
Sugar. *See* Market organisations.

Tariff quotas, 21-17
external relations, rules governing in, 37-31
Tariff rates,
harmonisation of, 32-15
Taxation, 30-01 *et seq.*
capital duty, harmonisation of, 30-26
cascade system of,
average rates, establishment of, 30-12
companies, of,
accounts, harmonisation of, 30-30
classical system, 30-29
harmonisation of, 30-28 *et seq.*
imputation system, 30-29
mergers, 30-30
subsidiary in different Member States, where, 31-12
withholding tax, 30-28, 30-30
customs duties, charges equivalent to, internal taxes distinguished from, 30-07 *et seq.*
direct, 30-27 *et seq.*
definition, of, 30-27
harmonisation of, 30-14, 30-28 *et seq.*
Segré Report on, 30-28, 30-30
equivalent charge, 21-03, 21-13
excise duties, 30-25
harmonisation of, object of, 21-02
import licence charge, status of, 30-07
indirect, 30-03 *et seq.*
decisions of Court on, 30-03 *et seq.*
direct applicability of prohibition on, 30-03 *et seq.*
discrimination by means of, 30-03
harmonisation of, 30-14 *et seq.*, 30-26, 32-14
refunds on exports, prohibition on, 30-11
internal,
charges equivalent to customs duties, distinguished from, 30-07 *et seq.*
mergers, on, 30-30, 31-12
national fiscal policies, co-ordination of, 30-28

509